Namibia

THE BRADT TRAVEL GUIDE

THE BRADT STORY

The first Bradt travel guide was written by Hilary and George Bradt in 1974 on a river barge floating down a tributary of the Amazon in Bolivia. From their base in Boston, Massachusetts, they went on to write and publish four other backpacking guides to the Americas and one to Africa.

In the 1980s Hilary continued to develop the Bradt list in England, and also established herself as a travel writer and tour leader. The company's publishing emphasis evolved towards broader-based guides to new destinations – usually the first to be published on those countries – complemented by hiking, rail and wildlife guides.

Since winning *The Sunday Times* Small Publisher of the Year Award in 1997, we have continued to fill the demand for detailed, well-written guides to unusual destinations, while maintaining the company's original ethos of low-impact travel.

Travel guides are by their nature continuously evolving. If you experience anything which you would like to share with us, or if you have any amendments to make to this guide, please write; all your letters are read and passed on to the author. Most importantly, do remember to travel with an open mind and to respect the customs of your hosts – it will add immeasurably to your enjoyment.

Happy travelling!

Hilary Bradt

Hilary Bradt

19 High Street, Chalfont St Peter, Bucks SL9 9QE, England
Tel: 01753 893444; fax: 01753 892333
Email: info@bradt-travelguides.com
Web: www.bradtguides.com

Namibia

THE BRADT TRAVEL GUIDE

Second Edition

Chris McIntyre

Bradt Travel Guides Ltd, UK
The Globe Pequot Press Inc, USA

Second edition 2003
Reprinted with amendments April 2004
First published 1998

Bradt Travel Guides Ltd
19 High Street, Chalfont St Peter, Bucks SL9 9QE, England
www.bradt-travelguides.com
Published in the USA by The Globe Pequot Press Inc, 246 Goose Lane,
PO Box 480, Guilford, Connecticut 06475-0480

ISBN 1 84162 062 9

British Library Cataloguing in Publication Data
A catalogue record for this book is available from the British Library

Photographs
Front cover Meerkats in the southern Kalahari (Chris McIntyre)
Text Chris McIntyre (CM), Tricia Hayne (TH), Rebecca Johnson (RJ)

Illustrations Annabel Milne, Carole Vincer
Maps Steve Munns

Typeset from the author's disc by Wakewing
Printed and bound in Italy by Legoprint SpA, Trento

Author and Contributors

AUTHOR

Chris McIntyre went to Africa in 1987, after reading physics at Queen's College, Oxford. He taught with VSO at a rural school in Zimbabwe for almost three years and travelled around extensively. In 1990 he co-authored the UK's first *Guide to Namibia and Botswana* (published by Bradt), before spending three years as a shipbroker in London.

Since then, Chris has concentrated on what he enjoys most: Africa. In 1996 he wrote the first guidebook to Zambia, for Bradt, and has since written *Botswana: The Bradt Travel Guide*, which was published in 2003. Whilst keeping his guides updated, he is now managing director of Sunvil Africa – a specialist tour operator which organises a variety of high-quality trips throughout southern Africa, including Namibia.

Chris maintains a keen interest in development and conservation issues, is a Fellow of the Royal Geographical Society, and contributes photographs and articles to various publications, including *The Times*, *Wanderlust*, *BBC Wildlife* and *Travel Africa*. Based in west London, he spends two or three months each year researching in Africa, but can usually be contacted by email on africa@sunvil.co.uk.

MAJOR CONTRIBUTORS

This book, just as much as the previous edition, has been a team effort, and many have devoted their energy to it. Largest amongst the contributions to this second edition are from:

Tricia and Bob Hayne updated sections on Windhoek, Swakopmund and most of southern Namibia in great detail. As editorial director of Bradt Travel Guides, Tricia is only too familiar with the minutiae of putting together a guidebook, although the distances of Namibia are in marked contrast to those covered for her own Bradt guide, to the Cayman Islands. When not researching obscure corners of the globe, both Tricia and Bob have a real interest in outdoor pursuits and the environment.

Chantal Pinto is Namibian, but was born and raised in Cape Town, South Africa. She moved to Namibia in 1987, whilst still at college, and later took an opportunity in the travel business as tourism to Namibia took off. Throughout the 1990s Chantal travelled extensively in the wildest corners of Botswana, Zimbabwe, South Africa and, especially, Namibia – whilst keeping on top of tourism developments at work. In 2002 she moved to London, to join Sunvil Africa and develop its Namibian programme. In her spare time she loves nature and the outdoors, and disappears into the country, or back to Africa, at every possible opportunity.

However, it's been built very much on the solid foundations laid by contributions for the first edition from:

Philip Briggs, Africa expert and author, who kindly gave an extensive and scholarly basis for the original *Wildlife Guide*; **Purba Choudhury**, arts, press and PR professional, who researched and wrote the *Arts and crafts* section; **David Else**, expert author and old Africa hand, who kindly gave route descriptions for the Naukluft hiking section; **Sue Grainger**, traveller and writer, who wrote much original material for the *Kaokoveld* chapter, and commented on more besides; **Jonathan Hughes**, ecologist, who wrote most of the *Survival in the Namib* boxes, and gave other valuable critiques; and **Rob McDowell** and **Heather Tyrrell**, who have both worked at Sunvil Africa over the years, and contributed to many sections, checked proofs and described many places seen on their travels.

DEDICATION

For my parents: Peter and Elizabeth McIntyre.
Without their unfailing love and support,
nothing would have been possible.

Contents

x

LIST OF MAPS

NOTE ON DATUM FOR GPS COORDINATES

For GPS coordinates given in this guide, note that the datum used is WSG 84 – and you must set your receiver accordingly before copying in any of these coordinates.

All GPS coordinates in this book have been expressed as degrees, minutes, and decimal fractions of a minute.

Acknowledgements

This second edition couldn't have been written without the help of many – some whose names I have forgotten, others I never knew. I hope those who aren't named here will forgive me, but some who stand out for their help and input include:

The NTS team – Dave van Smeerdik, Anna Cassim, Sabina Hekandjo, Regina Visher and especially Sue Camp, who always came to the rescue with exactly the right information that made all the difference; Neil Sylvester and the team at SAA, for their support and helping to make this book more colourful; Blythe Loutit, and the SRT team; the community at the remarkable Torra Conservancy, including Anna and Franz Coetzee; the team at Ground Rush, and Beth Sarro at Alter-Action, in Swakopmund; Jeanne Meintjes of Eco-Marine; Helen and Mike Warren from Erongo; Donna, Rosalea and Lisa at Okonjima; and, as ever, Kate and Bruno Nebe – without whom Swakopmund and its surroundings just wouldn't be the same.

Also Anja at Logufa, Gordon Campbell, Jenny Carvill, Hennie Fourrie, Retha Louise Hofmeyr, Dr Margaret Jacobsohn, Ruud Klep, Toya Louw, Ilvia McAdam, Arno Oosthuysen, Barbara-Anne Parfitt, Leon and Anita Pearson, Nick Santcross, Kurt Schlenther, Amy and Marie Schoeman, Peter Ward and Dr Polly Wiessner.

The team at Sunvil Africa sends about 500 people to Namibia every year, and many of these have helped me with their personal perspectives on the country – through both discussions and reports after they return. Eric Carter, Michael Jones, and Andrew Pearson stand out, though for this edition special thanks are due to Irene & Alan Jessop, who have travelled regularly to Bushmanland; their feedback and comments have been invaluable. When I last visited the same area, Estelle Oosthuysen was generous with her time, and provided very detailed and accurate information that is the base for the map of Khaudum. (Sunvil's travellers Paul Rankin and Debbie Shaw also take a bow here, for taking such a long trip to help Estelle to map the park!)

Meanwhile, back in the office, Claire Scott and David MacCallum-Price were always on hand to help with much information and experience, whilst the support of John, Noel and Dudley with my writing is always appreciated

For the second edition, Bob & Tricia Hayne are particularly indebted to all those whose hospitality made travelling around Namibia so memorable, including Bruno and Kate Nebe, Piet Swiegers and Sam Eggar, and to Chantal Pinto for support on so many fronts.

Immense gratitude, as usual, to those who worked on producing the book: Hilary Bradt, Sally Brock, Henry Stedman, Steve Munns and, especially, Tricia Hayne – whose hard work made this book possible. It wouldn't have happened without her. That which is good and correct owes much to their care and attention, while errors and omissions remain my own.

KEY TO STANDARD SYMBOLS

Symbol	Meaning	Symbol	Meaning
—·—·—	International boundary	♟	Statue or monument
······	District boundary	∴	Archaeological or historic site
------	National park boundary	🏰	Historic building
✈	Airport (international)	✝	Church or cathedral
✈	Airport (other)	⚑	Golf course
✛	Airstrip	🏃	Stadium
🚁	Helicopter service	▲	Summit
▬▬▬	Railway	△	Boundary beacon
----------	Footpath	⊙	Outpost
--🚗--	Car ferry	⨯—⨯	Border post
--🚢--	Passenger ferry	⌒	Rock shelter
⛽	Petrol station or garage	═══	Mountain pass
P	Car park	○	Waterhole
🚌	Bus station etc	☀	Scenic viewpoint
🚲	Cycle hire	❀	Botanical site
M	Underground station	⚘	Specific woodland feature
⌂	Hotel, inn etc	☆	Lighthouse
⚑	Campsite	⸬	Marsh
⬆	Hut	⚘	Mangrove
♀	Wine bar	➤	Bird nesting site
✗	Restaurant, café etc	✦	Turtle nesting site
✉	Post office	∽∽	Coral reef
☎	Telephone	➢	Beach
@	Internet café	🤿	Scuba diving
✚	Hospital, clinic etc	🐟	Fishing sites
⚱	Museum		
🐘	Zoo		
i	Tourist information		
$	Bank		

*Other map symbols are sometimes shown in
separate key boxes with individual
explanations for their meanings.*

Introduction

I first visited Namibia in 1989, as the South African administration started to relinquish its grip and the country prepared for independence. By then I had lived in southern Africa for several years and travelled widely. Namibia was rumoured to be wonderful; but nobody seemed to know any details. The world knew South West Africa (Namibia) only as a troubled place from news bulletins, nothing more.

So I hired a VW Golf and drove from Namibia's northeastern tip to its southern border in 12 days. Overseas tourism simply didn't exist then. Sesriem had one campsite with just 11 pitches for tents; the Fish River Canyon was deserted. The trip was terribly rushed, but Namibia captivated me. The scale of its wilderness was enchanting, and travelling was remarkably easy.

Six months later I returned to explore – and to research the first English guidebook. Whilst I was there, Namibia's independence arrived, putting the country's troubles into the past. Optimism was tangible, justified by democracy, an implausibly reliable infrastructure and rich mineral resources. I delved a little deeper into its magic. Elsewhere in the world, Namibia disappeared from the television news.

Only in the late 1990s did it return – featuring on holiday programmes. Fortunately, though, Namibia is far from Europe or the Americas. It has no white sandy beaches, warm tropical waters or big hotels, so it has never appealed to mass tourism. However, it does have huge tracts of pristine wilderness, home to some stunning wildlife. Glance around. The Namib Desert has plants and animals found nowhere else on earth. Here is the world's oldest desert, where endemic wildlife has evolved to survive – like the contorted *Welwitschia mirabilis* that live for millennia, the elusive golden mole and the unique fog-basking beetles.

Namibia's population has always been tiny, a sprinkling of settlements founded by different peoples: some ancient, some colonial. Around these outposts, vast open areas remain protected as national parks, supplemented by conservancies where scattered local communities protect the wildlife in their own areas. Namibia has little industry and virtually no pollution, so you look up at the clearest stars you'll ever see.

Best of all, Namibia's wilderness is still easy to explore independently. Choose backroads here and you can drive for hours through endless plains, huge mountain massifs and spectacular canyons without seeing a soul. Even in Etosha, one of Africa's top game parks, driving around is easy, and you can stop beside the waterholes for as long as you like. As animals wander all around, you just sip a cold drink and focus your camera.

Namibia's not an ideal country for backpacking. However, if you can afford to hire a car, then the country is your oyster – and it's not expensive. Good food, wine, beer and cheap camping make the cost of living in Namibia lower than anywhere else in southern Africa. With just a little more cash to spare, and advanced bookings, you'll find Namibia's lodges, camps and guest farms cost a fraction of the price of similar places elsewhere in southern Africa. Here you can afford comfort and expert guides who will help you discover their own areas, instructing you in everything from tracking black rhino to understanding the native flora.

Over the last 14 years I've been lucky enough to make dozens of trips back to Namibia. I've watched tourism gradually develop and change – and on the whole it's done so positively. While there are more visitors now, these are exploring more destinations within Namibia, so the country still seems empty. There are many new lodges and guest farms, but these are spread widely and most remain small, offering personal attention and unique attractions. Namibia is still not a mass-market destination, and there's no sign that it will be.

The contribution to the economy made by visitors is increasing, and the government recognises its importance – which is vital if the wild areas that attract visitors are to be conserved. Namibia's villagers, too, are benefiting from tourism. The Kaokoveld, in particular, is home to some thriving community projects – successes that are rare in most parts of Africa. Elsewhere, new conservancies are sprouting up, where neighbouring farms join forces and return wild game to their land, replacing domestic animals.

Just as Namibia is evolving, so are the ways to travel. Until recently, flying around was strictly the preserve of those who could afford to charter their own plane. They knew that Namibia's landscapes are often most spectacular from the air, and that flying around gives a whole new perspective on the country. Now it's becoming less expensive, with tour operators tailor-making fly-in trips around the country, and charging per seat, not per plane. These hops between lodges remain more costly than driving, but they are breathtaking, and allow easy access to even the remotest corners of the Skeleton Coast and Kaokoveld.

So Namibia and trips there are changing. But every time I go, I am again surprised at how easy the travelling is, and how remarkable the country.

THE NEXT EDITION

Our readers play a vital part in updating books for the next edition. If you have found changes, or have a story to tell, do write. The most helpful contributions will receive a free guide of their choice. Write to:

Namibia, Bradt Travel Guides, 19 High Street, Chalfont St Peter, Bucks SL9 9QE, UK; email: info@bradt-travelguides.com

The author can be emailed directly on africa@sunvil.co.uk

Part One

General Information

NAMIBIA AT A GLANCE

Location Southwest Africa, astride the Tropic of Capricorn and beside the South Atlantic Ocean. Its main borders are with South Africa, Botswana, and Angola, though it also adjoins Zambia.

Size 824,292km^2

Climate Subtropical desert climate

Time GMT +2

Electricity 220 volts

Weights and measures Metric

International telephone code +264

Status Republic

GDP $6,600 per capita (2000)

Currency Namibian dollar (N$), equivalent to South African rand. £1 = N$14.00; US$1 = N$8.50, €1 = N$9.10 (February 2003)

Population 1,827,000 (2001)

Population growth per year just under 3%

Life expectancy in years at birth 65

Economy Major earners: mining, including uranium, diamonds and other minerals; agriculture; tourism

Capital Windhoek

Main towns Swakopmund, Walvis Bay, Lüderitz

Language English (official), Afrikaans, German, several ethnic languages (most in Bantu and Khoisan language groups)

Religion Christianity; traditional beliefs

Flag Diagonal red stripe bordered by narrow white stripes separates two triangles – one green, one blue with a yellow sun motif.

Public holidays New Year's Day (January 1), Independence Day (March 21), Good Friday, Easter Monday, Workers' Day (May 1), Cassinga Day (May 4), Africa Day (May 25), Ascension Day (40 days after Easter Sunday), Heroes' Day (August 26), Human Rights Day (December 10), Christmas Day (December 25), Family Day (December 26)

History and Economy

HISTORY
Pre-history
Namibia's earliest inhabitants

Palaeontologists looking for evidence of the first ancestors of the human race have excavated a number of sites in southern Africa. The earliest remains yet identified are Stone-Age tools dated at about 200,000 years old, which have been recovered in gravel deposits around what is now the Victoria Falls. It is thought that these probably belong to *Homo erectus*, whose hand-axes have been dated in Tanzania to half a million years old. These were hunter-gatherer people, who could use fire, make tools, and had probably developed some simple speech.

Experts divide the Stone Age into the middle, early, and late Stone Ages. The transition from early to middle Stone-Age technology – which is indicated by a larger range of stone tools often adapted for particular uses, and signs that these people had a greater mastery of their environment – was probably in progress around 125,000 years ago in southern Africa. The late Stone Age is characterised by people who used composite tools, those made of wood and/or bone and/or stone used together, and by the presence of a revolutionary invention: the bow and arrow. This first probably appeared about 15,000 years ago, by which time the original Namibians were already roaming the plains of Damaraland and painting on the rocks at Twyfelfontein.

Africa's iron age

Around 3000BC, late Stone-Age hunter-gatherer groups in Ethiopia, and elsewhere in north and west Africa, started to keep domestic animals, sow seeds, and harvest the produce: they became the world's first farmers.

By around 1000BC these new pastoral practices had spread south into the equatorial forests of what is now Congo, to around Lake Victoria, and into the northern area of the Great Rift Valley, in northern Tanzania. However, agriculture did not spread south into the rest of central/southern Africa immediately. Only when the technology, and the tools, of iron-working became known did the practices start their relentless expansion southwards.

The spread of agriculture and iron-age culture seems to have been a rapid move. It was brought south by Bantu-speaking Africans who were taller and heavier than the existing Khoisan-speaking inhabitants of southern Africa.

Bantu colonisation
Khoisan coexistence

By around the time of Christ, the hunter-gatherers in Namibia seem to have been joined by pastoralists, the Khoi-khoi (or Nama people), who used a similar language involving clicks. Both belong to the Khoisan language family, as distinct from the Bantu language family. These were pastoralists who combined keeping sheep, goats and cattle with foraging.

These stock animals are not native to southern Africa and it seems likely that some Khoisan hunters and gatherers acquired stock, and the expertise to keep them, from early Bantu tribes in the Zimbabwe area. As the Bantu spread south, into the relatively fertile Natal area, the Khoisan pastoralists spread west, across the Kalahari into Namibia. Their traditional gathering knowledge, and ability to survive on existing plant foods, meant that they didn't depend entirely on their stock. Hence they could expand across areas of poor grazing which would have defeated the less flexible Bantu.

By around the 9th century another group, the Damara, are recognised as living in Namibia and speaking a Khoisan language. They cultivated more than the Nama, and hence were more settled. Their precise origin is hotly debated, as they have many features common to people of Bantu origin and yet speak a Khoisan language.

The first Bantu people

By the 16th century the first of the Bantu-speaking peoples arrived from the east, the Herero people. Oral tradition suggests that they came south from East Africa's great lakes to Zambia, across Angola, arriving at the Kunene River around 1550. However they got here, they settled with their cattle in the north of the country and the plains of the Kaokoveld. (Note that the Himba people living in the Kaokoveld today are a sub-group of the Herero, speaking the same language.)

Where the Herero settled, the existing people clearly had to change. Some intermarried with the incoming groups; some may even have been enslaved by the newcomers. A few could shift their lifestyles to take advantage of new opportunities created by the Herero, and an unfortunate fourth group (the Bushmen of the time) started to become marginalised, remaining in areas with less agricultural potential. This was the start of a poor relationship between the cattle-herding Herero and the Bushmen.

These iron-working, cattle-herding Herero people were very successful, and as they thrived, so they began to expand their herds southwards and into central Namibia.

The early explorers

Meanwhile, in the 15th century, trade between Europe and the East opened up sea routes along the Namibian coast and around the Cape of Good Hope. The first Europeans recorded as stepping on Namibian soil were the Portuguese in 1485. Diego Cão stopped briefly at Cape Cross on the Skeleton Coast and erected a limestone cross. On December 8 1487, Bartholomeu Diaz reached Walvis Bay and then continued south to what is now Lüderitz. However, the coast was so totally barren and uninviting that even though the Portuguese had already settled in Angola, and the Dutch in the Cape, little interest was shown in Namibia.

It was only in the latter half of the 18th century when British, French and American whalers began to make use of the ports of Lüderitz and Walvis Bay, that the Dutch authorities in the Cape decided in 1793 to take possession of Walvis Bay – the only good deepwater port on the coast. A few years later, France invaded Holland, prompting England to seize control of the Cape Colony and, with it, Walvis Bay.

Even then, little was known about the interior. It wasn't until the middle of the 19th century that explorers, missionaries and traders started to venture inland, with Francis Galton and Charles John Andersson leading the way.

THE OORLAM PEOPLE

Originating from the Cape, the Oorlam people were a variety of different groups, all speaking Khoisan languages, who left the Cape because of European expansion there. Some were outlaws, others wanted space far from the Europeans. Many broke away from fixed Nama settlements to join roving Oorlam bands, led by *kapteins* – groups which would hunt, trade, and steal for survival.

Oorlam incursions

By the latter half of the 18th century, the Dutch settlers in the Cape of South Africa were not only expanding rapidly into the interior, but they were also effectively waging war on any of the indigenous people who stood in their way. In *Africa: A Biography of a Continent*, John Reader (see *Further Reading*) comments:

> Khoisan resistance hardened as the frontier advanced during the 18th century. [The] Government [of the Cape's] edicts empowered [commando groups of settlers]... to wage war against all the region's Khoisan, who were now to be regarded as vermin. Slaughter was widespread. Official records show that commandos killed 503 Khoisan in 1774 alone, and 2,480 between 1786 and 1795. The number of killings that passed unrecorded can only be guessed at.

By 1793 the settler population in the Cape totalled 13,830 people, who between them owned 14,747 slaves.

With this pressure from the south, it is no wonder that mobile, dispossessed bands of Khoisan, known as Oorlam groups, pressed northwards over the Orange River and into southern Namibia. They often had guns and horses, and had learned some of the European's ways. However, they still spoke a Khoisan language, and were of the same origins as the Nama pastoralists who had already settled in southern Namibia.

At that time, the Nama in southern Namibia seem to have been settled into a life of relatively peaceful, pastoral coexistence. Thus the arrival of a few Oorlam groups was not a problem. However, around the start of the 19th century more Oorlams came, putting more pressure on the land, and soon regular skirmishes were a feature of the area.

In 1840 the increasingly unsettled situation was calmed by an agreement between the two paramount chiefs: Chief Oaseb of the Nama, and Jonker Afrikaner of the Oorlam people. There was already much intermingling of the two groups, and so accommodating each other made sense – especially given the expansion of Herero groups further north.

The deal split the lands of southern Namibia between the various Nama and Oorlam groups, whilst giving the land between the Kuiseb and the Swakop rivers to the Oorlams. Further, Jonker Afrikaner was given rights over the people north of the Kuiseb, up to Waterberg.

Nama–Herero conflict

By around the middle of the 18th century, the Herero people had expanded beyond Kaokoland, spreading at least as far south as the Swakop River. Their expansion south was now effectively blocked by Oorlam groups, led by Jonker Afrikaner, who won several decisive battles against Herero people around 1835 – resulting in his Afrikaner followers stealing many Herero cattle, and becoming the dominant power in central Namibia. From 1840, Jonker Afrikaner and his Oorlam followers created a buffer zone between the Hereros expanding from the north, and the relatively stable Nama groups in the south.

European colonisation
The missionaries

In the early 1800s, missionaries were gradually moving into southern Namibia. The London Missionary Society and the German Rhenish and Finnish Lutheran Mission societies were all represented. These were important for several reasons. Firstly, they tended to settle in one place, which became the nucleus around which the local Nama people would permanently settle. Often the missionaries would introduce the local people to different ways of cultivation: a further influence to settle in permanent villages, which gradually became larger.

Secondly, they acted as a focal point for traders, who would navigate through the territory from one mission to the next. This effectively set up Namibia's first trade routes – routes that soon became conduits for the local Nama groups to obtain European goods, from guns and ammunition to alcohol. It seems that the missionaries sometimes provided firearms directly to the local people for protection. Whilst understandable, the net effect was that the whole area became a more dangerous place.

In 1811, Reverend Heinrich Schmelen founded Bethanie, and more missions followed. By December 1842, Rhenish missionaries were established where Windhoek now stands, surrounded by about 1,000 of Jonker Afrikaner's followers. The settlement soon started trading with the coast, and within a few years there was a steady supply of guns arriving.

Nama conflict

In 1861 Jonker Afrikaner died, whilst returning from a raid he had mounted on the Owambo people (a group of Bantu origin who had settled in the far north of the country and displaced some of the Hereros). Jonker's death left a power vacuum in central Namibia.

There were many skirmishes for control during the rest of the 1860s, and much politicking and switching of alliances between the rival Nama groups (some of Oorlam descent). The main protagonists included the Witboois from around Gibeon, the Afrikaners based in Windhoek, the Swartboois, the Blondelswarts, the Topnaar and the Red Nation.

The traders

By around 1850 many hunters and traders were penetrating Namibia's interior, in search of adventure and profit – usually in the form of ivory and ostrich feathers. Amongst these, Charles John Andersson was particularly important, both for his own role in shaping events, and also for the clear documentation that he left behind, including the fascinating books *Lake Ngami* and *The River Okavango* (see *Further Reading*) – chronicling his great journeys of the late 1850s.

In 1860 he bought up the assets of a mining company, and set up a centre for trading at Otjimbingwe, a very strategic position on the Swakop River, halfway between Walvis Bay and Windhoek. (Now it is at the crossroads of the D1953 and the D1976.) In the early 1860s he traded with the Nama groups in the area, and started to open up routes into the Herero lands further north and east. However, after losing cattle to a Nama raid in 1861, he recruited hunters (some the contemporary equivalent of mercenaries) to expand his operations and protect his interests.

In 1863 the eldest son of Jonker Afrikaner led a foolish raid on Otjimbingwe. He was defeated and killed by Andersson's men, adding to the leadership crisis amongst the Nama groups. By 1864 Andersson had formed an alliance with the paramount Herero chief, Kamaherero, and together they led a large army into battle with the Afrikaner Namas at Windhoek. This was indecisive, but did clearly mark the end of Nama domination of central Namibia, as well as inflicting a wound on Andersson from which he never fully recovered.

The peace of 1870

During the late 1860s the centre of Namibia was often in a state of conflict. The Hereros under Kamaherero were vying for control with the various Nama clans, as Charles Andersson and his traders became increasingly important by forming and breaking alliances with them all.

After several defeats, the Nama kaptein Jan Jonker led an army of Afrikaners to Okahandja in 1870 to make peace with Kamaherero. This was brokered by the German Wesleyan missionary Hugo Hahn – who had arrived in Windhoek in 1844, but been replaced swiftly after Jonker Afrikaner had complained about him, and requested his replacement by his missionary superiors.

This treaty effectively subdued the Afrikaners, and Hahn also included a provision for the Basters, who had migrated recently from the Cape, to settle at Rehoboth. The Afrikaners were forced to abandon Windhoek, and Herero groups occupied the area. Thus the Basters around Rehoboth effectively became the buffer between the Herero groups to the north, and the Namas to the south.

The 1870s was a relatively peaceful era, which enabled the missionaries and, especially, the various traders to extend their influence throughout the centre of the country. This most affected the Nama groups in the south, who began to trade more and more with the Cape. Guns, alcohol, coffee, sugar, beads, materials and much else flowed in. To finance these imports, local Nama chiefs and kapteins charged traders and hunters to cross their territory, and granted them licences to exploit the wildlife.

The Hereros, too, traded; but mainly for guns. Their social system valued cattle most highly, and so breeding bigger herds meant more to them than the new Western goods. Thus they emerged into the 1880s stronger than before, whilst the power of many of the Nama groups had waned.

The scramble for Africa

In the last few decades of the 19th century the Portuguese, the British, the French, and Leopold II of Belgium were starting to embark on the famous 'Scramble for Africa'. Germany had long eschewed the creation of colonies, and Bismarck is widely quoted as stating: 'So long as I am Chancellor we shan't pursue a colonial policy.'

However, in March 1878 the English government of South Africa's Cape formally annexed an enclave around Walvis Bay. (The British had been asked earlier by missionaries to help instil order in the heartland of Namibia, but they didn't feel that it was worth the effort.)

In late 1883 a German merchant called Adolf Lüderitz started to buy land on the coast. He established the town named Lüderitzbucht – usually referred to now as Lüderitz – and began trading with the local Nama groups. (It was news of this act that was said to have finally prompted Britain to make Bechuanaland a protectorate.)

Faced with much internal pressure, Bismarck reversed his policy in May 1884. He dispatched a gunboat to Lüderitz and in July claimed Togo and Cameroon as colonies. By August Britain had agreed to Germany's claims on Lüderitz, from which sprang the German colony of South West Africa. Lüderitz itself was bought out a few years later by the newly formed German Colonial Company for South West Africa, and shortly after that the administration of the area was transferred directly to Germany's control.

In May 1884, Portugal proposed an international conference to address the territorial conflicts of the colonial powers in the Congo. This was convened in Berlin, with no Africans present, and over the next few years the colonial powers parcelled Africa up and split it between them. Amongst many territorial dealings, mostly involving pen-and-ruler decisions on the map of Africa, a clearly defined border between Britain's new protectorate of Bechuanaland and Germany's South West Africa was established in 1890 – and Britain ceded a narrow corridor of land to Germany. This was subsequently named after the German Chancellor, Count von Caprivi, as the Caprivi Strip.

German South West Africa

After a decade of relative peace, the 1880s brought problems to central Namibia again, with fighting between the Hereros, the Basters, and various Nama groups, notably the Afrikaners and the Swartboois. However, with German annexation in 1884 a new power had arrived. For the first five years, the official German presence in South West Africa was limited to a few officials stationed at Otjimbingwe. However, they had begun the standard colonial tactic of exploiting small conflicts by encouraging the local leaders to sign 'protection' treaties with Germany.

The Hereros, under chief Maherero, signed in 1885, after which the German Commissioner Göring wrote to Hendrik Witbooi – the leader of the Witbooi Namas who occupied territory from Gibeon to Gobabis – insisting that he desist from attacking the Hereros, who were now under German protection. Witbooi wrote to Maherero, to dissuade him from making a 'pact with the devil' – he was, perhaps, ahead of his time in seeing this German move as an opening gambit in their bid for total control of Namibia.

In 1889 the first 21 German soldiers, *Schutztruppe*, arrived. More followed in 1890, by which time they had established a fort in Windhoek. That same year Maherero died, which enabled the German authorities to increase their influence in the internal politics of succession which brought Samuel Maherero to be paramount chief of the Herero. By 1892 the first contingent of settlers (over 50 people) had made their homes in Windhoek.

A fair trade?

The 1890s and early 1900s saw a gradual erosion of the power and wealth of all Namibia's existing main groups in favour of the Germans. Gradually traders and adventurers bought more and more land from both Nama and the Herero, aided by credit-in-advance agreements. A rinderpest outbreak in 1897 decimated the Herero's herds, and land sales were the obvious way to repay their debts. Gradually the Herero lost their lands and tension grew. The Rhenish Missionary Society saw the evil, and pressurised the German government to create areas where the Herero *could not* sell their land. Small enclaves were thus established, but these didn't address the wider issues.

The 20th century
Namibian war of resistance 1904–07

As land was progressively bought up, or sometimes simply taken from the local inhabitants by colonists, various skirmishes and small uprisings developed. The largest started in October 1903 with the Blondelswarts near Warmbad, which distracted most of the German Schutztruppe in the south. See *Further Reading* for details of Mark Cocker's excellent *Rivers of Blood, Rivers of Gold* which gives a full account of this war.

The Herero nation had become increasingly unhappy about its loss of land, and in January 1904 Samuel Maherero ordered a Herero uprising against the German colonial forces. Initially he was clear to exclude as targets Boer and English settlers and German women and children. Simultaneously he appealed to Hendrik Witbooi, and other Nama leaders, to join battle – they, however, stayed out of the fight.

Initially the Hereros had success in taking many German farms and smaller outposts, and in severing the railway line between Swakopmund and Windhoek. However, later in 1904, the German General Leutwein was replaced by von Trotha – who had a reputation for brutal oppression after his time in East Africa. Backed by domestic German opinion demanding a swift resolution, von Trotha led a large German force including heavy artillery against the Hereros. By August 1904 the Hereros were pushed back to their stronghold of Waterberg, with its permanent waterholes. On August 11, the Germans attacked, and the battle raged all day. Though not decisive, the Hereros' spirit was beaten by the superior firepower and they fled east, into the Kalahari. Many perished. Sources conflict about exactly how many Hereros lost their lives, but the battle at Waterberg certainly broke their resistance to the Germans.

Thereafter, somewhat late to be effective, Hendrik Witbooi's people also revolted against the Germans, and wrote encouraging the other Nama groups to do the same. The Red Nation, Topnaar, Swartbooi and Blondelswarts joined in attacking the Germans, though the latter were largely incapacitated after their battles the previous year. The Basters stayed out of the fight.

For several years these Nama groups waged an effective guerrilla campaign against the colonial forces, using the waterless sands of the Kalahari as a haven in which the German troops were ineffective. However, in 1905 Hendrik Witbooi was killed, and January 1907 saw the last fighters sue for peace.

German consolidation

With South West Africa under stable German control, there was an influx of German settler families and the colony began to develop rapidly. The settlers were given large plots of the country's most productive lands, the railway network was expanded, and many of the towns began to grow. The non-European Namibians were increasingly marginalised, and simply used as a source of labour.

The building of the railway to Lüderitz led to the discovery of diamonds around there in 1908, and the resulting boom encouraged an influx of prospectors and German opportunists. By that time the mine at Tsumeb was already thriving, and moving its copper produce south on the newly built railway.

The German settlers thrived until the declaration of World War I, and between 1907 and 1914 the colonists were granted self-rule from Germany, a number of the main towns were declared as municipalities, and many of Namibia's existing civic buildings were constructed.

World War I

At the onset of World War I, Britain encouraged South Africa to push north and wrest German South West Africa from the Germans. In July 1915, the German Colonial troops surrendered to South African forces at Khorab – a memorial now marks the spot. At the end of the war, Namibia became a League of Nations 'trust territory', assigned to the Union of South Africa as 'a sacred trust in the name of civilisation' to 'promote to the utmost the material and moral well-being of its inhabitants'. The Caprivi Strip was incorporated back into Bechuanaland (though it was returned 20 years later).

The final colonists
South African rule
After overcoming their initial differences, new colonists from South Africa and the existing German colonists soon discovered a common interest – the unabashed exploitation of the native population whose well-being they were supposed to be protecting.

Gradually more and more of the land in central Namibia was given to settler families, often Boers from South Africa rather than Germans from Europe. The native population was restricted to various 'native areas' – usually poor land which couldn't be easily farmed by the settlers: Bushmanland and Hereroland in the Kalahari, Damaraland and Kaokoland bordering on the Namib. Much of the rest of the black population was confined to a strip of land in the north, as far from South Africa as possible, to serve as a reservoir of cheap labour for the mines – which South Africa was developing to extract the country's mineral wealth.

In 1947, after World War II, South Africa formally announced to the United Nations its intention to annex the territory. The UN, which had inherited responsibility for the League of Nations trust territories, opposed the plan, arguing that 'the African inhabitants of South West Africa have not yet achieved political autonomy'. Until 1961, the UN insisted on this point. Year after year it was systematically ignored by South Africa's regime.

The struggle for independence
Between 1961 and 1968, the UN tried to annul the trusteeship and establish Namibia's independence. Legal pressure, however, was ineffective and some of the Namibian people led by the South West African People's Organisation (SWAPO) chose to fight for their freedom with arms. The first clashes occurred on August 26 1966.

In 1968, the UN finally declared the South African occupation of the country as illegal and changed its name to Namibia. Efforts by the majority of the UN General Assembly to enforce this condemnation with economic sanctions were routinely vetoed by the Western powers of the Security Council – they had vested interests in the multinational companies in Namibia and would stand to lose from the implementation of sanctions.

The independence of Angola in 1975 affected Namibia's struggle for freedom, by providing SWAPO guerrillas with a friendly rearguard. As a consequence the guerrilla war was stepped up, resulting in increased political pressure on South Africa. But strong internal economic factors also played heavily in the political arena. Up to independence, the *status quo* had preserved internal inequalities and privileges. Black Africans (90% of the population) consumed only 12.8% of the Gross Domestic Product (GDP). Meanwhile the inhabitants of European origin (10% of the population) received 81.5% of the GDP. Three-quarters of the agricultural production was in the hands of white farmers. Although average per-capita income was (and remains) one of the highest in Africa, whites earned on average over 17 times more than blacks. The white population clearly feared they had a great deal to lose if a majority government came to power and addressed itself to these racially-based inequalities.

However, external South African economic factors had perhaps the greatest effect in blocking Namibian independence. South African and multinational companies dominated the Namibian economy and carried massive political influence. Prior to independence, the Consolidated Diamond Mines Company (a subsidiary of Anglo-American) contributed in taxes 40% of South Africa's administrative budget in Namibia. Multinationals benefited from extremely generous facilities granted to them by the South African administration in Namibia. According to one estimate, the independence of Namibia would represent costs for South Africa of US$240 million in lost exports, and additional outlays of US$144 million to import foreign products.

In South Africa the official government view stressed the danger that a SWAPO government might present to Namibia's minority tribes (since SWAPO membership is drawn almost exclusively from the Owambo ethnic group), whilst taking few serious steps towards a negotiated settlement for Namibian independence.

On the military side, South Africa stepped up its campaign against SWAPO, even striking at bases in southern Angola. It also supported Jonas Savimbi's UNITA (National Union for the Total Independence of Angola) forces in their struggle against the Soviet/Cuban-backed MPLA (Popular Movement for the Liberation of Angola) government in Luanda. Meanwhile, Cuban troops poured into Angola and aggravated the situation further by threatening the South African forces in Namibia.

Resolution 435

On the diplomatic front, a proposal (Resolution 435) put forward by the UN security council called for, amongst other things, the cessation of hostilities, the return of refugees, the repeal of discriminatory legislation and the holding of UN-supervised elections. South Africa blocked this by tying any such agreement to the withdrawal of Cuban troops from Angola, and demanding guarantees that its investments in Namibia would not be affected. SWAPO refused to agree to special benefits for the European population and other minority groups, nor would it accept predetermined limitations to constitutional change following independence.

By 1987, all the states involved in the conflict were showing clear signs of wanting an end to hostilities. After 14 years of uninterrupted war, Angola's economy was on the brink of collapse. (The war is calculated to have cost the country US$13 billion.) On the other side, South Africa's permanent harassment of Angola, and military occupation of Namibia were costing the regime dearly both economically and diplomatically.

In December 1988, after prolonged US-mediated negotiations, an agreement was reached between South Africa, Angola and Cuba for a phased withdrawal of Cuban troops from Angola to be linked to the withdrawal of South African troops from Namibia and the implementation of Resolution 435.

Independence

The independence process began on April 1 1989, and was achieved with the help of the United Nations Transition Assistance Group (UNTAG). This consisted of some 7,000 people from 110 countries who worked from nearly 200 locations within the country to ensure free and fair elections and as smooth a transition period to independence as was possible.

In November 1989, 710,000 Namibians (a 97% turn-out) voted in the members of the National Assembly which would draft the country's first constitution. SWAPO won decisively, but without the two-thirds majority it needed to write the nation's constitution single-handedly, thereby allaying the fears of Namibia's minorities. The 72 elected members (68 men and four women) of the Constituent Assembly, representing between them seven different political parties, soon reached agreement on a constitution for the new Namibia, which was subsequently hailed as one of the world's most democratic. Finally, at 00.20 on March 21 1990, I watched as the Namibian flag replaced South Africa's over Windhoek, witnessed by Pérez de Cuéllar, the UN Secretary-General, F W de Klerk, the South African President and Sam Nujoma, Namibia's first president.

The country's mood was peaceful and, on the day, ecstatic. There was a tremendous feeling of optimism, as (arguably) Africa's last colonial territory had earned its independence – after sustained diplomatic pressure and a bitter liberation struggle that stretched back to the turn of the century.

Politics since independence

Since the start there has been every indication that Namibia would stand by its constitution and develop into a peaceful and prosperous state. Walvis Bay, previously disputed by South Africa, was transferred to Windhoek's control on February 28 1994, and its relations with neighbouring countries remain good.

In December 1994 general elections for the National Assembly returned SWAPO to power, with 53 out of 72 seats, and extended Sam Nujoma's presidency for a further five years. The main opposition continues to be the Democratic Turnhalle Alliance (DTA), although it is still haunted by the stigma of its co-operation with the former South African regime.

GOVERNMENT

The Republic of Namibia's modern constitution, adopted on independence in 1990, was hailed as one of the world's most democratic. Its entrenched Bill of Rights provides for freedom of speech, press, assembly, association and religion. It also set up a bicameral Westminster-style parliament, with a strong executive and independent judiciary.

General elections for the first House of Parliament, the National Assembly, are held every five years. The members of the second House of Parliament, the National Council, are drawn from 13 Regional Councils, which are elected every six years. The constitution limits the president to a maximum of two terms of office.

ECONOMY

Before independence, the South African administration controlled the economy along traditional colonial lines. The country produced goods it did not consume but imported everything it needed, including food. Namibia still exports maize, meat and fish, and imports rice and wheat. However, although about 60% of the workforce is employed in agriculture, the country's commercial agriculture is limited by water, while large sections of wetter northern regions are already farmed intensively by subsistence farmers.

Namibia inherited a well-developed infrastructure and considerable remaining mineral wealth. Mining is the mainstay of the economy, accounting for about 25% of the country's GDP. There are important reserves of uranium, lead, zinc, tin, silver, copper and tungsten, as well as very rich deposits of alluvial diamonds. There are plans, too, to tap into the Kudu gas field, in the South Atlantic Ocean off Namibia's southern coast.

THE GUANO TRADE

A poem quoted in *The River Okavango* by CJ Andersson:

There's an island that lies on West Africa's shore,
Where penguins have lived since the flood or before,
And raised up a hill there, a mile high or more.
This hill is all guano, and lately 'tis shown,
That finer potatoes and turnips are grown,
By means of this compost, than ever were known;
And the peach and the nectarine, the apple, the pear,
Attain such a size that the gardeners stare,
And cry, "Well! I never saw fruit like that 'ere!"
One cabbage thus reared, as a paper maintains,
Weighed twenty-one stone, thirteen pounds and six grains,
So no wonder Guano celebrity gains.

Tourism also plays an important role in the formal economy. Tourism to Namibia remains small-scale, but has been growing steadily by about 15% per year since 1993. Statistics for arrivals from overseas in 1997 indicate about 28,000 visitors from the UK, 14,000 from the USA, and 80,000 from Germany. Namibia has tremendous potential for sustained growth in tourism, provided the increases are steady and well managed.

Namibia's main attractions for visitors are stunning scenery, pristine wilderness areas and first-class wildlife. As long as the country remains safe and its wilderness areas are maintained, then the country's potential for quality tourism is unrivalled in Africa. Already tourism is a powerful earner of foreign exchange and a vital support for numerous local community development schemes.

Economically, Namibia remains dependent on South Africa; its other main trading partners are Germany, Switzerland and the UK.

Since the country is still establishing its own industries, it meets most if its needs for manufactured goods by importing them from South Africa. Realistically, the economy is likely to stay closely involved with that of South Africa, especially while Namibia continues to peg its currency to the value of the South African rand.

The revenue and foreign exchange from mining provides the financial muscle for the government's agenda. The government is developing structural changes to make the economy more equitable, and to diversify its components. Better living conditions for the majority of Namibians are being realised by increasing the productivity of the subsistence areas, particularly in the populated north. However, there remains an enormous gap between the rich and the poor, which must be closed if the country is to have a secure and prosperous future.

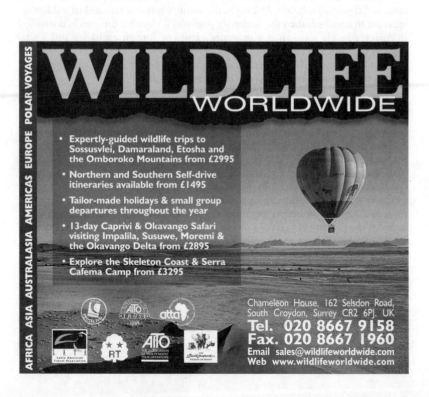

People and Culture

PEOPLE
The population
Recent statistics (the preliminary findings of the 2001 census) suggest that Namibia's population stands at about 1,827,000 and has increased by around 29% over the last decade. That's a growth rate of a little less than 3% per year. If this rate continues, the population can be expected to be over 3 million by around 2020. The population is densest in the north (near the Angolan border), where rainfall is heaviest.

About 44% of Namibia's population is under 15 years of age, whilst only 4% is over 65.

Statistics indicate that the average life expectancy for a Namibian is 65 years. Around 86% of the population is black African in origin, and the remaining 14% is mostly of European or mixed race.

Namibia's doctor/patient ratio is one of the best in Africa, with one doctor for every 3,650 people. There are about five hospital beds per 1,000 people, which is the third best ratio in Africa.

However, the statistics say nothing of the charm of many Namibians, and if you venture into the rural areas you will often find that Namibians are curious about you. Chat to them openly and you will find most to be delightful. They will be pleased to help you where they can, and as keen to help you learn about them and their country as they are interested in your lifestyle and what brings you to their country.

A note on 'tribes'
The people of Africa are often viewed, from abroad, as belonging to a multitude of culturally and linguistically distinct 'tribes' – which are often portrayed as being at odds with each other. Whilst there is certainly an enormous variety of different ethnic groups in Africa, most are closely related to their neighbours in terms of language, beliefs and way of life. Modern historians eschew the simplistic tags of 'tribes', noting that such groupings change with time.

Sometimes the word tribe is used to describe a group of people who all speak the same language; it may be used to mean those who follow a particular leader or to refer to all the inhabitants of a certain area at a given time. In any case, 'tribe' is a vague word that is used differently for different purposes. The term 'clan' (blood relations) is a smaller, more precisely defined, unit – though rather too precise for our broad discussions here.

Certainly groups of people or clans who share similar languages and cultural beliefs do band together and often, in time, develop 'tribal' identities. However, it is wrong to then extrapolate and assume that their ancestors will have had the same groupings and allegiances centuries ago.

In Africa, as elsewhere in the world, history is recorded by the winners. Here the winners, the ruling class, may be the descendants of a small group of intruders who achieved dominance over a larger, long-established community. Over the years, the history of that ruling class (the winners) usually becomes regarded as the history of the whole community, or tribe. Two 'tribes' have thus become one, with one history – which will reflect the origins of that small group of intruders, and not the ancestors of the majority of the current tribe.

Ethnic groups

When the colonial powers carved up Africa, the divisions between the countries bore virtually no resemblance to the traditional areas of the various ethnic groups, many of which therefore ended up split between two or more countries. As you will see, there are cultural differences between the groups in different parts of Namibia, but they are only a little more pronounced than those between the states of the USA, or the regions of the (relatively tiny) UK.

There continues to be a great deal of inter-marriage and mixing of these various peoples and cultures – perhaps more so than there has ever been, because of the efficiency of modern transport systems. Generally, there is very little friction between these communities (whose boundaries, as we have said, are indistinct) and Namibia's various peoples live peacefully together.

In Namibia, which is typical of any large African country, historians identify numerous ethnic groups. The main ones are detailed below, arranged alphabetically. Apart from Afrikaans, their languages fall into two main families: Khoisan and Bantu. The population sizes given are based on surveys done during the 1980s, and adjusted according to estimated average growth rates since then.

Basters

These Afrikaans-speaking people are descendants of indigenous Hottentot women and the Dutch settlers who first arrived at the Cape in the early 17th century. The original 'coloured' or 'bastard' children found themselves rejected by both the white and the black communities in the Cape, so keeping together they relocated themselves further north away from the colonialists. Proudly calling themselves 'Basters', they set up farming communities and developed their own distinct social and cultural structures.

During the 1860s, white settlers began to push into these areas so, to avoid confrontation, the Basters crossed the Orange River in 1868 and moved northwards once again. Trying to keep out of the way of the warring Hereros and Namas, they founded Rehoboth in 1871 and set up their own system of government under a Kaptein (headman) and a Volksraad (legislative council). Their support of the German colonial troops during the tribal uprisings brought them later protection and privileges.

Demands for self-rule and independence were repressed throughout this century until the Rehoboth Gebiet was granted the status of an independent state in the 1970s. This move by the South African administration was made with the aim of reinforcing racial divisions amongst the non-whites – rather like in the South African 'independent homelands'.

Today, Namibia's Basters still have a strong sense of identity and make up just under 3% of the population. Most still live and work as stock or crop farmers in the good cattle-grazing land around Rehoboth. Their traditional crafts include products like karosses (blankets), rugs, wall-hangings and cushion covers made of cured skins.

Bushmen

There is not another social/language group on this planet which has been studied, written about, filmed and researched more than the Bushmen, or San, of the

Kalahari, although they currently comprise only about 3% of Namibia's population. Despite this, or indeed because of it, popular conceptions about them, fed by their image in the media, are often strikingly out of step with the realities. Thus they warrant a separate section devoted to them here.

The aim of these next few pages is to try and explain some of the roots of the misconceptions, to look at some of the realities, and to make you think. Although I have spent a lot of time with Bushmen in the Kalahari, it is difficult to separate fact from oft-repeated, glossy fiction. If parts of this discussion seem disparate, it's a reflection of this difficulty.

Recent scientific observations on the Khoisan

Our view of the Bushmen is partly informed by some basic anthropological and linguistic research, mostly applying to the Khoisan, which is worth outlining to set the scene.

Anthropology

The first fossil records that we have of our human ancestors date back to at least about 60,000 years ago in East Africa. These are likely to have been the ancestors of everyone living today.

Archaeological finds from parts of the Kalahari show that human beings have lived here for at least 40,000 years. These are generally agreed to have been the ancestors of the modern Khoisan peoples living in Botswana today. (The various peoples of the Khoi and the Bushmen are known collectively as the Khoisan. All have relatively light golden brown skin, almond shaped eyes and high cheekbones. Their stature is generally small and slight, and they are now found across southern Africa.)

Language research

Linguists have grouped all the world's languages into around 20 linguistic families. Of these, four are very different from the rest. All these four are African families – and they include the Khoisan and the Niger-Congo (Bantu) languages.

This is amongst the evidence that has led linguists to believe that human language evolved in Africa, and further analysis has suggested that this was probably amongst the ancestors of the Khoisan.

The Khoisan languages are distinguished by their wide repertoire of clicking sounds. Don't mistake these for simple: they are very sophisticated. It was observed by Dunbar (see *Further Reading*) that, 'From the phonetic point of view these [the Khoisan languages] are the world's most complex languages. To speak one of them fluently is to exploit human phonetic ability to the full.'

At some point the Khoisan languages diverged from a common ancestor, and today three distinct groups exist: the northern, central and southern groups. Languages gradually evolve and change as different groups of people split up and move to new areas, isolated from their old contacts. Thus the evolution of each language is specific to each group, and reflected in the classifications described later in this chapter.

According to Michael Main (see *Further Reading*), the northern group are San and today they live west of the Okavango and north of Ghanzi, with representatives found as far afield as Angola. The southern group are also San, who live in the area between Kang and Bokspits in Botswana. The central group is Khoe, living in central Botswana, and extending north to the eastern Okavango and Kasane, and west into Namibia, where they are known as the Nama.

Each of these three Khoisan language groups has many dialects. These have some similarities, but they are not closely related, and some are different to the point where there is no mutual understanding. Certain dialects are so restricted that only a small family group speaks them; it was reported recently that one San language died out completely with the death of the last speaker.

This huge number of dialects, and variation in languages, reflects the relative isolation of the various speakers, most of whom now live in small family groups as the Kalahari's arid environment cannot sustain large groups of people living together in one place as hunter-gatherers.

In Namibia, the three main groups are the Haixom in the northern districts of Otavi, Tsumeb and Grootfontein; the !Kung in Bushmanland; and the Mbarankwengo in west Caprivi.

Genetic discoveries

Most genetically normal men have an X- and a Y-chromosome, whilst women have two X-chromosomes. Unlike the other 22 pairs of (non-sex) chromosomes that each human has, there is no opportunity for the Y-chromosome to 'swap' or 'share' its DNA with any other chromosome. Thus all the information in a man's Y chromosome will usually be passed on, without change, to all of his sons.

However, very rarely a single 'letter' in the Y-chromosome will be altered as it's being passed on, thus causing a permanent change in the chromosome's genetic sequence. This will then be the start of a new lineage of slightly different Y-chromosomes, which will be inherited by all future male descendants.

In November 2000, Professor Ronald Davis and a team of Stanford researchers (see *Further Reading*) claimed to have traced back this lineage to a single individual man, and that a small group of East Africans (Sudanese and Ethiopians) and Khoisan are the closest present-day relatives of this original man. That is, their genetic make-up is closest to his. (It's a scientific 'proof' of the biblical Adam, if you like.)

This is still a very contentious finding, with subsequent researchers suggesting at least ten original male sources ('Adams') – and so although interesting, the jury remains out on the precise details of all these findings. If you're interested in the latest on this, then you'll find a lot about this on the web – start searching with keywords: 'Khoisan Y chromosome.'

Historical views of the Bushmen

Despite much evidence and research, our views of the Bushmen seem to have changed relatively little since both the Bantu groups and the first Europeans arrived in southern Africa.

The settlers' view

Since the first Bantu farmer started migrating south through East Africa, the range of territory occupied by the foragers, whose Stone-Age technology had dominated the continent, began to condense. By the time the first white settlers appeared in the Cape, the Khoisan people were already restricted to Africa's southwestern corners and the Kalahari.

All over the world, farmers occupy clearly demarcated areas of land, whereas foragers will move more and often leave less trace of their presence. In Africa, this made it easier for farmers, first black then white, to ignore any traditional land rights that belonged to foraging people.

Faced with the loss of territory for hunting and gathering, the foragers – who, by this time were already being called 'Bushmen' – made enemies of the farmers by killing cattle. They waged a guerrilla war, shooting poison arrows at parties of men who set out to massacre them. They were feared and loathed by the settlers, who, however, captured and valued their children as servants.

Some of the Khoisan retreated north from the Cape – like the ancestors of Namibia's Nama people. Others were forced to labour on the settlers' farms, or were thrown into prison for hunting animals or birds which had been their traditional prey, but which were now designated property of the crown.

This story is told by Robert J Gordon in *The Bushman Myth: The Makings of a Namibian Underclass* (see *Further Reading*). He shows that throughout history the hunter-gathering Bushmen have been at odds with populations of settlers who divided up and 'owned' the land in the form of farms. The European settlers proved to be their most determined enemy, embarking on a programme of legislation and massacre. Many Bushmen died in prison, with many more shot as 'vermin'.

Thus the onslaught of farmers on the hunter-gatherers accelerated between the 1800s and the mid-1900s. This helped to ensure that hunter-gathering as a lifestyle only continued to be practical in marginal areas that couldn't be economically farmed – like the Kalahari. Archaeological evidence suggests that hunter-gatherer peoples have lived for about 60,000 years at sites like the Tsodilo Hills.

Western views of the Bushmen in the 1800s

Though settlers in the Cape interacted with Khoisan people, so did Europe and the US, in a very limited way. Throughout the 1800s and early 1900s a succession of Khoisan people were effectively enslaved and brought to Europe and the US for exhibition. Sometimes this was under the guise of anthropology, but usually it didn't claim to be anything more than entertainment.

One of the first was the 'Hottentot Venus' – a woman who was probably of Khoisan extraction who was exhibited around London and Paris from 1810 to 1815, as an erotic curiosity for aristocrats.

A string of others followed. For example, the six Khoisan people exhibited at the Coney Island Pleasure Resort, beside New York, and later in London in the 1880s and billed as the 'missing link between apes and men', and the 'wild dancing Bushman' known as Franz brought to England around 1913 by Paddy Hepston (see Parsons' piece in *Botswana Notes & Records*, detailed in *Further Reading*).

Impressions of the Bushmen from the 1950s

In the 1950s a researcher from Harvard, John Marshall, came to the Kalahari to study the !Kung San. He described a peaceful people living in harmony with nature, amidst a land that provided all their needs. The groups had a deep spirituality and no real hierarchy: it seemed like the picture of a modern Eden (especially when viewed through post-war eyes). Marshall was a natural cameraman and made a film that follows the hunt of a giraffe by four men over a five-day period. It swiftly became a classic, both in and outside of anthropological circles.

Further research agreed, with researchers noting a great surfeit of protein in the diet of the !Kung San and low birth rates akin to modern industrial societies.

Again the Bushmen were seen as photogenic and sources of good copy and good images. The lives were portrayed in romantic, spiritual terms in the book and film *The Lost World of the Kalahari* by Laurens van der Post (see *Further Reading*). This documentary really ignited the worldwide interest in the Bushmen and led to subsequent films such as *The Gods Must be Crazy*. All the images conveyed an idyllic view of the Bushmen as untainted by contact with the modern world.

The reality

The reality was much less rosy than the first researchers thought. Some of their major misconceptions have been outlined particularly clearly in chapter 13 of John

Reader's *Africa: A Biography of the Continent* (see *Further Reading*). He points out that far from an ideal diet, the nutrition of the Bushmen was often critically limited, lacking vitamins and fatty acids associated with a lack of animal fat in their diet. Far from a stable population with a low birth rate, it seems likely that there had been a decline in the birth rate in the last few generations. The likely cause for this was periods of inadequate nourishment during the year when they lost weight from lack of food, stress and the great exertions of their lifestyle.

In fact, it seems likely that the San, whom we now see as foragers, are people who, over the last two millennia, have become relegated to an underclass by the relentless advance of the black and white farmers who did not recognise their original rights to their traditional land.

The Bushmen today and the media

Though scientific thought has moved on since the 1950s, much of the media has not. The Bushmen are still perceived to be hot news.

The outpost of Tsumkwe is the centre for many of the Bushmen communities in Namibia. It's a tiny crossroads with a school and a handful of buildings, in a remote corner of northeastern Namibia. Despite its isolation, in 2001 this desert outpost hosted no less than 22 film crews. Yes, really, that's an average of almost two each month – and I'm not counting a whole host of other print journalists and photographers.

Talk to virtually any of the directors and you'll realise that they arrive with very clear ideas about the images that they want to capture. They all think they're one of the first, they think they're original, and they want to return home with images which match their pre-conceived ideas about the Bushmen as 'the last primitive hunter-gatherers'.

As an example, you'll often see pictures in the media of Bushmen hunters in traditional dress walking across a hot, barren salt pan. When asked to do these shoots the Bushman's usual comment is, 'Why, there's no point. We'd never go looking for anything there.' But the shots look spectacular and win prizes ... so the photographers keep asking for them. From the Bushmen's perspective, they get paid for the shots, so why not pose for the camera? I'd do the same!

Thus our current image of the Bushmen is really one that *we* are constantly re-creating. It's the one that we expect. But it's doesn't necessarily conform to any reality. So on reflection, popular thinking hasn't moved on much from Marshall's first film in the 1950s.

Current life for the Bushmen

Looking at the current lifestyle of the Bushmen who remain in the more remote areas of the Kalahari, it's difficult not to lapse into a romantic view of ignoring present realities. There are too many cultural aspects to cover here, so instead I've just picked out a few that you may encounter.

Nomads of the Kalahari

Perhaps the first idea to dispel is that the Bushmen are nomads. They're not. Bushman family groups have clearly defined territories, called a *n!ore* (in the Ju/'hoansi language), within which they forage. This is usually centred on a place where there is water, and contains food resources sufficient for the basic subsistence of the group.

Groups recognise rights to the *n!ore*, which is passed on from father to first-born son. Any visiting people would ask permission to remain in these. Researchers have mapped these areas, even in places like the Central Kalahari.

Hunter-gatherers

Any hunter-gatherer lifestyle entails a dependence on, and extensive knowledge of, the environment and the resident fauna and flora found there. In the Kalahari, water is the greatest need and the Bushmen know which roots and tubers provide liquid to quench thirst. They create sip wells in the desert, digging a hole, filled with soft grass, then using a reed to suck water into the hole, and send it bubbling up the reed to fill an ostrich egg. Water-filled ostrich eggs are also buried at specific locations within the groups 'area'. When necessary the Bushmen will strain the liquid from the rumen of a herbivore and drink that.

Researchers have observed that any hunting is done by the men. When living a basic hunting and gathering lifestyle, with little external input, hunting provides only about 20% of their food. The remaining 80% is provided largely by the women, helped by the children, who forage and gather wild food from the bush. By age twelve a child might know about 200 plant species, and an adult more than 300.

Social system

The survival of the Bushmen in the harsh environment of the Kalahari is evidence of the supreme adaptability of humans. It reflects their detailed knowledge of their environment, which provides them not only with food, but with materials for shelter and medicine in the form of plants.

Another very important factor in their survival is the social system by which the Bushmen live. Social interaction is governed by unwritten rules that bind the people in friendship and harmony, which must be maintained. One such mechanism is the obligation to distribute the meat from a large kill. Another is the obligation to lend such few things as are individually possessed, thereby incurring a debt of obligation from the borrower.

They also practise exogamy, which means they have an obligation to marry outside the group. This creates social bonds between groups. Such ties bind the society inextricably together, as does the system of gift exchange between separate groups.

Owing to the environmental constraints a group will consist of between 80 and 120 people, living and moving together. In times of shortage the groups will be much smaller, sometimes consisting of only immediate family – parents, grandparents and children. They must be able to carry everything they possess. Their huts are light constructions of grass, and they have few possessions.

Because no one owns property, no one is richer or has more status than another. A group of Bushmen has a nominal leader, who might be a senior member of the group, an expert hunter, or the person who owns the water rights. The whole group takes decisions affecting them, often after vociferous discussions.

Hunting

The Bushmen in the Kalahari are practised hunters, using many different techniques to capture the game. Their main weapons are a very light bow, and an arrow made of reed, in three sections. The arrowhead is usually poisoned, using one of a number of poisons obtained from specific plants, snakes and beetles. (Though most Bushmen know how to hunt with bows and arrows, the actual practice is increasingly uncommon when it's not done to earn money from observing visitors.)

All the hunters may be involved in the capture of large game, which carries with it certain obligations. The whole group shares in the kill and each member is entitled to a certain portion of the meat.

There are different methods for hunting small game, which only the hunter's family would usually share. One method for catching spring hares involves long, flexible poles (sometimes four metres long) made of thin sticks, with a duiker's horn (or more usually now a metal hook) fastened to the end. These are rammed into the hare's hole, impaling the animal, which is then pulled or dug out.

Trance dancing

Entertainment for the Bushmen, when things are good, usually involves dancing. During some dances, which may often have overtones of ritual or religion, the dancers may fall into a trance and collapse.

These trances are induced by a deliberate breathing technique, with a clear physiological explanation. Dances normally take place in the evening, around a fire. Then the women, children and old people will sit around and clap, whilst some of the younger men will dance around the circle in an energetic, rhythmic dance. Often this is all that happens, and after a while the excitement dies down and everyone goes to sleep.

However, on fairly rare occasions, the dancers will go into a trance. After several hours of constant exertion, they will shorten their breathing. This creates an oxygen deficiency, which leads to the heart pumping more strongly to compensate. Blood pressure to the brain increases; the dancer loses consciousness and collapses.

Caprivian

The Caprivi people live in the fertile, swampy land between the Chobe and Zambezi rivers – at the eastern end of the Caprivi Strip. Their language is of the Bantu family. Like the Kavango and the Owambo, they farm a variety of crops, raise livestock, and fish. The agricultural potential of the area is one of the highest in Namibia. However, this potential has been largely unrealised. Before the war with Angola, and the heavy involvement of South African troops (which brought roads and infrastructure), the whole of the Kavango and Caprivi region was one of the least developed in Namibia.

Caprivians make up about 4% of Namibia's population, and most can be considered as members of one of five main groups: the Masubia and Mafwe groups, and the smaller Mayeyi, Matotela and Mbukushu. Their traditional crafts include extensive use of baskets (especially fish traps, and for carrying grain), wooden masks and stools, drums, pottery, leather goods and stone carvings.

Damara

Along with the Nama and the Bushmen, the Damara are presumed to be the original inhabitants of Namibia, speaking a similar 'Khoi' click language (Khoisan family). Like the Nama, the Damara were primarily hunting people, who owned few cattle or goats. Traditionally enemies of the Nama and Herero, they supported the German colonial forces at Waterberg against the Herero uprisings and were awarded for their loyalty by an 'enlarged' homeland from the German authorities: Damaraland, the area adjacent to the Skeleton Coast (now the southern part of the Kunene province). Of the 80,000 Damara today, only a quarter manage to survive in this area – the rest work on commercial farms, in mines or as labourers in the towns. Damara women share the same Victorian style of dress as the Herero and Nama women.

They make up about 7.5% of Namibia's population, sharing their language with Namas. Traditionally Damara people have been thought of as miners, smelters, copper traders, stock farmers and tobacco growers; until the end of the 19th century when they moved to Damaraland and started practising agriculture.

Their traditional crafts include leather goods, glass and metal beadwork, wooden bowls and buckets, clay pipes and bowls, and more recently 'township art' such as wire cars.

Herero

In 1904, the Herero and the Hottentots staged a massive uprising against the German colonial troops in South West Africa. It ended in a bloody massacre of over half the total Herero population at the battle of Waterberg. The few Herero that survived fled into the Kalahari, some crossing into what is now Botswana. The recently formed Herero People's Reparation Corporation, based in Washington, is currently suing the German government and two companies for £2.6 billion, with the case expected to be heard in the US courts during 2003.

Today, the Herero constitute the third largest ethnic group in Namibia, after the Owambo and Kavango – about 8% of the present population. Their language is Bantu based. In Botswana, they are a minority group inhabiting Ngamiland, south and west of the Okavango Delta.

Traditionally pastoralists, the Herero prefer raising cattle to growing crops – prestige and influence are dependent on the number of cattle possessed. Today, the majority of Namibian Hereros use their cattle-handling skills on commercial farms.

Herero women wear very distinctive long, flowing Victorian gowns and head-dresses. Multiple layers of petticoats made from over 12m of material give a voluminous look (two women walking side by side occupy the whole pavement!). Missionaries, who were appalled by the Hereros' semi-nakedness, introduced this style of dress in the 1800s. Now the Hereros continue to wear these heavy garments and it has become their traditional dress – though they will admit just how hot it is if asked.

Traditional Herero crafts include skin and leather products, basketry, jewellery and ornaments, and dolls in traditional Victorian-style dress, which are a very popular curio for visitors.

Himba

The Himba people share a common ethnic origin with the Hereros, having split from the main Herero group on the Namibia/Botswana border and moved west to present-day Kaokoland in search of available land. The place they found, however, is mountainous, sparsely vegetated and very arid. Cattle are central to their way of life, with the size of the herd an indication of wealth and prestige – but overgrazing of the poor soils is a major problem. The Himba are a minority group in Namibia (less than 1% of the population), and live almost entirely in their traditional areas in remote Kaokoland.

Traditional Himba crafts include work in skin and leather (head-dresses, girdles and aprons), jewellery (copper-wire neck-bands and bracelets), musical instruments, wooden neck-rests, basketry and pottery.

Kavango

The Kavango people share their name with the Okavango River, which forms the northern border of Namibia with Angola. Not surprisingly, they have based their traditional agricultural and fishing existence on the fertile land and good water supply afforded by this environment.

Many of the Kavango, who used to live on the northern side of the Okavango River in Angola, came south of the river into Namibia during the 1970s, 80s and early 90s. They fled from the civil war between South African-backed UNITA rebels and the Soviet/Cuban-backed MPLA regime. As a consequence, the Kavango population in Namibia more than doubled in size during the 1970s, and now forms the second largest ethnic group in the country, making up almost 10% of the population.

Closely related to the Owambos, the Kavango people are traditionally fishermen, and crop and stock farmers. Their craftwork includes woodcarving (bowls, spoons, mortars, masks, boxes and furniture), basketry, pottery, jewellery (grass bracelets and copper-bead necklaces), mats, spears, daggers, pipes, musical instruments and head-dresses.

Nama/Hottentot

The Nama people are perhaps the closest in origin to the Bushmen, traditionally sharing a similar type of 'click' or Khoisan language, the same light-coloured yellow skin, and a hunter-gatherer way of life. One of the first peoples in Namibia, their tribal areas were traditionally communal property, as indeed was any item unless it was actually made by an individual. Basic differences in the perception of ownership of land and hunting grounds led in the past to frequent conflicts with the Herero people. The 50,000 or so Nama today live mostly in the area that was Namaland, north of Keetmanshoop in the south of Namibia, mainly working on commercial farms. Nama women share the same Victorian traditional dress as the Herero and Damara women.

The Nama people make up about 5% of Namibia's population, and are traditionally stock farmers. Their crafts include leatherwork (aprons and collecting bags), karosses (mantle of animal skins) and mats, musical instruments (eg: reed flutes), jewellery, clay pots and tortoise-shell powder containers.

Owambo

The Owambo people (sometimes called Ovambo) are by far the largest group in Namibia and make up just over half the population. Their language, Oshivambo (sometimes known as Ambo or Vambo in Namibia), is Bantu based. The great majority live in their traditional areas – Owamboland – away from the main transport arteries in the remote far north of the country, straddled on the border with Angola. The area receives one of the highest rainfalls in the country, and supports a range of traditional crops as well as allowing good grazing for the extensive cattle herds.

Before independence, the existence of half a million indigenous Namibians on the border with (socialist) Angola seriously perturbed the South African administration. By investing money into the region, the administration hoped to establish a protective buffer against Angola to protect the areas in the interior. The policy backfired – Owamboland became the heartland of SWAPO during the struggle for independence. The consequent harassment by the South African Defence Force, and a rapid population increase (exacerbated by a large influx of refugees from Angola), have left the area over-pressurised and undeveloped. The SWAPO government has long pledged to redress this imbalance.

Most of the Owambo belong to one of eight tribes: the Kwanyama, Ndongo, Kwambi, Ngandjera, Mbalantu, Kwaluudhi, Nkolokadhi and Eunda. Most still live in Owamboland, and have traditionally been traders and businessmen.

Traditional Owambo craftwork includes basketry, pottery, jewellery, wooden combs, wood and iron spears, arrows and richly decorated daggers, musical instruments, fertility dolls, and ivory buttons (ekipa) – worn by women and conveying their status and indicating their husband's/family's wealth.

Other Namibians
Coloured Namibians
The term 'Coloured' is generally used in southern Africa to describe people of mixed (black-white) origin. These Coloured people maintain a strong sense of identity and separateness from either blacks or whites – though they generally speak either Afrikaans or English (or frequently both) rather than an ethnic 'African' language. They are very different in culture from any of Namibia's ethnic groups, white or black.

Most Coloureds in Namibia live in the urban areas – Windhoek, Keetmanshoop and Lüderitz. Those in Walvis Bay are mainly fishermen, and some in the south are stock farmers. Their traditional crafts centre mainly on musical instruments, like drums and guitars.

White Namibians
The first whites to settle in Namibia were the Germans who set up trading businesses around the port of Lüderitz in 1884. Within a few years, Namibia formally became a German colony, and German settlers began to arrive in ever-increasing numbers. Meanwhile, white farmers of Dutch origin (the Boers, who first settled on the African continent at the Cape in 1652), were moving northwards in search of land free from British interference, following the cession of the Dutch Cape Colony to the British government.

Following the transfer of German Namibia to South African control after World War I, Boers (Afrikaners) moved into Namibia, and soon significantly outnumbered the German settlers. The Namibian whites collectively refer to themselves as 'Southwesters' after Namibia's colonial name of South West Africa.

Namibians of European descent live mainly in urban, central and southern parts of the country – though they also own and run most of the commercial farming operations. Virtually all of the tourism industry is managed by white Namibians. They came as missionaries, traders and hunters, though are now found throughout the economy. Perhaps a legacy of colonialism, they are normally amongst the more affluent members of society.

The crafts currently produced by the whites include leatherwork (shoes, handbags, belts), German Christmas and Easter decorations, needlework (including embroidery, patchwork and clothing), printed T-shirts, costume jewellery, greeting cards and various classical European art-forms.

Expatriates
Distinct from white Namibians, there is a significant 'expat' community in Namibia. These foreigners usually come to Namibia for two or three years, to work on short-term contracts, often for either multinational companies or aid agencies. Most are highly skilled individuals who come to share their knowledge with Namibian colleagues – often teaching skills that are in short supply in Namibia.

LANGUAGE
English is the official language and is taught throughout the education system, though Afrikaans is still the lingua franca amongst many of the older generation. The main ethnic languages fall into the Bantu and Khoisan language groups. Virtually all black Namibians also speak one or more African languages, and many will speak several. Many white Namibians (especially those in the commercial farming communities) regard German as their first language, though they will normally understand English and Afrikaans as well. Linguistics experts have

CULTURAL GUIDELINES

Comments here are intended to be a general guide, just a few examples of how to travel more sensitively. They should not be viewed as blueprints for perfect Namibian etiquette. Cultural sensitivity is really a state of mind, not a checklist of behaviour – so here we can only hope to give the sensitive traveller a few pointers in the right direction.

When we travel, we are all in danger of leaving negative impressions with local people whom we meet: by snapping that picture quickly, whilst the subject is not looking; by dressing scantily, offending local sensitivities; or by just brushing aside the feelings of local people, with the high-handed superiority of a rich Westerner. These things are easy to do, in the click of a shutter, or flash of a large dollar bill.

However, you will get the most representative view of Namibia if you cause as little disturbance to the local people as possible. You will never blend in perfectly when you travel – your mere presence there, as an observer, will always change the local events slightly. However, if you try to fit in and show respect for local culture and attitudes, then you may manage to leave positive feelings behind you.

One of the easiest, and most important, ways to do this is with greetings. African societies are rarely as rushed as Western ones. When you first talk to someone, you should greet him or her leisurely. So, for example, if you enter a shop and want some help, do not just ask outright, 'Where can I find ...' That would be rude. Instead you will have a better reception (and better chance of good advice) by saying:

Traveller: 'Good afternoon.'
Namibian: 'Good afternoon.'
Traveller: 'How are you?'
Namibian: 'I am fine, how are you?'
Traveller: 'I am fine, thank you. (*pause*) Do you know where I can find ...'

This approach goes for anyone – always greet them first. For a better reception still, learn these phrases of greeting in the local language. English-speakers are often lazy about learning languages, and, whilst most Namibians understand English, a greeting given in an appropriate local language will be received with delight. It implies that you are making an effort to learn a little of their language and culture, which is always appreciated.

identified at least 28 different languages and numerous dialects amongst the indigenous population. Although these different language groupings do loosely correspond to what might be described as Namibia's 'tribes', the distinctions are blurred by the natural linguistic ability of most Namibians. While it is normal to speak Afrikaans plus one local language, many Namibians speak a number of local languages fluently; thus ethnic groupings provide only a rough guide to the many languages and dialects of Namibia's people.

EDUCATION

Literacy is estimated at about 40%. Since independence, the government has poured resources into an expansion of the education system, and at present about 89% of children (aged 6–16) attend school. There are small primary schools in the most rural of areas and large secondary schools in the regional centres. To help with this expansion, many foreign teachers came to Namibia with the help of NGOs and overseas aid agencies.

Very rarely in the town or city you may be approached by someone who doesn't greet you, but tries immediately to sell you something, or hassle you in some way. These people have learned that foreigners aren't used to greetings, and so have adapted their approach accordingly. An effective way to dodge their attentions is to reply to their questions with a formal greeting, and then politely, but firmly, refuse their offer. This is surprisingly effective.

Another part of the normal greeting ritual is handshaking. As elsewhere, you would not normally shake a shop-owner's hand, but you would shake hands with someone to whom you are introduced. Get some practice when you arrive, as there is a gentle, three-part handshake used in southern African which is easily learnt.

Your clothing is an area that can easily give offence. Skimpy, revealing clothing is frowned upon by most Namibians, especially when worn by women. Shorts are fine for the bush or the beach, but dress conservatively and avoid short shorts, especially in the more rural areas. Respectable locals will wear long trousers (men) or long skirts (women).

Photography is a tricky business. Most Namibians will be only too happy to be photographed – provided you ask their permission first. Sign language is fine for this question: just point at your camera, shrug your shoulders, and look quizzical. The problem is that then everyone will smile for you, producing the type of 'posed' photograph which you may not want. However, stay around and chat for five or ten minutes more, and people will get used to your presence, stop posing and you will get more natural shots (a camera with a quiet shutter is a help). Note that care is needed near government buildings, army bases and similar sites of strategic importance. You must ask permission before snapping photographs or you risk people taking offence.

The specific examples above can teach only so much; they are general by their very nature. But wherever you find yourself, if you are polite and considerate to the Namibians you meet, then you will rarely encounter any cultural problems. Watch how they behave and, if you have any doubts about how you should act, then ask someone quietly. They will seldom tell you outright that you are being rude, but they will usually give you good advice on how to make your behaviour more acceptable.

Children in secondary school study for the IGCSE (General Certificate of Secondary Education) and then move on to the HIGCSE. Lessons are taught almost exclusively in English, although some indigenous languages may also be taught.

RELIGION

Some 80–90% of the population follows a Christian religion. Dutch Reformed, Roman Catholic, Lutheran, Methodist and Presbyterian churches are all common. However, most people will also subscribe to some traditional African religious practices and beliefs.

ARTS AND CULTURE

Namibia boasts some of the world's oldest rock paintings and engravings, which have been attributed to ancestors of Bushmen. The scenes are naturalistic depictions of animals, people, hunting, battles and social rituals. Local geology determined the usage of colour in the paintings. Some are monochrome pictures in red, but many are multicoloured, using ground-up earth pigments mixed with animal fat to produce 'paints' of red, brown, yellow, blue, violet, grey, black and white.

Rock engravings have also been found, often in areas where there is an absence of smooth, sheltered rock surfaces to paint on. Some of the best examples of paintings and engravings are in the Brandberg, Twyfelfontein and Erongo areas.

However, there is more to Namibian creativity than just rock paintings. Traditional arts and crafts include basketry, woodcarving, leatherwork, beadwork, pottery, music-making and dancing. More contemporary arts and crafts encompass textile weaving and embroidery, sculptures, print-making and theatre.

For up-to-date information on cultural events, buy a copy of *The Namibian* and read its 'Arts and Entertainment' section.

Crafts and visual arts

To access the whole range of Namibian regional arts and crafts in one place, visit the Namibia Craft Centre (see pages 147–8). Housing over 25 stalls under one roof, as well as the Omba Gallery, this is perfect for buying crafts if time is short. Many towns have street markets selling curios, and numerous lodges have small outlets selling local arts and crafts, albeit sometimes at a rather inflated price.

For more details of Namibian arts and crafts, it may be worth contacting the Arts and Crafts Guild of Namibia (PO Box 20709, Windhoek; tel: 061 223831/252468/251422; fax: 061 252125), which was established in 1992 to unite the various craftspeople under one umbrella group for promotional purposes.

Basketry

Most baskets are made from strips of Makalani palm leaves coiled into a shape that is determined by its purpose: flat plate shapes for winnowing baskets, large bowl-shaped baskets for carrying things, small closed baskets with lids and bottle shapes for storing liquids. Symbolic geometric patterns are woven into a basket as it is being made, using strips of palm leaves dyed in dark browns, purples and yellows.

Recently, baskets have been made using strips of recycled plastic bags to wind around the palm-leaf strips or grasses. Baskets are typically woven by women and are part of the crafts tradition of the northern Namibian peoples – Caprivi, Himba, Herero, Kavango and Owambo.

The best examples are found in the northern arts and crafts cooperatives, like Khorixas Community Craft Centre; Opuwo Art Promotions (PO Box 6, Opuwo); Oshana Environment and Art Centre, in Oshiko near Oshakati; Caprivi Art Centre (page 481); Mashi Crafts, beside the B8 in Kongola (page 473); and Tsumeb Arts and Crafts (page 421).

Woodcarving

Woodcarving is usually practised by men in Namibia. Wooden objects are carved using adzes, axes and knives; lathe-turned work is not traditional. Carving, incising and burning techniques are used to decorate the wood. A wide range of woodcarving is produced: sculptural headrests, musical instruments such as drums and thumb pianos; masks, walking-sticks, toys, animal figurines, bows, arrows and quivers; domestic utensils including oval and round bowls and buckets as well as household furniture.

The northern Namibian peoples – Bushmen, Caprivians, Damara, Himba, Kavango and Owambo – have woodcarving traditions. Naturally the northern arts and crafts cooperatives have a good selection (see above), especially the Mbangura

Cooperative (see page 460) which also specialises in wooden furniture. In addition the two street markets in Okahandja act as a national selling point for woodcarvings.

Leatherwork

Leatherwork is practised by all the peoples of Namibia. The skins of cattle, sheep and game are tanned and dyed using vegetable materials, animal fat and sometimes red ochre. The goods crafted include carrying skins and bags, tobacco pouches, karosses (to be used as rugs or blankets) and traditional clothing – head-dresses, girdles/aprons and sandals as well as more contemporary fashion accessories like shoes, boots, handbags, belts and jackets. The leatherworkers are usually women, though men also participate if large, heavy skins are being tanned or dyed. Swakopmund Tannery (see page 297) is an interesting place to visit to see how the hides are treated and also to buy crafted leatherwork.

Beadwork

Beadwork is traditionally the domain of the Bushman and Himba peoples. The Bushmen make beads from ostrich-egg shells, porcupine quills, seeds, nuts and branches; and also use commercially produced glass beads. The Himba people use iron beads and shells. In both peoples, men tend to make the beads and the women weave and string them into artefacts. These include necklaces, bracelets, armlets, anklets and headbands. The Bushmen also use beadwork to decorate their leatherwork bags, pouches and clothing – a particularly striking traditional design being the multicoloured circular 'owl's-eye'.

Bushman crafts are best bought either locally in the Tsumkwe area or the Tsumeb Arts and Crafts Centre (page 421). Alternatively, a more commercial outlet with a good selection is Bushman Art (179 Independence Avenue, Windhoek; tel: 061 228828; fax: 061 228971). Failing that, check for new outlets with the Nyae Nyae Development Foundation of Namibia at PO Box 9026, Eros, Windhoek tel: 061 236327; fax: 061 225997.

The Himba people also make a traditional iron-bead and leather head ornament (oruvanda) that all women wear and belts (epanda) that only mothers wear. Authentic Himba crafts are easiest to find in Kaokoland, where you will often be offered crafts by local villagers.

Pottery

Namibia's more renowned potters are women from the Caprivi, Kavango and Owambo peoples. Traditionally, geometric patterns of various colours decorate the vessels of different shapes and uses. Contemporary potters are experimenting with decoration by textures and a variety of sculptural motifs. The best selection of pottery is found at the Caprivi Arts Centre (see page 481).

Textiles

Nama women traditionally used patchwork techniques when making dresses and shawls. Now these women utilise their sewing skills in the art of embroidery and appliqué, making table and bed linens, cushion covers and wall-hangings depicting Namibian animals and village scenes. Good places to buy these items include:

Penduka Gallery PO Box 7635, Katutura, Windhoek; tel/fax: 061 257210
Gibeon Folk Art PO Box 101, Gibeon; tel: 063 251098/264668/264698

Textiles made by women involved in the **Anin** project near Uhlenhorst (see page 198) can be purchased both at Anib Lodge near Mariental (see page 196), and at

KARAKULS, SWAKARA AND NAKARA

Karakuls are Central Asian sheep, the young of which have long been prized for their pelts. In 1902, a German fur trader called Paul Thorer shipped 69 of these from Uzbekistan to Germany in the hope of breeding them there. The damper European climes did not suit them, but in 1907 twelve of those animals were shipped out to German South West Africa – as Namibia's climate was thought to be similar to that of the dry Central Asian areas from where they had come.

They did well, and two years later 278 more animals were brought out from Asia. Later, the South Africans continued the work started by the Germans, when they took over as the reigning colonial power in Namibia. An experimental farm was started near Windhoek, to investigate the farming and breeding of karakuls.

Over the next 50 or 60 years Namibia gradually became one of the three main producers of karakul fur, or 'Persian lamb' as it is often known. Early on, selective breeding in Namibia had developed white pelts, which were not produced in either the USSR or Afghanistan – the competing countries. Then Namibia marketed its fur under the trade name of *Swakara*, for **S**outh **W**est **A**frican **kara**kul. Since independence one firm now markets these as *Nakara*, for *Namibian karakul*. See page 148.

This trade grew rapidly, and as early as 1937 the country exported over a million pelts for over £1,200,000. It grew to its peak in 1976, when about 2.8 million pelts earned some 50 million rand – before the anti-fur campaigns of the late '70s and '80s slashed the demand for fur, and the prices paid for pelts.

Then the market crashed, and the biggest single source of income for many farmers in southern Namibia was removed. Given that the fur came only from the slaughter of very young lambs (it is said to be at its softest when they are 36 hours old), it's not surprising that people felt unhappy about buying it.

However, these are tough sheep, well suited to Namibia's extremes of temperatures and semi-desert climate, so the loss of the market for their lambs' pelts was a major blow. Karakul wool carpets, woven in Swakopmund, are increasing the demand for the wool of adults. You can accelerate this trend by buying one as a souvenir, then perhaps karakuls will again be common in Namibia.

House Sandrose in Lüderitz (see page 235). Other embroidered textiles, made by women involved with the **Tuyakula** project in Katutura, may be bought at Zoo Café in Windhoek (see pages 140 and 158–9).

Another textile craft that has recently developed is the hand-weaving of pure karakul wool into wall-hangings and rugs. The designs are usually geometric patterns or Namibian landscapes, though almost any design can be commissioned. Among the best places to see and buy these rugs and wall-hangings are Karakulia in Swakopmund (page 297) and Dorka Teppiche in Dordabis (see page 185).

Painting, sculpture and prints

The work of contemporary Namibian artists, sculptors and print-makers is on display (and often available for sale) in the many galleries in the urban areas. The country's biggest permanent collection is at the National Art Gallery of Namibia (see page 157). This has over 560 works of art dating from 1864 to the present day. There are many landscapes and paintings of wild animals amongst the earlier works. Every two years the winning entries of the Standard Bank Biennale are exhibited here. Contemporary Namibian visual arts are exhibited at the following:

Omba Gallery within Namibia Crafts Centre, 40 Tal Street, Windhoek; tel: 061 242 2222; fax: 061 221 1273. Exhibits work of Namibian and international artists and craftspeople
John Muafangejo Art Centre The Former Kitchen, Parliament Gardens, PO Box 994, Windhoek; tel: 061 231160; fax: 061 240930. This art school exhibits the work of young Namibian artists, as well as housing a small studio theatre
Centre for Visual and Performing Arts University of Namibia, Mandume Ndemufayo Road, Pioniers Park, Windhoek; tel: 061 206 3804; fax: 061 206 3835
The Wilderness Gallery Frans Indongo Gardens, PO Box 30815, Windhoek; tel: 061 238207. This promotes up-and-coming artists and has a good collection of photographs
Spot On Gallery PO Box 22541, Windhoek; tel: 061 225634; fax: 061 225283. This up-market gallery has a shop which sells a wide range of arts and crafts
Reflections Art Gallery Moltke Street, Swakopmund; tel/fax: 064 405484. This buys and sells Namibian artwork

Finally, note that many professional artists choose to sell their work at street markets rather than pay a gallery commission on any items sold. So high-quality arts and crafts can be found by the roadside and on the pavements.

Performing arts
Dance
Traditional dancing in Namibia is a participatory activity at community gatherings and events like weddings. Hence, a visitor is unlikely to witness any, unless invited by a Namibian. However, some public performances of traditional dancing are to be seen at the Caprivi Arts Festival (held between September and November in Katima Mulilo at the Caprivi Arts Centre) and at Lizauli Traditional Village (see pages 476–7).

In Bushmanland, in villages surrounding Tsumkwe, traditional Bushman dances are performed for tourists – usually for a fee. This is generally a relaxed, uncontrived affair.

Afkawandahe and the African Performing Arts Group also perform traditional Namibian dances at the College for the Arts auditorium in Windhoek (see page 145). Performances of European dance, including ballet, take place at either the National Theatre of Namibia or at Franco-Namibian Cultural Centre (see page 145).

Music
Most of the Namibian peoples have a music-making tradition – singing, and playing drums, bows, thumb pianos and harps. The Namas also have a tradition of religious singing in four-part harmony. Oruuano, the Namibian Artists' Union, recently held the first Oruuano of Namibia Arts Festival at Soweto Market, in Katutura (Windhoek), involving Namibian artists and musicians. It is hoped that this festival will become a regular occurrence.

Pre-Independence colonial influences have resulted in many Namibian musicians performing in the Western tradition. Concerts are regularly performed by Namibia National Symphony Orchestra, National Youth Choir, and touring foreign musicians in the main auditorium of the National Theatre of Namibia (page 145). This is also the venue for the Namibian Broadcasting Corporation's biennial Music Makers' Competition.

Many smaller-scale concerts take place at the Franco-Namibian Cultural Centre (see page 145). Cantare Audire Choir is a classically trained chorus which performs regularly at Christus Kirche, Windhoek (ask at the church for concert details).

Jazz, reggae, mbaganga and pop bands perform at the 150-seater Warehouse Theatre (see page 145) and at the various bars, restaurants and clubs in Windhoek such as Club Thriller (see page 145). Bands and rock groups with a larger following usually perform at the Independence Arena in Katutura, which has the capacity for 4,000 people, or alternatively at the Windhoek Country Club (see page 119) which can accommodate audiences of over 1,000 people. Out of Windhoek, the national tour circuit includes large venues in Swakopmund, Walvis Bay and Okahandja.

Theatre

There are many Namibian theatre companies including the Rossko Cultural Group, Dalma Productions and Caprivi Cultural Troupe. Several South African theatre companies also tour Namibia. Apart from the National Theatre of Namibia and the Warehouse Theatre, there are small studio-theatres at the John Muafangejo Arts Centre and the Space Theatre at the University of Namibia's Centre for Visual and Performing Arts. Both host avant-garde and experimental theatre performances.

The best of Namibian theatre (and other arts and crafts) can be seen at the National Arts and Cultural Festival, which takes place every December in a different region each year. Between September and November there are smaller festivals held throughout the country to choose the regional entries.

SPORT

Sport is popular in Namibia, with football, rugby, hockey and netball all played in schools. The introduction of basketball in recent years has proved hugely successful as well.

Athletics aficionados will be familiar with the name of Frankie Fredericks, the Namibian sprinter who has made his mark in the 200m event. Slightly overshadowed by Michael Johnson, he has nevertheless brought home a string of international medals, the most recent of which was in the Commonwealth Games held in Manchester in July 2002.

The Natural Environment

PHYSICAL ENVIRONMENT

The Republic of Namibia is located in southwest Africa, astride the Tropic of Capricorn and beside the South Atlantic Ocean. Its main borders are with South Africa, Botswana, and Angola, though it also adjoins Zambia. Covering about 824,292km², the country is much larger than Kenya, and more than twice the size of Zimbabwe. In Western terms, Namibia is more than a third larger than the UK and Germany *combined*, or twice the size of California.

Climate

Most of Namibia is classified as an arid to semi-arid region (the line being crossed from semi-arid to arid when evaporation exceeds rainfall). Most of it has a sub-tropical 'desert' climate, characterised by a wide range in temperature (from day to night and from summer to winter), and by low rainfall and humidity. The northern strip follows the same pattern, but has a more moderate, less dry climate. Note that although the terms 'summer' (November to April) and 'winter' (May to October) are sometimes used, they are not as applicable as, say, in a European maritime climate.

Temperatures range widely from very hot to very cold, depending on the height of the land above sea level and the month. From April to September, in the 'dry season', it is generally cool, pleasant, clear and dry. Temperatures average around 25°C during the day, but nights are much colder. Frost is possible in the higher areas and the deserts. October and November are still within the 'dry season' but then the temperatures are higher, especially in the lower-lying and more northerly areas.

Most of Namibia's rain falls in the summer, from around December to March, and it can be heavy and prolonged in the northern regions of Owamboland and Caprivi. The further south or west you go, the drier it becomes, with many southern regions of the Kalahari and the whole of the coastal Namib Desert receiving no rainfall at all some years. In this 'rainy season' temperatures occasionally reach 40°C, and sometimes you may find it humid in the north.

Weather

The beginning of the year, in **January** and **February**, is midsummer. Then it's hot and fairly damp with average maximum temperatures around 25–35°C and average minima around 10–20°C (depending exactly where you are). These averages, however, hide peaks of well over 45°C in the desert.

On a typical day during the rains, the sky will start blue and by early afternoon the clouds will appear. In the late afternoon there will be an hour's torrential rain on some days. Such tropical storms are spectacular; everything feels terrifically fresh afterwards. However, you wouldn't want to be caught outside. By the early evening the sky will usually begin to clear again.

The frequency of the rains decreases, and they cease around **March** or **April**. From then the heat is waning and the land gradually cools and dries out. The nights quickly become cooler, accentuating the temperature difference between the bright, hot days and the clear nights. **May** is a lovely month: there is minimal chance of rain, nights are not yet too cold, and many of the summer's plants are still lush and green.

By **June** the nights are cold, approaching freezing in desert areas where night game drives can be bitter. **July** and **August** are winter, when the average maximum temperatures are around 15–25°C and the average minima are around 0–10°C. That said, you'll still find yourself wearing shorts and a T-shirt during the day, and getting sunburnt if you are not careful. Clouds will be a rare sight for the next few months.

September is another super month, dry and clear, yet not too hot. By then most green vegetation is fading as the heat begins to build. Everything is dry. All through **October** the heat mounts, and by November it is very hot during the day. However, the humidity is still exceedingly low, so even the high temperatures feel quite pleasant.

By **November** the air seems pregnant with anticipation. Everything is dry, awaiting the rains. Though the clouds often build up in the afternoon, they won't usually deliver until at least **December**. When (and if) the rains do arrive, they are a huge relief, dropping the temperatures at a stroke, clearing the air and reviving the vegetation.

The coastal strip

Temperatures on the Namibian coast follow a similar overall pattern, though it may seem very different from one day to the next. Here the climate is largely determined by the interaction between warm dry winds from inland and the cold Benguela Current. The sea is too cold for much evaporation to take place and, consequently, rain-bearing clouds don't form over the coast. Most of the coast is classified as desert – rainfall is an extremely low 15mm per annum on average, and in some years there may be none.

However, hot air from the interior mixes regularly with cold sea air to produce a moist fog that penetrates up to 60km inland. This happens regardless of season, and has done for millennia. It is this periodic morning fog which provides the desert's only dependable source of moisture, and the Namib's endemic flora and fauna have evolved to take advantage of it.

Geology

Geologically, Namibia forms part of an extremely old region, with Pre-Cambrian granitic and metamorphic rocks dating back over two billion years. These shield or 'basement' rocks are usually covered by more recent sedimentary rocks, mostly deposited during the Mesozoic era (65 to 235 million years ago). Tectonic activity or movement in the earth's crust over the last 100 million years or so created a number of rifts through which magma was able to reach the surface (see box, *Kimberlite (diamond) pipes*) and resulted in the uplifting of most of the area above sea level.

Topography

The topography of Namibia can be divided into four regions. At 2,000m, the highest land is the central plateau that runs roughly from north to south, from south of Keetmanshoop to north of Otjiwarongo. This is hilly, verdant country where most of Namibia's best farmland is concentrated.

KIMBERLITE (DIAMOND) PIPES

Diamond is a crystalline form of ordinary carbon created under conditions of extreme pressure and temperature. In nature, such conditions are only found deep below the earth's surface in the lower crust or upper mantle. Under certain circumstances in the past (usually associated with tectonic activity) the rock matrix in which diamonds occurred was subjected to such great pressure that it became fluid and welled up to the earth's surface in a volcanic pipe of fluidised material. The situation is similar to a conventional volcanic eruption, except that instead of basaltic magma being erupted through fissures in the crust, the volcanic material is a peculiar rock called kimberlite. This contains a wide assortment of minerals (including diamond) in addition to large chunks of other rocks that have been caught up in the process.

The pipes are correctly termed kimberlite pipes, and occur throughout southern Africa from the Cape to Zaire. However, only a small proportion of those discovered have proved to contain diamonds in sufficient abundance to be profitably worked. Namibia's diamonds derive not from primary kimberlite pipes, but from secondary diamond deposits – areas where diamonds have been washed down and deposited by old rivers, which have eroded kimberlite pipes in the interior on their way.

To the west of this plateau, the land falls off in a dramatic escarpment down to the Namib Desert, one of the world's oldest deserts which stretches for 1,600km beside the Atlantic Ocean. The escarpment, and the incisions that have been cut through it by river action over the years, provides some of Namibia's most spectacular scenery. Below, the Namib is a flat coastal plain whose profile is broken only by shifting dunes and the odd towering inselberg (see page 253).

East of the central plateau, the land slopes off much more gradually, merging into the great sand-sheet of the Kalahari Desert. A plateau standing at about 1,000m, stretching from Namibia into Botswana and even beyond, this is rolling country with vegetated sand-dunes.

Sand-dunes

Barchan, or crescentric, dunes arise wherever sand-laden wind deposits sand on the windward (up-wind) slopes of a random patch on the ground. The mound grows in height until a 'slip-face' is established by sand avalanching down on the sheltered leeward (downwind) side. The resulting dune is therefore in a state of constant (if slow) movement – sand is continuously being deposited and blown up the shallow windward slope and then falling down the steep leeward slope. This slow movement, or migration, is more rapid at the edges of the dune (where there is less wind resistance) than in the centre, which results in the characteristic 'tails' of a mature barchan.

Fairly constant winds from the same direction are essential for the growth and stability of barchan dunes, which can migrate from anything up to six metres a year for high dunes to 15 metres a year for smaller dunes. Probably the best examples of barchan dunes occur in Namibia's Skeleton Coast, where some of the dune crests are highlighted by a purple dusting of garnet sand. You'll see them 'marching' across the road near where the D2345 turns from the main C34 coastal road.

Seif dunes

Where the prevailing wind is interrupted by crosswinds driving in sand from the sides, a long seif or longitudinal dune is formed, instead of a swarm of barchans. The shape of seif dunes is that of a long ridge with high crests, parallel to the direction of the prevailing wind. They commonly occur in long parallel ranges, such as those south of the Kuiseb River which show up so clearly on satellite photographs.

Sand-sheets

Sand-sheets occur when the land is vegetated with grass and scrub, or is covered with rocks and pebbles. Then the force of the wind is broken and it becomes less homogenous. In such situations poorly developed seif dunes or irregular barchans form, and may often join together to some extent, making an undulating sand sheet. From this platform of coarser sand, more erratic dunes often rise.

Sand-sheets, in one form or another, are the most common dune formation in southern Africa, since the 'text book' conditions needed to form perfect barchan or seif dunes are rare. However, the principles remain the same and 'imperfect' dunes of barchan or seif origin are widespread throughout the Kalahari and Namib deserts.

FLORA AND FAUNA

Despite its aridity, Namibia is full of fascinating wildlife. Its national parks and concession areas have protected their flora and fauna effectively and offer some superb big game, far from the tourist hordes of more conventional safari countries. Namibia has been the most successful country in the world at protecting its black rhino population, and has Africa's largest population of cheetahs.

Because the Namib is one of the world's oldest deserts, the extraordinary way that plants, animals and even human populations have adapted and evolved in order to survive here is fascinating. There are many endemic species; animals and plants not found anywhere else. From beetles and birds to big game like the famous 'desert elephants' and strange *welwitschia* plants – Namibia has unique and varied wildlife.

Vegetation types

As with animals, each species of plant has its favourite conditions. External factors determine where each species thrives, and where it will perish. These include temperature, light, water, soil type, nutrients, and which other species of plants and animals live in the same area. Species with similar needs are often found together, in communities which are characteristic of that particular environment. Namibia has a number of such communities, or typical 'vegetation types', within its borders – each of which is distinct from the others. East of the desert, some of the more common include:

Mopane woodland

The dominant tree here is the remarkably adaptable mopane (*Colophospermum mopane*), which is sometimes known as the butterfly tree because of the shape of its leaves. It is very tolerant of poorly drained or alkaline soils and those with a high clay content. This tolerance results in the mopane having a wide range of distribution throughout southern Africa; in Namibia it occurs mainly in the higher, slightly wetter areas including Etosha, the northern Kaokoveld, Caprivi and the Kalahari.

Mopane trees can attain a height of 25m, especially if growing on rich, alluvial soils. However, shorter trees are more common in areas that are poor in nutrients,

THE FOSSIL DESERT
Though the Namib is one of the world's oldest deserts, many insist that the Kalahari doesn't qualify for the title 'desert' as it receives much more than 100mm of rain per year. However, the sand sheet that covers the Kalahari results in virtually no surface water, and evidence suggests that it may once have been much more arid than it is now. So although it is commonly called a desert, a better description of it would be 'a fossil desert'.

or have suffered from extensive fire damage. Stunted mopane will form a low scrub, perhaps only 5m tall. All mopane trees are deciduous, and the leaves turn beautiful shades of yellow and red before falling in September and October.

Ground cover in mopane woodland is usually sparse, just thin grasses, herbs and the occasional bush. The trees themselves are an important source of food for game, as the leaves have a high nutritional value – rich in protein and phosphorus – which is favoured by browsers and is retained even after they have fallen from the trees. Mopane forests support large populations of rodents, including tree squirrels (*Peraxerus cepapi*), which are so typical of these areas that they are known as 'mopane squirrels'.

Savannah
This all-encompassing category refers to those areas of dry, thorny woodland that occur when trees and shrubs have invaded open grassland, often because of some disturbance like cultivation, fire or over-grazing. It could be subdivided further into *Thorntree*, *Bush* and *Mixed Tree and Shrub Savannah*.

Some form of savannah covers much of the Namibian highlands, and the dominant families of trees and bushes are the Acacia, Terminalia (bearing single-winged seeds) and Combretum (bearing seeds with four or five wings), but many others are also present.

Teak forest
In a few areas of the Kalahari (including some within Khaudum National Park), the Zambezi teak, *Baikaea plurijuga*, forms dry semi-evergreen forests on a base of Kalahari sand. This species is not fire-resistant, so these stands occur only where slash-and-burn cultivation methods have never been used. Below the tall teak is normally a dense, deciduous thicket of vegetation, interspersed with sparse grasses and herbs in the shadier spots of the forest floor.

Moist evergreen forest
In areas of high rainfall, or near main rivers and swamps where a tree's roots will have permanent access to water, dense evergreen forest is found. This lush vegetation contains many species and is characterised by having three levels: a canopy of tall trees, a sub-level of smaller trees and bushes, and a variety of ground-level vegetation. In effect, the environment is so good for plants that they have adapted to exploit the light from every sunbeam. In Namibia, this occurs only as *riparian* forest (sometimes called *riverine* forest), which lines the country's major rivers.

Vlei
A 'vlei' is a shallow grass depression, or small valley, that is either permanently or seasonally wet – though Namibia's vleis are drier than the areas that one would call

vleis in countries further east. These open, verdant dips in the landscape usually support no bushes or trees. In higher valleys amongst hills, they sometimes form the sources of streams and rivers. Because of their dampness, they are rich in species of grasses, herbs and flowering plants. Their margins are usually thickly vegetated by grasses, herbs and smaller shrubs.

Floodplain

Floodplains are the low-lying grasslands on the edges of rivers, streams, lakes and swamps that are seasonally inundated by floods. Namibia has only a few floodplains, in the Caprivi area. The best examples are probably beside the Okavango in Mahango, and near the Chobe and Zambezi rivers in the Impalila area. These contain no trees or bushes, just a low carpet of grass species that can tolerate being submerged for part of the year.

Pan

Though not an environment for rich vegetation, a pan is a shallow, seasonal pool of water with no permanent streams leading into or from it. The bush is full of small pans in the rainy season, most of which will dry up soon after the rains cease. The Etosha and Nyae Nyae pans are just much larger versions, which attract considerable numbers of migrant birds when full.

Desert flora

Weighty tomes have been written on the flora of the Namib Desert, with its endemic plants and multitude of subtly different vegetation zones. One of the easiest to read (see *Further Reading*, page 507) is Dr Mary Seely's excellent book *The Namib*, which is widely sold in Namibia. This is well worth buying when you arrive, as it will increase your understanding and enjoyment of the desert immensely.

Distance from the coast and altitude are crucial to note when looking at the Namib's flora, as both are factors in determining how much moisture a plant receives by way of the fog. This is maximised at an altitude of about 300–600m above sea level, and extends up to about 60km inland. Thus the communities of vegetation can differ widely over very small distances: the plains full of delicate lichens in one place, and empty a kilometre away. Adaptations to the extremes are all around: wax-covered leaves to reduce transpiration, hollow stems to store water, low growth to avoid the wind, slow growth to take advantage of the infrequent moisture.

The species differ too widely to describe here, but are mentioned in the relevant chapters. Many will become familiar to even a casual observer; none could forget the prehistoric welwitschia (*Welwitschia mirabilis*), the kokerbooms silhouetted on rocky mountainsides, or the strange halfmen seen in the far south.

Animals

Namibia's large mammals are typical of the savannah areas of southern Africa, though those that rely on daily water are restricted in their distributions. With modern game-capture and relocation techniques, you may well find animals far out of their natural ranges. (Bontebok and black wildebeest, for example, are native to South Africa but are now found on many ranches in Namibia.) Thus what you may see in a given area may be different from what 'naturally occurs'.

The large predators are all here in Namibia. Lion are locally common, but largely confined to the parks and the Caprivi area away from dense habitation.

Leopard are exceedingly common throughout the country, and the central highlands provide just the kind of rocky habitat that they love. They are, however, very rarely seen naturally. Cheetah do exceptionally well in Namibia, which is said to have about 40% of Africa's population. This is mainly because commercial farmers eradicate lion and hyena relatively easily, and allow smaller buck, the cheetah's natural prey, to coexist with cattle. Hence the cheetahs thrive on large ranches – having problems only if the farmers suspect them of killing stock and try to eradicate them also.

Wild dog have a stronghold in the wild areas around Khaudum, but are seldom seen elsewhere. They need huge territories in which to roam, and don't survive well on commercially farmed land. Recent attempts to reintroduce them to Etosha have failed; it is hoped that some may succeed in the future.

The social spotted hyena is common in the north and northwest of the country, and even occurs down into the Namib's central desert areas and the Naukluft mountains – though it is not common here. Much more common and widespread is the solitary, secretive brown hyena, which is common by the coast, where it can even be seen scavenging amongst the seal colonies.

Buffalo occur in protected national parks in the Caprivi, and have been re-introduced to Waterberg from South Africa, but are not found elsewhere in Namibia.

Elephant occur widely in the north, in Khaudum, Caprivi and Etosha. A separate population has its stronghold in the Kaokoveld. Many venture right down the river valleys and live in desert areas: these are the famous 'desert elephants'. They survive there by knowing exactly where the area's waterholes are, and where water can be found in the rivers. This ancestral knowledge, probably passed down the generations, is easily lost, although in recent years various conservation/ development schemes in the area have been so successful that these 'desert-adapted' elephants are now thriving.

Black rhino occur in similar areas, but poaching now effectively limits them to some of the main national parks, and the less accessible areas of the Kaokoveld. Their numbers also are doing very well, and those in the Kaokoveld form one of Africa's only increasing black rhino populations: success indeed for an area outside any national park where only community conservation schemes stand between the poachers and their quarry. White rhino have been re-introduced to Waterberg and Etosha, where they seem to be thriving.

Antelope are well represented, with springbok, gemsbok or impala being numerically dominant depending on the areas. The rare endemic black-faced impala is a subspecies found only in northwestern Namibia and southern Angola.

Roan antelope are found in the Caprivi, Waterberg and Etosha. Sable occur only in the Caprivi, with excellent numbers often seen on the Okavango's floodplains on the edge of Mahango. In the Caprivi's wetter areas there are also red lechwe and the odd sitatunga.

Red hartebeest are widespread in the north and east, though common nowhere. Blue wildebeest are found in Etosha and the north, as are giraffe. Eland occur in Etosha and the Kalahari, whilst Kudu seem the most adaptable of the large antelope, occurring everywhere apart from the coastal desert strip – and also eastwards to the Indian Ocean.

Amongst the smaller antelope, duiker are common everywhere apart from the desert, as are steenbok. Klipspringer occur throughout Namibia's mountains. Namibia's smallest antelope, the Damara dik-dik, is endemic to the area around the Kaokoveld and Etosha.

For further details of wildlife, see *Appendix 1*, page 487.

TRACKS

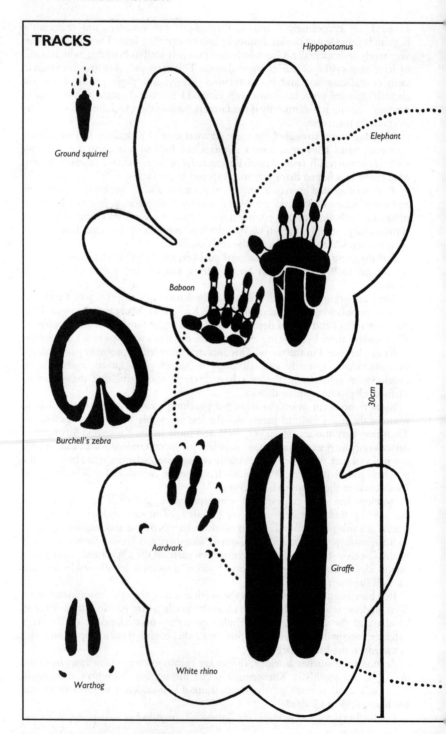

Hippopotamus

Ground squirrel

Elephant

Baboon

Burchell's zebra

30cm

Aardvark

Giraffe

White rhino

Warthog

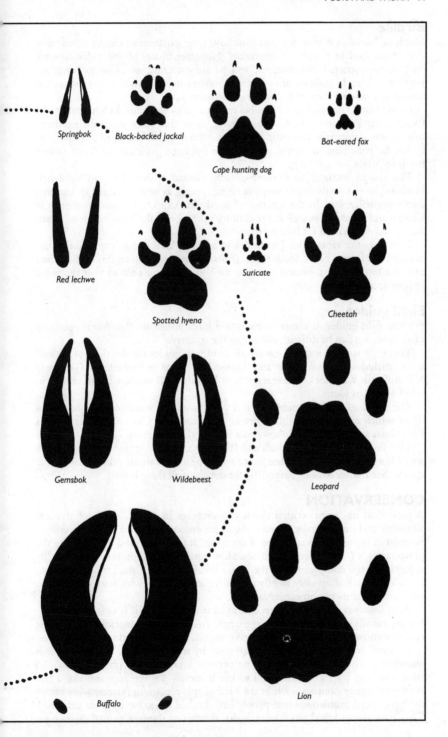

Springbok

Black-backed jackal

Cape hunting dog

Bat-eared fox

Red lechwe

Spotted hyena

Suricate

Cheetah

Gemsbok

Wildebeest

Leopard

Buffalo

Lion

Birdlife

Much of Namibia is very dry, and thus hasn't the variation in resident birds that you might find in lusher environments. However, many of those dry-country birds have restricted distributions, and so are endemic, or close to being so. Further, where Namibia's drier interior borders on to a wetter area, as within Mahango National Park, the species count shoots up.

In addition to its residents, Namibia receives many migrants. In September and October the Palaearctic migrants appear (ie: those that come from the northern hemisphere – normally Europe), and they remain until around April or May. This is also the peak time to see the intra-African migrants, which come from further north in Africa.

The coastal wetland sites, most notably around Walvis Bay and Sandwich Harbour, receive visits from many migrating species, as well as seabird species that aren't normally seen in the interior of southern Africa. So visits including the Caprivi and the coast, as well as the country's interior, make Namibia an excellent and varied destination for birding trips.

Inevitably the rains from December to around April see an explosion in the availability of most birds' food: seeds, fruits and insects. Hence this is the prime time for birds to nest, even if it is also the most difficult time to visit the more remote areas of the country.

Field guides

Finding field guides to plants, animals and birds whilst in Namibia is relatively easy; though it can be difficult outside of the country.

There are some comprehensive little hardback guides on the flora of various areas, including *Namib Flora* and *Damaraland Flora* published by Gamsberg Macmillan in Windhoek. These are sold in Namibia and marketed with visitors in mind as well as locals.

The standard birding guide to travel with is still Newman's *Birds of Southern Africa,* which is widely available overseas. For mammals, Chris and Tilde Stuart's *Field Guide to Mammals of Southern Africa* is generally very good.

The Shell guides to *The Namib* and *Waterberg* are excellent for appreciating the area's flora and fauna. Doubtless more will appear for various other areas in due course. See *Further Reading* (page 507) for details of all these books.

CONSERVATION

A great deal has been written about conservation in Africa, much of it over-simplistic and intentionally emotive. As an informed visitor you are in the unique position of being able to see some of the issues at first hand, and to appreciate the perspectives of local people. So abandon your preconceptions, and start by appreciating the complexities of the issues involved. Here I shall try to develop a few ideas, touched on only briefly elsewhere in the book, which are common to most current thinking on conservation.

First, *conservation* must be taken within its widest sense if it is to have meaning. Saving animals is of minimal use if the whole environment is degraded, so we must consider conserving whole areas and ecosystems, not just the odd isolated species.

Observe that land is regarded as an asset by most societies, in Africa as it is elsewhere. (The Bushmen used to be perhaps a notable exception to this.) To 'save' the land for the animals and to use it merely for the recreation of a few privileged foreign tourists – whilst the local people remain in poverty – is a recipe for huge social problems. Local people have hunted game for food for centuries. They have always killed those animals that threatened them or ruined their crops.

If we now try to proclaim animals in a populated area as protected, without addressing the concerns of the people, then our efforts will fail.

The only pragmatic way to conserve Namibia's wild areas is to see the *conservation* of animals and the environment as inseparably linked to the *development* of the local people.

In the long term one will not work without the other. Conservation without development leads to resentful local people who will happily, and frequently, shoot, trap and kill animals. Development without conservation will simply repeat the mistakes that most developed countries have already made: it will lay waste a beautiful land, and kill off its natural heritage. Look at the tiny areas of natural vegetation which survive undisturbed in the UK, the USA, or Japan, to see how unsuccessful they have been at long-term conservation over the last 500 years.

As an aside, the local people in Namibia – and other developing countries – are sometimes wrongly accused of being the only agents of degradation. Observe the volume of tropical hardwoods imported by the industrialised countries to see that the West plays no small part in this.

In conserving some of Namibia's natural areas, and helping its people to develop, the international community has a vital role to play. It could use its aid projects to encourage the Namibian government to practise sustainable long-term strategies, rather than grasping for the short-term fixes which politicians seem universally to prefer. But such strategies must have the backing of the people themselves, or they will fall apart when foreign funding eventually wanes.

Most Namibians are more concerned about where they live, what they can eat, and how they will survive, than they are about the lives of small, obscure species of antelope that taste good when roasted. To get backing from the local communities, it is not enough for a conservation strategy to be compatible with development: it must actually promote it and help the local people to improve their own standard of living. If that situation can be reached, then rural populations can be mobilised behind long-term conservation initiatives.

Governments are the same. As one of Zambia's famous conservationists once commented, 'governments won't conserve an impala just because it is pretty'. But they will work to save it *if* they can see that it is worth more to them alive than dead.

The best strategies tried so far on the continent attempt to find lucrative and sustainable ways to use the land. They then plough much of the revenue back into the surrounding local communities. Once the people see revenue from conservation being used to help them improve their lives – to build houses, clinics and schools, and to offer paid employment – then such schemes stand a chance of getting their backing and support. It can take a while...

Carefully planned, sustainable tourism is one solution that can work effectively. For success, the local people must see that visitors pay because they want the wildlife. Thus, they reason that the existence of wildlife directly improves their income, and they will strive to conserve it.

It isn't enough for them to see that the wildlife helps the government to get richer; that won't dissuade a local hunter from shooting a duiker for dinner. However, if he benefits directly from the visitors, who come to see the animals... then he has a vested interest in saving that duiker.

It matters little to the Namibian people, or ultimately to the wildlife, whether these visitors come to shoot the wildlife with a camera or with a gun – as long as any hunting is done on a sustainable basis, so that is only a few of the oldest 'trophy' animals are shot each year, and the size of the animal population remains largely unaffected. Photographers may claim the moral high ground, but should

IRDNC

The Integrated Rural Development and Nature Conservation (IRDNC) is a small organisation directed by Garth Owen-Smith, a Namibian nature conservator, and Dr Margaret Jacobsohn, a Namibian anthropologist who worked amongst the Himba people for years.

Their goal is to ensure the sustainable social, economic and ecological development of Namibia's communal areas, and they have been working towards it since the mid-1980s. The directors have received several international environmental prizes, and the IRDNC now employs a staff of over 30 and more than 130 rural community workers.

The IRDNC was one of the pioneers of the community game-guard scheme in the Kaokoveld, involved as early as 1983, and later helped to set up some of the community campsites there. It facilitated the important projects to return money from lodges to local communities at Lianshulu and Etendeka, and was also involved with setting up the joint venture between the community and Wilderness Safaris which is behind Damaraland Camp.

Typical of the organisation's low-key approach, when asked they emphasise how they have always worked as part of a team with the government, various NGOs, community groups and like-minded organisations in the private sector. (Namibia's Save the Rhino Trust is another notable player in much of this work.)

remember that hunters pay far more for their privileges. Hunting operations generate large revenues from few guests, who demand minimal infrastructure and so cause little impact on the land. Photographic operations need more visitors to generate the same revenue, and so may have greater negative effects on the country.

National parks and private reserves

In practice, there is room for both types of visitors in Namibia: the photographer and the hunter. The national parks are designated for photographic visitors, where no hunting is allowed.

Many private ranches now have game on their land and style themselves as 'hunting farms'. They are used mainly by overseas hunters (primarily from Germany and the USA) who pay handsomely for the privilege. The livelihood of these farms depends on hunting, and so it must be practised sustainably.

There are very few countries in Africa where land is being returned to a more natural state, with fewer livestock and more indigenous game, so Namibia is a great success story.

Government conservation policy

In March 1995 the Namibian Cabinet passed a new policy on wildlife management, utilisation and tourism in communal areas (areas occupied by subsistence farmers rather than large-scale commercial ranches). This followed five years of consultations, and much study.

Many interested groups, including the Integrated Rural Development and Nature Conservation (IRDNC) have been closely involved with the formulating of this policy, and it enabled a whole new type of community project like Damaraland Camp to get off the ground.

The new policy finally encouraged the linking of 'conservation with rural development by enabling communal farmers to derive financial income from the sustainable use of wildlife and from tourism'. It also aimed to 'provide an incentive to the rural people to conserve wildlife and other natural resources, through shared decision-making and financial benefit'.

Put simply, this gave a framework for local communities to take charge of the wildlife in their own areas for sustainable utilisation – with decisions made by the local communities, for the community.

Community Game Guard scheme

This scheme (originally called the Auxiliary Game Guard scheme) started in the 1980s and has been behind the phenomenal recovery of the desert-adapted populations of elephant and black rhino in the area. In its simplest form, a community game guard is appointed from each community, and is paid to ensure that no member of the community hunts anything that they are not allowed to hunt.

Community campsites

These aim to enable local communities to benefit very directly from passing tourists. The community sets up a campsite, and then a central community fund receives the money generated – and the whole community decides how that revenue is spent. Once the tourists have stopped to camp, it also gives the community a chance to earn money by guiding the visitors on local walks, selling curios or firewood, or whatever else seems appropriate in the area.

There are now several community campsites in the Kaokoveld, and an increasing number in the Caprivi area.

Tourism

Namibia lies far from Africa's 'original' big-game safari areas of East Africa, Kenya and Tanzania, and from the newer destinations of Zimbabwe and Zambia. Aside from Etosha and Caprivi, Namibia doesn't have the density of game that visitors would expect for such a trip, or the warm tropical shores that they would expect for a beach holiday (anyone who has been to Lüderitz will surely agree).

Thus Namibia doesn't generally attract first-time visitors who simply want to tick off game, or see game and lie on a beach. This combination accounts for much volume in the travel business. Therefore few cheap charter planes arrive in Namibia, and there is only a handful of large hotels, most of which aim more for business people than tourists.

The main area of growth in Namibia's tourism is in self-drive individual trips and small-group tours. These are perfect for the small lodges and guest farms, which can't take big groups anyhow. It is allowing many small-scale tourist ventures to develop and thrive – utilising not only the few famous national parks, but also old cattle ranches and otherwise unproductive sections of desert.

In the long term, this is a huge advantage for the country. Tourism is set to continue growing slowly but steadily – but without the boom-then-bust experienced by countries like Kenya. Every month new small camps, lodges and guest farms open for visitors; most try hard to retain that feeling of 'wilderness' which is so rare in more densely populated countries, and much sought after by visitors. Namibia has so much space and spectacular scenery that, provided the developments remain small-scale and responsible, it should have a very long and profitable career in tourism ahead.

Perhaps Namibia's most promising developments in this field are its successes in linking tourism with community development projects. The Community Game

Guard scheme has already safeguarded the populations of desert-adapted elephants and black rhino in the Kaokoveld, whilst a number of community campsites are thriving in the area.

Both projects are now extending their reach in the Caprivi area, assisted by trail-blazing individuals and organisations like the IRDNC. Tourism is a vital source of revenue for many of these projects and, if it helps to provide employment and bring foreign exchange into Namibia, this gives the politicians a reason to support environmental conservation.

The tourist's responsibility

Visitors on an expensive trip to Namibia are, by their mere presence, making some financial contribution to development and conservation in Namibia. There are several things that they can do to maximise this.

If camping, they can seek out the community campsites, and support them. They can use the local people there for guides, and pay for the facilities. Even travellers on a lower budget can thus have a direct impact on some of Namibia's smaller, rural communities.

If staying in lodges, they can ask the lodge operator, in the most penetrating of terms, what he or she is doing to help local development initiatives. How much of the lodge's revenue goes directly back to the local community? How do the people benefit directly from the visitors staying at *this* camp? How much of a say do they have about what goes on in the area where *these* safaris are operated?

If enough visitors did this, it would make a big difference. All Namibia's operators would start to place development initiatives higher on their list of priorities. At present, a few operators have really excellent forward-thinking ways of helping their local communities – Damaraland Camp being a real flagship, and the focus for much attention.

Some others make a form of 'charity' donation to local communities, but otherwise only involve local people as workers. Whilst this is valuable, much more is needed. Local people must gain greater and more direct benefits from tourism if conservation is going to be successful in Africa, and Namibia is no exception.

Hunting

Big-game hunting, where visiting hunters pay large amounts to kill trophy animals, is a practical source of revenue for many 'hunting farms' which accept guests. Some also accept non-hunters or 'photographic' guests.

It is interesting that the rich killing animals for sport is usually regarded as 'hunting', whilst the poor killing them for food is generally termed 'poaching'. That said, though many find hunting distasteful, it does benefit the Namibian economy greatly, and encourages farms to cultivate natural wildlife rather than introduced livestock. Until there are enough photographic guests to fill all the guest farms used for hunters, pragmatic conservationists will encourage the hunters.

If you don't hunt, but choose to stay at these places, ensure either that you are comfortable with hunting *per se*, or that there are no hunters on the farm whilst you are there. Arguments over dinner are surprisingly common.

Planning and Preparation

Until 1990, most of Namibia's tourists were from South Africa. They came in their own vehicles, for the sea fishing and the game parks – which still have well-organised facilities. Following independence, greater number of visitors have arrived from overseas every year, many using the restcamp facilities which were developed for the South Africans. Generally, the overseas visitors have more money to spend; they want small lodges rather than large camps, and restaurants rather than self-catering facilities.

Thus Namibia is seeing a real boom in lodges and bush-camps, and many economically marginal farms are thriving again as guest farms. Such small, individual places don't suit large tours or high-volume tour operators, who use only large hotels for their big groups. Thus the future for Namibia, the way that tourism is growing, is in self-drive trips by independent visitors who visit the smaller lodges and farms with their own vehicle, and don't rely on being part of a large touring group. Even those who first visit as part of a large group often return for their own individual self-drive trip.

Namibia is fortunate: its roads are good, its attractions well-signposted, and its national parks well-managed. Even the centralised booking system for the parks, based at Namibia Wildlife Resorts (NWR) in Windhoek, generally works well for advance bookings.

Despite its phenomenal growth, tourism to Namibia is still on a very small scale, a fraction of that found in, say, South Africa or Kenya. So the feeling of wilderness has not been lost; you will still be the only visitors in many corners of the country.

WHEN TO GO

There really are neither any 'bad' nor any 'ideal' times to visit Namibia, but there are times when some aspects of the country are at their best. You must decide what you are primarily interested in, and what's important to you, and then choose accordingly. See the *Climate* section, pages 33–4, for a more detailed discussion of the weather – perhaps the biggest influence on your decision. Then consider your own specific requirements, which might include some of the following:

Photography

For photography, Namibia is a stunning country in any month. Even with the simplest of camera equipment you can get truly spectacular results. My favourite time for photography is April to June. Then the dust has been washed out of the air by the rains, the vegetation is still green, and yet the sky is clear blue with only a few wispy white clouds.

Game viewing

The latter parts of the dry season are certainly the best time to see big game. Then, as the small bush pools dry up and the green vegetation shrivels, the animals move closer to the springs or the waterholes and rivers. So the months between July and late October are ideal for game.

During and after the rains, you won't see much game, partly because the lush vegetation hides the animals, and partly because most of them will have moved away from the waterholes (where they are most easily located) and gone deeper into the bush. However, many of the animals you see will have young, as food (animal or vegetable) is at its most plentiful then.

Birdwatching

The last few months of the year witness the arrival of the summer migrant birds from the north, anticipating the coming of the rains. Further, if the rains are good the natural pans in Etosha and Bushmanland will fill with aquatic species, including huge numbers of flamingos. This is an amazing spectacle (see box on *Flamingos*, page 319). However, bear in mind that Namibia's ordinary feathered residents can be seen more easily during the dry season, when there is less vegetation to hide them.

Walking

Daytime temperatures occasionally top 40°C in October and November, and heavy rainstorms are likely during the first two or three months of the year. Hence walkers should try to come between about May and September, when the temperatures are at their coolest, and the chances of rain are minimised. Note that most of the long trails in the national parks are closed between November and March.

Driving around

Driving usually presents few problems at any time of year. However, visitors in January and February, and occasionally even March or exceptionally April, may find that flooding rivers will block their roads. These usually subside within a matter of hours, and certainly within a day or so, but do provide an extra hazard. A 4WD is occasionally useful here, although taking another route is usually a cheaper alternative!

Those mounting 4WD expeditions to the more remote corners of the country should certainly avoid these months. Large tracts of Bushmanland, for example, become totally impassable in any vehicle. For detailed coverage of driving in Namibia, see *Chapter 6*, page 79.

Other visitors

Namibia is never crowded. Compared with the hordes of tourists that go to South Africa or Kenya, Namibia always seems deserted. That said, it becomes busier around Easter and from late July to early September. Then advanced bookings are *essential*. Many of the lodges and restcamps in and around Etosha, and in the Namib-Naukluft area, are fully booked for August as early as the end of April.

Avoid coming during the Namibian school holidays if possible. These are generally around April 25–May 25, August 15–September 5 and December 5–January 15. Then many places will be busy with local visitors, especially the less expensive restcamps and the national parks.

The main season when overseas visitors come is from around mid-July to late October. Outside of this, you'll often find the lodges delightfully quiet and have some of the attractions to yourself.

HOW TO TRAVEL

Obviously your style of travel around Namibia depends on your budget, though more expensive doesn't always guarantee a better trip.

Backpacking

Backpacking around Namibia is very limiting. You need private transport to see most of the national parks, and will be missing out on a lot if you don't have it. However, if you can splash out on a few days' car hire here, and a couple of guided trips from a lodge there, you might get by on £20/US$32 per day for the rest of your time.

Self-drive trips

The best way to see the country is certainly to have your own vehicle. Whether you opt to use camps, lodges and restcamps, or bring your own camping kit, is then merely a matter of style. The questions of what, how and where to hire a vehicle, and how much it will cost, are extensively covered in *Chapter 6*.

If you have a tight budget, a much better bet than backpacking would be to find four people to share the car, and camp everywhere. Then you could keep costs to around £40/US$64 per person per day.

For a less basic self-drive trip, with two people sharing the car and staying in a variety of small lodges and restcamps, expect a cost of about £80/US$128 each. If you choose more expensive lodges, with guided activities included, then this might rise to about £120/US$190 per day each – but should guarantee a first-class trip.

Group tours

Another option is to take a guided group tour around the country. These suit single travellers as they provide ready-made companions, and also the elderly, who may not feel confident driving. In either case, provided that you are happy to spend your whole holiday with the same group of people, such a trip might be ideal. Guided trips are generally more expensive than self-drive trips which follow the same itinerary.

Generally, the smaller the vehicle used, the better and the more expensive the trip becomes. On a cheaper trip, expect to camp, with a group size of 12–15 people, for around £65/US$100 per day, based on a 12-day itinerary. For something less basic, using smaller minibuses, a trip of one to two weeks will cost around £120/US$190 per person sharing, including all meals and activities. Several of the better operators run small-group trips in Land Rovers, with professional guides rather than simply drivers. These can be excellent, but will cost more than a self-drive trip around the same itinerary. Expect to pay upwards of £150/US$240 per person per night.

Fly-in trips

Finally if your budget is flexible (and especially if your time is very limited), then consider doing some or all of your trip as a fly-in safari. Small private charter flights can be arranged to many of the smaller lodges and guest farms; it's a very easy way to travel. It is also the only way to get to some of the more inaccessible corners, like the northern section of the Skeleton Coast.

A very popular combination is to fly down to the Sesriem area for three or four nights, hop up to Swakopmund, and then pick up a hire car to drive yourself north to Damaraland and Etosha. Another place commonly visited on short fly-in trips is the Fish River Canyon.

Expect to pay upwards of about £250/US$400 per person per night for a full fly-in trip, and note that your choice of lodges will be restricted to those that can arrange all your activities for you.

ORGANISING YOUR TRIP

Most visitors who come to Namibia for a holiday use the country's guest farms, lodges and restcamps – often combining them together into a self-drive tour around the country.

Such trips are quite complex, as you will be using numerous hotels, camps and lodges in your own particular sequence. Many of these places are small (and so easily filled), and organise their own logistics with military precision. Finding space at short notice is often difficult.

To arrange everything, it's best to use a reliable, independent tour operator based in your own country. Although many operators sell trips to Namibia, few really know the country well. Insist on dealing directly with someone who does. Namibia changes so fast that detailed local knowledge is vital in putting together a trip that runs smoothly and suits you. Make sure that whoever you book with is fully bonded, so that your money is protected if they go broke; and, ideally, pay with a credit card. Never book a trip from someone who doesn't know Namibia personally: you are asking for problems.

Trips around Namibia are not cheap, though they are currently cheaper (and also better value in many cases) than in any other country in southern Africa. Expect to pay around the same to an operator as you would have to pay directly: about £550–900/US$880–1,440 per person per week, plus airfares. At this price you can expect a good level of service whilst you are considering the options and booking the trip. If you don't get it, go elsewhere.

Booking directly with Namibian safari operators or agencies is possible, but communication is more difficult and you will have no recourse if anything goes wrong. European/US operators usually work on commission for the trips that they sell, which is deducted from the basic cost that the visitor pays. Thus you should end up paying about the same whether you book through an overseas operator or talk directly to someone in Namibia, but the former is a lot easier.

Tour operators

Until the last few years, most tour operators overseas have overlooked Namibia. Few have featured it. Now that it is better known, many are hastily putting together programmes without knowing what they're doing. Often they are just selling tours that someone in Namibia has designed and marketed. Few have spent much time in the country themselves, and fewer still can give detailed first-hand guidance on all of the country, let alone a wide range of guest farms, camps and lodges.

Don't be talked into thinking that there are only a handful of places to visit and a few camps to stay in. There are many, all individual and different. Ask about ones mentioned in these chapters; a good operator will know the vast majority of them and be able to describe them to you.

Here I must, as the author, admit a personal interest in the tour-operating business: I organise and run the southern African operations of the UK operator Sunvil Africa (tel: 020 8232 9777; email: africa@sunvil.co.uk). In Namibia our flexible fly-drives start at about £1,600/US$2,560 per person for two weeks, including flights from London, car hire, all accommodation and some meals. I believe that Sunvil Africa have the best and most interesting programme to Namibia – and will happily send you a detailed map of Namibia and our brochure, to demonstrate this. Just call us. For a fair comparison, other UK tour operators that feature Namibia include:

Aardvark Safaris RBL House, Ordnance Rd, Tidworth, Hants SP9 7QD; tel: 01980 849160; fax: 01980 849161; email: mail@aardvarksafaris.com; web: www.aardvarksafaris.com. Recently founded, small upmarket operator featuring much of Africa and Madagascar.

Abercrombie & Kent Sloane Square House, Holbein Place, London SW1W 8NS; tel: 020 7559 8500; fax: 0845 070 0608; web: www.abercrombiekent.co.uk. Long-established, large and posh operator worldwide, with a wide choice of Africa trips – though often focuses on selling its own lodges in Africa.

Africa Explorer 5 Strand on the Green, London W4 3PQ; tel: 020 8987 8742; fax: 020 8994 6264; email: africa.explorer@easynet.co.uk; web: www.africa-explorer.co.uk. Tiny but knowledgeable company, run by the jovial John Haycock, that has unusual, and enormous, six-wheeled self-contained vehicles for hire.

Africa Travel Centre Leigh St, London WC1H 9EW; tel: 020 7387 1211; fax: 020 7383 7512; email: sales@africatravel.co.uk; web: www.africatravel.co.uk. Featuring East and southern Africa, the Africa Travel Centre has a special emphasis on golfing holidays, and trips for sportspeople to Africa.

Bridge Travel Group Bridge House, 55–59 High Rd, Broxbourne, Herts EN10 7DT; tel: 0870 191 7168; fax: 01992 456 609. A member of the UK's large My Travel Group, Bridge has a programme concentrating on South Africa, including trips to Namibia.

Cazenove & Loyd 3 Alice Court, 116 Putney Bridge Rd, London SW15 2NQ; tel: 020 8875 9666; fax: 020 8875 9444; web: www.caz-loyd.com. Old-school, established tailormade specialists to East/southern Africa, the Indian Ocean Islands, and Central/South America.

Cedarberg Travel 16a High St, Hampton, Middx TW12 2SJ; tel: 020 8941 1717; fax: 020 8979 3893; email: info@cedarberg-travel.com; web: www.cedarbergtravel.com. South African specialist with some knowledge of Namibia.

Cox & Kings Gordon House, 10 Greencoat Place, London SW1P 1PH; tel: 020 7873 5000; email: africa.sales@coxandkings.co.uk; web: www.coxandkings.co.uk. Old company renowned for India, now also featuring Latin America, Indian Ocean, Middle East, China, Asia and Africa, including some Namibian trips.

Dragoman Camp Green, Debenham, Stowmarket, Suffolk IP14 6LA; tel: 01728 861133; fax: 01728 861127; email: info@dragoman.co.uk; web: www.dragoman.co.uk. Budget overland truck tours worldwide, including Africa.

Exodus 9 Weir Rd, London SW12 0LT; tel: 020 8675 5550; fax: 020 7673 0779; web: www.exodus.co.uk. Budget overland truck tours worldwide, including Africa, now branching out into set trips that don't involve trucks.

Explore Worldwide 1 Frederick St, Aldershot, Hants GU11 1LQ; tel: 01252 760000; fax: 01252 760001; email: res@exploreworldwide.com; web: www.exploreworldwide.com. A relatively large specialist company concentrating on small-group escorted tours throughout the world, including Namibia, using local operators and transport.

Footloose Adventure Travel Services 3 Springs Pavement, Ilkley, West Yorks LS29 8HD; tel: 01943 604030; fax: 01943 604070; email: info@footlooseadventure.co.uk; web: www.footlooseadventure.co.uk.

Gane and Marshall 98 Crescent Rd, New Barnet, Herts EN4 9RJ; tel: 020 8441 9592; fax: 020 8441 7376; email: holidays@ganeandmarshall.co.uk; web: www.ganeandmarshall.co.uk. Offers small group trips to South and Central America and the Galápagos, plus the Far East and most of Africa, from Ethiopia to Namibia.

Guerba Wessex House, 40 Station Rd, Westbury, Wilts BA13 3JN; tel: 01373 826611; fax: 01373 858351; email: info@guerba.co.uk; www.guerba.com. Long-standing overland truck company that's branched out in recent years into other trips worldwide; takes a very responsible approach to African travel.

Hartley Safaris The Old Chapel, Chapel Lane, Hackthorn, Lincs LN2 3PN; tel: 01673 861600; fax: 01673 861666; web: www.hartleys-safaris.co.uk. Old-school, established tailormade specialists to East/southern Africa, and Indian Ocean Islands.

Nomad African Travel Smugglers Cottage, Church Rd, Westbourne, Emsworth, Hants PO10 8UA; tel/fax: 01243 373929; email: info@nomadafricantravel.co.uk; web: www.nomadafricantravel.co.uk

Okavango Tours and Safaris Marlborough House, 298 Regents Park Rd, London N3 2TJ; tel: 020 8343 3283; fax: 020 8343 3287; email: info@okavango.com; web:

www.okavango.com. Small, long-established specialists to East/southern Africa, Madagascar and the Indian Ocean islands.

Rainbow Tours 64 Essex Rd, London N1 8LR; tel: 020 7226 1004; fax: 020 7226 2621; email: info@rainbowtours.co.uk; web: www.rainbowtours.co.uk. Established specialists to South Africa and Madagascar with a strong ethical streak, and a programme in Namibia.

Safari Consultants Orchard House, Upper Rd, Little Cornard, Suffolk CO10 0NZ; tel: 01787 228494; fax: 01787 228096; email: bill@safariconsultantuk.com; web: www.safari-consultants.co.uk, web: www.safariconsultantuk.com. Old school tailormade specialists to the Indian subcontinent, East/central/southern Africa, including Namibia, and the Indian Ocean islands.

Safari Drive The Trainers Office, Windy Hollow, Sheepdrive, Lambourn, Berks RG17 7XA; tel: 0870 240 6305; fax: 01488 71311; email: safari_drive@compuserve.com; web: www.safaridrive.com. Operate trips using equipped Land Rovers, mainly in Botswana and Tanzania though also covers Namibia.

Scott Dunn World Fovant Mews, 12 Noyna Rd, London SW17 7PH; tel: 020 8682 5010; fax: 020 8682 5090; email: world@scottdunn.com; web: www.scottdunn.com. Worldwide luxury operator featuring Asia, Latin America, ski chalets, Mediterranean villas and Africa, including Namibia.

Somerville Wood (Drive Africa) The Nightingale Centre, 8 Balham Hill, London SW12 9EA; tel: 020 8675 3974; fax: 020 8675 3913; email: mail@driveafrica.com; web: www.driveafrica.com. Relatively new company concentrating on sub-Saharan Africa, with a variety of offerings including fully equipped 4WDs.

Steppes Africa The Travel House, 51 Castle St, Cirencester, Glos GL7 1QD; tel: 01285 650011; fax: 01285 885888; email: safari@steppesafrica.co.uk; web: www.artoftravel.co.uk. Originally founded as 'Art of Travel', this posh tailormade specialist now features much of Asia, as well as most of East, central and southern Africa, plus Mauritius and the Seychelles.

Sunvil Africa Upper Square, Old Isleworth, Middlesex, TW7 7BJ; tel: 020 8232 9777; fax: 020 8568 8330; email: africa@sunvil.co.uk; web: www.sunvil.co.uk/africa. Sunvil started trips to Namibia in 1992, and now have the most comprehensive programme to the country, run by Chris McIntyre – this book's author.

Tim Best Travel 68 Old Brompton Rd, London SW7 3LQ; tel: 020 7591 0300; fax: 020 7591 0301; email: info@timbesttravel.com; web: www.timbesttravel.co.uk. Bespoke operator concentrating on South America, the Indian Ocean Islands and Africa – including Namibia.

Tribes Travel 12 The Business Centre, Earl Soham, Woodbridge, Suffolk IP13 7SA; tel: 01728 685971; fax: 01728 685973; email: bradt@tribestravel.co.uk; web: www.tribes.co.uk. Not a Namibian specialist, though an interesting selection of trips worldwide, based on fair-trade principles, including some innovative options.

Wildlife Worldwide 170 Selsdon Rd, South Croydon, Surrey CR2 6PJ; tel: 020 8667 9158; fax: 020 8667 1960; email: sales@wildlifeworldwide.com; web: www.wildlifeworldwide.com. Wide-ranging small operator with programmes across the globe, including options that feature Namibia.

National parks

Namibia Wildlife Resorts (NWR) is the government department responsible for all the national parks. It is generally efficient, if sometimes apparently over-zealous about its bureaucracy. Its system insists that advance bookings for accommodation are made through the Windhoek office.

You can, theoretically, reserve accommodation by post or fax. However, you must pay for it in advance. From overseas this can require a telex transfer of money. To start this process, write to the Director of Tourism, RESERVATIONS,

P Bag 13267, Windhoek; tel: 061 236975–8; fax: 061 224900. (See page 118 for Windhoek directions.) If you are booking less than 25 days ahead, then you must pay for everything in full. This system is most easily mastered by visiting the office in person in Windhoek. Alternatively book in advance through a tour operator that understands the system.

Entry permits for most parks are available at the gates, provided you're there before they close and there is space left. The exceptions are permits for the Naukluft, Terrace Bay and Torra Bay, which can only be obtained from Windhoek. Permits to drive through the Namib section of the Namib-Naukluft Park are available at most tourist offices.

Public holidays

During Namibia's public holidays the towns shut down, though the national parks and other attractions just carry on regardless.

New Year's Day	January 1
Independence Day	March 21
Good Friday	
Easter Monday	
Workers' Day	May 1
Cassinga Day	May 4
Africa Day	May 25
Ascension Day	40 days after Easter Sunday
Heroes' Day	August 26
Human Rights Day	December 10
Christmas Day	December 25
Family Day	December 26

GETTING THERE
By air
From Europe

There are several airlines flying to Namibia from Europe. Some are direct, and all are reliable. Most fly overnight, so you can fall asleep on the plane in London, and wake in southern Africa ready to explore. The time difference between western Europe and Namibia is minimal, so there's no jet lag.

One option to Windhoek is Air Namibia (tel: 01293 596657), which offers services from Frankfurt, with connections to London on British Airways. Currently flights depart from Frankfurt for Windhoek on Monday, Tuesday, Thursday and Saturday evenings. Northbound they leave Windhoek for Frankfurt on Tuesday morning, and also Wednesday, Friday and Sunday evenings. Air Namibia also operates connecting flights to/from Johannesburg and Cape Town to link up with most of these intercontinental flights to/from Windhoek.

From London, it is normally easiest and cheapest to use one of the major carriers to Johannesburg (11 hours), and then connect through to Windhoek. If you consider flying via Johannesburg, then there are a whole host of other options, from many European airports. British Airways and South African Airways have frequent services, and both operate add-on connections to Windhoek, run by their subsidiaries. Virgin also services the Johannesburg route, though their add-on prices for flights to Windhoek are not usually as competitive.

Expect to pay from around £550/US$825 return. Prices rise significantly for departures in July, August, and mid-December to mid-January, when you can expect to pay up to £950/US$1,425. The quietest periods are mid-April to end-June, and November.

Finding cheap tickets, and the right flights, is an art in itself. All the airlines will help you with information, but they sell their own seats at the 'published' fares. These are considerably above what you can expect to pay if you shop around. If you plan to hire a car or arrange some accommodation in advance, then speak to one of the UK's specialist tour operators (see page 51) *before* you book your flights. They will often offer to arrange everything together, and quote one cost for your whole trip – flights, car and accommodation. This may seem a lot, but compare it with the cost and hassle of putting the various components together yourself and you'll find that the better operators offer excellent deals.

However, if you're on a very tight budget and want to fly in and backpack around, then talk to a flight-only specialist. In the UK, start by looking in the classified adverts in the Sunday papers (start with *The Sunday Times*). You'll quickly learn what's available and how much the tickets cost. Flight specialists usually know nothing about Namibia; they just want to sell you flight tickets quickly. In London, they include Trailfinders (tel: 020 7938 3366), Travel Bag (tel: 020 0870 902 0179) and Bridge the World (tel: 020 7813 3350).

From the Americas

South African Airways operates direct flights between Atlanta and Johannesburg, codesharing with Delta, which connect with numerous regional flights to Windhoek. Alternatively, many travellers from the US approach southern Africa using connections via Europe, joining Air Namibia's flights in Frankfurt, or travelling on one of the many carriers servicing Johannesburg, and then connecting through to Windhoek. Start your research by looking in the classified section of the *New York Times*, which has a good section on discount flight specialists.

Given the duration of these flights, travellers often include a few days in Europe as they transit. This highlights the possibility of booking a return USA–London flight (from US$200 return) with an American travel specialist, and a return London–Windhoek flight (from US$1,000 return) with a London specialist. This means that you can use discounted fares for both legs and make a considerable saving. However, do allow a day or so in London between the flights, as your flights will not technically 'connect' – and if one is late you don't want to miss the other.

Travellers in Central and South America might use the Atlanta or European gateways, or the direct flights between São Paulo and Johannesburg, run by South African Airways (codeshare with Varig) five times a week.

From elsewhere

From the Far East, there are flights between Johannesburg and most of the major centres in the region, including Hong Kong (with South African Airways or Cathay Pacific) and Singapore (South African Airlines and Singapore Airlines). From Australasia, the best route is probably one of the flights from Perth to Johannesburg, with South African Airways or Qantas, connecting to Windhoek.

By land

If you are not flying in, then entering over one of Namibia's land borders is equally easy. Namibia has fast and direct links with South Africa – good tarred roads and railway service.

Crossing borders

Namibia's borders are generally hassle-free and efficient. If you are crossing with a hired car, then remember to let the car-hire company know as they will need to provide you with the right paperwork before you set off. Opening hours at the borders are currently as follows (see also www.namibweb.com/gi.htm):

With Botswana

Buitepos – on the Gobabis–Ghanzi road	08.00–17.00
Impalila Island – over the river from Kasane	07.00–18.00
Ngoma Bridge – between Caprivi and Kasane	06.00–18.00
Mohembo – on the southern side of Mahango	08.00–17.00

With Zambia

Wenella – just north of Katima Mulilo	07.00–18.00

With Angola

Oshikango – on the main road north	08.00–18.00
Ruacana – near the hydro-electric station	08.00–18.00
Rundu – cross the river to go north	08.00–17.00

With South Africa

Hohlweg – on the D622 southeast of Aroab	08.00–16.30
Klein Menasse – Aroab–Rietfontein road	08.00–16.30
Ariamsvlei – on the Karasburg–Upington road	24 hours
Noordoewer – on the Windhoek–Cape Town road	24 hours
Oranjemund – the bridge over the Orange River	06.00–22.00
Velloorsdrif – on the C10 southeast of Karasburg	08.00–16.30

VISAS AND ENTRY REQUIREMENTS
Documents
Currently all visitors require a passport which is valid for at least six months after they are due to leave, and an onward ticket of some sort. In practice, the second requirement is rarely even considered if you look neat, respectable and fairly affluent.

Currently, if you are a national of one of the following countries, you do not need a visa to enter Namibia: Angola, Australia, Austria, Belgium, Botswana, Brazil, Canada, Cuba, France, Germany, Iceland, Ireland, Italy, Japan, Kenya, Lesotho, Liechtenstein, Luxembourg, Malaysia, Mozambique, the Netherlands, New Zealand, Portugal, Russia and the CIS, Scandinavian countries, Singapore, South Africa, Spain, Swaziland, Switzerland, Tanzania, UK, USA, Zambia and Zimbabwe.

That said, it is *always* best to check with your local Namibian embassy or high commission before you travel. If you have difficulties in your home country, contact the Ministry of Home Affairs in Windhoek on the corner of Independence Av and Kasino St (P Bag 13200, Windhoek; tel: 061 292 9111).

The maximum tourist visa is 90 days, but this can be easily extended by application in Windhoek. You will then probably be required to show proof of the 'means to leave', like an onward air ticket, a credit card, or sufficient funds of your own. The current cost of a tourist or business visa is N$138.

Namibian embassies and high commissions
A list of the foreign embassies in Windhoek can be found on pages 151–2. Namibia's diplomatic representatives overseas include:

Angola Rua Dos Coqueiros, PO Box 953, Luanda; tel: (244) 2 395483; fax: (244) 2 339234; email: embnam@netangola.com
Belgium Av de Tervuren 454, B1150 Bruxelles; tel: (32) 2 771 1410; fax: (32) 2 771 9689; email: nam.emb@brutele.be
Botswana PO Box 987, 2nd Floor, Debswana House, Gaborone; tel: (267) 390 2181; fax: (267) 390 2248; email: nbc.gabs@info.bw

France 80 Av Foch, 17 Square de l'Avenue Foch, Paris 75016; tel: (33) 1 4417 3265; fax: (33) 1 4417 3273; email: namparis@club-internet.fr
Germany 5 Wichmannstrasse, 10787 Berlin; tel: (49) 30 254 0950; fax: (49) 30 254 09555
Russia 2nd Kazachy Lane, House No 7, Moscow; tel: (7) 95 230 3275; fax: (7) 95 230 2274; email: namibemb@online.ru
South Africa PO Box 29806, Sunnyside 0132, 702 Church St, Arcadia, Pretoria; tel: (27) 12 483 9100; fax: (27) 12 344 2998; email: secretary@namibia.org.za
Sweden Luntmakargatan 86–88, PO Box 26042, 111 22 Stockholm; tel: (46) 8 612 7788; fax: (46) 8 612 6655
UK 6 Chandos St, London W1N 0LQ; tel: (44) 20 7636 6244; fax: (44) 20 7637 5694; email: namibia-highcomm@btconnect.com
USA 1605 New Hampshire Av NW, Washington DC 20009; tel: (1) 202 986 0540; fax: (1) 202 986 0443; email: embnamibia@aol.com
Zambia 30A Mutende Rd, PO Box 30577, Woodlands, Lusaka; tel: (260) 1 260407/8; fax: (260) 1 263858; email: namibia@coppernet.zm
Zimbabwe 31A Lincoln Rd, Avondale, Harare; tel: (263) 4 885841; fax: (263) 4 885800; email: namhighcom@primenet.co.zw

Imports and exports

Being a member of the Southern African Customs Union (SACU) means that there are few restrictions between Namibia and either Botswana or South Africa. If you wish to export animal products, including skins or legally culled ivory, make sure you obtain a certificate confirming the origin of every item bought. Remember: even with such a certificate, the international CITES convention prohibits the movement of some things across international borders. Do consider the ethics of buying any animal products that might be covered by CITES.

MONEY AND BANKING
Currency

The Namibian dollar (N$) is divided into 100 cents. This is freely convertible in Namibia; there's no black market and no customs regulations applicable to moving it across borders. It is currently tied to the South African rand (R) so that N$1=R1. Rand can be used freely in Namibia – nobody even notices – though it is often difficult to change Namibian dollars once you leave Namibia. Even in South Africa, you must change the dollars at a bank, and may be charged a small premium for doing so.

Many banks overseas know only the exchange rate for rand, and don't supply Namibian dollars, or even quote a rate for it. If that's the case, you can bring rand to Namibia, and use that instead.

If the rand plummets in the future, perhaps as the result of negative developments in South Africa, then Windhoek may take full control of its currency, and allow it to float free from the rand. Its economy is probably strong enough to make this a very positive move. Check the latest situation with one of the bigger banks before you leave.

The last few years have seen the rand become progressively weaker against sterling and the US dollar, although there has been a considerable upturn in recent months. Nevertheless, travel in Namibia for the western visitor remains very good value.

Rates of exchange in March 2003:

£1 = N$12.70 = R12.70
US$1 = N$7.90 = R7.90
€1 = N$8.75 = R8.75

How to take your money

Namibian dollars are essential for buying petrol and small items, whilst most hotels, restaurants and larger shops accept credit cards.

Many travellers take most of their money as travellers' cheques (sterling or US dollars). Banks in the cities will cash any travellers' cheques, but American Express and Barclays Visa are well recognised, and prompt replacements are issued if cheques are stolen. (By carrying AMEX cheques you are eligible to use their customer mail-drop facilities in Windhoek.)

The major credit cards (Visa, MasterCard, and Diners Club) are widely accepted, and often transactions in Namibia take time to appear on your statement. There are reports, though, that American Express cards are increasingly difficult to use in both shops and banks, Drawing money at a bank via credit cards is easy, but it will take a few minutes longer than changing travellers' cheques.

The best system is always to have some cash Namibian dollars (or rand – remember they are interchangeable) with you, whilst conserving these by using credit cards where you can. You can gradually withdraw more money from your credit cards, or by cashing travellers' cheques, as your trip progresses. However, always make sure that your Namibian dollars will last out until you can get to a bank. For details of changing money, see pages 149–50.

Banking

Changing money at any of the commercial banks is as easy and as quick as it is in Europe. Normal banking hours are 08.30–15.30 weekdays and sometimes 08.30–11.00 Saturdays, depending upon the town, though there are a few places that are open seven days a week. Banks will cash travellers' cheques or give cash advances on credit cards, though the clearance required for a cash advance may take 30 minutes or so. Note that you may need to take a passport, even just to change currency.

BOB tills (auto-teller machines, or ATMs) work with Visa and MasterCard cards, though whether you are using a direct-debit card or a credit card, you should enter 'credit card account' and not 'bank account' when prompted about where you want your money to come from.

Away from the banks, Visa, MasterCard and American Express cards are usually accepted by lodges, hotels, restaurants, and shops, but travellers' cheques which are not in Namibian dollars or South African rand can be difficult to use. In the remoter areas cash is essential. Wherever you are, petrol stations always require cash. Note that at the end of the month, when many government employees are paid, the queue at the bank can be several hours long.

WHAT TO TAKE

This is difficult advice to give, as it depends upon how you travel and your own personality. If you intend to do a lot of hitching or backpacking, then you should plan carefully what you take in an attempt to keep things as light as possible. If you have a vehicle for your whole trip, then weight and bulk will not be such an issue.

Clothing

Most of your days you will want light, loose-fitting clothing. Cotton (or a cotton-rich mix) is cooler and more absorbent than synthetic fibres. For men, shorts (long ones) are usually fine, but long trousers are more socially acceptable in towns and especially in rural settlements and villages. For women, knee-length skirts or culottes are best. Namibia has a generally conservative dress code. Revealing or scruffy clothing isn't respected or appreciated by most Namibians.

For the evenings, especially for chilling rides in the back of safari vehicles, you will need something warm. Night-time temperatures in the winter months can be very low, especially in desert areas. If possible, dress in layers, taking along a light sweater (polar-fleeces are ideal) and a long-sleeved jacket, or a tracksuit, and a light but waterproof anorak. Note that some excellent cotton safari-wear is produced and sold locally. Try the department stores in Windhoek.

Finally, don't forget a squashable sun-hat. Cotton is perfect. Bring one for safety's sake, even if you hate hats, as it will greatly reduce the chance of your getting sunstroke when out walking.

Other useful items

See *Camping and walking in the bush*, page 102, for a discussion on what type of camping equipment to take. In addition, here are a few of my own favourites and essentials, just to jog your memory.

- sunblock and lipsalve for vital protection from the sun
- sunglasses – essential – ideally dark with a high UV absorption.
- insect repellent, especially if travelling to the north or during the rains
- 'Leatherman' multi-purpose tool. Never go into the bush without one of these amazing assistants
- electrical insulating tape – remarkably useful for general repairs
- binoculars – essential for watching game and birds
- camera, film and long lenses (see *Photography*, pages 59–60)
- basic sewing kit, with at least some really strong thread for repairs
- cheap waterproof watch (leave expensive ones, and jewellery, at home)
- couple of paperback novels
- large plastic 'bin-liner' (garbage) bags, for protecting your luggage from dust
- simple medical kit (see page 69)
- magnifying glass, for looking at some of the smaller attractions

And for backpackers, useful extras might include:

- concentrated, biodegradable washing powder
- long-life candles
- nylon paracord (20m) for emergencies and washing lines
- good compass and a whistle
- more comprehensive medical kit (see pages 69–70)
- universal plug

Maps and navigation

A reasonable selection of maps is available in Europe and the USA from specialised outlets. The Michelin map of East and southern Africa (sheet 995) sets the standard for the whole subcontinent, but is not really detailed enough for Namibia. The Freytag & Berndt map of Namibia looks good, though adds little to the free map issued by the tourist board.

Imported maps are obtainable in Europe from Stanfords, London (tel: 020 7836 1321) or Geocenter, Stuttgart, Germany (tel: 711 788 9340). In the USA try Map Link, Santa Barbara, California (tel: 805 965 4402).

Namibia has an excellent range of detailed 'Ordnance Survey' type maps available cheaply in Windhoek, from the Surveyor General's office on Robert Mugabe Avenue. See *Windhoek*, page 116, for details. If you are planning a 4WD expedition, then you may need to buy some of these before you head out into the bush. Expeditions to Kaokoland should also pick up a copy of the Shell map of

Kaokoland. It's better than anything else to that area, and does have good general information about the area in the back.

However, for most normal visitors on self-drive or guided trips, all the Ordnance Survey maps are *far* too detailed and unwieldy to use. Much better is the map distributed by the tourist board, which is perfect for self-drive trips using Namibia's roads. It really is the best map available, and has a useful distance table, and a street plan of Windhoek. It is available free at most tourist centres and information offices in Namibia. Overseas, most Namibian tourist offices will supply them, as will some of the better specialist tour operators (page 51).

GPS systems

If you are heading into the more remote parts in your own vehicle, then consider investing in a small GPS: a Global Positioning System. Under an open, unobstructed sky, these can fix your latitude, longitude and elevation to within about 100m, using 24 American military satellites that constantly pass in the skies overhead. They will work anywhere in the world.

Commercial units now cost from around £100/US$160 in Europe or the USA, although their prices are falling (and features improving) as the technology matures. Even the less expensive models will store 'waypoints', enabling you to build up an electronic picture of an area, as well as working out basic latitude, longitude and elevation. So, for example, you can store the position of your camp, and the nearest road, enabling you to leave with confidence and be reasonably sure of navigating back. This is invaluable in remote areas where there are few landmarks.

Beware though: a GPS isn't a substitute for good map-work and navigation. Do not come to rely on it, or you will be unable to cope if it fails. Used correctly, a GPS will help you to recognise minor errors before they are amplified into major problems. Finally, note that all these units use *lots* of battery power, so bring spares with you and/or a cigarette-lighter adaptor.

PHOTOGRAPHY
Cameras

The greatest flexibility is offered by 35mm SLR cameras with interchangeable lenses. For general photography, a mid-range zoom lens (eg: 28–70mm) is recommended – it is more flexible than the 'standard' (50mm) lens. For wildlife photography, you will need at least a 200mm lens to allow you to see the animal close up. Alternatively (or in addition), compact cameras take up little space and are excellent to have handy for quick shots of people or scenes – though they are of no use for animals. Digital cameras are becoming much more widespread and getting cheaper and better all the time.

Film

Film is expensive in Namibia, but print films are readily available in main towns, as are the more common slide films. Anything out of the ordinary can be impossible to find.

Bring a range of film speeds depending on what type of photography you are most interested in. For most landscape shots, where you will have plenty of light, a 'slow' film (100ISO or less) will give the best results. Most of the photographs in this book have been taken on Fuji Velvia, 50ISO. For wildlife photography, you will need a 'faster' film (200–400ISO) to enable you to use your telephoto lens without fear of camera-shake.

Films, especially when exposed, can deteriorate very quickly in the heat. Keep all films (and therefore your loaded camera) away from direct sunlight. Buying one polystyrene cool box just for films is a great investment.

Pictures taken at dusk or dawn will have the richest, deepest colours, whilst those taken during the middle of the day are usually pale and washed-out. Beware of the very deep shadows and high contrast in strong light during the middle of the day. Film cannot capture the huge range that your eye can. By restricting your photography to mornings and evenings, you will encounter fewer problems.

A polarising filter can be remarkably successful in extending the periods during which you can shoot and get good results.

Other camera equipment

A tripod, or a monopod, is invaluable. If you are shooting from a vehicle, then make sure you have a rest – bring a beanbag or fill a small bag with dry sand, to sit between your camera and the windowsill.

If you want to take pictures of people (or any showing full shadow details) in very bright conditions, then it's worth investing some time learning how to deal with these situations. Fill-in flash photography can capture black faces well, but usually needs practice.

Camera equipment should be carefully protected from dust, using plastic bags if necessary. Bring some lens tissues and a blower brush to clean the dust from your lenses. Also brush any dust from the back pressure-plate of your camera each time you change a film, as anything caught here causes long straight scratches along the length of your film.

Camera insurance

Most travel insurance policies are poor at covering valuables, including cameras. If you are taking a valuable camera abroad, then include it in your house insurance policy, or cover it separately with a specialist.

ACCOMMODATION
Hotels, pensions, lodges and camps

The hotels here are without exception fairly clean and safe. Unless you choose a really run-down old-style hotel in one of the smaller towns, you're unlikely to find anywhere that's dirty. Generally you'll get what you pay for, and only in Windhoek and Swakopmund will you find a real choice.

Establishments are graded by stars, from one to five, but the system is more a guide to their facilities and size than the quality or service. The 'T' that appears alongside the star rating indicates that the place has been judged suitable for tourists, while the number of Ys reflects the type of licence to serve alcohol (three Ys being a full licence).

Most bush camps and lodges are of a high standard, though their prices – and atmosphere – vary wildly. Price is a guide to quality here, though not a reliable one. Often the places that have better marketing (ie: you've heard of them) cost more than their less famous neighbours which are equally good.

Guest farms

These are private farms which host small numbers of guests, usually arranged in advance. They are often very personal and you'll eat all your meals with the hosts and be taken on excursions by them during the day.

Most have some game animals on their land and conduct their own game drives. One or two have interesting rock formations, or cave paintings to visit. Some encourage mainly 'photographic' visitors – that is visitors with a more general interest in the place and its wildlife. Most of these guest farms have been included in this guide. Others, which concentrate mainly on hunters coming to shoot trophy animals, have generally not been included.

Many guest farms concentrate on German-speaking visitors, though those mentioned in this guide also welcome English-speaking guests (and many will make enormous efforts to make you feel at home).

Their prices vary, but are rarely less than N$450 per person – and usually nearer N$650. They generally include all your meals, and often some trips around their farm.

Camping

Wherever you are in Namibia, you can usually find a campsite nearby. In the more remote areas, far from settlements, nobody bothers if you just sleep by the road. The campsites which are dotted all over the country generally have good ablution blocks, which vary from a concrete shed with toilets and cold shower, to an immaculately fitted-out set of changing rooms with toilets and hot showers. The more organised ones will also have facilities for washing clothes.

Prices are frequently per site, which theoretically allows for 'a maximum of eight persons, two vehicles and one caravan/tent'. In practice, if you've a couple of small tents you will not often be charged for two sites, so travelling in a small group can cut costs considerably.

FOOD AND DRINK
Food

Traditional Namibian cuisine is rarely served for visitors, so the food at restaurants tends to be European in style, with a bias towards German dishes and seafood. It is at least as hygienically prepared as in Europe, so don't worry about stomach upsets.

Namibia is a very meat-orientated society, and many menu options will feature steaks from one animal or another. However, there is usually a small vegetarian selection in most restaurants, and if you eat seafood you'll be fine. If you are camping then you'll be buying and cooking your own food anyway.

In the supermarkets you'll find pre-wrapped fresh fruit and vegetables (though the more remote the areas you visit, the smaller your choice), and plenty of canned foods, pasta, rice, bread, etc. Most of this is imported from South Africa. You'll probably be familiar with some of the brand names.

Traditional foodstuffs eaten in a Namibian home may include the following:

eedingu	dried meat, carrots and green beans
kapana	bread
mealie pap	form of porridge, most common in South Africa
omanugu	also known as mopane worms, these are fried caterpillars, often cooked with chilli and onion
oshifima	dough-like staple made from millet
oshifima ne vanda	millet with meat
oshiwambo	spinach and beef

Drink
Alcohol

Because of a strong German brewing tradition, Namibia's lagers are good, the Hansa draught being a particular favourite. In cans, Windhoek Export is one of a number to provide a welcome change from the Lion and Castle which dominate the rest of the subcontinent.

The wine available is mainly South African, with little imported from elsewhere. At its best, this matches the best that California or Australia has to offer, and at considerably lower prices. You can get a bottle of palatable wine from a *drankwinkel* (off licence) for N$55, or a good bottle of vintage estate wine for N$80.

Soft drinks

Canned soft drinks, from Diet Coke to sparkling apple juice, are available ice cold from just about anywhere – which is fortunate, considering the amount that you'll need to drink in this climate. They cost about N$2 each, and can be kept cold in insulating polystyrene boxes made to hold six cans. These cheap containers are invaluable if you have a vehicle, and are not taking a large cool box with you. They cost about N$50 and are available from some big hardware or camping stores. If you are on a self-drive trip, these are an essential buy in your first few days.

Water

The water in Namibia's main towns is generally safe to drink, though it may taste a little metallic if it has been piped for miles. Natural sources should usually be purified, though water from underground springs and dry riverbeds seldom causes any problems. (See *Chapter 5*, pages 70–1, for more detailed comments.)

TIPPING

Tipping is a very difficult and contentious topic – worth thinking about carefully; thoughtlessly tipping too much is just as bad as tipping too little.

Ask locally what's appropriate; here I can only give rough guidance. Helpers with baggage might expect a couple of Namib dollars for their help. Restaurants will often add an automatic service charge to the bill, in which case an additional tip is not usually given. If they do not do this, then 10% would certainly be appreciated if the service was good.

At upmarket lodges, tipping is not obligatory, despite the destructive assumptions of some visitors that it is. If a guide has given you really good service, then a tip of about N$40 (US$5/£2–3) per guest per day would be a generous reflection of this. If the service hasn't been that good, then don't tip. Always tip at the end of your stay, not at the end of each day/activity, which can lead to the guides only trying hard when they know there's a tip at the end of the morning. Such camps aren't pleasant to visit and this isn't the way to encourage top-quality guiding. Give what you feel is appropriate in one lump sum, though before you do this find out if tips go into one box for all of the camp staff, or if the guides are treated differently. Then ensure that your tip reflects this – with perhaps as much again divided between the rest of the staff.

HANDICRAFTS AND WHAT TO BUY

With rich deposits of natural minerals, Namibia can be a good place for the enthusiast to buy **crystals and gems** – but don't expect many bargains, as the industry is far too organised. For the amateur, the desert roses (sand naturally compressed into forms like flowers) are unusual and often cheap, while iridescent tiger's eye is rare elsewhere and very attractive. If you're really interested, forget the agates on sale and look for the unusual crystals – in Windhoek the House of Gems (see page 148) is a must, and in Omaruru Johnston's Gems is fascinating (see page 393).

In Kavango and Caprivi, you'll find good **woodcarvings** sold by the side of the road on small stalls. However, the best selection is at the cooperative which has huge stands either side of Okahandja. There are also some good buys to be had in Windhoek, both behind the Grab-a-phone kiosk and in Post Street Mall.

In the Kalahari regions, **Bushmen crafts** are some of the most original and unusual available on the continent, often using ostrich eggshell beads with very fine workmanship. Outside a few expensive shops in the major towns, by far the best source for this is the mission in Tsumkwe.

For details of other crafts, see *Chapter 2*, pages 28–30.

COMMUNICATIONS AND MEDIA
Communications
Post

The post is efficient and reasonably reliable. A postcard to Europe or the US costs N$2.50, and an airmail letter N$2.60 (N$2.80 to the US); delivery to Europe takes about a fortnight. For larger items, sending them by sea is much cheaper, but it may take up to three months and isn't recommended for fragile items.

Telephone, fax and email

Dialling into Namibia, the country code is 264. Dialling out, the international access code is 00. In both cases, omit the first 0 of the area code. You can dial internationally, without going through the operator, from any public phone box, provided you've enough coins or a phonecard (although note that most public phones take only cards). Phonecards (Telecards) are available in denominations of N$10, N$20 and N$50 from post offices and several shops, including many supermarkets.

Namibia's telephone system has been almost entirely upgraded, with many remote areas converted from old manual exchanges to direct-dial numbers. Generally three-digit area codes – like 061, 064 and 063 – are exceedingly easy to reach, whilst some of the remaining manual country exchanges, and party lines, can prove a nightmare.

If faxing from abroad, always dial the number yourself, with your fax machine set to manual. Wait until you are properly connected (listen for a high-pitched tone), and then try to send your fax.

Note that 'a/h' written next to a phone number means 'after hours' – ie: a number where the person is reachable in the evenings and at weekends. Often this is included for emergency contact, not for casual enquiries.

GSM cellphones will work in many areas of central Namibia, though not in the more remote corners of the country. You may need to 'enable' this function with your service provider before leaving home.

Email is common, but don't expect swift responses to all your emails to Namibia. There are plenty of **internet cafés** in major towns, and many hotels and backpackers' lodges have internet facilities too.

Media
The press

There are no official press restrictions in Namibia, and generally there's a healthy level of debate and criticism in some of the media, although that's not to say that important issues don't sometimes escape public scrutiny because of powerful pressures on editors. In short, it's just like back home!

There is a choice of about seven commercial newspapers, which are easiest to obtain in the larger cities. Getting them elsewhere often means that you will be a few days out of date. The *Namibian* and the *Windhoek Advertiser* are probably the best during the week, and the *Windhoek Observer* on Saturday is also good. One or two of the others are written in Afrikaans and German.

Radio and TV

The government-sponsored Namibia Broadcasting Corporation (NBC) accounts for most of the radio and all of Namibia's normal TV stations. They broadcast radio in six languages from Windhoek, and in three languages from transmitters in the north of the country.

There are currently two local commercial radio stations in Windhoek: Radio Energy and Radio 99. Away from Windhoek and the larger centres, the radio and public TV can be difficult to receive. If you're travelling around in a car, make sure you bring lots of music tapes.

NBC broadcasts one public TV channel, and there are several commercial networks on offer. These satellite channels offer a variety of international news, sport and movie channels – the same the world over. By far the most common is the South African based Mnet TV, which is installed in many of the larger hotels.

ELECTRICITY

Sockets usually supply alternating current at 220/240V and 50Hz. The plugs are the old standard British design, with three round pins. These are available in all the towns, though adapters are less easy to find. Often taking a screwdriver to rewire your appliance on to a local plug is the easiest way to ensure that it will work.

Health and Safety

with Dr Jane Wilson-Howarth and Dr Felicity Nicholson

There is always great danger in writing about health and safety for the uninitiated visitor. It is all too easy to become paranoid about exotic diseases that you may catch, and all too easy to start distrusting everybody you meet as a potential thief – falling into an unfounded us-and-them attitude toward the people of the country you are visiting.

As a comparison, imagine an equivalent section in a guidebook to a Western country – there would be a list of possible diseases and advice on the risk of theft and mugging. Many Western cities are very dangerous, but with time we learn how to assess the risks, accepting almost subconsciously what we can and cannot do.

It is important to strike the right balance: to avoid being excessively cautious or too relaxed about your health and your safety. With experience, you will find the balance that best fits you and the country you are visiting.

BEFORE YOU GO
Travel insurance
Visitors to Namibia should always take out a comprehensive medical insurance policy to cover them for emergencies, including the cost of evacuation to another country within the region. Such policies come with an emergency number (often on a reverse-charge/call collect basis). You would be wise to memorise this, or indelibly tattoo it in as many places as possible on your baggage.

Personal effects insurance is also a sensible precaution, but check the policy's fine print before you leave home. Often, in even the best policies, you will find a limit per item, or per claim – which can be well below the cost of a replacement. If you need to list your valuables separately, then do so comprehensively. Check that receipts are not required for claims if you do not have them, also that the excess which you have to pay on a claim is reasonable.

Annual travel policies can be excellent value if you travel a lot, and some of the larger credit-card companies offer excellent policies. However, it can often be better to get your valuables named and insured for travel using your home contents insurance. These year-round policies will try harder to settle your claim fairly as they want your business in the long term.

Immunisations
Having a full set of immunisations takes time, normally at least six weeks, although some protection can be had by visiting your doctor as late as a few days before you travel. Ideally, see your doctor or travel clinic (see page 68) early on to establish an inoculation timetable.

Legal requirements
No immunisations are required by law for entry into Namibia, unless you are coming from an area where **yellow fever** is endemic. In that case, a vaccination

certificate is mandatory. To be valid the vaccination must be obtained at least ten days before entering the country.

Recommended precautions

Preparations to ensure a healthy trip to Namibia require checks on your immunisation status: it is wise to be up-to-date on **tetanus** (ten-yearly), **polio** (ten-yearly) and **diphtheria** (ten-yearly). Most travellers should have **hepatitis A** immunisation with Havrix Monodose or Avaxim. The course comprises two injections given about a year apart (total cost about £100) and lasts for ten years.

The newer **typhoid** vaccines (eg: Typhim Vi) last for three years and are about 85% effective. They should be encouraged unless the traveller is leaving within a few days for a trip of a week or less when the vaccine would not be effective in time.

Immunisation against cholera is considered ineffective and is not required for trips to Namibia.

Vaccination against **rabies** is unnecessary for most visitors, but would be wise for those who travel for extended periods (four weeks or longer), or stay in rural areas. Ideally three injections taken over a four-week period prior to travel are advised. But there is some benefit to be gained from even one injection if time is short.

Hepatitis B vaccination should be considered for longer trips (two months or more) or for those working with children or in situations where contact with blood is likely. Three injections are needed for the best protection and can be given over a four-week period if time is short. Longer schedules give more sustained protection and are therefore preferred if time allows.

A BCG vaccination against tuberculosis (TB) is also advised for trips of two months or more.

Malaria prophylaxis

Malaria is the most dangerous disease in Africa, and the greatest risk to the traveller. It occurs in northern, and occasionally central, Namibia (see map, page 67), so it is essential that you take all possible precautions against it.

Prophylaxis regimes aim to infuse your bloodstream with drugs that inhibit and kill the malaria parasites which are injected into you by a biting mosquito. This is why you must start to take the drugs *before* you arrive in a malarial area – so that they are established in your bloodstream from day one. Unfortunately, malaria parasites continually adapt to the drugs used to combat them, so the recommended regimes must adapt and change in order to remain effective. None is 100% effective, and all require time to kill the parasites – so unless there is a medical indication for stopping, it is important to complete the course after leaving the area as directed (usually one to four weeks depending on the regime).

It is vital that you seek current advice on the best antimalarials to take. If mefloquine (Lariam) is suggested, start this two weeks before departure to check that it suits you; stop it immediately if it seems to cause depression or anxiety, visual or hearing disturbances, severe headaches, fits or changes in heart rhythm. Side effects such as nightmares or dizziness are not medical reasons for stopping unless they are sufficiently debilitating or annoying. Anyone who is pregnant, has been treated for psychiatric problems, is epileptic, has suffered fits in the past, or who has a close blood relative who is epileptic should avoid mefloquine. The usual alternative is chloroquine (Nivaquine) weekly plus proguanil (Paludrine) daily. The latter is the most likely regime to be offered for Namibia at the time of writing. However, if your trip includes visits to other African countries where

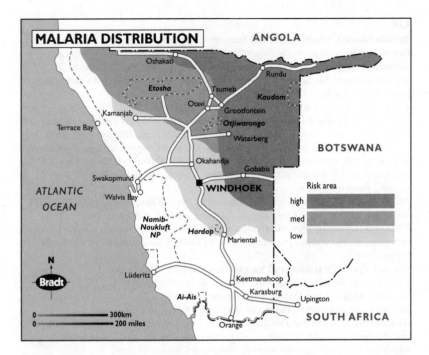

there is a higher prevalence of more resistant falciparum malaria, then other prophylactic drugs may be suggested. These include mefloquine (as described above), doxycycline (a daily antibiotic) or Malarone (also taken once daily, but needing to be continued for only one week after leaving the area). Malarone has the advantage of having few side effects, but as it is expensive it tends to be reserved for shorter trips, although it is licensed for up to three months' use. Paediatric Malarone is now available for children under 40kg. The number of paediatric tablets required is calculated by weight. Malarone may not be suitable for everyone, so always seek advice from a doctor.

Prophylaxis does not stop you catching malaria, but it significantly reduces your chances of fully developing the disease and will lessen its severity. Falciparum (cerebral) malaria is the most common in Africa, and usually fatal if untreated, so it is worth your while trying to avoid it.

It is unwise to travel in malarial parts of Africa whilst pregnant or with young children: the risk of malaria in many areas is considerable and such travellers are likely to succumb rapidly.

Because the strains of malaria, and the drugs used to combat them, change frequently, it is important to get the latest advice before you travel. Normally it is better to obtain this from a specialist travel clinic than from your local doctor, who may not be up-to-date with the latest drugs and developments. For details of relevant clinics, see below.

Travel clinics and health information

A full list of current travel clinic websites worldwide is available on www.istm.org/. For other journey preparation information, consult ftp://ftp.shoreland.com/pub/shorecg.rtf or www.tripprep.com. Information about various medications may be found on www.emedicine.com/wild/topiclist.htm.

UK

British Airways Travel Clinic and Immunisation Service There are now just two BA clinics, both in London. At 156 Regent St, W1B 5LB, tel: 020 7439 9584, there is a walk-in service Mon–Sat; visits to 111 Cheapside, EC1V 6DT, tel: 020 7606 2977, are by appointment only. See also www.britishairways.com/travelclinics. Also sell a variety of health-related goods.

Fleet Street Travel Clinic 29 Fleet St, London EC4Y 1AA; tel: 020 7353 5678

Hospital for Tropical Diseases Travel Clinic Mortimer Market Centre, 2nd Floor, Capper St (off Tottenham Court Rd), London WC1E 6AU; tel: 020 7388 9600; web: www.thhtd.org. Offers consultations and advice, and is able to provide all necessary drugs and vaccines for travellers. Runs a healthline (09061 337733) for country-specific information and health hazards. Also stocks nets, water purification equipment and personal protection meaures.

MASTA (Medical Advisory Service for Travellers Abroad) Keppel St, London WC1 7HT; tel: 09068 224100. This is a premium-line number, charged at 50p per minute.

NHS travel website, www.fitfortravel.scot.nhs.uk, provides country-by-country advice on immunisation and malaria, plus details of recent developments, and a list of relevant health organisations.

Nomad Travel Pharmacy and Vaccination Centre 3–4 Wellington Terrace, Turnpike Lane, London N8 0PX; tel: 020 8889 7014; email: sales@nomadtravel.co.uk; website: www.nomadtravel.co.uk. As well as dispensing health advice, Nomad stocks mosquito nets and other anti-bug devices, and an excellent range of adventure travel gear.

Thames Medical 157 Waterloo Rd, London SE1 8US; tel: 020 7902 9000. Competitively priced, one-stop travel health service. All profits go to their affiliated company InterHealth which provides health care for overseas workers on Christian projects.

Trailfinders Immunisation Centre 194 Kensington High St, London W8 7RG; tel: 020 7938 3999.

Irish Republic

Tropical Medical Bureau Grafton Street Medical Centre, Grafton Buildings, 34 Grafton St, Dublin 2; tel: 1 671 9200. Has a useful website specific to tropical destinations: www.tmb.ie

USA

Centers for Disease Control 1600 Clifton Rd, Atlanta, GA 30333; tel: 877 FYI TRIP; 800 311 3435; web: www.cdc.gov/travel. The central source of travel information in the USA. Each summer they publish the invaluable *Health Information for International Travel*, available from the Division of Quarantine at the above address.

Connaught Laboratories PO Box 187, Swiftwater, PA 18370; tel: 800 822 2463. They will send a free list of specialist tropical-medicine physicians in your state.

IAMAT (International Association for Medical Assistance to Travelers) 736 Center St, Lewiston, NY 14092. A non-profit organisation which provides lists of English-speaking doctors abroad.

Canada

IAMAT (International Association for Medical Assistance to Travellers) Suite 1, 1287 St Clair Av W, Toronto, Ontario M6E 1B8; tel: 416 652 0137; web: www.sentex.net/~iamat.

TMVC (Travel Doctors Group) Sulphur Springs Rd, Ancaster, Ontario; tel: 905 648 1112; web: www.tmvc.com.au

Australia, New Zealand, Thailand

TMVC Tel: 1300 65 88 44; web: www.tmvc.com.au. 20 clinics in Australia, New Zealand and Thailand, including:

Auckland Canterbury Arcade, 170 Queen Street, Auckland City; tel: 373 3531
Brisbane Dr Deborah Mills, Qantas Domestic Building, 6th floor, 247
Adelaide St, Brisbane, QLD 4000; tel: 7 3221 9066; fax: 7 3321 7076
Melbourne Dr Sonny Lau, 393 Little Bourke St, 2nd floor, Melbourne, VIC 3000; tel: 3 9602
5788; fax: 3 9670 8394.
Sydney Dr Mandy Hu, Dymocks Building, 7th Floor, 428 George St, Sydney, NSW2000;
tel: 2 221 7133; fax: 2 221 8401.

South Africa
SAA-Netcare Travel Clinics PO Box 786692, Sandton 2146; fax: 011 883 6152; web:
www.travelclinic.co.za or www.malaria.co.za. Clinics throughout South Africa
TMVC (Travel Doctor Group) 113 DF Malan Drive, Roosevelt Park, Johannesburg; tel:
011 888 7488; web: www.tmvc.com.au. Consult the website for details of clinics in South
Africa.

Switzerland
IAMAT (International Association for Medical Assistance to Travellers) 57 Voirets, 1212
Grand Lancy, Geneva; web: www.sentex.net/~iamat

Medical kit
Pharmacies in the main towns in Namibia generally have very good supplies of
medicines, but away from these you will find very little. If you're venturing deep into
the wilds, then you should take with you anything that you expect to need. If you are
on an organised trip, an overlanding truck, or staying at hotels, lodges or safari camps,
then you will not need much, as these establishments normally have comprehensive
emergency kits. In that case, just a small personal medical kit might include:

- antihistamine tablets
- antiseptic
- aspirins or paracetamol
- blister plasters (if you plan any serious walking)
- condoms and contraceptive pills
- insect repellent
- lipsalve (ideally containing a sunscreen)
- malaria prophylaxis
- Micropore tape (for closing small cuts – and invaluable for blisters)
- moisturising cream
- sticking plaster (a roll is more versatile than pre-shaped plasters)
- sunscreen

However, if you are likely to end up in very remote situations, then you should
also consider taking the following – and know how to use them:

- burn dressings (burns are a common problem for campers)
- injection swabs, sterile needles and syringes
- lint, sterile bandage and safety pins
- oral rehydration sachets
- steristrips or butterfly closures
- strong painkiller (eg: codeine phosphate – also use for bad diarrhoea)
- tweezers (perhaps those on a Swiss army knife)
- water purification equipment (2% tincture of iodine and dropper is ideal)
- several different malaria treatment courses and broad-spectrum antibiotics –
  plus a good medical manual (see *Further Reading*, page 507).

If you wear glasses, bring a spare pair. Similarly those who wear contact lenses should bring spare ones, also a pair of glasses in case the dust proves too much for the lenses. If you take regular medication (including contraceptive pills) then bring a large supply with you – much easier than hunting for your usual brand in Namibia. Equally, it's worth having a dental check-up before you go, as you could be several painful days from the nearest dentist.

Hospitals, dentists and pharmacies in Namibia

Should you need one, Namibia's main hospitals are good and will treat you first and ask for money later. However, with comprehensive medical insurance as part of your travel cover, it is probably better go to one of the private clinics. The main ones are in Windhoek and Otjiwarongo, and these are capable of serious surgery and a good quality of care. Outside of these, there are private medical facilities in Karibib, Swakopmund, Tsumeb and Walvis Bay.

If you've a serious problem outside of Windhoek, then **MediRescue (MRI)** organise medical evacuations from anywhere, and can be contacted on tel: 061 230505, radiopage: 252222, cell: 081 124 0012. They do insure individual travellers, but many lodges are members, covering you whilst you are staying there, and the best car-hire firms, like Avis, will automatically cover you with MediRescue if you have one of their cars. Finally, it may be that your insurers overseas would ultimately pick up the MediRescue bills if their services were needed.

Pharmacies in the main towns stock a good range of medicine, though often not in familiar brands. Bring with you a repeat prescription for anything you may lose or run out of.

STAYING HEALTHY

Namibia is probably the healthiest country in sub-Saharan Africa for visitors. It has a generally low population density and a very dry climate, which means there are comparatively few problems likely to affect visitors. The risks are further minimised if you are staying in good hotels, lodges, camps and guest farms, where standards of hygiene are generally at least as good as you will find at home.

The major dangers in Namibia are car accidents caused by driving too fast on gravel roads, and sunburn. Both can also be very serious, yet both are within the power of the visitor to avoid.

The following is general advice, applicable to travelling anywhere, including Namibia:

Food and storage

Throughout the world, most health problems encountered by travellers are contracted by eating contaminated food or drinking unclean water. If you are staying in safari camps or lodges, or eating in restaurants, then you are unlikely to have problems in Namibia.

However, if you are backpacking and cooking for yourself, or relying on local food, then you need to take more care. Tins, packets, and fresh green vegetables (when you can find them) are least likely to cause problems – provided that clean water has been used in preparing the meal. In Namibia's hot climate, keeping meat or animal products unrefrigerated for more than a few hours is asking for trouble.

Water and purification

Tap water in Namibia's major towns and borehole water used in many more remote locations is perfectly safe to drink. However, even the mildest of the local microbes may cause slight upset stomachs for an overseas visitor. Two-litre bottles of mineral water are available from most supermarkets; these are perfect if you're in a car.

If you need to purify water for yourself in the bush, then first filter out any suspended solids, perhaps by passing the water through a piece of closely woven cloth or something similar. Then bring it to the boil, or sterilise it chemically. Boiling is much more effective, provided that you have the fuel available.

Tablets sold for purification are based on either chlorine, iodine or silver, and normally adequate. Just follow the manufacturer's instructions carefully. Iodine is the most effective, especially against the resilient amoebic cysts which cause amoebic dysentery and other prolonged forms of diarrhoea.

A cheaper alternative to tablets sold over the counter is to travel with a small bottle of medical-quality tincture of iodine (2% solution) and an eye dropper. Add four drops to one litre of water, shake well, and leave to stand for ten minutes. If the water is very cloudy (even after filtering) or very cold, then either double the iodine dose, or leave to stand for twice as long.

This tincture of iodine can also be used as a general external antiseptic, but it will stain things deep brown if spilt – so seal and pack its container exceedingly well.

Heat and sun
Heatstroke, heat exhaustion and sunburn are often problems for travellers to Namibia, despite being easy to prevent. To avoid them, you need to remember that your body is under stress and make allowances for it. First, take things gently; you are on holiday, after all. Next, keep your fluid and salt levels high: lots of water and soft drinks, but go easy on the caffeine and alcohol. Thirdly, dress to keep cool with loose-fitting, thin garments – preferably of cotton, linen or silk. Finally, beware of the sun. Hats and long-sleeved shirts are essential. If you must expose your skin to the sun, then use sun blocks and high factor sun screens (the sun is so strong that you will still get a tan).

Avoiding insect bites
The most dangerous biting insects in parts of Namibia (see map, page 67) are mosquitoes, because they can transmit malaria, yellow fever, and a host of other diseases.

Research has shown that using a mosquito net over your bed, and covering up exposed skin (by wearing long-sleeved shirts, and tucking trousers into socks) in the evening, are the most effective steps towards preventing bites. Bed-net treatment kits are available from travel clinics; these prevent mosquitoes biting through a net if you roll against it in your sleep, and also make old and holey nets protective. Mosquito coils and chemical insect repellents will help, and sleeping in a stream of moving air, such as under a fan, or in an air conditioned room, will help to reduce your chances of being bitten.

DEET (diethyltoluamide) is the active ingredient in many repellents (Repel have an excellent range), so the greater the percentage of DEET, the stronger the effect. However, DEET is a strong chemical. Just 30% is regarded as an effective, non-toxic concentration. It will dissolve some plastics and synthetic materials, and may irritate sensitive skin. Because of this, many people use concentrated DEET to impregnate materials, rather than applying it to themselves. An alternative to this is to use Bug Guards – wrist and ankle bands containing 100% DEET in capsule form. The capsules break on movement, but the chemical never touches the skin. One pack contains four bands, which when used, last for two weeks. Mosquito nets, socks, and even cravats can be impregnated and used to deter insects from biting. Eating large quantities of garlic, or cream of tartar, or taking yeast tablets, are said to deter some biting insects, although the evidence is anecdotal – and the garlic may affect your social life.

Dengue fever

This mosquito-borne disease may mimic malaria but there is no prophylactic medication available to deal with it. The mosquitoes that carry this virus bite during the daytime, so it is worth applying repellent if you see any mosquitoes around. Symptoms include strong headaches, rashes and excruciating joint and muscle pains and high fever. Dengue fever only lasts for a week or so and is not usually fatal. Complete rest and paracetamol are the usual treatment. Plenty of fluids also help. Some patients are given an intravenous drip to keep them from dehydrating. It is especially important to protect yourself if you have had dengue fever before. A second infection with a different strain can result in the potentially fatal dengue haemorrhagic fever.

Snakes, spiders and scorpions...

Encounters with aggressive snakes, angry spiders or vindictive scorpions are more common in horror films than in Namibia. Most snakes will flee at the mere vibrations of a human footstep whilst spiders are far more interested in flies than people. You will have to seek out scorpions if you wish to see one. If you are careful about where you place your hands and feet, especially after dark, then there should be no problems. You are less likely to get bitten or stung if you wear stout shoes and long trousers. Simple precautions include not putting on boots without shaking them empty first, and always checking the back of your backpack before putting it on.

Snakes do bite occasionally, and you ought to know the standard first-aid treatment. First, and most importantly, *don't panic*. Most snakes are harmless and even venomous species will only dispense venom in about half of their bites. If bitten, you are unlikely to have received venom; keeping this fact in mind may help you to stay calm.

Even in the worst of these cases, the victim has hours or days to get to help, and not a matter of minutes. He/she should be kept calm, with no exertions to pump venom around the blood system, whilst being taken rapidly to the nearest medical help. The area of the bite should be washed to remove any venom from the skin, and the bitten limb should be immobilised. Paracetamol may be used as a painkiller, but never use aspirin because it may cause internal bleeding.

Most first-aid techniques do more harm than good: cutting into the wound is harmful and tourniquets are dangerous; suction and electrical inactivation devices do not work. The only effective treatment is antivenom. In case of a bite, which you fear may be both serious and venomous then:

- Try to keep calm. It is likely that no venom has been dispensed.
- Stop movement of the bitten limb by applying a splint.
- If you have a crepe bandage, firmly bind up as much of the bitten limb as you can. Release the bandage for a few minutes every half-hour.
- Keep the bitten limb *below* heart height to slow spread of any venom
- Evacuate the victim to a hospital that has antivenom
- *Never* give aspirin. You may offer paracetamol, which is safe.
- *Do not* apply ice packs.
- *Do not* apply potassium permanganate.

If the offending snake can be captured without any risk of someone else being bitten, take it to show the doctor. But beware, since even a decapitated head is able to dispense venom in a reflex bite.

When deep in the bush, heading for the nearest large farm or camp may be quicker than going to a town: it may have a supply of antivenom, or facilities to radio for help by plane.

DISEASES AND WHEN TO SEE A DOCTOR
Travellers' diarrhoea
There are almost as many names for this as there are travellers' tales on the subject. Firstly, do resist the temptation to reach for the medical kit as soon as your stomach turns a little fluid. Most cases of travellers' diarrhoea will resolve themselves within 24–48 hours with no treatment at all. To speed up this process of acclimatisation, eat well but simply: avoid fats in favour of starches, and keep your fluid intake high. Bananas and papaya fruit are often claimed to be helpful. If you urgently need to stop the symptoms, for a long journey for example, then Lomotil, Imodium or another of the commercial anti-diarrhoea preparations will do the trick. They stop the symptoms, by paralysing the bowel, but will not cure the problem. They should only be used as a last resort and never if you have bad abdominal cramps with the diarrhoea.

If the diarrhoea persists for more than two days, or the stools contain blood, pus or slime, and/or you have a fever, you must seek medical advice. There are as many possible treatments as there are causes, and a proper diagnosis involves microscopic analysis of a stool sample, so go straight to your nearest hospital. The most important thing, especially in Namibia's climate, is to keep your fluid intake up. If it is not possible to reach medical help quickly then take 500mg of ciprofloxacin repeating the dose six to twelve hours later if you still haven't reached help. If the diarrhoea is greasy and bulky and is accompanied by sulphurous (eggy) burps the likely cause is giardia. This is best treated with tinidazole (four x 500mg in one dose, repeated seven days later if symptoms persist).

The body's absorption of fluids is assisted by adding small amounts of dissolved sugars, salts and minerals to the water. Sachets of oral rehydration salts give the perfect biochemical mix you need to replace what is pouring out of your bottom but they do not taste so nice. Any dilute mixture of sugar and salt in water will do you good so, if you like Coke or orange squash, drink that with a three-finger pinch of salt added to each glass. The ideal ratio is eight level teaspoons of sugar and one level teaspoon of salt dissolved in one litre of water. Palm syrup or honey make good substitutes for sugar, and including fresh citrus juice will not only improve the taste of these solutions, but also add valuable potassium.

Drink two large glasses after every bowel action, and more if you are thirsty. If you are not eating you need to drink three litres a day *plus* whatever you are sweating *and* the equivalent of what's going into the toilet. If you feel like eating, take a bland diet; heavy greasy foods will give you cramps.

If you are likely to be more than a few days from qualified medical help, then come equipped with a good health manual and the selection of antibiotics which it recommends. *Bugs, Bites & Bowels* by Dr Jane Wilson-Howarth (see *Further Reading*, page 507) is excellent for this purpose.

Malaria
You can still catch malaria even if you are taking anti-malarial drugs. Classic symptoms include headaches, chills and sweating, abdominal pains, aching joints and fever – some or all of which may come in waves. It varies tremendously, but often starts like a bad case of flu. If anything like this happens, you should first suspect malaria and seek immediate medical help. A definite diagnosis of malaria is normally only possible by examining a blood sample under the microscope. It is

best to get the problem properly diagnosed if possible, so don't treat yourself if you can easily reach a hospital first.

If (and only if) medical help is unavailable, then self-treatment is fairly safe, except for people who are pregnant or under twelve years of age. There are a number of treatments available that can be obtained before you leave. Currently the most likely to be prescribed are quinine and fansidar or Malarone. It is always best to ask a doctor at a travel clinic for the most up to date advice. In Namibia you should always be able to get experienced local advice to tell you which will be the most effective.

Quinine is very strong, but often proves to be an effective last defence against malaria. Include it in your medical kit, as occasionally rural clinics will have the expertise to treat you, but not the drugs. Quinine's side effects are disorientating and unpleasant (nausea and a constant buzzing in the ears), so administering this whilst on your own is not advisable.

Sexually transmitted diseases

AIDS is spread in exactly the same way in Africa as it is at home, through body secretions, blood, and blood products. The same goes for the dangerous hepatitis B. Both can be spread through sex.

Remember that the risks of sexually transmitted disease are high, whether you sleep with fellow travellers or locals. About 40% of HIV infections in British people are acquired abroad. Use condoms or femidoms. If you notice any genital ulcers or discharge, get treatment promptly.

Hepatitis

This is a group of viral diseases which generally start with Coca-Cola-coloured urine and light-coloured stools. It progresses to fevers, weakness, jaundice (yellow skin and eyeballs) and abdominal pains caused by a severe inflammation of the liver. There are several forms, of which the two most common are typical of the rest: hepatitis A (or infectious hepatitis) and hepatitis B (or serum hepatitis).

Hepatitis A, and the newly discovered hepatitis E, are spread by the faecal-oral route, that is by ingesting food or drink contaminated by excrement. They are avoided in the same ways you normally avoid stomach problems: by careful preparation of food and by only drinking clean water. But as there are now excellent vaccines against hepatitis A (Havrix Monodose or Avaxim) it is certainly worth getting inoculated before you travel. See *Recommended precautions* on page 66.

In contrast, the more serious but rarer Hepatitis B is spread in the same way as AIDS (by blood or body secretions), and is avoided the same way as one avoids AIDS. There is a vaccine which protects against Hepatitis B, but three doses are needed over a minimum of four weeks. It is usually only considered necessary for medical workers, people working closely with children or if you intend to travel for eight weeks or longer. There are no cures for hepatitis, but with lots of bed rest and a good low-fat, no-alcohol diet most people recover within six months. If you are unlucky enough to contract hepatitis of any form, use your travel insurance to fly straight home.

Rabies

Rabies is contracted when broken skin comes into contact with saliva from an infected animal. The disease is almost always fatal when fully developed, but fortunately there are excellent post-exposure vaccines. It is possible, albeit expensive, to be immunised against rabies before you travel. You are advised to take this if you intend working with animals or you are travelling for four weeks or more to remote areas. Rabies is rarely a problem for visitors, but the small risk is further minimised by avoiding small mammals. This is especially true of any animals acting strangely. Both mad dogs in town and friendly jackals in the bush should be given a very wide berth.

If you are bitten, scratched or licked over an open wound, clean and disinfect the wound thoroughly by scrubbing it with soap under running water for five minutes, and then flood it with local spirit or diluted iodine. Then seek medical advice. At least two post-exposure rabies injections are needed even in immunised people. But for those who are unimmunised even more injections are needed together with rabies immunoglobulin (RIG). RIG is expensive (around $900 a dose) and is also in very short supply. Another good reason for taking pre-exposure vaccine.

You should always seek help immediately, ideally within 24 hours, but since the incubation period for rabies can be very long it is never too late to bother. The later stages of the disease are horrendous – spasms, personality changes and hydrophobia (fear of water). Death from rabies is probably one of the worst ways to go.

Bilharzia or schistosomiasis

Though a very low risk in Namibia, bilharzia is an insidious disease, contracted by coming into contact with contaminated water. It is caused by parasitic worms which live part of their lives in freshwater snails, and part of their lives in human bladders or intestines. A common indication of an infection is a localised itchy rash – where the parasites have burrowed through the skin – and later symptoms of a more advanced infection may include passing bloody urine. Bilharzia is readily treated by medication, and only serious if it remains untreated.

The only way to avoid infection completely is to stay away from any bodies of fresh water. Obviously this is restrictive, and would make your trip less enjoyable. More pragmatic advice is to avoid slow-moving or sluggish water, and ask local opinion on the bilharzia risk, as not all water is contaminated. Generally bilharzia snails do not inhabit fast-flowing water, and hence rivers are free of it. However, dams and standing water, especially in populated areas, are usually heavily contaminated. If you think you have been infected, don't worry about it – just get a test done on your return at least six weeks after your last possible exposure.

Sleeping sickness or trypanosomiasis

This is really a cattle disease, which is rarely caught by people. It is spread by bites from the distinctive tsetse fly – which is slightly larger than a housefly, and has pointed mouth-parts designed for sucking blood. The bite is painful. These flies are easily spotted as they bite during the day, and have distinctive wings which cross into a scissor shape when they are resting. They are not common in Namibia, but do occur occasionally in Bushmanland and the Caprivi. Note that not all tsetses carry the disease.

Prevention is easier than cure, so avoid being bitten by covering up. Chemical insect repellents are also helpful. Dark colours, especially blue, are favoured by the flies, so avoid wearing these if possible.

Tsetse bites are nasty, so expect them to swell up and turn red – that is a normal allergic reaction to any bite. The vast majority of tsetse bites will do only this. However, if the bite develops into a boil-like swelling after five or more days, and a fever starts two or three weeks later, then seek immediate medical treatment to avert permanent damage to your central nervous system. The name 'sleeping sickness' refers to a daytime drowsiness which is characteristic of the later stages of the disease.

Because this is a rare complaint, most doctors in the West are unfamiliar with it. If you think that you may have been infected, draw their attention to the possibility. Treatment is straightforward, once a correct diagnosis has been made.

RETURNING HOME

Many tropical diseases have a long incubation period, and it is possible to develop symptoms weeks after returning home (this is why it is important to keep taking anti-malaria prophylaxis for the prescribed duration after you leave a malarial zone). If you do get ill after you return home, be certain to tell your doctor where you have been. Alert him/her to any diseases that you may have been exposed to. Several people die from malaria in the UK every year because victims do not seek medical help promptly or their doctors are not familiar with the symptoms, and so are slow to make a correct diagnosis. Milder forms of malaria may take up to a year to reveal themselves, but serious (falciparum) malaria will usually become apparent within four months.

If problems persist, get a check-up at one of the hospitals that specialise in tropical diseases. Note that to visit such a hospital in the UK, you need a letter of referral from your doctor.

For further advice or help in the UK, ask your local doctor to refer you to the Hospital for Tropical Diseases, (see page 68), or in the US to the Centers for Disease Control (see page 68).

SAFETY

Namibia is not a dangerous country, and is generally amazingly crime-free. Outside of the main cities, crime against visitors, however minor, is exceedingly rare. Even if you are travelling on local transport on a low budget, you are likely to experience numerous acts of random kindness, but not crime. It is certainly safer for visitors than the UK, USA, or most of Europe.

To get into a difficult situation, you'll usually have to try hard. You need to make yourself an obvious target for thieves, perhaps by walking around at night, with showy valuables, in a less affluent area of the city. Provided you are sensible, you are most unlikely to ever see any crime here.

Most towns in Namibia have townships, and often these are home to many of the poorer sections of society. Generally they are perfectly safe to visit during the day, but tourists would be wise to avoid wandering around with valuables. If you have friends or contacts who are local and know the areas well, then take the opportunity to explore with them a little. Wander around during the day, or go off to a nightclub together. You'll find that they show you a very different facet of Namibian life from that seen in the more affluent areas. For women travellers, especially those travelling alone, it is important to learn the local attitudes about how to behave acceptably. This takes some practice, and a certain confidence. You will often be the centre of attention, but by developing conversational techniques to avert over-enthusiastic male attention, you should be perfectly safe. Making friends of the local women is one way to help avoid such problems.

Theft

Theft is rarely a problem in Namibia – which is surprising given the poverty levels amongst much of the population. The only real exception to this rule is theft from unattended vehicles, which is common in Windhoek (especially) and the larger towns. If you leave your vehicle with anything valuable on view, then you will probably return to find a window smashed and items stolen. Aside from this, theft is really very unusual.

SAFETY FOR WOMEN TRAVELLERS
Janice Booth

When attention becomes intrusive, it can help if you are wearing a wedding ring and have photos of 'your' husband and children, even if they are someone else's. A good reason to give for not being with them is that you have to travel in connection with your job – biology, zoology, geography, or whatever. (But not journalism, that's risky.)

Pay attention to local etiquette, and to speaking, dressing and moving reasonably decorously. Look at how the local women dress, and try not to expose parts of yourself that they keep covered. Think about body language. In much of southern Africa direct eye contact with a man will be seen as a 'come-on'; sunglasses are helpful here.

Don't be afraid to explain clearly – but pleasantly rather than as a put-down – that you aren't in the market for whatever distractions are on offer. Remember that you are probably as much of a novelty to the local people as they are to you; and the fact that you are travelling abroad alone gives them the message that you are free and adventurous. But don't imagine that a Lothario lurks under every bush: many approaches stem from genuine friendliness or curiosity, and a brush-off in such cases doesn't do much for the image of travellers in general.

Take sensible precautions against theft and attack – try to cover all the risks before you encounter them – and then relax and enjoy your trip. You'll meet far more kindness than villainy.

Reporting thefts to the police
If you are the victim of a theft then report it to the police – they ought to know. Also try to get a copy of the report, or at least a reference number on an official-looking piece of paper, as this will help you to claim on your insurance policy when you return home. However, reporting anything in a police station can take a long time, and do not expect any speedy arrests for a small case of theft.

Arrest
To get arrested in Namibia, a foreigner will normally have to try quite hard. Though most Namibians are not paranoid about spies, it is always wise to ask for permission to photograph near bridges or military installations. This simple courtesy costs you nothing, and may avoid a problem later.

One excellent way to get arrested in Namibia is to try to smuggle drugs across its borders, or to try to buy them from 'pushers'. Drug offences carry penalties at least as stiff as those you will find at home – and the jails are a lot less pleasant. Namibia's police are not forbidden to use entrapment techniques or 'sting' operations to catch criminals. Buying, selling or using drugs in Namibia is just not worth the risk.

Failing this, argue with a policeman or army official – and get angry into the bargain – and you may manage to be arrested. It is *essential* to control your temper; stay relaxed when dealing with officials. Not only will you gain respect, and hence help your cause, but you will avoid being forced to cool off for a night in the cells.

If you are careless enough to be arrested, you will often only be asked a few questions. If the police are suspicious of you, then how you handle the situation will determine whether you are kept for a matter of hours or days. Be patient, helpful, good-humoured, and as truthful as possible. Never lose your temper, it will only aggravate the situation. Avoid any hint of arrogance. If things are going badly after half a day or so, then start firmly, but politely, to insist on seeing someone in higher authority. As a last resort you do, at least in theory, have the right to contact your embassy or consulate, though the finer points of your civil liberties may end up being overlooked by an irate local police chief.

Bribery

Bribery may be a fact of life in some parts of Africa, but in Namibia it is very rare. Certainly no normal visitor should ever be asked for, or offer, a bribe. It would be just as illegal as offering someone a bribe back home.

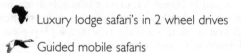

Getting Around Namibia

DRIVING IN NAMIBIA

Driving yourself around Namibia is, for most visitors, by far the best way to see the country. It is much easier than driving around Europe or the USA: the roads are excellent, the traffic is light, and the signposts are numerous, clear and unambiguous.

Further, if you choose to visit private camps or concession areas, you can then use the skills of the resident guides to show you the wildlife. You're not restricted to the car, to be in it every day. Driving yourself gives you freedom to explore and to go where you like, when you like.

It's generally easiest to hire a vehicle for your whole time in Namibia, collecting it at the airport when you arrive, and returning it there when you depart. This also removes any worries that you may have about bringing too much luggage (whatever you bring is simply thrown in the boot on arrival).

However, if your budget is very tight then you may think about just taking a vehicle for a few days, perhaps from Windhoek to Swakopmund via the Sesriem area, or to drive around Etosha. However long you keep the vehicle, the type you choose and the company you hire from can make an enormous difference to your trip.

Hiring a vehicle

Think carefully about what kind of vehicle to hire, and where to get it from, well before arriving in the country. It is usually better to organise this in advance. Check out the deals offered by overseas operators *before* you buy your flights. Arranging flights, car and accommodation with one operator, based in your home country, can sometimes be cheaper and easier than making all the bookings separately. The normal minimum age to hire a car is 23, though the occasional operator will accept drivers of 21.

Hiring a car in one city and dropping it off elsewhere is perfectly possible with the major car-hire companies. Expect to pay a drop-off fee. Although these vary widely, you'll probably be looking at somthing in the region of N$200.

There are four big car-hire companies in Namibia: Avis, Budget, Europcar and Imperial (which is associated with Hertz). Their prices tend to be similar, as do their conditions of hire, which leaves quality and availability as appropriate criteria for choosing between them.

Having used all three, I now generally hire from Avis. They have the youngest and largest fleet, as well as a wide back-up network in Namibia, so any problems get sorted out fast. There is the further advantage that they are well represented throughout the subcontinent, so it is easy to arrange one-way trips between South Africa or Botswana and Namibia – which adds a lot of flexibility to your choice of route.

Aside from these three large firms, there is a plethora of smaller, local car-hire companies in Windhoek (see page 83), some of which are good. Others have more dubious reputations, and even buy their cars from the big companies, which dispose of their vehicles after one or two years. This makes their rates cheaper. However, compromising on the quality of your vehicle is crazy when you rely upon it so completely. Economise on accommodation or meals – but rent the best vehicle you can.

Hiring a 4WD requires similar logic to the above, but more money. Most car-hire companies offer 4WDs, but because of their expense fleets are often much smaller, and so they must be booked even further in advance.

Typical 'per day' on-the-road prices from the more reputable companies, based upon unlimited mileage and their maximum insurance (see *Insurance, CDWs and gravel roads*, page 82), are:

Group A	Toyota Corolla 1.3 or similar	£31/US$46
Group B	Corolla 1.6	£35/US$52
Group C	VW Jetta	£44/US$65
Group J	Single cab 4WD	£66/US$98
Group N	Double cab 4WD	£76/US$113

Slightly cheaper deals are available from smaller local firms, but none has the same back-up support as the big companies. Neither will you have the same chance of redress if there are any problems. The cost of adding in a second driver is usually N$50.

If time is not in short supply but money is, consider just hiring for a few days at a time to see specific sights – which would not be too expensive if you are planning on sitting by waterholes in Etosha all day.

No matter where you hire your vehicle, do give yourself plenty of time when collecting and dropping it off to ensure that it is properly checked over for damage etc. Make sure, too, that you get the *final* invoice before you leave the vehicle, or you may return home to an unexpected credit-card bill.

A warning before you sign up for any car hire: see the section on insurance and CDWs on page 82. There is often fine print in these agreements which may mislead the unwary.

2WD or 4WD?

Whether you need to hire a 2WD or a 4WD vehicle depends on where you want to go. For virtually all of the country's main sights and attractions, and many of the more off-beat ones, a normal saloon **2WD** car is ideal.

The only real exception to this advice is if you're travelling anywhere during the rains, around January to March, when you might consider taking a **4WD,** just in case you need to ford any shallow rivers that block the road. Additional advantages of a 4WD vehicle are:

- You relax more on gravel roads, knowing the vehicle is sturdier.
- You may be higher up, giving a slightly better view in game parks.
- It's easier to cross shallow rivers or sand patches if you encounter them.
- At Sossusvlei, you can drive beyond the 2WD car park into Sossusvlei itself (if you're proficient in sand-driving techniques!).

However, the main disadvantages are:

- The cost of hiring a 4WD is about double that of hiring a 2WD.
- 4WDs are generally heavier to handle, and more tiring to drive.
- A 4WD's fuel consumption is much higher.

- 4WDs have higher centres of gravity, and so tend to roll more easily.
- There's usually no secure boot (trunk), where luggage is not on view, so you can't safely leave bags in the 4WD when you are not there.

Despite the disadvantages, if you want to get up to the northern Kaokoveld, further than Tsumkwe in Bushmanland, or to any of the really offbeat areas in the Caprivi – then you'll *need* a high-clearance 4WD. The main point to remember is that in most of these areas, just one 4WD vehicle simply isn't enough. Your party needs to have a *minimum* of two vehicles for safety, and you should have with you a couple of experienced bush-drivers. These areas are very dangerous if you drive into them alone or ill-equipped.

What kind of 2WD?

This is really a question of budget. A simple 'Group A' – usually a basic 1.3 or 1.6 VW Golf, Toyota Corolla or Mazda Midge – is fine for two adults and most trips. (The harder suspension of the Golf is probably best on Namibian roads.)

If you've any flexibility in your budget, then get one up from the basic car if you can. A 'Group B' normally comes with air conditioning and a radio/tape player, both of which can be useful. A larger vehicle is superfluous for two people, unless you need an automatic gearbox, want the sheer luxury of the space, or plan to drive *huge* distances.

For three or four people, look to a larger saloon, typically a Group C, like a VW Jetta 1.6. This has a cavernous boot (trunk) for luggage, and power steering is added to its refinements. If budget allows, then the Toyota Camry is excellent – and in many ways better than the more expensive Mercedes 220 which is sometimes offered.

Five or six people on a budget should consider a Toyota Venture, which is very spacious, or something similar. However, do get the more recent 2.2, rather than the older 1.8 model, as the latter are lamentably under-powered. If your budget is flexible, then consider either two small cars, or a VW Microbus (combi). Two cars will give more flexibility if the group wants to split up on occasions. These combis have lots of space to move around, and six window seats for game viewing. Their main disadvantage is that they lack a secure, hidden boot. Like most 4WDs, you can't safely leave the vehicle alone with any luggage in it.

What kind of 4WD?

In order of increasing cost, the choice normally boils down to a single-cab Toyota Hilux, a double-cab Toyota Hilux, or a Land Rover 110. Occasionally you'll find Mazdas used instead of Toyotas, but their design and limits are very similar. The only relevant difference is that Toyotas are more common, and hence their spares are easier to obtain.

For two people, the single-cab Toyota Hilux is fine. This has just two seats (sometimes a bench seat) in the front and a fibreglass canopy over the pick-up section at the back. This is good for keeping the rain off your luggage, but it will not deter thefts. It's worth noting that a twin-cab will afford you a lot more space to move around and enable you to store cameras and drinks within easy reach.

For three or four people, you'll need the double-cab or the Land Rover. The double-cabs are lighter vehicles, generally more comfortable and faster on tar. However, the Land Rovers are mechanically more simple, and easier to mend in the bush – *if* you know what you're doing. Further, your luggage is inside the main cab, and so slightly safer, easier to access, and will remain a little less dusty. Five or more people will need the flexibility of two vehicles – more than four people in either of these is really quite squashed.

Insurance, CDWs and gravel roads

Wherever you hire your vehicle, you must read all the fine print of your hire agreement very carefully. The insurance and the Collision Damage Waiver (CDW) clauses are worth studying particularly closely. These spell out the 'excess' that you will pay in the event of an accident. These CDW excesses vary widely, and often explain the difference between cheap rental deals and better but more costly options.

In the last decade, Namibia has proved to be a very bad country for accidents. The problem is that the gravel roads are too *good*. If they had lots of potholes, then people would go slowly. But instead they are smooth, even, and empty – tempting people to speed. This results in an enormous damage and write-off rate amongst the car hire fleets. One large company with 70 cars complained to me that clients had written off 10% of its fleet *in the last month*.

Generally this isn't due to collisions, but to foreign drivers going too fast on gravel roads and losing control on a bend, or losing concentration and falling asleep on a long, straight, tar road. There is usually no other reason than carelessness and ignorance. This phenomenon affects 2WDs and 4WDs equally, and under some circumstances the latter can roll more easily because they have a higher centre of gravity.

Because of this, car hire companies have very high excesses (ie: the amounts that you pay if you have a major accident). A maximum 80% CDW is normal – which means that you will always pay 20% of the cost of any damage. The bill for a major accident in a small Group A or B would normally be £1,300/US$2,080.

However, beware: the fine print will often state that you will still pay for *all* of the damage if you have an accident due to *negligence, or where no other vehicles are involved and you are driving on a gravel road*.

Some companies will offset some of this risk for you for an additional cost – the extra charge of their Additional Collision Damage Waiver (ACDW). Even after you have paid that, many will still hold you liable for 20% of the cost of any damage which occurs on an untarred road – and all of the cost if the accident is caused by 'negligence'. In short: the Namibian companies simply can't get totally comprehensive cover for their rental cars.

The only way around this is the solution found by a UK company that specialises in fly-drive trips to Namibia: Sunvil Africa (London, tel: 020 8232 9777). They offer their travellers a full 100% CDW – with no excesses in the event of a major accident, even if it occurs on a gravel road with no other vehicle involved. They insure their vehicles in the UK, not in Namibia, hence they can get this full cover.

This also gives them the lowest rental rates around, whilst using the best car hire companies in Namibia. Sunvil Africa offer this to UK-based clients who book a whole trip with them: flights, car hire and accommodation. Their trips are flexible, good value, and well worth considering.

Driving over borders

If the car-hire companies have offices in Botswana and South Africa, then you can *usually* take cars into these countries. You will need to advise the company in advance, as they need a few days to apply for the right permits and insurances – which may cost an extra N$150 or so.

If you want to do a one-way hire, this is also possible, but expect a one-way drop-off fee of around N$1,000–1,500. Note that car hire is generally cheaper in South Africa, and about the same price in Botswana. Thus for a long trip a one-way hire from South Africa into Namibia is usually slightly cheaper than vice-versa.

Previous page Balloon over the dunes near Sesriem (CS)

Above Namibia's well-maintained roads are usually long, straight and empty (CM)

Right Aus daisy, *Arctotis fastiosa*, found only within 30km of Aus (TH)

Below Helmeted guineafowl drinking from a puddle in the road (CM)

Below right A freak shower of hailstones near Otjiwarongo, October 18 1997 (CM)

Taking vehicles across Zimbabwe's borders is trickier, and has only become possible in the last few years. It is generally very expensive to do one-way hires that pick up or drop off in Zimbabwe (though Botswana's Kasane is very close).

Car-hire companies

The contact details for Namibia's larger car-hire companies are:

Avis PO Box 2057, Eros Airport, Windhoek; tel: 061 233166; fax: 061 223072
Budget PO Box 1754, Windhoek; tel: 061 228720; fax: 061 227665
Imperial PO Box 1387, Windhoek; tel: 061 227103; fax: 061 222721

The many smaller local companies include:

Andes P Bag 13231, Windhoek; tel: 061 256334; fax: 061 228552
Asco PO Box 40214, Windhoek; tel: 061 233064/232245; fax: 061 232245
Bonanza PO Box 5153, Windhoek; tel: 061 240317; fax: 061 240318
Britz PO Box 23800, Windhoek; tel: 061 250654; fax: 061 250653
Camel PO Box 80763, Windhoek; tel: 061 248818; fax: 061 222375; email: info@camelcarhire.com.na
Camping PO Box 5526, Windhoek; tel: 061 237756; fax: 061 237757
Caprivi PO Box 1837, Windhoek; tel: 061 232871; fax: 061 232374
Eyandi PO Box 5590, Windhoek; tel: 061 255103; fax: 061 255477
Fürst PO Box 90164, Windhoek; tel: 061 236037; cell: 081 128 6088
Hertz PO Box 90135, Windhoek; tel: 061 252690; fax: 061 253083
Kalahari PO Box 1525, Windhoek; tel: 061 252690; fax: 061 253083
Leopard PO Box 90633, Windhoek; tel: 061 236113; fax: 061 236111
Into Namibia PO Box 31551, Windhoek; tel: 061 253591; fax: 061 253593
Kessler PO Box 1837, Windhoek; tel: 061 256323; fax: 061 256333
Odyssey PO Box 20938, Windhoek; tel: 061 223269; fax: 061 228911; email: carhire@odysseycarhire.com; web: www.odysseycarhire.com
Pegasus PO Box 21104, Windhoek; tel/fax: 061 251451; fax: 061 223423; email: pegasus@nam.lia.net
RK 4x4 PO Box 31076, Windhoek; tel/fax: 061 223994
Tempest PO Box 24075, Windhoek; tel: 061 239163; fax: 061 230722
Woodway PO Box 11084, Windhoek; tel: 061 222877; fax: 061 220335; email: woodway@namib.com

There is a voluntary grouping of the more responsible members of the car-hire trade, the Car Rental Association of Namibia (CARAN). This lays down guidelines for standards and, if you use one of CARAN's members, then they can provide an informal arbitration service if things go wrong. They can be contacted at PO Box 807098, Windhoek.

On the road

Almost all of Namibia's major highways are tarred. They are usually wide and well-signposted, and the small amount of traffic on them makes journeys easy. Less important roads are often gravel, but even these tend to be well maintained and easily passable. Most of the sights, with the exception of Sandwich Harbour, are accessible with an ordinary saloon car (referred to as 2WD in this book). Only those going off the beaten track – into Khaudum, Bushmanland or the Kaokoveld – really need to join an organised group.

The only safe alternative to such a group trip is a convoy of two 4WDs with at least as many experienced bush drivers. Don't be fooled into thinking that a 4WD will get you everywhere, and solve all your problems. Without *extensive* experience of using one *on rough terrain*, it will simply get you into dangerous situations which you have neither the skill nor the experience to cope with. See *4WD driving*, page 86, for further discussion.

Consider getting yourself an International Driving Permit before you arrive in Namibia, as some sources advise that one is required if you wish to drive here. (That said, driving on a normal overseas driving licence with the requisite passport generally seems to be fine.) With a British licence, an international permit can be obtained in the UK from the RAC, or in the USA from Triple A. Driving is on the left.

Equipment and preparations

Driving around Namibia is usually very easy – much easier than driving at home. But because the distances are long, and some areas remote, a little more preparation is wise.

Fuel

Petrol and diesel are available in all the major towns, and many more rural corners too. For most trips, you just need to remember to fill up when you have the opportunity. Unleaded petrol costs around N$3.80 per litre. In a major emergency, many farms will be able to help you – but you shouldn't let yourself finish up in need of such charity.

If you are taking a small expedition into the northern Kaokoveld, Bushmanland, or the more obscure corners of the Caprivi, then you will need long-range fuel tanks and/or a large stock of filled jerrycans. It is essential to plan your fuel requirements well in advance, and to carry more than you expect to need. Remember that using the vehicle's 4WD capability, especially in low ratio gears, will significantly increase your fuel consumption. Similarly, the cool comfort of a vehicle's air conditioning will burn your fuel reserves swiftly.

It's worth knowing that if you need to transfer petrol from a jerrycan to the petrol tank, and you haven't a proper funnel, an alternative is to roll up a piece of paper into a funnel shape – it will work just as well.

Spares

Namibia's garages are generally very good, and most larger towns have a comprehensive stock of spares for most vehicles. (Expect to pay over about £60/US$96 for a new tyre for a small 2WD saloon.) You'll often find several garages specialising in different makes of vehicle. In the bush you'll find that farm mechanics can effect the most amazing short-term repairs with remarkably basic tools and raw materials.

Navigation

See the section on *Maps and navigation* in *Chapter 4* for further comments. The free map of the country issued by the tourist board is probably the best for driving, though expeditions may want to think about buying more detailed maps from the Surveyor General's office (see page 116). If you are heading off on to the sand tracks of Bushmanland or the wilds of eastern Caprivi, then consider taking a GPS system.

Driving at night

Never drive at night unless you have to. Both wild and domestic animals frequently spend the night by the side of busy roads, and will actually sleep on quieter ones. Tar roads are especially bad as the surface absorbs all the sun's heat by day, and then radiates it at night – making it a warm bed for passing animals. A high-speed collision with any animal, even a small one like a goat, will not only kill the animal, but will cause very severe damage to a vehicle, and potentially fatal consequences to you.

2WD driving
Tar roads
All of Namibia's tar roads are excellent, and a programme of tarring is gradually extending these. Currently they extend to linking most of Namibia's larger towns. Most are single carriageways (one lane in either direction), and it's an effort to rein back the accelerator to remain within the speed limit of 120km/h.

Remember that even on these you will find hazards like animals crossing. They are not as insulated from the surrounding countryside as the motorways, freeways and autobahns back home. So don't be tempted to speed.

On main roads, regular picnic sites with a shaded table and benches give the opportunity to stop for a break on long journeys.

Strip roads
Very occasionally there are roads where the sealed tar surface is only wide enough for one vehicle. This becomes a problem when you meet another vehicle travelling in the opposite direction...on the same stretch of tar. The local practice is to wait until the last possible moment before you steer left, driving with two wheels on the gravel adjacent to the tar, and two on the tar. Usually, the vehicle coming in the opposite direction will do the same, and after passing each other both vehicles veer back on to the tar. If you are unused to this, then slow right down before you steer on to the gravel.

Gravel roads
Most roads in Namibia are gravel, and most of these are very good. Virtually all are fine for 2WD vehicles. They don't normally suffer from potholes, although there may be slight ruts where others have driven before you.

You will occasionally put the car into small skids, and with practice at slower speeds you will learn how to deal with them. Gravel is a less forgiving surface on which to drive than tar. The rules and techniques for driving well are the same for both, but on tar you can get away with sloppy braking and cornering which would prove dangerous on gravel.

The main problem with Namibia's gravel roads is that they are too good. Drivers are lulled into a false sense of security; they believe that it is safe to go faster, and faster. Don't fall for this; it isn't safe at all. See the *Insurance, CDWs and gravel roads* section on page 82, and promise that you'll never drive faster than 80km/h on gravel. That way you'll return from a self-drive trip still believing how safe and good the roads are! A few hints for gravel driving in a 2WD vehicle may be helpful:

- **Slowing down** If in any doubt about what lies ahead, always slow down. Road surfaces can vary enormously, so keep a constant lookout for potholes, ruts or patches of soft sand which could put you into an unexpected slide.
- **Passing vehicles** When passing other vehicles travelling in the opposite direction, always slow down to minimise both the damage that stone chippings will do to your windscreen, and the danger in driving through the other vehicle's dust cloud. If the dust cloud is thick, don't return to the centre of the road too fast, as there may be another vehicle behind the first.

- **Using your gears** In normal driving, a lower gear will give you more control over the car – so keep out of high 'cruising' gears. Rather stick with third or fourth, and accept that your revs will be slightly higher than they might normally be.
- **Cornering and braking** Under ideal conditions, the brakes should only be applied when the car is travelling in a straight line. Braking whilst negotiating a corner is dangerous, so it is vital to slow down before you reach corners. Equally, it is better to slow down gradually, using a combination of gears and brakes, than to use the brakes alone. You are less likely to skid.

Salt roads
For details of driving on salt roads, see page 323.

4WD driving
If you have a high-clearance 4WD, it can extend your options considerably. However, no vehicle can make up for an inexperienced driver – so ensure that you are confident of your vehicle's capabilities *before* you venture into the wilds with it. You really need extensive practice, with an expert on hand to advise you, before you'll have the first idea how to handle such a vehicle in difficult terrain. Finally, driving in convoy is an *essential* precaution in the more remote areas, in case one vehicle gets stuck or breaks down. Some of the more relevant techniques include:

Driving in sand
If you start to lose traction in deep sand, then stop on the next piece of solid ground that you come to. Lower your tyre pressure until there is a distinct bulge in the tyre walls (having first made sure that you have the means to re-inflate them when you reach solid roads again). A lower pressure will help your traction greatly, but increase the wear on your tyres. Pump them up again before you drive on a hard surface at speed, or the tyres will be badly damaged.

Where there are clear, deep-rutted tracks in the sand, don't fight the steering wheel – just relax and let your vehicle steer itself. Driving in the cool of the morning is easier than later in the day because when sand is cool it compacts better and is firmer. (When hot, the pockets of air between the sand grains expand and the sand becomes looser.)

If you do get stuck, despite these precautions, don't panic. Don't just rev the engine and spin the wheels – you'll only dig deeper. Instead stop. Relax and assess the situation. Now dig shallow ramps in front of all the wheels, reinforcing them with pieces of wood, vegetation, stones, material or anything else which will give the wheels better traction. Lighten the vehicle load (passengers out) and push. Don't let the engine revs die as you engage your lowest ratio gear, and use the clutch to ensure that the wheels don't spin wildly and dig themselves further into the sand.

Sometimes rocking the vehicle backwards and forwards will build up momentum to break you free. This can be done by intermittently applying the clutch and/or by getting helpers who can push and pull the vehicle at the same frequency. Once the vehicle is moving, the golden rule of sand driving is to keep up the momentum: if you pause, you will sink and stop.

Driving in mud
This is difficult, though the theory is the same as for sand: keep going and don't stop. That said, even the most experienced drivers get stuck. Some areas of Namibia (like the omurambas in Khaudum National Park) have very fine soil known as 'black-cotton' soil, which can become totally impassable when wet.

Push-starting when stuck

If you are unlucky enough to need to push-start your vehicle whilst it is stuck in sand or mud, then there is a remedy. Raise up the drive wheels, and take off one of the tyres. Then wrap a length of rope around the hub and treat it like a spinning top: one person (or more) pulls the rope to make the axle spin, whilst the driver lifts the clutch, turns the ignition on, and engages a low gear to turn the engine over. This is a difficult equivalent of a push start, but it may be your only option.

Rocky terrain

Have your tyre pressure higher than normal and move very slowly. If necessary passengers should get out and guide you along the track to avoid scraping the undercarriage on the ground. This can be a very slow business, and is often the case in the highlands of the northern Kaokoveld.

Crossing rivers

The first thing to do is to stop and check the river. You must assess its depth, its substrate (type of riverbed) and its current flow; and determine the best route to drive across it. This is best done by wading across the river (whilst watching for hippos and crocodiles, if necessary). Beware of water that's too deep for your vehicle, or the very real possibility of being swept away by a fast current and a slippery substrate.

If everything is OK then select your lowest gear ratio and drive through the water at a slow but steady rate. Your vehicle's air intake must be above the level of the water to avoid your engine filling with water. It's not worth taking risks, so remember that a flooded river will often subside to much safer levels by the next morning.

Overheating

If the engine has overheated then the only option is to stop and turn the engine off. Don't open the radiator cap to refill it until the radiator is no longer hot to the touch. Even then, keep the engine running and the water circulating, while you refill the radiator – otherwise you run the risk of cracking the hot metal by suddenly cooling it. Flicking droplets of water on to the outside of a running engine will cool it.

In areas of tall grass keep a close watch on the water temperature gauge. Grass stems and seeds will get caught in the radiator grill and block the flow of air, causing the engine to overheat and the grass to catch fire. You should stop and remove the grass seeds every few kilometres also, depending on the conditions.

Driving near big game

The only animals which are likely to pose a threat to vehicles are elephants (see box *Driving near elephants: avoiding problems* page 88 for details). So, treat them with the greatest respect and don't 'push' them by trying to move ever closer. Letting them approach you is much safer, and they will feel far less threatened and more relaxed. Then, if the animals are calm, you can safely turn the engine off, sit quietly, and watch as they pass you by.

If you are unlucky, or foolish, enough to unexpectedly drive into the middle of a herd, then don't panic. Keep your movements, and those of the vehicle, slow and measured. Back off steadily. Don't be panicked, or overly intimidated, by a mock charge – this is just their way of frightening you away. Professionals will sometimes switch their engines off, but this is not for the faint-hearted.

DRIVING NEAR ELEPHANTS: AVOIDING PROBLEMS

Elephants are the only animals that pose a real danger to vehicles. Everything else will get out of your way, or at least not actively go after you, but if you treat elephants wrongly there's a chance that you might have problems.

To put this in perspective, most drivers who are new to Africa will naturally (and wisely) treat elephants with enormous respect, keeping their distance – simply out of fear. Also, in the more popular areas of Etosha, where the elephants are habituated to vehicles, you'd have to really annoy an already grumpy elephant for it to give you trouble.

To give specific advice is difficult, as every elephant is different. Each is an individual, with real moods and feelings – and there's no substitute for years of experience to tell you what mood they're in. However, a few basics are worth noting.

Firstly, keep your eyes open and don't drive too fast. Surprising an elephant on the road is utterly terrifying, and dangerous for both you and the elephant. Always drive slowly in the bush.

Secondly, think of each animal as having an invisible 'comfort zone' around it. (Some experts talk of three concentric zones: the fright, flight, and fight zone – each with a smaller radius, and each more dangerous.) If you actively approach then you breach that zone, and will upset it. So don't approach too closely: keep your distance. How close depends entirely on the elephants and the area. More relaxed elephants having a good day will allow you to get within 25m of them, bad-tempered ones that aren't used to cars may charge at 250m! You can often approach more closely in open areas than in thick bush. That said, if your vehicle is stationary and a relaxed, peaceful elephant approaches you, then you should not have problems if you simply stay still.

Thirdly, *never* beep your horn or flash your lights at an elephant (you shouldn't be driving yourself at night anyhow!). Either is guaranteed to annoy it. If there's an elephant in your way, just sit back, relax and wait; elephants always have right of way in Africa! The more sound and fury – like wheel spins and engine revving – the more likely that the elephant will assume that you are attacking it, and this is especially the case with a breeding herd.

Finally, look carefully at the elephant(s):

Are there any **small calves** around in the herd? If so expect the older females to be easily annoyed and very protective – keep your distance.

Are there any **males in 'musth'** around? These are fairly easy to spot because of a heavy secretion from penis and temporal glands and a very musty smell. Generally these will be on their own, unless they are with a cow on heat. Such males will be excitable; you must spot them and give them a wide berth.

Are there any elephants with a lot of seepage from their **temporal glands**, on the sides of their heads? If so, expect them to be stressed and easily irritable – beware. This is likely to have a long-term cause – perhaps lack of good water, predator pressure or something as random as toothache – but whatever the cause that animal is under stress, and so should be given an extra-wide berth.

DISTANCE CHART
Distances in kilometres

Distances between towns are only one part of the equation when calculating travelling times. More important are the type of road (tar, gravel, salt) and the terrain, both of which must be taken into consideration.

```
Aus
989  Buitepos
898  115  Gobabis
1145 777  657  Grootfontein
798  786  630  645  Henties Bay
1156 783  688  425  345  Kamanjab
346  1010 895  1142 1115 1153 Karasburg
876  501  388  403  242  414  873  Karibib
1422 1533 1418 767  1404 1156 1901 1252 Katima Mulilo
211  802  687  934  907  945  208  665  1693 Keetmanshoop
1149 777  662  419  234  113  982  317  1150 982  Khorixas
125  1136 1021 1268 923  1279 471  999  2027 208  1150 Lüderitz
249  692  498  824  549  835  540  555  1583 332  829  374  Maltahöhe
432  381  466  713  686  724  429  444  1472 221  718  555  111  Mariental
1226 863  738  167  506  677  1223 484  926  1015 500  1286 609  636  Namutoni
442  1101 991  1238 1211 1249 147  969  1997 304  1273 471  905  794  1319 Noordoewer
764  393  381  395  392  761  112  553  1140 430  889  443  332  487  857  Okahandja
1128 753  640  397  579  221  1125 386  1128 917  256  1253 807  696  123  1221 364  Okaukuejo
937  562  339  342  254  353  934  61   1101 726  256  1060 616  505  173  1030 325  173  Omaruru
1401 913  852  681  1398 659  989  1190 675  1524 1080 969  245  1494 637  368  598  345  Oshakati
1174 683  568  87   507  336  1053 404  846  845  330  1179 735  524  170  1449 292  308  253  345  Otavi
938  565  450  207  389  218  935  197  966  727  212  1061 617  506  288  1031 174  190  135  463  118  Otjiwarongo
1011 638  523  280  462  145  1008 269  1011 800  139  1134 690  576  361  1104 247  117  208  436  191  73   Outjo
606  407  292  539  512  550  603  270  1298 395  544  729  285  174  620  699  158  522  331  795  450  405  Rehoboth
1553 1180 1065 494  1143 272  1550 686  1253 1342 377  1676 1232 1121 469  1646 798  534  750  152  497  688  876  Ruacana
1393 1020 905  248  893  645  1390 741  511  1182 639  1516 1072 961  415  1486 629  617  590  335  455  500  405  742  Rundu
1389 1016 921  658  578  233  1386 647  1389 1178 346  1512 1068 957  739  1482 625  495  586  451  569  378  323  783  878  Sesfontein
434  877  771  356  709  725  472  530  517  615  559  185  296  852  821  390  754  533  992  682  564  261  981  1019 1015 Sesriem
1051 676  563  578  67   412  1048 175  1337 840  318  731  482  619  1121 287  561  236  489  445  513  308  876  787  783  261  645  Swakopmund
1237 746  631  60   570  399  1116 377  819  907  367  1242 798  687  107  1241 355  345  316  282  63   181  228  876  323  878  297  632  745  Tsumeb
1401 1028 913  256  901  581  1398 659  974  1190 675  1524 1080 969  423  1494 637  653  598  563  343  463  536  914  795  1015 552  632  745  824  Tsumkwe
700  709  594  690  98   443  1079 206  1458 814  349  938  451  650  1175 318  593  267  866  521  403  476  715  750  947  476  266  552  745  316  673  Walvis Bay
693  320  205  452  466  463  690  181  1211 482  816  372  261  533  786  435  71   242  363  363  245  318  87   700  708  860  318  696  319  356  426  708  389  Windhoek
```

Suggested itineraries

If you're organising a small 4WD expedition, then it is assumed that you know exactly what you're doing, and where you want to go, and hence no 4WD itineraries have been included here.

The suggested itineraries here, for 2WDs, are intended as a framework only, and the time spent at places is the *minimum* which is reasonable – if you have less time, then cut places out rather than quicken the pace. With more time to spare, consider taking the same routes, and exploring each area in greater detail.

When planning your own itinerary, try to intersperse the longer drives between more restful days. Avoid spending each night in a new place, as shifting your base can become tiring. Try to book hire cars and accommodation as far in advance as you can; that way you'll get the places you want, exactly when you want them.

Included here are two very loose categories: 'budget' and 'indulgent'. These broadly reflect the cost of the choices made. Most of the places on the budget itinerary allow camping. The odd place that doesn't, like Zebra River Lodge, is such good value that it'd be wasteful not to use it.

Two weeks
Southern–central Namibia

Night		Budget	Indulgent
1	Fly overnight to Namibia		
2	In/near Windhoek	Cori Guest House	Eningu Lodge
3–4	Mariental area	Hardap Restcamp	Intu Afrika
5–6	Fish River Canyon area	Ai-Ais Restcamp	Canyon Lodge
7–8	Lüderitz	Kratzplatz	The Nest
9	Helmeringhausen area	Duwisib Restcamp	Dabis G'stfarm
10–11	Namib-Naukluft area	Zebra River Lodge	Wolwedans
12–13	Namib-Naukluft area	Desert Homestead	Sossusvlei W'ness Camp
14	Fly overnight out of Namibia		

There is a wide choice of places in the NamibRand, Sesriem and Naukluft areas for the last four nights of this trip. It really depends on how much time you want to spend exploring the mountains and walking, compared with investigating the area's dunes and desert.

Central Namibia–Etosha

Night		Budget	Indulgent
1	Overnight flight to Namibia		
2	In/near Windhoek	Pension Handke	Ozombanda
3–4	Swakopmund	Secret Garden	Hansa
5	Skeleton Coast	Die Oord Restcamp	Cape Cross Lodge
6–7	Damaraland	Khorixas Restcamp	Damaraland Camp
8	Etosha/Damaraland	Okaukuejo Restcamp	Damaraland Camp
9	Etosha	Okaukuejo Restcamp	Ongava Lodge
10	Etosha	Halali Restcamp	Ongava Lodge
11–12	Etosha	Namutoni Restcamp	Etosha Aoba
13	En route to Windhoek	Waterberg's Restcamp	Okonjima
14	Fly overnight out of Namibia		

This trip is better in a 'clockwise' direction, as below, because then the best game-viewing (at Etosha) is saved until near the end. This route could easily be expanded by a few days to visit the Sesriem area, by slotting it in after Windhoek and before Swakopmund.

Even on an unrestricted budget, many would rather stay *inside* Etosha, at the basic Okaukuejo and Halali restcamps, rather than *outside* it – regardless of how comfortable the outside lodges are.

Three weeks
Southern–central–Etosha

Night		Budget	Indulgent
1	Overnight flight to Namibia		
2–3	Mariental area	Hardap Restcamp	Intu Afrika
4–5	Fish River Canyon area	Ai-Ais Restcamp	Canyon Lodge
6–7	Lüderitz	Kratzplatz	Zum Spergebiet Sea View
8	Namib-Naukluft area	Duwisib Restcamp	Wolwedans
9	Namib-Naukluft area	Desert Homestead	Wolwedans
10–11	Namib-Naukluft area	Desert Homestead	Kulala Lodge
12–13	Swakopmund	Pension Rapmund	Swakopmund Hotel
14–15	Damaraland	Twyfelfontein Lodge	Etendeka Mountain Camp
16–17	Etosha	Okaukuejo Restcamp	Ongava Lodge
18–19	Etosha	Halali Restcamp	Mushara Lodge
20	En route to Windhoek	Waterberg Restcamp	Waterberg Wilderness Lodge
21	Fly overnight out of Namibia		

Trans-Caprivi Strip

Night		Budget	Indulgent
1	Overnight flight to Victoria Falls		
2–3	Victoria Falls area	Waterfront	Tongabezi
4–6	Chobe River area	Camping in Kasane	Impalila Island
7–8	Katima–Mudumu area	Hippo Lodge camping	Lianshulu
9–10	Popa Falls area	Popa Falls Restcamp	Suclabo Lodge
11	Rundu	Sarasungu camping	Sarasungu
12–13	Etosha	Namutoni Restcamp	Etosha Aoba
14–15	Etosha	Okaukuejo Restcamp	Ongava Lodge
16	Southern Kaokoveld	Khorixas Restcamp	Huab Lodge
17	Southern Kaokoveld	Ongongo campsite	Huab Lodge
18	Southern Kaokoveld	Ongongo campsite	Etendeka
19	Southern Kaokoveld	Brandberg Restcamp	Etendeka
20	En route to Windhoek	Ozombanda	Okonjima
21	Fly overnight out of Namibia		

This trans-Caprivi route is intrinsically more expensive than spending the same length of time just in Namibia. Victoria Falls and the Chobe/Kasane are both relatively costly, Botswana's national park fees are relatively high, and there would also be a one-way drop-off fee levied on the car hire. Such a trip is better suited to a second or third visit to Namibia, rather than the first.

BY AIR
Namibia's internal air links are good and reasonably priced, and internal flights can be a practical way to hop huge distances swiftly. The scheduled internals are sufficiently infrequent that you need to plan your trip around them, and not vice versa. This needs to be done far in advance to be sure of getting seats, but does run the risk of your trip being thrown into disarray if the airline's schedule changes. Sadly, this isn't as uncommon as you might hope.

CLASSIC AIR FLIGHTS

Walking over the tarmac in the late 1990s at Hosea Kutako Airport to board your flight to Victoria Falls, you may have been surprised to find a silver, black, white and turquoise *Fish Eagle* in front of you – a glistening old propeller-driven plane. Aviation enthusiasts would recognise this as a vintage Douglas DC-6B, powered by four Pratt & Whitney R-2800 engines. It is one of two classic DC-6Bs which belonged to the privately owned Namibia Commercial Aviation (NCA).

In fact these two were the very last aircraft to roll off the production line in 1958. Initially they had a little less than three years of European commercial operations with JAT, of Belgrade, before they were transferred to the Yugoslav Air Force. The *Fish Eagle* was then used exclusively as the personal transport of the Yugoslav leader, Marshall Tito. For this it was fitted out in style with wood and leather, extra soundproofing, a kitchen/galley, and even six beds.

Over a decade later, in 1975, both aircraft were donated to the Zambian Air Force, where Marshall Tito's plane became President Kaunda's personal transport for several years, before falling out of favour. Then it was left to languish on the ground in Lusaka for 15 years, unused. Finally, in 1992, the Zambian Air Force decided to sell 40 tons of DC-6 spares, and a condition of sale was that the buyers would agree to take away and dispose of these two aircraft.

NCA bought the spares and, after a week working on the first of the planes, the engineers had restored one of the aircraft, the *Fish Eagle*, sufficiently for it to be flown out to Rundu, their base in Namibia. This has now been sold, but the second aircraft, the *Bateleur*, was restored during 1998 and is still in use for private charters all over Namibia.

Increasingly private charter flights are being used for short camp-to-camp flights. These are expensive, though the Dune Hopper, mentioned below, is an attempt to cut these prices. See *Chapter 10*, page 149, for the contact details of airline head offices in Windhoek.

Regional flights

Air Namibia operates regular and reliable flights around the region. One-way fares from Windhoek include £183/US$275 to Maun, £277/US$416 to Victoria Falls, £245/US$368 to Luanda and £145/US$218 to Johannesburg or Cape Town. In general, you will find these to be the same price if you buy them locally or overseas. However, if you travel between Europe and Namibia with Air Namibia, and book your regional flights at the same time, then these routes become much cheaper.

South African Airways and **Comair** (a subsidiary of **British Airways**) also operate links to Jo'burg and Cape Town, and **Air Botswana** links Maun with Windhoek.

Internal flights
Scheduled internal flights

Namibia has a good network of scheduled internal flights, run by **Air Namibia**, which link the outlying towns to the hub of Windhoek. The main regional airports (with their useful international city codes) are Cape Town (CPT); Johannesburg (JNB); Katima Mulilo, M'pacha (MPA); Livingstone, Zambia (LVI); Lüderitz (LUD);

Maun, Botswana (MUB); Mokuti Lodge, Etosha (OKU); Ondangwa (OND); Oranjemund (OMD); Rundu (NDU); Swakopmund (SWP); Victoria Falls, Zimbabwe (VFA); Walvis Bay (WVB); Windhoek, International (WDH) and Eros (ERS).

Prices and timetables of internal flights change regularly. Generally, though, these flights are not expensive; even Lüderitz to Windhoek costs only £85/US$128.

Chartered internal flights
Namibia Commercial Aviation (tel: 061 223562; fax: 061 234583) runs a superb DC6 dating from 1958. Currently in use for private charters, it used to form part of Air Namibia's normal schedule on the routes to/from Victoria Falls.

Flexible fly-in trips
In the last few years, there have been an increasing number of light aircraft flights around Namibia, arranged by small companies using small four- and six-seater planes. These are particularly convenient for linking farms and lodges which have their own bush airstrips. If you have the money, and want to make the most of a short time in the country, then perhaps a fly-in trip would suit you. Now it's possible to visit Namibia in the same way that you'd see Botswana's Okavango Delta, by flying from camp to camp. This is still the only way to see the northern wilderness area of the Skeleton Coast. Any good tailor-made specialist tour operator (see pages 50–1) could put together such a trip for you – but expect it to cost at least £250/US$375 per person per night.

One particularly popular option is to take one of the scheduled flights that link Windhoek and Swakopmund with the properties around Sesriem and Wolwedans. This is usually arranged as part of a package through a tour operator, or one of the lodges. It's not cheap, but is a fast way to get in to the dunes if time is limited. For pleasure flights, see also page 314.

Of course, if you've a private pilot's licence and an adventurous streak, then Namibia's skies are marvellously open and free of hassles – but you'll have to spend a day in Windhoek sorting out the paperwork and taking a test flight.

BY RAIL
Generally, Namibia's trains cater better for freight than visitors (*Desert Express* excepted). Although there is an extensive network of tracks connecting all of Namibia's main towns, there is no through service into South Africa – the only passenger train to cross the border terminates at Upington, where there is no through connection into the South African rail network (the next mainline station, De Aar, is 415km away).

The dedicated Starline passenger rail service is run by TransNamib. Trains are pleasant and rarely full, but they are slow and stop frequently. Travelling by train is not for those in a hurry, and most travellers without their own vehicle prefer long-distance coaches or hitchhiking.

With the exception of the routes from Keetmanshoop to Upington, and Otjiwarongo to Tsumeb, all train journeys are overnight. This means that there's no chance of enjoying the view, but, on the plus side, it allows travellers to get a night's sleep while in transit, saving on accommodation costs and perhaps 'gaining' a day at their destination. Carriages are divided into economy and business sections. There are vending machines dispensing snacks and soft drinks on most trains, and videos are shown through the journey.

Passengers need to check-in half an hour before the train departs. Only two pieces of luggage may be carried free of charge; bicycles are not allowed. There are sleeper beds on the Windhoek–Keetmanshoop line.

Fares

Overall, fares for TransNamib's trains or buses are low, averaging around N$54 for 500km on the trains, but the tariff can appear amazingly complex. There are various combinations of two classes of travel, three different tariffs (off-peak periods, peak periods and high-peak periods), and occasional discounts (33%) for travel on Tuesdays and Wednesdays. There is in fact a grid that underlies the pricing structure; once you have decided on the various components, then it's just a matter of checking your journey against that grid. Copies are available at the station in Windhoek.

The most expensive permutation, for travel between Windhoek and Keetmanshoop during a high-peak period, in business class, would cost N$81, while economy is N$65. All train prices quoted are for one-way fares.

Schedules

The following show departures and arrivals to and from Windhoek and other railway stations:

	Windhoek departures	Windhoek arrivals
	Sun/Tue/Thu	Tue/Thu/Sat
Windhoek	17.45	05.30
Okahandja	↓ 20.25	03.30 ↑
Karibib	23.00	00.50
Omaruru	↓ 01.10	21.35 ↑
Otjiwarongo	05.35	17.45
Otavi	↓ 08.20	12.15 ↑
Tsumeb	09.40	10.25
	Mon/Wed/Fri	Mon/Wed/Fri
	Tsumeb arrivals	**Tsumeb departures**

	Windhoek departures	Windhoek arrivals
	daily except Sat	daily except Sun
Windhoek	↓ 19.00	06.20 ↑
Rehoboth	21.31	03.45
Kalkrand	↓ 23.15	01.50 ↑
Mariental	01.55	23.40
Gibeon	03.02	21.50
Asab	↓ 03.40	21.00 ↑
Tses	04.40	20.10
Keetmanshoop	↓ 06.30	18.30 ↑
	daily except Sun	daily except Sat
	Keetmanshoop arrivals	**Keetmanshoop departures**

On just two days per week this links into a short service between Keetmanshoop and Upington, across the South African border:

	Keetmanshoop departures	Keetmanshoop arrivals
	Wed/Sat	Sun/Thu
Keetmanshoop	08.50	16.30
Grünau	↓ 13.10	12.25 ↑
Karasburg	14.30	11.20
Ariamsvlei	↓ 18.25	09.00· ↑
Upington	21.30	05.00
	Wed/Sat	Sun/Thu
	Upington arrivals	**Upington departures**

	Windhoek departures daily except Sat	**Windhoek arrivals** daily except Sun
Windhoek	↓ 20.00	07.00 ↑
Okahandja	22.05	05.10
Karibib	↓ 00.40	02.20 ↑
Usakos	↓ 01.50	00.45
Swakopmund	05.30	20.35
Walvis Bay	↓ 07.00	19.00 ↑
	daily except Sun **Walvis Bay arrivals**	daily except Sat **Walvis Bay departures**

	Windhoek departures Sun/Tue/Thu	**Windhoek arrivals** Tue/Thu/Sat
Windhoek	↓ 22.00	04.25 ↑
Omitara	↓ 02.15	00.01
Witvlei	04.00	22.20
Gobabis	↓ 05.25	21.00 ↑
	Mon/Wed/Fri **Gobabis arrivals**	Mon/Wed/Fri **Gobabis departures**

	Tsumeb departures Mon/Wed/Fri	**Tsumeb arrivals** Wed/Fri/Mon
Tsumeb	↓ 10.25	09.40 ↑
Otavi	12.15	08.20
Otjiwarongo	↓ 16.45	05.35 ↑
Omaruru	↓ 20.35	00.25
Usakos	↓ 22.55	21.55
Arandis	↓ 00.55	19.45 ↑
Swakopmund	02.35	18.05
Walvis Bay	↓ 04.00	16.15 ↑
	Tue/Thu/Sat **Walvis Bay arrivals**	Tue/Thu/Sun **Walvis Bay departures**

Aside from the above train services, Starline also run some passenger services by bus. See pages 98–9 for details.

Booking

All Starline trains and buses may be booked at any station. Main station telephone numbers are as follows:

Gobabis tel: 061 298 2305
Grootfontein tel: 067 249 2210
Karasburg tel: 063 270090
Keetmanshoop tel: 063 229202/229230
Lüderitz tel: 063 201200
Mariental tel: 063 249202/249200
Okahandja tel: 062 503315

Omaruru tel: 064 570006
Otjiwarongo tel: 067 305202
Swakopmund tel: 064 208512
Tsumeb tel: 067 298202
Walvis Bay tel: 064 208504
Windhoek tel: 061 298 2032;
     fax: 061 298 2495

The *Desert Express*

The *Desert Express* was introduced in 1998, the result of years of planning and work. The whole train was designed, built and fitted for this trip. It offers a luxurious overnight trip with interesting stops en route, and currently makes the journey between Windhoek and Swakopmund twice a week, with different stops in each direction.

Check-in is 90 minutes before departure, and if you've free time around Windhoek station then take advantage of the free entry to the Transport Museum (see page 156).

Westbound, it leaves Windhoek on Tuesday and Friday afternoon at 14.30 (15.30 in summer). After about an hour it reaches the Okapuka Ranch, where travellers disembark for a short excursion to see the ranch lions being fed. Continuing on the train, a sundowner drink and nibbles are served before an impressive dinner, after which the train stops in a siding, Friedrichsfelde, for the night. It starts moving early in the morning, catching the spectacular sunrise over the desert and passing through the Khan Valley before stopping in the dunes between Swakopmund and Walvis Bay, for travellers to take a short walk in the desert. It arrives in Swakopmund at 10.00 after a good breakfast.

Eastbound, it departs from Swakopmund on Wednesday and Saturday afternoon at 13.00 in winter (first Sunday in April to first Sunday in September), or 14.00 in summer. After a few hours it stops at Ebony siding from where passengers are transported to Spitzkoppe, where there's a chance to explore in search of rock paintings, or have a sundowner drink. Everyone is back on the train about three hours later, after which dinner is served. At 08.00, the train reaches Okapuka Ranch for an hour's stop to see the ranch lions being fed, before continuing with breakfast and arriving at Windhoek station by 10.00.

The *Desert Express* has 24 air-conditioned cabins (making advance booking vital). Each is small but ingeniously fitted: beds that pull down from the walls, washbasins that move, and various switches cleverly hidden away. Each has its own en-suite facilities and will sleep up to three people, though two in a cabin is perfect. It's a super way to be whisked between Windhoek and Swakopmund in comfort, perfect for a trip's start or end.

Bookings can be made through good overseas operators, local agents, or direct to Desert Express, P Bag 13204, Windhoek; tel: 061 298 2600; fax: 061 298 2601; email: dx@transnamib.com.na.

Rates: N$1,950 single, N$1,500 per person for two people sharing a cabin, and N$1,080 per person for three people sharing a cabin. This includes excursions, dinner and breakfast.

BY BUS

In comparison with Zimbabwe, East Africa or even South Africa, Namibia has few cheap local buses that are useful for travellers. Small Volkswagen combis (minibuses) do ferry people between towns, providing a good fast service at about N$16 (£2/US$3) per 100km, but these operate only on the busier routes between centres of population. Visitors usually want to see the more remote areas – where local people just hitch if they need transport.

Coaches
Intercape Mainliner
There is one company, Intercape Mainliner, which operates luxury vehicles on long-distance routes covering most of the main towns. These are comfortable, with refreshments available, music, videos, toilets and air conditioning.

Reservations
Reservations for all coaches should be made at least 72 hours in advance, either via Mainliner's website, intercape.co.za, or at one of their offices, or through one of the agents listed below. The exception to this is the journey between Windhoek and Rehoboth, where tickets may be bought only on the bus prior to departure. Tickets for Intercape Mainliner services may be bought online with a credit card at

www.intercape.co.za, or through their reservations office at the Galilei Street depot in Windhoek, off Jan Jonkers, tel: 061 227847; fax: 061 228285. Alternatively, get in touch with one of their booking agents:

Gobabis Boekhou & Sekretariële, tel: 061 562470
Karibib Ströblhof Hotel, tel: 062252 81
Keetmanshoop Du Toit Motors, tel: 063 223912 or Jonneys Auto Electric, tel: 063 222442
Otjiwarongo Welwitschia Travel, tel: 0651 303437
Swakopmund Ritz Reise, tel: 064 405151
Tsumeb Tourism Centre, tel: 067 220728 or Tsumeb Aviation Services, tel: 067 220520
Walvis Bay Flamingo Travel, tel: 064 207268 or Ultra Travel, tel: 064 207997
Gobabis Boekhou & Sekretariële, tel: 062 562470
Karibib Ströblhof Hotel, tel: 064 550081
Keetmanshoop H&J, tel: 063 223063
Otjiwarongo Welwitschia Travel, tel: 067 303437
Swakopmund Ritz Reise, tel: 064 405151
Tsumeb Tourism Centre, tel: 067 220728 or Tsumeb Aviation Services, tel: 067 220520
Walvis Bay Flamingo Travel, tel: 064 207268

and in South Africa:

Cape Town Intercape, tel: (27) 21 386 4400.
Johannesburg Intercape, tel: (27) 11 333–5231

Timings given for Mainliner services are local time, and not, as previously, in South African time.

Schedules have changed little over the years, though the fares increase often. Use timings included here as a rough guide only. Up-to-date schedules and fares may be obtained on the website, www.intercape.co.za. Fares are quoted one way, but for return fares there is a discount of N$15 discount for journeys that are totally within Namibia. The discount does not apply to cross-border journeys. The following gives an indication of one-way fares:

Windhoek to Rehoboth	N$50 approx (must be purchased on the bus)
Windhoek to Okahandja	N$70
Windhoek to Swakopmund	NS$120
Windhoek to Walvis Bay	N$130
Windhoek to Otjiwarongo	N$180
Windhoek to Grünau	N$245
Windhoek to Rundu	N$350
Windhoek to Cape Town	N$430
Windhoek to Johannesburg	NS$545
Windhoek to Victoria Falls	N$500

Windhoek–Walvis Bay

City (pick-up point)	Windhoek departures Mon/Wed/Fri/Sat	Windhoek arrivals Mon/Wed/Fri/Sun
Windhoek (Grab-a-phone)	↓ 05.55	16.25 ↑
Okahandja (Shell Ultra)	06.55	15.35
Karibib (Ströblehof Hotel)	↓ 08.05	14.25 ↑
Usakos (Shell Ultra)	08.55	13.55
Swakopmund (Talk Shop on Roon St)	↓ 10.35	12.10
Walvis Bay (Spur restaurant)	↓ 11.10	11.30 ↑
	Walvis Bay arrivals	Walvis Bay departures

Windhoek–Victoria Falls

This service runs twice every week.

City (pick-up point)	Windhoek departures Fri/Mon	Windhoek arrivals Mon/Thu
Windhoek (Grab-a-phone)	↓ 18.55	02.55 ↑
Okahandja (Shell Ultra)	19.55	01.55
Otjiwarongo (Marina Toyota)	22.10	00.10 ↑
Otavi (4-way stop – Toyota)	↓ 23.25	22.55
Grootfontein (Maroela Motors)	01.10	21.25
Rundu (Engen main road)	↓ 04.10	18.40 ↑
Katima Mulilo (Shell service station)	11.55	12.10
Victoria Falls (post office)	↓ 10.45	08.00 ↑
	Sat/Tue	Sun/Wed
	Victoria Falls arrivals	**Vic. Falls departures**

Windhoek–Cape Town

Note that tickets between Windhoek and Rehoboth cannot be prebooked.

City (pick-up point)	Windhoek departures Sun/Mon/Wed/Fri	Windhoek arrivals Mon/Wed/Fri/Sat
Windhoek (Grab-a-phone)	↓ 16.55	05.25 ↑
Rehoboth (Echo service station)	17.55	04.10
Mariental (Engen station)	↓ 20.00	02.15
Keetmanshoop (BP Du Toit station)	↓ 22.35	00.00 ↑
Grünau (Shell truck stop)	00.25	21.40
Cape Town (Station Tourist Centre)	↓ 13.30	10.00 ↑
	Mon/Tue/Thu/Sat	Sun/Tue/Thu/Fri
	Cape Town arrivals	**Cape Town depart.**

Windhoek–Upington

Note that tickets between Windhoek and Rehoboth cannot be prebooked.

City (pick-up point)	Windhoek departures Mon/Wed/Fri/Sun	Windhoek arrivals Mon/Wed/Fri/Sat
Windhoek (Grab-a-phone)	↓ 16.55	05.25 ↑
Rehoboth (Echo service station)	17.55	04.10
Mariental (Engen station)	↓ 20.10	02.25
Keetmanshoop (BP Du Toit station)	↓ 22.40	00.00 ↑
Grünau (Shell truck stop)	00.25	21.40
Upington (Intercape Lutz St)	↓ 06.30	17.45 ↑
	Tue/Thu/Sat/Mon	Sun/Tue/Thu/Fri
	Upington arrivals	**Upington departures**

Starline services

Part of the TransNamib group, which operates most of the country's railway service, Starline also operate buses on 25 routes nationwide, linking areas that used to be serviced more regularly by the rail network. These often leave from railway stations, and most of the routes are designed for local traffic, often with just one service a week and a minimal length of time at the destination. For visitors, the most useful service is that linking Lüderitz with Keetmanshoop:

Railway station	Keetmanshoop departures	Keetmanshoop arrivals	
	daily	daily	
	except Sun	except Sat	Sun
Keetmanshoop	07.30	17.30	16.30
Goageb	↓ 08.45	16.20 ↑	15.20 ↑
Bethanie	09.20	15.40	14.40
Aus	↓ 10.55	14.00 ↑	13.00 ↑
Lüderitz	12.15	12.30	11.30
	Lüderitz arrivals	**Lüderitz departures**	

For booking details and costs, see TransNamib's rail stations, pages 94–5.

Namib-Naukluft Lodge Shuttle

African Extravaganza run a useful minibus shuttle service between Windhoek, Swakopmund and their Namib-Naukluft Lodge, near Solitaire (see page 269). Though in practical terms this limits you to staying at their lodge, unless you can arrange for another to collect you, it is a convenient way to see part of the desert if you don't want to drive.

The shuttle departs from both towns at 14.00 (13.00 June–Sept), arriving at the lodge just before sunset. Then it departs from the lodge early in the morning to reach Windhoek or Swakopmund at 13.00 (12.00 June–Sept). It costs N$2,500 per person sharing, N$2,800 single, for a return trip; or N$2,900 per person sharing, N$3,200 single, if you want to start from Windhoek and end at Swakopmund, or vice versa.

BY TAXI

Private taxis do operate in the larger towns, and are useful for getting around Windhoek, Swakopmund and Walvis Bay. They are normally summoned by phoning, rather than being hailed from the street.

Township taxis are rather different, being minibuses that serve the routes between the townships and the centre, usually leaving when full and carrying a very full load of passengers. Unless you know where you are going, and have detailed local advice about which ones to take, you're unlikely to find these very useful.

HITCHHIKING

Hitchhiking is a feasible way to travel independently around Namibia, provided that you're patient and don't have a tight schedule to keep. It is certainly one of the best ways to meet people, and can be speedy and cheap. How fast you get lifts is determined by how much traffic goes your way, where you stand, and how you dress. Some of the gravel roads have very little traffic, and you will wait days for even a single car to pass. The important part is to set off with enough food and (especially) water to be able to wait for this long, or to choose very carefully the lift that you take, and where they leave you.

For the sake of courtesy, and those who come after you, it's important not to abuse people's kindness. Offer to help with the cost of fuel (most people will refuse anyhow) or pay for some cold drinks on the way. Listen patiently to your host's views and, if you choose to differ, do so courteously – after all, you came to Namibia to learn about a different country.

Camping and Walking in the Bush

CAMPING

Many manuals have been written on survival in the bush, usually by military veterans. If you are stranded with a convenient multi-purpose knife, then these useful tomes will describe how you can build a shelter from branches, catch passing animals for food, and signal to the inevitable rescue planes which are combing the globe looking for you – whilst avoiding the attentions of hostile forces.

In Namibia, camping is usually less about surviving than about being comfortable. You will usually have much more than the knife: at least a bulging backpack, if not a loaded vehicle. Thus the challenge is not to camp and survive, it is to camp and be as comfortable as possible. Only practice will teach you this, but a few hints might be useful for the less experienced African campers.

Where you can camp

In national parks and areas that get frequent visitors, there are designated camping sites, usually at restcamps. Most people never need to venture away from these.

Outside the parks, you should ask the local landowner, or village head, if they are happy for you to camp on their property. If you explain patiently and politely what you want, then you are unlikely to meet anything but warm hospitality from most rural Namibians. They will normally be as fascinated with your way of life as you are with theirs. Company by your camp fire is virtually assured.

Choosing a site

Only experience will teach you how to choose a good site for pitching a tent, but a few points may help you avoid problems if you're in a very remote area:

- Avoid camping on what looks like a path through the bush, however indistinct. It may be a well-used game trail.
- Beware of camping in dry riverbeds: dangerous flash floods can arrive with little or no warning.
- Near the coast, and in marshy areas, camp on higher ground to avoid cold, damp mists in the morning and evening.
- Camp a reasonable distance from water: near enough to walk to it, but far enough to avoid animals which arrive to drink.
- If a storm with lightning is likely, make sure that your tent is not the highest thing around.
- Finally, choose a site that is as flat as possible; it will make sleeping much easier.

Camp fires

Camp fires can create a great atmosphere and warm you on a cold evening, but they can also be damaging to the environment and leave unsightly piles of ash and blackened stones. Deforestation is a cause for major concern in much of the developing world, including parts of Namibia, so if you do light a fire then use wood as the locals do: sparingly. If you have a vehicle, then consider buying firewood in advance from people who sell it at the roadside in the more verdant areas.

If you collect it yourself, then take only dead wood, nothing living. Never just pick up a log: always roll it over first, checking carefully for snakes or scorpions.

Experienced campers build small, highly efficient fires by using a few large stones to absorb, contain and reflect the heat, and gradually feeding just a few thick logs into the centre to burn. Cooking pots can be balanced on the stones, or the point where the logs meet and burn. Others will use a small trench, lined with rocks, to similar effect. Either technique takes practice, but is worth perfecting. Whichever you do, bury the ashes, take any rubbish with you when you leave, and make the site look as if you had never been there. (See *Further Reading* for details of Christina Dodwell's excellent *Travel, Survival and Bush Cookery*.)

Don't expect an unattended fire to frighten away wild animals – that works in Hollywood, but not in Africa. A camp fire may help your feelings of insecurity, but lion and hyena will disregard it with stupefying nonchalance.

Finally, do be hospitable to any locals who appear – despite your efforts to seek permission for your camp, you may effectively be staying in their back gardens.

Using a tent (or not)

Whether to use a tent or to sleep in the open is a personal choice, dependent upon where you are. In an area where there are predators around (specifically lion and hyena) then you should use a tent – and sleep *completely* inside it, as a protruding leg may seem like a tasty take-away to a hungry hyena. This is especially true at organised campsites, where the local animals have got so used to humans that they have lost much of their inherent fear of man. At least one person has been eaten whilst in a sleeping bag next to Okaukuejo's floodlit waterhole, so always use a tent in these restcamps.

Outside game areas, you will be fine sleeping in the open, or preferably under a mosquito net, with just the stars of the African sky above you. On the practical side, sleeping under a tree will reduce the morning dew that settles on your sleeping bag. If your vehicle has a large, flat roof then sleeping on this will provide you with peace of mind, and a star-filled outlook. (Hiring a vehicle with a built-in roof-tent would seem like a perfect solution, until you want to take a drive whilst leaving your camp intact.)

Camping equipment

If you intend to camp in Namibia, then your choice of equipment will be affected by how you are travelling; you'll have more room in a vehicle than if you just carry a backpack. A few things to consider are:

Tent Mosquito-netting ventilation panels, allowing a good flow of air, are essential. Don't go for a tent that's small; it may feel cosy at home, but will be hot and claustrophobic in the desert. That said, strength and weatherproofing are not so important, unless you're visiting Namibia during the height of the rains.

Mat A ground mat of some sort is essential for comfort, warmth and protecting the tent's groundsheet from stony ground (put it underneath the tent). The ubiquitous closed-cell foam mats are good and readily available. Genuine Karrimats and Therm-a-Rests (combination air-mattress/foam mats) are quite expensive, but much stronger and more durable – worth the investment.

Sleeping bag A three-season down sleeping bag is ideal, being the smallest and lightest bag that is still warm enough for winter nights. Synthetic fillings are cheaper, but for the same warmth are heavier and more bulky. They do have the advantage that they keep their warmth when wet, unlike down, but clearly this is not so vital in Namibia's dry climate.

Sheet sleeping bag Thin pure-cotton sheet sleeping bags (eg: YHA design) are good protection for your main sleeping bag, keeping it cleaner. They can, of course, be used on their own when your main sleeping bag is too hot.

Stove 'Trangia'-type stoves, which burn methylated spirits, are simple to use, light, and cheap to run. They come complete with a set of light aluminium pans and a very useful all-purpose handle. Often you'll be able to cook on a fire with the pans, but it's nice to have the option of making a brew in a few minutes while you set up camp. Canisters for gas stoves are available in the main towns if you prefer to use these, but are expensive and bulky. Petrol- and kerosene-burning stoves are undoubtedly efficient on fuel and powerful – but invariably temperamental, messy, and unreliable in the dusty desert. If you're going on a long hike then take a stove and fuel, as firewood may not always be available in the drier areas.

Torch (flashlight) This should be on every visitor's packing list. Find one that's small and tough, preferably water- and sand-proof. Head-mounted torches leave your hands free (useful when cooking) but some people find them bulky. The small, strong and super-bright torches (such as Maglites) are excellent, but their bulbs are difficult to buy in Namibia. Bring several spares with you.

Water containers For everyday use, a small two-litre water bottle is invaluable – however you are travelling. If you're thinking of hiking, you should bring a strong, collapsible water-bag for times when you will be away from a close source of water. Ten litres is a useful size, and probably the most you'll ever consider carrying on top of your normal kit. (Ten litres of water weighs 10kg.) Large plastic containers for the car can be bought when you arrive.

See *Planning and Preparations*, pages 57–8, for a memory-jogging list of other useful items to pack.

Dangers from wildlife

Camping in Africa is really *very* safe, though you may not think so from reading this. If you have a major problem whilst camping, it will probably be because you did something stupid, or because you forgot to take a few simple precautions. Here are a few general basics, applicable to anywhere in Africa and not just Namibia.

Large animals

Big game will not bother you if you are in a tent – provided that you do not attract its attention, or panic it. Elephants will gently tiptoe through your guy ropes whilst you sleep, without even nudging your tent. However, if you wake up and make a noise, startling them, they are far more likely to panic and step on your tent. Similarly, scavengers will quietly wander round, smelling your evening meal in the air, without any intention of harming you.

- Remember to use the toilet before going to bed, and avoid getting up in the night if possible.
- Scrupulously clean everything used for food that might smell good to scavengers. Put these utensils in a vehicle if possible, suspend them from a tree, or pack them away in a rucksack inside the tent.

- Do not keep any smelly foodstuffs, like meat or citrus fruit, in your tent. Their smells may attract unwanted attention.
- Do not leave anything outside that could be picked up – like bags, pots, pans, etc. Hyenas, amongst others, will take anything. (They have been known to crunch a camera's lens, and eat it.)
- If you are likely to wake in the night, then leave the tent's zips a few centimetres open at the top, enabling you to take a quiet peek outside.

Creepy crawlies
As you set up camp, clear stones or logs out of your way with extreme caution: underneath will be great hiding places for snakes and scorpions. Long moist grass is ideal territory for snakes and Namibia's many dry, rocky places are classic sites for scorpions.

If you are sleeping in the open, it is not unknown to wake and find a snake lying next to you in the morning. Don't panic; it has just been attracted to you by your warmth. You will not be bitten if you gently edge away without making any sudden movements. (This is one good argument for using at least a mosquito net!)

Before you put on your shoes, shake them out. Similarly, check the back of your backpack before you slip it on. Just a curious spider, in either, could inflict a painful bite.

WALKING IN THE BUSH
Walking in the African bush is a totally different sensation from driving through it. You may start off a little unready – perhaps even sleepy for an early morning walk – but swiftly your mind will awake. There are no noises except the wildlife, and you. So every noise that isn't caused by you must be an animal; or a bird; or an insect. Every smell and every rustle has a story to tell, *if* you can understand it.

With time, patience, and a good guide you can learn to smell the presence of elephants, and hear when impala are alarmed by a predator. You can use ox-peckers to lead you to buffalo, or vultures to help you locate a kill. Tracks will record the passage of animals in the sand, telling what passed by, how long ago, and in which direction.

Eventually your gaze becomes alert to the slightest movement, your ears aware of every sound. This is safari at its best. A live, sharp, spine-tingling experience that's hard to beat and very addictive. Be careful: watching animals from a vehicle will never be the same for you again.

Walking trails
Namibia has several long hikes suited to those who are both fit and experienced in Africa. These include unaccompanied trails along the Fish River Canyon, in the Naukluft Mountains and on Waterberg Plateau, and guided trails on Waterberg and along the Ugab River.

There are also hundreds of shorter hikes, varying from half an hour's stroll to a few days, and many areas which cry out to be explored on foot. None involve much big game, though you may come across larger animals; all are more about spending time in the environments to increase your understanding of them.

Safety of guided walks
In many areas where guided game walks are undertaken, your chances of being in a compromising situation with seriously dangerous game – namely lion, buffalo or elephant – are almost zero. There are many first-class guided walks in the desert

and the mountains, showing you superb scenery and fascinating areas, which don't have these risks to contend with.

Generally Namibia isn't the place for a walking safari which concentrates on big-game (as always, there are exceptions – Hobatere springs to mind). Hence many guides don't need to carry a gun, or know how to use one. This is fine for most of Namibia.

However, in areas where you may meet lion, buffalo or elephant, you need extra vigilance. A few lodges will take chances, and send you out walking with a guide who doesn't have big game experience. Don't let them. If lion, buffalo or elephant are present, then you need a professional guide who carries a loaded gun *and* knows how to use it.

This applies especially in Mahango, Mamili and Mudumu, which have thick vegetation cover and healthy game populations. Don't accept the logic that 'experience and large stick' will be good enough. It will be for 99.9% of the time... but you don't want to become the 0.1%. Don't walk in such areas unless your guide has experience of big game and a rifle.

Further east, in Zambia and Zimbabwe where walking safaris have been refined, the guides must pass stringent exams and practical tests before they are licensed to walk with clients.

Guided walking safaris

If you plan to do much walking, and want to blend in, try to avoid wearing any bright, unnatural colours, especially white. Muted shades are best; greens, browns and khaki are ideal. Hats are essential, as is sun-block. Even a short walk will last for two hours, and there's often no vehicle to which you can retreat if you get too hot.

Cameras and binoculars should be immediately accessible – ideally in dust-proof cases strapped to your belt. They are of much less use if buried at the bottom of a camera bag.

With regard to safety, your guide will always brief you in detail before you set off. S/he will outline possible dangers, and what to do if they materialise. Listen carefully: this is vital.

Face-to-face animal encounters

Whether you are on an organised walking safari, on your own hike, or just walking from the car to your tent in the bush, it is possible that you will come across some of Africa's larger animals at close quarters. Invariably, the danger is much less than you imagine, and a few basic guidelines will enable you to cope effectively with most situations.

Firstly, don't panic. Console yourself with the fact that animals are not normally interested in people. You are not their normal food, or their predator. If you do not annoy or threaten them, you will be left alone.

If you are walking to look for animals, then remember that this is their environment, not yours. Animals have been designed for the bush, and their senses are far better attuned to it than your are. To be on less unequal terms, remain alert and try to spot them from a distance. This gives you the option of approaching carefully, or staying well clear.

Finally, the advice of a good guide is more valuable than the simplistic comments noted here. Animals, like people, are all different. So whilst we can generalise here and say how the 'average' animal will behave – the one that's glaring over a small bush at you may have had a *really* bad day, and be feeling much more grumpy than average.

Here are a few general comments on how to deal with some potentially dangerous situations.

Buffalo

This is probably the continent's most dangerous animal to hikers, but there is a difference between the old males, often encountered on their own or in small groups, and large breeding herds.

Lone male buffalo are easily surprised. If they hear or smell anything amiss, they will charge without provocation – motivated by a fear that something is sneaking up on them. Buffalo have an excellent sense of smell, but fortunately they are short-sighted. Avoid a charge by quickly climbing the nearest tree, or by side-stepping at the last minute. If adopting the latter, more risky, technique then stand motionless until the last possible moment, as the buffalo may well miss you anyhow.

The large breeding herds can be treated in a totally different manner. If you approach them in the open, they will often flee. Occasionally though, they will stand and watch, moving aside to allow you to pass through the middle of the herd. Neither encounter is for the faint-hearted or inexperienced, so steer clear of these dangerous animals wherever possible.

Black rhino

The Kaokoveld has one of the world's best populations of black rhino – a real success story for Namibian conservation. However, if you are lucky enough to find one, and then unlucky enough to be charged by it, use the same tactics as you would for a buffalo: tree-climbing or dodging at the last second. (It is amazing how fast even the least athletic walker will scale the nearest tree when faced with a charging rhino.)

If there are no trees in the vicinity, you have a problem. Your best line of defence is probably to crouch very low, so you don't break the skyline, and remain motionless.

Elephant

Normally elephants are only a problem if you disturb a mother with a calf, or approach a male in musth (state of arousal). So keep well away from these. However, after decades of persecution, Namibia's 'desert elephants' have a reputation for almost unprovoked aggression. Many people (mostly local villagers) are killed by them each year. The moral is to give these elephants a very wide berth, and to be extremely cautious when in areas where they are likely to be found.

Normally, if you get too close to an elephant, it will first scare you with a 'mock charge': head up, perhaps shaking; ears flapping; trumpeting. Lots of sound and fury. This is intended to be frightening, and it is. But it is just a warning and no cause for panic. Just freeze to assess the elephant's intentions, then back off slowly.

When elephants really mean business, they will put their ears back, their head down, and charge directly at you without stopping. This is known as a 'full charge'. There is no easy way to avoid the charge of an angry elephant, so take a hint from the warning and back off slowly as soon as you encounter a mock charge. Don't run. If you are the object of a full charge, then you have no choice but to run – preferably round an anthill, up a tall tree, or wherever.

Lion

Tracking lion can be one of the most exhilarating parts of a good walking safari. Sadly, they will normally flee before you even get close to them. However, it can be a problem if you come across a large pride unexpectedly. Lion are well camouflaged; it is easy to find yourself next to one before you realise it. If you had been listening, you would probably have heard a warning growl about twenty metres ago. Now it is too late.

The best plan is to stop, and back off slowly, but confidently. If you are in a small group, then stick together. *Never* run from a big cat. Firstly, they are always faster than you are. Secondly, running will just convince them that you are frightened prey worth chasing. As a last resort, if they seem too inquisitive and follow as you back off, then stop. Call their bluff. Pretend that you are not afraid and make loud, deep, confident noises: shout at them, bang something. But do not run.

John Coppinger, one of Africa's most experienced guides, adds that every single compromising experience that he has had with lion on foot has been either with a female with cubs, or with a mating pair, when the males can get very aggressive. You have been warned.

Leopard
Leopard are very seldom seen, and would normally flee from the most timid of lone hikers. However, if injured or surprised, they are very powerful, dangerous cats. Conventional wisdom is scarce, but never stare straight into the leopard's eyes, or it will regard this as a threat display. (The same is said, by some, to be true with lion.) Better to look away slightly, at a nearby bush, or even at its tail. Then back off slowly, facing the direction of the cat and showing as little terror as you can. As with lion – loud, deep, confident noises are a last line of defence. Never run from a leopard.

Hippo
Hippo are fabled to account for more deaths in Africa than any other animal (ignoring the mosquito). Having been attacked and capsized by a hippo whilst in a dug-out canoe on the Okavango, I find this very easy to believe. Visitors are most likely to encounter hippo in the water, when paddling a canoe or fishing. However, as they spend half their time grazing ashore, you'll sometimes come across them on land. Out of their comforting lagoons, hippos are even more dangerous. If they see you, they will flee towards the deepest channel nearby – so the golden rule is never to get between a hippo and its escape route to deep water. Given that a hippo will outrun you on land, standing motionless is probably your best line of defence.

Snakes
These are really not the great danger that people imagine. Most flee when they feel the vibrations of footsteps; only a few will stay still. The puff adder is responsible for more cases of snakebite than most other venomous snakes because, when approached, it will simply puff itself up and hiss as a warning, rather than slither away. This makes it essential always to watch where you place your feet when walking in the bush.

Similarly, there are a couple of arboreal (tree dwelling) species which may be taken by surprise if you carelessly grab vegetation as you walk. So don't.

Spitting cobras are also encountered occasionally; they will aim for your eyes and spit with accuracy. If the spittle reaches your eyes, you must wash them out *immediately* and thoroughly with whatever liquid comes to hand: water, milk, even urine if that's the only liquid that you can quickly produce.

CANOEING
There is comparatively little canoeing done in Namibia, though operations do run on the country's borders: down the Orange River, on the eastern side of the Kunene, and occasionally on the Kwando, the Chobe and the Zambezi. The main dangers for canoeists are:

Hippo

Hippos are strictly vegetarians, and will only attack a canoe if they feel threatened. The technique for avoiding hippo problems is first of all to let them know that you are there. Bang your paddle on the side of the canoe a few times (most novice canoeists will do this constantly anyhow).

During the day, hippopotami congregate in the deeper areas of the river. The odd ones in shallow water, where they feel less secure, will head for the deeper places as soon as they are aware of a nearby canoe. Avoiding hippos then becomes a simple case of steering around the deeper areas. This is where experience and knowing the river become useful.

Trouble starts when canoes inadvertently stray over a pod of hippos, or when a canoe cuts a hippo off from its path of retreat. Either situation is dangerous, as hippos will overturn canoes without a second thought, biting them and their occupants.

Crocodiles

Crocodiles may have sharp teeth and look prehistoric, but are of little danger to a canoeist... unless you are in the water. Then the more you struggle and the more waves you create, the more you will attract their unwelcome attentions. They become a major threat when canoes are overturned by hippos – making it essential to get out of the water as soon as possible, either into another canoe or on to the bank.

When a crocodile attacks an animal, it will try to disable it. It does this by getting a firm, biting grip, submerging, and performing a long, fast barrel-roll. This disorients the prey, drowns it, and probably twists off the bitten limb. In this dire situation, your best line of defence is to stab the reptile in its eyes with anything sharp that you have. Alternatively, if you can lift up its tongue and let the water into its lungs whilst it is underwater, then a crocodile will start to drown and will release its prey.

There is one very reliable report of a man surviving an attack in the Zambezi. The crocodile first grabbed his arm and started to spin backwards into deep water. The man wrapped his legs around the crocodile, to spin with it and avoid having his arm twisted off. As it spun, he tried to poke his thumb into its eyes, but this had no effect. Finally he put his free arm into the crocodile's mouth, and opened up the beast's throat. This worked. The crocodile left him and he survived with only a damaged arm. Understandably, anecdotes about tried and tested methods of escape are rare.

MINIMUM IMPACT

When you visit, drive through, or camp in an area and have 'minimum impact' this means that that area is left in the same condition as – or better – than when you entered it. Whilst most visitors view minimum impact as being desirable, spend time to consider the ways in which we contribute to environmental degradation, and how these can be avoided.

Driving

Use your vehicle responsibly. If there's a road, or a track, then don't go off it – the environment will suffer. Driving off-road leaves unsightly tracks which detract from the 'wilderness' feeling for subsequent visitors. In the drier western areas these tracks can also crush fragile desert plants, and scar the desert for decades.

Hygiene

Use toilets if they are provided, even if they are basic long-drop loos with questionable cleanliness. If there are no toilets, then human excrement should always be buried well away from paths, or groundwater, and any tissue used should be burnt and then buried.

If you use rivers or lakes to wash, then soap yourself near the bank, using a pan for scooping water from the river – making sure that no soap finds its way back into the water. Use biodegradable soap. Sand makes an excellent pan-scrub, even if you have no water to spare.

Rubbish

Biodegradable rubbish can be burnt and buried with the camp fire ashes. Don't just leave it lying around: it will look very unsightly and spoil the place for those who come after you.

Bring along some plastic bags in which to remove the rest of your rubbish, and dump it at the next town. Items which will not burn, like tin cans, are best cleaned and squashed for easy carrying. If there are bins, then use them, but also consider when they will next be emptied, and if local animals will rummage through them first. Carrying out all your own rubbish may still be the sensible option.

Host communities

Whilst the rules for reducing impact on the environment have been understood and followed by responsible travellers for years, the effects of tourism on local people have only recently been considered. Many tourists believe it is their right, for example, to take intrusive photos of local people – and even become angry if the local people object. They refer to higher prices being charged to tourists as a rip-off, without considering the hand-to-mouth existence of those selling these products or services. They deplore child beggars, then hand out sweets or pens to local children with outstretched hands.

Our behaviour towards 'the locals' needs to be considered in terms of their culture, with the knowledge that we are the uninvited visitors. We visit to enjoy ourselves, but this should not be at the expense of local people. Read *Cultural guidelines*, pages 26–7, and aim to leave the local communities better off after your visit.

Local payments

If you spend time with any of Namibia's poorer local people, perhaps staying at one of the community campsites, then take great care with any payments that you make.

Firstly, note that most people like to spend their earnings on what *they* choose. This means that trying to pay for services with beads, food, old clothes or anything else instead of money isn't appreciated. Ask yourself how you'd like to be paid, and you'll understand this point.

Secondly, find out the normal cost of what you are buying. Most community campsites will have a standard price for a campsite, an hour's guided activity, or whatever. Find this out before you sleep there, or accept the offer of a walk. It is then important that you pay about that amount for the service rendered – no less, and not too much more.

As most people realise, if you try to pay less you'll get into trouble – as you would at home. However, many do not realise that if they generously pay a lot *more*, this can be equally damaging. Local rates of pay in rural areas can be very low, and a careless visitor can easily pay disproportionately large sums. Where this happens, local jobs can lose their value overnight. (Imagine working hard to become a game scout, only to learn that a tourist has given your friend the equivalent of your whole month's wages for just a few hours guiding. What incentive is there for you to carry on with your regular job?)

If you want to give more – for good service, a super guide, or just because you want to help – then either buy some locally made produce (at the going rate), or donate money to one the organisations working to improve the lot of Namibia's most disadvantaged. The Nyae Nyae Foundation (page 433), IRDNC (page 44), and Save the Rhino Trust (Knobloch St, Swakopmund; tel: 064 403829; email: srtrhino@ iafrica.com.na) would all be delighted to suggest a worthwhile home for your donation – where every cent of your money will be put to good use, without causing any damage to the people that you are trying to help.

Part Two

The Guide

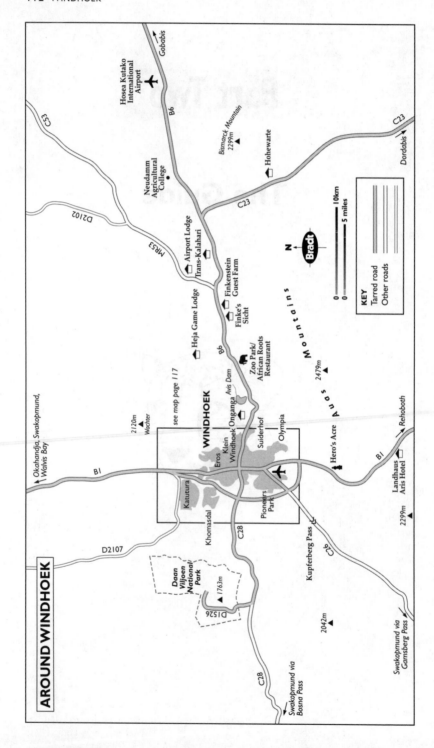

AROUND WINDHOEK

Windhoek

Namibia's capital spreads out in a wide valley between bush-covered hills and appears, at first sight, to be quite small. Driving from the international airport, you pass quickly through the suburbs and, reaching the crest of a hill, find yourself suddenly descending into the city centre.

As you stroll through this centre, the pavement cafés and picturesque old German architecture conspire to give an airy, European feel, whilst street-vendors remind you that this is Africa. Look upwards! The office blocks are tall, but not sky scraping. Around you the pace is busy, but seldom as frantic as Western capitals seem to be.

Leading off Independence Avenue, the city's main street, is the open-air Post Street Mall, centre of a modern shopping complex. Wandering down it, between its bright, pastel-coloured roofs, you'll find shops selling everything from fast food to fashion. In front of these, street-vendors crouch beside blankets spread with jewellery, crafts and curios for sale. Nearby, the city's more affluent residents step from their cars in shaded parking bays to shop in air-conditioned department stores.

Like many capitals, Windhoek is full of contrasts, especially between the richer and poorer areas, but it lacks any major attractions. For casual visitors the city is pleasant; many stop for a day or two, as they arrive or leave, though few stay much longer. It is worth noting that the city all but closes down on Saturday afternoons and all day Sunday, so be aware of this if you plan to be in town over a weekend. Note, too, that during the holiday season from Christmas to around January 10, large numbers of locals leave for the coast, leaving many shops, restaurants and tourist attractions closed. That said, this is the centre of Namibia's administration, and the hub of the country's roads, railways and communications. If you need an embassy, good communications, or an efficient bank, then Windhoek is the right place for you. And to prepare for a trip into the bush, Windhoek is by far the best place in Namibia to get organised and buy supplies.

HISTORY

At an altitude of about 1,650m, in the middle of Namibia's central highlands, Windhoek stands at the head of the valley of one of the Swakop River's tributaries. The Nama people named this place Ai-gams ('fire-water') and the Herero called it Otjomuise ('place of steam'), after the group of hot (23–27°C) springs, now situated in the suburb of Klein Windhoek.

The springs were long used by the original Khoisan hunter-gatherer inhabitants. However, the first recorded settlement here was that of the important chief Jonker Afrikaner and his followers, around 1840. (Jonker had gradually moved north from the Cape, establishing himself as the dominant power in the centre of the country, between Nama groups in the south and Herero to the north.) Many think that the name Windhoek was bestowed on the area by him, perhaps after Winterhoek, his birthplace in the Cape. Others suggest that Windhoek is simply a corruption of the German name for 'windy corner'. Jonker Afrikaner certainly used the name 'Wind Hoock' in a letter to the Wesleyan Mission Society in August 1844, and by 1850 the name 'Windhoek' was in general use.

By December 1842, Rhenish missionaries Hans Kleinschmidt and Carl Hahn had established a church and there were about 1,000 of Jonker's followers living in this valley. The settlement was trading with the coast, and launching occasional cattle-rustling raids on the Herero groups to the north. These raids eventually led to the death of Jonker, after which his followers dispersed and the settlement was abandoned.

The Germans arrived in 1890, under Major Curt von François. They completed the building of their fort, now known as the Alte Feste – Windhoek's oldest building. This became the headquarters of the *Schutztruppe*, the German colonial troops. Gradually German colonists arrived, and the growth of the settlement accelerated with the completion of the railway from Swakopmund in 1902.

In 1909 Windhoek became a municipality. The early years of the 20th century saw many beautiful buildings constructed, including the landmark Christus Kirche, constructed between 1907 and 1910. Development continued naturally until the late 1950s and '60s, when the South African administration started implementing policies for racial separation: the townships began to develop, and many of Windhoek's black population were forced to move. This continued into the '70s and '80s, by which time rigid separation by skin colour had largely been implemented. The privileged 'whites' lived in the spacious leafy suburbs surrounding the centre; black residents in Katutura, which means 'the place where we do not like to live'; and those designated as 'coloured' in Khomasdal. Even today, these divisions are largely still in place.

The 1990s, following independence, saw the construction of new office buildings in the centre of town. More recently, impressive new government buildings, including a new Supreme Court building, have been constructed on the east side of Independence Avenue, while the open spaces between the old townships and the inner suburbs are gradually being developed as modest, middle-income housing.

GETTING THERE

Most visitors passing through Windhoek are either driving themselves around or are members of a group trip. Relatively few will need to rely on the local bus, coach or train services detailed here, despite their efficiency.

By air

Windhoek has excellent international air links with the UK, Germany, South Africa, Zimbabwe and Zambia, as detailed in *Chapter 4, Planning and Preparation*, pages 53–4. More general information on air travel around Namibia is also included in *Chapter 6*, pages 91–3. From Windhoek there are regular flights to:

Katima Mulilo	N$1,249
Lüderitz	N$1,059
Mokuti Lodge	N$830
Ondangwa	N$819
Oranjemund	N$1,179
Rosh Pinah	N$1,129
Swakopmund	N$489
Walvis Bay	N$489

Travellers should note that Windhoek has two airports, and check which one is used for each of their flights. Hosea Kutako International Airport tends to be for larger aircraft and most international flights, while Eros, near the Safari Hotel, caters mostly for internal flights and light aircraft, and just a few international flights. Both are small by international standards and are modern and pleasant – at least as airports go.

Windhoek's Hosea Kutako International Airport is 42km east of town, along the B6 towards Gobabis. The larger car-hire companies have their own offices at the airport, and others will meet you there on request, so picking up a hired car on arrival is straightforward (see pages 79–80).

If you don't plan to have your own vehicle, and have made no other arrangements, you can prebook one of the services run by local companies. Operators include Marenko Shuttle Services (tel/fax: 061 226331), and Transfer Excellence (tel/fax: 061 244949). Alternatively, a taxi to/from the airport should cost from around N$130, depending on the number of passengers. In the passenger area inside the airport are a small bank with bureau de change facilities open for incoming flights, a post office, a bureau for making international telephone calls (with fax facility), and a café which overlooks the arrivals hall. Inside the departure lounge, beyond customs, there's plenty of seating, a bar, a small souvenir shop, and a slightly larger duty-free shop. This last accepts Namibian dollars, credit cards and some foreign currency. You will probably get your change in South African rand, and the staff here will also exchange N$100 notes for the equivalent in rand, if asked.

If you've asked a porter to carry your bags to your car or taxi, a tip of around N$2 is about right.

Eros International Airport stands near the main B1 road on the way south to Rehoboth, about 500m from the Safari Hotel. It is even smaller than the international airport – positively *bijou*. Eros is used for most of Air Namibia's internal flights, a few regional services (and sometimes Cape Town flights), and a steady stream of light aircraft traffic. It has an Avis desk, a small café and a curio shop, and is usually refreshingly informal. There's no public transport to/from here, but as it's relatively close (4km) to the centre of town, taxis are easily summoned by phone. Failing that, the Safari Court Hotel and its cheaper partner, the Safari Hotel, are just five minutes' walk away.

By coach

Intercape Mainliner (tel: 061 227847; fax: 061 228285; web: www.intercape.co.za) coaches depart from the big parking area behind the Grab-a-phone kiosk opposite the Kalahari Sands Hotel. These head south for Upington (with connections to Jo'burg) and Cape Town at 16.55 on Mondays, Wednesdays, Fridays and Sundays. They also travel west to Walvis Bay via Okahandja, Karibib, Usakos, and Swakopmund, departing at 05.55 on Mondays, Wednesdays, Fridays, Saturdays and Sundays. See *Chapter 6*, pages 96–9, for more precise details and costs.

By train

Windhoek is at the hub of TransNamib's relatively slow services around the country. Departures to Tsumeb are on Sunday, Tuesday and Thursday at 17.45; to Keetmanshoop daily (except Saturday) at 19.00; to Swakopmund and Walvis Bay daily (except Saturday) at 19.55; to Gobabis on Sunday, Tuesday and Thursday at 21.50, and to Upington on Tuesday and Friday at 19.00. See *Chapter 6*, pages 93–5.

The capital is also a terminus for the *Desert Express*'s trips (see pages 95–6) across the Namib, aimed specifically at visitors. This leaves from Windhoek station on Sunday, Tuesday and Friday afternoon at 14.30 (15.30 in summer), arriving in Swakopmund at 10.00 the following morning. Its air-conditioned cabins have en-suite facilities and cost N$1,500 per person sharing a twin cabin. This includes excursions, dinner and breakfast.

Windhoek's railway station is just off Bahnhof Street; tel: 061 298 2032.

ORIENTATION

Under South African rule, Windhoek grew like most large South African cities, forming an 'atomic' structure. Its nucleus was the central business district and shopping areas, surrounded by leafy, spacious suburbs designed for whites with cars. Beyond these, the sprawling, high-density townships housed Windhoek's non-white population.

In modern Windhoek, 12 years after independence, this basic structure is still in place, though the colour divisions have blurred. The leafy suburbs are still affluent, though are now more mixed. Meanwhile, Khomasdal and Katutura remain crowded, poorer and have very few white residents.

In common with other towns in Namibia, Windhoek undergoes occasional road-name changes to reflect the prominence of local or international figures. One such change in 2002 is that Peter Müller Street, in the centre of town, was renamed Fidel Castro Street. It's likely, though, that both names will be in use for a considerable period of time.

Maps

For most visitors, the free map available from the tourist board is the best around. Overall, it is good and reasonably accurate.

For detailed maps, head for the Surveyor General's on Robert Mugabe Avenue, between Dr May and Lazarett Street (tel: 061 245056/7/8/9; fax: 061 227312). Ordnance Survey maps are around N$50 each. The 1:1,000,000 map of the whole country is wall-sized and shows all commercial farms and their names. The 1:250,000 maps are good for vehicle navigation in the wilder areas. The 1:50,000 series suits walkers. Most of the surveys were originally made in 1979, so despite being recently printed these maps are old. However, they are the best available.

Getting around
Private taxis

In and around Windhoek it's usually best to walk, as everything is central and close together. If you need a taxi then **Windhoek Radio Taxis**, at 452 Independence Avenue (near the Grab-a-Phone kiosk and bus terminal), is the largest taxi company (tel: 237070). Alternatively **White Rhino Taxi** (tel: 221029) is small but very reliable. Others include, **Prime Radio Taxis** (tel: 272307) and **Express Taxis** (tel: 239739). It's not a good idea to hail a taxi on the street, particularly for women on their own. In general, agree the fare before you take the taxi.

For independent drivers, using cellphones, it's best to ask your hotel or pension to suggest someone reliable. Otherwise, those who can currently be recommended include Elton (Eltons Radio Taxi, tel: 081 2505565), Lito (Kalahari Radio Taxi, tel: 081 249 2522), and A Kasera Radio Taxi (tel: 081 127 0557).

Hired car

Windhoek is extremely easy to navigate, with just a few main roads, good signposting, and surprisingly little traffic, even at so-called 'peak' times of the day.

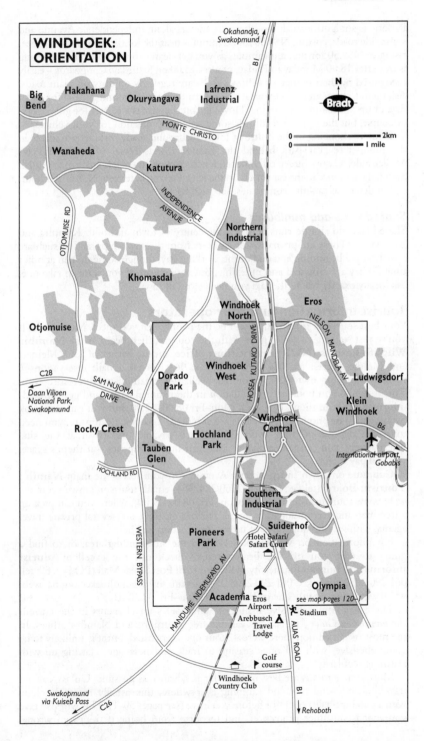

WINDHOEK: ORIENTATION

Okahandja, Swakopmund

B1

N

Bradt

0 — 2km
0 — 1 mile

Big Bend

Hakahana

Okuryangava

Lafrenz Industrial

MONTE CHRISTO

Wanaheda

Katutura

OTJOMUISE RD

INDEPENDENCE AVENUE

Northern Industrial

Khomasdal

Windhoek North

Eros

Otjomuise

C28

SAM NUJOMA DRIVE

Daan Viljoen National Park, Swakopmund

Dorado Park

Windhoek West

HOSEA KUTAKO DRIVE

NELSON MANDELA AV

Ludwigsdorf

Klein Windhoek

B6

Windhoek Central

Rocky Crest

Hochland Park

Tauben Glen

HOCHLAND RD

International airport, Gobabis

Southern Industrial

Suiderhof

WESTERN BYPASS

Pioneers Park

Hotel Safari/ Safari Court

MANDUME NDEMUFAYO AV

Academia

Eros Airport

Arebbusch Travel Lodge

Stadium

Olympia

see map pages 120–1

AUAS ROAD

Golf course

B1

Windhoek Country Club

Swakopmund via Kuiseb Pass

C26

Rehoboth

Parking is straightforward, too: there are meters along Independence Avenue and some side roads, costing N$0.50 for 20 minutes near the tourist information office, rising to N$0.50 for just ten minutes as you get nearer to the post office, Parking is free after 18.00 Monday to Friday, or after 13.00 on Saturday. Car guards – easily recognised by their orange or yellow vests – are regularly on duty on main roads. Ask them to keep an eye on your car in return for a tip of around N$1–2 for half a day, or up to N$4 in the evening. How vigilant they are is a matter for guesswork, of course, but their presence affords some sense of protection for your vehicle.

If you're shopping in the centre of town, secure and shady parking is available in the multi-storey car park behind the Kalahari Sands Hotel (turn down Peter Müller/Fidel Castro Street off Independence Avenue, then left again into Stübel Street; the entrance to the car park is on the left). Parking here costs N$2.60 per hour.

For details of car-hire companies, see page 83.

Shared taxis and minibuses

Shared taxis do shuttle runs between the centre of town and both Katutura and Khomasdal. These are primarily for workers from the townships, and as such are mostly at the beginning and end of the working day, though some do run at other times. They are crowded and inflexible, but very cheap. If you want to take one, ask locally exactly where the taxi you need stops in town.

Tourist information and tour operators

Your best source of information will be the people that you meet. Meanwhile, if you're just starting to get to grips with the country, then begin at the **Namibia Wildlife Resorts (NWR) reservations office,** on the corner of John Meinert and Moltke streets; tel: 061 236975–8; fax: 061 224900; email: reservations@ mweb.com.na or nwr@mweb.com.na; web: www.namibiawildliferesorts.com. This is where you book accommodation in the national parks, and get (limited) information about them. It is open Mon–Fri 08.00–17.00, but you can also book by fax, email or phone. Credit cards are accepted. To book a campsite, you need to pay a deposit of 10%, with the balance payable on arrival at the site. Alternatively, you can take a chance and turn up at campsites – if there's space, you can pay direct.

Continue on down Independence Avenue. On your left is the main **Namib i Tourism Board** (tel/fax: 061 2842360/2842364; email: tourism@mweb.com.na; web: www.tourism.com.na; open Mon–Fri, 08.00–17.00), where you can pick up a free map and accommodation guide. Further on there are several private travel agents, with varying quantities of useful information and help,.

For information on Windhoek itself, and the surrounding area, or to find a guide to take you off the beaten track, check out the excellent **tourist information bureau** for the city in the centre of Post Street Mall (PO Box 59; tel: 061 290 2092/2058; fax: 061 290 2203/2546; email: maj@windhoekcc.org.na; web: www.windhoekcc.org). The office is open Mon–Fri, 07.30–16.30.

There is a comprehensive listing of Windhoek's travel agents in the current *Accommodation Guide for Tourists*, available free at airports and Namib i offices. In the most recent edition there were 42 tour operators listed, but it is unlikely to be comprehensive, with old ones ceasing to trade and new ones starting up with alarming regularity.

Most arrangements are best made as far in advance as possible. Unless you are travelling independently and camping everywhere, this usually means booking with a good specialist operator before you leave (see pages 50–1). This will also give you added consumer protection, and recourse from home if things go wrong.

However, if you are in Windhoek, and need to arrange something on the spot, then try to get a personal recommendation of a good local company. Failing that, try one of the following general agents:

African Extravaganza corner of Rossini and John Meinert St, PO Box 22028, Windhoek; tel: 061 263082/3/6; fax: 061 215356; email: afex@afex.com.na; web:www.natron.net/afex

Ondese Travel & Safaris PO Box 6196, Windhoek; tel: 061 220876; fax; 061 239700

Namib Travel Shop/Wilderness Safaris PO Box 6850, Windhoek; tel: 061 274500; fax: 061 239455; email: info@nts.com.na; web: www.wilderness-safaris.com

Namibia Safari Centre PO Box 20498, Windhoek; tel: 061 251212; fax: 061 251212

Sand Rose PO Box 40263, Windhoek; tel: 061 245255; fax: 061 245454; email: sandrose@sandrose.com.na; web: www.sandrose.com.na

Sense of Africa PO Box 2058, Prosperita, Windhoek; tel: 061 275300; fax: 061 263417; email: Lleach@sense-of-africa.com.na; web: www.sense-of-africa.com

Tourist Junction 40 Fidel Castro (Peter Müller) St, Windhoek; tel: 061 231246; fax: 061 231703; email: info.ritztours@galileosa.co.za

For budget options, which for two or three people may work out no more expensive than self-drive, the following are recommended:

Cardboard Box Travel Shop 15 Johann Albrecht St; PO Box 5142, Windhoek; tel: 061 256580; fax: 061 256581; email: namibia@bigfoot.com; web: www.namibia.addr.com/travel

Chameleon Safaris 22 Wagner St, Windhoek West, PO Box 6107, Windhoek; tel: 061 247668; email: chamnam@chameleon.com.na or info@chameleon.com.na; web: www.chameleonsafaris.com. Small-group adventure camping safaris, from 3 to 18 days, with weekly departures.

Crazy Kudu PO Box 99031, Windhoek; tel: 061 222636; fax: 061 255074; email: namibia.safaris@crazykudu.com; web: www.crazykudu.com

Wild Dog PO Box 26188, Windhoek; tel: 061 257642; fax: 061 240802; email: info@wilddog-safaris.com; web: www.wilddog-safaris.com

WHERE TO STAY

Windhoek has a range of places to suit different budgets, from four-star hotels to backpackers' dorms. Hardly any are run down or seedy, so you are unlikely to find yourself in a dive. Prices range upwards from about N\$150 per person, sharing a double room with its own toilet and bathroom. Single travellers will usually pay about 30–50% more. Dormitory beds at backpackers' lodges cost around N\$40–50.

The dividing line between hotels and pensions/guesthouses used here is somewhat artificial: one of atmosphere rather than title or price. Hotels tend to be larger and more expensive, but often have more amenities: you can be more anonymous and blend into the scenery. Windhoek's pensions and guesthouses are smaller, often family-run, and usually more friendly and personal. See also the general comments in *Chapter 4*, pages 60–1. The larger hotels invariably put on extensive spreads for their meals. Eat-as-much-as-you-can buffet meals, especially breakfasts, are the norm.

Hotels

Windhoek Country Club Resort and Casino (152 rooms) Western Bypass, Pioneers Park; PO Box 3077, Windhoek; tel: 061 205 5911; fax: 061 252797; email: hrwcc@legacyhotels.co.za.

Managed by the South African chain Legacy Hotels & Resorts, the Country Club is Windhoek's grandest hotel. It is situated on the B1 bypass that skirts the city, about 1.5km off the road to Rehoboth. Until Windhoek expands further, this is in the middle of nowhere.

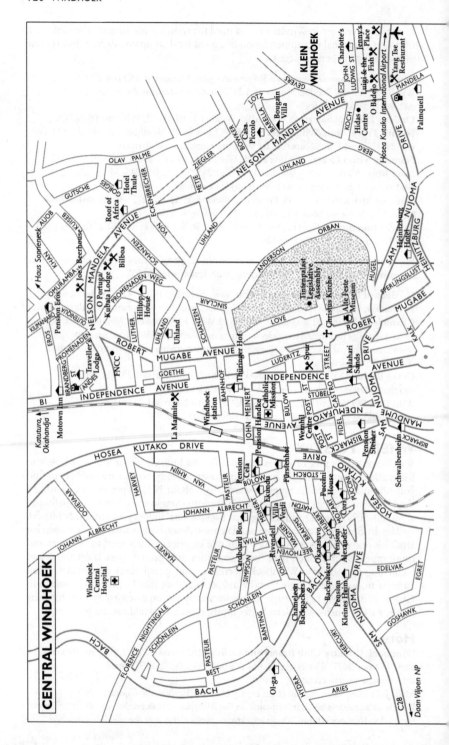

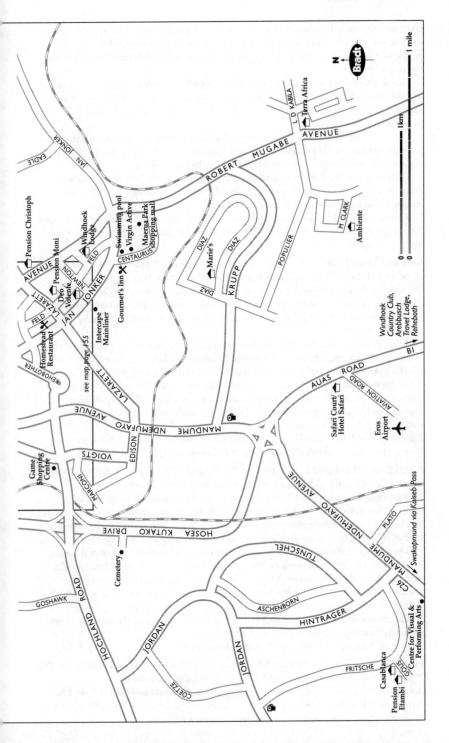

Its cavernous, vaulted entrance hall is made of mock-stone blocks, and lined with various small shops. Opposite reception is the cave-like entrance to the casino, where rows of people fill slot machines with money or gamble at tables from 10.00 right through to 04.00 the next morning.

The resort's rooms are plush and well designed, with air conditioning, heating, Mnet TV, minibar/fridge, phone, hairdryer, safe, and a balcony or patio. Each has a toilet, and separate bath and shower en suite. In the public areas, surveillance systems have been installed for added security.

Outside, at the back of the hotel, there's a fast-flowing circular river, surrounding a pool and poolside bar, shaded by another design in rough-hewn rocks. Beyond is an 18-hole golf course, with special rates for guests: 9 holes N$70 , 18 holes NS140.

Buffet lunch in the main restaurant, the Kokerboom, is N$65 (N$105 on Sunday); dinner is N$115. Above the casino is a very good Chinese restaurant, Chez Wou, which attracts a busy trade from outside the hotel for both lunch and dinner.

The Country Club is a good hotel, but it is expensive and could be anywhere in the world. *Rates: single from N$840, double from N$990, up to the Presidential Suite at N$4,900 per night, including breakfast.*

Kalahari Sands Hotel (173 rooms) Gustav Voigts Centre, 129 Independence Av, PO Box 2254; tel: 061 2800000; fax: 061 222260; email: ksands@sunint.co.za
Dominating the city's skyline in the centre of Independence Avenue, the Kalahari Sands Hotel is a large hotel owned by the Sun International group. Escalators whisk you through the shopping arcade below and into its lobby, which is pretty much like the lobby of any other four-star hotel.

The rooms are above the lobby, reached by one of several lifts, so most have good views of the city. All are carpeted and well-furnished, with air conditioning, direct-dial phones, Mnet TV, and en-suite toilet, bath and shower. Twin beds, or a king-size double, are the norm. Facilities include the Dunes restaurant, Oasis bar, Sands Casino, a small gym and a rooftop pool. Generally regarded as Windhoek's best hotel, the Kalahari Sands lacks character and feels like a good Sheraton. That said, it works well and is convenient for walks around the centre of town.
Rates: single from N$890, double from N$1,110, executive suite N$2,370, all including breakfast. Breakfast for non-residents is N$79, lunch buffet N$95, dinner N$110.

Safari Court Hotel (252 rooms) Aviation Rd, PO Box 3900, Windhoek; tel: 061 240240; fax: 061 235652; email: safari@safarihotel.com.na; web: www.safarihotel.com.na
This international-standard hotel has grown up alongside the older Hotel Safari over the past few years (see below). Although it still shares the Safari's entrance from the road, and guests may take advantage of the expansive pool, the Safari Court is altogether more exclusive than its lowlier sibling, with its own vaulted reception area, and a separate restaurant and bar.

The Safari Court's modern, elegant rooms are of a high standard, with en-suite toilets, baths and superb, powerful showers. They also have tea/coffee-making facilities, a fridge with minibar, direct-dial phones, TVs with Mnet and a large lockable section to the wardrobes. If you're arriving in the morning, perhaps from nearby Eros Airport, then an early check-in is normally possible here.

The elegant **Acacia** restaurant is open for dinner only, serving an international cuisine including Namibian oysters, ostrich steak and seafood.
Rates: single N$498–518, double N$598–618, including breakfast.

Hotel Safari (192 rooms) Aviation Rd, PO Box 3900, Windhoek; tel: 061 240240; fax: 061 235652; email: safari@safarihotel.com.na; web: www.safarihotel.com.na
About 3km from the centre of town, just off the B1 road to Rehoboth and close to Eros Airport, the Hotel Safari covers several acres and includes a large pool set in the grounds. Its younger (and larger) sister-hotel, the Safari Court, is adjacent.

The Safari has two styles of accommodation. Budget rooms are laid out motel style, while slightly more expensive 'flats' are housed in a separate two-storey block.

All the Safari's rooms are a good standard, with en-suite toilet and shower/bath, direct-dial telephone, minibar/fridge, tea/coffee maker, and a TV. An excellent breakfast is included, and drinks and snacks (tasty toasted sandwiches, burgers, etc) are served beside the pool throughout the day – making this a popular venue for a mid-afternoon bite to eat. The hotel also has its own restaurant and grill bar.

If you've no transport, then the complimentary minibus is convenient for trips to/from town, leaving opposite the Kalahari Sands, on Independence Avenue.

Rates: single around N$298–398, double N$348–478, triple N$462, all including breakfast.

Hotel Fürstenhof (33 rooms) Bülow St, PO Box 316, Windhoek; tel: 061 237380; fax: 061 228751; email: fuerst@iafrica.com.na
Less than 1km west of the centre, the Fürstenhof is perched slightly above the city off Bülow St. It has changed hands in recent years, but retains lots of individuality and a traditional German character – emphasised by heavy velour fabrics, old furnishings and lots of deep, dark colours. Its spacious rooms all have air conditioning, minibar/fridges, phones, TV with Mnet, and en-suite toilets with a shower or bath. Fifteen rooms have been added recently, so take care when booking: rooms in the older section are very basic compared with the deluxe new ones. The hotel now has a swimming pool.

The restaurant is good but expensive (see page 141), and has changed little in recent years.

Rates relate to standard and deluxe rooms: single N$430/580, double N$560/760, family room (2 adults/2 children) N$1,520, including breakfast.

Heinitzburg (Castle) Hotel (16 rooms) 22 Heinitzburg St, PO Box 458, Windhoek; tel: 061 249597; fax: 061 249598; email: heinitz@mweb.com.na; web: www.heinitzburg.com
This distinctive white turreted fort, built at the turn of the 19th century, is a member of the Relais et Châteaux group. Set high on a hill, it is quiet and secluded, yet easily seen from Independence Avenue. Drive about 1km from the centre, along Sam Nujoma Drive, towards the airport. Take a right on to Heinitzburg Street and the Castle, No 22, is reached via a short but steep drive on the right.

Owned by Jürgen and Beate Raith, previously proprietors of the Fürstenhof, this is one of the most stylish places in town. Its rooms are all different; alongside amenities such as satellite TV and fridge/minibar and gilded bathrooms, expect impressive furniture with expanses of beautiful, solid wood and lots of space. With four-poster beds, dreamy white quilts and sumptuous fabrics, this is a truly romantic hideaway. Outside, a rose terrace commands super views of the city below – an attraction in its own right for non-residents who come for afternoon tea and cakes – and there is a sheltered pool area with sun loungers.

The Heinitzburg's new restaurant, Leo's, offers a contrast in style. Small, modern and sophisticated, its menu is the creation of the hotel's own French chef (see page 141). Lunch is served on the terrace.

Rates: single N$770–840, double from N$1,150, up to the Honeymoon Castle Tower at N$1,300. All rates include breakfast. Payment may be made in euros.

Hotel-Pension Thule (12 rooms) 1 Gorges St, PO Box 166, Windhoek; tel: 061 250146; fax: 061 250759; email: thule@mweb.com.na
In spite of the appellation, the German-owned Thule is clearly aiming at the hotel market. Opened in April 2002, it is situated in a prime spot high on the hill above Eros, with sweeping views across the city. To get here from the airport, follow Nelson Mandela Av to the traffic lights after the BP garage, then turn right into Metje St. Take the third left into Olav Palme St, then left at the top of the hill into Gorges (later Gutsche) St. At the top of the next hill, turn left again, and the Thule is behind the imposing gates on the left.

From its flag-festooned entrance past tall palms, the Thule oozes style, although the entrance is decidedly at odds with the almost stark modernity of the interior. Airy, light and very modern, its carpeted rooms are a blend of chrome and glass with opulent soft furnishings that would make a film star feel at home. Each room has AC/heating and boasts two double beds, with a safe, TV, phone, minibar/fridge, coffee and tea facilities, hairdryer. En-suite facilities have both bath and shower, with underfloor heating for maximum comfort. In addition, VIP rooms have a sofa and dressing room. There is also one room designed specifically for the disabled. Views come as standard, either across the mountains at the back, or over the central fountain to the city beyond.

In the main building, and the surrounding grounds, no expense has been spared to maximise the impact of the hotel's location. This is not a place for vertigo sufferers, nor for families with young children. Varying levels feature a pool with elegant tables and chairs, a small formal courtyard, the restaurant and – at the top – the Sundowner Bar. While the restaurant , with its wide curved expanse of glass and terrace beyond, is open only for breakfast at present, plans are in hand to bring in a chef from Germany. In the meantime, dinner is available to guests on request. Not so the bar, which is open to the public from 16.30 to 21.30 – it's a great place for a sundowner. And if you look over the edge of the hill at sunset, you may even spot guinea fowl in the trees below.

Namibian managers Hugo and Roswitha have several years of experience in the tourist trade, having owned and run their own lodge. This new venture will certainly offer a challenge.

Rates: single N$580, double N$850, VIP room N$900, including breakfast.

Hotel Thüringer Hof (40 rooms) Independence Av, PO Box 112, Windhoek; tel: 061 226031; fax: 061 232981; email: thurhof@mweb.com.na
Towards the north end of Independence Avenue, near Bahnhof Street, this is a member of the Namib Sun chain. It is opposite the tourist information office, very close to the national parks booking office and the railway station, and across the road from the main police station. Popular with the German and local markets, it tends to be quite noisy.

Inside, the Thüringer Hof is rather dark and old-fashioned, but the staff are friendly. Its double or twin rooms are clean and functional, if generally unremarkable. All have direct-dial telephones, tea/coffee-making facilities, and TV with Mnet. One attraction of the hotel is its lively beer garden. Here you can order food as well as drinks, and choose from the Thüringer Hof's pub-grub menu, with daily specials around N$32.

If you want to sleep somewhere basic and convenient, the Thüringer Hof might fit the bill. It's mainly used by local business travellers.

Rates: single N$320, double N$490, suite with 3 beds N$610, including breakfast.

Continental Hotel (60 rooms) Independence Av, PO Box 977, Windhoek; tel: 061 237293; fax: 061 231539; email: contintl@mweb.com.na
Very central, the Continental aims mainly at business people, and feels dark and musty in comparison with most of the newer, smaller places further out of town. Like the Thüringer Hof, the Continental is uninspiring. En-suite rooms are clean and functional, with TV and phone. In an attempt to cater for all tastes, there is a café at the rear of the hotel, next to the Esplanada Restaurant, and a bar area with a pool table and slot machines, Next door is a separate nightclub, the Diplomat. There is also secure parking.

Rates: single N$315–360, double N$406–510, including breakfast. There are still a few single rooms with shared facilities for N$160.

Motown Inn (60 rooms) corner of Brandberg and Independence Av; tel: 061 234646; cell: 081 128 1871; fax: 061 234646; email: reservations@motown.namibia.na; web: www.motown.namibia.na
Located at the northern end of Independence Av, this new inn focuses primarily on the backpacker market and those looking for no-frills accommodation at a sensible price.

Clean and comfortable, it offers good security – rooms are accessed with a swipe card, there is a security guard on duty round the clock, and every room has a safe. Internet facilities are also exceptional, with four computers in the reception area, and a free daily internet slot for guests.

Rooms cater for a range of accommodation needs. Some have shared bathrooms, others are en suite; some have fans, others have AC. All except economy rooms have TV. The hotel has its own pizza restarant, a cafeteria and lounge, with room service available. There are also laundry facilities, and a coin-operated laundrette. Outside, there is secure parking. *Rates: single economy room N$140–165; luxury N$250; executive N$320; self-catering N$280. Self-catering apartment (sleeps 6 in 2 rooms) N$350.*

Pensions and B&Bs

The proliferation of pensions and guesthouses in recent years has spawned plenty of lookalike establishments each catering for the same market. Most are situated in the suburban areas surrounding Windhoek. The more centrally located are mostly clustered in the area just to the west of Independence Avenue (helpfully known as West Windhoek), within a reasonable walking distance of shops and other facilities. One of the most popular areas for visitors is to the northeast, incorporating Eros and Klein Windhoek. Here, in addition to plenty of accommodation, there is a good choice of restaurants and bars. In Olympia, to the southeast of the city, pensions are relatively scarce. Those that are here are usually quiet, often with views over the rolling hills to the south. Then to the southwest are the open spaces of Pioneers Park.

Unless otherwise stated, all rooms have en-suite shower and toilet facilities.

Central Windhoek and Windhoek West

Hotel-Pension Alexander (13 rooms) 10 Beethoven St, PO Box 1911; tel/fax: 061 240775 Between Schubert and Mozart streets, Pension Alexander is 15 minutes' walk from the centre, and is owned and run by Alexander.

It aims for simple, affordable accommodation, and rooms all have cool tiled floors, fans, direct-dial telephones, TV with Mnet, and a bath or shower. There's a small but pleasant pool outside and the rooms are quite spread out, with safe off-street parking available. *Rates: single N$210, double N$290, family N$350 (4 people), including breakfast.*

Hotel-Pension Cela (17 rooms) 82 Bülow St, PO Box 1947, Windhoek; tel: 061 226295/4; fax: 061 226246; email: cela@mweb.com.na or cela@iway.na; web: www.natron.net/tour/cela/start.html This suburban pension, just beyond the Handke near John Meinert St, seems rather jaded, but its rooms are reasonably well equipped, with fridge/minibar, phone and Mnet TV.

With a small swimming pool at the back, and off-street parking, it makes a fairly central base, though it is a shame that the seating areas outside the rooms are dominated by concrete rather than plants and lawns. *Rates: single N$215, double N$310, triple N$415, quadruple N$525, including breakfast.*

Cori Guest House (12 rooms) 8 Puccini St, Olympia, PO Box 80698, Windhoek; tel: 061 228840, 081 124 5650; fax: 061 225806; email: cori@cyberhost.com.na; web: www.e-tourism.com.na/cori It's not difficult to spot this lilac and blue pension near the corner of Hosea Kutako Drive and Puccini St, some 10–15 minutes' walk from the centre of Windhoek.

Owners Cobie and Rini are Namibian Germans who live on the premises and have run this hospitable pension for the last three years. Each well-appointed twin room has a private entrance from the garden, and features a TV, radio/alarm, coffee/tea-making facilities and a fan.

The attractive garden offers plenty of shady trees, with a small swimming pool, and a thatched seating area and braai. Dinner – usually a braai – is available on request, or guests may make use of the grill facilities for their own cooking. There is secure parking for guests' vehicles. Airport collection can be arranged for N$150 per trip, or Cobie will collect you from the airport shuttle stop in Windhoek. He also organises small group tours around Namibia.

Rates: single N$220, double N$300 including full breakfast.

Ekundu Guesthouse (8 rooms) 10 Johann Albrecht St, PO Box 3799, Windhoek; tel: 253440, 081 255 7815; fax: 064 230729; email: rosist@iafrica.com.na
Opened in 1999, this small, central guesthouse with its distinctive green-and-cream colour scheme has bright, modern rooms with pine furniture and Mnet TV. It's inexpensive, there's a cheerful breakfast area, and the kitchen is also available for guest use. Secure parking is available, too. The drawback? It's on a busy road, so can be noisy.

Rates: single N$195, double N$290, family (up to 3) N$360, up to 4 N$400, including continental breakfast.

Hotel-Pension Handke (10 rooms) 3 Rossini St, PO Box 20881, Windhoek; tel: 061 234904; fax: 061 225660; email: pensionhandke@iafrica.com.na
Just out of the centre, the inexpensive Handke is within about five minutes' walk of the centre of town – ideal if you've no car. A dedicated mother-and-son team, Amanda and Ernst Kipka, offer a warm welcome. Handke's rooms are small and simple, yet good value, particularly those at the back which are quieter than the others All have en-suite shower/toilet, ceiling fan and a direct-dial telephone. There's little space around the rooms, but the tree-shaded garden is a pleasant place to sit, and the TV lounge and breakfast area offer real home comfort. Convenient off-street parking in front of the pension is a major advantage if you do have a car (if so, approach via John Meinert St).

Rates: single N$250, double N$350, family room N$150 per person (min 3 people) including breakfast; 10% surcharge on credit cards.

Hotel-Pension Kleines Heim (14 rooms) 10 Volans St, Windhoek West, PO Box 22605; tel: 061 248200; fax: 061 248203; email: kleiheim@iafrica.com.na; web: http://kleinesheim.hypermart.net
Kleines Heim is just off Sam Nujoma Drive, about five minutes' drive from the centre of town, or a 15-minute walk. To reach it, take Sam Nujoma Drive west, then right on to Bach Street, left on to Mercury Street, and left again on to Volan St. Parking is off the street and within the pension's grounds.

Run by Henk and Adrée Mudge, Kleines Heim has a beautiful setting. Its individually decorated rooms, with many personal touches, lead on to lawns, which surround a swimming pool under impressive palm trees. All the rooms are very comfortable and spacious, with direct-dial phones, TVs, tea/coffee-making facilities, en-suite shower/toilets (three with bath), and all have underfloor heating for winter (a big bonus, when many small pensions can be cold), and ceiling fans for summer. Dinner can be provided on request, at N$70 for 3 courses, though most visitors eat out.

Rates: single N$390, double N$620, including full breakfast.

Okarusuvo (3 rooms) 17 Beethoven St, PO Box 96337, Windhoek; tel: 061 232252; cell: 081 241 7817; email: riben@mweb.com.na; web: www.natron.net/tour/okarusuvo
Erda Iben opened this small guesthouse, which is a 15–20 minute walk from the city centre, in 2000. This is very much a B&B establishment, suitable for holidaymakers rather than backpackers. Erda will arrange transfers to the airport and lifts into town.

Rates: double N$260

Ol-ga (4 rooms) 91 Bach St, PO Box 20926, West Windhoek; tel: 235853; fax: 255184; email: metzger@mweb.com.na

Gesa Oldach has been welcoming visitors from all over the world to her home for eight years, and claims it is one of the oldest B&Bs in Windhoek. Located about 2.5km west of the centre of the city, this is a guesthouse that will appeal particularly to birdwatchers, for numerous species are attracted to its mature trees.

Pine-furnished rooms are small but well appointed, with local art adorning the walls, and TV, kettle with tea and coffee and mosquito nets. There is a barbecue available for guests, or grills can be prepared on request for N$25 per person.

Rates: single N$150, double N$200, including breakfast.

Rivendell (8 rooms) 40 Beethoven St, PO Box 5142, Windhoek; tel: 061 250006; fax: 061 250010; email: ahj@iafrica.com.na

This guesthouse opened in 1998 and offers a comfortable, clean and relaxed place to stay to the west of the city, about 15–20 minutes' walk from the centre. Four of the rooms have en-suite bathrooms, while the remainder have shared bathrooms. Some are situated around a small swimming pool. Prices do not include breakfast, but guests are welcome to use the kitchen.

Rates: single with shared facilities N$135, en-suite double N$165–200, breakfast N$20.

Schwalbenheim (8 self-catering apartments) 14 Bismarck St, PO Box 6455, Windhoek; tel: 061 222 829; email: info@schwalbenheim.com.na; web: www.schwalbenheim.com.na

Opened in 1998, this Namibian-run accommodation, in a quiet location, comprises 5 apartments with 4 beds, 2 with 2 beds and 2 singles. Each apartment has its own self-catering facilities, en-suite bathroom and small patio and grassed area. Although some guests stay for longer periods, the owner is happy to cater for overnight stops. It's a good place for families.

Rates: single N$220, double N$265, triple N$320, 4 adults N$380, biggest apartment N$415.

Hotel-Pension Steiner (16 rooms) 11 Wecke St, PO Box 20481, Windhoek; tel: 061 222898; fax: 061 224234; email: steiner@iafrica.com.na; web: www.steiner.com.na

This small, quiet pension, built on several levels, is a convenient short walk from the centre, squeezed into a cul-de-sac off Trift Street, between Sam Nujoma Drive and Peter Müller (Fidel Castro) St. Its recently renovated rooms have tiled floors, Mnet and German TV channels, phones, minibar/fridges, ceiling fans, and radios, as well as en-suite toilets and either baths or showers.

Behind the building is a thatched bar overlooking a deep swimming pool, around which tables for light lunches are set. In winter months, the open fire in the lounge bar is particularly welcome.

Steiner is particularly popular with German and French visitors, and its atmosphere is one of helpful efficiency.

Rates: single N$270, double N$420, triples N$490, quadruples N$535, including breakfast.

Villa Verdi (14 rooms, including honeymoon suite, 3 flats) 4 Verdi St, PO Box 6784, Windhoek; tel: 061 221994; fax: 061 222574; email: villav@mweb.com.na; web: www.villa-verdi.com

In many ways this place off John Meinert St set the standards for small hotels in Windhoek in 1994. The stylish use of ethnic décor and African art broke the mould of the standard, traditional German pensions, and made this instantly into Windhoek's artiest and, arguably, best small pension. Although still owned by André Louw, it is now managed by Yvonne and Craig.

All the rooms have a different theme, mostly following Namibia's different tribes. All are non-smoking. Each has double or twin beds, bath or shower, TV with Mnet, direct-dial phones, minibar/fridge, and electric blankets for the winter. AC is planned in the near future for half the rooms. Snacks are available all day by the small splash-pool, and dinner – at N$95 for a 3-course meal – is available in the evening if you request it in advance. As

Villa Verdi is often booked up, advance reservations are essential.
Rates: single N$410, double N$680, including breakfast.

Eros and Klein Windhoek

Pension BougainVilla (5 rooms) 66 Barella St, Klein Windhoek, PO Box 9131, Windhoek, tel: 061 252266, 081 127 469; fax: 061 252260; email: bougainvilla@mweb.com.na; web: www.namibeye.com/bougainvilla, www.swiftcentre.com/bougainvilla
On the corner of Nelson Mandela St, just after the turning into Barella St beyond the traffic lights as you come into Windhoek from the airport, this is the large white building with dark pink decoration; it's not difficult to spot, though the name is painted very small.
Double rooms with queen-sized beds each have TV, AC, phone with internet connection, private bar and hairdryer, Outside, tranquil, flower-decked gardens surround the swimming pool. There's secure parking for those with a car (though the centre of town is just 15 minutes' walk away), and barbecue facilities as well. Evening meals are available by arrangement.
Rates: single US$50, double US$60, including breakfast.

Casa Piccolo (9 rooms) 6 Barella St, Klein Windhoek, PO Box 11728, Windhoek; tel: 061 221155; fax: 061 221187; email: casapiccolo@iafrica.com.na; web: www.natron.net/tour/casapiccolo
Opposite Pension BougainVilla, the bright yellow of Casa Piccolo's walls gives the place a sunny atmosphere that permeates through the tiled floors and simple white décor of its twin-bedded rooms. Claudia Horn has run this place for three years, mostly catering for the South African business market, though holidaymakers would be just as much at home with bright, clean facilities that include fan, fridge, coffee and tea, phone and TV. Off-street parking will add to peace of mind if you have a vehicle.
Rates: single N$270, double N$340, including breakfast.

Charlotte's Guesthouse (3 rooms) 2A John Ludwig St, PO Box 4234, tel: 061 228846; fax: 061 253503; email: charlott@mweb.com.na
Tucked behind the post office at Klein Windhoek, Charlotte's (now owned by Christine Archer) caters predominantly for business people, with a TV and phone in each room and a separate lounge area. Prices are on the high side for accommodation that is quite cramped.
Rates: single N$350, double N$385, including breakfast.

Hotel-Pension Eros (21 rooms) 21 Omuramba Rd, Eros Park, PO Box 9607, Windhoek; tel: 061 227020, 081 242 0676; fax: 061 242919; email: eros@iway.na
Just south of Eros St, this successful pension near Joe's Beerhouse is very good value. Modern rooms, in several blocks adjacent to a padlocked parking area, all have direct-dial phone, TV and minibar/fridge. Efficiency is the hallmark here, as you would expect from a pension that is geared almost exclusively to the business market.
Rates: single N$230, double N$310, including full breakfast.

Hilltop House (6 rooms) 12 Lessing St, PO Box 4327, Windhoek; tel/fax: 061 249116; email: hilltop@iafrica.com.na
This spacious, airy B&B overlooking Windhoek's rolling northern suburbs was opened just a couple of years ago, but already has a reputation as one of the best of its kind in the city. From the airport, turn right off the B6 into Nelson Mandela Av, then left into Robert Mugabe Av and immediately left again into Promenaden Weg. Head up the hill, and bear second right into Lessing St; number 12 is on the left. From here, the centre of Windhoek is just a 15-minute stroll, or a couple of minutes by car.
Each of the wooden-floored bedrooms looks out over the secluded garden and beyond to the surrounding hills. Tasteful cream décor, offset by dark-wood furniture, is enlivened

by numerous personal touches: traditional woodcarvings, hand-filled jars of handcream and shampoo, plants and wrought iron give a hint of Africa juxtaposed with real comfort. All rooms have a luxurious en-suite stone-tiled shower with two washbasins and hairdryer, and other mod cons include TV with Dstv, AC, coffee/tea-making facilities, and fridge with (affordable) minibar.

Breakfast at Hilltop is a meal to be savoured, served in your room or by the small pool in the early morning sun. Diehard aficionados of bacon and egg will not be disappointed, but for the very best try the 'healthy eating' option – it's unbeatable. Innovative light meals are also available on request if you're too tired to venture out.

Rates: single N$495, double N$795, triple N$1,190 including breakfast.

Haus Sonneneck (5 rooms) 1 Robyn St, Eros, PO Box 86234, Windhoek; tel/fax: 061 225020, cell: 081 1273353; email: haussonneneck@mweb:com.na; web: www.haussonneneck.com

Located beyond the MediClinic at Eros, on the corner of Eros Way and Robyn St (but with the main entrance on Eros Way), Haus Sonneneck is rapidly gaining a reputation as one of Windhoek's best pensions. Not only does each spacious room have AC, minibar/hot drinks, wall safe, satellite TV and phone, but it also has its own private garden with table and chairs.

Beyond this individual sanctuary is the pool, overhung by trees and surrounded by the gardens which are the hallmark of the place. Birds, too, appreciate the welcome; there's plenty of scope for birdwatchers here.

Overseen by owners Gisela and Rudolf, all is calm and peace, yet the centre of Windhoek is just a few minutes' drive away, and there's secure parking.

Rates: single N$425, double N$645, family (3) N$785, family (4) N$895, including breakfast.

Kubata Lodge (10 rooms) 151 Nelson Mandela Av, PO Box 6842, Windhoek; tel: 061 224608, 081 240 3713; fax: 061 224610; email: kubata@iway.na

Right next door to Portuga's restaurant, the secure entrance to Kubata Lodge leads through a cool passage between twin ranks of thatched rooms. The strong Portuguese influence here is blended with a hint of Africa, with tiled floors, ornate heavy doors and wildlife printed bedcovers. Rooms are quite dark, but are well appointed, with a TV, fan, fridge/minibar, and coffee and tea; luxury rooms have an extra couch, which will convert into a double bed.

Beyond the rooms, sun loungers are set around a small pool, and there's a breakfast area with bar. There is no hint of personality about the place, but it's efficiently run and in a convenient location for restaurants and the airport.

Rates: single N$280, double N$310–410, additional person N$30, all including breakfast. Air conditioning N$30 per night.

Hotel-Pension Palmquell (10 rooms) 60 Jan Jonker Rd, PO Box 6143, Windhoek; tel: 061 234374, cell: 081 1271036; fax: 061 234483; email: hotel.palmquell@iafrica.com.na; web: www.palmquell.com

If you're coming from the airport, the Palmquell is clearly signposted to the left off Sam Nujoma Drive. Follow Jan Jonker Rd past the junction with Nelson Mandela Av, and you'll find it on the right. It's a bit too far to walk into Windhoek, but ideal if you have a car – there is secure parking available.

Austrian-owned, this upmarket pension offers a quiet setting among the palm trees that give it its name. Relax in the sauna, lounge by the pool, or take a cool dip, perhaps followed by a drink at the bar. Double and family rooms are simply furnished, but very well equipped, with AC and underfloor heating, telephone, TV and a wall safe; paintings by Namibian artists provide an individual touch. Although meals are not available in the evening, there are plenty of restaurants locally. And the hotel *does* boast a good range of South African wines!

Rates: single N$485, double N$790, family N$790–890, including breakfast..

Hotel-Pension Uhland (12 rooms) 147 Uhland St, PO Box 96284, Windhoek; tel: 061 229859; fax: 061 229108; email: uhland@mweb.com.na; web: http://natron.net/tour.uhland
Situated on the northeast side of town, off Independence Avenue, this friendly, pink-painted pension stands on the side of a hill, making it an airy spot when it's hot. The centre of town is a 10–15-minute walk away, though Uhland has plenty of secure parking if you have a car.
The new owners are completely renovating this small pension, with evident pride. Cane furniture complements the carpeted rooms, which each have Mnet TV, clock/radio, phone, mosquito nets, fans, tea/coffee-making facilities and minibar/fridge. Renovations are expected to be complete in 2003. The comfortable living room with TV and stereo adjoins the breakfast room, while outside is a patio with a pool, and a thatched bar area. Some rooms have a couch which turns into two beds, and even small kitchens, all for the same price, so ask what's available when you book or check in.
Rates: N$270 single, N$380 double, N$485 for 3/4 people, including breakfast.

Also in this area are:

Home in Town B&B Caprivi St (corner of Nelson Mandela) tel: 061 233622, 081 129 9556
Le Suricate B&B (5 rooms) 22 John Ludwig St, Klein Windhoek, PO Box 11646, Windhoek; tel/fax: 061 226612; email: panupanu@iway.na
Pension Nouveau 1 Heoiodoor St, Eros, PO Box 8047, Windhoek; tel/fax: 061 264319; email: nouveau@iway.na; web: www.natron.net/nouveau

Olympia and southeast Windhoek

Ambiente Guesthouse (4 rooms) 18 Marjorie Clark St, Olympia, PO Box 11106, Windhoek; tel: 061 252505, cell: 081 128 2505; fax: 061 217130; email: ambiente@mweb.com.na
Owned by Carola and Stephan Werner, this guesthouse offers a quiet retreat away from the bustle of town. Two of the double rooms can be used as triples and all have en-suite bathroom, minibar, TV, safe, AC and a kitchenette. They all have their own patios and have a light airy atmosphere. There is a swimming pool and a large thatch-covered area with wonderful views across the countryside. This area also seems to be a playground for some local meercats. Carola also holds craft markets in her garden at various times during the year. Tranfers from the airport can be arranged for N$140.
Rates: single N$320, double N$440, N$60 extra for triple.

Hotel-Pension Christoph (10 rooms) 33 Heinitzburg St, PO Box 6116, Windhoek; tel: 061 240777; fax: 061 248560: email: christoph@mweb.com.na
Recently taken over by a friend of the eponymous Christoph's daughter, the atmosphere here has changed. Situated on the southeast corner of Robert Mugabe and Heinitzburg Streets, the pension is 10–15 minutes' walk from the centre. At the heart of Christoph is a pool, surrounded by lawns to laze on (with loungers) and overlooked by the rooms.
Nearby is a bar for sundowners, complete with sizeable woodcarvings and space to park off-road. Christoph's well-equipped rooms have tiled floors, ceiling fans, shower/toilet, tea/coffee makers, Mnet and satellite TV, minibar/fridges, safe-boxes, phones, and small digital clocks to wake you from your slumber. It will be interesting to see the direction in which the pension heads in the future.
Rates: single N$250, double N$350, triple N$450, all exclusive of VAT, but including breakfast.

Marie's Guesthouse (7 rooms) 156 Diaz St, PO Box 90366, Windhoek; tel: 061 251766; fax: 061 251787; email: afriquedirect@namibnet.com or afriquedirect@mweb.com.na; web: www.travel.com.na
Some way out of Windhoek, Marie's is easily spotted by the animal and bird murals on the outside wall. You'll need your own vehicle to find the place: head south on Robert Mugabe Av, then turn right after the railway into Krupp Street, and right again into Bable.

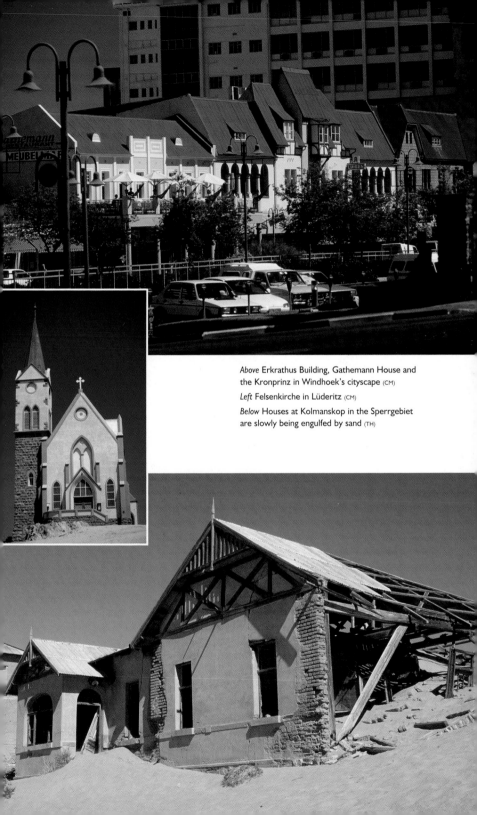

Above Erkrathus Building, Gathemann House and the Kronprinz in Windhoek's cityscape (CM)

Left Felsenkirche in Lüderitz (CM)

Below Houses at Kolmanskop in the Sperrgebiet are slowly being engulfed by sand (TH)

Above Looking over the
Namib Desert from
Hartmann's Mountains (CM)

Right Pearl-spotted owl
in acacia tree (CM)

Below Pelicans on the beach
at Sandwich Harbour (CM)

Diaz is a circular street that crosses this – turn right and Marie's is on the right. There's secure parking.

The pension was taken over and extensively renovated by Natascha Dorna in 2003. Each of the en-suite rooms now has TV and phone. Outside there are barbecue facilities and an inviting pool. Natascha also organises tours and safaris through her own company, Quelea Travel.

Rates: single N$190, double N$290.

Hotel-Pension Moni (12 rooms) 7 Rieks van der Walt St, PO Box 2805, Windhoek; tel: 061 228350; fax: 061 227124; email: pensionmoni@hgud.de; web: www.pensionmoni.hgud.de
About 2km from the centre, Pension Moni is easiest to reach from the Ausspannplatz roundabout (recently renamed the August Neto Gardens), at the south end of Independence Avenue. From there take Jan Jonker, and first left on to Lazarett, first right on to Feld, and then first left into Rieks van der Walt St.

Everything in this quiet, friendly pension, run by the affable Sven Schmidt, is immaculately kept – from the gardens to the accommodation, which overlooks a central pool area. Recently redecorated rooms are bright and cheerful, with original paintings on the walls, and direct-dial phones, radio/alarms, fans, TV with Mnet and tea/coffee-making facilities. Dinner is not automatically available, but can be prepared for groups, and sandwiches or snacks are also available on request.

Rates: single N$325, double N$455, triple N$575, quadruple N$650, including breakfast. Children aged 3–11 sharing with adults pay half-price.

Terra Africa (6 rooms) 6 Kenneth McArthur St, Olympia, PO Box 97164, Windhoek; tel: 061 252100, 081 249 2520; fax: 061 252020; email: terra@africaonline.co.na
Dutch husband-and-wife team Liesbeth and Sebastian van der Schoof have set out to create something different in guesthouse accommodation. Opened in May 2001, Terra Africa is set in a residential road behind a gate adorned with bougainvillaea. The rather utilitarian square building belies the care that is being lavished on the modern interior. Stone-flagged floors lead into a spacious lounge with dining area for breakfast and dinner, and big picture windows overlooking tree-shaded gardens with a small pool and courtyard area.

Each of the four carpeted twin rooms has en-suite bath or shower and is themed to a relevant design – Morocco is complete, while others, including Bushman, are well in hand. Two self-catering rooms also have a sink/hotplate, and the larger of these has a couch and business area as well. Be careful when you're booking: although most of the rooms overlook the hills, those upstairs (both self catering) are not cushioned from traffic noise on Robert Mugabe Av.

Dinner is available on request, both for guests and non-residents, and is cooked by master chef Sebastian himself. There are ambitious plans to build a further four rooms and to landscape the garden; this is one to watch.

Rates: single N$475, double N$600, family room (up to 4) N$265 per person, all including breakfast.

Windhoek Town Lodge (20 rooms) Ballot St, PO Box 6586, Windhoek; tel/fax: 061 252536; email: windhoektownlodge@webmail.co.za
The angular design of this quiet lodge just 15 minutes' walk from Windhoek centre, or 5 minutes from Maerua Park, reflects its no-frills attitude. To get here, follow Independence Avenue to Ausspannplatz, then turn left into Lazarett St, right into Feld St, and left into Ballot St. The lodge is on the right.

Run by Alec and Ronell Williams, it is particularly popular with business people and families. En-suite double and family rooms are located on two storeys. Their simple pine furniture is offset by tiled floors; each room has a free-standing fan, TV and tea/coffee-making facilities, while family rooms are self-catering, with fridge, two-plate stove, sink and table and chairs. No food is available. Outside is secure parking.

Rates: single N$180, double N$225, family N$280. No breakfast served.

Pioneers Park and southwest Windhoek

Hotel-Pension Etambi (11 rooms) 6 Gous St, PO Box 30547, Windhoek; tel: 061 241763; fax: 061 242916; email: etambi@iway.na or etambi@africaonline.com.na; web: www,africaonline.com.na/etambi or www.etambihotelnamibia.com
As Etambi is ten minutes' drive from the city centre, you really need your own vehicle to stay here. To get there, take Marconi Street westwards, before turning on to Jordan Street, following the signs for Pioneers Park. The road sweeps around to the right, and after about 1km you take the third left on to Hintrager Street. After a further kilometre, take first right on to Fritsche Street, and the left after the shopping centre on to Gous Street. Etambi is on the right.

Run by Peter and Elke Young, Etambi caters a lot for independent business people – so has phones and TVs in the rooms, each of which has its own entrance off the garden. It's a friendly and efficient little pension, with the owners' hallmark clearly imposed. The rooms are large and comfortable with modern furnishings. Each has a kettle, minibar/fridge, and a room safe. There is an outside braai for guests to use, a small pool, and a cool, vine-covered terrace area. Dinner (N$50–60 for three courses, or a barbecue on Sundays) is served on request on the terrace or in the restaurant, which has an open fire. Secure parking is available.
Rates: single N$300, double N$410, triple N$510, quadruple N$600, including breakfast.

Hotel-Pension Casablanca (6 rooms) Fritsche St (corner of Gous St), Pioneers Park, PO Box 30547, Windhoek; tel: 061 241763; fax: 061 242916; email: etambi@iway.na or etambi@africaonline.com.na; web: www.casablancahotelnamibia.com
Just next to Etambi (see below), and under the same ownership, the turreted Casablanca with wrought-iron finishing has a slightly classier atmosphere. Still geared to the business market, and with a small conference room/bar, it is located on the main road so at busy periods rooms at the front can be quite noisy.

Comfortable, stylish rooms, grouped round a small, Italian-style courtyard, have kings or twin beds with carefully chosen curtains and furnishings, and examples of Peter's photography adorn the walls. Each also has its own desk with plug for a laptop computer. To the front is Elke's domain: a mature garden with numerous indigenous plants and areas where guests can relax, while at the side is a small pool and bar area. Meals are available at Etambi on request.
Rates: single N$360, double N$480, including breakfast.

Other pensions and B&Bs in this area include:

Mahali 9 Tunschel St, Pioneers Park, PO Box 6371, Windhoek; tel: 061 256946; fax: 061 256945; email: mpengu@iafrica.com.na; web: www.natron.net/tour/mahali/index.main
Pension Shumba 14 Jordan St, Pioneers Park; tel/fax: 061 240774; email: shumba.pension@africa.com.na
Villa Tiziana 29 Goshawk St; tel: 061 222943

Smaller B&Bs

Even smaller than the above, several local homes offer 'bed and breakfast', including:

Riverside Home Accommodation 7 Veronica St, Ludwigsdorf, PO Box 3257, Windhoek; tel: 061 233500; fax: 061 206 3806 (mark for the attention of Haacke); email: whaake@unam.na
Camelthorn Guesthouse Pioneers Park, PO Box 30064, Windhoek; tel: 061 241936; fax: 061 241183
Little Angel Guesthouse 106 Jan Jonker, Klein Windhoek; tel: 061 231639
The Guesthouse (5 rooms) 163 Uhland St, PO Box 194, Windhoek; tel: 061 255458/234438; cell: 081 128 4900; fax: 061 234438; email: bazz@iafrica.com.na

Hostels and camping

Windhoek has a thriving number of backpackers' hostels. Until recently, these were mostly confined to the north and west suburbs, but the opening of the new Chameleon City Lodge is likely to create quite a stir. While the Cardboard Box is still the favourite choice of younger travellers, Chameleon, Puccini and Backpacker, recently joined by Roof of Africa, are all increasingly successful. Being newer and, generally, better equipped, they often demonstrate a willingness to help visitors (with free lifts from the city, and the like) and tend to have one eye on a more mature market. The city's only dedicated campsite, Arebbusch, is just south of town, so only of benefit to those with vehicles. Campers without transport can pitch a tent at some of the backpackers' hostels.

Arebbusch Travel Lodge (50 chalets, 8 double rooms) Olympia, PO Box 80160; tel: 061 252255; fax: 061 251670; email: atl@iwwn.com.na; web: www.iwwn.com.na/arebbusch
Less than 10km south of the centre, between the Safari Hotel and Windhoek Country Club, this is Windhoek's only dedicated campsite; it is clean, spacious and very impressive. There are 12 pitches for caravans, and 40 for tents.

The chalets have small, well-equipped kitchens, TVs, direct-dial phones, linen, en-suite shower/toilet, air conditioning and an outside braai. The rooms are more basic, having just beds, a cupboard and a washbasin. They share toilets and showers with the campers. Both types of rooms are clean, comfortable, and serviced daily. Arebbusch's security is tight – with an electric fence and guard on the gate – so it is proving a safe place to stay.

There's also a spotless restaurant on site, with a good range of steaks and salads, some vegetarian options and a kids' menu (closed Sundays except for breakfast). Added to this are a laundry, a bar and a good pool. The only snag is, you need a car to get here.
Rates: double N$200 per person (sharing facilities), 2-bed chalet N$275 per person (self-catering) or N$350 B&B, N$400 for a 4- or 5-bed chalet. Camping N$50 per person.

Backpacker Unite (37 beds) 5 Greig St, Windhoek; tel: 061 259485; cell (day): 081 129 8093; email: magicbus@iafrica.com.na
Between Bach and Beethoven streets, Backpacker Unite in Greig Street is about ten minutes' walk from the centre. The zebra-striped exterior walls may be appealing, but the razor wire hanging from them certainly isn't. This is a rather soulless establishment, with simple, clean rooms and four bathrooms. Visitors can use the pool and sauna, and there is a pool table, too.

The place is run by Hermann and Erica Viljoen. Hermann offers a free pick-up service within the city, and also runs one- and two-night trips to Sossusvlei (N$1,330/N$1,600) which depart on Saturday, and two-night trips to Etosha (N$1,400) departing on Tuesdays.
Rates: N$40 for dorm bed, N$80 for a double room, N$30 for camping.

Cardboard Box (43 beds, camping) 15 Johann Albrecht St, PO Box 6406; tel: 061 228994; fax: 061 256581, email: ahj@iafrica.com.na; web: www.namibian.org
On the corner of Johann Albrecht and John Meinert streets, a short uphill walk from town, this large and rather scruffy backpackers' lodge has been the capital's favourite for younger independent travellers for quite a while – despite its size and noisy dorms. Visitors have use of a small pool, pool table, washing machines, internet access, and crockery/cutlery in the kitchen. There's secure parking, too. As you might expect, it acts as agent for several cheap car-hire companies, and has its own travel shop.
Rates: N$40 for beds in large dorm, N$50 for small dorm, N$120 for double room, camping N$30 per person.

Chameleon Backpackers (26 beds) 22 Wagner St, PO Box 6107, Windhoek; tel/fax: 061 247668; email: chamnam@chameleon.com.na, chamnam@namib.com; web: www.chameleonbackpackers.com

Just west of Beethoven St, Chameleon is about 15 minutes' walk from the centre (some of it uphill, but you can circumnavigate the steep bits). It is a clean, pleasant and well-run backpackers' lodge catering predominantly for the young, professional traveller, and it certainly sets the trend. Residents are offered free tea/coffee and bed linen in dorms for four people, or in twin rooms, either sharing bathrooms or en suite. Use of an equipped kitchen, pool, and Mnet TV lounge is also part of the deal, and laundry facilities are available. There is a free shuttle to the centre to meet bus arrivals and departures. Chameleon also run scheduled camping safaris, and are happy to arrange car hire.
Rates: N$50 for dorm beds, N$120 for twin rooms (shared bath), or N$150 (en suite), all including breakfast.

Chameleon City Lodge (18 dorm beds, 3 double rooms) 5 Voight St, Windhoek Central, PO Box 6107, Windhoek; tel: 061 244347; fax: 061 247668; email: chamnam@chameleon.com.na, chamnam@namib.com; web: www.chameleonbackpackers.com
An offshoot of the established Chameleon Backpackers, City Lodge was opened in 2001 and is already proving a success. Guests are collected at any time of day or night off incoming buses at the terminal by the Grab-a-phone kiosk in central Windhoek. Those who are walking from the stop should head north up Independence Avenue, then turn right on Sam Nujoma and left on to Daniel Mandume, where the Chameleon sign will be above you to the left (turn left, then left again into Trift St, and finaly left into Voight St).

City lodge is set to become the benchmark for backpackers' hostels. Bright, cheerful and clean, its small, well-decorated dormitories are comfortable and well thought out, while double rooms offer a degree of privacy, with their own washbasins. Facilities include a fully equipped kitchen, TV and video, a safe for valuables and a secure cage for luggage, not to mention phone, bar, and internet access. There's a barbecue area too, with umbrellas set out on the grass for shade. And for N$25 they'll do your laundry! Secure parking is also available.
Rates: dorm beds N$40 in six-bed room, N$50 in four-bed room, double N$120 per room, rooftop tent N$30 per person, all including breakfast.

Deo Volente (9 rooms) 154 Jan Jonker Weg, PO Box 80103, Windhoek; tel: 061 234301/252057; cell: 081 124 2293; fax: 061 258220; email: leonivr@mweb.co.za
The smart terracotta exterior and palm-fringed entrance of this guesthouse close to the Intercape Mainliner offices near Maerua Park is the best bit. Inside, the rather functional rooms are gloomy and not particularly welcoming, and rates seem very high by these standards.
Rates: N$95 for bed in 6-bed dorm, N$150 in 3-bed room. Breakfast N$25.

Hakuna Matata (15 dorm beds, 9 double rooms, self-contained flats) 78 John Meinert St, PO Box 30984; tel: 061 245444, cell: 081 1282594; email: hakunam@iafrica.com.na; web: hakunabackpackers.com
This rambling complex, situated on the right past the junction of Freud St, offers a variety of rooms.

Dorms have lockable lockers in the rooms, and there's secure parking inside its distinctive beige walls. Best described as very basic, it provides travellers with cheap accommodation, fairly close to the centre of Windhoek.
Rates: dorm bed N$60, single N$120, double N$140, flats N$ 240–320.

Puccini House also known as **Puccini International Hostel** (47 dorm beds, 9 double rooms) 4 Puccini St; PO Box 31396, Windhoek; tel/fax: 061 236355; email: puccinis@mweb.com.na
Between Sam Nujoma and Hosea Kutako drives, just beyond the railway, Puccini St is less than ten minutes' walk from town. A very popular backpackers' lodge, this has a pool,

sauna, secure parking, and a well-equipped kitchen, including a pizza oven. Rates include bed linen and a light breakfast, though more substantial fare can be provided at extra cost. The owner, Christabella, together with her Jack Russells, provide a relaxed atmosphere and can help with booking trips or hire cars.
Rates: dorm bed N$55, single N$85, double N$150.

Roof of Africa (42 dorm beds, 24 double rooms, camping) 124 Nelson Mandela Av, Klein Windhoek, PO Box 11745, Windhoek; tel: 061 254708, cell: 081 124 4930; email: info@roofofafrica.com.na or roofof@mweb.com.na; web: www.roofofafrica.com
Clearly visible as you're entering Windhoek on Nelson Mandela Av, Roof of Africa has its main entrance in Gusinde St. This friendly and efficiently run establishment seems to cater for most requirements. Simple and clean double rooms range from those with shared bathrooms to deluxe rooms with AC; all have TV and telephones. Other facilities include a well-equipped self-catering kitchen, internet (expensive at N$25 per half-hour), secure lockers and off-street parking. Terri and Torsten have plans to build a new swimming pool and sauna, while at present guests can relax under the cool thatched bar area. There is a small camping area for 5 tents.
Rates: dorm bed N$50; double room N$165 (shared facilities), N$295 (en-suite), N$350 (deluxe); camping N$40 per person. Breakfast is included for en-suite and deluxe rooms; otherwise a cooked breakfast costs N$25. An evening meal will cost about N$30.

Tramper's Haven (16 beds, 1 single, 1 double) 78 Bülow St, PO Box 20222, Windhoek; tel/fax: 061 223669; email: trampers@iway.na
Margot Theisinger brings a touch of maternal care to this small, central, backpackers' hostel, just five minutes' walk from the centre of town. Brightly painted dormitories (to match the colourful outside walls) with wooden floors have six or ten beds, and their own showers and toilet en suite. There is a self-catering kitchen, a barbecue area and lockers in the large room. Guests are collected free of charge from the bus terminal.
Rates: dorm bed N$50, single N$120, double N$150; breakfast N$25 per person on request.

Travellers' Lodge (18 beds) Corner of Andes and Johnson streets; tel: 061 249099
About 1km north of town, just off Independence Avenue, and first right after Nelson Mandela Drive, this is a particularly unfriendly backpackers' place, albeit the cheapest around – which might explain why guests find themselves sleeping in the kitchen. Facilities are much the same as at the others – with shared bathroom/toilets, crockery/cutlery supplied and a communal kitchen. The outside door is normally locked, which doesn't add warmth to the welcome, and there is limited off-street parking.
Rates: N$25 for dorm bed, N$30 including linen. N$70 for a double room.

Just outside town
Lodges and guest farms have proliferated in the area around Windhoek, and many of these make good alternatives to staying in the city on the way to or from the airport.

To the east (towards the airport)
There are quite a few places to stay along road between Windhoek and Hosea Kutako International Airport. The benefits of staying out of town in relatively rural surroundings are self evident, and there are many different styles of accommodation from which to choose. Those below are listed in order of their distance from Windhoek:

Hotel-Pension Onganga (10 rooms) 11 Schuckmann St, Avis, PO Box 90668, Windhoek; tel: 061 241701, cell: 081 127 3494; fax: 061 241676; email: onganga@mweb.com.na; web: www.onganga.de

This simple, modern new pension (opened in 2001) is near Avis Dam. Signposted to the left off the B6 airport road, shortly after leaving Windhoek, it is built on several levels. Each of the quiet twin and double rooms has en-suite shower, TV with Dstv, phone, minibar/fridge and tea/coffee-making facilities. Screened doors and windows mean that guests can take advantage of the breeze afforded by Onganga's hillside position. Owner Steffi has decorated the place in a cheerful yellow and white, with cane furniture in the breakfast room, and an open fire for those chilly winter evenings.

Outside, the small pool facing the mountains is surrounded by a grassy area set with umbrellas, overlooked by a rustic bar with a barbecue, while behind the pension is a 20-minute walking trail. There's also a small craft shop with postcards. Light meals are available on request. Airport collection is N$180 for up to four people, while trips to Windhoek cost N$30.

Rates: single N$320, double N$440, including breakfast.

Heja Game Lodge (20 rooms, 6 self-catering chalets) PO Box 588, Windhoek; tel: 061 257151/2; fax: 061 257148; email: heja@namib.net.com
Signposted off the B6 airport road, just 13km from Windhoek, this family-run lodge is 3km along a tarred road past Otjihase Mine, then a further 3km on a gravel track through land grazed by a variety of game animals. Wildebeest, springbok, blesbok, oryx, ostrich and warthog are just some of the animals to be spotted as you drive through.

Rooms are functional, with AC, TV and phone, while chalets also have a kitchenette, braai and small patio. Activities include game drives, and one-hour horse rides with a guide, and there's the possibility of longer drives into Namibia's third highest mountain. The restaurant is open daily, with an à la carte menu except on Sundays. There is even a private church on site for weddings etc. That said, this is not a place to linger, but it makes a carefree stopover for families and is well frequented by the German market. Airport transfers cost N$50 per person.

Heja is particularly popular with day-trippers on Sundays, when the buffet lunch from 12.00 to 14.00 costs N$75 (children under 12 N$35) and you'll need to book. Game drives at N$50 for about an hour, (very) short horse rides and the swimming pool overlooking the dam are added Sunday attractions, and there's a trail around the dam that takes about an hour to walk.

Rates: Rooms N$280 single, N$495 double, chalets N$380 single, N$640 double, extra bed N$80, all including breakfast

Finke's Sicht (6 rooms, 2 flats) Farm Bellerode, Plot 3, PO Box 90671, Windhoek; tel: 061 238978, cell: 081 124 4714; fax 061 238890
Just beyond Finkenstein on the way in to Windhoek, this bed and breakast was originally the overspill for Finkenstein, but is now trading in its own right. Trips around the farm, as well as hunting, birdwatching and horseriding, can be arranged in advance, or guests are welcome to explore the area on foot. Cooking is based on farm produce, including homemade jams and pickles, and game.

Rates: single N$220, double N$400, flat for 4–5 people N$560, including breakfast. 'Backpackers' special' N$85, including breakfast. Packages available for half and full board.

Finkenstein Guest Farm (5 rooms) PO Box 167, Windhoek; tel: 061 234751; fax: 061 238890
Conveniently situated on the main road between Windhoek and the airport (about halfway between), Finkenstein is an old-style guest farm run by Annegret and Helmut Finke, though all but the most ardent dog lovers are likely to find the 'welcome' a bit overwhelming. The five guest rooms have en-suite facilities and traditional furnishings, but a greater attraction are home-cooked three-course meals with wine. Get talking to the housekeeper, Oti, and you'll find out more about Namibia in an hour than you thought possible!

Rates: N$390 single, N$350 per person sharing, including breakfast.

Hotel Kapps Farm Although this hotel was closed in 2002, it would be surprising if, with its prime location on the main road to the airport, it were not snapped up soon, so keep an eye out if you're passing.

Airport Lodge (6 bungalows, 1 2-bedroom house) PO Box 5913, Windhoek; tel: 061 231491/243192; fax: 061 236709; email: airport@mweb.com.na; web: www.natron.net/tour/airport
Run by Brian and Hermine Black, Airport Lodge is signposted halfway between Windhoek's main international airport and the city, about 600m from the B6 main road, down the MR53 turning. Set well apart in extensive bush, each of the lodge's ethnic-décor thatched bungalows has three single beds (children will love the third, set high up in its own 'loft' area), en-suite toilet/shower, mini-kitchen, satellite TV, direct-dial telephone, mosquito nets and AC/ceiling fan, not to mention a small veranda. There's a large swimming pool with outside and inside bars, a braai, and an open fire for winter evenings. This is a peaceful and convenient stop before and after flights. Airport transfers cost N$40 per person (N$80 minimum).
Rates: 3-bed bungalow N$330, house N$600. Breakfast N$25; dinner N$30–45.

Trans Kalahari Caravan Park (6 rooms) PO Box 11084, Windhoek; tel: 061 222877; fax: 061 220335; email: woodway@namibnet.com; web: www.mietwagen-namibia.de
Set back above the main airport road, just 21km from the airport (a little closer than Airport Lodge), this is more than just a caravan park, with large, simply furnished, en-suite rooms, some with AC, catering mainly for the German market.
The main building features a rustic bar and restaurant with lounge area and a good range of crafts for sale – ideal for last-minute souvenirs – and the restaurant serves Namibian-German cuisine, with the emphasis on game. Some may be put off by the owner's dogs, which include a Doberman, or by the lack of television; others will appreciate the privacy. Airport transfers are N$110.
Pitches at the campsite have electricity, water and a grill area, and a toilet block with hot-water showers.
Rates: single N$280, double N$320, triple N$400, breakfast N$27.50, camping N$25 per person and N$50 per pitch.

Hohewarte Guest Farm PO Box 11281, Windhoek; tel/fax: 062 540420; email: howarte@mweb.com.na
Follow the airport road for about 28km, then turn right towards Dordabis. Hohewarte is 15km down this road, to the left.
Once a German colonial police station, Hohewarte farm now stands in an area of some 10,000 hectares, at the foot of the 2,299m Bismarck Mountain.
Rates: single N$360, N$300 per person sharing.

To the north and west
Eagles Rock Leisure Lodge (5 Rooms) PO Box 6176, Windhoek; tel: 061 234542; fax: 061 234542
Forty-five minutes' drive (38km) west of Windhoek, Eagles Rock is 3km along the D1958, after its junction with the C28. See *Chapter 9*, page 167, for more details.
Rates: single N$365, double N$580.

Elisenheim Guest Farm (9 rooms, 5 campsite pitches) PO Box 3016, Windhoek; tel/fax: 061 254429; email: awerner@mweb.com.na; web: www.natron/net/tour/elisenheim
Just 15km north of the centre of Windhoek, Elisenheim is signposted to the left of the main B1 as it leaves the city. Follow the track for a further 6km, then turn right just before Namibia tannery.
The farm, set in grounds of some 5,000 hectares at the foot of the mountains, offers German hospitality under the care of Andreas and Christina Werner, and a place to relax.

The comfortable rooms all have en-suite showers and toilets, while outside is a tree-shaded swimming pool surrounded by a grassy area. Weaver birds nest in the bamboo that shelters the house. Close by is a small campsite, with its own pool. Campers need to be totally self-sufficient, as nothing is available here except firewood.

Dinner – usually a two-course set menu based on game – is available for N$70 per person, and lunches can also be prepared. Visitors are welcome to explore the area, which is home to kudu, warthog and steenbok, and plenty of baboons 'looking for work'. A sundowner trip into the mountain for a minimum of four people costs N$55, including drinks.

Rates: N$280 single, double N$450, including breakfast. Camping N$35 per person (children N$20).

Sundown Lodge (11 rooms) PO Box 5378, Windhoek; tel: 061 232566; fax: 061 232541; email: sundown@iafrica.com.na

Opened in the mid-90s, and run by Bob and Silke Sinclair, Sundown Lodge is a purpose-built stopover, providing a basic night's rest in attractive surroundings near Windhoek. It is well signposted just off the main B1, about a 25km drive north of the city, on the D1474. (Though this has been omitted from some maps, it's easy to find as it's right by the police roadblock.)

Expect your room to have its own telephone/desk, fridge, kettle and tea/coffee facilities, en-suite toilet and shower, and a small patio for sitting outside. Lunch and dinner are available at N$45 and N$60 respectively; alternatively, there are braai facilities. Guests are welcome to use the swimming pool with adjacent bar, or to explore the surrounding bush. Transfers to Windhoek International Airport cost N$280 per trip.

Rates: N$250 single, double N$360, including breakfast.

Immanuel Wilderness Lodge (9 rooms) PO Box 3305, Windhoek; tel: 061 260901; cell: 081 245 0112; fax: 061 260903; email: immanuel@wilderness-namibia.de; web: www.wilderness-namibia.de

Marianne and Ralph Eder and their three children came to Namibia from Germany with the intention of opening their new home to disadvantaged children, but things didn't go according to plan. Instead, they are now welcoming tourists to this attractive thatched lodge, approached down the same drive as Sundown Lodge (above), and set in 10 hectares of land. Goats, dogs and horses are part of the homestead, and horseriding is a possibility. There's also a pool to cool off.

Double and twin rooms are in three separate thatched bungalows, with simple rustic furniture – some of it homemade – and en-suite showers. Each has a ceiling fan and, outside, a small patio with chairs. Lunch and dinner are available on request at N$35 and N$53 respectively, and teenage daughter Julia's cakes are excellent! Don't come here expecting luxury, but for genuine hospitality and warmth, it would be hard to beat.

Rates: single N$250, double N$420, double with extra single bed N$490, double with 2 extra singles N$550, all including breakfast.

Additional options in this direction, but within relatively easy reach of Windhoek, are:

Okapuka (see pages 173–4)
Dürsternbrook (see page 173)

To the south

Gravel Travel Mountain Lodge (9 rooms, camping) PO Box 80603, Windhoek; tel/fax: 061 250147; cell: 081 127 0666; email: gravel@iafrica.com.na; web: www.namibialodge.com or www.graveltravel.de

About 15km south of Windhoek, Gravel Travel Mountain Lodge is 4km along the D1504, just beyond the Harmony Seminar Centre, which is signposted from the main road. Take this road, pass Raleigh International, and the track to the lodge is the next on the left.

High up in the Auas Mountains, the lodge was opened in 2001 to cater for guests taking part in motorbike tours of Namibia. You can forget concerns about noise, though, since none of the biking takes place in this region. Instead, visitors can expect thatched rooms with pine furnishings, stone floors and en-suite showers, set around a rectangular pool with open views across the mountains. There's a bar and dining room, with dinner available on request. While everything still seems very new, the place certainly has the potential to attract visitors seeking a rural environment within easy reach of the capital.
Rates: single N$350, double N$500, including breakfast; camping N$50 per person. Dinner N$85.

Landhaus Aris (5 rooms) PO Box 5199, Windhoek; tel: 061 236006; fax: 061 234507 About 25km south of the city, to the right of the main road to Rehoboth, Aris was bought at the end of 2001 after standing empty for over two years. Although the place is now open, rooms remain basic and old-fashioned, the pool could do with some serious attention and hunting tropies on the walls may not appeal to many readers. On the positive side, weaver birds have colonised trees in the large, rather neglected grounds, and kudu can be seen in the hills to the front. The bar and restaurant are open all day till late, serving meals and snacks, with a Sunday buffet at N$55.
Rates: single N$150, double N$250, including breakfast.

Auas Game Lodge (16 rooms) PO Box 80887, Windhoek; tel: 061 240043; fax: 061 248633; cell: 081 127 0043; email: auas@iafrica.com.na; web: www.auas/lodge.com Auas is a German-run lodge, about 44km southeast of Windhoek into the Kalahari. To reach it, take the B1 or the C23 roads heading south, then turn left on to the gravel D1463 – the road is not always viable in a 2WD, so do check in advance if this is likely to be a problem. The lodge is 22km from the B1, or 16km from the C23.
Auas stands on a game farm, whose residents include black wildebeest (from South Africa) and crocodiles in a separate enclosure. The active will appreciate the swimming pool and tennis court, and opportunities for mountain-bike rides, while more sedentary guests can relax on their own veranda or at the bar. Day visitors are welcome for lunch or dinner, with advance reservation.
Rates: single N$460, double N$680, including breakfast, coffee and cake, and game drive. With dinner, N$593/946.

Other accommodation possibilities to the south of Windhoek include the following:

Amani Lodge (6 rooms) PO Box 9959, Eros; tel: 061 239564; fax: 061 235614; email: amani@e-tourism.com.na; web: www.discover-africa.com.na
This French-owned lodge 26km southwest of Windhoek on the C26 offers an excellent dinner for both non-residents and its own guests.

Eningu Clayhouse Lodge For a stylish lodge within an hour of the airport, this should be top of your list (see page 185).

WHERE TO EAT
Windhoek has lots of cafés and restaurants, though you'll often have more success searching for European cuisine than African specialities. Note that many places are closed on Sundays. Not surprisingly, as a spin-off from the burgeoning restaurant scene, there are plenty of fast-food places, particularly in the new shopping malls. Pies, burgers and the like are freely available at points right across the city, including Nando's on Independence Avenue near the station, while in the shopping malls, pizza parlours proliferate.

Cafés and light meals

For coffee or snacks in town, the two cafés in the Levinson Arcade (off Independence Avenue, and parallel to the Post Street Mall), the **Schneider** and the **Central,** are ideal, and great places to watch the world go by. Buy a local paper from the street sellers to find out what's going on. A little further down, **Le Bistro** on the corner of Independence Avenue and the Post Street Mall is a very trendy, popular place for the local crowd to grab a coffee and a bite, or have an early-evening drink.

On the other side of Independence Avenue in Zoo Park (where, perversely, there is no zoo) are two cafés. **Zoo Café** (tel: 061 215169), overlooking Independence Avenue, is an elegant establishment that specialises in cakes and light meals. The embroidered fabrics here have been worked by women involved in the TB project at Katutura (see pages 158–9). Up the hill, at the top of the park, is a small café with a shaded seating area, which sells drinks and snacks.

The **Cauldron**, under the Kalahari Sands Hotel, is convenient for light lunches of burgers or omelettes (expect to pay less than N$20 for a drink and a toasted sandwich), and serves a memorable banana split. It's closed Saturday afternoon and Sunday. At the western end of Post Street Mall, on the ground floor of the Wernhil Park Shopping Centre, is the decidedly eastern **Tim Sum** (tel: 061 232312), which offers a cheap and excellent range of Taiwanese vegetarian foods – set lunches N$25–30. It serves until 18.30, though it's closed Saturday and Sunday afternoons. Close by is a traditional German coffee-shop, **Ins Wiener**, which also serves light lunches; expect to pay about N$30 for Greek, tuna or chicken salad. Just round the corner is the **Craft Centre Café**, usually busy with locals and visitors alike for its homemade quiches, cakes and puddings, and serving a range of coffees.

Out at Klein Windhoek, close to Luigi & the Fish, is the popular **Jenny's Place**, a licensed coffee and gift shop that serves everything from excellent cakes to sandwiches and light meals in a surprisingly spacious, tree-shaded courtyard. Freshly squeezed fruit juice and a range of coffees and milkshakes are also on offer throughout the day. Jenny's has a good gift and craft shop on site, too.

There are plenty of cafés at Maerua Park Mall, near the swimming pool, including the **Brazilian**, which serves coffee and light snacks daily until 20.00 (closed Saturday afternoon and Sunday).

Restaurants

Like any capital, Windhoek has dozens of restaurants to choose from – you should have no problem finding something good to eat. Until the late 1990s, most served fairly similar fare, often with a German bias, but now there is a lot more variety. There are Italian, Greek, Portuguese and Chinese and even Ethiopian specialities, to name just a few. Many reach a very high standard, and none is expensive in European or American terms.

Eating at the very best, and without restricting your choices, you would have to try very hard to make a meal cost more than N$200 per person. Here's a selection of favourites:

Abyssinia Feld St; tel: 061 254891/2
Opposite the well-established Homestead, this very smart restaurant was opened in 2001. It specialises in Ethiopian cuisine, complete with the traditional coffee ceremony, with meals served either in Ethiopian style or at Western tables. It's an excellent option for vegetarians, with plenty of choice on offer.
Costs: selection for 1 person N$65, 2 people N$120. Salads N$15–20, mains N$45–70, vegetarian meals N$30–35 (or a selection at N$50 per person).

Restaurant Africa Alte Feste, Robert Mugabe Av; tel: 061 247178
The setting, in one of Windhoek's historical buildings and with a balcony overlooking the city, is part of the attraction here. With traditional dishes from Namibia and the rest of Africa – including Ghana, Kenya, Zambia and Zimbabwe and little concession to Western ideas of tender meat, the service and food can be somewhat hit-and-miss, so it's an authentic experience! Delicacies include – for the truly adventurous – *omanugu*, or mopane worms.
Costs: around N$80 for a full meal with a few beers.

O Badejo Seafood Restaurant Sam Nujoma Drive; tel: 061 255503
Although the food here is not dissimilar to that served at the neighbouring Luigi & the Fish, with an emphasis on seafood but serving meat dishes as well, prices are considerably higher, reflecting an atmosphere that is altogether more elegant and formal.
Costs: Starter N$25–45, main N$40–180. Closed Sunday evening.

Bilboa Bar, Grill and Shellfish Restaurant 145 Nelson Mandela Av; tel: 061 237922, cell: 081 128 9365
This restaurant is relatively new and specialises in seafood. In addition to seating inside there is a large, pleasant courtyard. The restaurant opened in 2001 and has stiff competition from the popular O Portuga's and Joe's Beerhouse close by. It remains to be seen whether the cuisine can match the standards of its near neighbours.
Costs: starters N$25–45, main N$40–80.

Cattle Baron Maerua Park, tel: 61 254154; fax: 61 254156
Situated within this new shopping complex, the Cattle Baron has two restaurants next to each other, namely the Lounge and Grill House. The former has a more formal setting with round tables encircled by black-leather seating, while the Grill House has a more relaxed family atmosphere. The menu is primarily grills, with steaks between N$40–70. There is a children's menu.

La Cave Carl List Bldg, Fidel Castro (Peter Müller) St; tel: 061 224173
The unprepossessing entrance opposite the Sanlam Centre is more akin to a storeroom than a smart restaurant. But continue downstairs and you'll find a tiled, modern restaurant with separate sports bar and a couple of slot machines. The smallish eating area is cool and modern, but the adjoining bar maintains the original décor so appears somewhat old fashioned. The menu is along German lines with fish and game prominent.
A lunchtime special is available most days at about N$30; otherwise you can expect to pay N$15–30 starters, N$40–75 main, N$15–20 desserts. Closed on Sundays.

Chez Wou see page 122 (Windhoek Country Club).

La Dolce Vita Kaiserkrone, off Post Street Mall; tel: 061 170147. In the small Kaiserkrone Centre, on the left of Post Street Mall as you walk from Independence Av, La Dolce Vita is open for breakfast, lunch and dinner, with an impressive range of pizza and pasta dishes and salads served either indoors or in the pleasant, shady courtyard. Closed Saturday evening and Sunday. No credit cards.
Costs: N$10–25 for a starter, N$30–45 for main, and N$10–20 for sweet.

Dros Post Office Mall; tel: 061 242740
Open from 08.00 to midnight every day, this chain restaurant offers burgers, pizzas and grills. There is a terrace outside, the staff are friendly and the food is just what you would expect from this type of establishment.
Costs: burgers N$20–30, pizzas N$17–46, grills N$30–50.

Hotel Fürstenhof Romberg St, PO Box 316, Windhoek; tel: 061 237380; fax: 061 228751
West of the centre, one of Windhoek's grandest restaurants has quite a formal atmosphere.

For men, a jacket and tie isn't out of place. The food is classic French/German style, varying from seafood through to game and a daily vegetarian dish. The wine list is grouped by grape variety, and most bottles are around N$80. The choice is competent, but neither inspired nor outstanding value. The Fürstenhof seems to be resting on its laurels. *Costs: N$30–40 for a starter, N$65–90 for main, and N$30 for sweet.*

Gathemann 175 Independence Av; tel: 061 223853
This must have the best position of the capital's restaurants, on a first-floor balcony, opposite the park, with commanding views over Independence Avenue. Sadly, though, this grand old establishment has lost its edge. The traditional German cuisine (with a bias towards game) remains good, but standards of service have slipped heavily (though prices have not), with dirty, scruffy tablecloths, warm wine and a lack of professionalism. The wine list is extensive, and therefore good in parts. *Costs: starters N$25–50, main courses N$58–110.*

Gourmet's Inn 195 Jan Jonker Rd; tel: 061 232360/232882
At the corner of Jan Jonker and Centaurus, Gourmet's Inn looks from the outside like a transport café, but don't be put off, for beyond the doors all is warm terracotta and yellow décor, with a pleasant terrace, and air conditioning. Although it has a reputation for top-class, expensive, rich European fare, prices are not excessive. Its wine list is good, though not cheap, and the atmosphere is quite intimate. Book ahead. *Costs: starters N$20–40, mains N$40–70, vegetarian dishes N$30–45.*

Grand Canyon Spur 251 Independence Av; tel: 061 231003
Situated above street level on Independence Avenue, opposite the Bank of Windhoek, the Spurs offers American burgers, steaks, and a host of side orders together with Windhoek's best serve-yourself salad bar. The atmosphere is lively, similar to a Hard Rock Café, and it's open 7 days a week from early until late. *Costs: starters N$10–20, light meals during day N$15–30, main courses N$40–60.*

Homestead Restaurant 53 Feld St; tel: 061 221958/90; fax: 061 221846.
Very near Ausspannplatz (now called the August Neto Gardens) off Lossen St, this is a spacious, airy restaurant whose tables are spread over its veranda (during the summer) and several rooms. Inside are large pot-plants, a superb feature aquarium and a good selection of 'choose-yourself, from the rack' estate wines from South Africa – ranging from N$60 to N$200 a bottle. Many are good value.
   The Homestead's excellent food is continental cooking in large portions, with inventive vegetarian options. This is still one of Windhoek's best restaurants. *Costs: starters N$20–30, vegetarian mains around N$50, steaks N$55–70.*

Hunter's Moon Hidas Centre, junction Nelson Mandela & Sam Nujoma, Klein Windhoek; tel: 061 252400
This large sports bar upstairs in the Hidas Centre offers a fairly standard steak-and-grills menu, with no frills. Daily specials are around N$25. Live music can occasionally be heard. Open Mon–Sat, 11.00–23.30.

Joe's Beerhouse 160 Nelson Mandela Av; tel: 061 232457; email: joes@iafrica.com.na; web: www.joesbeerhouse.com
The cavernous thatched premises that house the new Joe's Beerhouse seat over 200 people in a rustic environment set around a large bar area. Joe's cuisine is good value and strictly for serious carnivores, with lots of game and huge portions, though its service can be slow and lackadaisical. Beers and spirits are excellent, but wines are mediocre. There's also a small craft shop with postcards. Joe's reputation goes before it, and the place is almost always full; booking is usually essential. *Costs: starters N$22–30, mains N$32–88.*

Leo's at the Castle 22 Heinitzburg St; tel: 061 249597
The Heinitzburg's new restaurant, Leo's, is one for the elite. Small, modern and sophisticated, it is open for dinner only, masterminded by the hotel's French chef. In addition to the carefully selected à la carte menu, which is dominated by fish and game (but vegetarians are well catered for on request), there is a four-course gourmet menu at N$220. The Heinitzburg boasts the largest wine cellar in Namibia, so be prepared to linger over the winelist.
Costs: starters N$38–68, mains N$86–136 (for a shellfish platter).

Luigi & the Fish 90 Sam Nujoma Drive; tel: 061 228820; email: luigi@iafrica.com.na
About 2.5km from the centre, Luigi's is on the left of Sam Nujoma Drive, about 100m after the junction with Nelson Mandela Av, at Klein Windhoek. Its atmosphere is relaxed, with plenty of seating both inside and out under the trees. Food here is a feast for fish lovers (though there's plenty of meat and some good veggie options as well), while starters have a Mexican slant. Service is friendly, but can be slow when it's busy.
There is sometimes live music in the courtyard, and upstairs is a popular bar that's open till late.
Costs: starters N$20–30, mains N$30–60 (seafood platter N$80).

La Marmite 383 Independence Av; tel: 061 248022, cell: 081 244 5353
This small, friendly restaurant opposite Trés Supermarket specialises in West and central African food. Owned and run by its Camerounian chef, Martial, it's well worth a visit, though it's normally closed on Sunday.
Prices are very reasonable, even by Namibian standards.

Plaza Pizzeria & Bistro Maerua Park
Modern, trendy and popular, this new bistro is open daily from 17.00 till late, with the standard fare of pizzas at standard prices balanced by a cocktail menu.

O Portuga 151 Nelson Mandela Av; tel: 061 272900
This friendly and relaxed Portuguese/Angolan restaurant at Eros has a Mediterranean flavour. The wide-ranging menu is particularly strong on seafood, and you can expect huge portions, South African wines are fairly standard; Portuguese are very expensive. It's a popular place with a mixed clientele, but service can be very slow when the place is busy.
Costs: N$20–40 starter, N$45–60 main.

Saddle Steak Ranch Maerua Park
An informal restaurant with a children's play area, it offers steaks, burgers, pizzas, pasta dishes and some seafood, all at reasonable prices.

Sardinia Pizzeria 39 Independence Av; tel: 061 225600
This is a relaxed café/restaurant serving genuine Italian cuisine that's both popular and good value. Owned and run by the Solazzi family, it's worth a second glance, for behind the café-style front is a simple restaurant area – though you'll have to book to get a table here in the evenings. The wine list is reasonable, although Italian favourites come at a price. Closed Tuesdays.
Costs: pizzas and pasta dishes N$30–40.

Windhoek Brauhaus Mandume Ndemufayo (corner of Fidel Castro St/Peter Müller); tel: 061 226981
A large, reasonably central *brauhaus* with hearty German cuisine – and plenty of beer!
Costs: starters N$15–30, mains N$ 40–60.

Yang Tse Sam Nujoma Drive; tel: 061 234779.
A large, efficient restaurant, situated above Spar near the junction with Nelson Mandela Av, this prepares probably the best Chinese food in town. Equally well suited to a business

lunch or a relaxing dinner, it also has a takeaway service. Open daily till 23.00.
Costs: expect around N$100–130 for a complete meal with a few drinks.

Just outside Windhoek, towards the airport, is the **African Roots Restaurant**, well worth a trip in its own right or as part of an excursion to its adjacent zoo (see page 16). Also try **Amani** (see page 139).

ENTERTAINMENT AND NIGHTLIFE

Windhoek is not famous for its nightlife. Most visitors choose to go to a restaurant for a leisurely dinner and perhaps a drink, and then retire for an early start the next day. But if you feel livelier, there are cinemas and a few nightclubs. Friday is usually the best night, better than Saturday. Similarly, weekends at the start/end of the month, when people have just been paid, are busier than those in the middle.

Bars

Namibia doesn't have the 'pub' culture of the UK. In the poorer areas, especially in the old townships, there are some illegal *shebeens* (so-called *cuca-shops*), geared purely to serious drinking. It's worth noting that here, as in most traditional cultures in southern Africa, respectable women are rarely seen in bars.

If you're intent on finding somewhere relaxing to drink, then look no further than the hotel bars. All of the bigger hotels have bars, includng the relaxed beer garden at the **Thüringer Hof**, though places like the **Fürstenhof**, or smaller establishments, may restrict their use to residents only. One of the best places for a sundowner is the bar of the new Thule Hotel. See the section on *Hotels*, pages 119–25.

If you're thinking of somewhere with more life, then **Joe's Beerhouse** is your best bet, or – more central – **Dros** on Post Street Mall. Slightly further out, at Klein Windhoek, there's a popular bar known as **Explorers** above Luigi & the Fish. It is open every day – and there is also a PlayStation and video area for kids of all ages.

In the other direction, Maerua Park Mall off Centaurus Avenue is quite a hive of activity in the evenings, with many shops open till quite late, and several bars, cafés and informal restaurants where you can while away the evening. Among these, **Saddles** bar stands out as a comfortable place for a relaxed evening, while the more trendy can try the cocktails and chrome of the nearby **Plaza Pizzeria**. Just outside the mall, in a small wooden building, near the corner of Robert Mugabe Avenue and Jan Jonker Road, is **O'Hagan's Irish Pub**, which sometimes plays host to a less than liberal crowd.

Nightclubs

Windhoek normally has a couple of clubs running at any one time, some of them cosmopolitan and fun. As in most cities, clubs go in and out of fashion in a matter of months, so anything written here is probably already out of date. Ask for up-to-date local advice on what's currently good and safe. If you're thinking of a club in one of the townships, you should go with a local, or get a reliable taxi that will take you and collect you. At the time of writing, the best venues are:

Pentagon Entertainment Centre This large, popular venue with big-screen TV is in the southwest of Windhoek, near Keppler Street. Live bands play outside till late in the evening, and from 22.00 on Wednesday, Friday and Saturday nights it operates as a nightclub until the small hours. Fridays is particularly busy.

Ladidas, off Lazarett St, plays good music and is particularly popular with the local community.

M3 on Lazarett St attracts crowds from the Angolan and Portuguese communities.

Club Thriller in Katutura, tel: 061 216669, is an old favourite, which has operated since before independence. It now plays mostly rumba, with the odd guest band. Expect a thorough security search at the door, and thereafter a relaxed atmosphere. There's a cover charge of about N$25, and it's open almost till dawn. You should have a guide and/or taxi to come here.

Tower Bar Old Breweries Building, Tal St; tel: 081 249 8455. Next to the Namibia Craft Centre, the aptly named Tower Bar is located at the very top of the Old Breweries Building, so be prepared for a hike up some stairs. Live bands play on Wednesday, Friday and Saturday with opening times 18.00–02.00. Prices vary but expect to pay N$10–15.

Kiepies, close to the Pentagon, specialises in country music.

Although there are numerous so-called 'casinos' that flaunt row upon row of one-armed bandits, there are only two real **casinos**, one at the Windhoek Country Club, the other at the Kalahari Sands Hotel. Both are open until the small hours.

Cinemas

Windhoek's three-screen multiplex, the **Maerua Park Cinema** (tel: 061 248980 or 249267) in the Maerua Park Mall on Centaurus Road (where Robert Mugabe Avenue meets Jan Jonker), is set to expand to five screens during 2002. Although this is the capital's only cinema, prices are low compared with Europe or the US: tickets are N$22 (N$26 on Friday and Saturday), but on Wednesdays they're just N$11. Pensioners and under-12s pay N$14 before 18.00. Films shown are very much the latest Hollywood releases, and drinks and snacks are available too.

Theatres

Windhoek's most relaxed venue for the performing arts and live theatre is the **Warehouse Theatre** at 48 Tal Street, tel: 061 225059, fax: 061 220475. Housed in the Old Breweries Building, you'll find a modern mix of local and visiting artists, with music from jazz and funk to rock and roll. It's a safe place, with a relaxed atmosphere – trendy, arty and highly recommended. Cover charge varies with the band. Snacks are available, but eat elsewhere before you arrive, and there's a bar open until late. See the papers for the latest information.

There are several more formal options. Concerts, opera, theatre, ballet and contemporary dance are performed at the **National Theatre of Namibia**, on the corner of Robert Mugabe Avenue (12 John Meinert Street; tel: 061 237966; fax: 061 237968) and the **College of the Arts** auditorium (contact the principal at 41 Fidel Castro (Peter Müller) Street, PO Box 2963; tel: 061 225841; fax: 061 229007). The **Franco-Namibian Cultural Centre** (FNCC, 118 Robert Mugabe Av, PO Box 11622, Windhoek; tel: 061 222122; fax: 061 224927; email: fncc@mweb.com.na) is primarily a language centre, but has a small cinema and holds various concerts and cultural events, usually with a francophone bent. All three are worth checking to see if there are any productions whilst you're around. Information is advertised at the back of newspapers, especially the Friday *Windhoek Observer* which covers the weekends. Otherwise, ask at your hotel or pension for details.

For more unusual and experimental theatre, try the **Space Theatre** at the University of Namibia's Centre for Visual and Performing Arts at Pioneers Park, close to the Country Club (contact Ann Namupala on tel: 061 206 3802), or the small studio theatre at the **John Muafangejo Art Centre** (page 32).

Twice a month, **Theatre in the Park**, under the auspices of the College of the Arts, puts on live shows in Parliament Gardens. In addition, they have initiatives that range from children's theatre to the promotion of African films. Ad-hoc performances at lunchtime and weekends may also take place. Details are available at the Windhoek City information office.

SHOPPING

Shopping in Windhoek is easy and fun, and being able to park very near to the shops, and even on Independence Avenue, makes it all the easier if you've a car. However, if you want something specific, then phone around first – it's much quicker than scouring the city by foot or car.

Books and music

Imported books are generally expensive in Namibia, and even those published locally are subject to a heavy sales tax. But if you want something specific on Namibia, then often you'll get titles here which are difficult to find abroad. The best places to look are:

CNA Gustav Voigts Centre, 129 Independence Av. A large department store with a section on the latest titles. Very mainstream.

Der Bücherkeller Carl List House, Fidel Castro (formerly Peter Müller) St, PO Box 1074; tel: 061 231615; fax: 061 236164. Recently under new management, and now linked to Swakopmund Buchhandlung, this large shop has plans to broaden its stock considerably from the current selection, which is dominated by novels and coffee-table books, but with some Namibia-specific natural history books. Many of the books are in German, but there's a reasonable selection in English.

Onganda Y'Omambo Books On the north of Post Street Mall (tel: 061 235796; fax: 061 235278), this shop has a wide selection of books (new and secondhand), with a particularly good selection both on Namibian history and culture, and by Namibian authors.

RC Bookshop Bülow St (corner of Stubel St). This bookshop is in front of St Mary's Cathedral and sells mainly religious books. It also has a small coffee bar.

Uncle Spike's Book Exchange Garten St, on the corner of Tal St (tel: 061 226722). Has a more eclectic range. Good for swapping paperbacks.

Windhoek Book Den Frans Indongo Gardens, Bülow St, tel: 061 239976

Zum Bücherwurm 11 Kaiserkrone; tel/fax: 061 255885; email: bucherwurm@namibnet.com. Although this specialises in German books, there's a small but interesting selection of books on Namibia in English.

For a selection of African music CDs, try **Universal Sounds** next to Le Bistro (tel: 061 227037).

Cameras, film and optics

Most of the main brands of film are now available in Windhoek, including a range of slide film. Ideally, buy film from the specialists in Windhoek, rather than waiting until you're at a remote game lodge, whose limited film supplies are out-of-date, having been on a hot shelf for years. If you're looking for anything outside the 100/200/400 ISO range, or have very specific needs, then bring all your own supplies with you.

Similarly, most popular cameras can be found here, though they are often more expensive than they would be in Europe or the US. There are numerous places that will develop your snaps – often within the hour – or sell you a film, but Windhoek's best specialists are:

Nitzsche-Reiter at the front of the Sanlam Centre, on Independence Av; tel: 061 231116

Photo World 246 Independence Av, opposite Bülow St; tel: 061 223223

Gerhard Botha Independence Av, opposite Sardinia Restaurant; tel: 061 235551

Camping kit
To rent
It is easy to arrange to hire camping kit in Windhoek, provided that you can return it there at the end of your trip. Both the following companies have a comprehensive range, from tents and portable toilets to full 'kitchen packs', gaslights and jerry cans. They are best contacted at least a month in advance, and can then arrange for a pack incorporating what you want to be ready when you arrive. The minimum rental period is three days. They usually request a 50% deposit to confirm the order, with full payment due on collection of equipment.

Camping Hire Namibia 78 Malcolm Spence St, Olympia, PO Box 80029, Windhoek; tel: 061 251592 or tel/fax: 061 252995; email: camping@natron.net; web: http://natron.net/tour/camping/hired.html. Payment may be made either in cash or by credit card (Visa or MasterCard).

Adventure Camping Hire 20 Beethoven St, PO Box 20179, Windhoek; tel: 061 242478; fax: 061 223292; email: adventure@natron.net; web: www.natron.net/tour/adventure

To buy
If you need to buy camping kit in Namibia, then Windhoek has the best choice. Items from South Africa are widely available, but kit from Europe or the US is harder to find. The best places are:

Safari Den in the middle of Post Street Mall. In their plush shop they've binoculars, knives (including Swiss Army and Leatherman tools), and a useful range of tents, sleeping bags and other camping kit. Their main branch is at 20 Bessemer St (tel: 061 231934), in the southern industrial area.

Trappers Trading Co Wernhil Park, PO Box 9953; tel: 061 223136. Has an outlet on the mall, close to Safari Den. It's good for practical bush wear – cotton clothes are cheaper here than Europe, and the quality's reasonable though rarely excellent. Also has a small shop at the Windhoek Country Club Hotel (tel: 061 233749).

Safariland (Holtz) Gustav Voigts Centre, 129 Independence Av, PO Box 421, Windhoek; tel: 061 235941. Has a similar variety of safari and bush wear.

Cymot 60 Mandume Ndemufayo Av; tel: 061 234131; fax: 061 234921; email: greensport@cymot.com.na; web: www.cymot.com.na. Cymot get bigger every year, and their expanding range is the best around: everything from spare parts for cars (tel: 061 226242), to a good range of cycles and spares (tel: 061 236536), to tents and outdoor equipment.

Le Trip at the bottom of the Wernhil Park Centre; tel/fax: 061 233499. They have roof-tents and bicycle equipment, and also the invaluable polystyrene containers that cost only a few dollars, but keep canned drinks refreshingly cold.

Cape Union Mart Maerua Park Mall; tel: 061 220424. Has a wide range of camping equipment, safari clothes and shoes.

Crafts and curios
The Post Street Mall normally hosts one of the capital's largest craft and curio displays, as street traders set out their wares on blankets in front of the shops. Similarly, sellers of basketwork and carvings can usually be found on Fidel Castro (Peter Müller) St near the Grab-a-phone kiosk, which is almost opposite the Kalahari Sands on Independence Avenue. There is also a wide variety of commercial craft shops in the centre of town, all aiming at tourists and often presenting similar crafts in a more upmarket setting, with higher prices.

Namibia Craft Centre 40 Tal St (next to the Warehouse Theatre); tel: 061 242 2222; fax: 061 221 1273

Well worth a visit. This houses the Omba Gallery, with regular exhibitions of Namibian and other African art, a café and a number of stalls selling different arts and crafts including paintings, sculptures, designs in copper, hand-painted fabrics, jewellery and much else. Many of the exhibitors are members of NACOBTA – the Namibia Community-Based Tourism Association – that was founded in 1995 with the aim of improving living standards among Namibia's rural communities. Members welcome visitors to their sites without advance notice. For details, contact them direct (PO Box 86099, Windhoek; tel: 061 250558; fax: 061 222647; email: nacobta@iafrica.com; web: www.nacobta.com.na). *Open: Mon–Fri 09.00–17.30, Sat 09.00–13.30.*

Master Weavers Wernhil Park shopping centre, PO Box 21886; tel: 061 221895 Offer a fine variety of handmade rugs for sale, though many visitors buy these direct from the factories in Swakopmund or Lüderitz.

Penduka Craft Co-operative tel: 061 257210; email: penduka@namib.com. Out beyond Katutura, overlooking Goreangab Dam, this co-operative employs local women in a village setting to produce a range of crafts, including textiles and baskets. To get there, follow Independence Avenue north through Katutura, cross over Otjomuise, then bear left on to Green Mountain Dam. The centre is down a dirt track to the left. Alternatively, join one of the half-day excursions that cover this area (see page 159). Visitors may watch crafts being made, and there is a shop on site.

Gemstones

Given the incredible minerals and precious stones that are mined in Namibia, it's a wonder that there aren't better gemstones for sale as curios. Sadly many of the agates and semi-precious stones seen in curio shops on Independence Avenue are imported from as far as Brazil.

The exception to the rule is **House of Gems** (tel: 061 225202; fax: 061 228915). Tucked away at 131 Stübel Street, near John Meinert Street, it is run by Sid Peters (one of the country's leading gemmologists). It is a real collector's place, packed with original bits and pieces. Even if you're not buying, it is worth visiting. Some of the stones are from Sid's own tourmaline mines (claimed to produce the world's best tourmaline). Here you can see them sorted, cut, faceted and polished on the premises.

Leatherwork

Windhoek is a good place to buy leatherwork. You'll see lots of ostrich, game and karakul leathers. Don't expect any give-aways, but if you know what you want then there are good deals to be had. The standard varies greatly; you will find some local work aiming at export markets of a very high standard, while other products are not so good. As with anywhere, shop around. The highest-quality sources are in the centre of town, like **Pelzhaus** on Independence Avenue, over the road from the main post office, and **Nakara** for **Na**mibian **kara**kul leathers, near Gathemann Restaurant on Independence Avenue. (Previously this was *Swakara*, for *South West African kara*kul leathers!)

It's also worth visiting the **Okapuka Tannery**, about 20km north of Windhoek. To find it, take the main road to Okahandja, then turn off at the signs for Elisenheim, and follow this road for about 6km.

Food and drink

The age of the supermarket has certainly reached Namibia, though there remain some good small food shops around town. If you are stocking up for a long trip into the bush, then seek out the best large stores. Most central is **Checkers** in the basement of the Gustav Voigts centre on Independence Avenue – the car park is behind the Kalahari Sands Hotel (see page 122). A little further away is **Shoprite** on Independence Avenue itself, almost opposite the information centre. Further out of town, but most convenient for drivers, are the large supermarket in the new **Game** shopping centre at the junction of Bismarck and Hochland Roads, and Checkers at **Maerua Park Mall**. For those staying at Klein Windhoek, the most convenient store is probably OK Foods in the **Hidas Centre**, at the junction of Sam Nujoma and Nelson Mandela.

Pharmacies

There are numerous pharmacies throughout the city, many of them open seven days a week, and most with a range of goods and drugs that is equal to anything in western Europe or the USA. The pharmacy in the Erkrathus Building on Independence Avenue is on 24-hour call, tel: 081 129 4422.

PRACTICALITIES
Airlines

Most of the airlines have town offices somewhere around the Sanlam Centre, near the Kalahari Sands Hotel. **Air Namibia** (PO Box 731, Windhoek; web: www.airnamibia.com.na) is at the front, on Independence Avenue. Although this is convenient for personal visits, it is better to contact them at the airports if you wish to reconfirm tickets or book flight seats:

General reservations Tel: 061 299 6333
Eros International Airport Tel: 061 299 6500
Hosea Kutako International Airport Tel: 061 299 6600 (note: this is the main airport for international arrivals and departures)
Town office Tel: 061 299 6444

British Airways Sanlam Centre, 154 Independence Av; tel: 061 248528; fax: 061 245529
Comair, the South African regional carrier is now owned by **British Airways** and shares the same premises in the Sanlam Centre; tel: 061 226662; fax: 061 227923
Lufthansa Sanlam Centre, 154 Independence Av; tel: 061 226662; fax: 061 227923; email: wdhgg@dlh.de
LTU 'Germany's other airline', Kuehne & Nagel Bldg, 5 Mac Adam St; tel: 061 238205; fax: 061 222350
South African Airways (SAA) is just north of Air Namibia's office, in Carl List House, Independence Av; tel: 061 273340; fax: 061 235200
TAAG Angolan Airlines are near SAA, in the Sanlam Centre, Independence Av; tel: 061 226625/236266; fax: 061 227724

Banks and money

The centre of town has all the major banks in the country. These are generally very efficient and certainly quicker than the smaller branches in the suburbs, or outside the capital. If you need anything complex, like an international money transfer, go to the largest branch possible. In any event, remember to take your passport with you.

Changing money

Rates for exchanging money are the same at all banks, though expect to get considerably lower rates from a hotel. Outside of normal banking hours, the bureau de change at the Commercial Bank of Namibia on Independence Avenue, opposite the Grab-a-phone kiosk, is open Saturday and Sunday, 08.00–19.00 (and also accepts American Express cards), while the bureau de change at the airport is opened for incoming flights.

Banks

The city's main branches of Namibia's largest four banks are all very near the centre:

First National Bank PO Box 195, 209 Independence Av; tel: 061 299 2101; fax: 061 225994; email: info@fnbnamibia.com.na; web: www.fnbnamibia.com.na. This is in the centre of Independence Av, opposite the post office. It has close links to Barclays in the UK, and is best for Visa transactions.

Standard Bank PO Box 3327, Mutual Platz, Post Street Mall, tel: 061 294 2283; fax: 061 294 2583; email: info@standardbank.com.na; web: www.standardbank.com.na. If you're using MasterCard rather than Visa, then Standard is probably the best bank to deal with.

Bank of Windhoek PO Box 15, 262 Independence Av; tel: 061 291267; fax: 061 299 1287; email: info@bankwindhoek.com.na; web: www.bankwindhoek.com.na

Commercial Bank of Namibia PO Box 1, 12 Bülow St; tel: 061 295 2121; fax: 061 295 2120; email: EsmarieB@nedcor.com; web: www.c-bank.com.na

American Express

The American Express agents in Namibia are located in the Bank Windhoek Building on Kaiserkrone, just off Post Street Mall (tel: 061 249517; fax 061 229654). There is also an American Express office at Hosea Kutako International Airport.

If you have either an American Express card or AMEX travellers' cheques, you can have your mail sent here. Mail addresses should be formated: McINTYRE, Chris, c/o American Express Client Mail, at the above address.

Thomas Cook

The local office is at Namibia Bureau de Change in the Levison Arcade just off Independence Avenue (tel: 061 229667).

Hospitals

In an emergency, phone **211111** in Windhoek, which will put you through to an operator who can reach the ambulance or fire services. In case of difficulty getting through, phone 1199. If you have a cellphone, then call 112. For an ambulance from the private MediRescue, call 061 230505, radiopage: 252222, or cell: 081 124 0012. The police can be reached on 10111.

The city's main public hospital is Windhoek Central Hospital, on Florence Nightingale St; tel: 061 222886. This is good, but with huge demands from the local population, it can become very busy. However, if you've a serious medical condition then it's better to use your medical travel insurance, and contact one of the private hospitals (each of which is open 24 hours and has an accident and emergency department):

Medi Clinic Heliodoor St, Eros Park; tel: 061 222687. Windhoek's most expensive clinic, reached via Nelson Mandela Drive and then Omuramba Road.
Catholic Mission Hospital 92 Stübel St (between Bülow St and John Meinert St); tel: 061 237237. Much more central, but not quite so plush.
Rhino Park Private Hospital on Hosea Kutako Drive; tel: 061 225434. This aims to provide affordable healthcare, but has no casualty department.

If you've a serious problem outside Windhoek, then contact **MediRescue (MRI)** (see page 70).

Post and communications

The **main post office** is in the centre of Independence Avenue, between Daniel Munamava and Zoo Park. It has an efficient post restante facility, and a place to make international phone calls or send faxes, plus access to the internet. It's cheap and easy to send packages overseas from here. The office is open Mon–Fri 08.00–16.30, and Sat 08.30–12.00. There's a machine for dispensing phonecards just outside the main office, though it accepts only notes, not coins.

The Independence Avenue landmark, **Grab-a-phone** (tel: 061 220708; fax: 061 220820), on the corner of Fidel Castro (Peter Müller) Street, has recently reopened following renovation; it's a private (more expensive) office where you can also make calls or send faxes.

The area telephone code for Windhoek is 061; don't use it when phoning within the city.

Internet facilities

The proliferation of internet facilities worldwide is not lost on Windhoek. In addition to dedicated internet cafés such as those listed below, many backpackers' hostels and hotels allow internet access to their guests.

Communication Service Centre & Internet Café Independence Av N$15 for ½ hour. Open Mon–Sat 08.00–20.00, Sun 09.00–21.00.

Fabulous Telecom Services Opposite Le Bistro in Post Street Mall. N$10 for 15 minutes, or N$15 for half an hour. Open Mon–Fri 08.30–19.00, Sat 09.00–16.00.

Post office Internet facilities in the main post office on Independence Av cost N$11 for half an hour. Opening hours are as for the post office itself.

Tourist Junction 40 Fidel Castro (Peter Müller) St; tel: 061 231246; fax: 061 231703; email: info.ritztours@galileosa.co.za. N$15 for ½ hour, or N$25 for an hour. Open Mon–Sat 08.00–17.00.

Cell phones

Cell phones may be rented for your trip from a number of locations, including Windhoek International Airport, and Walvis Bay Airport. In Windhoek, contact Mutual Platz Shop 13; tel: 061 245225/6/7; fax: 061 245288; email: gsmrent@iafrica.com.na, or drop in to Tourist Junction (see above).

Visas and immigration

For visa extensions or anything to do with immigration, you need the Department of Civic Affairs, within the Ministry of Home Affairs. This is currently in the Cohen Building, on the corner of Kasino Street and Independence Avenue, tel: 061 292 9111. Office opens Mon–Fri 08.00–13.00.

Foreign embassies and high commissions

Namibia's diplomatic missions abroad can be found on page 55. Foreign missions in Namibia, all of which are in Windhoek, include:

Angolan Embassy Angola House, 3 Dr Agostinho Neto St, P Bag 12020, Windhoek; tel: 061 227535; fax: 061 221498; telex: 897 WK

Belgian Consulate Stewart Scott Bldg, Ground floor, 36 Franciska St, PO Box 22584, Windhoek; tel: 061 238295; fax: 061 236531

Botswana Embassy 101 Nelson Mandela Av, PO Box 20359, Windhoek; tel: 061 221941/7; fax: 061 236034; telex: 894 WK

Brazilian Embassy 52 Bismarck St, Windhoek West, PO Box 24166, Windhoek; tel: 061 237368; fax: 061 233389; telex: 498 BREMB WK

British High Commission 116 Robert Mugabe Av, PO Box 22202; tel: 061 223022; fax: 061 228895

Canadian Consulate 8th floor Metje-Behnsen Bldg, Independence Av, PO Box 239, Windhoek; tel: 061 227417; fax: 061 222859

Cuban Embassy 31 Omuramba Rd, Eros, PO Box 23866, Windhoek; tel: 061 227072; fax: 061 231584; telex: 406 WK
Egyptian Embassy 10 Berg St, PO Box 11853, Windhoek; tel: 061 221501/2
Danish Consulate 7 Best St, PO Box 24236, Windhoek; tel: 061 237565; fax: 061 237614
French Embassy 1 Goethe St, PO Box 20484, Windhoek; tel: 061 229021; fax: 061 231436; telex: 715 WK
German Embassy 6th Floor, Sanlam Centre, 154 Independence Av, PO Box 231, Windhoek; tel: 061 223100; fax: 061 22 2981; telex: 482 WK
Ghanaian High Commission 5 Nelson Mandela Av, Klein Windhoek, PO Box 24165; tel: 061 220536; fax: 061 221343
Italian Embassy corner Anna and Gervers St, PO Box 24065, Windhoek; tel: 061 228602; fax: 061 229860; telex: 620 WK
Kenyan High Commission 5th floor, Kenya House, Robert Mugabe Av, PO Box 2889, Windhoek; tel: 061 226836
Royal Netherlands Embassy 2A Cron St, PO Box 564, Windhoek; tel: 061 223733; fax: 061 223732; telex: 412 WK
Nigerian High Commission 4 Omuramba Rd, Eros, PO Box 23547, Windhoek; tel: 061 232103; fax: 061 221639
Norwegian Consulate 10th Floor, Sanlam Centre, 154 Independence Av, PO Box 9936, Windhoek; tel: 061 258278; fax: 061 230528
Portuguese Embassy 24 Robert Mugabe Av, PO Box 443, Windhoek; tel: 061 228736; fax: 061 237929; telex: 409 WK
South African Embassy RSA House, corner Jan Jonker and Nelson Mandela Av, PO Box 23100, Windhoek; tel: 061 501 7111; fax: 061 224140
Spanish Embassy 58 Bismarck St, PO Box 21811, Windhoek; tel: 061 223066; fax: 061 223046; telex: 672 ESNAM WK
Swedish Embassy 9th Floor, Sanlam Centre, 154 Independence Av, PO Box 23087, Windhoek; tel: 061 222905; fax: 061 222774; telex: 463 WK
Swiss Consulate 2nd Floor, Southern Life Tower, Post Street Mall, PO Box 22287, Windhoek; tel: 061 222359; fax: 061 227922; telex: 869 WK
USA Embassy 14 Lossen St, P Bag 12029, Windhoek; tel: 061 221601; fax: 061 229792
Zambian High Commission 27 Sam Nujoma Drive, PO Box 22882, Windhoek; tel: 061 237610; fax: 061 228162
Zimbabwean High Commission corner Independence Av and Grimm St, PO Box 23056, Windhoek; tel: 061 228134; fax: 061 226859; telex: 886 WK

WHAT TO SEE AND DO

Although Windhoek isn't the planet's liveliest capital, there are some beautiful old buildings, a couple of museums and art galleries, and some tours worth taking.

Windhoek's historical buildings

Most of Windhoek's historical buildings date from around the turn of the century, and are close to the centre of town. Walking is the obvious way to see these. Starting in the Post Street Mall, here is one suggested sequence, taking about two or three hours:

Gibeon meteorites On the middle of the mall is a sculpture, incorporating 33 meteorites that fell around Gibeon, some 300km south of Windhoek. These were part of what is thought to have been the world's heaviest shower of meteorites, which occurred around 600 million years ago. About 77 meteorites, with a total mass of 21 tons, have been recovered so far; many of these are in museums around the globe.

Clocktower At the junction of the Mall with Independence Avenue is a replica of the clocktower that was once on the old Deutsche-Afrikabank. The original was constructed in 1908.

Now turn southeast, towards Christus Kirche, and cross Independence Avenue into Zoo Park. From here, you can get a good view of three fine buildings on the west side of Independence Avenue. They were designed by Willi Sander, a German who designed many of Windhoek's older landmarks. The right one of the three, **Erkrathus Building**, was built in 1910: a business downstairs, and a place to live upstairs. **Gathemann House**, the building in the middle, was designed for Heinrich Gathemann, who was then the mayor of Klein Windhoek, and built in 1913 to a basically European design, complete with a steep roof to prevent any accumulation of snow! Again, it originally had living quarters above the business. **Kronprinz Hotel** was designed and built by Willi Sander in the years 1901 and 1902. It was extended in 1909, and refurbished and extended in 1920. It is now overshadowed by the Sanlam building, but a plan has been made to modernise the shops (one of which is Nakara, see page 148) whilst preserving the façades.

Continuing into **Zoo Park**, on green lawns under its palm trees (among the Christmas decorations!) you will find two features of note:

Elephant Column A sculptured column over a metre high marks the place where primitive tools and elephant remains, dated to about 5,000 years ago, were found. Scenes of an imagined elephant hunt kill are depicted in bas-relief (by Namibian sculptress Dörte Berner), and a fossilised elephant skull tops the column.

War memorial On the south side of the elephant column is this memorial, about a century old, crowned by an eagle, and dedicated to German soldiers killed whilst fighting the Nama people led by Hendrik Witbooi. As yet there is no memorial for the Nama people, led by Hendrik Witbooi. (Recently the Namas killed have been remembered as part of the general monument at Heroes' Acre; see page 164.) Now head south on Independence Avenue a short way until your first left turn, up Fidel Castro (Peter Müller) Street. On the other side of the corner are Windhoek's best street-sellers for baskets, and the Grab-a-phone/bus/taxi terminus. On the left, on the far corner of Lüderitz Street, you will see:

Hauptkasse Used as the house of the Receiver of Revenue, as well as officers' quarters and even a hostel, it is now the Directorate of Extension Services, within the Ministry of Agriculture.

Ludvig Van Estorff House Opposite the Hauptkasse, on the south side of Fidel Castro (Peter Müller) Street, this was simply built in 1891, as a canteen, and is named after a commander of the Schutztruppe who lived here in 1902–10. It is now the National Reference Library.

Christus Kirche In a commanding position, now on its own roundabout, this 'fairytale' Evangelical Lutheran Church is Windhoek's most famous building. It was designed, by Gottlieb Redecker, in art nouveau and neo-Gothic styles, and built between 1907 and 1910 of local sandstone. Kaiser Wilhelm II donated the stained-glass windows; his wife, Augusta, gave the altar bible. Originally this church commemorated the peace at the end of various wars between the German colonists and the indigenous people of Namibia, and inside are plaques dedicated to the German soldiers who were killed. (As yet, there's no mention of the losses of the indigenous people...) The church is normally open 07.30–14.30 during the week. However, if it is closed and you wish to see inside, the key can be borrowed during office hours from the church offices, just down the hill at 12 Fidel Castro (Peter Müller) Street.

Kaiserliche Realschule On the west side of Robert Mugabe Avenue, just near Christus Kirche, this is now part of the National Museum. However, it was built in 1907–8 as a school, and became Windhoek's first German high school.

Walking further south along Robert Mugabe Avenue, you'll see the new Bank of Namibia building. On your right, just before crossing Sam Nujoma Drive, is:

Office of the Ombudsman Built as a dwelling for the chief justice and his first clerk, this was originally erected in 1906–7, and has much decorative work typical of the German 'Putz' style of architecture. The original stables are now a garage and outbuilding.

Now turn around and walk back towards Christus Kirche, on the right (east) side of Robert Mugabe Avenue.

Alte Feste The large building on the right is the old fort, built by the first Schutztruppe when they arrived here around 1890. It is strategically positioned, overlooking the valley, though its battlements were never seriously besieged. A plaque on the front maintains the colonial view that it was built to 'preserve peace and order' between the local warring tribes – which is as poor a justification for colonialism as any. Inside is now the main historical section of the National Museum (see page 156 for details).

The **Equestrian Statue** To the left of the Alte Feste is a large statue of a mounted soldier, commemorating the German soldiers killed during the wars to subdue the Nama and Herero groups, around 1903–7. (Here, too, there's no mention of the Nama or Herero people who died.)

Parliament (formerly Tintenpalast) Once back at the Christus Kirche, turning right (east) leads you to what were originally the administrative offices of the German colonial government. The building became known as the Tintenpalast, or Ink Palace, for the amount of bureaucracy that went on there, and has housed successive governments since around 1912. The Germans occupied it for only about a year, before losing the colony to South Africa after World War I. Now this beautiful double-storey building is home to Namibia's parliament. When the assembly is not in session, you can book a place on a 45-minute tour by phoning 061 288 2627, which integrates well into this short walking tour, perhaps 1½–2 hours after the start.

State House As you continue north along Robert Mugabe Avenue, on the left is the president's official residence. This was built as recently as 1958, on the site of the old German governor's residence. Until 1990, this was used by South Africa's administrator general.

It is now a short walk left, down Daniel Munamava Street, back to join Independence Avenue by the main post office.

Museums, galleries and libraries
Windhoek has, perhaps after Swakopmund, some of the country's best museums, galleries and libraries, though even these state collections are limited. The South African regime, which controlled the museums until 1990, had a polarised view of the country's history, understandably, and undesirably, slanted towards their involvement in it. It remains difficult to find out much of the history of Namibia's indigenous peoples. That said, the museums are gradually redressing the balance.

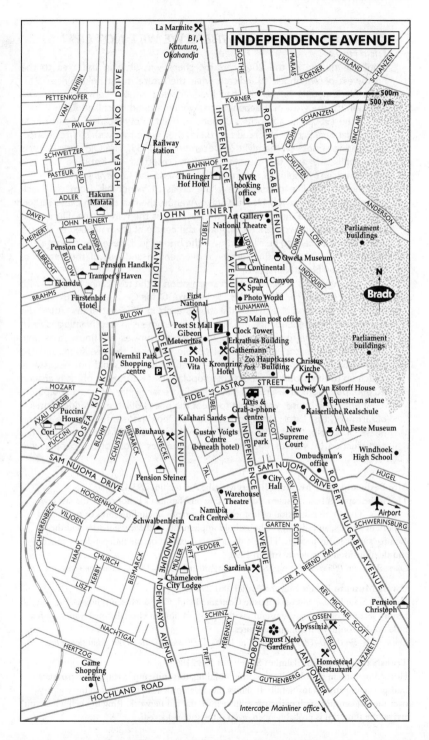

KATUTURA: 'THE PLACE WHERE WE WILL NOT LIVE'

Tricia Hayne

Until the middle of the 20th century, there was little in the area to the northwest of Windhoek to indicate what the future might hold. Since 1913, most black people in the city had lived in what is now known as the Old Location, to the west of Independence Avenue around Hochland Park. When, during the 1950s, the authorities decided to build a new location as part of the Union National Party's enforced apartheid, they were met with stiff resistance, culminating in riots on the night of December 10 1959. The Old Location was duly abolished, and the people forcefully resettled to Katutura and the neighbouring townships of Khomasdal, Wanaheda and Okuryangava.

Although the line dividing the white areas of Windhoek from the black townships was effectively Hosea Kutako Avenue, the real division came earlier, at the point where Independence Avenue crosses the railway line. During the years of apartheid, workers heading into the centre of town needed to show a *kopf* (or 'head') card to be allowed over the bridge; in the evening, the gate was closed at 18.00, preventing further movement in and out of the centre of Windhoek by black Namibians.

In the early days, there was strict segregation in the townships by tribe, with houses labelled D for Damara, H for Herero, O for Owambo etc. Even now, house numbers indicate tribal affiliations, each in different areas. After the declaration of independence in 1990, the government invited Namibians from the north to come to the capital to work, with promises of a house, a garden, a job and even a car. Thousands of people accepted the invitation, and the population of the townships swelled – even if the reality did not necessarily match up to the promises. Today, the population of Katutura is officially around 40,000, but unofficial estimates place that figure far higher, at up to 200,000.

At first, long houses were built to meet the needs of large, extended families of farmworkers. Later, small corrugated-iron 'box' houses formed the second phase of development. The third phase, with the best of intentions, was the construction by various NGOs of modern houses. Most of the people who

Alte Feste and State Museum Robert Mugabe Av; tel: 061 293 4362
This is the capital's best museum, concentrating on Namibia's history over the last few centuries. There's an exhibition of historical photographs, including shots of many important leaders, and displays of household implements of the missionaries and the country's indigenous peoples. There's also a special exhibit on the independence process, and the transition to majority rule in 1990.
Open: Mon–Fri 09.00–18.00, Sat, Sun 10.00–12.30 and 15.00–18.00. Admission is free.

Owela Museum Robert Mugabe Av; tel: 061 293 4358
North of State House, almost opposite Conradie Road, Owela Museum houses the natural history sections of the State Museum, with a good section on cheetah conservation, and a little on the country's traditional cultures.
Open: Mon–Fri 09.00–18.00, Sat and Sun 10.00–12.30 and 15.00–18.00. Admission is free.

TransNamib Museum Bahnhof St; tel: 061 298 2186
Housed upstairs in the old railway station building, this museum is run by the parastatal transport company, TransNamib. It shows the development of transport in the country over the last century, with particular emphasis on the rail network. Ring the bell when you arrive; the museum is probably open, even if the gate is locked!

moved into the area came from traditional kraals in the north of the country, and were ill-equipped to cope with the challenges of urban life. Where there were small houses, families of eight to 12 people would move in, and Western-style kitchens were left empty as the tradition of cooking in the open air was continued in the small yards.

It would be unsurprising if the streets of Katutura were strewn with litter, but by and large the reverse is the case. It is striking that, in spite of the sprawling nature of the township, and the density of housing, it is both orderly and clean. Water pipes are stationed every 300–400m. In some areas, bougainvillaea lines some of the streets, and there are occasional sunflowers in the gardens. Maize, too, is grown, though this is almost exclusively for *tombo* – maize beer – not to eat. There is little in the way of cultivation of food, and malnutrition is rife.

Perhaps unexpectedly, there is no shortage of schools. These are government run, but most were built by donations from overseas charities and governments. Although, in theory, education is compulsory, the reality is not so straightforward. Schooling alone costs around N$15 a term, and then each child must have a uniform. As wages in the black community are significantly lower than for white workers, many families cannot afford to provide this uniform, and their children remain on the streets. For the post-school generation, there are a number of training opportunities provided by the church, hospitals and schools, as well as the government, in fields that include nursing and waitressing.

For the visitor, streets in the township are very confusing. and it's easy for an outsider to get lost, so it's best to stick to the main thoroughfares. Nevertheless, it's safe enough here in the daytime, though at night it is not advisable to come without a guide. There are two markets in Katutura: Soweto on Independence Avenue, and Kakukaze Mungunda Market on Mungunda Street. To find out about opening times for the markets, contact the Windhoek City information office in Post Street Mall, or phone 061 290 2565. Beyond the townships is the Penduka Cooperative (see page 148).

Open: Mon–Fri 08.00–13.00 and 14.00–17.00. Admission is N$5 per adult. Closed weekends and public holidays.

National Art Gallery of Namibia Robert Mugabe Av and John Meinert St; tel: 061 231160; fax: 061 240930
Namibia's small National Gallery (also see page 157) has a permanent exhibition of Namibian art – some historical, some contemporary – and also hosts a variety of visiting exhibitions. It's well worth checking out.
Open: Tue–Fri 09.00–17.00, Sat 09.00–14.00. Closed Sun, Mon. Admission is free.

National Reference Library 11 Peter Müller (Fidel Castro) St; tel: 061 293 4203
Housed in Ludvig Van Estorff House (see page 157), this is really of more relevance to serious researchers than casual visitors.

Bushman Art Gallery Erkraths Bldg, 187 Independence Av; tel: 061 228828/229131; email: bushmanart@iafrica.com.na; web:www.bushmanart.com
At the front this is purely a curio/gift shop, with a good selection of books on Namibia (in German and English), as well as T-shirts, jewellery, gemstones, cards, hats, and even socks. Behind, through the shop, a museum area displays Bushman tools, clothing etc,

TUYAKULA – PEOPLE HELP PEOPLE
Tricia Hayne

With the increasing incidence of AIDS among the local population, and poor standards of hygiene, there is a parallel increase in TB, which strikes as the immune system is lowered by HIV. And the problem is growing.

Lack of education means that there is almost total incomprehension about AIDS – put simply, it can't be seen, so it can't be there. This, in turn, means that many people are totally unaware that they have contracted the disease. When, on top of this, TB is diagnosed, and medication is handed out, many patients will take all the tablets at once without understanding the implications for their health. Inevitably, complications set in, and many patients have died.

When Petra Illing first arrived, from Germany by way of Bosnia and Zaire, to work with a small medical organisation known as Tuberculosis Wurtzburg, she was confronted with a tuberculosis problem of epidemic proportions. In the ensuing seven years, she has put into practice her belief that 'people help people' – *tuyakula* – creating a scheme whereby TB patients are treated holistically. In essence, her aim was to offer patients a way out of the cycle of disease and poverty through a series of garden projects, which would then work outwards for the good of the community as a whole.

With the opening of the first of her 'garden clinics' in 1996, the *mosumbo* – 'white lady' – was deemed to be crazy. At that stage, standards of hygiene were so low that patients would simply defaecate in the grounds of the clinic. Today, though, those grounds are transformed into neat rows of fruit, herbs and vegetables, such as cabbages, spinach, onions, lemons, oranges, grapefruits, grapes and tomatoes. Each is tended by a former TB patient, who is employed in return for both remuneration and fresh fruit and vegetables.

There are now seven garden clinics in the Tuyakula scheme in Windhoek, each with its own garden and children's play area, and there is sufficient food grown for everyone concerned with the projects. Directly related to the garden projects, three of the clinics now run feeding programmes for about 40 people at any one time. Each morning, at 08.30, patients on the feeding programme receive breakfast of bread, jam and butter, followed by their medication. At lunch, the process is repeated.

On average, TB patients weigh around 40–55kg when they first start attending hospital, and many can hardly stand. With good food and proper medication, they usually gain some 5–6kg in the following months. Most

various African masks and Karakul carpets. Many items on display are for sale, except the Bushman tools.

Open: Mon–Sat 09.00–17.30, Sun 10.00–13.00. Admission is free.

Other options
City tours

Various small agencies offer tours of the city, some walking, some by vehicle. Often an afternoon tour will be combined with driving out on to some of the mountains overlooking Windhoek for a sundowner drink. It is also possible to visit the township of Katutura as part of a Windhoek city tour, though these aren't as popular as Jo'burg's tours of Soweto. The companies running day trips seem to change often. Current favourites are:

attend for about six months, first as inpatients in the TB hospital, next to the main Katutura hospital, then as outpatients at one of the city's clinics. Each of these clinics caters for up to 500 patients a day, with every conceivable ailment and complaint. It is here that TB patients become involved with the garden clinics.

In addition to those working in the gardens, other former patients are employed producing embroidery for sale locally – have a look at the cushions on sale in Windhoek's Zoo Café for examples of their work. At present, there are ten gardeners, a further ten people working in the kitchen, and 12 involved with needlework projects, each working for about six months under the supervision of other ex-patients who are employed on a permanent basis.

With an improvement in health and a greater understanding of the importance of a good diet, former patients go out into the community to spread the news. Many have started to cultivate the land around their houses with food crops, and sometimes their neighbours follow suit, creating pockets of neatly tended vegetable plots.

The seven clinics receive funding to the tune of N$130,000 per year from the German-based Johanniter International, while a further N$4.5 million has been allocated for the construction and maintenance of three similar projects in Rundu. Yet all is not as rosy at it might appear. Security guards patrol the clinics and theft is a problem – of food, soap, drugs, toilet paper, almost anything. The unions do not always see eye to eye with their boss on this, since theft is not necessarily considered the crime that it would be in the West. But Petra is adamant that money is not an issue for her existing clinics; if there were more, she would use it to establish new feeding programmes.

As well as TB and AIDS, alcohol abuse is a real problem and teenage pregnancy is rife, a result of lack of education, the breakdown of traditional family units, and even boredom. Gradually, sex education is being introduced into schools, taking over the role traditionally held by older women in the kraals.

With her common-sense approach, Petra is convinced that the key to improving the lives of the people of Katutura is in their hands. She would like to see more residents become guides, encouraging visitors into the townships and breaking the cycle of fear and apathy that currently exists. It remains to be seen if her vision will prove to be a reality.

Petra Illing may be contacted at maroilling@yahoo.de

Face to Face Tours PO Box 22389, Windhoek; tel: 061 265446
A three-hour trip at N$150 per person covers the centre of Windhoek and out to Katutura, including stops at the markets, local homes to see how food is prepared, a shabeen, and the co-operative at Penduka.

Gourmet Tours PO Box 2148, Windhoek; tel/fax: 061 231281
Half-day city tours in the morning or evening take in the centre of Windhoek, a viewpoint looking over the city, a drive through Katutura and coffee at the Heinitzburg Hotel. Tours cost N$180 per person. Other half-day options include trips to the leopards at Dürstenbrook (N$310 per person), Daan Viljoen (N$210), Okapuka (N$290), and Auas Game Lodge (N$310). Full-day tours feature Midgard (N$450) and Oropoko (N$480), while longer tours to Gamsberg and Etosha are available on request.

Pack Safari 109 Papageienweg, PO Box 29, Windhoek; tel: 061 231603, cell: 081 124 6956; fax: 061 247755; email: info@packsafari.com; web: www.packsafari.com
Pack Safari runs a range of day tours, including a 3-hour city tour (N$240 per person) taking in historical buildings, the affluent suburb of Ludwigsdorf and the less affluent Katutura, where a development project is visited. Other options include a half-day visit to Daan Viljoen (N$280), a full day to Rehoboth and Oanab Dam (N$690), the Gamsberg Trail (N$1,320), or a visit to the leopards of Dürsternbrook (N$590). Rates are per person, with a minimum of two people per trip normally required. Pack Safari also offers scheduled and guided tours through the region.

If you prefer to drive yourself, and want to head off the beaten track, it is worth contacting the Windhoek tourist information office in Post Street Mall (see page 118), who can arrange for a local community guide to accompany you. Guides are accredited by the City of Windhoek,

SPORTS FACILITIES
Gym
Virgin Active On Centaurus Rd, just off Jan Jonker, and by Maerua Mall, this has a big indoor pool, plus a large gym with lots of training machines, an aerobics studio, several glass-backed squash courts, and steam and sauna rooms. Day membership as a casual visitor is N$50, so if you need to relax and have a shower in town before travelling, this is the perfect place. The club is open Mon–Thu 05.00–21.00, and Fri/Sat 07.00–20.00. Note that the car park is not patrolled, so don't leave your luggage unattended in a car outside.
Nucleus Centrally located in the Old Brewery Building on Tal St, by the Namibia Craft Centre, this fitness gym has been operating for 12 years. The gym is at the top of several flights of stairs (getting there is a workout in itself), and offers full changing facilities, basic running/cycling machines and general fitness apparatus. It is open Mon–Thu 06.00–21.00, Fri 06.00–20.00, Sat/Sun 09.00–13.00, 16.00–19.00. The daily rate is N$50, monthly N$120.

Swimming
Immediately next to Virgin Active is the stunning open-air Olympic-size 50m swimming pool and a professional diving pool, which is run by the municipality. The latter was closed for refurbishment in 2002, with no date available for its re-opening. Surrounded by grassed areas with shaded picnic benches, this is a great place to unwind. Officially it's open Nov–Mar, Mon–Fri 10.00–20.00, and weekends 10.00–18.00; Aug–Nov and Apr/May, 10.00–18.00; closed Jun/Jul. In reality, it usually closes every year at the end of April, and reopens Sept 1. Costs: under 16s N$0.50, adults N$1.50 (N$1.50/3 weekends and holidays).

Golf
Windhoek Golf and Country Club PO Box 2122, Windhoek; tel: 061 205 5223; fax: 061 205 5220; email: wcc@iafrica.com.na; web: www.wccgolf.com.na
This 18-hole golf course next to Windhoek Country Club Hotel offers the usual facilities you might expect from such an upmarket club: a resident professional, motorised caddies, a driving range and a well-equipped pro-shop. The clubhouse has a bar area and a restaurant, the Eagle's Nest (tel: 061 205511), which is open Wed–Sun. Next door is the Windhoek Bowls Club, which has its own clubhouse, bar and swimming pool.
Golf rates for visitors: non-affiliated N$90 (9 holes), N$180 (18 holes); hotel residents N$70 (9 holes), N$140 (18 holes); driving range N$15 (30 balls), N$30 (60 balls).

Horseriding
Guided rides into the mountains around Windhoek, including breakfast and sundowner rides, may be taken with **Auas View Trails** (PO Box 80312,

Windhoek; tel: 061 223865; fax: 061 214901). Costs are from N$160 per person for an hour and a half, to N$280 for three hours. Transfers from Windhoek cost N$50 per trip. Hard hats are available on request. There are also several game farms that offer horseriding to guests.

EXCURSIONS OUTSIDE WINDHOEK
Wildlife Impressions

Just outside Windhoek on the road to the airport, near Avis, Wildlife Impressions is also named Zoo Park, which is not to be confused with the municipal park of the same name in the centre of Windhoek. Outside, the emphasis is very much on the 'zoo', affording an opportunity to see many of Namibia's smaller inhabitants close up. Snakes, suricats and other small creatures are in enclosures at ground level, while various species of bird have the freedom of a large netted area across the complex.

Inside, over a moat complete with resident crocodile, is an exhibition of stuffed animals that's great for children – and just as interesting for adults. Here are all Namibia's indigenous mammals, displayed in a setting that reflects their natural habitats, and giving an idea of their relative sizes.

The adjacent display of African wood carvings, featuring work from Kenya down to the south of the continent, is claimed to be the largest in southern Africa. Be that as it may, there's plenty to look at here. And when you've seen enough, complete your visit with a meal at the **African Roots Restaurant** (tel: 061 232796). Swakopmund-born owner Leon Rousseau is also the chef here (except for Sunday lunch, when he hands over the reigns to his wife). Guests to this large restaurant overlooking the zoo area are welcomed with a secret-formula traditional drink, then can select from a menu that ranges from *aioru* – a West African fish pot – and other African-influenced specialities to game, plus a few vegetarian choices, all served with homemade bread. Occasionally, ad hoc live music enhances the atmosphere. Prices are reasonable, with starters at N$17–26, and main courses from N$29 for vegetarian noodles to N$77 for a game kebab. The restaurant is closed Sunday evening and Monday lunch. Over the next couple of years, Leon has plans to build guest accommodation here.

Avis Dam

Also on the airport road, to the left on Avisweg (signposted 'Swiss Chalets') as you leave Windhoek, Avis Dam is something of a let down. As you would expect, there's a man-made lake here, created by a dam across the Klein Windhoek River, and it's popular with locals for fishing, birdwatching, picnics, canoeing and bike rides, but there's little of any scenic interest to attract visitors. On the other hand, it's a pleasant spot for a picnic on the way to or from the airport. If you've more time, Daan Viljoen National Park is a far better bet.

Canoes are sometimes available for hire at weekends from Nokki's Canoe Hire at the thatched building on the opposite side of the main road (tel: 081 128 5231).

Daan Viljoen National Park

Entrance fees for day visitors: N$10 per person per day (under 16s N$2), plus N$20 per car, all payable at the park.

This small game park, some 20km west of the city, has good facilities, is accessible all year to 2WD vehicles and makes a close, easy, half-day excursion from the capital (though you'll need longer for some of the hikes). It encompasses some of the hills of the Khomas Hochland and, with its thorn trees and dry scrub vegetation, the environment is typical of the central highland area around Windhoek. This rolling landscape has been a park since 1962, and even before then some parts were protected.

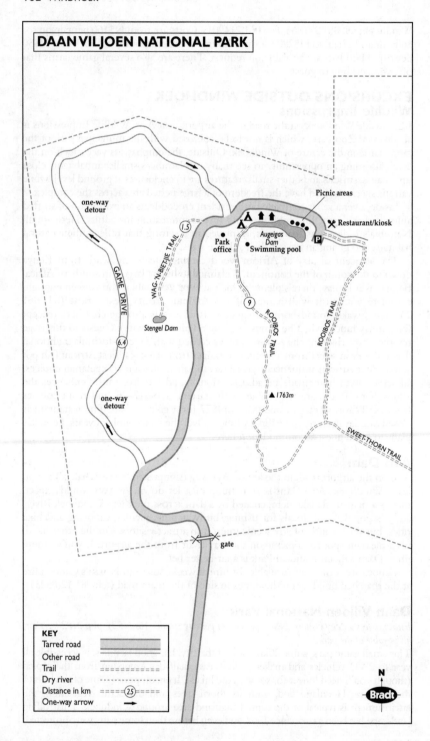

DAAN VILJOEN NATIONAL PARK

one-way detour

GAME DRIVE

WAG-'N-BIETJIE TRAIL

1.5

6.4

Stengel Dam

one-way detour

Park office

Augeigas Dam

Swimming pool

Picnic areas

Restaurant/kiosk

P

9

ROOIBOS TRAIL

ROOIBOS TRAIL

▲ 1763m

SWEET-THORN TRAIL

gate

KEY

Tarred road	
Other road	
Trail	
Dry river	
Distance in km	25
One-way arrow	→

N

Bradt

The park has good populations of Hartmann's mountain zebra, blue wildebeest, kudu, gemsbok and springbok, as well as klipspringer (as you would expect from the hilly terrain), red hartebeest, impala and even eland. Baboons and rock hyrax (dassies) are often quite visible, and you may spot a family of warthog too.

Over 200 bird species have been recorded here, and Daan Viljoen is a good place for several species endemic to this north-central area of Namibia. These include the lively rockrunner, or Damara rockjumper, which warbles a distinctive song in the morning and evening, and is often seen jumping around with its tail high in the air. The white-tailed shrike is black, white and grey and tends to bounce along the ground, often in groups making lots of noise. Montiero's hornbill is quieter, and more difficult to spot, and Rüppel's parrot and the rosy-faced lovebird are particularly 'cute' species often seen here.

During the middle of the week – and even sometimes at weekends – Daan Viljoen is quiet, attracting just a few locals out from Windhoek to sit by the lake formed by Augeigas Dam, perhaps with a barbecue. There's a **6.5km game drive** marked on the ground as 'Detour' – it's a one-way route, leading from the entrance up to the park office, so if time is tight you'd be better to do this when you arrive. On the other hand, as there is no really dangerous game here, take the opportunity to walk around by yourself, following one of the shorter of the park's three marked trails (see below). Your chances of spotting some game are good.

Getting there

Take Sam Nujoma Drive out of town, then follow the signs on to the C28 towards Swakopmund. The park is well signposted, about 24km from town, on a good tar road. If you don't have a vehicle, call one of the companies running city tours; most offer day trips here (see pages 158–60). The park is open daily from sunrise to sunset, but day visitors must leave by 18.00.

Facilities

Accommodation needs to be booked in advance at the NWR in Windhoek, but for day visits you can complete the formalities at the gate.

Accommodation is set around the shores of the lake. Rondavels have two single beds with hotplates, fridges, bedding, washbasins and towels, and shared showers and toilets. They cost N$280 for two people, or N$210 single, including breakfast. Three or more visitors are charged at N$85 per person. Luxury suites cost N$550 per night. Camping is N$125 per site, for a maximum of eight people, two vehicles and one caravan or tent. Both rates include park entrance fees for up to four people (additional group members pay the standard N$10 per person entrance fee).

There's a restaurant which opens for meals, 07.00–09.15, 11.30–13.45 and 18.30–21.00, as well as a small kiosk selling snacks and soft drinks and absolute essentials – oil, soup, sugar and corned beef (perversely, it's closed at lunchtimes during the week). Some distance from these is a large swimming pool of somewhat dubious cleanliness, though it's popular enough for all that. There is no petrol station.

Hiking

The game park excludes elephant, buffalo and lion, so you can safely walk alone on the short game trails. There are now three routes:

Wag-'n-biet-jie Trail is an easy 3km stroll, following the Augeigas River. It's named after the Afrikaans name for the *buffalo thorn*, meaning 'wait-a-bit'. This common tree is all around, and can be distinguished by the curved thorns pointing backwards on its branches. These snag anyone who is caught by the tree's main thorns and tries to pull free – forcing them to 'wait a bit'. The trail follows the river upstream until it reaches a lookout point over the Stengel Dam, after which it returns along the same route back to the camp.

Rooibos Trail is a more strenuous 9km hike, starting at the swimming pool from where it winds up to the region's highest point (1,763m) after about 3km. The views are worth the climb, and you can usually see Windhoek in the distance. Then it gradually descends to cross part of Choub River, and wind round across it again, though there is apparently an alternative route which follows the riverbed left until the trail rejoins it.

Sweet-thorn Trail is a relatively new 32km two-day hike, which must be booked in advance through Windhoek's NWR. Only one group of 3–12 people is allowed on the trail per day, starting at 09.00 from the restcamp office. This trail also follows the dry Choub River for part of the time, but strikes out into the otherwise unseen north and east sections of the park. It costs N$75 per person, and you must supply your own food and equipment, though there is a simple hut halfway along for the overnight stop.

Alternatively, you can just follow the wild game trails from the restcamp area. You are unlikely to get lost unless you try to. Before you set off walking, see if you can get a copy of the guide to the local birdlife, *Birds of Daan Viljoen National Park,* from the park's kiosk. This excellent little booklet contains a species checklist, an identification guide to some of the more common birds, and short descriptions of the habitats found in the park.

Heroes' Acre

About 15km south of the city, to the left of the B1 as you head south from Windhoek, Heroes' Acre is a N$61 million monument to 'the Namibian peoples' struggle for independence and self-emancipation'. It was completed in August 2002, in time for the annual Heroes' Day, August 26, and boasts a restaurant, a pavilion with a seating capacity of 5,000 people and a platform for dignitaries.

One of its main features is an 8m-high wall-panel, depicting various scenes from Namibia's popular revolts and uprisings, including the Nama people's uprising under Kaptein Hendrik Witbooi, resistance to the forced removal of people to Katutura, and the armed liberation struggle. Whilst only Namibian stones were used in the site's construction, the panel and various bronze statues, including one of a soldier weighing about four tonnes, were imported from North Korea.

Game lodges and guest farms

Even if you're staying in Windhoek, you may like to spend half a day or so visiting a local game lodge or guest farm. Places within easy reach of the centre that welcome day visitors include Heja Game Lodge (see page 136), Midgard (see page 172), Auas Game Lodge (see page 139), and Hohewarte Guest Farm (see page 137).

Other possibilities

Within relatively easy reach of Windhoek is Okahandja (about 1½ hours by car), with its woodcarvers' markets and the nearby ostrich farm. See page 174. Or if you just want to escape the city for a day, you could try some watersports at Lake Oanob Resort (see page 188).

The Central Corridor

Despite Windhoek's dominance of the country's central region, remember that it occupies only a small area. The city doesn't sprawl for miles. Drive just 10km from the centre and you will be on an open highway, whichever direction you choose. The recent completion of the trans-Kalahari Highway means that you can drive directly from Walvis Bay right across this region to South Africa's northern heartland, without leaving tarmac. In time, this may have a major impact on the area.

This chapter concentrates on this central swathe of Namibia, working outwards from Windhoek – to the edges of the Namib-Naukluft National Park in the west, and to the border with Botswana in the east.

FROM WINDHOEK TO THE COAST

Travelling from Windhoek to the coast, there's a choice of three obvious roads: the main tarred B2, the C28 and the more southerly C26. If speed is important, then you *must* take the B2: about four hours of very easy driving. Both the 'C' road options are gravel, and will take at least six hours to drive. However, they are more scenic.

Note that some of the side-roads off these three main roads are used very little. The D1412, for example, is a narrow, slow road whose crossing of the Kuiseb is wide and sandy. It would probably be impassable during the rainy season.

Guest farms and lodges

Between the B2 to the north and the C26 to the south are several good guest farms and lodges. Details of these are given under the route itself, or under the relevant town.

Between the C28 and the B2, Tsaobis-Leopard Nature Park (page 177) and Etusis Lodge (page 178) are probably better as stops when travelling north–south, as they are somewhat off-piste between Windhoek and Swakopmund. In contrast, Rooisand (page 270), at the foot of the Gamsberg Pass, would make an excellent stop on the C26.

In the same area around the Gamsberg as Rooisand are several farms which cater to parties in their own 4WD vehicles, who want challenging 4WD driving and hiking. Some allow you to follow trails across their land and neighbouring farms, and on to the Gamsberg itself.

Farm Weener, 17km down the D1278 from the C26, is at the foot of the Gamsberg and offers basic camping for N$30 per person per day, plus a fee of N$30 per vehicle to drive around the farm's marked 4WD trails. There are also hiking trails. Book with Mrs Rosalie, tel: 062 572108.

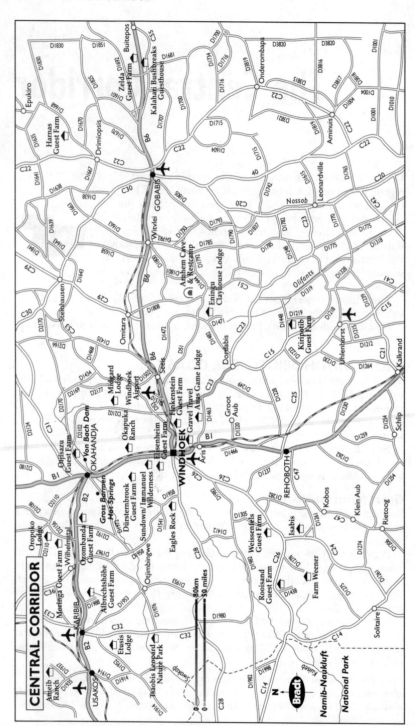

Isabis, 16km south of the C26 on the D1265 (signposted Nauchas and Rehoboth), has some beautiful riverbed campsites for N$30 per person per day including firewood, water and a 4WD trail through the farm. There's a N$80 per vehicle per day access fee for this area. Book with Joachim Cranz on tel: 061 228839, or cell: 081 1245588 – and contact him if you want further information on the hiking and 4WD trails in this region.

Hakos Guest Farm (7 rooms and two private campsites) Tel: 062 572111; fax in Windhoek: 061 256300; email: hakos@mweb.com.na; web: www.natron.net/tour/hakos
Run by Johann Straube, this small guest farm is signposted 7km to the left (if you're heading east) from the top of the Gamsberg Pass. There are great views over the surrounding mountains, various hiking trails on the farm and a 4WD route over the mountains. More unusual attractions include the indoor swimming pool and a small observatory with a 'roll-off roof' which has mirror and lens telescopes on a heavy mount with automatic tracking. That said, Johann encourages amateur astronomers to bring their own equipment, and enthuses about the clarity of the night sky.
Rates: doubles N$420 per person sharing, singles N$510, including dinner and breakfast.

The C28
The shortest of the gravel roads, the C28, is very beautiful and, around halfway along, you drive (slowly!) through the steep gradients (20%) of the Bosua Pass – where the central Namibian Highlands start to give way to granite kopjes of rounded boulders before the low, flat Namib.

Guest farms and lodges along the C28
Eagles Rock Leisure Lodge (9 bungalows and 10 rooms) PO Box 6176, Windhoek; tel/fax: 061 257116; fax: 061 257122; cell: 081 127 9531; email: info@eaglesrocklodge.com; web: www.eaglesrocklodge.com
Forty-five minutes' drive (38km) west of Windhoek, Eagles Rock is 3km along the D1958, after its junction with the C28. Being so close, Eagles Rock makes a good stop for those who want to stay near, but not actually in, Windhoek – and Matthias and Rosanna Bleks are fascinating hosts.

The lodge is set amidst trees and lawns, with a pool for the heat, and a cosy (and eclectic) library inside for cool winter evenings. The rooms have twin beds, en-suite shower/toilet and plenty of space. Rosanna's Italian background influences the food, which is excellent.

If you are staying for a few days then game drives, visits to nearby Bushman paintings, and even horse riding can be organised. Matthias has been at Eagles Rock since childhood and is involved in a training centre nearby, run by his father, Helmut Bleks. This includes vocational training for weaving, tannery, brick-laying, market gardening, and the hospitality industry – and visits here can be arranged if you have a special interest in what's going on.
Rates: N$485 single, N$400 per person sharing, including breakfast and dinner.

The C26
The C26 is much longer than the C28, but just as scenic. Just after its start, it drops steeply through the Khomas Hochland Mountains (the Kupferberg Pass), then later passes through the remarkable folded mountains of the Gamsberg Pass, which itself involves 20km of twists and turns, and 40 minutes' driving if you go gently (admiring the fine views). Further on still, the Kuiseb Pass sees the road wind down into the river's valley, cross on a small bridge, and then gradually climb back on to the desert plain (discussed in *Chapter 12*).

Note that some of the side-roads off these three main roads are used very little. The D1412, for example, is a narrow, slow road whose crossing of the Kuiseb is wide and sandy. It would probably be impassable during the rainy season.

Guest farms and lodges along the C26

Amani Lodge (6 rooms) PO Box 9959, Windhoek; tel: 061 239564; fax: 061 235641; email: amani@e-tourism.com.na

Twenty-three km southwest of Windhoek on the C26, just over the Kupferberg Pass, Amani Lodge stands at an altitude of 2150m. It's perhaps best known as the highest lodge in Namibia. Amani's run by Alain Houalet, who is originally from France. The accommodation has been built to a high standard – with touches of French style: three thatched chalets and another three fairly luxurious twin rooms. The main house includes a breakfast area, and there's also a communal bar and lounge/dining area.

Activities include 4WD nature drives, horseriding (N$70 per hour), bow shooting, hiking in the mountains and spending time with the habituated leopard and cheetah which are kept here. (I'm told that these cats at Amani are 'registered' with the Africat Foundation.)
Rates: N$465 per person sharing, N$565 single, including dinner and breakfast.

Corona Guest Farm (10 rooms) PO Box 11958, Windhoek; tel/fax: 062 572127; fax: 062 572147; email; corona@iway.na; web: www.natron.net

Corona is about half-way between Windhoek and Walvis Bay, twenty minutes south of the C26. To reach it, take the D1438 turn-off (which is about 31km east of the C14/C26 junction north of Solitaire) south for 18km.

Corona was burnt down in 1995, but has since risen from its ashes and now boasts 4 family-sized suites and 6 double rooms – each with its own bathroom. There are also several verandas, small lounges, a bar (with satellite TV), a reading corner, and an outdoor swimming pool with sundeck under some lovely jacarandas.

Activities include various farm activities plus horseriding, nature drives, and hiking. There are various shelters containing rock art on the farm, and from here it's possible for hikers to climb the Gamsberg Mountain, making use of Corona's 'mountain hut' at their base for a night if they wish. At the other extreme, adventurous guests are encouraged to join the hosts for a night camping at the bottom of the Gaub Canyon.
Rates: N$670–890 single, N$550–650 per person sharing, full board.

Weissenfels Guest Farm (11 rooms and campsites) PO Box 2907, Windhoek; tel: 062 572112; fax 062 572102; email: rowins@iafrica.com.na; web: www.orusovo.com/weissenfels

Weissenfels is 120km west of Windhoek on the C26 – just west of the D1265, and east of the Gamsberg Pass. It covers 40km² acres of rolling highlands and has been a guest farm since 1992. Now its run by Winston Retief and Rosi Rohr, who have retained a fairly traditional feel to it.

Accommodation is in one of five 'budget' double rooms, which share bathrooms, or six en-suite double rooms. There's also one larger family room, and one small room for tour guides. (Because of its location, Weissenfels does cater for occasional small tour groups.)

Weissenfels makes a good stop-over for a snack or lunch if you're travelling on the C26, but if you decide to stay for longer then there are some pleasant hiking trails (which you can follow with a guide, or on your own), and there's a fair amount of game around. Alternatively, 4WD game drives and horseriding are possible, as are picnics at the farm's various rock pools, and a trip to the top of the Gamsberg in a specially-converted 4WD.
Rates: N$480 per person sharing (half board in en-suite rooms), N$375 per person sharing in the budget rooms, N$80 per person camping.

Horse trails

One Namibian company, **Reit Safari** (PO Box 20706, Windhoek; tel: 061 217940; fax: 061 256300; email: reitsaf@cyberhost.com.na) run by Albert and Waltraut Fritzsche, organise adventurous nine-day trips on horseback, from the central highlands to Swakopmund. They travel across the escarpment and through the desert. With a few nights to get used to the horses, and one at the end to relax, these are full 12-day trips. Participants *must* be fit, have extensive experience of riding and horses, and be totally at ease on the back of a cantering horse.

Riders camp throughout the trip and trucks transport the equipment ahead of the party.

Rates: U$2,525 per person for the whole trip, including all meals, but excluding drinks. (Residents of southern Africa may be eligible for a discount.)

The main B2

The B2 heads north from Windhoek to Okahandja, about 71km, before turning west for the coast. Although the distance to Swakopmund is 358km, the road is flat and the tarred surface means that it is around four hours of very easy driving.

Okahandja

This small town is 71km north of Windhoek. It has some good shops, a couple of banks, 24-hour fuel, two of the country's best open markets for curios, an excellent shop for biltong (dried meat), and quite a lot of old buildings and history – if you've the time to stop and take a look around.

History

Okahandja is the administrative centre for the Herero people (see *Chapter 2*, page 23), despite being considerably southwest of their main settlements. Missionaries first reached the area in the late 1820s, but it wasn't until 1849 that the first of them, Friedrich Kolbe, settled here. He remained for less than a year, driven away by the attacks of the Namas, under Jonker Afrikaner.

He fled with good reason as, on August 23 of the following year, about 700 men, women and children were killed by the Namas at the aptly named Blood Hill. It is said that after the massacre, the women's arms and legs were chopped off in order to take their copper bangles.

The small kopje of Blood Hill can be seen just to the east of the main Windhoek–Swakopmund road. Jonker Afrikaner lies peacefully in his grave, next to several Herero chiefs, opposite the church on Kerk Street.

Getting there

Most overseas visitors coming through Okahandja are driving, but the town is also served by both coach and train services.

By coach

Intercape Mainliner's services from Windhoek to Walvis Bay stop at Okahandja's Shell Ultra, at 08.00 on Mon, Wed, Fri and Sat, and those from Walvis Bay to Windhoek at 16.30 on Mon, Wed, Fri and Sun. These cost around N$60 to Windhoek, and N$100 to Walvis Bay. See *Chapter 6*, pages 96–9, for more details.

By train

Trains depart from Okahandja for Windhoek at 03.30 on Tue, Thu and Sat, also at 05.10 daily except Sundays. They also leave for Tsumeb at 20.25 every Tue, Thu and Sun. They are very slow – see *Chapter 6*, pages 94–5, for details.

Where to stay and eat

Okahandja has few places to stay, and most visitors stay at one of the surrounding guest farms instead.

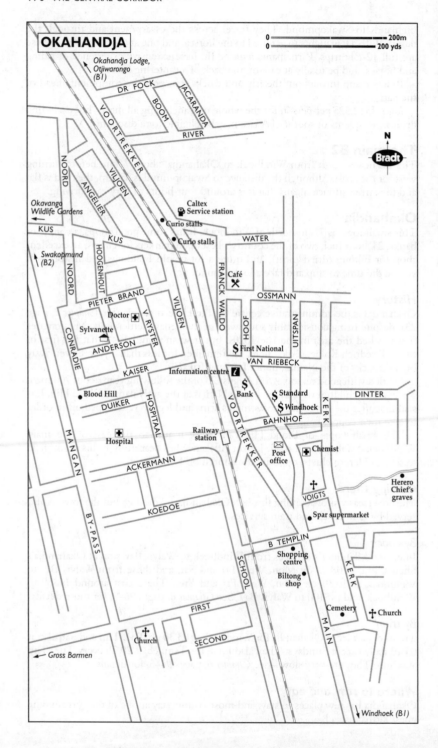

OKAHANDJA

0 ———————— 200m
0 ———————— 200 yds

N

Bradt

Okahandja Lodge,
Otjiwarongo
(B1)

DR FOCK
BOOM
JACARANDA
RIVER
VOORTREKKER
VILJOEN
ANGELIER
NOORD
KUS

Okavango
Wildlife Gardens

KUS
HOOGENHOUT
NOORD

Swakopmund
(B2)

PIETER BRAND
V RYSTER
VILJOEN

Doctor
Sylvanette

CONRADIE
ANDERSON
KAISER

Blood Hill

DUIKER
HOSPITAAL

Hospital

MANGAN
BY-PASS

ACKERMANN

KOEDOE

Caltex
Service station
Curio stalls
Curio stalls

WATER

Café

OSSMANN

FRANCK WALDO
HOOF
UITSPAN

First National
VAN RIEBECK

Information centre

Bank
Standard
Windhoek

DINTER

BAHNHOF

Railway
station

VOORTREKKER

Post
office
Chemist

Herero
Chief's
graves

VOIGTS

Spar supermarket

KERK

B TEMPLIN
Shopping
centre
Biltong
shop

SCHOOL

FIRST
SECOND

Church

Gross Barmen

Cemetery
Church

MAIN
KERK

Windhoek (B1)

Okahandja Lodge (22 rooms and 2 family units) PO Box 1524, Okahandja; tel: 062 504299; fax: 062 502551; email: okalodge@africaonline.com.na
About 2km north of town, to the east of the road just after the turn off to the Okahandja Wildlife Gardens, this is one of a number of lodges around Namibia's towns that cater for coach parties. Its rooms are in large blocks set around an open lawn and pond area. They are pleasant inside, if somewhat unoriginal.
Rates: single N$470, double N$720, including breakfast.

Sylvanette Guesthouse (7 rooms) 311 Hoogenhout St, PO Box 529, Okahandja; tel: 062 501213/501078, cell: 081 127 3759; fax: 062 501852; email: sylvanet@iafrica.com.na
In the suburbs close to town, Sylvanette has seven double rooms with en-suite facilities, an airy lounge where sundowners are served, cosy breakfast room and a swimming pool. There's a fully equipped kitchen for self caterers, and dinner can be arranged if you request it in advance.
Rates: single N$200, double N$350, including breakfast.

To eat in Okahandja there are several good small take-aways dotted along Main Street, including Marie's, on B Templin. Just on the northern outskirts of town (at the turn-off of the D2110 from the B1) is the **Okavango Wildlife Gardens**. This is an established plant nursery – perfect if you need to buy a house plant during your travels – which also has a restaurant which overlooks a small area set aside for game. It makes a good stopover and the busy car-park seemed a relatively safe place to leave things – though you might be wise to ask the security guard to keep a special watch on your car if there's any luggage on view.

Okahandja's grocery shops are known for having some of the best fresh vegetables available in the country, and there's also a renowned outlet for biltong on the eastern side of Main Street south of B Templin Road, near the Bäckerei Dekker – another good bakery.

Nearby guest farms
Around Okahandja lies some of the best farmland in the country. Some of the local farms accept guests, and some of those are good. The best include:

Otjisazu Guest Farm (13 rooms) PO Box 1505, Okahandja; tel: 062 501259; fax: 062 501323; email: otjisazu@iafrica.com.na
Having recently changed hands, Otjisazu is now run by Herbert and Monica Lauenroth. It's an hour's drive from Windhoek. Take the D2102 signposted to the Von Bach Dam about 1km south of the bridge over the Okahandja River. After about 4.5km and again at about 16.5km there are very sharp bends, and the road crosses a number of dry riverbeds. (This isn't a road to drive for the first time when it's dark.) It reaches Otjisazu after about 27.5km. The area around is rolling acacia scrub/bush – typical of the central plateau around Windhoek.
The farm stands in pleasant, well-watered gardens with a good stone braai and stone counter, and shaded tables. There is also a separate outside boma dining area and bar, overlooking a good-size pool. Inside, the farmhouse is comfortable and spacious. The furniture's neither antique nor very modern – despite the building dating from 1878, when it was originally built as a mission. The twin rooms are comfortable, solidly constructed and all en suite: most seem purpose-built.
Nature drives are available around the farm – lasting an hour or so in the evening. With luck you'll spot a few of the farm's kudu, gemsbok, springbok, duiker, steenbok, or (it is claimed) eland. Horseriding is available on request. Otjisazu has always been quite a nice guest farm, and its new owners seem determined to make staying here good value.
Rates: N$495 single, N$470 per person sharing, including dinner and breakfast.

Midgard Lodge (46 rooms) PO Box 16, Windhoek; tel: 062 503888; fax: 062 503818; email: midgard@mweb.com.na
Run by the Namibi Sun Hotel group, Midgard is about 85km from Windhoek on the D2102. It covers 65km², which includes a large swimming pool, tennis courts, horseriding and hiking trails. Midgard is popular for an outing from town for Sunday lunch – though it is better suited to conferences than casual visitors.
Rates: single N$490 (VIP single N$600), double NS690 (VIP double N$900), including breakfast.

Oropoko Lodge (33 twin rooms, 3 suites) PO Box 726, Windhoek; tel: 062 503871; fax: 062 503842; email: oropoko@iafrica.com.na; web: www.oropoko.com
Oropoko is reached by taking the main B2 west from Okahandja for about 41km, before turning north on to the D2156. It is well signposted 18km along this road.

Oropoko is a grand lodge with a stunning situation on a small mountain, whose top was flattened to make way for it. Its large outdoor pool has an impressive view, and the lodge's bar and dining room are of a similar scale. Meals are extensive affairs: large buffet breakfasts, and heavy à la carte dinners. The bar has numerous large leather armchairs. Guestrooms at Oropoko are large, luxurious and square. Each has an en-suite bathroom, minibar/fridge, telephone, and its own safe.

The lodge aims for the most affluent travellers – which might explain the zeal of the security force manning the gate. If film fans imagine James Bond approaching a villain's isolated estate, surrounded by a veritable private army, then Oropoko offers them the perfect chance to act out that fantasy. Just try to drop in here.

The game area surrounding the lodge buildings is about 110km², and it protects seven white rhino, half a dozen giraffe, waterbuck and nyala, as well as the more normal antelope for this area like gemsbok, kudu, and steenbok. Game drives can sometimes be organised for N$100 per vehicle, in the morning or the evening.
Rates: single U$70, double U$105, including breakfast.

Ozombanda Guest Farm (4 rooms) PO Box 449, Okahandja; tel: 062 503870; fax: 062 503996; email: ozombanda@natron.net
Ozombanda is easily reached on the south side of the B2, about 30km west of Okahandja. It started accepting guests in early 1997, and its owners, Volker and Monika, remain refreshingly enthusiastic. This is a typical Namibian farm, where you can relax whilst gaining an insight into how it all works.

Ozombanda has four palatial thatched chalets made to identical (and unexpectedly) high standards, with tiled floors, large twin/king-size beds and en-suite shower and toilet. These stand near the large swimming pool, which is just behind the farmstead. It's a lovely place to relax – provided that you can talk Volker out of taking you on a long farm drive to show you things.

The farm stretches for about 120km², some of which has cattle on it, some just game – primarily kudu, gemsbok, and springbok, with a few smaller antelope, baboon, and the odd spotted and even brown hyena. On one side of the farm there's a kopje, perfect for short climbs or seeking leopard in the twilight. Ozombanda's located conveniently enough for a one-night stopover, but ideally allow two nights here to relax and take a farm drive or two. It's outstanding value.
Rates: N$575 single, N$495 per person sharing, including full board.

Moringa Guest Farm (5 bungalows) PO Box 65, Okahandja; tel/fax: 062 503872 or 062 501106; email: moringa@iway.na; web: www.moringasafaris.com
Just west of Oropoko, and reached along the same D2156, Moringa is run by the Böhmcker family (who have been here since 1905) in a traditional style. It is typical of the country's adaptable farms, having farmed karakul for many years, before the market for the pelts crashed. Then it turned to beef, then became involved in hunting, and most recently tourism.

Moringa was one of the earliest farms to re-introduce game onto the land, and this has paid real dividends. Around 100km² of the farm is now devoted to game, which is relatively relaxed and plentiful. Here you'll find giraffe, blesbok, kudu, springbok, leopard, cheetah, and more besides – and driving or walking around Moringa feels much more like a game reserve than most guests farms. Don't miss seeing, and perhaps exploring on foot, the large hillside stands of *Moringa ovalifolia* (it's the same contorted species that's well known from the Haunted Forest, in Etosha) from which the farm takes its name.

One game drive is included in the farm's normal full-board rate, below. The farmhouse itself has a bar, a good small pool and a very welcoming conservatory for the winter. The cooking is traditional, with a strong German influence, and so if you are looking to relax at a pleasant traditional guest farm, this could be perfect.

Rates: N$420 per person sharing full board, including one game drive.

Dürsternbrook Guest Farm (5 rooms, 2 luxury tents and camping) PO Box 870, Windhoek; tel: 061 232572; fax: 061 234758/232572; email: dbrook@mweb.com.na; web: www.durstenbrook.net
To reach Dürsternbrook, turn west off the B1, about 30km north of Windhoek, on to the D1499, and then follow the clear signs for another 18km. Dürsternbrook's venerable main claim to fame is its leopards, which are kept in a large enclosure, and can be viewed from a vehicle, or on foot. It also has a much larger area of land for drives and walks to view less dangerous game, including hartebeest, giraffe, eland, oryx, kudu and smaller buck. Horseriding is an additional attraction.

Dürsternbrook's main building is a large old colonial farmhouse dating from 1910. Its walls are adorned with hunting trophies, a practice it encourages with limited trophy hunting. It was one of Namibia's first guest farms, and its owners speak English, German, French and Afrikaans.

Rates: N$658–804 double, including dinner, breakfast, and leopard/cheetah viewing and game drive. Single supplement N$203.

Okapuka Ranch (20 rooms and camping) PO Box 5955, Windhoek; tel: 061 234607/227845; fax: 061 234690; email: okapuka@iafrica.com.na; web: www.natron.net/okapuka
Okapuka has an imposing set of gates on the eastern side of the main B1 road, about 40km south of Okahandja and 30km north of Windhoek. Its 2.5km drive winds through 120km² of well-stocked game ranch, protecting herds of sable, giraffe and blue wildebeest as well as gemsbok, kudu, ostrich and crocodile. The 120km self-drive game trail through the area is an attraction in its own right, as is the 3km² enclosure containing a pride of lion, which are fed regularly for the benefit of observers. Here I'll ignore any discussion of the ethics of keeping, and breeding from, a pride of lion described by the owner as 'problem animals'. It's very sad, but unsurprising, to note that they recently killed one of the staff.

The lodge itself has been stylishly built on a rise above the surrounding country, and lavishly equipped with a sauna, tennis courts, and a chic swimming pool. Accommodation has been extended in recent years, with the lodge now catering on part of its site for conference guests, while independent visitors live in a separate area. Individual en-suite rooms are carpeted and comfortable, each boasting AC/heating, satellite TV, minibar, kettle and telephone, as well as a private terrace. The separate campsite, with its own pool, has both permanent luxury tents, with adjoining shower and toilet, and sites for caravans and visitors' own tents.

The large, thatched, bar/lounge area is beautiful, though more imposing than relaxing, and the sight of leopard and cheetah skins draped over the furniture isn't to everybody's taste. Alongside, the restaurant caters for both residents and day visitors. On Sundays, there is a three-course buffet for N$75 (children N$45) and excellent dinner for N$170 per person. At other times, the à la carte menu, focusing on game, is reasonably priced at N$22–30 for starters, or N$50–70 for main courses.

Okapuka encourages day visitors, offering daily 1½-hour game drives at N$90, as well as lion feeding, helicopter flights, horseriding and other activities. There are also two walking trails. Note that the ranch regularly hosts guests from the *Desert Express* train (see pages 95–6) to watch a lion-feed, which inevitably brings the occasional influx of visitors.

In spite of the grand attractions of the place, it's a shame that the evident attention paid to detail doesn't extend to the rather curt style of management.

Rates: N$580 single, N$820 per person sharing, including breakfast and lion-feeding tour. Dinner N$85, lunch and dinner N$150.

Getting organised

The town's **post office** is almost opposite its pharmacy, and if you need a **bank** then there are branches of Standard Bank and First National on Main Street, along with a scattering of 24-hour **fuel stations** beside the town's main roads.

If you're stopping for longer then seek out the small **information centre** (near the corner of Van Riebeck Road), which has the usual glossy brochures and an interesting, if brief, leaflet to guide you around the town's historical sites (see below).

In an emergency, the police are reached on tel: 062 10111, whilst the ambulance is on 062 503030, the hospital on 062 503039, and the fire service on 062 5001051/4, 502194 or 502041.

What to see and do

By the side of the railway line, on Voortrekker Street, is a large open-air **curio market** run by the Rundu-based Namibian Carvers Association. This, and its sister outlet on the southern side of town, are probably the two best places in the country for carvings. See *Chapter 2*, pages 28–9.

Craftsmen here specialise in large wooden carvings. These include some beautiful thin, wooden giraffes (some 2m or more high), huge 'tribal' heads, cute flexible snakes, and wide selections of more ordinary carved hippos and bowls. Do stop for a wander around as you pass, especially if you're on the way to Windhoek airport to leave – this is the perfect spot for last-minute present shopping, and it's open on Sundays.

Ombo Ostrich Farm PO Box 1364, Okahandja; tel: 062 501176; fax: 062 502315; email: ombo@iafrica.com.na
About 3km out of Okahandja, on the D2110 northwest, this ostrich farm is signposted from the turning to the Okavango Wildlife Gardens. They have 45-minute tours (N$15 per adult, N$10 per child) covering everything you ever wanted to know about these amazing birds, as well as snacks, refreshments, crafts and curios.

If you're in town for an evening, then check to see if the Nau-Aib Community Hall (tel: 062 501041/51; fax: 062 501746) has any performances, as it is sometimes a venue for touring bands.

Historical sites

The town has many historical sites, including the **graves** of a number of influential leaders, including: Jonker Afrikaner, the powerful Oorlam leader; Chief Hosea Kutako, an influential Herero leader who campaigned against South African rule in the 1950s; and Chief Clemens Kapuuo, once president of the DTA, who was assassinated in 1978. Note that casual visitors cannot access these graves.

Close by is the **Church of Peace**, a Lutheran-Evangelistic church built in 1952, and also the **house of Dr Vedder**, one of the oldest in town.

Just south of the post office, on Hoof Street, is a building known as **the old stronghold**, or the old fort. This was the town's old police station, started in 1894, though now it is empty and falling into disrepair. Meanwhile to the west, **Blood Hill**, scene of the 1850 massacre, is found between Kaiser and Duiker streets, although there's little to see now.

Around Okahandja

There are two resorts close to Okahandja, both run by the NWR. These are primarily used as weekend get-aways by the local urbanites – though if you are passing and need somewhere cheap to stay, they are fine.

Von Bach Recreational Resort

Von Bach Dam supplies most of the capital's water, and is surrounded by a nature reserve. It is signposted a few kilometres along the D2102 just south of Okahandja, and 1km south of the bridge over the Okahandja River. The environment here is thorn-scrub and particularly hilly, supporting game including kudu, baboon and leopard, as well as Hartmann's mountain zebra, springbok, eland and even ostrich. However, with only one road through the park they are all very difficult to spot. Don't come here just for the game.

If you are camping, then there are campsites and a couple of very basic two-bed huts, without bedding or facilities (you must use the campers' communal ablution blocks). Reservations can be made through the NWR in Windhoek, and day-visitors must phone 062 501457 in advance if they want to drop in.
Rates: camping N$110 per pitch. The huts are N$120 per hut. Entrance fees: N$10 per adult (N$2 per child) per day, plus N$10 entry per car. Open: all year – though gates open at sunrise and close at sunset.

Gross Barmen Hot Springs

This busy resort has a shop, restaurant, filling station and tennis courts, as well as the mineral spa fed by the hot thermal springs. It is built around a dam about 25km southwest of Okahandja, on the banks of the Swakop River, and is easily reached from the town's southern side along the C87.

What to see and do

Gross Barmen's main attraction is its mineral spring, and swimming baths. The fountain here, clearly visible, wells up at about 65°C. It feeds the inside 'thermal hall' with its sunken baths for overnight visitors, as well as the cooler outside pools (for children and adults) which are used mainly by the day-visitors, who are especially numerous at weekends.

Additional attractions are some gentle walks in the surrounding hillsides and, especially for birdwatchers, a good little path cut right through the reedbeds. These all make pleasant strolls, and a couple of benches make good vantage points over the dam whilst you rest.

Where to stay

Accommodation here includes five-bedded bungalows, two-bed bungalows or rooms, and campsites. All have a fridge/kettle, hot-plate, en-suite shower and toilet, and linen and bedding is provided. The two-bed bungalows also have field kitchens.

Book these through the NWR in Windhoek, and note that day visitors must phone 062 501091 in advance, to arrange their visits.
Rates: N$360 for a 5-bed and N$220 for a 2-bed bungalow, N$140 for a 2-bed room, or N$690 for a luxury suite. Camping sites N$110 per day, for up to 8 people. Entry fee: N$20

per adult (N$10 child) per day, plus N$10 entry for a car. Open: all year – gates always open for those with reservations.

Karibib

For over 90 years, this small town on the railway line from Windhoek to Swakopmund, 112km from Okahandja on the B2, has been known mainly for the very hard, very high-quality marble which comes from the Marmorwerke quarry nearby. This produces about 100 tonnes of finished stone per month – mainly kitchen/bathroom tiles and tombstones.

More recently, in the late 1980s, South Africa's Anglo-American Corporation opened the open-cast Navachab Gold Mine on the south side of town, to mine low-grade ore.

There's a lot of small-scale mining in the area, especially for gemstones. Amethyst, tourmaline, aquamarine, quartz, silver topaz, citrine and garnets are just some of the minerals found in the region around here. See the tumbled stones on the floor display of the Namib i centre (see Henckert Tourist Centre, below) for an idea of what is around – they all come from the local area.

Where to stay and eat

In town there are just two hotels, both with small restaurants where you can stop for a snack, a steak house (on the main road) and a country club.

Hotel Erongoblick (15 rooms) PO Box 67, Park St, Karibib; tel: 064 550009
Situated on Park Street, most of the Erongoblick's rooms have en-suite facilities, and there's off-street parking at the back of the hotel. It also has a squash court, a pool and sauna – and is the better of the two town hotels.
Rates: N$160 single, N$270 per person sharing, including breakfast.

Hotel Stroblhof (11 rooms) PO Box 164, 310 Main St, Karibib; tel: 064 550081; fax: 064 550240
With only some of its rooms having en-suite facilities, this basic hotel has some simple rooms as well as dormitory-style accommodation for backpackers.
Rates: double N$230 per person, single N$370, triple N$460 per room, including breakfast. Dormitory accommodation is N$95 per person.

Country Club Tel: 081 1248760
Near the mountainous outcrop known as Klippeneberg, this is signposted on the main road. It has tennis courts, squash, a swimming pool, a small golf course and a bar/restaurant that is popular with some of Karibib's residents. It's not really geared to tourists, but is hospitable enough if you drop by.

Nearby guest farms

There are several guest farms and lodges in this area, including:

Albrechtshöhe Guest Farm (5 rooms) PO Box 124, Karibib; tel/fax: 062 503363; email: meyer@nam.lia.net
Albrechtshöhe is off the D1988, about 2km south of the main B2, 92km west of Okahandja, and 26km from Karibib. It's a traditional guest farm, run by Paul-Heinz and Ingrid Meyer, which started life as a railway station. Because of the natural springs of the area, the Schutztruppe completed Albrechtshöhe in 1906 to provide water for horses and steam trains. Today these historic, fortified buildings house a guest farm. Activities here include bush walks and game drives as well as expeditions to search for gems and explore the local mountains. Like many Namibian guest farms, this is also a hunting farm.
Rates: N$500 per person, sharing or single, including dinner and breakfast.

Tsaobis Leopard Nature Park (10 bungalows, camping) PO Box 143, Karibib; tel: 064 550811/241191; fax: 064 550954/272791; email: tsaobis@iafrica.com.na
This is a private game reserve in beautiful hilly country 11km west of the C32, on the south bank of the Swakop River. The animals here include leopard, cheetah, wild dog, aardwolf, caracal, zebra and gemsbok. The lodge also supports a research project into the baboons that inhabit this area.

The reserve covers a large area of 370km² and many animals are kept in enclosures near the main house and bungalows, so they can often be seen. This is a good area for hiking; there are several trails and two-way radios are available. A number of activities are currently planned, including geological excursions, a mountain-bike trail, and a 4WD route.

Tsaobis is more like a restcamp than a guest farm and accommodation is in simple self-catering bungalows, or at the adjacent campsite. Meals are available on request. Outside, a new lapa offers welcome shade in the heat of the day, and there is a swimming pool for cooling off. Note that there is no fuel or supplies at Tsaobis, and neither the activities (hiking tours of the animals) nor the meals are automatically available: all should be pre-arranged when you first book your accommodation here.

Rates: self-catering bungalows N$290–504 for two people, camping N$46 per person and N$200 per campsite.

Etusis Lodge (7 bungalows, 6 tents) Farm Etusis No 75, PO Box 5, Karibib; tel: 064 550826; fax: 064 550961; email: etusis@natron.net; web: www.etusis.com
The turning for Etusis is signposted from the C32, about 19km south of Karibib. The lodge itself is 16km from the road, standing at the foot of the Otjipatera Mountains: a range of white marble.

There are seven solid, comfortable bungalows here with en-suite toilets and showers, and each has two beds designed for children also. Each has 220V electricity, solar-heated water and a ceiling fan – as well as exposed wooden beams and attractive thatch. The 'luxury' tents each stand nearby on a concrete base, and share clean communal facilities.

Central to the lodge is a bar and dining area, with small curio shop and TV/lounge– all under a large thatched building overlooking a small swimming pool. The lodge also has limited conference facilities.

Activities centre on morning and evening game drives – in search of impala, kudu, mountain zebra, leopard, jackal, and blesbok – and the opportunity to hike unguided in the mountains behind the lodge. There are also options for horseriding, kite-flying, target shooting, and various other sports.

Rates: bungalows N$1250 single, N$1100 per person sharing; tents N$850 single, N$750 per person sharing. Full board and activities are included.

Getting organised

In an emergency, the police are reached on tel: 064 10111, whilst the ambulance and fire service are on 064 550016 – or 550126 after hours. The small private clinic behind the First National Bank is tel: 064 550073 or 550329.

What to see and do

Your first stop here should be the **Henckert Tourist Centre and shop**, but if you have more time then the town is dotted with several **historic buildings** dating from the early 1900s. Then Karibib was an important overnight stop on the railway between Windhoek and Swakopmund, as well as a trade centre. Ask at the information centre for their brief guide to the town.

There is a small **shooting range** and a few **hiking trails** into the rolling landscapes south of town, behind the country club. In town itself, the Club Western Gambling and Entertainment Centre, and its adjacent Club Western

Restaurant, seem to be the focus of local excitement, although as an alternative, the town's cemetery is beautifully lit at night!

The local branch of the Wildlife Society has a '**vulture restaurant**' with twice-weekly feedings, and the **gold mine** has occasional site tours. Horseriding trips may also be available. For any of these, enquire at the information centre (in advance, if possible), which is the main stop for visitors passing through.

Henckert Tourist Centre PO Box 85, Karibib; tel: 064 550028/64; fax: 064 550230
On the main street, this is a landmark – a first-class curio shop that doubles as a **Namib i** information centre. This fascinating shop began as a small gem shop in 1969. Now it has a very large range of carvings and curios, one of the country's best selections of Namibian semi-precious stones and gemstones, a facility to change money if necessary, and a generous line in tea and coffee. There's even a children's corner with eye-catching stones.

There is also a weaving centre, employing about 25 people in making craftwork, about 70% of which is bought by visitors. This demonstrates the importance of tourism here, and the vital role that you play in the local economy when you spend money in Namibia.

Usakos

This small town, 147km from Swakopmund, used to be the centre of the country's railway industry, though now it's little more than a stop on the line, with banks and fuel to tempt those who might pass right through. If you linger here then the old station is worth a brief look, and the Namib information office is useful if you're planning to do much exploration of the local area.

Where to stay and eat

For casual snacks as you pass through on your way to Swakopmund, **Namib Wuste Farm Stall** is the best in town. It is almost always open (closing at 20.00, even on Sundays) for a good range of take-away foods, biltong and chilli bites.

Most visitors staying in the area will use the guest farms around here and Karibib, but if you need to stay in Usakos itself, your two options are:

Bahnhof Hotel (14 rooms) Theo-Ben Gurirab St, PO Box 43, Usakos; tel: 064 530444; fax: 064 530765; email: websmith@iway.na; web: http://hop.to/namiba
This two-star hotel, located next to the post office, is fully licensed with an à-la-carte restaurant, bar, beer garden and undercover off-street parking. All rooms have air conditioning, satellite TV, telephones and en-suite bathrooms. Internet and conference facilities are available. Birdwatching and local Bushman art are on offer at the nearby Mansfield farm, next to Usakos.
Rates: single N$195, double N$280, including breakfast.

Usakos Hotel (10 rooms) Bahnhof St, PO Box 129, Usakos; tel: 064 530259; fax: 064 530267
This plain hotel has a simple restaurant, and off-street parking. All the rooms have en-suite bathroom and some have air conditioning. If you've no transport then you can arrange day trips from here to Spitzkoppe (see page 345) with the owner.
Rates: N$145 per person sharing or single, including breakfast.

Nearby guest farms

Ameib Ranch (10 rooms plus camping) PO Box 266, Usakos; tel: 064 530803; fax: 064 530904
Ameib has been accepting guests for years, and is quite idiosyncratic, but it does have superb rock formations and excellent rock art, so is worth a visit.

Approaching from Windhoek or Otjiwarongo, turn right towards Swakopmund in the centre of town, then immediately right again, on to the D1935. This turning can be inconspicuous: there's a small sign to Ameib on your right as you turn, and a hospital on your left. (From Swakopmund on the B2, look for a small sign to the left. If you reach the main junction in the centre of town, you have missed it.)

Then follow the gravel D1935 for 12km to a signposted right turn on to the D1937. The landscape is beautiful: a little like Damaraland's vegetation, with sparse cover on the hillsides, and lush river valleys. About 5km further (on poor gravel) you reach Ameib's imposing gates. Then 11km later, the ranch is set amongst rounded granite boulders in the Erongo Mountains.

Its rooms are large and clean, with en-suite facilities, but the decor is uninspiring. They are functional, but not beautiful. However, visitors come here mainly for the excellent rock paintings. Many are within Phillip's Cave, a large eyelash-shaped cave made famous by Abbé Breuil's book of the same name (see *Further Reading*). It's a classic site for Bushman art, and the paintings here include a famous elephant, giraffe, and red stick-like people. Getting there is a 1.8km drive from the ranch itself, followed by a 30-minute trail (15mins at a fast, serious hiking pace). If possible, do this in the cool of the morning.

There are also unusual rock formations, like the Bull's Party – a group of large rounded boulders which (allegedly) look like a collection of bulls talking together. These are about 5.2km from the main ranch, and around them are lots of unusually shaped rocks, including mushroom-shaped and balancing boulders – worth exploring for an afternoon.

Unfortunately, Ameib still has a small 'zoo' next to the ranch, complete with native animals and birds in small cages.

Rates: N$480 single, N$460 per person sharing, including dinner and breakfast. N$50 per person camping.

Getting organised

If you need money then there's a First National Bank, and for supplies try Engers Mini-Market or the Usakos Selfhelp (which is a shop, not a therapy group). Next to the Padstal Take-away, Rainbow Curios sells gemstones and various curios. Like everything else, it's on Bahnhof Street.

In an emergency, the police are reached on tel: 064 10111, whilst the ambulance and fire service are on 064 530023 – or 530095 after hours. The hospital is tel: 064 530013 or 530067.

EAST FROM WINDHOEK
Gobabis

This busy town, standing at the centre of an important cattle farming area on the western edges of the Kalahari, forms Namibia's gateway into Botswana via the Buitepos border post, about 120km east. It's an ideal place to use the banks, fill up with fuel or get supplies before heading east towards Ghanzi, where most goods aren't so easily available. However, it's less interesting as a stopover.

Getting there
By car

The main tar road, west to Windhoek and east into Botswana, is part of the trans-Kalahari route designed to link Walvis Bay with South Africa's Gauteng Province (the area around Johannesburg and Pretoria). This means that shipments from Europe or the USA can be sent via Walvis Bay, and trucked across this road to Gauteng – which should be far faster than shipping them to Durban, and moving them by road from there.

Whilst certainly helping Gauteng's economy, its benefit for Namibia or the

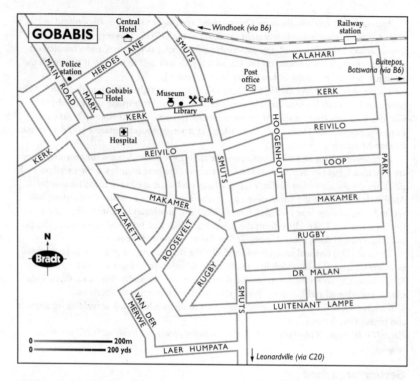

Kalahari is less obvious. It is expected to herald an increase in traffic on this route over the next few years.

By coach

Intercape Mainliner used to run a good service linking Windhoek and Jo'burg, which stoped at Gobabis. However, this has now stopped – it runs through Upington instead – so there are currently no coaches passing through Gobabis.

By train

Gobabis is linked to Windhoek by a train service, which arrives from there around 05.43 on Monday, Wednesday and Friday, and departs again at 21.00 on the same days. It is very slow, taking almost eight hours to get to Windhoek. See *Chapter 6*, pages 93–5, for details, or call the TransNamib in Gobabis on tel: 061 2982305.

Where to stay and eat

For snacks during the day there is a pleasant little café, complete with menu in German, at the back of the general store – just to the right of the Municipal Offices on the main street. If you want to stay in the area for a few days, then consider Arnhem Restcamp, or the excellent Eningu Clayhouse Lodge, just west of here, near Dordabis: see page 185. However, if you need to be nearer town, then there are three possibilities:

Central Hotel (15 rooms) PO Box 233; tel: 061 562094/5; fax: 061 562092
This old town hotel on Heroes' Lane has basic en-suite rooms, and a small breakfast/dining room and bar.
Rates: N$150 single, N$120 per person sharing, including breakfast.

Gobabis Hotel (17 rooms) PO Box 924; tel: 061 562568/563068; fax: 061 562641
Pretty similar to the Central Hotel, the Gobabis is on Mark Street and boasts a small
central plunge-pool. Its lack-lustre rooms have Mnet TV – useful if you wish to forget
where you are. The bar is reputed to be the highpoint of the local social scene.
Rates: N$150 single, N$120 per person sharing, including breakfast.

Doll's House Hotel (6 rooms and camping) PO Box 13, Witvlei; tel: 0683 570038; fax:
067 221575
Run by the same people as the Makalani Hotel in Tsumeb, it's small, clean and efficient,
though only two rooms have en-suite facilities and the rest share. With food always available,
this makes a good stop for a night's sleep if you're rushing across the Botswana border.
Rates: from N$100 single, N$70 per person sharing, including breakfast. Camping N$20 per person.

Gobabis Guest House (6 rooms) PO Box 123, 8 Lazarett St, Gobabis; tel: 062 563189;
fax: 062 564125; email: gghnam@iafrica.com.na
To find this from the main road, turn right down Kerk St, then left down Lazarett St; the
guesthouse is on the right. The rooms are clean and modern with small verandas, and
parking is secure.
Rates: single N$220, double N$300, including breakfast.

Getting organised
The main **banks** are all here, Bank of Windhoek and First National are both on
Church Street, whilst Standard Bank is on Heroes' Lane. As you drive around the
small centre, Gobabis will strike you as a prosperous community, with many small,
busy shops and businesses. This means that it's a good place to stop for last-minute
supplies if you are on the way to Botswana. Several **24-hour fuel stations** line the
main road, and **garages** include the useful Gobabis Toyota on Heroes' Lane and
Motorama for Volkswagen on Church Street.

There's a small, new information centre in town, called the **Eastern Tourism
Forum**, though at time of press its permanent location was uncertain. It can
probably be reached on tel: 061 562551; fax: 061 563012.

In an emergency, the police are reached on tel: 061 10111, whilst the
ambulance and hospital are on 061 562275, and the fire service on 061 566666. If
you can't get through anywhere else, then try 061 1199 as an emergency number
of last resort.

Nearby guest farms
There is an assortment of fairly offbeat guest-farms within reach of Gobabis, and
several places geared up to catch people taking overnight stops on the Trans-
Kalahari highway. These include:

Kiripotib Guest Farm (5 rooms) P Bag 13036, Windhoek; tel: 062 581419; email:
kirikara@mweb.com.na; web: www.kirikara.com
The engaging Hans and Claudia von Hase run this friendly guest farm. It's the base not
only for a thriving little arts and crafts business, but also for African Kirikara Safaris –
which offers various mobile safaris around the subcontinent. Kiripotib has three pleasant,
spacious rooms with en-suite bathrooms, and also two twin-bedded safari-style tents that
each have open-air en-suite shower facilities. Meals are served in a thatched Lapa, or
around the fire under the stars.

Perhaps the most interesting aspects of Kiripotib are the variety of arts and crafts
practised on site. There's a spinning workshop and weavery, where the team on the farm
produces a variety of unique Namibian carpets made from karakul wool. You can see all the
stages between the sheep and the carpets, and there's a small exhibition of these that are for
sale. If you're planning on buying a carpet, then it costs no more to bring colours and fabric

samples to Kiripotib, and the team here can then make up one of their designs, matching your colours and sizes as closely as possible. (Obviously this takes time, but they do send regular shipments to Europe, and so delivery is easily arranged.)

Secondly there's a well-equipped small jewellery workshop which, when in full production, makes fascinating viewing.

More distant activities include farm drives (usually integrated with a general tour of the weavery), and trips to nearby farms with their own attractions. For example, with a little advanced notice, you can visit Tivoli Star Lodge, based on the neighbouring farm, Tivoli, which has a small observatory with a sliding roof and a computer-controlled reflecting telescope. Alternatively one nearby farm has plenty of game in a classic Kalahari landscape (shame the big cats are caged), or it's possible to arrange a drive and half-day walk in the Karubeams Mountains. There it takes about 30 minutes to climb on to a lovely plateau, and there's a fair chance of seeing oryx, kudu and klipspringers.

From an arts and crafts perspective, one of the most interesting trips is to the farm, Jena, which is about 80km south of Kiripotib. See comments under Uhlenhorst, on page 198, on the embroidery work done there.

Rates: N$510/585 (N$405 for a tent) per person sharing/single including breakfast and dinner. Open: 21 Jan–15 Dec.

Rust Mijn Ziel Guestfarm (2 chalets) PO Box 5545, Windhoek; tel: 062 581655; fax: 062 581667; email: erholungsfarm@iway.na; web: www.erholungsfarm.iway.na
This tiny guestfarm on the D1790 between Dordabis and Gobabis is run by Lothar and Sabine Ruchel. It's a working farm with sheep and goats, and they've just two Swiss-style wooden chalets. The separate cozy lounge has a fire for winter and no TV – though there is a rather marvellous reel-to-reel tape recorder.

There are about 25–30km of nature trails for walking in the bush, and visitors can explore these whilst taking hand-held radios in case of emergency. Horseriding is also possible, always accompanied by one of the team from the farm, although they don't yet have all the safety equipment that a modern stable in Europe would have (eg: no hard hats at all when I visited).

Rates: from N$440 per person sharing, including all meals. Open: all year.

Kalahari Bushbreaks Guesthouse (7 rooms) all reservations via Logufa, PO Box 21783, Windhoek; tel: 062 658936; fax: 062 569001; email: enquiries@kalaharibushbreaks.com; web: www.kalaharibushbreaks.com. Contact the lodge directly on tel: 062 568936; fax: 062 569001
About 87km east of Windhoek, and 26km west of the border with Botswana at Mamuno, Kalahari Bushbreaks is about 3km south of the main B6 road. It is owned and run by Ronnie and Elsabe Barnard, who have lived here since 1982. The lodge has 40km^2 under game, including eland, oryx, giraffe, kudu, red hartebeest, warthog, zebra (both Burchell's and Hartmann's mountain) and blue wildebeest. Several species of antelope which wouldn't normally be found in the Kalahari are also here, including waterbuck and blesbok (both normal and albino). The predators include cheetah, leopard and caracal.

Accommodation is currently in one of seven bedrooms, all with en-suite facilities, and when I last visited there was talk of two new bungalows which each have two twin rooms. The standard of the accommodation here is generally good, with lots of wood, reeds and leather.

The main lodge building consists of a warm, enclosed lounge and dining area with high thatched ceiling. Above this are three en-suite bedrooms. There's also a large, doughnut-shaped thatched boma area, with a fireplace in the middle, which is used for outdoor eating when temperatures are warm. Reflecting Ronnie's profession of architecture, it's all been well and carefully designed with solid wood on a large scale. Be aware that there is a sprinking of animal trophies on the walls, and that the farm is occasionally used for hunting.

Although many visitors simply stop over here, activities can be arranged revolving around game and birdwatching drives. They can also encompass visiting rock paintings (some San, and some alleged to be of a different origin), bush walks with a guide and horseriding for experienced riders (who don't mind riding feisty working horses) without a hard hat.

Rates: N$375/455 per person sharing/single, including dinner and breakfast. Activities cost about N$35 per person (minimum 4 people) for a 90-minute game drive, or N$75 per hour per group (maximum 4 people) for a guided walk. Open: all year

Kalahari Bushbreaks Tented Camp & Campsite all reservations via Logufa, PO Box 21783, Windhoek; tel: 062 658936; fax: 062 569001; email: enquiries@kalaharibushbreaks.com; web: www.kalaharibushbreaks.com or contact the lodge on tel: 062 568936; fax: 062 569001
Accessed via the same turn-off as the guesthouse, Kalahari Bushbreaks also runs a simple camp of a few pre-erected dome tents and a campsite within a few hundred metres of the road. Both are deigned as stopovers for travellers on the Trans-Kalahari, though there is always the opportunity to join (and pay for) activities from the lodge if you wish.

The tented camp is immediately adjacent to the gate, and consists of three simple, bow-tents. The campsite is on the right, just beyond the gate and the tented camp.
Rates: N$115 per tent plus N$15 per person for bedding. N$30 per person camping. Open: all year.

Zelda Game and Guest Farm (10 rooms) PO Box 75, Gobabis; tel: 062 560427; fax: 062 560431; email: zelda.guestfarm@iafrica.com.na
Zelda is about 90km east of Gobabis, and 20km west of the Buitepos border, on the north side of the main B6 Trans-Kalahari Highway. This farm started in 1946, and started accepting guests in 1997. It covers about 100km², of which half is dedicated to game, and the rest to cattle farming.

Most people use it as a stop-over, complete with the 'Baboona' bar (with pool table), a restaurant, a souvenir shop and a pleasant, leafy garden – with swimming pool for those hot Kalahari days. Activities are limited, but it's possible to do nature/farm drives, and to help with the feeding of the animals!
Rates: around N$230/350 per person sharing/single, including breakfast. Open: all year.

Good Hope Country House (4 rooms) PO Box 1100, Gobabis; tel/fax: 062 563700; email: sanworld@iafrica.com.na; web: www.sanworld.com.na/
Run by James and Christine Chapman – descendants of James Chapman, the famous Victorian Explorer – this is a small guesthouse often used as a base for safaris run by the family.

When researching I wasn't able to get in touch with Good Hope, although when available it seems to have a generally good reputation. I'd welcome news about it from passing visitors…

Harnas Guestfarm (6 wooden cottages and 3 igloos) PO Box 548, Gobabis; tel: 062 568788/568879; fax: 062 5688887; email: harnas@iwwn.com.na; web: www.namibweb.com/harnas.htm
Almost 100km drive northeast of Gobabis, Harnas is probably has the highest profile of any guest farm in the region. To get here, take the B6 east from Gobabis and turn left after about 6km onto the C22. The first 12.5km of this is tar, but then it reverts to being a wide gravel road for about 30km until it reaches a Harnas sign at Drimiopsis, when you take a right. About 7.5km further on the road branches and you keep left. Continue for a further 38km and the entrance to Harnas is on the left.

Harnas farm was once a cattle farm, but has gradually changed into a sanctuary for injured and orphaned animals – now housing over 200 of them. That's why it's so well known, and in recent years, Harnas Wildlife Foundation has been established for the

TO SAVE OR NOT TO SAVE

Several farms, often driven by kind individuals with the very best of motives, have set up 'orphanage' or 'rehabilitation' programmes in Namibia for injured/unwanted animals. Harnas, Kaross and Okonjima spring to mind as the high-profile examples – but they are not the only ones.

Before visiting, it's perhaps worth considering the logic of some of the arguments for this, and perhaps discussing the issues with your hosts whilst there.

Some aim just to keep alive damaged or orphaned animals, some of which can be rehabilitated and released, though others can't be. The problems of keeping, say, a small orphaned antelope like a bushbuck are minimal. However, the problems caused by big cats are more major. Keeping such carnivores is difficult, as they need to be in very secure pens. Further, animals need to be killed to feed them. If it's a kindness to keep an injured lion alive, what about the horses, cows or antelope that have to be slaughtered to feed it? Why is the lion's life more valuable than the herbivores?

Demand for visitors to see big cats, and other 'sexy' species, close up make keeping habituated big cats a potentially lucrative draw for one's guest farm. (Note that I don't use the term 'tame' as neither lions nor leopards ever seem to become anything like truly tame.)

So is this why it's done?

Cynics claim that it's far from pure compassion. They question why there's a paucity of rescue centres for, say, black-faced impala? They're a species that are seriously endangered and rare. Very beautiful and well-worth preserving – but are they sexy enough to attract guests? Probably not, the cynics observe.

Pragmatic conservationists have lots of time for projects to preserve *species*, but many argue that individual animals are much less important. And as neither lions nor leopards are anything like rare – nor will they be in the near future – they really don't fall into this bracket at all. Most conservationists don't see the point in spending time and money keeping a lion alive when the same money could go towards preserving a whole ecosystem elsewhere.

One could argue, however, that when well-run such projects generate large incomes from visitors. This cash can then be used to fund serious, necessary (but perhaps less attractive) research programmes, or education programmes, which really do benefit Africa's wildlife on a much broader scale. That's a fine argument – but if it's the case, and this is their rationale for keeping caged animals as an attraction to raise money, then the cynics argue that it's time such organisations came clean.

purpose of supporting activities of the orphanage and controlling donations.

There's a variety of accommodation here – basically a total of about 16 beds in 6 wooden cottages which are well equipped with small refrigerators, tea and coffee making facilities, and braai areas. There are also some igloo-style tents with en-suite facilities, and all are spread around quite a large grassy area. Visitors also have use of a restaurant (with simple set menus), though many self-cater, and there's a large swimming pool available. Activities centre around game drives and animal feeding tours.

Rates: N$605/550 per person sharing for a cottage/igloo, including breakfast. N$135 for a campsite. Game drives N$90 per person, and animal feeding tours range from N$70-135 per tour. Open: all year.

Crossing the border into Botswana

The Buitepos border opens 07.00–17.00 and is suitable for 2WD vehicles. There's little on the other side apart from a border post until you reach the small Kalahari cattle-farming town of Ghanzi.

Hitching

Gobabis is probably the best place for hitching from Namibia into Botswana, as many trucks pass this way. Don't accept anything that will stop short of the border at Buitepos, and do carry plenty of food and water.

Dordabis and environs

The small town of Dordabis, at the end of the tarred C23 to the southeast of Windhoek, is closer to the capital than Gobabis. There's a police station and petrol station here, and a small township just outside the centre, all in a beautiful valley covered with tall acacia trees, between rounded, bush-covered hills.

In recent years the area has attracted attention as the base for several artists and craftspeople, especially weavers. **Dorka Teppiche**, situated on the farm Peperkorrel 294 (PO Box 9976, Dordabis; tel: 061 573581; fax: 061 229189) welcomes visitors, and here you can see how the textiles are woven, as well as buy the results.

Where to stay

Most of the guest farms in the area around Dordabis and Gobabis promote hunting rather than just watching game, though there are two excellent exceptions. Both are unusual, and worth a visit:

Eningu Clayhouse Lodge (8 twin rooms) PO Box 9531, Windhoek; tel: 062 581880; fax: 062 581577; email: logufa@mweb.com.na; web: natron.net/tour eningu.htm. Central reservations tel: 061 226979; fax: 061 226999

Just an hour's drive (65km) south of the international airport, Eningu is surrounded by bush-covered dunes on the fringes of the Kalahari. Expect lots of masked weaverbirds in hanging nests, round eroded hills … and perhaps a little Kalahari sand when the grass dies down. It is one of Namibia's most original small lodges, winning the country's 'Best Lodge' award in 1997.

Each of its large, spacious rooms has stylish wooden furniture and two single beds with mosquito nets. Rugs cover parts of the painted, polished floors and the en-suite bathrooms have showers rather than baths. Outside each is a veranda on which to relax, with a few chairs.

Eningu is consciously arty – though in a relaxed way without being pretentious. Its design seems to owe as much to New Mexico as Africa, and the work of many artists can be seen here, including that of the owner's mother, a well-known sculptress.

Activities include archery, volleyball and badminton, though relaxing in the hammocks amongst the banana trees (or the swimming pool and whirlpool-jacuzzi) is also popular. If you stay for more than one night, then you may also do trips to a local sculpture studio, a local leatherworking shop and craft centre, or even Arnhem Cave. This is a super, offbeat lodge, perfect for a first/last night in Namibia (if you're flying in/out).
Rates: N$524 per person, full board.

Arnhem Cave and Restcamp (4 chalets and camping) PO Box 11354, Windhoek; tel/fax: 061 581885; email: arnhem@mweb.com.na

Arnhem is signposted from the D1808, about 4km south of its junction with the D1506. From the airport take the B6–C51–D1506–D1808; from Gobabis turn left at Witvlei on to the D1800–D1808.

The main attraction here is a cave system. It's claimed to be the longest in Namibia and the sixth longest so far discovered in Africa, with about 4,500m of passages. It's thought to have been a home for bats for around 9,500 years, and still probably contains about 15,000 tons of bat guano, despite it being mined on and off for the last 70 years. Six species of bat have been identified here, including the giant leaf-nosed bat – the world's largest insectivorous bat. There are also shrews, spiders, beetles, water-shrimps and various invertebrates, some of which are endemic to the cave.

Though very dusty, and not at all fun for claustrophobics, there's a marked trail through the cave. Visitors are advised to dress in old clothes and bring torches (which can be hired for N$8 each).

The small restcamp here has good, purpose-built, thatched four-bed chalets (with fridges) as well as grassy camping sites and a swimming pool. Wood is for sale, and braai facilities are provided, but meals should be booked in advance.

Rates: self-catering chalet N$300, bed and breakfast N$230 per person, camping N$60 per person. Day visitors to cave (min 4 people) N$70.

SOUTH FROM WINDHOEK
Rehoboth
Just north of the Tropic of Capricorn and 87km south of Windhoek on the tarred B1, Rehoboth is the centre of the country's Baster community (see *People and Culture*, page 16), which is quite different from any of Namibia's other ethnic groups, and jealously guards its remaining autonomy. However, there are few reasons to stop here, other than the museum, and most people just pass on through.

Getting there
Most visitors just slow down as they drive through on the main road, but you can also arrive by train or coach. Note that long-distance coaches won't pre-book the short Windhoek–Rehoboth legs, but you may be able to board on a stand-by basis. Perhaps this explains the relative prevalence of hitchhikers around Rehoboth.

By coach
Intercape Mainliner's services from Windhoek to South Africa stop here, at the Echo service station, at 18.45 on Sun, Mon, Wed and Fri, then from South Africa to Windhoek (stand-by only) at 05.00 on Mon, Wed, Fri and Sun. These cost around N$305 to Cape Town and N$25 from Windhoek. See *Chapter 6*, pages 96–8, for more details.

By train
Trains depart from Rehoboth for Windhoek at 03.45 daily, except Sunday, and for Keetmanshoop at 21.31 daily except Saturday. They are very slow – see *Chapter 6*, pages 94–5, for details. Do note, though, that the station is a considerable distance north of the town – too far to walk – so this is rarely a good option for visitors.

Where to stay
There are two hotels in town, the **Rio Monte** (PO Box 3257; tel: 062 522572), and the **Suidwes Hotel** (PO Box 3300; tel: 062 522238). Both are in the centre of town, just to the east of the main road, and appear as if they rent their rooms by the hour or the night. Neither is recommended unless you're desperate, though both are very cheap. Better options are Reho Spa and Lake Oanob Resort:

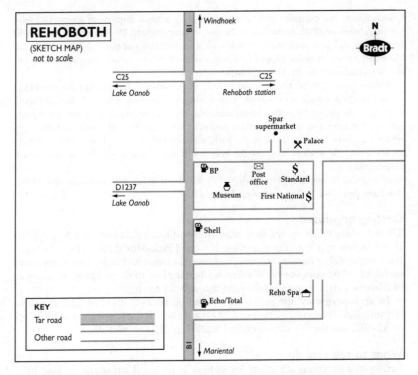

REHOBOTH
(SKETCH MAP)
not to scale

↑ Windhoek

C25 → Rehoboth station
← Lake Oanob C25

Spar supermarket

× Palace

⊞ BP

☒ Post office

$ Standard

D1237
← Lake Oanob

Museum

First National $

Shell

Reho Spa

Echo/Total

KEY
Tar road
Other road

↓ Mariental

Reho Spa (21 bungalows, camping) P Bag 1025, Rehoboth; tel: 062 522774; fax: 062 522769; email: reservations@mweb.com.na; web: www.namibiawildliferesorts.com
Run by the NWR, this small restcamp is built around the town's hot-water springs. Although it's signposted from the B1, it's not quite as easy to find as you'd expect.

The simplest approach is to turn east off the B1 at the Echo/Total garage. Follow this to the end, then turn left; Reho Spa is on the left. There's a memorable indoor jacuzzi of thermal spring water the size of a swimming pool, as well as a large outdoor pool and some good bungalow accommodation. The place can be marvellously empty if you avoid the weekends and holidays. All the bungalows here have a fridge, cooker, washbasin, toilet, and bath or shower, and campsites are available.

Rates: N$200 for a 4-bed bungalow, N$220 for 5-bed, and N$280 for 6-bed,; luxury 4-bed bungalow N$325. Camping is N$90 per site, with powerpoint, up to four people, plus N$10 per additional person up to a maximum of eight.

Lake Oanob

West of Rehoboth is Lake Oanob, created by the construction of the highest dam in Namibia. Completed in 1990, it is also one of the country's newest dams. There is a display at the lookout point showing 'before' and 'after' photos of the dam's construction, as well as some of the technical drawings used. It's an amazing thought that such a small body of water as this has a catchment area of about 2,700km².

To reach the dam, take the D1280 west of the B1, about 8km before Rehoboth, and follow this road for around 7km. There is a small entrance fee of N$10 per person.

Lake Oanob Resort (10 rooms, 5 chalets, camping) PO Box 3381, Rehoboth; tel: 062 522370; fax: 062 524112; email: oanob@iafrica.com.na
Built to cater for the numerous city-dwellers who use the place as a weekend escape, Lake

Oanob Resort has expanded in recent years, adding a small number of rooms and self-catering chalets overlooking the lake to the simple campsite here. En-suite rooms have rustic furnishings, and each has a small veranda – ideal for checking out the night sky – while the chalets are extremely well equipped for a longer stay. There's an outside bar/restaurant on site that is relaxed and friendly, albeit chilly in winter.

Fishing is available on the lake, and watersports enthusiasts are catered for with a range of facilities that include water-skiing, aqua-biking and kayaking. On land, there are short walking trails and bridle paths (horses available) around the lake. It's a pretty good place for birdwatching, too, with fish eagles and pelicans frequenting the area, and plans are under way to reintroduce game to the park, with springbok, blesbok and ostrich already in residence. As a short stop on the way south from Windhoek, this is well worth investigating.

Rates: single N$360, double N$450, family N$580, including breakfast; 2-bedroom chalet from N$500, 3-bedroom chalet from N$600. Camping N$100–160.

Getting organised

Though there's less choice here than in Windhoek, Rehoboth has a couple of shops, including a Spar, the marvellously named Pick-Mor Bazaar, a First National Bank in the Rekor Business Centre, and several casinos and nightclubs – none very exclusive. Most visitors find Windhoek a better place to shop. There are a couple of 24-hour petrol stations on the road through the town.

In an emergency, the police are reached on tel: 062 10111 or 523223, whilst the ambulance is on 062 523811 or 522006 after hours, the hospital on 062 22006/7 or 524502, and the fire service on 062 522091, 522532 or 522950.

What to see and do

Rehoboth's only real attraction for visitors is its small **museum** (P Bag 1017, Rehoboth; tel: 062 522954), just behind the post office. It's small, but has good local history exhibits on the origins of the Baster community, and the flora and fauna in the surrounding area, as well as an interesting section on bank notes. Opening hours are 10.00–12.00 and 14.00–16.00 Monday to Friday, and 09.00–12.00 Saturday.

If you're heading towards Sesriem, then note that south of Klein Aub (on the C47 southwest of Rehoboth) is a road sign showing a cup and saucer, 1km off the road. This is Connie's Restaurant, which serves excellent coffee, biscuits and light snacks.

The Southern Kalahari and Fish River Canyon

If you have journeyed north from South Africa's vast parched plateau, the Karoo, or come out of the Kalahari from the east, then the arid landscapes and widely separated towns of southern Namibia will be no surprise. Like the towns, the region's main attractions are far apart: the Fish River Canyon, Brukkaros, the Quivertree Forest, and scattered lodges of the Kalahari.

Perhaps because of their separation, they receive fewer visitors than the attractions further north, so if you want to go hiking, or to sleep out in a volcano, or just to get off the common routes – then this southern side of the country is the perfect area to visit.

MARIENTAL

Despite being the administrative centre of the large Hardap Region, which stretches from the Atlantic coast to Botswana, Mariental still avoids being a centre of attention by having remarkably few attractions. It is central and pleasant, with a sprinkling of efficient businesses serving the prosperous surrounding farmlands... but contains very little of interest. Visitors view it as a place to go through, rather than to, often skirting around the town on the main B1 – stopping only for petrol and cold drinks, if they stop at all.

Standing on the edge of the Kalahari Desert, in an area which has long been a centre for the Nama people of Namibia, Mariental's current name originated from the area's first colonial settler, Herman Brandt, who named it Marie's Valley, after his wife.

Agriculturally, Mariental is succeeding by changing with the times. The shrinking trade in pelts of karakul sheep – once so important to southern Namibia – seems to be concentrating around here. Also a new ostrich abattoir has established the town as an important centre for the country's ostrich farming, which is expanding rapidly as markets open up around the world for the ostrich's lean, low-fat meat.

With virtually no rain some years, Namibia's successful commercial farmers have diversified in order to survive. The (welcome) current trend towards managing native game rather than farm animals, and earning income directly from tourism, is just an example of this – like the boom in ostrich farming.

Getting there
By car
Approaching by car you can't miss Mariental. It's set slightly back, adjacent to the main B1. The turnings for the town centre are around the Trek garage, which has an excellent Wimpy and small supermarket adjacent to it. These are south of the

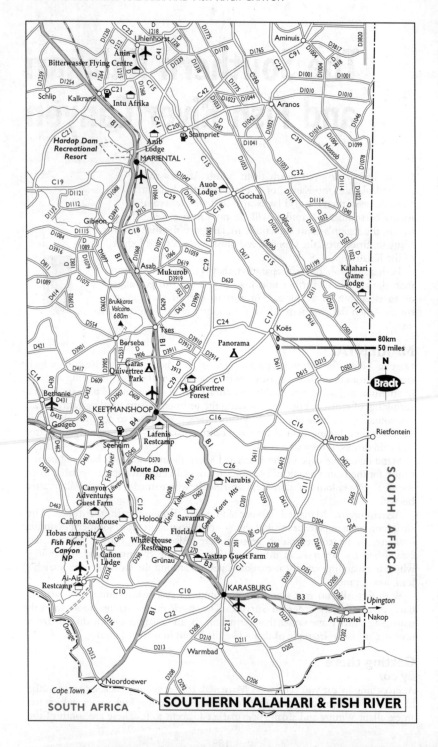

SOUTHERN KALAHARI & FISH RIVER

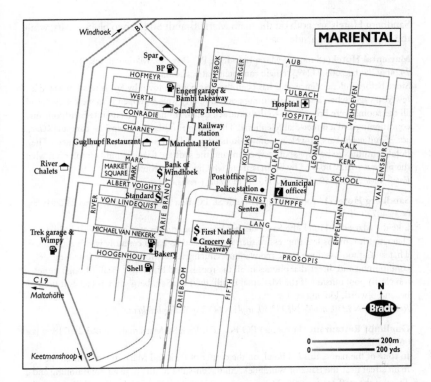

larger side-roads to Stampriet and Hardap Dam, and just north of the tarred C19 to Maltahöhe.

By coach

Intercape Mainliner run a good service linking Windhoek and Cape Town, which stops at Mariental, at the Engen station, at 20.00 – Sun, Mon, Wed and Fri – heading south, and then at 02.15 Tue, Thu, Fri and Sun going north. It costs N$345 to Cape Town, N$170 to Keetmanshoop, and N$130 to Windhoek, and must be booked in advance. See pages 96–8 for details.

Starline buses link Mariental with Gochas on Wednesday, leaving Mariental at 08.00 and returning at 15.30. There are also buses on Monday and Thursday to Maltahoe, departing at 08.00 and returning at 15.00.

By train

Mariental is linked to Windhoek and Keetmanshoop by a slow, overnight train service. It departs daily except Saturday for Keetmanshoop at 01.50 and for Windhoek at 23.50. See *Chapter 6*, pages 94–5, for details, or call TransNamib on tel: 066 29202.

Where to stay

If distances dictate that you stop around Mariental, then the hotels in town are convenient and generally cheaper than the nearby lodges. If you've more time, or are on a pre-arranged itinerary, then either Anib Lodge, Intu Afrika, or the resort at Hardap Dam are possibilities. See below for all three. Note that, without an advanced booking, you're more likely to find rooms in town. The Mariental and

Sandberg Hotels are both on the main Marie Brandt Street, two blocks apart, while the Guglhupf is on a side road.

Mariental Hotel (18 rooms) Marie Brandt St, PO Box 619, Mariental; tel: 063 242466/7/8; fax: 063 242493; email: mnhotel@iafrica.com.na
Since before independence, this has been the best hotel in town by far. It was renovated a few years ago, when a small swimming pool and fairly well-equipped gym were added, and all the rooms were brought up to the same standards. All now have en-suite bathroom, air conditioning and a direct-dial telephone. The hotel promises three separate bars: the *ladies*, *action*, and *public* bars. (I welcome news on how these live up to their various names.) The hotel continues to be kept spotlessly clean, and the staff are friendly and helpful, even when the place is totally booked by businessmen, which is not uncommon.
Rates: single N$264.50, double N$356.50, including breakfast.

Sandberg Hotel (14 rooms) Marie Brandt St, PO Box 12, Mariental; tel: 063 242291; fax: 063 240738
Like the Mariental Hotel, the Sandberg has been around for years and changed little in character. It remains less impressive than its rival, and its bar is certainly worth avoiding. That said, it too has done some renovation, reducing its number of rooms, installing air conditioning and direct-dial phones in all the rooms, and building a small (though none too clean) pool outside. If the Mariental is full, then the Sandberg's not as bad as it used to be, and is worth looking at.
Rates: single N$230, double N$333.50, triple N$437, including breakfast.

Guglhupf Restaurant (11 rooms) PO Box 671, Park St, Mariental; tel: 063 240718/9; fax: 063 242525.
In spite of the name, this *is* a hotel, on the corner of Park and Mark streets, behind the main street near the Bank of Windhoek. All the en-suite rooms have air conditioning and a TV, and the staff are friendly. The restaurant is open for breakfast, lunch and dinner, with main meals including steaks, pizza and pasta.
Rates: single N$185, double N$295; breakfast is à la carte and extra.

River Chalets (6 rooms) PO Box 262, Mariental; tel: 063 240515, cell: 081 128 2601; fax: 063 242418
The cheerful yellow and blue building that is the River Chalets is on the west side of the main B1 as it effectively bypasses Mariental. Its self-catering rooms each accommodates three or five people, and all have braai facilities.
Rates: single N$230, double N$315, 3-bed room N$346, 5-bed room N$460 per night. Breakfast N$17.

Where to eat
If you're staying at one of the hotels, then it is easiest to eat there: all three have restaurants in keeping with their general styles. If you're just passing through, then the three main garages have facilities to bite-and-run. The Engen garage at the north end of town has the **Bambi** take-away adjacent to it, serving pies and simple meals, whilst on the main road the Trek garage has a more extensive **Wimpy** with tables and menus. This serves what you'd find in any Wimpy across the world, and opens late into the evening. And at the BP station at the main entrance to town, the so-called ice-cream parlour also offers pies and other snacks.

Getting organised
Mariental is an efficient place if you need to do business here, with banks, garages, post office, police station and a couple of supermarkets, including a large Spar at the entrance to town by the BP garage – all you expect in a small market town.

The railway line from Windhoek south bisects the town, allowing only one crossing point (Michael van Niekerk Street). Two of the banks, the **Bank of Windhoek** and the **Standard Bank**, are on the western side, whilst the **First National Bank** is just over the tracks. Most of the **garages** are on the west, though to reach the **police station** (tel: 063 10111) and the municipal offices, where there is a **tourist information office** (open Mon–Fri only), you must cross the tracks, take a left on to Drieboom Street, then right on to Ernst Stumpfe Road. They are four–five blocks down here, on your left. Turn left on to Khoicas Street, just before the police station, to reach the **post office**, and turn left just after the police (on to Wolfaardt Street) to get to the **hospital** (tel: 063 242092).

HARDAP DAM RECREATIONAL RESORT

Entry: N$20 per adult per day, N$2 per child per day, and N$20 per car.
About 250km from Windhoek, and less than 25km from Mariental, lies the Hardap Dam, creating Namibia's largest man-made lake. This dams the upper reaches of the Fish River to provide water for Mariental and various irrigation projects. It is surrounded by a small reserve, complete with restcamp.

Getting there

Hardap has clear signposts from the main B1, about 10km north of Mariental. The entrance gate is 6km from the road, and then the office is a further 3km. There is no public transport here, though in the high season hitchhiking in and out of the restcamp from the B1 turn-off should prove straightforward.

The dam

The origin of Hardap's name is uncertain. It is probably derived from a Nama name for a big pool that was flooded by the dam, though the word also means

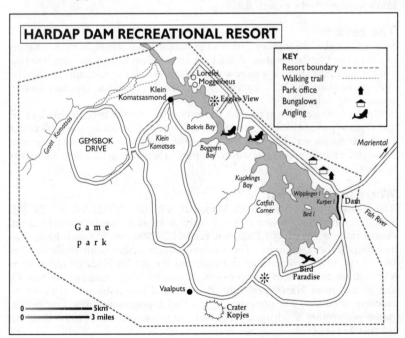

nipple (or possibly *wart*) in the Nama language – and one of the rounded hills around the dam is said to resemble a female breast.

The dam wall is 39.2m high and 865m long and was completed in 1963. It holds a maximum of about 300 million cubic metres of water, and covers around 25km². Though it doesn't often fill, it will when the rains are exceptional. It filled to 97.7% of its capacity in early 1997, forcing the sluice gates to be opened at 09.00 on Wednesday 22 January – for the first time in 20 years. If they had remained shut, it would have flooded Mariental with the next rains. (This same 1997 season also saw Sossusvlei flooded for the first time in a decade.)

Flora and fauna

Hardap stands in the central highlands of Namibia, and its rolling hilly landscape is mostly covered in low-growing bushes and stunted trees. Its river-courses tend to be thickly vegetated, often having dense, taller stands of camelthorn and buffalo-thorn trees.

The most interesting birds to be seen here are often Cape species, at the northern edge of their range, like the cinnamon-breasted warbler, the Karoo eremomela, or the uncommon Sclater's lark. Others are Namibian species towards the southern edge of their ranges, like the delightful rosy-faced lovebirds.

Hardap's larger game includes Hartmann's mountain zebra, oryx, kudu, springbok, eland and red hartebeest. Cheetah used to occur, but they thrived and escaped on to neighbouring farms, so now they have been excluded. This is classic leopard country, hilly and thickly bushed – so these are the dominant predators, though they are seldom seen. There are no lion, elephant or buffalo.

A handful of black rhino were relocated to Hardap from Damaraland in 1990, and they have settled up towards the north of the park. They were introduced to the west side of the lake, but one has been reported as crossing the lake to settle into a territory on the eastern side.

The resort

Surrounding the lake is about 251km² of protected national park, home to a variety of game. The lake itself is about 30km long, and effectively splits this area into two. On the northeast shore is a narrow strip within which the restcamp perches, on cliffs overlooking the lake. A scenic drive links several picnic sites and lookout points along its length.

On the southwest side of the lake, the reserve stretches far from the lake's shore, and is game park, veined by game drives and a few short hiking trails. Note that Hardap becomes very hot during the summer, and very cold during the winter. From chilly recollections of its windy campsite in September, I'd hate to camp here when it's *really* cold!

Where to stay and eat

The restcamp here (P Bag 2020, Mariental; tel: 063 240381; fax: 063 242285; email: reservations@mweb.com.na; web: www.namibiawildliferesorts.com; central reservations tel: 061 236975–8; fax: 061 224900) has 50 simple bungalows and there's also a campsite. The accommodation ranges from small two-bed bungalows with kitchen, fridge, hotplate and shower for N$220 a night, up to VIP suites with four beds in two rooms, air conditioning, equipped kitchen, TV and phone, from N$500 per night. Bedding and towels are provided, but no crockery or cutlery. The campsite charges N$110 per site for up to four people. Additional visitors are charged N$10 each, up to a maximum of eight. Breakfast is available for N$17.

The restaurant has superb views over the lake. It opens 07.00–09.00, 12.00–14.00 and 18.00–21.00, though meals must be ordered at least 30 minutes before closing time. A kiosk by the adjacent pool sells drinks and crisps 08.00–17.00.

Getting organised
Unlike some resorts, Hardap is open all year and doesn't lock its guests out at night. You can enter and leave at any hour of the day or night – though you can only pay for accommodation during office hours.

There's a fuel station, a small shop, and the kiosk mentioned above. However, if you intend to cook, then stock up in Mariental.

What to see and do
Hardap can get busy at the weekend, with city-dwellers escaping for a weekend of fishing or relaxing, but it's generally quiet during the week. The game park is small but quite good, and the hike is excellent.

Lake trips
Trips on the lake are run by Oasis Ferries (tel: 063 240805; cell: 081 249 4200) and last around 1½ hours. Fares are N$60 per person (children N$35), although these are less for a larger group (up to a maximum of 25). For information, contact Mr Bamberger on the above numbers.

Namibia's native fish
When paying your entry fees at reception, don't forget to take a glance at the aquaria there – displaying some of Namibia's freshwater fish, including those in the lake.

If you have a special interest in fish, then Namibia's Freshwater Fish Institute is just near the park entrance, on the left as you drive in. This is not a tourist sight, but a research and breeding centre, where the scientists sometimes welcome visitors who are fascinated by fish. Given that several Namibian species are endemic to small areas, even just to one lake or pan, this work of protecting and monitoring fish species is important.

The game park
If larger vertebrates are of more interest, then head for the game park. This means leaving the restcamp and taking a right turn before getting to the gates to the park – then driving over the dam wall. Get a map from the park office, as there are over 60km of gravel roads for game drives.

Branching off the far circular game drive in the Great Komatsas area (the Gemsbok Drive) is a marked hiking trail of 15km. This isn't strenuous and takes about 4–5 hours – though there is a shorter variation, using a shortcut, of 9km which takes 2–3 hours. There is no dangerous game around apart from a few black rhino – so keep vigilant for the thud of heavy feet, and read the *Rhino* section on page 106 before starting.

EAST OF MARIENTAL AND THE B1: THE KALAHARI
The Kalahari Desert often surprises people when they first see it. It is very different from the Namib. First of all, remember that the Kalahari is not a true desert: it receives more rain than a true desert should. The Kalahari is a *fossil* desert. *Chapter 3*, page 37, gives a more complete explanation, but don't expect to find tall Sossusvlei-style dunes devoid of greenery here. The Kalahari's dunes are very different. They

are often equally beautiful, but usually greener and less stark – and with this vegetation comes the ability to support more flora and fauna than a true desert.

Thus a few days spent in a Kalahari environment adds another dimension to a trip to Namibia, and provides game viewing away from the ever-popular Etosha, or the lush reserves of the Caprivi.

Guest farms and lodges

To the east of Mariental, on the Kalahari side, there are several excellent lodges/guest farms, as well as the flying centre at Bitterwasser, which is a major attraction in its own right for accomplished glider pilots.

When the Namibian–South African border is re-opened at Mata Mata, then the area southeast of Mariental will open up to guests, as more people pass though. The huge Kgalagadi Transfrontier Park is Africa's first 'Peace Park' – a truly integrated trans-national wildlife reserve – although perhaps to the chagrin of the Kalahari Gemsbok's small band of existing devotees, who have always regarded this out-of-the-way corner as one of the best national parks on the subcontinent.

Anib Lodge (10 rooms, camping) PO Box 800, Mariental; tel: 063 240529; fax: 063 240516; email: anib@natron.net; web: www.natron.net/tour/anib/lodgee.htm
About 34km from Mariental, Anib is around 23km east of the B1, on the C20 towards Stampriet and Aranos. It's run by Viktoria and Ernst Dukes, a vivacious Austrian couple who previously spent several years at the Etosha Garden Hotel, and have now brought this experience to create a homely and very personal atmosphere in their own lodge. Simple but comfortable double and family rooms feature stone floors and locally produced Anin textiles; each has an en-suite shower, as well as air conditioning/heating. One of the rooms has wheelchair access. The small campsite gets the five-star treatment, with each of the four pitches having electricity and a private bathroom with hot water.

Chairs and tables are set out in a flower-decked garden with a swimming pool, affording plenty of opportunity for relaxation. Two hours before sunset, guests are taken out on a sundowner game drive to experience for themselves the attractions of the Kalahari.

Food is an important aspect of life here, for Viktoria not only produces home-cooked meals but also bottles her own produce under the label 'Kalahari Gourmet'. This, along with local pottery and the Anin textiles, are sold in the shop on site. The Anin project itself is based some 100km north of Anib, between Hoachanas and Uhlenhorst (see page 198).

There are marked walks around the farm, and game drives are included in the price. Anib offers visitors the opportunity to experience all that the Kalahari has to offer, and is well worth a stay of a couple of nights.
Rates: N$621 per person, including dinner, bed and breakfast, and a game drive. Children 6–12 half price. Camping N$85 per person.

Intu Afrika Kalahari Game Reserve PO Box 40047, Windhoek; tel: 061 248741; fax: 061 226535; email: intu@iafrica.com.na; web: www.thirstlandadventures.namibia.na
Intu Afrika is a small (18,000 hectare) private reserve now owned by Thirstland Adventures. It has been fortunate in having backing to promote and sustain a sizeable wildlife reserve, as well as to develop an interesting project with the help of a small Bushman community.

Intu Afrika is on the D1268, 110km north of Mariental just south of the C21 (or north of the C20), and is clearly signposted from the B1 whether heading north or south There are now three distinct accommodation options (Zebra Lodge and Dune Lodge operate as one) as well as a separate campsite. Each is run individually, with its own kitchen, bar and management, though activities are common to all.

The original **Zebra Lodge** building is substantial, with comfortable furniture in its large airy lounge, a well-stocked bar, and enormous tree-trunk carvings adorning the reception area. At the front is a stylish swimming pool, overlooked by some marvellously knurled old *Acacia erioloba* trees.

There are four twin rooms on either side of the main building, each modern and functional with a minimum of clutter. The floors are tiled, the bathroom's en suite, and there's a phone in each room. Set a short distance away are five luxurious split-level bungalows (**Dune Lodge**), each with a sitting area and a bedroom – popular with small families, or as suites.

A few kilometres away lies the exclusive **Camelthorn Lodge**, its 10 rustic chalets dotted individually in the bush surrounding a central lapa with comfortable bar area and small swimming pool. Meals are taken in or alongside an outdoor boma. Visitors here are paying for privacy and seclusion, not luxury.

Less luxurious – but better value – is **Suricate Tented Camp**, signposted off the D1268 some 11km to the south. Here, 11 large, walk-in tents are lined up on the top of a long dune, flanking a central bar and dining area, with uninterrupted views across the reserve. These are more basic than the lodge, with no electricity, but each is self-contained with its own en-suite shower and a small veranda.

Finally, there is a **campsite** for touring vehicles and tents, with ablution blocks, kitchen and bar area, and a central fireplace.

The landscape at Intu Afrika is classic Kalahari: deep red longitudinal dunes, usually vegetated, separated by lighter clay inter-dune valleys covered in grass, trees and shrubs. The area's larger game includes giraffe, oryx, blue and black wildebeest, Burchell's zebra, and springbok – but it is the smaller animals that are the stars. The reserve seems to have a high density (or at least a visible number) of bat-eared foxes, and some entertaining groups of meerkats (suricats); the sight of a group of meerkats foraging under the guard of 'sentries' is a real delight. The sentries balance upright on their hind legs, while their keen eyes scan the area around. Neither of these social creatures is common, yet they seem to thrive here. Game-drives and related activities such as birdwatching trips are available from all parts of the reserve, including the campsite.

One other aspect of the lodge that it promotes is its Bushman project – set up and managed by anthropologists Bets and Michael Daiber. In late 1996, a small community of about 40 !Xoo Bushmen decided to support this project, and relocated to the reserve. The project's aim was to:

> 'empower the [Bushmen] community to regain their dignity and pride by
> creating employment and cultural activities which utilise traditional
> Bushmen skills in order to generate money for their community ...
> including game guiding, tracking, camp supervising and craft making.'

For the visitor, interactions with Bushmen start by being guided on early morning walks by community members, who not only can point out some of the wildlife, but also explain their traditional way of life, including collecting and storing food. You can also buy their crafts at Zebra Lodge. Six families now live here, and many of the children go to a nearby school, while other members of the community are employed on the reserve.

Compared with other lodges in the region, rates at Intu Afrika are very high, a reflection as much on its location in a beautiful private reserve as on the standards that prevail overall.

Rates per person sharing, per night (low–high season): Dune Lodge and Camelthorn N$1,160–1,450, Zebra Lodge N$960–1,200, including all meals, activities, drinks and house wine at dinner. Suricate N$835 (fully inclusive) or N$420, including breakfast. Single supplements apply at the lodges and tented camp. Campsite N$100 camping only. High season July–October inclusive.

Bitterwasser Lodge and Flying Centre (30 bungalows, 13 rondavels) P Bag 13003, Windhoek; tel: 063 265300; fax: 063 265355; email: bitterwa@mweb.com.na; web: www.bitterwasser.com

South of Uhlenhorst, on the C15, about 59km from the B1, this specialist lodge caters to glider pilots up to world-class level. Note that this is not a school for gliding – it is a place for those who know how. Pilots often stay for weeks, and have broken so many records that there's an avenue of palm trees lining the way to the airfield, where each palm was planted to commemorate a record. Every year, the avenue grows.

Bitterwasser has three gliders, a single-seater Nimbus 2, an ASW 20 15m, and a DG 500M, all of which are available for hire, but most pilots prefer to ship out their own craft by container for the season, which runs from October to February (though the lodge is open all year round). Gliding aside, there are opportunities for swimming, hot-air ballooning and game drives.

The lodge's bungalows are comfortable, with en-suite facilities and 24-hour electricity. Some have air conditioning and even CD-radios. Rondavels are more basic, with simple furniture and a central ablution block. There are also rooms in the adjacent Dune House. If you're a serious glider, then email them for precise details of their facilities and prices, or check out their website.

Rates: Bungalows single N$785, double N$1,060, bed and breakfast. Rondavels N$415, for two people, including breakfast. Dinner N$75 per person.

Auob Lodge (25 rooms) PO Box 17, Gochas; tel: 063 250101; fax: 063 250102; email: auob@mweb.com.na; web: www. namibialodges.com. Central reservations tel: 061 240375; fax: 061 256 598
Situated on the C15, about 6km north of Gochas, Auob Lodge stands in the Kalahari, close to the dry River Auob, within 80km² of its own land. It also has its own airstrip, co-ordinates S24.49 E18.46. Despite the name, the place has the atmosphere of a Continental hotel, with heavy furniture, a bar, pool room, lounge and separate restaurant. Rooms, located around a swimming pool, are comfortable, with ceiling fans and en-suite shower and toilet, but don't expect much in the way of frills. The lodge offers horseriding (not suitable for novices), and game drives amongst typical Kalahari game species, including giraffe and wildebeest, plus blesbok, introduced from South Africa.

Rates: single N$375, double N$570, triple N$645, including breakfast. Dinner N$83. Game drive N$80 per person.

Uhlenhorst

North of Mariental, this dot on the map seems little more than a large farm. It marks a petrol station and a general farm store, even if the latter has the farm's own workers in mind, rather than the odd lost tourist. However, you might be surprised to learn that in the 1930s and '40s there were two hotels, several shops, a post office and a bank here. Uhlenhorst is typical of many small Namibian towns that were once important, but faded with the advent of communications and good roads into mere shadows of themselves. If you come this way, then stop at the store for excellent homemade biltong – and perhaps to see the owners' large collection of pet ducks and even a few swans. Not the obvious pets in the Kalahari. With more time to spare, seek out the nearby farm, Jena, which is on the west side of the C15 or MR33 between Uhlenhorst and Hoachanas. From here Heidi von Hase runs a cottage embroidery industry, the **Anin project** (*anin* means 'birds' in the local Nama language), employing about 300 women of the 'Red Nation' Nama people. They handmake a wide and intricate range of embroidery and linen, including bedlinen and tableware. All work from home and come from in and around the tiny village of Hoachanas – nearby at the junction of the C21 and C15 (MR33). Crafts like these are increasingly benefiting the economies of some of Namibia's poorer areas – so go on, buy something whilst you're here! For details, or to make an appointment to visit the farm shop, contact Anin Namibia, P Bag

13094, Windhoek; tel: 063 265331; fax: 063 265332; email: anin@mweb.com.na; web: www.anin.com.na. If you're not passing through, seek out their stall at the craft centre in Windhoek, or you can find their products both at Anib Lodge and at Haus Sandrose in Luderitz.

Stampriet to Gochas
Stampriet itself has nothing of interest to drivers except a small fuel station – useful should you be running low – and Gochas likewise, but the C15 road between the two small towns makes an interesting alternative to the B1 if you're driving south from one of the above lodges. Running parallel to the Auob River, it passes through a fertile stretch of farmland. Perhaps of greatest interest, though, are the ground squirrels that inhabit the banks lining the road; it's a great place to stop and watch these intriguing animals as they go about their daily routines. From Gochas, it is a straight drive on the C18, a good, empty road, to rejoin the B1 near Gibeon.

THE ROAD FROM MARIENTAL TO KEETMANSHOOP
Between Mariental and Keetmanshoop is a 221km stretch of tar road that most visitors see at speed. However, a few places are worth knowing about as you hurry past:

Gibeon
About 6km west of the B1, this sprawling community lies in a valley. Its sole claim to fame is as the site of what is thought to be the world's heaviest shower of meteorites some 600 million years ago. Many of these are now displayed in Windhoek's Post Street Mall (see page 152), while a smaller specimen may be seen at the museum in Rehoboth.

Asab
Almost halfway between Mariental and Keetmanshoop is a tiny place beside the road: Asab. There's a fuel station, the dirty, run-down **Asab Hotel** (tel: 063 242577), and a sparsely stocked shop. It's a useful spot for emergencies, and the place to branch off the main road if you are heading to Mukurob.

Mukurob
Known as 'the Finger of God', Mukurob was once an immense rock pinnacle, which balanced on a narrow neck of rock and towered 34m above the surrounding plains. It collapsed around December 8 1988, leaving a sizeable pile of rubble. Its demise caused much speculation at the time, as the finger's existence was linked to divine approval – and the country was in the process of becoming independent. Initially it was claimed that God was displeased with contemporary developments in this independence process. Later, right-wing extremists were blamed rather than God. Eventually, though, theories linked its fall firmly with the shock waves from the large Armenian earthquake of December 7. To drive to where it stood, turn east off the B1 on to the D1066, just south of Asab, and follow the signs for about 23km. To see it as it once was, drop into the tourist information office at Keetmanshoop and have a look at the replica.

Tses
Two-thirds of the way towards Keetmanshoop, opposite the turning to Berseba and Brukkaros, Tses is a small township on the east of the road. As in any small, poor country township, visitors passing through are treated as something of a curiosity, but made welcome. If you're travelling by bus, the service leaves for

Keetmanshoop on Monday and Friday at 13.15. There's a small trading store across the railway, and a Caltex petrol station open 07.00–20.00.

Brukkaros

Rising to 650m, the volcanic crater of Brukkaros towers over the expanse of bare, flat plains that surround it. It's a classic volcano shape, easily visible west of the B1. Early this century the Germans used the eastern side of the crater as the base for a heliograph. Then later, in the early 1930s, the Smithsonian Institute built a solar observatory on the western side, taking advantage of the clear air and lack of artificial lights nearby. Both the Germans and the observatory have now gone, and the skies are as clear as ever – so it's a great place to explore and possibly camp.

Getting there

About 80km north of Keetmanshoop, and just south of the turning to Tses, turn west on to the M98 (signposted simply 'Berseba'). The road crosses the Fish River after about 19km, and it's worth a short stop to check out the waterbirds, including sacred ibis, that congregate here. In late afternoon, you may even spot a family of baboon crossing the river. After a further 19km, just before you reach Berseba, turn north towards the volcano on to the D3904. Though this looks like a short distance, it'll be 9km or so on a flat road until you are at the gates, and only then do you start to climb the volcano near the end of the road. Getting here without your own vehicle would mean taking the twice-weekly bus to Berseba (arriving from Keetmanshoop at 11.00 on Monday and Friday, and departing at 12.15) but you'd almost certainly have to walk from there.

There's an entrance fee of N$15 per person for day visitors, or N$25 for those camping overnight, plus N$10 for a vehicle. The money collected benefits the people of the surrounding villages.

Where to stay

Before the road deteriorates, there's a small campsite (tel: 061 250558; fax: 061 222647) with individual barbecue places, basic toilets and bucket showers. Above this, you need a 4WD to reach the second camping area. Though wood and water are said to be available at the gates, don't bank on it – there's a basic store in Berseba if you're out of supplies. There's a public telephone at the gate in case of emergency.

What to see and do

From the 4WD campsite, a footpath leads to the eroded edge of the southern crater's southern lip. The path here was made whilst the observatory was being constructed, and it goes over the lip and into the crater, taking about 40 minutes, then continues up to the old observatory just below the western rim after an hour or so. The rim itself is a very short scramble away. Guided walks are in theory available for N$20 an hour.

You can hike around here, or just sit and watch the dust-devils twist their way for miles around as the sun goes down. It is a superb place to sleep out under the stars, which you will probably never see more clearly.

Berseba

The nearest town to Brukkaros, Berseba is one of the region's oldest settlements – notable for having had a Rhenish missionary, Samuel Hahn, based there as early as 1850. Now it remains a large though poor settlement, surviving by subsistence farming. This area often receives very little rain, and agriculture of any kind is difficult. There are a couple of shops for essentials and a fuel pump at the end of the road, though don't rely on the latter.

Continuing south on the B1, the road remains level and straight. If you're camping and hoping to stop before Keetmanshoop, it may be worth considering Susan Hulme's somewhat unusual site 22km to the north of the town:

Garas Quivertree Park and Restcamp PO Box 106, Keetmanshoop; tel/fax: 063 223217; email: morkel@namibnet.com. There's a great sense of humour here, with numerous model figures lining the 1km drive from the B1 to the campsite. Although there *is* a campsite, with some very basic (but nevertheless clean) toilet and shower facilities, the real appeal is the rather eclectic mix of traditional huts and other artefacts that are displayed around the place almost in junkyard fashion. There are quivertrees too, as you would expect from the name, and several aloe plants. Wood and water are available, but otherwise you need to be entirely self sufficient. *Rates: camping N$25 per person, plus N$5 per vehicle and N$5 per trailer. Day visitors N$5 each.*

KEETMANSHOOP

Pronounced 'Keet-mans-verp', which is often shortened in slang to just 'Keetmans', Keetmanshoop lies about 480km south of Windhoek at an altitude of 1,000m. The tar roads from Lüderitz, South Africa and Windhoek meet here, making it the hub of southern Namibia's road network, as well as the administrative centre of this region.

Originally there was a Nama settlement on the banks of the seasonal Swartmodder River here, also known as Swartmodder. Then, in 1866, the Rhenish Missionary Society sent Johan Schröder here from their established station at Berseba. He organised the building of a church and named it Keetmanshoop (which means 'Keetman's hope'), after Johan Keetman, one of the rich benefactors who had paid for the building.

In 1890 that church was swept away by a freak flood, but a new one, built on higher ground, was completed five years later. This was disused for years, but restored and declared a monument in 1978. Now it shelters the town's museum, so at least visit this, even if you see nothing else here.

Getting there
By air
Keetmanshoop's small airport is found by following Kaiser Street west and north through town, past the caravan park, and out the other side. There are currently no scheduled flights, although it is possible for charters to land here. In case the situation should change, it is worth checking with Air Namibia (see page 149).

By car
Keetmanshoop is situated at the hub of the road network in southern Namibia, linked to Windhoek, South Africa and Lüderitz by good tar roads.

By bus
Intercape Mainliner run a good service linking Windhoek and Cape Town, which stops at Keetmanshoop, at the BP Du Toit station on 5th Avenue, at 22.35 on Sun, Mon, Wed and Fri heading south, and then at midnight Tue, Thu, Fri and Sun going north. It costs N$320 from Cape Town and N$240 from Windhoek, and must be booked in advance, either at the local office at the Engen garage on 5th Avenue (tel: 063 223063) or through another agent (see pages 96–8 for details).

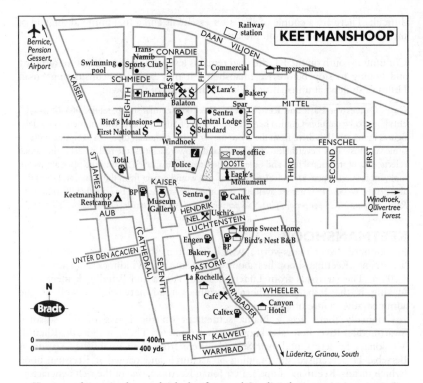

Keetmanshoop is also at the hub of several Starline bus services, connecting the town with, among others, Bethanie, Helmeringhausen, Aus, Lüderitz and Oranjemund – but note that unauthorised visitors may not visit Oranjemund as it lies within the Sperrgebiet. Lüderitz buses leave the town at 07.30 on Monday, Wednesday and Friday, with the return journey arriving back in Keetmanshoop at 13.00 on the same days. Buses for Bethanie and Helmeringhausen depart from Keetmanshoop on Tuesday at 08.10, arriving back at 18.00. Those for Goageb, Bethanie, Aus and Lüderitz run daily except Sunday, leaving at 07.30, with the return trip arriving back every day except Saturday at 17.30 (16.30 on Sunday). For details, phone TransNamib in Keetmanshoop on tel: 063 292202.

By train

Keetmanshoop is linked by train services to Windhoek and also to Ariamsvlei, on the South African border, and through to Upington. Trains run between Keetmanshoop and Windhoek every day except Saturday, arriving at 06.30 and departing at 18.25. On two days per week, Wed and Sat, trains depart for Ariamsvlei at 08.50, arriving back the following day at 16.30. See *Chapter 6*, pages 94–5, for details, or call TransNamib in Keetmanshoop on tel: 063 292202.

Where to stay

Central Lodge (13 rooms) Fifth Av, PO Box 661, Keetmanshoop; tel: 063 225850; fax: 063 223532; email: clodge@iway.na

George Roux has plugged a big gap in the market with the elegant Central Lodge, opened in 2001. A breath of fresh air in Keetmanshoop, the Central is just that – central. Its narrow entrance leads through the restaurant to a spacious courtyard, complete with fountain, around which are set light, welcoming rooms. Each is well appointed, with en-suite shower, TV, phone, air conditioning/heating, telephone and tea/coffee-making facilities. Three luxury rooms also boast a jacuzzi.

Beyond the courtyard is a swimming pool surrounded by a grassy area with tables and chairs. In the main building, the stylish and modern restaurant is open 12.00–14.00 and 18.30–21.00 daily, except Sunday evenings, serving the standard fare of steaks, fish and crayfish. Alongside is a small bar, while outside, secure parking is available for visitors' vehicles.

Rates: single N$200–225, double N$350–400, family from N$450, including breakfast.

Canyon Hotel (70 rooms) Warmbader Rd, PO Box 950, Keetmanshoop; tel: 063 223361; fax: 063 223714; email: canyon@iafrica.com.na; web: www.canyon-namibia.com
Time has not dealt kindly with Keetmanshoop's best hotel, and it's looking a little worn, although there's a rolling programme of renovation, and rooms downstairs have recently been redecorated. That said, the service remains friendly, and the rooms, whilst they could be anywhere in the world, are comfortable, with TVs, direct-dial telephones, air conditioning and simple coffee machines. En-suite bathrooms have showers and, downstairs, hairdryers.

Around the hotel you'll find a restaurant, a bar, curio shop, and large outdoor pool, as well as a separate coffee shop/bar serving light meals.

Rates (low/high season): single N$290/414, double N$450/644, including breakfast. Low season is November to March.

Bird's Mansions Hotel (22 rooms) Sixth Av, PO Box 460, Keetmanshoop; tel: 063 221711; fax: 063 221730; email: birdsmansions:iway.na; web: http://birdnest.hypermart.net or www.visitnambia.de
In the centre of town, Bird's Mansions was taken over three years ago by Riana Jacobs, owner of the Bird's Nest B&B, and friendly service is the hallmark here. Large rooms with new carpets and fans are off the courtyard at the back, while those in the main building remain old fashioned. All share the same facilities, though: TV, telephone and air conditioning. Construction at the rear of the hotel will result in a lapa with heated swimming pool, eating area and dance floor by August 2002.

There's off-street parking behind the hotel (entrance on Seventh St). The airy restaurant offers a varied menu of fish, game, steak and pasta, with prices in the N$40–75 bracket. Next door is an internet café.

Rates: single N$280, double N$400, family room N$550, including breakfast.

Bird's Nest B&B (10 rooms) 16 Pastorie St, PO Box 460, Keetmanshoop; tel: 063 222906; fax: 222261; email: birdnest@iafrica.com.na; web: http://birdnest.hypermart.net or www.visitnamibia.de
The Bird's Nest is an excellent little B&B close to the centre of Keet, and under the same ownership as Bird's Mansions, Rooms are fairly small, but light and modern, with attractive fabrics and en-suite showers or baths. All have air conditioning/heating, ceiling fans, TV, telephone and facilities for making hot drinks. Outside, the gardens are well tended, underlying the care that goes into this place.

Rates: single N$250, double N$380, family N$530 (up to 4 people, of which 2 under 12), including breakfast.

Home Sweet Home (7 rooms) 19 Luchtenstein St, PO Box 1164, Keetmanshoop; tel: 063 22607, cell: 081 127 5397; email: jrpanel@iway.na
Tucked away down a side street close to the centre of town, this vivid green and purple bed and breakfast is certainly eye-catching. Rooms are bright, light and modern, with combinations of double and bunk beds, basic self-catering facilities and en-suite shower, and there's secure parking. For all its attractions, though, the place didn't feel particularly welcoming when we visited.

Rates: single N$200, double N$280, 4 people N$380. Breakfast is not available, but costs around N$25 at Uschi's restaurant down the road.

La Rochelle (7 rooms) 12 Sixth Av, PO Box 582, Keetmanshoop; tel: 063 223845; fax: 063 229253
George and Elsa Brand bought this hundred-year-old house in 1997, painted it bright pink and converted it into a guesthouse, with some interesting results. Somewhat chintzy in décor, the rooms vary from the fairly luxurious, with air conditioning and TV, to the more standard, with a fan. Although all are en suite, check your room first if you're sharing – one has the toilet *in* the bedroom. Outside is a small pool and a pleasant rocky garden, plus secure parking.
Rates: single N$160–200, double N$260–300, including breakfast.

Pension Gessert (6 rooms) 138 13th St, Westdene, PO Box 690, Keetmanshoop; tel/fax: 063 223892; email: gesserts@iafrica.com.na
This quiet little residential B&B with its pretty garden is in the Westdene suburb. To reach it, head west and then northwest on Kaiser St, crossing the railway line. Then turn sharp left into Westdene, and right into 19th Av. 13th St is the third turning on the left. The place is friendly and professional.
    Attractive rooms have en-suite facilities and air conditioning, and there is a small swimming pool that you can use. Breakfast is provided, and other meals are available on request.
Rates: single N$240, double N$350, family N$460, including breakfast.

Bernice Beds (5 rooms) 129 10th St, PO Box 415, Keetmanshoop; tel: 063 222844; cell: 081 124 6278; fax: 063 223289
Also in the suburb of Westdene, this small pension set in attractive gardens was opened in 2001 by Laetitia Schröer. As for Pension Gessert, above, take the road to the northwest towards the airport, cross over the bridge and turn left at the lights, then left again into 10th St. Double and family rooms all have TV, air conditioning/heating and en-suite showers, and there's safe parking. Pleasant and welcoming, this place offers good-value accommodation.
Rates: single N$150, double N$250, family N$100 per person. Breakfast N$25 per person.

Keetmanshoop Restcamp Eighth Av, P Bag 2125, Keetmanshoop; tel: 063 223316 or 221265; fax: 063 222835
This has been one of Namibia's best municipal sites for years. Inside protective coils of razor wire lie clean ablution blocks surrounded by grass lawns (easily pierced by tent-pegs), and there's lots of space for cars and caravans on the gravel drives that surround the grass. It's a very good site, if you are happy to camp in town.
Rates: N$40.25 per site, plus N$19.55 per vehicle. Showers N$9.20.

Burgersentrum Backpackers (25 dormitory beds, 5 double rooms) 12 Schmiede St, PO Box 1381, Keetmanshoop; tel: 063 223454; fax: 063 225259
Keet's only backpackers' hostel is close to the junction with 3rd St, next door to the purple house. Rooms are basic but clean, with shared bathrooms and toilets, and a communal kitchen. A standard 'per person' rate makes this good value for double rooms.
Rates: N$70 per person.

Where to eat
Keetmanshoop's best place for a good meal is the **Central Lodge** (see page 202). Both the **Canyon Hotel** and **Bird's Mansions** also have restaurants, the former rather soulless and typical of a large hotel. Both have wide-ranging menus (mains N$45–60 and N$45–75 respectively) that include a couple of vegetarian options.

Once you've run the gauntlet of the very austere bar at the front, **Lara's Restaurant** (tel: 063 222233), at the corner of Fifth Avenue and Schmiede Street, is an unexpectedly cheerful spot without any pretensions. Portions are huge, and it's chips with everything, but the steaks are excellent and prices are reasonable, at around N$40–50 for mains. It's open 08.00–21.00 every day except Sunday. **Uschi's** (tel: 063 222445), at the corner of Hendrik Nel Street and Fifth Avenue, offers a variety of snacks and light meals, including an adventurous pizza menu at around N$30–45 – but don't come in a hurry for the latter. It's open 08.00–10.00 Monday to Saturday. **Balaton** (tel: 063 222539) on Mittel Street opens all day as a take-away and simple restaurant serving spicy Hungarian cuisine. Very warming; ideal for cold winter evenings. The Germanic **Trans-Namib Sports Club** on Schmiede Street serves pub grub and draught beer.

On the snack front, most of the proliferation of garages have some form of café attached, serving pretty standard fare of pies, burgers and cold drinks – useful if you're pushed for time.

Getting organised

Keetmanshoop could well be vying for the record for the greatest number of **fuel stations** per head of population! It's also a good place to visit banks and shops and get organised. If you enter on Kaiser Street, then you will find most of these one block over to your right, on Fenschel Street – which runs parallel to Kaiser Street. Here are the First National and Standard **banks**, and several **supermarkets**, including Sentra and Spar; next to Uschi's restaurant there's another branch of Sentra that remains open at lunchtime. **Camping supplies** are available from LTL on Fifth Avenue, opposite Central Lodge. For souvenirs, it may be worth checking out the craft stalls laid out by the side of the road as you leave the B1.

If you want to stop for a brief break, then the small grassy park standing between the tourist office and the post office is ideal. You can relax and watch both the townspeople and your vehicle at the same time.

In an emergency, the main hospital (tel: 063 223388) is on the main road as you're heading out of town. The town's pharmacy is on tel: 063 223309, and the police may be contacted on tel: 063 223359.

Tourist information

Southern Tourist Forum (STF) Fifth St; tel: 063 223316; fax: 063 223818; email: munkhoop@iafrica.com.na

Opposite the main post office, over a grassy square, this bears a grand name for a tourist office, but the lady who runs the place is keen and helpful, and aims to promote the whole region. So do stop in for a chat, and look out for the replica of Mukurob, the Finger of God (see page 199). It's open Mon–Fri, 07.30–12.30 and 13.30–16.30.

What to see and do

Like many of Namibia's provincial towns, Keetmanshoop doesn't have a wealth of attractions in the town, though you could while away a couple of lazy hours visiting its museum, and the tourist office, which resides in perhaps the town's most historic building, the **Kaiserliches Postamt** – or Imperial Post Office. This was built in 1910 and is now a national monument.

Museum Tel: 063 221256/11

In a central spot on Kaiser Street, this old Rhenish Mission Church was built in 1895 to replace the original one that the floods destroyed. Now it is surrounded by rockeries and used as the town's museum. Don't ignore these rockeries though, as they are dotted with native plants, as well as old wagons, machinery and even a Nama hut. If you're not visiting the Quivertree Forest, then take a close look at the small trees here in the museum's garden. Inside the church is a beautiful pulpit and an interesting collection of local memorabilia, including a selection of early cameras, photographs, and various implements which were used by past townspeople.

Open: Mon–Fri 07.30–12.30, 13.30–16.30. Admission is free, but donations are welcome.

Nearby guest farms and lodges

Quivertree Forest Restcamp (8 rooms, 8 bungalows, camping) PO Box 262, Keetmanshoop; tel/fax: 063 222835; email: quiver@iafrica.com.na

14km from Keetmanshoop is the Quivertree (or Kokerboom) Forest (see opposite), which stands on privately owned farmland. To get here, take the C16 road towards Koës, and turn off on to the M29 (marked just 29 on the road).

The farm itself is owned by Coenie and Ingrid Nolte, who are helpful and informative hosts. Accommodation consists of eight en-suite rooms in two separate houses, each with its own lounge and minibar, and one with a kitchen. In addition, there are eight comfortable self-catering bungalows, of a wonderful igloo design, all of which have en-suite facilities. Near by is a barbecue area, tree-house style. There is also a tree-shaded campsite adjacent to the Quivertree Forest.

It's also a great place for children, with a swimming pool, ingeniously converted from a large farm tank, and a trampoline, not to mention a family of meerkats and two pet warthogs. Rather less attractive is the stark cage behind the farm buildings where three cheetahs are housed. Staying here is a good alternative to Keetmanshoop, and makes it easier to see the forest and the rocks around dawn and dusk, when the light is at its best for photography.

Rates: single N$340, double N$600, including breakfast & dinner. Bed & breakfast only is N$235 single, N$440 double, and self-catering single N$200, double N$300. Camping N$55 per person (both dinner (N$80) and breakfast (N$35) are available by arrangement).

Panorama Campsite (4 pitches) Tel: 063 225050

Campers seeking something a little more remote may be interested in this simple site some 40km from Keetmanshoop on the C17 towards Koës. Each pitch has a table, hot water and braai, with ablution blocks close by and wood available on site, though you will need to bring all other provisions with you. There is a 16km 4WD trail around the site, and a guided fossil 'trail', taking in the fossils of the huge mesosaurus that inhabited the freshwater lakes of Gondwanaland 270 million years ago. Stands of quivertrees are also a feature of this landscape, as are the giant dolorite rock formations. Costs for the trail are around N$30 per person, depending on group size, or visitors may drive themselves.

Rates: N$40 per pitch, plus N$10 per person. Braai available on request at N$35 per person.

Lafenis Restcamp (21 bungalows and rooms, camping) P Bag 827, Keetmanshoop; tel/fax: 063 224316; fax: 063 224309; email: wheretostay@colourgem.co.za

Just south of Keetmanshoop on the B1, about 2km from the junction with the B4 for Lüderitz, this is a simple, friendly restcamp with a rather unlikely wild west theme. It caters adequately for overnight stops. There's a campsite with electric hook-ups, a swimming pool, and a small restaurant, and each of the small bungalows has air conditioning.

Rates: VIP rooms N$300 double; bungalows from N$180 (1-bed) to N$585 (7-bed), all including breakfast. Camping N$50 for the site, plus N$10 per adult, N$6 per child under 13.

Excursions from Keetmanshoop

If you prefer to base yourself in a town, then the **Fish River Canyon** and **Brukkaros** can both become day-trips from Keetmanshoop. However, each is a

QUIVERTREES

The quivertree, *Aloe dichotoma*, occurs sporadically over a large area of southern Namibia and the northern Cape, usually on steep rocky slopes. Its name refers to its supposed use by the Bushmen for making the quivers for their arrows – the inside of a dead branch consists of only a light, fibrous heart which is easily gouged out to leave a hollow tube.

The quivertree is specially adapted to survive in extremely arid conditions: its fibrous branches and trunk are used for water storage, as are its thick, succulent leaves, whilst water lost through transpiration is reduced by waxy coatings on the tree's outside surfaces. Additionally, in common with most desert-adapted flora, its growth rate is very slow.

destination in its own right, and so they are covered separately. The two obvious excursions from town, the Quivertree Forest and the Giant's Playground, are almost adjacent. A little further afield, on the way to the Fish River Canyon via Seeheim, is Naute Dam, recently declared a recreational area.

Quivertree Forest

Also known as the 'Kokerboomwoud', this is a dense stand of *Aloe dichotoma* tree-aloes, just 14km away from Keetmanshoop on the land of Gariganus Farm, owned by Coenie and Ingrid Nolte.

Take the B1 north for about one kilometre, then the C16 towards Koës, then left again on to the M29 shortly after this. These trees are found all over southern Namibia and the northern Cape, but in few places are so many seen together. (A second is a few kilometres south of Kenhardt, on the R27 in South Africa.)

Ideally drop in here around sunset or sunrise, when the light is at its best. These skeletal 'trees' make particularly striking photographs when the lighting of a fill-in flash is balanced against flaming sunset behind. Entry to the forest costs N$10 per person, plus N$20 for a vehicle, and includes entry to the Giant's Playground (see below).

Giant's Playground

Just 5km further down the M29 are some marvellous balancing basalt rocks known as the Giant's Playground. Reminiscent of formations in Zimbabwe's Matobo Hills, these are more limited but still interesting.

Naute Dam Recreational Resort

Surrounded by low hills, and overlooked by the Klein Karas mountains, the lake created by Naute Dam is about 26km long and, at its widest, some 7km.

Getting there

From Keetmanshoop, take the B4 west to Seeheim, then turn south on to the C12. The entrance to the resort is to the left, about 25km from Seeheim, just before the dam itself. Further south, just beyond the dam, is a second turning on to the D545, signposted Nautedam, which leads towards the southern lakeshore. This road heads straight towards the mountains for 13km, then you turn right by a farm, signposted 'camping area'. From here, you can choose whether to head for the lake (take the left fork) or the game park.

Entrance to the park is N$7 per vehicle (N$15 for a minibus) plus N$3 per person.

Where to stay

Although an area around the lake is officially designated as a campsite, there are no facilities here at all, so if you plan to camp you will have to bring everything with you. That said, it's a peaceful spot right by the lake, and a wonderful place for birdwatching. It is to be hoped, though, that the area's new-found protected status will bring about a clean up of the broken glass strewn among the boulders. Camping costs N$30, and fees must be paid at the main entrance.

What to see and do

The 470m-long Naute Dam was opened in 1972. Standing 37m above the riverbed, it holds back the water from the Naute River as it feeds into the Fish River to the southwest. From the main entrance, where there are picnic tables and a small snack kiosk, there is a good vantage point over both the dam itself and the lake beyond with its cluster of small islands.

Not surprisingly, the lake has become a focus for numerous birds. There are opportunities for birdwatching from the viewpoint, but it is the reed-fringed sandy lakeshore to the south of the main entrance that is the real haven for waterbirds, with pelicans, herons, little egrets, cormorants and sacred ibis all in evidence. On the margins can be seen plenty of other species, including the blacksmith plover, African darter and African red-eyed bulbul.

At present, the game park is in its infancy, but it is presumably just a matter of time before this becomes an attraction in its own right.

THE DEEP SOUTH

South and east of Keetmanshoop, Namibia's central highlands start to flatten out towards the South Africa's Karoo, and the great sand-sheet of the Kalahari to the east. Many of the roads here are spectacular: vast and empty with enormous vistas. The C10 between Karasburg and the B1, and the D608, are particular favourites.

The towns here seem to have changed little in years. They vary from small to minute, and remind the outsider of a typical South African *dorp* (a small town). Expect some of them to be on the conservative side.

Between Keetmanshoop and Grünau
Where to stay

The long straight road between the two towns is characterised by farmland, backed to the east by the Karas Mountains. In recent years, a number of guest farms along the road between Keetmanshoop and Grünau have opened their doors to visitors. The most established of these is the White House (which is also closest to Grünau), but others are worth considering. The following are listed in order of distance from Keetmanshoop:

Narubis Travel Lodge (6 rooms, 5 semi-private rooms) PO Box 1439, Keetmanshoop; tel/fax: 063 250700
East of the B1, and about 60km from Keetmanshoop, Narubis is set in open bush with views across to the Karas Mountains. Downstairs rooms are en suite, while those upstairs share a shower and toilet, and are separated from each other only by screens. There's a restaurant and bar, and a pool table for entertainment. This is a simple, no frills place to stay, but it's clean and bright, ideal for those on a tight budget.
Rates: N$130 per person in double room, N$10 per person in semi-private room, including breakfast. Lunch N$40, dinner N$50.

Savanna Guest Farm (5 rooms) PO Box 14, Grünau; tel/fax: 063 262070; email: savanna@iway.na. This 2,000ha farm in a beautiful setting at the foot of the Great Karas

Mountains is run by Erich and Zelda von Schauroth. The turning is off the B1, 42km north of Grünau, opposite the D203.

En-suite rooms are comfortable and air conditioned, though not luxurious, and have self-catering facilities. Many guests stay for days or even weeks at a time, for this is a place to discover for yourself the environment of a working sheep farm. Don't come expecting to be entertained, but if you enjoy walking and getting away from it all, this could be an ideal location. For added relaxation, there is a heated swimming pool, and a three-course dinner with traditional farm cooking is available by arrangement.

Rates: single N$440, per person sharing N$380, including dinner, bed and breakfast. Self-catering and long-term rates available on request.

Florida B&B (3 bungalows) PO Box 8, Grünau; tel/fax: 063 262069, cell: 081 129 8354; email: floridaa@iway.na

13km beyond Savanna, this newly opened place is very much an overnight stop, and as such offers good value. Its self-catering bungalows are set apart from the farmhouse and, though basic in structure, are fully equipped with some thoughtful touches.

Rates: N$90 per person. Breakfast N$20, dinner N$40.

White House Rest Camp (5 rooms, 3 bungalows) PO Box 9, Grünau; tel/fax: 063 262061; email: withuis@iway.na

The turn-off to the White House has a clear signpost, about 11km north of Grünau, on the B1. The house itself lies 4km from the main road, on a working 15,000ha sheep farm which stretches to the distant mountains.

The best accommodation here is in a stunning old farmhouse with Oregon pine floors, high wooden ceilings, wide verandas, a huge kitchen and even an old radiogram. It was built in 1912 for £2,500, and bought by the present owner's grandfather in 1926 for £3,500. After its being used as a school, amongst other things, and falling into disuse, the present owners, Dolf and Kinna De Wet, began to renovate the house in 1995. They have done a superb job. Just sit down quietly to soak up the atmosphere and journey back to the first half of the 19th century – it's incredible.

Guests normally stay in one of a handful of beautiful old rooms here on a self-catering basis, and the kitchen has large fridge, gas cooker, and all crockery and utensils. This isn't luxurious (though it would have been 60 years ago), but it is comfortable and very authentic. At the back, there's a small separate studio flat with its own fridge and dining table in the one room, and little shower-toilet adjacent.

In the grounds of the main house are three recently built self-catering bungalows. Comfortable and well equipped, each unit sleeps four people in a double bed and two bunks, with en-suite shower and outside braai, so is ideal for families. If you decide on this option, do ask for the single chalet – the double one has paper-thin walls.

Excellent meals are available, if requested in advance – come with a good appetite!

The White House is a beautiful old place which is excellent value and well worth a visit (though the historical aspect will pass you by if you're not in the main house). Those with an interest in geology will also be attracted by the rose quartz mine on the farm.

Rates: N$100 per person, under 12s half price. Breakfast N$30, dinner N$50, braai pack N$40.

Grünau

Grünau is a crossroads, where the railway from Upington in South Africa crosses the main B1. The little town also, more or less, marks the spot where the main tarred B3 from the central and eastern parts of South Africa meets with the B1 coming from the Cape. Thus it is strategically positioned for overnight stops between South Africa and Namibia – but isn't a destination of note in its own right.

Where to stay

There is a choice of places to stay in and around Grünau itself, including several on the B1 to the north (see above).

Grünau Country House (8 rooms, 4 bungalows, camping) 1 Main Rd, PO Box 2, Grünau; tel: 063 262001; fax: 063 262009; email: grunauch@iway.na
With a change of ownership comes a new name, and a facelift. Altus and Izane took over the former Grünau Hotel in 2001 and have plenty of plans for the place. Some of the rooms have already been renovated with en-suite showers, tea/coffee facilities and ceiling fans, and air conditioning is to be installed during 2003. Two of the rooms will also have wheelchair access. The campsite remains bare, with little shade. Work on the main building has so far been confined to structural repairs, and there is still a large, rather dated dining room, a bar area with a pool table and a lounge at the back, and outside is a swimming pool.
Rates: single N$180, double N$250, family room N$360, bungalows N$75 per person, camping N$30 per person. Breakfast and other meals available.

Grünau Motors (5 chalets, camping) PO Box 3, Grünau; tel: 063 262026; fax: 063 262017
Just on the north side of Grünau is a 24-hour Shell petrol station, with a simple restcamp attached. The small bungalows are clean and well appointed, with air conditioning, en-suite bathroom, TV and kitchenette. The surroundings, though, are flat and characterless, albeit with secure parking. The shop sells snacks and basic foodstuffs, and has a simple restaurant which closes at 20.00.
Rates: single N$145, double N$245; N$45 per extra person (maximum six in family room). Camping N$60 per pitch, plus N$10 per person..

Vastrap Guest Farm (7 rooms, 1 chalet) PO Box 26, Grünau; tel/fax: 063 262063; email: vastrap@mweb.com.na
Around 5km from Grünau on the B3 to Karasburg is a sign to Vastrap Restcamp, which is about 2km from the road, on a farms belonging to its owners, Rean and Hettie. The design is unusual, as these are rooms within old farmstead buildings that have been linked together rather than in separate bungalows, and the recent upgrade in status to a guest farm is well justified. Rooms are simple but cheerful, with en-suite showers. There is also a dining room where home-cooked meals are served, with a separate bar, and there is unlimited coffee available to guests.
Rates: single N$180, double N$250, family N$360. Dinner N$60, breakfast N$35.

Karasburg

Karasburg is really a bigger version of Grünau – a convenient overnight stop on a long journey. It has several 24-hour **fuel stations**, while **take-aways** include the Excel, and Hanzell's, next to the Engen garage. There's a **post office** on Park Street, a **Bank of Windhoek** on 9th Avenue and a **First National Bank** on Main Street – so if Namibia's dollar ever floats free from South Africa's rand, then expect these to be busy. The **hospital** is on tel: 063 270167. Signposts to Lordsville and Westerville point the way to Karasburg's old-style satellite townships.

For **supplies**, there is a Spar supermarket, and a branch of OK next to the BP garage.

Where to stay

There is just one hotel in town, plus a couple of B&Bs: **It's Coffee Time** (tel: 063 270378) and **Jeanie's Place** (tel: 063 270349) – a new establishment with three en-suite rooms and a small pool. There's also, unexpectedly, a small backpacker's hostel, **Pela-Pela** (tel: 063 270483).

Kalkfontein Hotel (17 rooms) PO Box 205, Karasburg; tel/fax: 063 270023/270172; email: kalkfont@iway.na

This is a typical, old, small-town hotel. The Kalkfontein's bar is the local meeting place, and its rooms are spread around yards and courtyards at the back. These are very basic and carpeted, and their furniture is old and somewhat battered – but they are clean and well kept. All the rooms have en-suite bath or shower. The restaurant is no longer operational.
Rates: single N$150, double N$250, family N$450, including breakfast.

Warmbad

About 48km south of Karasburg, Warmbad (the name means 'warm bath' in German) features some hot springs, as well as what is reputed to be the oldest existing house in Namibia.

Koës

This small outpost lies about 124km northeast of Keetmanshoop, deep in the Kalahari Desert. It is the centre for the local Afrikaans farming community, and has a **Bank of Windhoek**, a few small shops and a hotel.

Hotel Koës (8 rooms & 1 chalet) 2 Fontein St, PO Box 140, Koës; tel/fax: 063 252716
This tiny, basic hotel has eight rooms, of which five have en-suite facilities. It's perhaps not going to be the highlight of your holiday, but might be useful in an emergency.
Rates: single N$130, N$80 per person sharing.

Kalahari Game Lodge (8 chalets and camping) PO Box 22, Koës; tel: 063 693105, 061 259262; fax: 061 251556; email: afriquedirect@namibnet.com, africadirect@mweb.com.na
This simple restcamp on a 27,000-hectare estate is on the C15, almost 100km east of Koës, near the Mata Mata gate into the enormous Kgalagadi Transfrontier Park. If and when that gate re-opens, this is bound to become a popular spot to stop overnight, but for now it is hard to get to and rarely visited. This is a shame, as the estate has both lion and cheetah, with wild dog to be introduced in 2004.
Rates: N$700 per person, including dinner and breakfast. Self-catering N$300 per person. Camping N$30 per person.

Noordoewer

This small settlement on the Orange River stands a few kilometres from the main crossing point for Namibia–Cape traffic. With a ready supply of water, there are several large-scale irrigation projects – some producing table-quality grapes like those on the Orange further east in South Africa. This is also the embarkation point for several canoeing and rafting trips down the Orange – which are based in, and organised from, Cape Town (see page 228).
The border is open 24 hours, and there is reliable fuel.

Where to stay
Camel Lodge (16 rooms, camping) PO Box 1, Noordoewer; tel: 063 297171; fax: 063 297134; email: nih@mweb.com.na
In the centre of Noordoewer, 3km from the border with South Africa, this is a convenient stopover. Some rooms have en-suite facilities and TVs, while others share a bathroom. Breakfast and dinner are available on request.
Rates: single N$135 with shared bathroom, N$160 en suite, N$190 with TV; double N$195 sharing bathroom, N$250 en suite with TV. Camping N$50 per person.

Abiqua River Camp (35 pitches) Tel: 063 297255; fax: 063 297259; email: abiqua@iway.na
15.7km west of the South African border at Noordoewer, this grassy campsite is right on the Orange River. As you'd expect, river rafting and canoeing are popular, and there is plenty of scope for birdwatching. Pitches have electric hook ups, and meals are available on request.
Rates: N$35 per person, breakfast N$25, other meals N$35.

There is also **Fiddler's Inn**, located in the 'no-man's land' area between Noordoewer and the South African border.

FISH RIVER CANYON

At 161km long, up to 27km wide, and almost 550m at its deepest, the Fish River Canyon is probably second in size only to Arizona's Grand Canyon – and is certainly one of Africa's least-visited wonders.

This means that as you sit dangling your legs over the edge, drinking in the spectacle, you're unlikely to have your visit spoiled by a coach-load of tourists, or to leave feeling that the place is at all commercialised. In fact, away from the busier seasons, you may not see anyone around here at all!

Geology

The base rocks of the Fish River Canyon, now at the bottom nearest the river, are shales, sandstones and lavas which were deposited about 1,800 million years ago. Later, from 1,300 to 1,000 million years ago, these were heated and strongly compressed, forming a metamorphic rock complex, which includes intrusive granites and, later, the dolorite dykes which appear as clear, dark streaks on the canyon.

A period of erosion then followed, removing the overlying rocks and levelling this complex to be the floor of a vast shallow sea, covering most of what is now southern Namibia. From about 650 to 500 million years ago various sediments, limestones and conglomerates were deposited by the sea on to this floor, building up into what is now referred to as the Nama Group of rocks.

About 500 million years ago, the beginnings of the canyon started when a fracture in this crust formed a broad valley, running north–south. Southward moving glaciers deepened this during the Dwyka Ice Age, around 300 million years ago. Later faults and more erosion added to the effect, creating canyons within each other, until a mere 50 million years ago, when the Fish River started to cut its meandering way along the floor of the most recent valley.

History

Situated in a very arid region of Namibia, the Fish River is the only river within the country that usually has pools of water in its middle reaches during the dry season. Because of this, it was known to the peoples of the area during the early, middle and late Stone Ages. Numerous early sites dating from as early as 50,000 years ago have been found within the canyon – mostly beside bends in the river.

Around the beginning of this century, the Ai-Ais area was used as a base by the Germans in their war against the Namas. It was finally declared a national monument in 1962. Ai-Ais Restcamp was opened in 1971, though it has been refurbished since then.

Getting there

Detailed routes to the various lodges and camps are given below. Note that you can't drive between the west and east sides of the canyon quickly. If you are approaching the east side from the north during the rainy season, and the C12 is blocked by flooding, then try taking a shortcut from the B4, on to the D545 and then the C12. If the water pouring over the retaining wall is too fast to cross, then a detour to your left will bring you to a crossing on top of a dam wall – avoiding the need to ford the torrent. Alternatively, take the longer tar route on the B1 and C10.

The only option for those without their own vehicle, aside from hitchhiking, is to take one of the package trips offered by Canyon Adventures Guest Farm (see pages 214–15).

AFRICA'S LARGEST CANYON?
Pedants cite Ethiopia's Blue Nile Gorge as being Africa's largest canyon. It is certainly deeper than the Fish River Canyon, at about 1,000m, but it is also narrower (about 20km wide at its widest), and probably shorter as well. Like many vague superlatives, 'largest' is difficult to define. In this case, we would have to measure the volume of the canyon – and even then there would be questions about exactly where it begins and ends. Suffice to say that both are too large to take in at one sight, and both are well worth visiting.

Where to stay

Seeing the canyon as a day-trip from a base some way off is practical, particularly as the diagonal rays of early morning or late evening light do little for photographers' hopes of capturing the depths of the canyon. Keetmanshoop is one possibility, or for a less urban setting you could opt for somewhere around Karasburg or Grünau to the east, or Seeheim to the north. However, if only to minimise your driving, stay closer if you can – at Hobas Campsite, Ai-Ais or one of the private lodges nearby, offering a good range of choice.

Private lodges

Cañon Lodge (30 twin bungalows) PO Box 80205, Windhoek; tel: 061 230066; fax: 061 251863; email: nature.i@mweb.com.na; web: natron.net/canyonlodge or www.natron.net/canyon

Cañon Lodge is one of several accommodation options that lie within the 102,000ha Gondwana Reserve. The reserve, which borders on the national park, was established by Mannie Goldberg and Peter Wilson in 1996 from seven commercial sheep farms. Their aim: to reclaim the land from overgrazing and return it to its natural state. Close to the canyon's northern viewpoints, the lodge is just 2km off the D324, which itself is 7km south of the junction with the D601, near Hobas.

The lodge centres on an old farmhouse, built in 1904, which has been restored and now functions as the reception, well-stocked bar, coffee and restaurant area. Adjacent is an open terrace where tables are shaded by an old false pepper tree (the seeds of which must have been imported with horse feed for the German Schutztruppe).

All around the lodge are stone kopjes – small hills made from bare stone boulders. Amongst these, ingeniously spread out, are beautiful bungalows, containing double or twin beds, an en-suite toilet and shower or bath, within raw stone walls under thatched roofs. These are rustic, but comfortable and surprisingly cool during the heat of the day.

Both guests and day visitors are catered for in the large but intimate restaurant, which in summer spills out on to the terrace, but on chilly winter evenings is warmed by blazing open fires. Meals are substantial, with considerably more choice than you might expect in such an out-of-the-way place. Much of the reason for this lies in the lodge's self-sufficiency project, for a hefty proportion of the fresh food consumed comes from their own farm. Already, the place produces almost all its own bacon, milk, eggs and salad vegetables, not to mention fresh herbs, and homemade bread and salamis, thus obviating the necessity to bring in expensive and tired products from markets as far away as South Africa. While a significant aspect of trial and error lies behind this success, there is no doubting the value of the achievement, both in terms of local employment and the environment – not to mention the taste!

In addition to the obvious attractions of the canyon itself across the plain, there is plenty to do while here, and some visitors stay for several days. Climb up a kopje (which is easy) and you'll find a spot for a sundowner drink, overlooking a wide plateau and, 20km away, the main viewpoint of the canyon. Stay at the bottom, and you can spend time watching the colony of dassies on those same rocks as they bask in the evening sun. Guided walks and drives are offered around the reserve at various times of day, and, for the more adventurous, there are flights down the canyon (see box, page 215), as well as guided horseriding trips (hard hats are provided). There's even a small swimming pool set a short distance from the lodge itself where you can relax in complete privacy.

The owners of the Gondwana Reserve have plans to start work in 2003 on a small, exclusive lodge with just seven rooms. The new lodge will be about 7km from Cañon Lodge. Each room will be air conditioned, and guests will have their own meals prepared on the premises. For details, contact Cañon Lodge.

Rates: N$655 single, N$495 per person sharing, including breakfast. Dinner is N$130, lunch N$70, lunchpacks N$55.

Cañon Roadhouse (9 rooms, camping) Tel: 063 266031. Reservations as for Cañon Lodge, above

Cañon Roadhouse is run by the same partners as Cañon Lodge, and is also on land that forms part of the Gondwana Reserve. It is further north, signposted about 17km off the C12 at near Holoog (a large dot on the map, but a tiny settlement), along the D601.

If the name is a little off-putting, think of this as a comfortable roadside inn and you'll be near the mark. Its accommodation is set at the back, around a quiet, cactus-planted courtyard. Comfortable, modern rooms with en-suite bathrooms show the hand of a thoughtful designer, with décor picking out the rich reds and creams of the surrounding landscape. The campsite at the back has space for six pitches, and there is a swimming pool for guest use.

Many visitors are drawn here as if to an oasis by the reliable fuel station, and find themselves staying for a drink on the front terrace, or something to eat in the restaurant, which is adorned with old farm implements and related artefacts. The à la carte menu features light lunches in the N$20–45 range, or several more substantial dishes, including game. Activities are as for Cañon Lodge, above.

Rates: single N$402.50, double N$644, including breakfast. Camping N$20 per person plus N$60 per site.

Cañon Mountain Camp (contact details as for Cañon Lodge, above)

This simple converted sheep-shearing shed within driving distance of the lip of the canyon is a further offshoot of Cañon Lodge, and was opened in 2002. Visitors coming here should book in at the reception for Cañon Lodge, from where they will be directed to the camp. All meals and activities are shared with the lodge.

Accommodation is ideal for small groups or families who are self-catering. Basic but comfortable rooms are set around an enclosed courtyard, with separate toilets and showers, a communal kitchen and a large braai area overlooking the hills. There are plans under consideration to convert a small water reservoir into a swimming pool, but for now this remains a secluded spot with very few mod cons (there's no electricity), offering the opportunity to experience at first hand the peace of this unspoilt environment.

Rates: N$100 per person.

Canyon Adventures Guest Farm (6 rooms, 18 dorm beds, campsite) PO Box 1840, Keetmanshoop; tel: 063 693007, 063 266018; fax: 063 693006; email: frlodge@iafrica.com.na; web: www.fishrivercanyon.ws

About 33km south of Naute Dam on the C12 is a signpost to Fish River Lodge (recently renamed Canyon Adventures Guest Farm), which lies a further 23km west of the road. Its land includes a 32km stretch of the Fish River Canyon, as well as 12km of the adjacent Löwen River Canyon.

It is accessible by car, although visitors to the campsite in the canyon will need a 4WD. Owner Louis used to have the Chapel Inn in Keetmanshoop, but that is now closed and his energies are concentrated on the guest farm here.

FLIGHT OVER THE FISH RIVER CANYON
Tricia Hayne

The peace of the canyon is disturbed for just a few moments by the sound of a light aircraft as it sweeps across the apparently endless plateau to the east and suddenly soars over the edge of the canyon. Just five passengers share the tiny cockpit of the Cessna 210 with the pilot. Since this is a top-wing aircraft, everyone on board has unimpeded views over the landscape unfolding below and plenty of opportunity for photography.

This may be the Fish River, but from the air the word 'snake' comes more readily to mind as it winds down the canyon in a series of tortuous switchbacks. Even in the dry season, pools of green water reflect back the shadow of the plane as it follows the river on its course through towering canyon walls whose turreted edges have been eroded over countless millennia. Among the broad bands of browns and dull reds, the occasional bright flower clings to bare rock, but it is the sheer scale of the spectacle that makes a flight worthwhile. For all too brief a time, passengers have the chance to share the perspective of the magnificent black eagle that occasionally circles overhead.

As the plane weaves down the canyon, the edges soften and the landscape takes on the more familiar pattern of a mountainous environment. Towards Ai-Ais, the riverbed widens and the aircraft veers away, following parallel to the canyon before returning to Cañon Lodge.

Weather permitting, flights are run daily from Cañon Lodge. Prices in 2002 were N$480 per person for the half-hour flight, but rates are tied to the US dollar and thus fluctuate regularly. For details, and current prices, contact the lodge direct (see pages 213–14).

Accommodation at the lodge is geared to the middle market, with two triple and four double rooms, while for backpackers there are dormitory beds in the adjoining Stable. Dinner is available on request at N$70. There is also a campsite, Koelkrans, in the canyon itself, with six two-bedded, self-catering huts; no linen is provided.

One of the highlights of a stay here is the possibility to hike in the canyon without some of the restrictions that apply inside the national park's conservation area further south. Hiking remains restricted to April–September, since temperatures in the canyon soar in the summer months, but visitors may spend anything from one to five days hiking, making this an attractive option for those with less time to spare. Hikers will still need to be fully equipped, with sufficient food and water for the duration of their hike. The five-day, 85km hiking trail costs N$380 per person, which includes two nights' dormitory accommodation, and transport to the start of the trail 16km away.

Visitors without their own vehicle may arrange to be collected from Keetmanshoop at a cost of N$400 per person. The lodge also offers 4WD tours of the canyon at N$75 per person for a half day, and they have a 65km 4WD trail, for which a map is available.

There are two three-day (two-night) special packages available for backpackers from Keetmanshoop. The first, with self-catering accommodation in the Stable, costs N$700 per person, while those seeking farmhouse accommodation stay on a full-board basis at N$1,200 per person. Prices for both are based on a minimum of two people, and include transport to and from Keetmanshoop.

Rates: single N$280, double N$450, including breakfast. Dorm bed N$70 per person (summer only, no breakfast). Koelkrans huts/camping N$200 per vehicle and N$10 per person.

Within the conservation area
Ai-Ais Hot Springs
Ai-Ais Restcamp (PO Box 2012, Karasburg; tel: 063 262045; fax: 063 262047/8; email: reservations@mweb.com.na; web: www.namibiawildliferesorts.com) is open all year and recently renovated. The large restcamp sits at the bottom of the canyon, at the end of the C10 road. This is towards the southern end of the conservation area, and is the finishing point for the canyon's hiking trail.

Ai-Ais means 'burning water' in the local Nama language, a reference to the hot, sulphurous springs which well up here, the original reason for the siting of the restcamp. It's very much a little spa, with a large, naturally hot, outdoor pool and private hot tubs as well as the usual restcamp facilities that give it the air of a holiday camp.

Getting there
Ai-Ais is best reached from Keetmanshoop by driving south on the main B1, and then turning west on to the C10. (Try to avoid this in the late afternoon, as the sun is directly in your face.)

Alternatively, from Lüderitz, reach Seeheim on the B4 and take the gravel C12 south. Then turn right on to the D601 towards Hobas, left along the D324, and right on to the C10. Coming from the south, you can turn left off the B1 on to the D316 – though this road is quieter and perhaps less well graded than the C10.

However you reach it, the final few kilometres of the C10 spirals down, cut into the rock layers of the canyon's side, until it reaches the bed of the Fish River. It's a marvellous road, though steep in parts, with some sharp corners – so drive carefully. You can arrive at any time, so do not fear being locked out if you are late.

Accommodation
There's a choice of simple, clean restcamp accommodation here: luxury flats (two beds), flats (four beds), and huts (four beds). All have a fridge, kettle and hot-plate for self-catering, and bedding and towels are provided. The flats also have en-suite shower and toilet, whilst the huts or 'bungalows' share their ablutions with the campers. The luxury flats have a bath as well as a shower, plus air conditioning.
Rates: luxury flat N$360 (2 people), including entrance to the spa, standard flat N$300 (4 people), hut N$220, room only. Additional people are charged at N$85 each.
Camping N$125 per site for up to four people, two vehicles and one caravan or tent. Additional people are charged at N$10 each, up to a maximum of eight. Park fees are applicable on top (see page 217). Camping all year, but flats and restaurant open second Friday in March to October 31.

Facilities
The restcamp has a basic shop, post box and fuel station, as well as a restaurant that serves breakfast 07.00–08.30, lunch 12.00–13.30 and dinner 18.00–20.30. These are à la carte, but are still like school dinners.

Entrance to the pool or hot tubs is N$15 per adult, and N$10 per child, except where costs are included with your accommodation. The more active might bring tennis racquets, to play on the courts here, or wander off on a walk up the canyon – which is beautiful.

Hobas Campsite
Within the conservation area, and run by the NWR, Hobas (P Bag 2012, Karasburg; tel/fax: 063 266028; email: reservations@mweb.com.na; web: www.namibiawildlife resorts.com) is a busy campsite near the main viewpoint of

the canyon. The sites are spread out under shady, willowy trees and there are thatched sunshades for extra shelter during the intense midday sun, as well as tables and chairs for picnics, and a small swimming pool.

As the only convenient base in the area for overland groups, this site gets many large trucks stopping here – so can become festive at times. Competition for the quieter sites is high. Beside the gate is the park warden's station and office. The gate is open 06.00–22.00 every day, and inside you can buy a few curios and refreshments. Those just coming to see the canyon must stop here to pay their park entry fees.

Rates: camping N$125 per site for a maximum of eight people, two vehicles and one caravan or tent. Note that park fees are payable in addition to the campsite fees (see below).

The conservation area

Entry: N$20 per adult (N$1 per child) per day, plus N$20 per vehicle. Fees are payable by all visitors on entry to Ai-Ais and at Hobas campsite, and are in addition to any fees charged for accommodation.

In 1969 the area around the Fish River Canyon was proclaimed a conservation area, which made sense. The land was as poor in potential for agriculture as it is rich in potential for tourism, and this was a way of protecting the area from uncontrolled development. The 345,000-hectare conservation area now encompasses Ai-Ais and Hobas, whilst all the private lodges are outside.

Flora and fauna

Driving around you will probably see few larger animals, though there are many if you look hard. These include herds of Hartmann's mountain zebra, small groups of kudu and the smaller klipspringer antelope, which are usually seen in pairs. Baboon make no secret of their presence if around, whilst dassies (alias rock rabbits) are common but leopard, though certainly present, are very rarely seen. It's not unusual to drive for a few hours, and see no mammals at all.

Birds, too, are around but often not obvious. This isn't a centre for birdwatching, as only about 60 species are thought to live here, but look out for the majestic black eagle, as well as the rock kestrel and rock pigeon, and especially for the localised yellow-rumped eremomela which occur near Ai-Ais. Karoo bustards and ostrich are the highlights of the open plains above the canyon itself. Vegetation is sparse. Both on the top and on the canyon's slopes, the larger species are mostly *Euphorbias*, with the odd quivertree. However, parts of the canyon's base where there is water are quite lush – like the Sulphur Springs and Ai-Ais areas. There you can expect camel-thorn, wild tamarisk and ebony trees, amongst others.

What to see and do

Once in the area, a day is enough to see the canyon properly, unless you've arranged (in advance) to do the hike. Do note that, with the exception of those booked on the five-day hike (see below), no visitors are allowed to descend into the canyon from the lip at any time of year.

Start the morning by driving past Hobas to the **Main Viewpoint**. This is *the* classic view of Hell's Bend, featured in most of the photographs – and probably the only view that you'll see if you're on a bus tour. A 3km track leads off to the right, to the **Hiker's Viewpoint**, which lends a different perspective and is worth the wander if it is cool.

Then take the road that leads to the left of the Main Viewpoint. This is a continuation of the D324 which doubles back, to run roughly parallel to the canyon, generally keeping within a few hundred yards. There are several stops for viewpoints along its length, perhaps the best being the **Sulphur Springs**

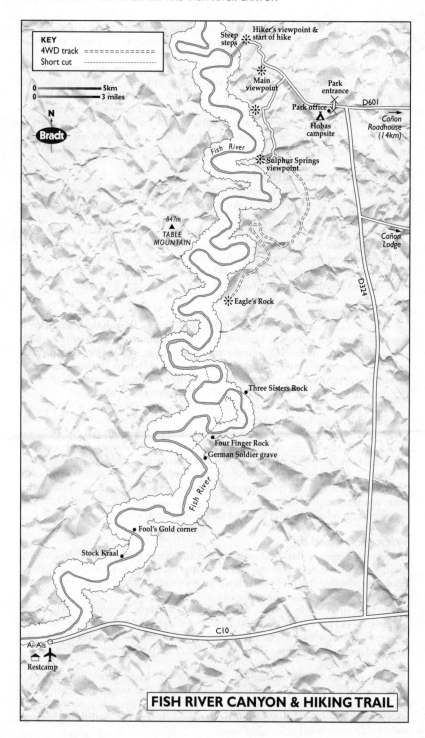

KEY
4WD track
Short cut

0 ——— 5km
0 ——— 3 miles

N

Bradt

Hiker's viewpoint &
start of hike
Steep steps

Main viewpoint

Park entrance
Park office
D601
Cañon Roadhouse (14km)
Hobas campsite

Fish River

Sulphur Springs viewpoint

Cañon Lodge

847m
TABLE MOUNTAIN

D324

Eagle's Rock

Three Sisters Rock

Four Finger Rock
German Soldier grave

Fish River

Fool's Gold corner

Stock Kraal

C10

Ai-Ais
Restcamp

FISH RIVER CANYON & HIKING TRAIL

Viewpoint (Palm Springs), which has a picnic table and a stunning view of another tight switchback in the river's course.

This road is little used and graded less, so it's bumpy in parts but suitable for a 2WD car driven slowly and carefully. The scenery is so spectacular that you won't want to rush. If you have a 4WD, you can continue past the Sulphur Springs Viewpoint to the southernmost viewpoint at Eagle's Rock – a further 12km of very rough, stony road, but offering a good view of the canyon further south. Either way, you'll eventually have to retrace your tracks to return on the D324, back past the Hobas gate and south.

Ai-Ais makes a great afternoon stop during the winter (see its opening dates, above), giving you time to relax in a mineral pool, or to take a gentle walk up the canyon, for a taste of what the hikers will experience. Note that permits to visit the conservation area for a day are valid at both the Ai-Ais and Hobas gates.

Hiking the Fish River Canyon

For very fit, experienced and self-sufficient backpackers, the Fish River Canyon is the venue for one of southern Africa's greatest hikes: a chance to follow the river where vehicles never venture, about 90km from Hiker's Point to Ai-Ais. However, numbers are limited to one group per day, which must be pre-arranged with the NWR in Windhoek months in advance, so you need to work out your logistics carefully long before you get here.

Regulations

Hiking trips are allowed from April 15 to September 15, and the NWR insists on the group being 3–40 people for safety, with no children under the age of 12. Hikers need to bring a medical certificate, which has been issued within 40 days of the hike and is signed by their doctor, stating that they are fit to do the hike.

The hike costs N\$100 per person, paid for in advance at the NWR in Windhoek, and hikers are responsible for all of their own food, equipment, safety and transport to/from the canyon. Hikers must stay at least one night in the national park, either at Hobas Campsite or at Ai-Ais Restcamp.

Preparations

This is a four- or five-day hike covering 80–90km in what can be some of the subcontinent's most extreme temperatures. There's no easy way out once you start; no chance to stop. So this isn't for the faint-hearted, or those without experience of hiking in Africa.

For those who come prepared, it's excellent. Your own large, comfortable backpack with your normal hiking equipment (see page 102) should include: at least a two-litre water bottle, with some method of purifying water; a sleeping roll and bag, though a tent is not needed; food and cooking utensils for at least six days (wood for fires is generally available on the second half of the hike). Also, each group should have at least one comprehensive medical kit, as help may be days away if there is an accident. A light rainproof jacket is also a good idea, in the unlikely event of a shower.

Finally, make sure that you've a good map. One rough route-plan with pretty colour pictures and lots of advice is usually available at Hobas, though it is best when used in conjunction with a more 'serious' version from the Surveyor General's office in Windhoek (see page 116).

Transport

If you're driving yourself in, leave your vehicle near the start of the hike at Hobas, since there is transport available from Ai-Ais back to the start point of the hike. If you are hitchhiking, remember that your arrival date will be unpredictable, and you might miss your start date.

The hike

The descent into the canyon is steep in parts, taking 45–90 minutes. Chains are provided on the more difficult sections. The first day is taxing, with stretches of loose river-sand between areas of large boulders. It can be slow going, and the trail stays mostly on the eastern side of the river. After 14km there is an 'emergency exit' up to the Sulphur (Palm)Springs Viewpoint, but most people eventually reach the area around Sulphur Springs and overnight there, 16km into the walk. The springs themselves are fast-flowing, hot (57°C), and apparently rich in fluorides, chlorides and sulphates.

It gradually gets easier after Sulphur Springs, traversing fewer stretches of boulders, and more sand and rounded river-stones. The river zigzags sharply, so most hikers cut the corners and get their feet wet. There are several more significant shortcuts, and an 'emergency exit' at 70km. Finally, 90km from the start (80km if you cut corners) you arrive at Ai-Ais.

Trail etiquette

The correct trail etiquette here is the same as sensible rules for responsible hiking anywhere in the bush (see pages 104–7). However, as groups cover the same trail regularly here, these guidelines are all the more vital. In particular:

- There are no 'official' fireplaces; use existing ones if possible. Use only dead wood for fires, and bring a stove as there's little wood at the start of the trail.
- Leave no litter in the canyon – even fruit peel will look unsightly.
- Use only biodegradable soap, and wash away from the main river from which people will be drinking.
- Never feed animals; baboons would be a problem here if fed.
- There are no toilets, so burn all toilet paper and bury it with the excrement, in a shallow hole far from the water.

Lüderitz and the Southwest

11

Though the European colonisation of Namibia started in this southwestern corner, this remains perhaps Namibia's least known area for visitors. At the end of a long road, Lüderitz is now being rediscovered, with its wonderful turn-of-the-century architecture, desolate beaches, and position as the springboard for trips into the forbidden area, the *Sperrgebiet*.

But there is more than Lüderitz in this area. Early historical sites from the 1900s are dotted throughout the region – and though places to stay are often far apart, most of the hotels and guest farms are excellent value. Best of all are the amazing landscapes. Rugged mountains and flowing desert sands make the empty roads spectacular – with the D707, the southern sections of the C13, and even the main B4 across the Koichab Pan ranking amongst the country's more dramatic drives.

THE ROADS TO LÜDERITZ
From Keetmanshoop

As you drive east from Keetmanshoop to Lüderitz, the main B4 road is now all tarred. After about 44km the C12 turns off left to the Fish River Canyon. A kilometre or so afterwards the B4 crosses the Fish River itself, which meanders down a broad, shallow, vegetated valley with few hints of the amazing canyon to the south.

To the north of the road are some spectacular flat-topped hills, capped by hard dolorite which erodes slowly. One of these has been named Kaiserkrone, the 'Kaiser's crown', as it is an unusual conical shape capped by a symmetrical crown of hard dolorite rock.

There are several small towns along this road. Most can supply fuel and essentials, but none are comparable in size with Lüderitz or Keetmanshoop, so few visitors stop at any for long. There's also a café, the **Kuibis Restaurant**, about halfway between Goageb and Aus, serving light meals between sunrise and sunset (closed Sat at 16.00; open Sun at 10.00). The main towns are:

Seeheim

About 45km from Keetmanshoop on the B4, Seeheim has accommodation that offers straightforward access along the C12 to the Fish River Canyon, passing Naute Dam on the way:

Seeheim Hotel (22 rooms, camping) PO Box 1338, Keetmanshoop; tel/fax: 063 250503; email: seeheim@iway.na
On the main B4, the Seeheim Hotel is something of a one-stop shop, since it also offers fuel, and a shop selling souvenirs, bread and soft drinks. Its accommodation, all in one building, is divided between luxury rooms, which have en-suite bathrooms and ceiling

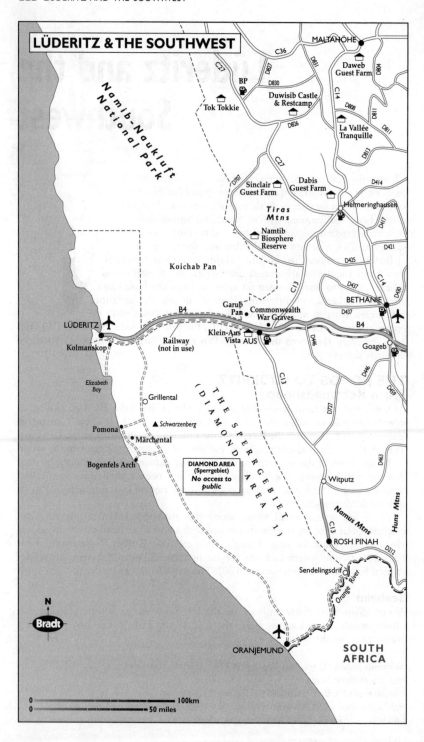

LÜDERITZ & THE SOUTHWEST

MALTAHÖHE

C36

D827

D831

Daweb
Guest Farm

D804

C27

BP

D830

Namib-Naukluft
National Park

Tok Tokkie

Duwisib Castle
& Restcamp

C14

D808

D811

D826

La Vallée
Tranquille

D811

D813

C27

D707

Sinclair
Guest Farm

Dabis
Guest Farm

D414

Helmeringhausen

Tiras
Mtns

D417

Namtib
Biosphere
Reserve

D421

D425

Koichab Pan

C13

D437

C14

D400

BETHANIE

Garub
Pan

D437

B4

Commonwealth
War Graves

B4

LÜDERITZ

Klein-Aus
Vista AUS

Goageb

Kolmanskop

Railway
(not in use)

D446

C13

Elizabeth
Bay

Grillental

THE SPERRGEBIET
(DIAMOND AREA 1)

D727

D446

D459

Schwarzenberg

Pomona

Märchental

DIAMOND AREA
(Sperrgebiet)
No access to
public

D463

Bogenfels Arch

Witputz

Namus Mtns

Huns Mtns

C13

ROSH PINAH

D212

Sendelingsdrif

Orange River

N

Bradt

ORANJEMUND

SOUTH
AFRICA

0 ———————— 100km
0 ———————— 50 miles

fans, and standard rooms with shared facilities. There is also a dining room with à la carte menu and a separate bar. Outside, there is a swimming pool, while around the hotel are some marked hiking trails, and horseriding is available by arrangement.

Rates: luxury single N$310, double N$420; standard single N$150, double N$280. Camping N$50 per person.

Goageb

The tiny community of Goageb, with fewer than 20 telephones, lies 106km west of Keetmanshoop. It has a fuel station, the Konkiep Handelshuis (tel: 063 283566), which also offers beds for the night, but you'd have to be pretty desperate to stop here. The region's only railway station is at Goageb, which could increase its importance when or if passenger trains run through here again. The Starline bus between Keetmanshoop and Lüderitz stops here at 08.45 every morning except Sunday, returning at 16.20 (15.20 on Sunday).

A convenient place to stop is the **Kuibis Restaurant**, shop and roadside café, 100km west of Goageb, serving light meals all day.

Bethanie

About 30km north of Goageb, Bethanie (also spelt Bethanien) is a larger town and centre for local administration. The main road into the small town is the tarred C14, just to the east of Goageb, but if you're coming from Lüderitz turn off on to the D435 about 20km further west. If you're tied to public transport, Starline runs a number of services that call at Bethanie. The bus between Keetmanshoop and Lüderitz stops here after Goageb at 09.20 each morning except Sunday, returning via Aus at 14.00 (13.00 on Sunday). Every Tuesday there is a bus to Helmeringhausen, arriving from Keetmanshoop at 10.30, and leaving Bethanie at 12.10; the return bus arrives at Bethanie at 15.10. The Thursday service from Keetmanshoop to Rosh Pinah and Oranjemund stops here at 11.00, returning on Friday at 14.00.

The town is dominated by the apparently modern Lutheran church, which was actually one of the first churches in Namibia. Originally built in 1859, it was restored by American evangelists in 1998. Rather more in keeping with the surroundings are several shops (including the gloriously named Pick a Dilly), an agency for the **Standard Bank**, a magistrate's office, village council, a take-away restaurant, two **fuel stations** (not 24 hours) and one hotel:

Bethanie Hotel (10 rooms, camping) PO Box 13, Bethanie; tel: 063 283013; fax: 063 283071
This is one of the country's oldest hotels, built around 1880, and it remains dark and old-fashioned. Nevertheless, the owner is helpful, and there's a bar, snooker room and dining room. Rooms are off a courtyard at the back. Doubles are en suite, but singles share a (clean) outside toilet block with the campsite. Four of the rooms have air conditioning.
Rates: single N$160, double N$280, including breakfast. Camping N$25 per person.

For those heading north, there's also a restcamp on the C14, 35km from Bethanie:

Konkiep Lapa Restcamp (9 cabins, camping) PO Box 133, Bethanie; tel: 063 283151/283072; fax: 063 283087
Self-catering two-bed cabins and a separate campsite share ablution facilities here. There's a bar and lapa, as well as an inside braai. Wood and water are available, but otherwise you'll need to bring everything with you.
Rates: cabins N$100 per person, camping N$60 per pitch, plus N$20 per person.

Aus

About 211km west of Keetmanshoop a slip-road turns left off the B4 to Aus, notable for its unpredictable weather and its history as a POW camp. Five hundred metres from the main road there's a police post (tel: 063 258005) on the left, and further on a **fuel station** stands in the heart of this small hillside town.

Aus's weather can be extreme, very cold in winter and hot in the summer. It is also unpredictable – which stems from its proximity to the Cape – although the winter rain, and its associated flora, is more pronounced in the area around Rosh Pinah. (The Cape has a different weather pattern from anywhere else in southern Africa, with winter rainfall from May to September, and gloriously warm, *dry* summer weather from November to February.)

Sometimes Aus's weather will follow a typically Namibian pattern; at others it will have the Cape's weather, with showers in winter, and occasionally even snow. If heavy or prolonged, this rain can cause a sudden flush of sprouting plants and blooms, rather like the 'flower season' in Namaqualand, south of the border. Many unusual plants have been catalogued here, including a rather magnificent species of bulb whose flowers form a large globe, the size of a football. When these seed, the globe breaks off and rolls about like tumbleweed. Endemic to this small area is the yellow-flowered Aus daisy, *Arctotis fastiosa*, which grows only within a 30km radius of the town (a slightly more orange sub-species is found at Rosh Pinah). In winter, the yellow *kuibi* or butter flower, *Papia capensis*, brightens up the plains at the foot of the mountains, interspersed with the blue sporry, *Felicia namaquana*, and the bright purple fig bush. Higher up, the mountain butter flower holds sway, the western slopes are scented by wild rosemary, and the Bushman's candle is to be found – although here it is yellow or, rarely, white, unlike its bushier pink cousin in the desert to the west.

When the German colonial troops surrendered to the South African forces in 1915, a camp for the prisoners of war was set up a few kilometres outside what is now Aus. At one point 1,552 German POWs were held here by 600 guards. It seems that the German prisoners worked hard to make their conditions more comfortable by manufacturing bricks, building houses and stoves, and cultivating gardens. They eventually even sold bricks to their South African guards. The camp, now marked by a monument 4km from town, closed shortly after the end of the war. Sadly, little remains of the buildings bar a few ruined huts. On a hill 1.3km to the east of town, however, there is a small cemetery maintained by the Commonwealth War Graves Commission. Here lie 61 prisoners of war, and a further 60 members of the garrison, most of them victims of a flu epidemic in 1918. If you're driving up here, keep to the right-hand track.

Getting there

Most visitors to Aus arrive by car. However, Starline buses stop here daily except Sunday at 10.55 on the journey between Keetmanshoop and Lüderitz, returning at 14.00 (13.00 on Sunday). Although a railway runs through the town, it has been closed for some time, and despite plenty of rumours, there are at present no plans to re-open it to passengers.

Where to stay

Klein-Aus Vista (4 rooms, 7 chalets, hikers' cabin, campsite) PO Box 25, Aus; tel: 063 258116; tel/fax: 063 258021; email: ausvista@iway.na or ausvista@namibhorses.com; web: www.namibhorses.com

About 3km west of Aus, the family farm Klein-Aus lies 1,400m up in the Aus Mountains, to the south of the main B4, with a big ranch-style sign over the entrance. Piet Swiegers and his brother grew up on the farm, and it is Piet's passion for the place that has led him to share the family farm with visitors. Their own land stretches for about 15,000 hectares, but added to this is a large concession into the Namib Naukluft Park to the north that

THE DESERT HORSES

On the edge of the Koichab Pan, around the Garub Pan, perhaps the world's only desert-dwelling horses are thriving. In 1996 there were about 134 horses, and '97 was a good year for them with at least ten new foals born. On average, though, the numbers fluctuate between 90 and 300 at any one time.

Their origins remain a mystery. They have possibly descended from farm animals that have escaped, or horses that the German *Schutztruppe* abandoned at the start of World War I. The most likely explanation, however, seems to be that they came from Duwisib Castle, near Maltahöhe.

By October 1908 Captain Von Wolf, Duwisib's owner, had assembled a herd of about 33 animals, namely '2 imported stallions, 17 imported mares, 8 Afrikaner mares, 6 year-old fillies'. He was a fanatical horseman, and by November 1909 he had expanded this collection to '72 horses. Mares: 15 Australians, 23 others, 9 thoroughbreds. Rest: Afrikaners and foals. 2 imported thoroughbred stallions'.

Von Wolf left Duwisib in 1914 and was later killed at the battle of the Somme. It is thought that the desert horses near Aus are descended from Von Wolf's herd, which was abandoned after he died. Certainly they seem to be used to roaming free across the Sperrgebiet, drinking at Garub, and eating when they can. Pass them in March, surrounded by a wavy sea of fine green grass, and their situation seems idyllic. But see them on the same desolate gravel plains on an October afternoon, and you'll appreciate their remarkable survival.

affords them a further 300,000 hectares. Here, the focus is on the desert horses that inhabit the plains, and Piet has ambitious plans to become more involved with the management and study of the horses. Historical interest comes from various German fortifications from the 1914–18 war, constructed to defend the area against attack from the railway. And from July to September, after winter rains, the whole area is lit up by the yellow flowers of the *kuibi*.

Set against this backdrop, accommodation is diverse, catering for pretty well every sector of the market – and with one eye on conservation. In the main house, or **Desert Horse Inn**, guests have comfortable and stylish double rooms with en-suite bathrooms (bath *and* shower), ceiling fans, and facilities for making tea and coffee. The décor of each is individual, with a selection of stunning black-and-white photographs by Stan Engelbrecht on the walls. Those seeking to enjoy the solitude and beauty of the mountains may be better served by the single or double chalets at **Eagle's Nest**, some 7km away and overlooked by a pair of nesting black eagles. With solid, rustic wooden furnishings, these, too, have private or en-suite bathrooms, and lack for nothing, from paraffin lamps to flush organic toilets, and a kitchenette with a gas cooker, beer and wine in the fridge, and a table and chairs. Set slightly apart and higher up is **The Rock**, an aptly named rock chalet that was opened in August 2002.

Small groups can take advantage of the **hikers' cabin** at *Geister Schlucht*, or 'Ghost Gully', named after the German stormtroopers who are said to patrol at full moon, having long ago defended the gully against an attack on their water supply. Inside, bunks and single beds are arranged to accommodate up to 14 self-catering visitors, with a kitchen/bar and living area. Finally, there is a ten-pitch **campsite** with spotless ablution blocks that could have been built yesterday rather than three years ago.

Hiking is a major attraction here, with a number of waymarked trails, including some four-hour circular walks starting at various points on the farm. Though the terrain is rugged, the trails (which are marked by the odd white footprint painted on to a rock) try to keep on an even level, and there are occasional springs and pools for cooling off. Alternatively, there is plenty of scope for striking out on your own to seek out wild flowers or choose a vantage point to watch the sunset.

Visitors also have the opportunity to go with Piet on tours ranging from sunset drives, through half-day trips, to full-day tours covering some 200km, taking in the feral horses and some spectacular desert and mountain scenery with a highly knowledgeable guide. Within the concession lies the extinct volcano Dikke Willem, looming above the desert plains and the Koichab riverbed. A full-day trip costs N$2,400 per vehicle (up to 4 people), including breakfast and lunch; a half-day is N$1,400, including breakfast; sunset tours are N$200 per person.

Although some of the accommodation allows for self-catering, breakfast at the house is available to all visitors, as is an excellent three-course dinner with a reasonable selection of wines. Also on offer are water and fruit juice bottled on the farm.

Rates: Rooms single N$635, double N$950; including breakfast. Chalets N$435 per person. Hikers' cabin N$75–105 per person, according to group size. Camping N$40 per person. Breakfast N$40, dinner N$95 per person.

Bahnhof Hotel (10 rooms) PO Box 89, Aus; tel: 063 258065; tel/fax: 063 258091
Masquerading behind a colourful exterior, this is a typical small-town hotel in the centre of Aus. Its rooms are old, carpeted and, though clean, in need of a new lease of life. Most have baths, though a couple have showers and a few share their facilities.

Rates: single N$180, double N$200, including breakfast.

Namib Garage (3 rooms, campsite) PO Box 29, Aus; tel: 063 258029; fax: 063 258017
Self-catering rooms here, one with an en-suite bathroom, are simple and clean, ideal for longer stays. The campsite with 7 pitches is enclosed by a wall. Accommodation enquiries should be made at the garage in Aus, which is open 08.00 to 17.00, and which also has a well-stocked shop and a small restaurant with bar. Meals at the restaurant must be prebooked.

Rates: single N$120, double N$180, camping N$20 per person, plus N$20 for power. Breakfast N$25.

Garub Pan

At the foot of the Aus Mountains, about 20km west of Aus, a sign 'feral horses' points north off the road. Follow the track for just 1.5km and you find Garub Pan, an artificial waterhole which sustains the desert horses and is popular with the local gemsbok as well.

There is a display about their origins, which is largely faded and illegible, and a shaded wooden observation hide – though staying in the car will give almost as good a view.

Koichab Pan to Lüderitz

Driving west from Garub, you enter the flat, gravel plains of the huge Koichab Pan, ringed by mountains in the distance. It's a vast and spectacular place where you'll be able to see any oncoming traffic on the straight road for perhaps 20km before you pass it.

About 52km from Aus, almost halfway to Lüderitz, is a lay-by containing a picnic table in the shade, and half a dozen well-watered trees. Don't miss the chance to stop here, as it must make one of the most bizarre and solitary picnic sites on the continent.

Above Sossusvlei in March, after the exceptional rains of 1987 (CM)

Right The dry, cracked surface of Nara Vlei (CM)

Below Devil thorn flowers (*Tribulus* species) beside the Tsauchab River (CM)

Above Fish River Canyon (CM)

Right Flowering aloe in the Namib-Naukluft, near Groot Tinkas (CM)

Below Kokerboom tree (*Aloe dichotoma*) on plains above the Fish River Canyon (CM)

Finally, as you draw much nearer to Lüderitz, the last 20km or so of the road cross a coastal dune-belt of marching barchan dunes – which are constantly being blown across the road from south to north. Ever-present bulldozers are constantly clearing these, but sometimes you will still encounter low ramps of sand on the tar. Drive very slowly for this last section, as hitting even a small mound of sand can easily wreck a vehicle's suspension.

From Ai-Ais or Noordoewer via Rosh Pinah

Noordoewer (see pages 211–12) is one of the main access points into Namibia from South Africa. But while most drivers head north on the fast B1 towards Keetmanshoop, there is a second road, the C13, that travels northwest, running more or less parallel to the country's southern border until it meets the Orange River, just south of the Ai-Ais and Fish River Canyon National Park.

For those coming from Ai-Ais, it is well worth considering taking the southerly route to Lüderitz, which eventually joins up with the C13 along the Orange River, and on to Aus via Rosh Pinah. Not for those in a hurry, it nevertheless affords some superb scenery to the south of the mountains, with fascinating plant-life, including many succulents and endemics. Note that, as there are no settlements along here, and very little traffic comes this way, you should take more than the usual 'emergency rations' of food and water.

Some 10km after leaving Ai-Ais on the C10, there is a turning to the right on the D316. Though a minor road, this is in good order, leading across open farmland, down to a small river and then uphill on its way – eventually – to join the main B1. If Lüderitz is your goal, though, look out for a sandy track on the right, a short way up the hill, signposted simply 'Rosh Pinah 4x4' (⊕ 28°09.775'S, 17°35.752'E). The signpost is slightly misleading, for when it's dry one of the tracks in this direction is passable, with care, for 2WD vehicles.

From here, the track winds back down through apparently barren terrain towards a dry riverbed, backed by mountains (⊕ 28°09.409'S, 17°31.338'E). Here, the white monotone of the sand is broken by low-lying bushes and, after the rain, flowering succulents which carpet the valley in a deep red, enlivened by splashes of bright yellow stonecrop. Some 19km from the D316, the track splits (⊕ 28°12.651'S, 17°26.292'E). Those with a 4WD can take their pick, but if you have a 2WD vehicle it's important that you take the left fork, through the gate, which continues on slightly higher land until it joins up with the C13 on the Orange River (⊕ 28°19.650'S, 17°23.268'E). The 4WD trail more or less follows the line of the river, coming out on the same road (⊕ 28°16.430'S, 12°22.097'E), just half a kilometre closer to Rosh Pinah.

As it twists and turns along the country's southern border, the C13 narrows and widens according to the proximity of mountains and river to either side. At times the vista opens out across the river, offering some excellent picnic spots and opportunities for birdwatching – particularly as it crosses the Fish River (⊕ 28°5.606'S, 17°10.306'E) – only to be restricted again as the road hugs close to the mountains to the north. Goats may be in their element, but drivers should take particular care along this stretch, for the road is unpredictable: many of the turns are sharp and hidden inclines may be unexpectedly steep. Eventually, the Orange River is left behind as the road heads northwest through desolate hills towards Rosh Pinah, along the border of the Sperrgebiet.

Along the Orange River

Forming the border between Namibia and South Africa, the Orange River tends to be overlooked by visitors. However, with South Africa's wild Richtersveld

National Park (now amalgamated with Ai-Ais National Park as one of the first 'peace parks' in the region) on its southern side, and very little access to its northern banks, it makes a perfect wilderness destination.

The flora in this area of the Namib is particularly unusual, because its proximity to the Cape leads it to receive some winter rainfall. This seems to promote the growth of succulents, including various *Lithops* and *Mesembryanthemum* species, several of which are endemic to this area. Visit in July, August or September and you may find whole areas in bloom, like Namaqualand just over the border to the south.

There are some fascinating larger plants here too, including *Aloe pillansii*, a close relative of the quivertree, which grows to 6–7m in the shape of a candelabra, and the rare, protected *Pachypodium namaquanum*, or half-man, a curious succulent which grows to 2m tall with a great girth. Its head always faces north.

Canoeing
Several companies run canoeing trips along the Orange River, most of which are based out of Cape Town. These are generally geared towards South African visitors, and work well for those driving across the border who want to stop for a few days' canoeing.

Unlike the Victoria Falls, this isn't a white-water experience at all, and neither is it a game experience, though you may catch glimpses of game as you paddle. Rather it is a gentle trip through a stunningly beautiful wilderness area, notable for its scenery and lack of people.

What to take
The arrangements with each canoeing company are different, but most will supply two-person mohawk canoes, paddles, lifejackets, all meals and cool boxes for your own drinks. They will also have watertight containers to keep limited luggage dry.

You must bring your sleeping bag, personal toiletries (preferably biodegradable), a set of clothes for the river and one for when you're away from the water. A hat, long cotton trousers and long-sleeved cotton blouse/shirt, as well as a bathing costume, are fine for the river, plus trainers and warm tracksuit (the temperatures can drop!) for wearing off the river. Many ask you to bring your own drinks (soft, alcoholic and bottled water). Note that glass bottles are not allowed down the river, and so you'll need to decant liquids before you start.

Some companies advise that you will also need your own knife, fork, spoon, mug, plate, torch, toilet paper and sleeping mat. Visitors sometimes take small tents and even folding chairs along, and often you'll be requested to bring large, strong plastic bin liners. The better companies, like Felix Unite, have stocks of all this kit available to hire for their trips.

Rafting companies
The southern Cape, around Cape Town, is the base for most of these trips, and companies to contact include:

Felix Unite PO Box 2807, Claremont 7700, Cape Town, South Africa; tel: + 27 21 670 1300; fax: + 27 21 683 6500; email: julie@felix.co.za. The most experienced and probably the largest of the companies currently running this river. A 4-day trip costs N$1,045 per person, 6-day N$1,295, including meals.

Aquatrails 4 Constantia Rd, Wynberg 7800, Cape Town, South Africa; tel/fax: + 27 21 762 7916; email: info@aquatrails.co.za

Which Way Adventures PO Box 2600, Somerset West 7129, South Africa; tel: + 27 21 852 2364; fax: + 27 21 852 1584; email: whichway@africa.com.za

Intrapid Rafting Tel: + 27 21 461 4918; fax: + 27 82 536 8842; email: raftsa@iafrica.com

If you need further information on rafting companies, then contact Captour, the Cape's tourist information centre, on tel: (27) 21 418 5202.

Where to stay
There are a couple of places to stay in Noordoewer itself (see pages 211–12). Otherwise, you'll be looking at camping en route. Even in winter this is can be an attractive option where the canyon walls provide shelter from the extremes of winter temperature. There's a good campsite, **Bo Plaas** (PO Box 32, Noordoewer; telephone connected via Radio 251 in Walvis Bay on 064 203581), between the Gamkab and Fish rivers (⊕ 28°8.378'S, 17°11.775'E). In a tranquil setting at the foot of the hills near the Huns Mountains, it is a rustic site right on the Orange River, with space for up to 40 people. Aside from wood and water, you will need to bring everything with you. Guests may use the pool, but the river is a far more appealing prospect for swimming, also offering opportunities for canoeing trips to Fish River. Horseriding is available on request. Rates are N$70 per vehicle.

A second campsite, **Namuskluft** (tel: 063 274134/274278; fax: 063 274277) lies some 14km east of the C13, about 1km before it reaches Rosh Pinah. It offers a swimming pool, walking trails, 4WD trips and even a bar.

Rosh Pinah
About 165km south of Aus, and a similar distance from Ai-Ais (171km) or Noordoewer (154km), the mining town of Rosh Pinah lies in a very remote corner of Namibia, almost on the eastern border of the Sperrgebiet.

A deposit of copper was discovered just south of here by a Prussian Jew, Mose Eli Kahan, who had fled Europe to escape persecution. By the 1920s this was being worked, but was abandoned when the price slumped in the 1930s. Thirty years later, in 1968, Kahan found a zinc deposit in the mountains, which he named Rosh Pinah. Though he died soon afterwards, his son eventually joined forces with the large South African mining company Iscor to develop it.

Production began in 1969, and the mine now employs over 400 people directly. It produces around 72,000 tonnes of zinc per year, as well as a lead concentrate, and also a little silver. A more recent discovery of better-quality zinc has led to the development of the nearby Scorpion mine, with an expected life of around 20 years. Once the mine is active, the zinc will be loaded on to trucks and taken by rail and road to Lüderitz, from where it will be shipped overseas. Before this can happen, however, significant investment is being made in the region's transport infrastructure.

As part of these improvements, the road between Rosh Pinah and Aus is being upgraded to tar; by mid-2002, a 13km stretch out of Rosh Pinah was finished, with completion of the whole road expected either in 2003 or shortly after. Even before this, the drive from Ai-Ais to Aus could be undertaken in around six hours or so; once the road is tarred, the journey time will be shorter still. In addition to work on the roads, the railway from Aus to Lüderitz is being repaired and improved, although information about completion dates of the project ranges from 2003 to 2006.

Few visitors pass through Rosh Pinah so there are no hotels, though if you've friends at the mine you may be able to use the company's guesthouse. There is, however, a small fuel station with a shop alongside that has a surprising varied stock, including fresh fruit and vegetables. It's also worth noting that there is mobile phone coverage in the town itself.

LÜDERITZ
Trapped between the desiccating sands of the Namib and the freezing waters of the South Atlantic's Benguela current, Lüderitz is a fascinating old German town, full

of character. It is usually sleepy and laid-back, with relaxed locals who often have time to talk. (Witness the number of public phones, which seem to be everywhere.) Around the centre of town, houses are painted in improbable pastel shades, which makes Lüderitz feel like a delightful toy town at times. The air here is tangibly clean, even on the foggiest of mornings. Local Namibians say that Lüderitz can have all four seasons in a day, as the weather can change in hours from bright, hot and sunny, to strong winds, to dark, cold and foggy – and then back to sunshine again. This variation, together with a cold sea and the prevailing southwest wind, rule out Lüderitz as a beach destination, though brave souls still take brief dips from the beach near the Nest Hotel or round on the peninsula.

In the evenings, there are a few lively bars, and a handful of quiet restaurants, notable for their seafood. But the entertainment here pales in comparison with Swakopmund. Because of its location, Lüderitz is not somewhere to 'drop in on' as you need to make a special journey to come here – but it's worth visiting for its architecture, its peninsula, and to see a part of Namibia which seems almost unaware of the outside world.

Tourism is having an impact here, but only gradually. Several new hotels have been opened in the last few years, and more guesthouses have opened their doors. Lüderitz's prosperity is likely to be increasingly based on tourism, with a trendy waterfront development near the harbour the most recent innovation. Over the next year or two, there are plans to develop the area alongside the old power station overlooking the sea near the Nest Hotel. Rumours abound as to the eventual use of this site, but luxury flats are almost certain to feature in the equation. Whether or not the town gets the sports centre that the locals would like may well be a matter of economics.

One dramatic recent development is the discovery of an enormous offshore gas-field in the South Atlantic – the Kudu field. If plans to tap that were put into action it could bring another boom to this quiet little port, and change its character irrevocably. However there are plans to use Oranjemund as the base for this, leaving Lüderitz unaffected. Of more immediate relevance to Lüderitz, however, is the use of the harbour as the export base for the new Scorpion zinc mine near Rosh Pinah. While construction of the warehousing is already complete, movement of the zinc cannot commence until the transport infrastructure between the two towns is in place, estimated at somewhere between 2003 and 2006.

Meanwhile, the only thing that seems to disturb the peace is a siren sounded at noon during the week, to remind the townspeople of the time! (The same sounded intermittently means that there's a fire somewhere.)

History

Stone-Age tools and artefacts found in the region confirm that Khoisan people knew the area centuries before any Europeans arrived. The first recorded visit by a European was that of Bartholomeu Dias, the great Portuguese explorer, who sheltered here in 1487. He returned the following year and erected a limestone cross at the spot now known as Diaz Point, naming the place Angra Pequena, or 'Little Bay'.

Passing mariners recognised it as one of the best natural harbours on the southwest coast of Africa – even if the land around the harbour was desolate, forbidding, and totally lacking in fresh water. The Dutch East India Company sent an emissary to start trading with Nama groups in the region. This failed. In 1793 the area was annexed by the Dutch authorities in the Cape... who proceeded to do nothing with it.

By the mid-1800s, whalers, sealers, fishermen and guano collectors were exploiting the area's rich marine life and there are reports of hundreds of ships around the harbour area. By 1862 some had set up shore bases here.

In March 1883 a German trader, Adolf Lüderitz, with help from Heinrich Vogelsang, a merchant from the Cape, bought a small ship, the *Tilly*, and surreptitiously set sail northwards from the Cape. They arrived at Angra Pequena on April 10, landed their supplies, and Vogelsang set off to Bethanie in the interior. By May 1 Vogelsang had bought the bay (and 8km around it) for Lüderitz from Nama Kaptein Josef Frederiks for £100 and 200 rifles.

On May 12 the German flag was hoisted in Angra Pequena, and in August Vogelsang returned to Kaptain Josef, buying a 32km-wide coastal belt from the Orange River to the 26th degree of latitude south for a further £100 and 60 rifles. He named the area Lüderitzland.

Whilst Vogelsang cultivated a business selling guns throughout the region, Lüderitz returned to the Cape in September to find his land rights challenged. Negotiations ensued, by which time Germany was waking up to the scramble for Africa, and sent a gunboat, the *Nautilus*, to what they called Lüderitz Bay. By August 1884 the British had agreed that Germany could found its first colony here – their first foothold which led to the eventual annexation of South West Africa.

Lüderitz himself made little money out of the venture, and disappeared a few years later whilst out prospecting. The town grew slowly, and was an important supply base for the German Schutztruppe during the war with the Nama people in 1904–7. The construction of a railway line to Keetmanshoop, between 1906 and 1908, promised more trade, but was overshadowed by the diamond boom that began as the railway was finished. (See *The diamond boom*, page 245.)

From then the town exploded, as the centre of supplies and operations of the diamond-mining company, CDM. Gradually the town's fishing industries developed, and an important export trade of rock lobster was established. However, the CDM headquarters moved to Oranjemund in 1943, precipitating the start of the town's slow decline. What does remain, though, is the significant diamond-diving industry (see page 232), and NAMDEB continues to have a considerable stake in the town, publishing the only local newsletter.

Only in the last few years, through tourism and fishing, has Lüderitz's economy started to look up again. Ironically tourism has been helped by the lack of development between the 1940s and the 90s – which preserved many of the beautiful buildings of the early 1900s.

Getting there

Most visitors drive to Lüderitz, between visiting the Namib-Naukluft National Park and the Fish River Canyon. Because the town is out on a limb, the drive takes time. Although the town is bisected by a railway, trains have not run for several years. That said, work is in hand to upgrade the track for the transport of zinc from the Scorpion mine near Rosh Pinah, so it is possible that passenger trains could again run on this route in the future.

If you choose to visit the area, allow yourself a minimum of two nights to appreciate it, and to see its surrounds properly.

By car

See *The roads to Lüderitz*, pages 221–9, for comments on the whole journey, but note that for the last 20km there is a 60km/h speed limit. This is because the fast tarmac road cuts through a field of shifting barchan dunes, which constantly march across it. Go slowly. Even a small pile of sand is hard when hit at speed.

DIVING FOR DIAMONDS

The wealth of southwestern Namibia may have been built on diamonds from the Sperrgebiet, but today the greatest proportion of the diamonds found in the area around Lüderitz are mined from under the sea rather than in the Sperrgebiet itself. These alluvial diamonds are found all along the Orange River and at its mouth, but over the years many have been swept farther north by the Benguela Current, with significant deposits now to be found in the seas around Lüderitz harbour.

The leading company in this field is NAMCO, which has been operational since 1994. Following the company's estimates that around 2.6 million carats of diamonds were to be found in these waters, large-scale operations went live in 1998, with some 650,000 carats now produced each year. Boats put out to sea regularly from the harbour in Lüderitz. On the larger diamond boats, robotic machines trawl in waters up to 150m deep, digging a trench in the sea bed then sucking up the material from depths of 10–16m, up to 25m, ready for processing on board. While the first bags collected contain little except sand, beneath this layer is gravel; it is among the gravel that diamonds are most likely to be found. NAMDEB, too, has considerable resources devoted to this sector within an area that extends 200km out into the Atlantic.

Smaller boats are owned and operated under licence to NAMDEB by diamond divers. Each boat is allocated a specific area, not more than 5km from the coast, in which to search. Theirs is a dangerous job, in unforgiving conditions, but the potential rewards are high: in 1999, 60,000 carats of diamonds were collected in this way.

When the boats return to port, the sacks are taken by officials from NAMDEB to their processing plant, where the contents are classified. All boats, including any personal luggage on board, are thoroughly checked and inspected for any gravel that may have been overlooked before they are declared 'clean'.

By air

Lüderitz has one flight per day, except Saturday, to Windhoek via Walvis Bay (N$950). The airstrip is about 9km east of the town, opposite Kolmanskop.

By bus

The only option is TransNamib's *Starline* bus service (tel: 063 202875/ 2021220) connecting Lüderitz with Keetmanshoop via Aus, Bethanie and Goageb once every day (except a few public holidays). It leaves the corner of Bahnhof Street and Bismarck Street at 12.30 (11.30 on Sunday), arriving in Keetmanshoop at 17.30 (16.30 on Sunday). The following day it leaves Keetmanshoop at 07.30, arriving in Lüderitz at 12.15, but there is no return service on a Sunday. See pages 98–9 for details.

Although Intercape Mainliner buses do not come to town, they have a booking agent at Lüderitz Safaris and Tours (see page 238), so you can plan onward journeys here.

By sea

There are no regular passenger boats calling at Lüderitz, but the town is a port of call for a number of cruise ships, usually between January and March.

Hitchhiking

Compared with many of Namibia's attractions, Lüderitz is relatively easy to reach by hitching. The tar road from Keetmanshoop has a steady trickle of traffic along it, and intrepid hitchhikers have even made it from Walvis Bay along the C14 via Sesriem – though taking food and water with you is essential if you try this route.

Getting around

If you don't have your own car, there are two options – hire a car, or use the service of one of the town's tour operators (see page 238). Transport from the airport or to Kolmanskop with one of the tour operators costs N$60, or N$30 per person, plus 15% VAT.

Car hire

Three of the big car-hire companies have offices in Lüderitz:

Avis Next to Caltex on Bahnhof St; tel: 063 203965, after hours 063 203966, cell: 081 124 1827; fax: 063 203967
Budget At J&A Trading on Bay Rd; tel/fax: 063 203692
Imperial Next to the museum on Diaz St; tel: 063 203884

Where to stay

Lüderitz has three fairly traditional hotels plus two sharp new ones. There are also a few small B&B-type guesthouses, a backpackers' lodge and a windswept campsite (complete with super lighthouse). It is best to book most of them in advance, as the town's rooms quickly fill up during the busier times of year (see *When to go*, pages 47–8).

Nest Hotel (73 twin rooms) 820 Diaz St, Ostend, PO Box 690, Lüderitz; tel: 063 204000; fax: 063 204001; email: nesthotel@natron.net; web: www.natron.net/tour/nest-hotel/main.html
Set on its own right on the sea to the southwest of town, with its own beach, the Nest is Lüderitz's largest hotel, and reputedly cost N$30 million to build. Rooms are built around a sheltered central courtyard with swimming pool, and each has a sea view. Facilities are as you would expect from a 4-star hotel: all rooms have en-suite shower or bath, TV, phone, AC/central heating, coffee- and tea-making facilities and hairdryer. Three have wheelchair access. Public rooms feature a rather small bar set off a considerably larger reception area, and a good waterfront restaurant. There's also a sauna, and a 'sundowner' bar that is rarely open – a casualty of the town's fabled cool breezes! Outside is a guarded parking area.
Rates (low/high season): single N$435/540, double N$635–790, family N$850–1,060, suite NS$1,120–1,400, including breakfast. (Low season is Dec–Mar, and Jun.)

Sea-View Hotel Zum Sperrgebiet (22 twin rooms) Woermann St, PO Box 373, Lüderitz; tel: 063 203411; fax: 063 203414; email: michaels@ldz.namib.com; web: www.natron.net/tour/sea view/seaviewd.htm
Owned by Mrs Ingrid Morgan, this modern hotel is compact, smart and very comfortable, albeit slightly out of the centre. Each of the small rooms is well designed, with a TV, a coffee and tea maker, a hairdryer, a small balcony with a view over either the harbour or the courtyard, and en-suite facilities including a good shower (some also have baths). The efficient-looking restaurant sits beside a small (but spectacular) indoor swimming pool, surrounded by banana trees and shaded glass walls, overlooking the harbour in the distance. A sauna and garden are tucked away, out of view.
Rates: single N$443, double N$701, triple N$932, family N$1,189, including breakfast.

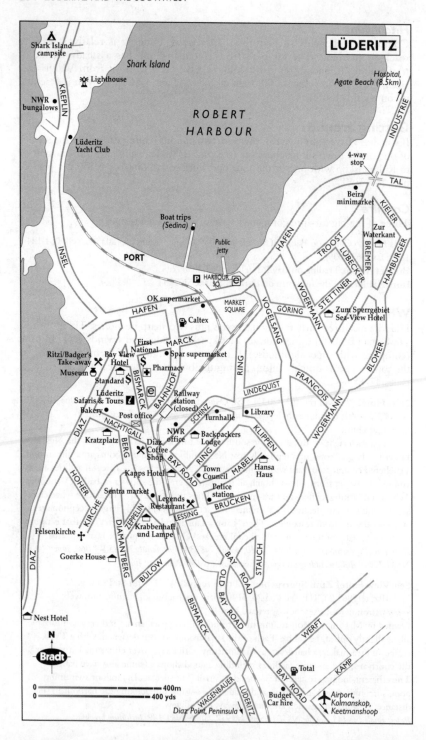

Bay View Hotel (21 rooms) Bismarck St, PO Box 100, Lüderitz; tel: 063 202288; fax: 063 202402; email: colourgem@iafrica.com; web: www.namibia.co.za
On the corner of Bismarck and Diaz streets, the Bay View is clean, comfortable and friendly. Reception is on Diaz St, opposite the museum. If you're looking for a hotel with a feel for the old town, the Bay View is the best there is. Despite being one of the town's larger hotels, it still feels small, perhaps because the rooms are built around a courtyard and swimming pool.
Each twin-bedded room has a TV and direct-dial phone. There is off-street parking at the back. A small, bright restaurant with adjoining bar serves breakfast, lunch, and dinner (you don't need to be a resident).
Rates: single N$280, N$460, triple N$590, including breakfast.

Kapps Hotel (140 rooms) Bay Rd, PO Box 218, Lüderitz; tel: 063 202345; fax: 063 202402; email: pmk@mweb.com.na
The Kapps is Lüderitz's oldest hotel, built in 1907 and once owned by the Lüderitz family. Rooms with telephones, kettles with tea and coffee and en-suite toilets and showers, are set around a brick-lined courtyard at the back. New fabrics help to alleviate their otherwise tired décor. It has its own restaurant, Rumours Grill, serving reasonable food in uninspiring surroundings.
Rates: single N$250, double N$390, family N$460 (up to 4), including breakfast.

Hotel Diamond Reef City (11 rooms) Bismarck St, PO Box 1300, Lüderitz; tel: 063 202851; fax: 063 203853; email: fotofun@iafrica.com.na
The high-ceilinged rooms (only two are en suite) at the Diamond Reef are basic, set around a stark courtyard at the back of the hotel. Bathrooms are large, with toilets and baths with shower attachments, but no way to mount these on the wall for a proper shower.
Inside the hotel is a slightly institutional-style dining room and a lounge for sitting with no TV. Adjacent is a fairly quiet bar with a pool table, but next door is a casino and bar under different ownership.
Rates: single N$210, double N$330, triple N$400, family N$445, including breakfast.

House Sandrose (1 room, 1 flat, 1 house) 15 Bismarck St, PO Box 109, Lüderitz; tel: 063 202630, cell: 081 241 5544; fax: 063 202365; email: clooser@africaonline.com.na
Christine and Erich Looser's centrally located accommodation is guaranteed to make visitors feel individual. Three entirely distinct styles pervade their three units, from the roomy Grosse Bucht self-catering house that sleeps up to 5, through the two-bed Bogenfels flat with shower and toilet across a small private courtyard, to the colourful double room featuring Anin bed linen (see page 198). Each has its own cooking facilities (the bedroom has just an egg boiler, kettle and toaster) and a secluded area of garden. There is also guarded street parking in front of the Sandrose gift shop (where Anin linen is available to purchase).
Rates: single N$220, double N$300, triple N$440, 4 people N$550, 5 people N$687. Breakfast N$40 on request.

Zur Waterkant (4 rooms, 2 flats) Bremer St, PO Box 1055, Lüderitz; tel/fax: 063 203145; email: zur-waterkant@raubkatzen.de; web: www.raubkatzen.de
Marlene and Hartmut Halbich's homely B&B offers comfortable accommodation, though if Hartmut is not in, you'll find a smattering of German is helpful. En-suite rooms are simply furnished with double beds, and each has a small, sea-facing balcony. There are also two self-catering flats. Dinner is available on request.
Rates: single N$280, double N$340, including breakfast. Self-catering N$200 per person.

Hansa Haus Guesthouse (4 rooms) Mabel St, PO Box 837, Lüderitz; tel/fax: 063 203581; email: mcloud@africaonline.com.na
Right at the top of Mabel St, this imposing blue house was built in 1909 with a commanding view of the town. It was renovated by the present owners, who live here with their children, and opened as a guesthouse in 2001. Double rooms with high ceilings are

attractively furnished and have basic cooking facilities. Guests share two bathrooms, with either shower or bath, and there's a separate TV lounge.
Rates: single from N$160, double N$280. No breakfast available.

Kratzplatz (10 rooms) 5 Nachtigal St, PO Box 885, Lüderitz; tel/fax: 063 202458, cell: 081 1292458
This friendly B&B run by Manfred and Monica Kratz stands on the continuation of Bay Rd after it crosses the railway line. The main building, a converted church, features white-washed, high-ceilinged rooms, five of which are en suite. A further three rooms share two bathrooms, and there's also a family room, and an apartment sleeping up to 9 people. Most rooms have TV, and the style and furnishings are modern and simple: this is a pleasant place to sleep, with secure parking. Dinner is available for groups.
Rates: single N$180, double N$270, triple N$320, including breakfast. Family (self-catering) N$400. Breakfast for self-catering visitors is N$30.

Krabbenhoft und Lampe (2 flats, 5 double rooms) 25 Bismarck St, PO Box 257, Lüderitz; tel: 063 202674/202466, cell: 081 129 2025; fax: 063 202549; email: taurus@ldz.namib.com; web: www.klguesthouse.com
This imposing place at the top of the town houses some unexpected guest accommodation. Constructed in 1880, the building used to be home to a carpet-weaving factory but is now simply a shop. Upstairs, however, the large, rather stark rooms retain many architectural features, with scarcely a nod in the direction of modernity. Two flats on the first floor are fully self-catering, while one flight further up are five twin-bedded rooms with shared bathrooms, toilets and kitchen facilities. It's certainly distinctive, and represents good value for money.
Rates: double N$220, 2-bed flat N$320, 6-bed flat N$650.

Backpackers Lodge (3 rooms, 16 beds) 7 Schinz St, opposite the Nature Conservation office; tel: 063 202000; tel/fax: 063 202445/202742
With an increasing number of backpackers finding Lüderitz, this good and very central lodge has a monopoly. It has simple twin rooms as well as dormitories (all clean and well-maintained), an equipped kitchen (free tea and coffee), a laundry service and a yard at the back for braais. Its large main room has lots of space and is used for watching TV and playing table tennis, also as an overflow for the truck groups that visit. There is an informative noticeboard at the front and Toya is also a mine of useful information about the area.
Rates: double N$140, dorm bed N$60

Shark Island Campsite (3 bungalows, lighthouse and 20 campsites) Book via the NWR in Lüderitz, PO Box 9, Lüderitz; tel: 063 202811; fax: 063 204188; email: reservations@mweb.com.na; web: www.namibiawildliferesorts.com
Along Hafen and Insel streets, beside the harbour and past the Caltex refinery, lies Shark Island, which is linked to the mainland by a causeway and a road. Here Lüderitz's only campsite has a superb location, with power and braai facilities, but is amazingly windy. If there's nobody on the gate then campers can just pitch their tents – try to find a site sheltered by the rocks – and the attendants will come over to collect money. The sites are overlooked by a lighthouse, with two bedrooms, kitchen, bathroom and living area, which can be rented for small groups – this must be Lüderitz's most imposing place to stay whilst visiting town. The nearby bungalows are good value, and are warmer than the campsites!
Rates: lighthouse N$580 per night, bungalows (sleep 6) N$300, camping N$95 per site, with powerpoint, up to a maximum of eight people. There is a standard entry fee of N$10 per person.

Where to eat and drink
There's not an endless choice of cuisine in Lüderitz, but seafood (and particularly lobster in season, best ordered in advance) is a speciality – it is what most visitors want, and what most places serve. If seafood is above your budget then steaks and

more usual Namibian fare are also available, while some good smaller take-aways serve burgers and bar food which can be excellent value.

Ritzi's Seafood Restaurant Diaz St; tel: 063 202818. Down from the museum and almost opposite the Bay View, Ritzi's has a decidedly unprepossessing entrance next to Badger's take-away. But those in the know brave the doorway, and the rather basic bar, heading straight for Lüderitz's best eatery – by far. Inside, all is warm, cosy and intimate, with a great atmosphere – and *no* piped music. As you'd expect, the menu majors on seafood, but with plenty of innovation – do try the prawn basket starter. If fish is not for you, there's a good choice of alternatives, and there are also several specials. Prices come as a very pleasant surprise, including a seafood platter at N$99, and the wine list is unbelievably good value. Open for lunch and dinner except Sunday – booking advisable.

Badger's Take-away Diaz St; tel: 063 202818. Badger's nowadays is simply a take-away, with an adjacent bar, its former restaurant now the domain of Ritzi's. Open Mon–Fri 09.00–midnight, Sat 09.00–14.00 and 17.00–midnight.

Legends Tel: 063 203110. On the corner of Bay Rd and Lessing St, opposite the police station, this informal but comfortable restaurant has its own bar alongside. Friendly staff serve the normal seafood and steak fare, as well as burgers and pizzas, and there are vegetarian options too – all in generous portions. Prices are around N$40–90, with crayfish at N$160. It is open daily, with a happy hour Sat 20.00–21.00.

Zum Sperrgebiet Sea-View Restaurant Tel: 063 31 3411; fax: 063 31 3414. In the hotel on Woermann St, this lacks character like many modern hotels, but is stylish, with good service, and there are ceiling fans for when (if?) the weather becomes hot. It serves good food at around N$15–30 for a starter, N$50–60 for steaks, N$125 for crayfish, and N$15–20 for dessert, and light meals are also available.

Bay View Restaurant Tel: 063 202288; fax: 063 202402. Light and airy, with polished wooden floors, pot plants, and watercolours on the walls, this first-floor restaurant serves à la carte food all day. For breakfast or lunch expect to pay around N$20 each, for dinner N$65. A blow-out meal of oysters to start, with crayfish and dessert to follow, might be N$140.

Rumours Grill Bay Rd; tel: 063 202345. The broad-ranging menu here features everything from burgers and steaks to seafood. Rumours is popular locally, but the restaurant surroundings are singularly depressing, and crayfish at N$135 is pretty expensive by these standards. It's open from 18.00 to late, and there's a separate, lively sports bar with large TV.

Diaz Coffee Shop Corner Bismarck and Nachtigal roads; tel: 063 203147. This well-positioned and relaxed café has snacks and cakes, as well as light meals. It's open Mon–Fri 07.00–17.00, Sat 08.00–15.00, and Sun 09.00–13.00.

The Fairies Coffee Nook Also on the harbour front, this is a simple but clean café, open Mon–Fri 07.30–17.00, Sat 07.30–14.00 and 15.30–18.00, and Sun 15.30–18.00. Signposts on the harbour in summer 2002 indicate that a new restaurant is likely to be opened upstairs.

Steve's Pizza Place Next to Legends, this is the place for take-away pizzas.

Captain Macarena (tel: 063 203958) serves fish and chips to take away from its premises in the new Harbour Square development.

Lüderitz doesn't major on nightlife, but locals congregate at the bars adjacent to Rumours or Legends, or at the German club above the Turnhalle. More expensive, but popular when the sun's out, is the Sundowner Bar at the Nest Hotel. There's a bowling alley, Kegelbahn, next to Rumours Grill.

Getting organised

In an emergency, the police are reached on tel: 063 10111, whilst the ambulance and hospital are on 063 202446, and the fire service on tel: 063 202255. There's a **pharmacy** on Bahnhof St (tel: 063 202806), next to the First National Bank.

Tour operators
If you merely need advice about enjoying yourself, there are several companies who might be able to help:

Lüderitz Safaris and Tours PO Box 76, Bismarck St, Lüderitz; tel: 063 202719/202622; fax: 063 202963
Run by Marion Schelkle, this is a convenient tour operator that also doubles as the tourist information office and is the booking agent for Intercape Mainliner. They can help with bookings in Lüderitz, or further afield, and can issue permits for Kolmanskop. There is also a small selection of books and crafts for sale.

Coastways Tours PO Box 77, Harbour Square, Lüderitz; tel: 063 202002, cell: 081 257 4118; fax: 063 202003; email: lewiscwt@iway.na. Coastways started up with self-drive 4WD trips to Saddle Hill and Spencer Bay to the north of Lüderitz, in the Namib-Naukluft Park, and plans are in hand to extend these as far as Walvis Bay. A three-day trip to Spencer Bay costs N$1,200; visitors should take all their own food, bedding etc, but no tents are required. In 2002, the company was granted a temporary concession to take trips to Pomona and Bogenfels in the Sperrgebiet (see pages 244–6) but no decision had been taken on the long-term licence holder.

Ghost Town Tours PO Box 305, Lüderitz; tel/fax: 063 204031, cell: 8112 84336; email: kolmans@iafrica.com.na. The company that administers Kolmanskop also runs trips there (see page 244) and issues permits for self-drive visitors. Longer trips to Elizabeth Bay include lunch, while the 'Elizabeth Bay special', for between four and eight people, takes in both the above, together with a guided tour of Lüderitz itself and the surrounding area, for a total of N$500 per person, including lunch at Kolmanskop. Tours leave Mon–Fri at 08.00, returning at around 15.00. For details of the Elizabeth Bay trip, see page 244.

Note that trips into the Sperrgebiet (except to Agate Bay and Kolmanskop) must be booked at least five working days in advance. You will need to provide names, passport numbers and nationalities for all who want to take part in order to get the right permits.

The **NWR** office is housed in the old post office building, dating back to 1907, on Schinz Street (tel: 063 202811; fax: 063 204188; email: reservations@mweb.com.na; web: www.namibiawildliferesorts.com).

Shopping
Lüderitz has three main supermarkets – of which the **Spar**, on the corner of Bahnhof and Moltke streets, and **Jose's OK Grocer**, on Hafen Street opposite the main harbour, are probably the best. Passing the harbour on the left, the **Beira Minimarket** is a few blocks away and has, as its name suggests, a Portuguese bias. There's also a Portuguese supermarket at the southern end of Bismarck Street.

The new harbour development provides a number of small shops catering for visitors, with curios, postcards and jewellery available alongside the more usual hair salons and food shops. Also well worth a visit are the craft shop that is part of House Sandrose on Bismarck Street, and that at Lüderitz Safaris and Tours further down the same street.

Internet cafés
There are two internet cafés in the town: **Extreme Communications**, on the harbour (tel: 063 204256; fax: 204295), and **Club Internet** on Bahnhof Street.

What to see and do
Even visitors with a limited attention span find enough to occupy themselves around Lüderitz for a day, whilst those who enjoy a more leisurely pace will take three or four to see the area's main attractions. At the end of August, a two-day German Festival takes place in Lüderitz and at Kolmanskop.

For the visitor, the focus of the town is the new harbourfront development, which was opened in 2002. With a small tower that affords a good overview of the town, and a public jetty, it is a pleasant place to while away an hour or so watching the boats in the harbour. There is also a café, and public toilets (with a nominal charge).

Shark Island
This erstwhile island is now joined to the mainland by a causeway, and most people visit only if they're staying at the campsite here – or in the lighthouse (see page 236).

Felsenkirche
If you approach the town from the sea, this small, rather stark Lutheran church is clearly visible. Located on a hill close to the Goerke Haus, it was built in 1912 and has some interesting stained-glass windows.
Open: Mon–Sat for just one hour in the afternoon.

Museum
Opposite the Bay View, on Diaz Street, this small museum (tel: 063 202532) has exhibits on the diamond-mining industry, including fake diamonds, an egg collection, a good section on the Bushmen, a variety of small exhibits on other indigenous cultures, and assorted cases of local flora and fauna.
Open: Mon–Fri 08.30–11.00, 15.30–17.00, Sat 09.00–11.00.
Costs: N$5 adults, N$3.50 children.

Goerke Haus
High up on Diamantberg, at the end of Zeppelin Street, Goerke House is the beautiful cream building with a blue roof that is built into the rocks above the level of the road. It is the town's best preserved historical building, visible from around town, and if you visit nothing else in Lüderitz, make sure you see this. (Note that the house has recently been repainted; references to the 'blue house' refer to this.)

Hans Goerke was born in Germany in 1874 and arrived in German South West Africa with the Schutztruppe in 1904. In 1907 he became provisions inspector for the German forces – just before diamonds were discovered near Kolmanskop. By the end of 1909 he had resigned from the army and was making a fortune in the diamond rush, which enabled him to have this house built between October 1909 and September 1910. It was then valued at 70,000 Deutschmarks (£3,500/ US$5,250). One of Lüderitz's so-called 'diamond palaces', it is thought to have been designed by a German architect, Otto Ertl. Although it was built during the art nouveau period (*jugendstil* in German), 1890–1920, and has many relevant features, it isn't typical of that style.

Goerke left Namibia for Germany in 1912. In 1920 the house was bought by Consolidated Diamond Mines (CDM), the forerunner of the present-day NAMDEB Diamond Corporation (which is now a partnership between South Africa's huge De Beers and the Namibian government). In 1944 they sold it back to the government of South West Africa for £2,404 (US$3,606), and the house became the residence of the local magistrate, and hence known as the Drostdy.

In 1981 the magistrate was recalled to Keetmanshoop – Lüderitz just didn't have enough crime – and the CDM repurchased the house and restored it for use as a VIP guesthouse.

There is an informative small leaflet about the house (see *Further Reading*). Get one from the curator before you look around if possible. It notes some of the interesting art nouveau details to look out for, including:

* The flamingo motifs used on the stained-glass windows. The side profile of the flamingos' necks is a wavy form typical of the art nouveau style.
* The decorative detail on either side of the hat and coat stand in the hall, resembling Egyptian papyrus bells. Early art nouveau took inspiration from the shapes of plants.
* The mix of artistic styles, which is typical of art nouveau: Roman arches over the stairwell, supported by an Egyptian lotus column, capped by a Grecian Doric capital.
* The posts at the foot of the stairs resembling dentilled Gothic spires.

Other interesting features of the house include:

* The carpets and curtains which, although new, are typical of the period around 1910.
* The light fittings, some of which are original, as seen in the old photographs on display, are classic examples of the art nouveau style.
* The stunning pine flooring which is original, though during Goerke's time it was covered in patterned linoleum, a little of which remains in the study.
* The original stained-glass windows at the entrance and on the stairs.
* The friezes on the walls which have been restored, and the kitchens and bathrooms which have been modernised so that guests of NAMDEB can stay here.

Moves are afoot to have the house's original furniture sent back from South Africa, where it was taken years ago. However, the current furniture, although not original, is beautiful, from the piano with ivory keys to marble-topped dressing tables in the bedrooms and oak furniture around the lounge. Don't miss it.

Open: Times limited to Mon–Fri: 14.00–16.00, Sat 16.00–17.00
Costs: N10 per person.

Diamantberg

Behind Goerke House, Diamantberg is the highest land around town. With a pair of stout shoes you can easily scramble up for a good view of the town and harbour beyond. Standing in the cool sea breeze, under desert sun, much about the landscape seems extreme. There is little vegetation to soften the parched land, whilst the sea beyond seems cold and uninviting. However, as if to compensate, the town's people have painted many of their buildings in soft pastel shades. Quaintly shaped wooden buildings, just a few storeys high and painted baby-blue, pink and green, all give Lüderitz the air of a pleasant, gentle town.

EXCURSIONS FROM LÜDERITZ

If you have your own transport then Lüderitz peninsula, Agate Beach and Kolmanskop are well worth visiting. To see some of the area to the south of Lüderitz, in the Sperrgebiet – the restricted diamond area – you must join an organised tour. There is also an excellent boat trip from the harbour.

Boat trips

Weather permitting, the small schooner, *Sedina*, leaves the harbour at 08.00 for a 2¼-hour trip – under sail if you're lucky – around Diaz Point to Halifax Island in search of penguins, seals and dolphins. While visitors are almost guaranteed to see these creatures, keep your eyes open and you'll spot plenty of birds as well, from scoters and various species of cormorant to oystercatchers and flamingos. The boat's skipper, Gunther, has sailed these waters for years, and is only too happy to share his considerable knowledge of marine wildlife. Trips cost cost N$170 per person (children half price) through Atlantic Adventure Tours, tel: 063 204030, or contact one of the local tour operators.

Lüderitz peninsula

To the southwest of the town lies the Lüderitz peninsula, surrounded by sea on three sides yet a rocky desert within. Here, the lower slopes are dotted with a surprising variety of salt-tolerant succulent plants. In winter, if there's been some good rain, many of these are in flower, affording scope for hours of plant spotting. Around the coast there are some rocky beaches and some sandy ones; all are worth exploring if you have a car.

Note that whilst the roads here are fine for 2WD cars, don't be tempted to follow tracks across soft sand made by local 4WD enthusiasts, or you'll need their help to pull your vehicle out.

To reach the peninsula, simply follow Bismarck Street into Lüderitz Street, keeping the railway line on your left. The most interesting parts of the peninsula are:

Radford Bay, shortly after leaving the town, is often home to a flock of flamingos.

Second Lagoon Also a popular spot with visiting flamingos, and sometimes the odd stranded motorist. Continuing to the right –

Griffith Bay Excellent views of the town across the cold, misty sea, plus a few crystal-clear rocks pools to dabble in. It is named after an American officer who sheltered here and was then killed during the American civil war.

Angra Club Believe it or not, there really is a golf course here, its nine holes played exclusively on sand. Although it's open to the public, locals advise visitors to go with someone who knows the course.

Sturmvogel Bucht The whaling station here can be visited from the *Sedina* (see *Boat trips*, above). Costs are N$170 per adult, N$85 per child.

Diaz Point Reached by a short wooden bridge is a granite cross, a replica of the one erected by Bartholomeu Dias, the first European explorer to enter the bay. He sheltered here in the late 14th century, referring to the bay as Angra Pequena, or 'Little Bay'. There are often seals sunning themselves on the rocks here. Just south of Diaz Point is a grave bearing a stark reminder: 'George Pond of London, died here of hunger and thirst 1906.' There is talk of establishing a campsite and café here in the future, but for now it remains a secluded spot.

Halifax Island The large jackass penguin colony here can be viewed with a good pair of binoculars from the cliffs and beaches on the western side of Guano Bay, or – closer up – from the deck of the *Sedina* – see above.

Guano Bay is another good place to spot flamingos, either from land or from the *Sedina*.

Essy Bay A number of very rocky little bays, each with a place for a braai. All are linked by a network of good sand roads. The beach to the south side has a toilet block.

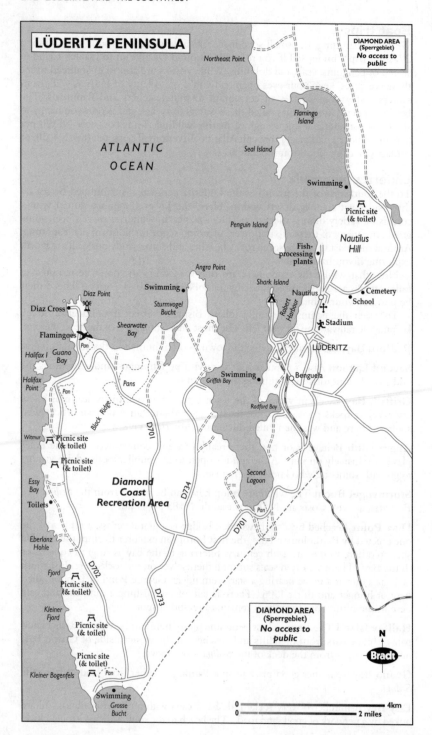

LÜDERITZ PENINSULA

DIAMOND AREA
(Sperrgebiet)
No access to public

Northeast Point

ATLANTIC OCEAN

Flamingo Island

Seal Island

Swimming

Picnic site (& toilet)

Penguin Island

Nautilus Hill

Fish-processing plants

Angra Point

Swimming

Shark Island

Diaz Point

Diaz Cross

Sturmvogel Bucht

Nautilus

Cemetery

School

Robert Harbour

Flamingos

Shearwater Bay

Pan

Stadium

Halifax I

Guano Bay

LÜDERITZ

Halifax Point

Pan

Pans

Swimming

Griffith Bay

Benguela

Black Ridge

Radford Bay

Witmur

Picnic site (& toilet)

D701

Picnic site (& toilet)

Diamond Coast Recreation Area

D734

Second Lagoon

Essy Bay

Toilets

Pan

Eberlanz Hohle

D702

Fjord

Picnic site (& toilet)

Kleiner Fjord

D733

Picnic site (& toilet)

DIAMOND AREA
(Sperrgebiet)
No access to public

Picnic site (& toilet)

N

Kleiner Bogenfels

Pan

Swimming

Grosse Bucht

Bradt

0 ———————— 4km
0 ———————— 2 miles

Eberlanz Höhle A cave cut deeply into the rock, about ten minutes' walk from the road. There's a path marked over the rocks, and even a small visitor's book in the cave!

Kleiner Fjord A small sandy beach with deep water and lots of kelp, so unsuitable for swimming.

Grosse Bucht A wide sandy beach with dark sand, long stranded pieces of kelp, plenty of kelp flies, and several turn-off points for stopping. The sand is dotted with mounds of salt-tolerant succulent plants in beautiful greens and reds, and the bay is perfect for accomplished windsurfers (strong winds). There are toilets here as well.

The Sperrgebiet: Diamond Area No 1

The Sperrgebiet, or 'forbidden zone', was first declared in 1908. Then mining was confined to within a few kilometres of the coast, whilst a coastal belt 100km wide was declared 'out of bounds' as a precaution to prevent unauthorised people from reaching the diamond fields.

At the height of restrictions there were two diamond areas: No 1 from the Orange River to 26° south, and No 2 from 26° south northwards to the Kuiseb, incorporating most of the Namibia's great dune-sea. Now these areas have shrunk, leaving only parts of No 1 as forbidden. This may not be for much longer, though, for discussions are currently underway to have the whole of this area, as far south as Oranjemund, designated as a national park. At present, the focus is on the type of activities that could be permitted in a region with such highly sensitive ecosystems, and the infrastructure that would be needed to support any development of this nature.

In the meantime, security here remains tight. Signs by the roadside threatening fines or imprisonment for just entering these areas are serious.

If you wish to visit Elizabeth Bay or Bogenfels then you must give your full names, passport or ID number, and nationality to the relevant tour operator (see page 238) at least five working days before the trip, as it takes NAMDEB that long to issue a permit for you. Therefore trips must be booked well in advance. Note that visitors may not take anything out of the area, including rock samples – take note all amateur geologists. Vehicles coming from the Sperrgebiet are subject to random searches by NAMDEB officials.

Increasing tourism is encouraging increased access, and several attractions within the Sperrgebiet are now easily visited:

Agate Beach

This windswept beach is signposted from the corner of Tal and Hamburger streets. It's a 5km drive north of Lüderitz, alongside fenced-off areas of the Sperrgebiet that add to the air of desolation, particularly in winter. There is, however, a small pond to the side of the road that attracts small numbers of flamingos and other waterbirds, while nearby the odd springbok or oryx takes advantage of a patch of green around the water-treatment plant. The almost-black sand on the beach is sprinkled with fragments of shining mica – and the occasional agate. It's hardly a picture-postcard spot, and the combination of wind and tide means that a fair amount of rubbish ends up here, but it stretches a long way and is fun for beachcombers. It's also popular locally for swimming. The occurrence of agates depends on the winds and the swell: sometimes you will find nothing, at others – especially at low tide – you can pick up a handful in a few hours.

Kolmanskop

This ghost town, once the principal town of the local diamond industry, was abandoned over 45 years ago and now gives a fascinating insight into the area's great diamond boom. A few of the buildings, including the imposing concert hall, have been restored, but many are left exactly as they were deserted, and now the surrounding dunes are gradually burying them. What a spectacular place this would be for a large party.

In a room adjacent to the concert hall, there is a simple café-style restaurant that is open 09.00–14.00 Monday to Saturday. The menu is simple, offering light lunches, snacks and drinks, but do make time to look at the photographs that adorn the walls, from early mining pictures to some chilling reminders of the far-reaching effects of Nazi Germany.

Getting there

Kolmanskop is just beside the main B4 road, 9km east of Lüderitz. You need a permit (issued at Lüderitz Safaris and Tours or Ghost Town Tours in Lüderitz; see page 238) to enter; without one, you will be turned away. They cannot be bought at Kolmanskop.

Permits cost N$30 per person (children N$15) to join one of the guided tours, which start at the museum in Kolmanskop at 09.30 or 10.45, Monday to Saturday, and take 40 minutes. Tours on Sunday and most public holidays are at 10.00 only. Alternatively, buy a photographer's pass for N$100, which includes a guided tour, and you can visit at any time of day (sunrise to sunset), for as long as you like, giving the chance to absorb the eerie atmosphere without other visitors. For the best photographs, set off with your camera to catch photos at first light, taking a snack breakfast to eat before one of the guided tours.

Tours outside these hours can be booked for groups of ten or more, for N$45 per person, through Ghost Town Tours (see page 238).

Elizabeth Bay

This south-facing bay, 40km south of Lüderitz, has a band of diamond-bearing coarse grits and sands measuring about 3km by 5km. It was mined from 1911 to 1948, and then reopened in about 1991, with a projected minimum lifespan of ten years.

Getting there

Guided tours run by Ghost Town Tours (see page 238) pass into the Sperrgebiet through the Kolmanskop gate, and from there to Elizabeth Bay. The scenery on the way is mostly flat gravel plains, with some dunes as you approach the coast. This is a chance to see the working diamond mine on top of the hill, as well as a disused one below. A visit to a local seal colony at Atlas Bay in the Sperrgebiet is normally included. Trips for between four and eight people run Mon–Fri from 08.30 to about 13.00, costing N$250 per person, including lunch. No children under 14 are permitted.

Pomona/Bogenfels

A day trip into the Sperrgebiet as far as Bogenfels covers some 265km on mostly good gravel roads, passing through areas of considerable historical, geological and botanical interest.

Where it has been untouched by diamond mining, much of the environment is pristine, but many of the diamond areas have been ravaged by the industry, leaving behind expanses of bare rock devoid of sand and without a hint of vegetation. The road passes through areas of shining dolomite rock, its colours varying in the sun

THE DIAMOND BOOM

Kolmanskop, or 'Kolman's hill', was originally a small hill named after a delivery rider, Kolman, who used to rest his horses there. In April 1908, Zacharias Lewala was working nearby when he picked a rough diamond from the ground. He took this to his German foreman, August Stauch, who posted a claim to the area, and then got the backing of several of the railway's directors to start prospecting. Stauch exhibited some of his finds in June 1908, prompting an immediate response: virtually everybody who could rushed into the desert to look for diamonds. Famously, in some places they could be picked up by the handful in the moonlight.

TV Bulpin (see *Further Reading*) records the story of one resident, Dr Scheibe, going prospecting:

> While he plotted his position on a map, he told his servants to look for diamonds. One of them simply went down on his knees, filled both hands with diamonds, and even stuffed some into his mouth. Dr Scheibe stared at the scene in amazement, repeating over and over again, '*Ein märchen, ein märchen*' (a fairytale, a fairytale).

This first large deposit at Kolmanskop lay in the gravel of a dry riverbed, so soon a mine and a boomtown developed there. Deposits were found all over the coastal region, all around Lüderitz. Quickly, in September 1908, the German colonial government proclaimed a *Sperrgebiet* – a forbidden zone – to restrict further prospecting, and to license what was already happening.

Between 1908 and the start of World War I over 5 million carats of diamonds were found, but the war disrupted production badly. At the end of it Sir Ernest Oppenheimer obtained options on many of the German mining companies for South Africa's huge Anglo American Corporation, joining ten of them into Consolidated Diamond Mines (CDM) of South West Africa. In 1922–23 CDM obtained exclusive diamond rights for 50 years over a coastal belt 95km wide, stretching 350km north of the Orange River, from the new South African administrators of South West Africa. These were later extended to the year 2010. This allowed CDM to control the country's diamond production until independence, and NAMDEB to do so now.

Meanwhile many small towns like Kolmanskop were flush with money. It had a butcher's, a baker's and a general shop; a large theatre, community hall and school; factories for furniture, ice, lemonade and soda-water; a hospital with the region's first X-ray machine; comfortable staff quarters, elaborate homes for the managers – and a sea-water pool fed by water pumped from 35km away. Yet Kolmanskop was fortunate: it was next to the main railway line. Often deposits were less accessible, far from water or transport – and many such early mines still lie half-buried in the Namib.

from blue or pink to pure white. In the occasional winter, if there has been some rain, areas of the Sperrgebiet are alight with colour from numerous plants, many of them seen only once every ten years or so, taking advantage of nature's brief bounty. Here, in amongst grey scrubby plants, are the soft green of new grasses, the bright pink Bushman's candle, and the milk bush, favoured by oryx; here too are the so-called 'window' plants, whose leaf tips feature tiny windows that allow light through to the main plant buried below, so that photosynthesis can take place inside the plant.

Getting there

Guided tours (currently run by Coastways Tours, see page 238) take a whole day to reach Bogenfels, in the Sperrgebiet, visiting the ghost town of Pomona and the Idatel or Märchental ('fairytale') valley, famous for the diamonds that were collected in the moonlight here. Trips depart at 09.00 and return at around 17.00, and include an excellent lunch at Pomona. Costs are N$725 per person, based on a minimum of four people, and are subject to changes in entry fees that may be imposed by NAMDEB.

Pomona

Pomona itself once housed over a thousand people, of whom some 300–400 were German, and the rest black Namibian workers, these latter living in huts that accommodated up to 50 people. While the black workers were on fixed-term contracts, whole families of Germans lived here, with their own school, church, hotel and even a bowling alley. Water was brought in by narrow-gauge railway from Grillen Tal, several kilometres away, where the crumbling ruins of the main pump station can still be explored.

In the early years, a claim could be bought for 60 Deutschmarks, rising to a staggering 6,000DM by 1917–18. Diamonds were not mined, but were sifted by hand with great trommel sieves, their rusting frames now good only for photographers.

Bogenfels

The third mining town in the area was at Bogenfels, where a small desalination plant is still to be seen right on the beach. The main attraction for visitors, though, is the spectacular rock arch that stands about 55m high beside the sea. Despite its inaccessibility, photographs have made it one of the south's better known landmarks.

Oranjemund

This is a prosperous mining town in the far southwest corner of Namibia, where the headquarters of NAMDEB are based. It is a closed town, where NAMDEB own all the property. Without an invitation from a resident, and the permission of NAMDEB, you cannot enter it. Even then, those leaving the mining area have to pass strict X-ray checks, which search for hidden diamonds. Living conditions there are reported (by NAMDEB!) to be very good; many of the workers come here from northern Namibia and are on lucrative 'six-months-on, six-months-off' contracts.

However, even here the diamond deposits are gradually being exhausted, and within 25 years operations are likely to be scaled down. Perhaps in a century tourists will be shown around this as another one of the Sperrgebiet's ghost towns...

NORTH OF THE B4
Helmeringhausen

Despite being a large dot on the map, this is just a farm that has grown into a village, in the middle of some very scenic roads. Just to the north are flat plains with little hills of balancing rocks – rather like the cairns found on Scottish mountains, only somewhat bigger.

Heading southwest on the C13 towards Lüderitz the road winds down and opens out into an immense valley – a huge plain lined by mountains with a clear escarpment on the east, and a more ragged array to the west. It is most spectacular, especially at sunset.

There's one bus a week to Helmeringhausen, from Keetmanshoop via Bethanie. Buses arrive on Tuesday afternoon at 13.10, and depart an hour later.

In Helmeringhausen itself there is a shop for basics, and a small agricultural museum displaying tools and machinery from around the turn of the century (get the key from the hotel: it's free for residents!). Also there is a vital fuel station which opens 08.00–18.00 Mon–Sat, and one hotel:

Helmeringhausen Hotel (9 rooms) PO Box 21, Helmeringhausen; tel/fax: 063 283083; email: hhhotel@natron.net
This super little place, started in 1938, is a classic example of a well-maintained local hotel. The rooms are simple, modern and spotlessly clean. Some have double beds, others twin beds, all are en-suite (some baths, some showers). There is safe parking at the back (though it's difficult to imagine a crime problem here), and a few tables and chairs around a small pool with a braai area,
    Lunch and dinner are available by arrangement, and even those passing through could stop for afternoon tea and a snack. The owners, Altna and Heinz ('Langer') Vollertsen, are very welcoming. They have plastered their bar wall with various currencies, underneath which is an excellent range of spirits.
Rates: single N$368, double N$561.20, including breakfast. Dinner is N$85.

Nearby guest farms
There are three excellent small guest farms around here. Dabis and Sinclair make natural overnight stops when driving between the Fish River Canyon and the Sesriem area, whilst Namtib is also a candidate if you are travelling between Lüderitz and Sesriem. Note that roads further west in this area, the C13, D707, D407 and D826, often run between mountains and the dunes of the Namib-Naukluft Park – and can be particularly spectacular.

Sinclair Guest Farm (6 rooms) PO Box 21783, Helmeringhausen; tel: 061 226979; fax: 061 226999; email: logufa@mweb.com.na; web: www.natron.net/tour/sinclair
Situated on the D407, about 59km northwest of Helmeringhausen, Sinclair's farmhouse is signposted clearly and is 3km from the road. All around are rolling hills, whose valleys are dotted with the odd camelthorn tree.
    Inside Sinclair is a shady, green oasis, with palms and a variety of fruit trees from pomegranate to orange, grapefruit, lemon, and mandarin. Looking on to these are various shady verandas outside with tables, chairs, and places to relax. It is a restful environment, perfect for a short stop.
    The rooms here are simple and carpeted, and all have en-suite facilities including showers (one also has a bath). If you're stopping for one night, then arrive for tea before 16.00, and spend a few hours wandering over to see the old copper mine, and perhaps up a nearby hill for sunset. If staying for two then join a farm drive, or walk around a little further – perhaps guided by the farm dogs.
    Sinclair is still run by Gunther and Hannelore Hoffmann as a working farm, though recent droughts have left it increasingly reliant on guests for income. Fortunately, it has good food and a pleasant, relaxed atmosphere, so is often full.
Rates: N$525 per person, includes dinner, bed and breakfast.

Dabis Guest Farm (7 twin rooms) PO Box 15, Helmeringhausen; tel: 063 62 6820. Reservations tel: 061 232300; fax: 061 249937; email: photographer@mweb.com.na; web: www.natron.net/tour/dabis
Dabis has been owned by the Gaugler family for three generations, since 1926, and is now run by Jo and Heidi Gaugler. It is just a few kilometres north of Helmeringhausen, about 7km off the main C14 down a track with some steep dips, and has achieved an effective balance between welcoming visitors and operating as a farm.
    Accommodation is in simple twin-bed rooms with en-suite shower (one has a bath instead) and toilet. Outside, guests also benefit from a newly built swimming pool and

tennis court (racquets available). One of the main attractions of staying here, however, is learning about the farm. Most guests arrive by 15.00, have tea at 16.00, and then go out on a farm drive with Jo for an hour or two. Jo will explain his techniques in depth, complete with information on the area's climate over the last four decades. Dabis now farms mainly sheep for lamb production – karakul and a cross breed – using advanced rotation techniques to survive on the meagre rainfall. Although the main emphasis is on farming, there are a number of bat-eared foxes around to be seen if you are lucky. Jo and Heidi are more than happy to share their farm with guests, and their knowledge can considerably enrich your stay.

Rates: single N$690, double N$1,173, triple N$1,795, for dinner, bed and breakfast, and the evening farm drive on arrival. Lunch packs are available for N$46 per person.

Namtib Biosphere Reserve (5 rooms) PO Box 19, Aus; tel: 063 866409; fax: 061 233597; email: namtib@iafrica.com.na; web: www.nam.lia.net/natron/tour/namtib/namtib.htm

Don't be put off by the new name – this is not a scientific project, but a welcoming guest farm run on ecological lines by Walter and Renate Theile. It lies 12km east of the scenic D707 road, which runs between the Namib's dunes on the west and jagged mountains on the east. Namtib is clearly signposted (Namtib Desert Lodge) about 86km south of the D407 junction, or 46km north of the C13.

The farmhouse nestles in an isolated valley surrounded by mountains, overlooking the edge of the desert plain. Its rooms are unusually designed, comfortable and clean but not luxurious: simple bungalows with double beds are separated from a private bathroom (with shower, toilet and washbasin) by a small open-air square, where many visitors choose to sleep in the heat of the summer. With one door on either side of the bedroom, airflow helps to keep this cool, too. There is no electricity, so after dark candles come to the fore. The main farmhouse has a comfortable veranda and a dining room where home-cooked meals are currently served, though in 2002 a new lounge and dining area were under construction.

This is a working farm, with cattle, sheep and game, and visitors are welcome to go out on farm drives with Walter. The Theiles aim to make a living from the land, whilst regenerating what they can of its natural flora and fauna. Certainly there are some inquisitive mongooses around, not to mention bat-eared fox, aardwolf and porcupine, while hidden in the surrounding hills are leopard, cheetah and lynx. Although Namtib is registered as an American Saddle Horse Stud, their horses are spirited and riding here is no longer available. But for guests who like walking, the beautiful red-granite Tiras Mountains are immediately behind the farm – and the nearest natural spring is only ten minutes' walk away.

Rates: N$450 per person, full board. Game drives are usually included for overnight guests, but other visitors will be charged N$45 per person.

The area around Namtib has been loosely designated by a group of local farmers as the **Tiras Berge Conservancy**. Various types of accommodation are available through members of the group, from basic campsites like Weissenborn (tel: 063 86522) to more upmarket establishments such as Landsberg (tel: 061 233872). Here Wilfried Izko has two bungalows and a self-contained house for guests at N$330 per person for dinner, bed and breakfast, and takes visitors on drives across his 75,000ha farm. Be warned, though, that the widely available leaflet that shows the P409 through the mountains is misleading – this is a private track, and visitors who are not staying overnight may well meet with a hostile reception.

MALTAHÖHE

This small town is an important crossroads, as it is linked by a tar road to the main north–south B1 artery, but it is too far from the desert to be a major centre for visitors in its own right. A Starline bus service connects the town with Mariental to the east on Monday and Thursday, with buses scheduled both to arrive and depart from here at 13.00.

Maltahöhe's most interesting attraction is virtually unknown. About 30km north of here, on the farm Sandfeld, is a fascinating valley which, when the rains are good, fills with shallow water to a depth of about 30cm. This doesn't happen every year, but when it does – normally between mid February and mid March – the shallow lake quickly becomes covered in a spectacular bloom of red, pink and white lilies, *Crinum crinum paludosum*. These last about a week, and are said to be endemic to the valley, which is known as the 'lily-veld'.

The town itself has several shops and garages, a post office, Standard and First National banks, and a useful information office, associated with the Namib Pappot Safari Company, who run trips around Sesriem and have a base here. There is just one hotel in town:

Maltahöhe Hotel (27 rooms) PO Box 20, Maltahöhe; tel: 063 293013; fax: 063 293133
Run by Manfred and Gerda Schreiner, this friendly little hotel has won an award as Namibia's best country hotel twice in recent years. Its simple, clean rooms all have a fan and a telephone (not direct-dial), and there's a small pool for cooling off. Manfred knows the region well, and can organise trips into the desert or around the local area if you don't have your own transport. So don't hesitate to stop here if you need a place to sleep: you'll be pleasantly surprised.
Rates: single N$250, double N$360, room only.

Nearby guest farms

There are several guest farms and restcamps in the area, including:

Duwisib Farm Restcamp (4 rooms, 3 bungalows) PO Box 21, Maltahöhe; tel: 063 293344; tel/fax: 061 223994. Reservations tel: 061 226119; fax: 061 220275
Adjacent to the west side of Duwisib Castle is a small private restcamp, on the D826. Meals can be arranged in advance if needed, and there's a basic farm store here.
Rates: N$320 per person half board.

Daweb Guest Farm (6 rooms, 3 pitches for camping) PO Box 18, Maltahöhe; tel/fax: 063 293088; email: daweb@natron.net; web: www.natron.net/tour/daweb
Run by the hospitable Rosemarie and Rolf Kirsten, Daweb is just 2km south of Maltahöhe on the C14 to Helmeringhausen. It is an 18,000ha cattle farm, which has been in the family's hands since 1896. Its guestrooms are built together in a small block, with whitewashed brick walls and a corrugated-iron roof. These are comfortable, if a little small, with en-suite (excellent) showers and toilets. The small campsite has braai facilities. Daweb is a pleasant stopover with a warm welcome and good family fare. If visitors arrive early enough, Rolf will usually take them out on a drive to explain the workings of the farm.
Rates: single N$460, double N$760, triple N$990, including dinner and breakfast. Camping N$40 per person.

La Vallée Tranquille (8 rooms) PO Box 70, Maltahöhe; tel/fax: 063 293508; email: valleet@iway.na; web: www.natron.net/tour/tranquille/premier.html
The French ownership of this small farmhouse some 60km south of Maltahöhe on the C14 is clear from the décor of the bedrooms, set in two separate buildings, and of the dining area, bar and comfortable lounge. There's a small pool outside, and the owners offer hiking, birdwatching and other activities on the farm.
Rates: single N$380, for dinner, bed and breakfast.

Duwisib Castle

Standing solidly amidst the rolling hills 72km southwest of Maltahöhe (beside the D286), the sandstone fortress of Duwisib Castle is another of those anachronisms in which Namibia seems to specialise. Look from a distance and you won't believe it: a small, square castle with fortified battlements and high turrets – in the middle of the African bush.

The castle itself is built around an open central quadrangle, where there is now a small lawn and fountain, shaded by a couple of beautiful jacaranda trees. Its rooms are sparsely furnished, though there are some excellent original pieces dating back to around the turn of the century, and interesting paintings and prints on the walls – many equestrian in theme.

Above the entrance hall is a steep set of stairs (easily missed) up to a small gallery overlooking the entrance, and there is also a cellar, which now seems to be a storeroom. Get a copy of Dr Mossolow's booklet (see *Further Reading*) for a more detailed description of the castle's contents.

History

The castle's history has been documented in an excellent booklet by Dr N Mossolow, available at the castle. It details how Hansheinrich von Wolf was born in 1873 into a military family in Saxony and served with the Royal Saxon Artillery near Dresden. He came to South West Africa as a captain in the Schutztruppe, when he volunteered after the outbreak of the Herero War. He was decorated in 1905, and returned to Germany where he married Miss Jayta Humphrey in 1907.

Later that year he and his wife returned to German South West Africa, and over the next few years bought up farming land in the area. By October 1908 he had '33 horses, 68 head of large stock and 35 head of small stock' on his farm, and two wells. An 'extravagant residence of undressed stone, with 22 rooms and a cellar' had reached 2m above its foundations. He bought up more farmland, up to 50,000ha, and by 1909 the castle was complete, with furnishings and paintings imported from Germany.

Von Wolf proceeded to enlarge the area under his control by buying more land. A fanatical horseman and breeder of horses, he spent much time and energy developing his stable. (See *The Desert Horses*, page 225.)

In 1914 he set off with his wife to England, to purchase another thoroughbred stallion, but on the way war broke out. The ship diverted to South America, where they were briefly interned before he arranged a secretive passage back to Europe. Eventually they arrived back in Germany where Von Wolf reported for duty as an officer. On September 4 1916 he was killed at the Battle of the Somme.

Getting organised

The castle opens daily from Monday to Friday, 08.00–13.00 and 14.00–17.00. Park around the back and you'll find a wonderful kiosk selling drinks and snacks. Excellent fresh coffee is served, and perhaps the best apple pie in Africa is baked on the premises by a superb Nama cook.

There is a campsite here run by the NWR, with ten pleasant camp pitches (number three is a favourite, under a great tree) which should be reserved in advance in Windhoek (PO Box 132, Maltahohe; tel/fax: 066 385303; reservations tel: 061 236975/6/7; fax: 061 224900; email: reservations@mweb.com.na; web: www.namibiawildliferesorts.com). Pitches are N$95 per night, for up to four people; additional people (up to a maximum of eight) are N$10 per person per night.

The Namib-Naukluft National Park

People have different reactions when they encounter a desert for the first time. A few find it threatening, too arid and empty, so they rush from city to city, through the desert, to avoid spending any time there at all. Some try hard to like it for those same reasons, but ultimately find little which holds their attention. Finally there are those who stop and give the place their time, delighting in the stillness, strange beauty, and sheer uniqueness of the environment. The desert's changing patterns and subtly adapted life forms fascinate them, drawing them back time after time.

Covering almost 50,000km², the Namib-Naukluft National Park is one of the largest national parks in Africa, protecting one of the oldest deserts on earth, South America's Atacama Desert being the other contender for this title. The Namib's scenery is stunning, and its wildlife fascinating; you just need to make the time to stop and observe it.

The sections in this chapter run roughly south to north. Note that the NamibRand, Sesriem, the Naukluft and Solitaire are very close together.

HISTORY
The park has grown gradually to its present size. In 1907 the area between the Kuiseb and Swakop rivers was proclaimed as 'Game Reserve No 3'. Later it was augmented by the addition of Sandwich Harbour in 1941.

In 1956 the Kuiseb Canyon and Swakop River Valley were added, along with the Welwitschia Plains, and in 1968 the park was renamed The Namib Desert Park. In 1979 a large area of what was the protected 'Diamond Area No 2' was added, including Sesriem and Sossusvlei, and the park was officially joined to the Naukluft Park, creating the Namib-Naukluft National Park.

Most recently, in 1986, the rest of 'Diamond Area No 2' was added, taking the park's southern boundary as far south as the main road to Lüderitz, and increasing its area to its present size of 49,768km² – larger than Switzerland, or about the same as Maryland and New Jersey combined.

FLORA AND FAUNA
Though the Naukluft's wildlife is discussed separately, the flora and fauna elsewhere in the Namib-Naukluft are similar, dependent more on the landscape than on precise location. (Dr Mary Seely's book, *The Namib*, is a superb and simple guide to this area, widely available in Windhoek and Swakopmund. See *Further Reading*, page 507.) The four basic types of environment found here, and some of their highlights, are:

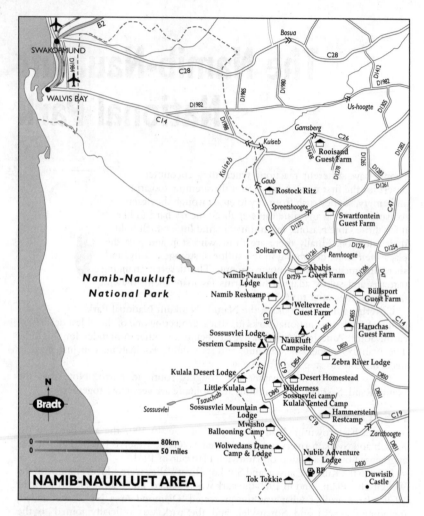

Sand-dunes

Dunes are everybody's idea of a desert, and generally thought of as being bare and lifeless. Whilst this is not inaccurate for many deserts, the Namib is sufficiently old for endemic species to have evolved.

Various grasses grow on some of the more stable dunes, but most of the vegetable matter comes from wind-blown detritus. This collects at the bottom of the dunes, to be eaten by fish-moths (silver-fish), crickets and the many tenebrionid beetles – or *tok tokkies*, as they are known – near the base of the food chain. Particular tenebrionid species occur in specific environments, with those in the coastal fog belt adapting ingeniously to harness the available moisture.

These then provide food for spiders, geckos, lizards, and chameleons which, in turn, fall prey to sidewinder snakes. Rare Grant's golden moles eat any small beetles or larvae that they can catch, and birds are mobile enough to move in and out of the dunes in search of the smaller animals. The dune lark is endemic to this region, and is seldom found outside the dune areas.

River valleys and pans

The river valleys that run through the Namib are linear oases. Though dry on the surface, their permanent underground water sustains trees and bushes, like the camelthorn, *Acacia erioloba*, and nara melon, *Acanthosicyos horrida*, found in the middle of the great dune-sea at Sossusvlei.

Other common river-valley trees include the anaboom, *Acacia albida*, shepherd's tree, *Boscia albitrunca*, easily identified by its white trunk, the wild green-hair tree, *Parkinsonia africana*, and the marvellously weeping false ebony, *Euclea pseudebenus*.

The lush vegetation found in these valleys makes them a favourite for numerous insects and birds, as well as larger mammals like gemsbok, kudu and springbok. These are the most likely areas to find nocturnal cats from leopard to caracal, especially where the rivers cut through mountains rather than dunes.

Gravel plains

Throughout the desert, and especially north of the Kuiseb River, the Namib has many expansive, flat plains of rock and stone. These come alive during the rains, when they will quickly be covered with tall thin grass and creeping yellow flowers, attracting herds of gemsbok, springbok and even Hartmann's mountain zebra. During drier times there are fewer large mammals around, but still at night black-backed jackal, aardwolf and the occasional aardvark forage for termites, while bat-eared and Cape foxes scavenge for insects, reptiles, and anything else edible.

Spotted hyena and even the rare brown hyena are sometimes recorded here. Both leave distinctive white droppings, but only the sociable spotted hyenas make such eerie, mournful calls.

Resident larger birds include ostrich, secretary birds, Rüppell's korhaan and Ludwig's bustard, while enthusiastic 'twitchers' will seek the pale, apparently insignificant Gray's lark (amongst other larks), which is endemic to the gravel plains of the Namib.

Inselbergs and mountain outcrops

Throughout the Namib there are mountains, often of granite or limestone. Some, like many between Sesriem and Sossusvlei, have become submerged beneath the great dune-sea. Others, especially north of the Kuiseb River, jut up through the flat desert floor like giant worm casts on a well-kept lawn. These isolated mountains surrounded by gravel plains are inselbergs (from the German for 'island-mountain') – and they have their own flora and fauna. *Euphorbia*, *Acacia*, *Commiphora*, *Zygophyllum* and *Aloe* species are common, whilst the succulent *Lithops* (often called living rocks, for their pebble-like shape) occur here, though less frequently.

Many inselbergs are high enough to collect moisture from morning fogs, which sustain succulents and aloes, and with their whole communities of invertebrates. Temporary pools in crevices can be particularly interesting, and there's a whole microcosm of small water creatures that lay drought-resistant eggs. These survive years of desiccation, to hatch when the pools do finally fill.

Being open land these make perfect perches for raptors – and lappet-faced vultures, greater kestrels, and red-necked falcons are typical of this environment. Also watch for sandgrouse, which congregate at water around dusk and dawn, and other well-camouflaged foraging birds.

NAMIBRAND NATURE RESERVE

Covering about 2,100km², an area equivalent to about half the size of Belgium, the NamibRand Nature Reserve is one of the largest private reserves in Africa. Lying south of Sesriem, it borders on to the main Namib-Naukluft National Park in the west, a boundary of about 100km, and in the east its extent is generally defined by the Nubib Mountains.

There are a wide variety of different desert landscapes and environments within this, from huge red sand-dunes to vegetated inter-dune valleys, sand and gravel plains, and some particularly imposing mountains. It's a spectacular area of desert.

There are several ways to visit this, all utilising small lodges and camps as bases for expert-led guided trips. If you want a detailed look at the central Namib, with guides who understand it, this is an excellent complement to a day or two of driving yourself around Sesriem and Sossusvlei.

History

Before becoming a nature reserve, this was a number of separate farms formed in the 1950s to eke out an existence farming in the desert. Several severe drought years in the 1980s demonstrated that farming domestic stock here just wasn't viable. There were allegations of farmers opening their fences to game from the Namib-Naukluft National Park, only to kill the animals for their meat once they left the park.

Game was the only option, and this survived well on the farm Gorrasis, owned by Albi Brückner (a businessman, rather than a farmer, who'd bought the farm for its landscapes).

In 1988 Brückner bought out two neighbouring farms, Die Duine and Stellarine, and gradually the reserve was broadened from that base. Now various shareholders have contributed money to the reserve, and different operators hold 'concession' areas which they utilise for tourism.

Flora and fauna

The NamibRand's flora and fauna are the same as that in the western areas of the Namib-Naukluft. However, there are also red hartebeest, which aren't usually found in the national park, and blesbok which have been introduced from South Africa.

What to see and do

What you see and do here depends entirely on where you stay, as many of the camps in the concession have a different emphasis:

Mwisho Ballooning Camp (4 tents) PO Box 197, Maltahöhe; tel: 063 293233; fax: 063 293241; email: namibsky@mweb.com.na
Opened in 1991, Mwisho was one of the first camps in this area, and it pioneered ballooning in the Namib. The turning to Mwisho, west off the C27, is about 52km to the north of the junction of the D827 and C27 (57km past the BP petrol station). Alternatively, coming from the north, it is 20km south of the C27-D845 junction. If you are approaching from Sesriem, that's about 30km south of the first NamibRand signboard south of Sesriem on the C27.

Accommodation is in walk-in Meru-style tents, with twin or double beds, a wardrobe, chairs, table, and en-suite toilet and shower. Dining is in the main farmhouse, and there's normally a nature drive at about 16.00, which stops somewhere spectacular to watch the sunset. If you're going ballooning and have just one night in this area, then Mwisho is perfect. *Rates: single N$1,275, N$995 per person sharing, including all meals. The compulsory ballooning is US$250 per person extra.*

Wolwedans Dune Camp (6 tents) PO Box 5048, Windhoek; tel: 061 230616; fax: 061 220102; email: info@wolwedans.com.na; web: www.wolwedans.com
Wolwedans Dune Camp has been the flagship operation in the reserve since it opened. Its turning, west off the C27, is about 32km to the north of the junction of the D827 and C27 (27km past the BP petrol station). Coming from the north, it is 50km south of the C27-D845 junction. If you are approaching from Sesriem, that's about 40km south of the first

NamibRand signboard south of Sesriem on the C27. The camp has its own airstrip as well. Once on the 'drive' to Wolwedans, ignore the small house on the left and continue about 20km from the gate to the Wolwedans Farmhouse, from where transfers into the Dune Camp are arranged. Beware of turning off this track, as you may become stuck in the sand.

The whole camp is built on wooden decks, raised above the sand. Each dome tent (about 3.5m square) has twin beds and solar-powered lights. Behind each is its own private hot shower and toilet, and in front is a veranda. There's a central open dining area and sun deck. Activities usually consist of afternoon and whole-day drives, including a picnic lunch, into the reserve with a professional guide. Meals come from the same kitchen as those for the Dune Lodge (see below); the standard is excellent.

Rates: single N$1,750, double N$2,500, including full board and activities. Closed Dec 1–Feb 28.

Wolwedans Dune Lodge (9 chalets) PO Box 5048, Windhoek; tel: 061 230616; fax: 061 220102; email: info@wolwedans.com.na; web: www.wolwedans.com
Just before this book was going to press, Wolwedans Dune Lodge was completely destroyed by fire, but the owners have pledged to rebuild it and have it open once more by June 2003. It is to be expected that the accommodation will remain at the same high standard as before the fire, to which the description below relates. (For directions, see its sister Dune Camp, above, but note that the two are some distance apart after leaving the farmhouse.)

Originally opened in 1998, Wolwedans Dune Lodge is run with all the courtesy and attention to detail of a country house, with an atmosphere of relaxed gentility. More luxurious than the Dune Camp, accommodation consists of purpose-built wooden chalets, each built on stilts with its own secluded veranda and en-suite shower and toilet. The real coup is the bedrooms. Solid wooden twin beds, draped with nets that give all the allure of a dreamy four-poster, face directly east through a canvas 'wall' that, when rolled up, affords unparalleled stargazing and a front-row view of sunrise over the mountains.

Simple walkways over the dunes lead to the hub of the camp, where a comfortable bar with leather armchairs, a separate library and a dining room all share that same view. Meals are taken around a large table in the dining room. Dinner is a relatively formal affair, with some of the best food to be had in Namibia, and good wines to match. And after dinner, what better than to while away the evening around the campfire on the deck. This is a place to relax, unwind and get a real feel for the surroundings. Guided activities follow the same pattern as those of the camp, usually returning in time for a civilised afternoon tea.

Rates: single N$2,730, double N$3,900, including full board and activities.

Sossusvlei Mountain Lodge (10 chalets) c/o P Bag X27, Benmore 2010, Johannesburg, South Africa; tel: +27 11 809 4300; fax: +27 11 809 4400; email: information@ccafrica.com; web: www.ccafrica.co.za or www.ccafrica.com. Windhoek office tel: 061 236276; email: wdh@afroventures.com
In the north of the NamibRand Reserve, about 32km south of Sesriem and 6km from the D826, Sossusvlei Mountain Lodge is probably the most stylish modern lodge in Namibia.

Spacious chalets, made largely of stone and glass, are built into the rocks overlooking a desert plain. Their graceful interiors use a mix of bright chrome and earthy, desert colours; these personal cocoons have minibars, CD systems and air conditioning. Most of their glass walls slide or fold away to open up the room to the desert, and at night an electric skylight can slide back above your bed allowing you to stargaze. Serious astronomers will also appreciate the large, computer-controlled telescope that's on hand.

The main lodge is similarly luxurious, with air conditioning (on despite the windows all being open during our last visit); there's a satellite TV, email and internet connection if you need them. The food is excellent; the wine cellar impressive – and there's a slightly surreal pool outside. Activities focus on Sossusvlei trips, although quad-biking excursions over nearby dunes are an unusual, and fun, addition to the normal walking and driving trips.

Rates : US$375 per person, including all meals and activities.

Toktokkie Trails (tents) PO Box 162, Maltahöhe; tel/fax: 06638 5230 or 061 235454 Owners Marc and Elinor Dürr have closed the former Die Duine Guest House to concentrate on Toktokkie Trails. The place is 11km west of the D827, its turning is signposted 400m or so north of the C27-D827 junction. Contact details are likely to change over the next few months.

If you stay here, then allow two nights. This is the ideal length of time for a desert walking trail. Walking is leisurely, concentrating on the flora and fauna, and their adaptations to the desert; it's not a route march, as Marc goes at the pace of the slowest. You need only carry your camera, binoculars and water.

A recommended option is to spend your second night sleeping out in the desert, under the stars. Any luggage that you need will be driven out to the overnight stop for you, and then collected in the morning. It's magical.

The desert landscape around here is a spectacular mix of wide plains, mountains, the odd tall sand-dune and many smaller vegetated ones. It's great country for walking, dotted with marvellously knurled old camelthorn trees.

Rates: N$1,200 per person sharing, including full board and guided activities.

Driver's note The D826, C27 and D707 are amongst the most scenic routes in the country. Sand-dunes line the west of these roads, and mountains overlook the east – spectacular stuff. However, they do tend to be quite slow going, and the gravel is sometimes not as good or as wide as the faster C36 or C14 routes, so allow plenty of time for your journey (an average of about 50km/h is realistic).

Surprisingly, there is a fairly reliable **BP fuel station** on the D826, called Boere-Diens, 5km to the north of the junction of the D827 and D826. They also sell cold drinks, if you ask.

NAUKLUFT MOUNTAINS

An hour's drive northeast of Sesriem, the main escarpment juts out into the desert forming a range known as the Naukluft Mountains. In 1968 these were protected within the Naukluft Mountain Zebra Park – to conserve a rare breeding population of Hartmann's mountain zebra. Shortly afterwards, land was bought to the west of the mountains and added to the park, forming a corridor linking these mountains into the Namib National Park. This allowed gemsbok, zebra and other game to migrate between the two, and in 1979 the parks were formally combined into the Namib-Naukluft National Park.

Geology

The uniqueness of the area stems from its geology as much as its geographical position. Separated from the rest of the highlands by steep, spectacular cliffs, the Naukluft Mountains form a plateau. Underneath this, to a height of about 1,100m, is mostly granite. Above this base are alternating layers of dolomites and shales, with extensive deposits of dark limestone, rising to about 1,995m. Over the millennia, rainwater has gradually cut into this massif, dissolving the rock and forming steep *kloofs*, or ravines, and a network of watercourses and reservoirs – many of which are subterranean. The name *Naukluft,* which means 'narrow ravine', is apt for the landscape.

Where these waters surface, in the deeper valleys, there are crystal-clear springs and pools – ideal for cooling dips. Often these are decorated by impressive formations of smooth tufa – limestone that has been re-deposited by the water over waterfalls.

Flora and fauna

Receiving occasional heavy rainstorms in summer that feed its network of springs and streams in its deeper kloofs, the Naukluft supports a surprisingly varied flora and fauna.

The high plateaux and mountainsides tend to be rocky with poor, if any, soil. Here are distinctive *Euphorbia*, *Acacia*, *Commiphora* and *Aloe* plants (including quivertrees – which are found in a dense stand in Quivertree Gorge). Most are low, slow-growing species, adapted to conserving water during the dry season. The variations of slope and situation result in many different niches suiting a wide variety of different species.

Down in the deeper kloofs, where there are permanent springs, the vegetation is totally different, with many more lush, broad-leaf species. Wild, cluster and sycamore figs are particularly prevalent, whilst you should also be able to spot camelthorn, buffalo thorn, shepherd's and wild olive trees.

The Naukluft has many animals, including large mammals, though all are elusive and difficult to spot. Hartmann's mountain zebra, gemsbok, kudu and klipspringer are occasionally seen fleeing over the horizon (usually in the far distance). Steenbok and the odd sunbathing dassie are equally common, and springbok, warthog, and ostrich occur, but are more often found on the plains around the mountains. The mountains should be a classic place for leopard, and the smaller cats, as there are many small mammals found here – though these are almost never seen.

Over 200 species of birds have been recorded here, and a useful annotated checklist is available from the park office. The Naukluft are at the southern limit of the range of many species of the northern Namib – Rüppell's parrot, rosy-faced lovebirds and Monteiro's all occur here, as do species typical of the south like the Karoo robin and chat. In the wetter kloofs, watch for species that you wouldn't find in the drier parts of the park, like the water-loving hamerkop, brubru and even African black ducks. Raptors are usually seen soaring above. Black eagles, lanner falcons, augur buzzards and pale chanting goshawks are common.

Getting there

The national park's entrance is on the D854, about 10km southwest of the C14, which links Solitaire and Maltahöhe. Approaching from Windhoek, pass Büllsport and take the D854 towards Sesriem.

Alternatively, Büllsport Guest Farm owns a section of the Naukluft Mountains, accessible from the farm without going into the national park, and Ababis borders on to the mountains.

What to see and do

Animals are seldom seen in this mountainous area, so hiking is the main activity here. A recent addition is the 4WD off-road driving trail, which takes two days and is aimed at local enthusiasts testing their vehicles to the limits.

Hiking

Naukluft has two circular day-hikes, the Waterkloof and Olive trails. Both can be started from the campsite, and don't need booking ahead, or any special equipment. That said, at least a day's water, snacks and a medical kit should be taken along, as rescue would be difficult if there was an accident. Walkers should be fit and acclimatised, and strong hiking boots are essential, as the terrain is very rocky.

There is also one long eight-day trail, rated as one of Africa's toughest hikes. Like the others, this is unguided, but simple diagrammatic maps are available from the park warden's office.

Waterkloof Trail

The Waterkloof is 17km long and starts near the campsite. It takes six or seven hours to walk comfortably, and is marked by white-painted footprints on the rocks. At first the trail follows the Naukluft River upstream, through some beautiful gorges, and in the early months of the year you'll often find pools here, complete with tadpoles and frogs.

After a gentle two hours you reach a painted rock marking the last water point (though bring water, don't rely on this), beyond which the canyon opens out. After about two hours more there's a marked halfway point, from where a steep climb leads you to the trail's highest point: a 600m peak with fine views all around.

From there the trail winds down through a stand of *Euphorbia* into a large valley, to follow the course of the (usually dry) river. It cuts off several of the bends, and keeps left to avoid some steep shelves, which form waterfalls in the rainy season. In this area some large cairns mark the route of the old German cannon road, which also follows the river valley for a while, before climbing steeply up to the main southern ridge of the plateau. Below those waterfalls, you meet the Naukluft River, and turn left to follow the trail for a few kilometres back to camp.

Olive Trail

This starts about 4km from the park office – clearly signposted off the track from the entrance gate. You can walk here, or drive and park in a small parking area.

The Olive Trail is 10km long and takes about four hours to complete. From the parking area it gradually climbs to the top of a small plateau, before descending through a series of river valleys and gorges (using chains in places), to meet a rough 4WD track which leads back to the parking area.

Naukluft Trail

This 120km trail starts from the park office, where there's a bunkhouse known as Hiker's Haven. Hikers can use this on their first and last nights. Initially it follows the (usually dry) Naukluft River south for a while, as it flows out of the mountains, before climbing up to the edge of the escarpment, with excellent views to the left over the plains. The Putte shelter is reached about 14km (6 hours) after starting.

On the second day the route covers 15km (6 hours), crossing a rolling plateau to the Bergpos junction, before dropping down the narrow Ubusis Kloof to reach Ubusis Hut. Day three starts by retracing your steps to Bergpos, and turning left across the plateau to Alderhost shelter (12km, taking 6 hours).

On day four the trail is level, before dropping down to a shelter at Tsams Ost for the evening – 17km later (6 hours). There's a rough 4WD track from here down and west to the main C36, and hikers doing only a four-day trip can be collected here.

Day five is steep and then undulating, though it levels out towards the end where it follows a tributary of the Die Valle River, to reach the Die Valle shelter about 17km (6 hours) later. Day six is a tough one, climbing up a narrow gorge to reach a high point called Quartz Valley, before dropping down the Arbeid Adelt Valley to the Tufa shelter, 16km and about 6 hours later.

On day seven the trail climbs steeply, using chains in places, back up to the plateau and some excellent views, to reach Kapokvlakte shelter after 14km (5 hours). Finally, on the last day, the trail descends gradually, then steeply, to meet the Waterkloof Trail and follow the Naukluft River back to camp. Energetic hikers could combine the last two days into a 30km walk which would take about 11 hours to complete. An early start from Tufa shelter is essential, and if there are less than five hours of daylight, then you should stop at Kapokvlakte shelter.

Open: from March 1 to the third Friday in October. Walks start every Tuesday, Thursday and Saturday for the first three weeks of each month. Book in advance at the NWR in Windhoek, group limited to 3–12 people.

Rates: N$100 per person, including space at the Hiker's Haven for the nights before and after the trail. These exclude park fees, paid separately.

4WD trail

This is a 73km two-day trail for those with a 4WD and the experience to use it properly. After the first 28km there is an overnight camp, where four stonewalled, partially open, A-frame shelters have built-in bunk beds. There are toilets here, water, a solar-heated shower and a braai area. Bring your own firewood, camping kit and supplies.

Open: all year, weather permitting. Book in advance at the NWR in Windhoek. Groups of 1–4 vehicles, with a maximum of four people per vehicle.

Rates: N$220 per vehicle, excluding park fees, which are paid separately.

Where to stay

The options are to camp at the basic national park's site, or to use one of these guest farms as a base. The mountains are also within a few hours' drive from most of the lodges in the Solitaire and Sesriem areas.

Büllsport Guest Farm (8 rooms including a family room) P Bag 1003, Maltahöhe; tel: 063 693371/693363; fax: 063 693372/293365; email: buellsport@natron.net; web: www.natron.net/tour/buellspt

About 230km from Windhoek (3 hours' drive), Büllsport has its own dot on the normal tourist board map of Namibia – which is puzzling. Apart from the farm's shop and garage (for punctures, fuel and small repairs), there's just the guest farm here.

Run by Johanna and Ernst Sauber, this is one of the best traditional guest farms in the country, attracting a wide range of nationalities to stay. You can expect good food (often braais in the evening), a comfortable (though not luxurious) twin room with en-suite shower and toilet, and a warm welcome. Outside is a lovely new swimming pool.

Many visitors use this as a base for visiting the Naukluft Mountains, as Büllsport owns a section of them. You can walk up them for a long day hike, or Ernst will drive you up in a 4WD for an afternoon stroll on the top of the plateau, or to the Quivertree Gorge, from where it's about 2½ hours' hike down to the farm. Within a short drive of the farmhouse there's an old German Schutztruppe post, and a few hours' walk from that is a large natural rock arch – which they call the 'Bogenfels of the Naukluft', after the original in the Sperrgebiet.

Johanna also offers short horseriding trails into the mountains, with even inexperienced riders welcome. These cost around N$132.25 per person per hour. For two or more experienced riders, she can arrange a two-day trail, including meals and an overnight bush-camp in the Naukluft. Alternatively, the farm is just under two hours' drive (115km) from Sesriem, so it makes a practical base for day-trips there, if closer accommodation is full. 4WD excursions to Sossusvlei are available by arrangement.

Rates: single N$634, double N$934, triple N$1,252, with dinner, bed and breakfast.

Zebra River Lodge (7 twin rooms) PO Box 11742, Windhoek; tel: 063 293265; fax: 063 293266; email: marianne.rob@zebrariver.com; web: www.zebrariver.com

Run by Rob and Marianne Field, Zebra River has established itself as one of the friendliest, most welcoming places in Namibia. It is situated in its own canyon in the Tsaris (aka Zaris) Mountains, reached by turning south from the D850 (between the D854 and the D855). Note that their driveway is several kilometres long, and crosses a sand river which, in exceptional years, flows across the road.

The guest rooms lead off a wide veranda around the plunge-pool, with a green garden around. All have en-suite shower and toilet, and plenty of space – apart from the 'honeymoon' suite which has a large stand-alone bath, a huge king-size bed, and even more space.

Marianne's cooking is superb, and the atmosphere is very relaxed and unpretentious. Everyone sits around the large table for dinner, with both wine and conversation often lasting late into the evening.

ZRL can be used as a base for driving yourself to Sesriem or the Naukluft, but don't ignore the lodge's own area. There are several clear trails around the canyons, two of which lead up to freshwater springs. Whilst they are only a day's hiking away, you can arrange to walk part of the way and have Rob drive you the rest. There were resident black eagles and rosy-faced lovebirds in the canyon on the author's last visit, and a day spent hiking here was a perfect introduction to the longer, and so more challenging, hiking in the Naukluft.

Alternatively, Rob loves the Sossusvlei area – that's what attracted him here first – and leads excellent 4WD trips to Sossusvlei. These last a full day, including a trip into the Dead Vlei, Sesriem Canyon and a picnic lunch, and cost N$520 per person (minimum 2 people). Book these in advance, when you make a reservation with the lodge.
Rates: single N$580, double N$980, full board.

Ababis Guest Farm (4 double rooms, 1 family room) PO Box 1004, Maltahöhe; tel: 063 293362; fax: 063 293364; email: ababis@lianam.lia.net
Ababis stands on the west side of the C14, opposite the junction with D1261, on the north side of the Naukluft Mountains. It has been a guest farm since 1993, and is quite traditional in character, though it has changed hands recently.

The farm has some cattle and a few ostriches, as well as areas devoted purely to wildlife including gemsbok, springbok, blesbok, ostrich, occasional zebra, a few kudu, and some bat-eared foxes. On the edge of the Naukluft, it is a good base for long hikes, while there's also a gentle walking trail around the farm which takes a few hours, down to a (usually) dry river.

If you're not driving yourself around, then there is a 4WD drive on to the Naukluft Plateau, lasting about eight hours, a morning or afternoon trip into Sossusvlei, or a half-day's drive encompassing local Bushman paintings, a spring and a small 'kokerboom forest' in the hills. Trips costs about N$950–1,800 per vehicle, for up to 4 people.
Rates: single N$755, N$605 per person sharing, full board.

Hammerstein Lodge and Camp (5 bungalows, 16 rooms) PO Box 250, Maltahöhe; tel: 063 693111; fax: 063 693112; email: hammerst@hammerstein.com.na
Situated on the C36, the turn-off north to Hammerstein has a clear signpost between the D854 (which goes past the Naukluft Mountains), and the D827. This is a well-established private restcamp, run by Anton and Gerty Porteus, mainly as a base for self-driving visitors. It has simple 2-bed and 4-bed self-catering bungalows, as well as rooms with en-suite facilities.
Rates: 2-bed bungalow N$391, 3-bed N$478. Rooms single N$640, N$552 per person sharing, including dinner and breakfast.

Haruchas Guest Farm (4 twin rooms, 1 family room) PO Box 80127, Windhoek; tel: 063 293399; fax: 061 251682; email: haruchas@natron.net; web: www.natron.net/tour/haruchas/index.htm Situated on the D855, between Büllsport and the D850, Haruchas is a typical farm (it covers 200km²!) set high up on the Tsaris Mountains. Wolfgang and Milena Sauber, who between them speak German, Afrikaans, English, Czech and Italian, run Haruchas.

The family unit has lovely thick walls as it was originally built in 1906, whilst the four other rooms are much newer, and purpose-built. All have verandas, en-suite toilet and bath (with shower attachment), pine furniture and lots of space. There are a couple of hiking trails which you can take from the farm, detailed in books in the rooms, and this would make a good writer's retreat.
Rates: single N$475, N$395 per person sharing, half board.

Naukluft Campsite About 10km southwest of Büllsport, on the D854, is the ornate entrance to the Naukluft section of the Namib-Naukluft National Park. Through the gates, a road winds up northwest into the Naukluft for about 12km before the NWR's restcamp. This has no bungalows, but eight beautifully situated camping spots, surrounded by mountains and trees. Only water, firewood and toilets/showers are provided, so bring all your supplies. In busy periods your stay is limited to three nights, and it's wise to book in advance at the NWR in Windhoek.

Rates: N$100 per site for up to eight people. Maximum stay is three nights during busy times
Namib-Naukluft Camping Sites PO Box 145, Maltahöhe; tel: 063 293245; fax 063 293244; email: reservations@mweb.com.na; web: www.namibiawildliferesorts.com. Central reservations, tel: 061 236975-8; fax: 061 224900; email and website as above.

Basic campsites are situated at Kuiseb Bridge, Homeb, Mirabib, Tinkas, Kriess-se-Rus, Vogelfederberg, Bloedkoppie, Gana and Welwitschia. The sites have communal ablution facilities.
Rates: N$90, excluding park fees.

SESRIEM AREA AND SOSSUSVLEI
When people speak of visiting the Namib Desert, this is often where they mean. The classic desert scenery around Sesriem and Sossusvlei is the stuff that postcards are made of – enormous apricot dunes with gracefully curving ridges, invariably pictured in the sharp light of dawn with a photogenic gemsbok or feathery acacia adjacent.

Sesriem and Sossusvlei lie on the Tsauchab River, one of two large rivers (the other being the Tsondab, further north) which flow westward into the great dunefield of the central Namib, but never reach the ocean. Both end by forming flat white pans dotted with green trees, surrounded by spectacular dunes – islands of life within a sea of sand.

Getting there
Sesriem is clearly signposted 12km southwest along the C27 from its junction with the C36. The best, easiest, and cheapest way to see the area is with your own car – so the vast majority of visitors drive. There is no public transport, and whilst hitching is possible it is difficult, as there are many possible routes here. (This also makes it easier to get away than to arrive.)

There's also a shuttle bus that links Namib-Naukluft Lodge with Windhoek and Swakopmund. This lodge runs day-trips into Sesriem and Sossusvlei which cost about N$300 per person.

Along similar lines, it's possible to fly by light aircraft into Sossusvlei Lodge or Wolwedans , from which there are guided tours around the area – though neither is a cheap option.

Best routes
The **quickest** route from Windhoek is normally south on the B1, then west on the C47 just after Rehoboth to Rietoog, right on to the D1206 to Büllsport (where the guest farm makes a good overnight stop if you're just off a plane). Then continue on the D854, almost in the shadow of the Naukluft Mountains, right on to the C36 and then left for 12km to Sesriem. This takes about four and a half hours.

The **most spectacular** route from Windhoek is via the C26, followed by the steep Spreetshoogte pass on the D1275 – which could easily be a six-hour drive. Swartfontein Lodge is the obvious stopover en route.

Approaching **from Keetmanshoop**, taking the main tar road to Maltahöhe is best, followed by the obvious C36, whilst **from Lüderitz**, Sesriem is really too far for comfort in one day. A stopover would be wise. This approach does allow you

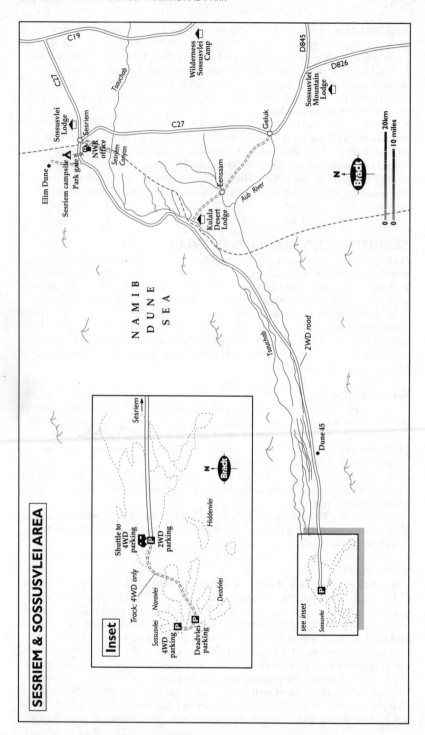

to take the D707 and the C27, which can both be slow going, but are certainly amongst the most spectacular roads in the subcontinent – with desert sands to their west, and mountain ranges on the east.

From **Swakopmund**, it is quickest to drive south to Walvis Bay and then take the C14, via the Kuiseb River's canyon. Allow at least four hours for this – more if you want to drive leisurely and stop for a picnic.

Rainy season access

For a few days each year, rain causes rivers to wash across certain roads – making them difficult, or impossible, to cross. (See advice on crossing rivers, page 87.)

The D854 is often badly affected, having three or more rivers flowing across it, fed by rains that fall on the Naukluft Mountains. The third of these, nearest Sesriem, usually seems the deepest – though this does depend on where the rain falls in the mountains.

Similarly, the Tsauchab River (which flows through Sesriem Canyon, and on to Sossusvlei) crosses the C36 between its junctions with the D854 and C27. It also crosses the C27 south of Sesriem (but north of the turn-off to Kulala). Both these river crossings look very wide, but are usually shallow and can be crossed with care in a normal 2WD.

If you anticipate problems, then approaching from Maltahöhe, on the C36, is probably the safest route – though it's a long way around from Windhoek. It is vital to ask reliable local advice before you set off.

What to see and do

Sesriem is the gateway to this part of the park, and the hub of the area. This has the NWR office, where everybody stops to buy their entry permits and fill up with fuel and supplies of cold drinks. From here a short road leads left to Sesriem Canyon, and another heads straight on, through a second gate, towards Elim Dune, Sesriem's small airfield and Sossusvlei.

Ballooning

Namib Sky Adventure Safaris run early morning ballooning trips over the desert – which are expensive but superb. You start from Sossusvlei Lodge, Kulala, or Mwisho, before dawn, and are driven to a take-off site, which varies with the winds and conditions.

The crew gradually unfurl the balloon, and inflate it with propane burners. When ready, everybody climbs into the basket, and it is inflated to take off. Gradually, the balloon sails higher over the surrounding dunes and mountains. Floating at wind-speed is travelling in still air – with only the occasional burst of gas interrupting the silence. It's an eerie experience, and an excellent platform for landscape photography.

Beneath the balloon a support vehicle follows as best it can, carrying a table, chairs and full supplies for a champagne breakfast – which is set up wherever the balloon lands. Eventually, everything is loaded on to the support vehicle and its trailer, and guests are returned to where they started, usually a little before midday.

Though a morning's ballooning costs US$250 per person, it is such an unusual and exhilarating experience that it is not only highly recommended, but also (arguably) quite good value.

Sesriem Canyon

About 4km from Sesriem, following the signs left as you enter the gates, is Sesriem Canyon. This is a narrow fissure in the sandstone, 30m deep in places, carved by the Tsauchab River. It was used by the early settlers, who drew water from it by knotting together six lengths of hide rope (called *riems*). Hence it became known as *ses riems*.

For some of the year, the river's bed is marked by pools of blissfully cool water, reached via an easy path of steps cut into the rock. It's a place to swim and relax – perfect for the heat of the day. At other times, though, the water can be almost stagnant and definitely not a place to bathe. It's also worth following the watercourse 500m up-river from the steps, where you'll find it before it descends into the canyon – another great place to bathe at times.

Beware of flash floods in the canyon itself. Heavy rain in the Naukluft Mountains occasionally causes these, trapping and drowning visitors.

Elim Dune

As you drive towards Sossusvlei, Elim Dune is about 5km from Sesriem. The turning off to the right is shortly after the entrance into the park, leading to a shady parking spot. It is the nearest sand-dune to Sesriem, and if you arrive late in the afternoon, then you may, like me, mistake it for a mountain.

From the parking spot you can climb it, though this takes longer than you might expect – allow at least an hour to get to the top. The views over plains towards the Naukluft Mountains on the east, and dune-crests to the west, are remarkable. It is especially worth the long climb at sunset, and conveniently close to the gates at Sesriem.

Sossusvlei area

As of 1997, entry permits for Sossusvlei are limited, to protect the area. In theory, only a certain number of vehicles are allowed to start along the road during each of three periods in each day. The first is from sunrise, the second in the middle of the day, and the third in the afternoon. Until now, the number of visitors arriving has rarely exceeded the quota, but this may change as the area receives more visitors. Permits cost N$30 per adult, plus N$20 for a car.

The road from Sesriem to Sossusvlei

After paying for your permit, continue southwest past Sesriem. The road is soon confined into a corridor, huge dunes on either side. Gradually, this narrows, becoming a few kilometres wide. This unique parting of the southern Namib's great sand-sea has probably been maintained over the millennia by the action of the Tsauchab River and the wind.

About 24km after leaving Sesriem, you cross the Tsauchab River. Although this seldom flows, note the green camelthorn, *Acacia erioloba*, which thrives here, clearly indicating permanent underground water.

Continuing westwards, the present course of the river is easy to spot parallel with the road. Look around for the many dead acacia trees that mark old courses of the river, now dried up. Some of these have been dated at over 500 years old.

Note that this road has always been fine, white gravel: photogenic, but very dusty (and easily driven in a normal 2WD car). Sadly, the dust from vehicles is thought to be harming the acacias, and other wildlife, so there are plans to tar the road in late 1998.

Along this final stretch of road are a few side-tracks leading to the feet of some of the dunes, numbered according to their distance along the road from the office. Dune 45, on the south side, is particularly photogenic. About 36km after crossing the Tsauchab, this road ends at the 2WD parking area.

Parking (2WD parking area)

Here low sand-dunes apparently form a final barrier to the progress of the river or the road. There is a large group of acacias, which shade a couple of picnic tables. Nearby are a few toilets of dubious cleanliness.

As we go to press, new regulations mean that this is now as far as you can drive yourself. To reach Sossusvlei, you must now either walk or take the shuttle bus. Alternatively, if you are staying at a nearby lodge and taking one of their guided excursions, the guide will usually be able to drive into the old 4WD parking area.

The first pan is only about 500m over the sandbar, though it'll take an hour or more to cover the 5km to the farthest pan, Sossusvlei itself. Shuttle 4WDs are run by Hobas Shuttle and Tours from 08.00 until 16.00. The return trip costs N$80 per person; it is not yet clear whether or not you can still buy a single and then walk back. The driver will collect you from Sossusvlei or Dead Vlei at a pre-arranged time – if you don't want to be rushed, allow around two or three hours.

Hidden Vlei

On the left of the (2WD) parking area, you'll see signs to Hidden Vlei – which is reached by climbing over the dunes. As at Dead Vlei, here you'll find old, dead acacia trees, which were deprived of water when the river changed course, but still stand to tell the tale.

Dead Vlei

Like Hidden Vlei, but perhaps more accessible, Dead Vlei is an old pan with merely the skeletons of trees left – some over 500 years old. Many consider it to be more starkly beautiful than Sossusvlei.

From the (2WD) parking area, walk over the sandbar following the 4WD track that will lead you into the large main pan. Keep over to the left-hand side, and you'll soon find the old parking area for Dead Vlei, your start point for the 500m hike over the dunes into Dead Vlei.

Sossusvlei and Nara Vlei

After about 4–5km the 4WD track bends round to the right, and ends in front of Sossusvlei. This is as far as the pans extend. Beyond here, only tall sand-dunes separate you from the Atlantic Ocean.

Most years, the ground here is a flat silvery-white pan of fine mud that has dried into a crazy-paving pattern. Upon this are huge sand mounds collected by nara bushes, and periodic feathery camelthorn trees, *Acacia erioloba*, drooping gracefully. All around the sinuous shapes of the Namib's (and some claims the world's) largest sand-dunes stretch up to 300m high. It's a stunning, surreal environment.

Perhaps once every decade, Namibia receives really torrential rain. Storms deluge the Naukluft's ravines and the Tsauchab sweeps out towards the Atlantic in a flash flood, surging into the desert and pausing only briefly to fill its canyon.

Floods so powerful are rare, and Sossusvlei can fill overnight. Though the Tsauchab will subside quickly, the vlei remains full. Miraculous lilies emerge to bloom, and the bright yellow devil thorn flowers (*Tribulus* species) carpet the water's edge. Surreal scenes reflect in the lake, as dragonflies hover above its polished surface. Birds arrive and luxuriant growth flourishes, making the most of this ephemeral treat.

These waters recede from most of the pan rapidly, concentrating in Sossusvlei, where they can remain for months. Whilst they are there, the area's birdlife changes radically, as waterbirds and waders will often arrive, along with opportunist insectivores. Meanwhile, less than a kilometre east, over a dune, the main pan is dry as dust, and looks as if it hasn't seen water in decades.

Where to stay

There are only a few possibilities if you want to stay near to Sesriem. Either camp there, or stay at one of the nearby lodges. None of these are cheap, but if you're prepared to travel 35km, then the new Desert Homestead is probably the least expensive. However, anywhere in the Naukluft, Solitaire or even northern NamibRand also makes a practical base for visits here, provided that you don't insist on being at Sesriem for sunrise. As tourism to this corner of the desert increases, brighter visitors are starting to move away from the busy Sesriem and Sossusvlei area, to find superb desert experiences in the private areas of desert that lie to the north and south – like Wolwedans and Die Duine. For the present, however, this remains an area where you must book well in advance to have any hope of finding good accommodation when you arrive.

Sossusvlei Lodge (45 twin tents) PO Box 6900, Windhoek; tel: 063 693223; fax: 063 693231; email: sossusvl@iafrica.com.na; web: www.sossusvleilodge.com
Situated at Sesriem, immediately on the right of the national park entrance, Sossusvlei Lodge has the most convenient possible location for anyone wanting to drive to Sossusvlei at first light, or leave the park as late in the day as possible. When built it caused quite a stir: a large luxury lodge so close to the restcamp and park. However, now it is accepted as part of the scenery, into which it blends surprisingly well.

Its construction is an innovative mix of materials and colours: concrete, ironwork, canvas and leather; reds, apricots, greens and whites. The 'tents' are elaborate, permanent constructions and each has an en-suite bathroom (with shower, toilet and washbasin) built as part of the solid base, which supports the canvas walls of the bedrooms. Inside is luxurious and spacious, with adjoining large single beds, bedside tables, lamps, easy chairs, a dressing table, etc – so banish any thoughts of camping when you read of 'tents' here. Although the bathrooms could do with a coat of paint, and there are signs of wear in the fabric of the canvas, this is still an extraordinary place to stay.

The lodge's bar is popular with campers as well as guests, and its restaurant is good, serving help-yourself breakfasts and light, modern, à la carte lunches. Dinner is buffet-style, with various meats (often including unusual game) cooked to order. The swimming pool faces the desert and feels sublime after a dusty day in the dunes.

The atmosphere here is that of a hotel, as you will be left to organise yourself, though morning and afternoon trips are available into the park using the nearby Namib-Pappot Safari Company.

The lodge has a 10" computer-controlled, light refraction telescope. This can be linked to a PC, to pinpoint any one of 281,000 objects in the night sky, including such southern-hemisphere 'specials' as Omega Centaurus and The Jewel Box, and even be programmed to track (or 'slew') them. The sky at Sesriem is clear for about 300 days per year, and there is virtually no pollution. Ask at reception if anyone is available to work the telescope for you; if not, climb the central water tower to see the stars at their best. (Clouds or rain are a cause for celebration here; don't expect sympathy if you can't see any stars.) Sossusvlei Lodge is not cheap, but is very comfortable and perfect for early starts into the Sossusvlei area of the national park.
Rates: N$1,460 single, N$1,700 double, for dinner, bed and breakfast.

Kulala Desert Lodge (12 twin chalets) Reservations PO Box 6850, 8 Bismarck St (corner Merensky & Schinz streets), Windhoek; tel: 061 274500, cell: 081 1243066; fax: 061 239455; email: info@nts.com.na; web: www.wilderness-safaris.com
Opened in 1996, Kulala is signposted off the C27 some 15km south of Sesriem (but north of the junction with the D845). The lodge is then about 14km from the road. Overlooking the national park from the southern banks of the Tsauchab River, Kulala is easily the closest lodge to Sossusvlei. However, its access to the vlei remains limited to the C27, and

the park entrance at Sesriem, thus the Sesriem campsite and Sossusvlei Lodge are effectively a shorter drive from the vlei.

Inside, Kulala's ethnic décor owes much to André and Coralee Louw –designers of Villa Verdi, in Windhoek – whilst its cool clay construction drew inspiration from North African designs. The chalets, or 'kulalas', are large tents built on wooden platforms overlooking the riverbed, topped with thatched roofs. Each incorporates an en-suite clay bathroom, complete with shower and toilet. Outdoors enthusiasts can put their mattresses on the roof, and sleep in the open – a fun option (though chilly in winter).

Sandwiched between the national park to the northwest, and the private NamibRand Nature Reserve to the south, Kulala has 32,000ha of its own land on which it operates balloon safaris and nature drives. The balloon safaris, organised by Eric and Nancy Hesemans, who started Namibia's first ballooning at Mwisho, begin at first light, before the heat of the sun stirs powerful thermals over the desert. They end some 60–90 minutes later with a champagne breakfast served wherever you land. In between, you float serenely above a rolling vision of mountains, plains and iridescent sand-dunes, observing the silent dawn as it rises over one of the earth's most beautiful landscapes. A wondrous experience – even at a cost of US$250 per person.

Morning drives into Sossusvlei (with the lodge's own guides) are N$595 per person, including drinks and park entrance fees. Shorter evening drives (lasting from about 16.00–19.00), take a closer look at some of the smaller fauna and flora in the desert and cost N$370 per person, including sundowner drinks and a spotlit night drive on the way back to the lodge. Alternatively, many guests drive themselves around the area using Kulala as merely a stylish base.

Rates: single N$1,525–2,080, N$985–1,400 per person sharing, for dinner, bed and breakfast.

Little Kulala (8 kulalas) Contact details as Kulala Desert Lodge, above.
Little Kulala is situated on the same farm as Kulala Desert Lodge, of which it is a mini replica. Here, there are just 8 kulalas, each with its own plunge pool and rooftop sleeping area.

Rates: single N$2,530–3,610; N$1600–N$2495 per person sharing, including all meals and activities.

Sesriem campsite (20 pitches and overflow field) PO Box 145, Maltahöhe; tel: 063 293245; fax: 063 293244; email: reservations@mweb.com.na; web: www.namibiawildliferesorts.com. Central reservations, tel: 061 236975–8; fax: 061 224900
In 1989, Sesriem campsite had just ten pitches, and was the only place in the area. Each was shaded by an old camelthorn tree, which boasted a tap sprouting beside its trunk, and was protected by a low, circular wall. It was stunning.

Times have changed. Now there are 20 pitches, an overflow field (on the left) which is often busy, and two ablution blocks. But it's still a marvellous place to camp, especially if you get one of the original pitches, on the edge of the campground. Fuel and wood are normally available at the NWR office, as are a few simple foodstuffs – though it's better to bring food with you. The neighbouring Sossusvlei Lodge welcomes campers to dinner, provided they book a table before midday, and don't become rowdy.

To guarantee camping space, especially in the high season, you should book at the NWR in Windhoek before arriving, although it's always worth checking on arrival to see if there's a space available. Gates into the park open only between sunrise and sunset, and entry to the road into the vlei is strictly controlled (see page 264).

Rates: N$160 per pitch per night, for up to 4 people, plus national park fees. Additional people N$10 up to a maximum of 8.

Sossusvlei Wilderness Camp (9 twin rooms) PO Box 6850, Windhoek; tel: 061 274500; fax: 061 239455. For other contact details, see Kulala Desert Lodge above.
This swish new lodge opened in mid-1998, catering to upmarket fly-in safaris using its own

landing strip. For those driving, it is about 30km from Sesriem on the 7,000ha farm named Witwater. Its entrance is on the west of the C36, just north of its junction with the D845. The camp has nine thatched guestrooms, which have been built from rock and timber. Each has an en-suite bathroom with shower and its own private wooden deck and small plunge pool. All are recessed into a low kopje, around which desert plains fade into mountains and distant dunes. There's a central lounge, dining room and bar that is linked to all the tents by raised wooden walkways. If cost is no object, then this camp is excellent and one of the most stylish in the area.
Rates: single N$2,715–3,610, N$1,895–2,495 per person sharing, including all meals and guided activities.

Kulala Tented Camp (6 Meru-style tents) Contact as for Kulala Desert Lodge.
This new tented camp is on the same property as its established sister-lodge, above. Its walk-in, Meru-style tents are on elevated decks, each with en-suite facilities. The main area consists of a thatched dining room, lounge, bar and swimming pool.
Rates: single N$1,345–1,525, N$985–1,300 per person sharing, including breakfast and dinner.

The Desert Homestead & Horse Trails (16 chalets) PO Box 24, Maltahöhoe; tel/fax: 063 293243; email: homestead@africaonline.com.na
Opened in 2001, this new lodge, just 35km from Sesriem, is owned by the same group that had Hilltop House in Windhoek, and it shares the same high standards. Each of the tastefully appointed rock chalets has en-suite facilities, and offers a sweeping view of the distant Nubib Mountains. The décor hints at a bygone era of Namibian farm living, with enamel basins, brass taps and beautifully draped mosquito nets. Traditional farm-cooked meals are prepared with a modern twist using vegetables and herbs grown in the gardens. Meals are usually taken on the veranda, while light meals, snacks and other goodies may be purchased from the lodge's old-fashioned trading store. A swimming pool for guests and email facilities bring the picture up to date, while beyond is a well-situated waterhole frequented by the small herd of wild desert horses imported to the area from Garub during the drought of 1994.

The main activity here is horseriding – across grassy plains and along ancient watercourses. Guests planning to ride will need to have an intermediate level of riding experience, for the horses here range from Arabs to Hanoverians; they are not riding-school ponies. There are two excursions daily, when the air is coolest, and desert wildlife is at its most active: at sunrise, the trip culminates in a champagne breakfast, while sundowners are served on the sunset ride. For non-riding guests, there are guided walks (day or night) in Sossusvlei, and an evening sundowner drive.

Enthusiasts seeking more time in the saddle won't be disappointed, for the optimum opportunity is the 'sleep-out package'. On this, up to six riders start with an early-morning ride, followed by a 4WD excursion to Sossusvlei, then a longer horse ride. Stay overnight in the desert with a campfire, evening meal and hot bucket shower, then wake up to a second long ride. The day finishes with either a sundowner ride or a drive – depending on the level of enthusiasm remaining.
Rates: single N$500, double N$825, triple N$1,150, family room N$1,450, all including breakfast. Dinner N$100, braai packs N$85, lunch packs N$55. Horse safaris N$100 per rider, per hour; sunrise N$400; sunset N$250; sundowner drive N$50. Guided trips to Sossusvlei (min 2 people) – N$290 (day walk); N$215 (night walk); N$460 (drive).

SOLITAIRE AREA
North of the Sesriem area, the C36 leads into the equally beautiful C13 road, often with dunes on one side and mountains on the other. These are the main routes from Sesriem to Swakopmund, so are relatively busy (typically a few cars per hour).

Solitaire

Solitaire is a large dot on the NWR's map, but a small place. It is just a few buildings, run by the helpful, if idiosyncratic, Percy; but is so atmospheric, so typical of a middle-of-nowhere stop in the desert, that it's been the location for several film and advert scenes.

There is a fuel station here that is pretty reliable, and it is still the best place for miles to have punctures mended. The shop behind the garage opens all hours, selling quite a wide range of supplies (the best around, though that's no great praise). Superb fresh bread is baked on the premises, as is apple crumble, and most people stop for a drink and a snack. The storeroom at the back has a surprising range of wine. There's a campsite, too, costing N$20 per person, plus N$50 for the site.

Where to stay

Around Solitaire are several good places to stay whilst visiting the desert. The Namib-Naukluft Lodge, Namib Restcamp and Weltevrede are mainly bases from which to explore the Sesriem area, whilst Rooisand and Swartfontein have spectacular mountainous scenery of their own worth seeing, and are useful stopovers on the way to/from Sesriem.

Solitaire Country Lodge (25 rooms) PO Box 6597, Windhoek; tel: 061 240375; fax: 061 256598; email: afrideca@mweb.com.na; web: www.namibialodges.com
Opened in June 2002, this new lodge right next to the fuel station and shop is aiming for the two–three-star slot, with comfortable, en-suite rooms. It is part of the Namibia Country Lodges group that includes Twyfelfontein near Damaraland.
Rates: single N$150, double N$215, including breakfast. Camping N$50. Dinner N$72.50 per person.

Solitaire Guest Farm (5 rooms) PO Box 4119, Walvis Bay; tel/fax: 062 572024; email: aswarts@mweb.com.na
Situated 6km east of Solitaire on the C14, this small guest farm has en-suite double rooms and a swimming pool.
Rates: single N$450, double from N$385 per person, including breakfast and dinner.

Namib-Naukluft Lodge (16 rooms) African Extravaganza, PO Box 22028, Windhoek; tel: 061 263082/3/6/7; fax: 061 215356; email: afex@afex.com.na; web: www.natron.net/afex
On the C36, south of Solitaire and just a few kilometres from the Namib Restcamp, the Namib-Naukluft Lodge is outwardly uninspiring, despite being designed by a well-known Namibian architect. However, it is plush inside, and if you are looking for 'normal' rooms, rather than trendy tents, perhaps this is the place for you.

Its modern rooms are built in line. Through sliding glass doors, leading on to a veranda, they face a huge desert plain. Each has adjacent twin beds, en-suite toilet and (powerful) shower. By reception is a large lounge-bar and a dining room, though meals are often eaten on the veranda facing the desert.

Behind the lodge, in the shade of a large kopje, is a braai area for moonlit dining, while at the far end of the row of rooms is a small (popular) swimming pool and a shaded area for relaxing. If you don't have a car whilst here, you can take short walks on the lodge's own land, and reserve a seat on their daily 4WD trips into Sossusvlei (N$300 per person).

The lodge is owned by a large company, African Extravaganza, and thus conveniently links up with a shuttle-service to/from Windhoek and Swakopmund (see page 99). This departs from both towns at 14.00 (13.00 June–Sept), arriving at the lodge just before sunset.
Rates: single N$775, N$625 per person sharing, including breakfast and dinner.

Namib Restcamp (13 bungalows and camping) PO Box 1075, Swakopmund; tel: 063 693376; fax: 063 693377; email: namibrescamp@mweb.com.na
The Namib Restcamp has been open for nine years, and is situated on the 17,000ha farm,

Dieprivier. It is about 27km from Solitaire on the C36, and 60km north of Sesriem. This farm was one of the area's first places to take visitors, and it is still run by Jannie and Gerda von Wielligh and their family. Its other residents include cattle, sheep, goats, ostrich, gemsbok and the odd meerkat.

Accommodation is in simple two- or four-bed bungalows, with en-suite showers and toilets – basic but adequate. Facilities include a swimming pool with a shaded area for pool-side buffets. Namib Rest Camp is primarily a base for making your own excursions around the area, though they do run their own excellent trips.

These normally visit their own range of petrified dunes – which make a stunning backdrop to the camp. Here the landscape has been eroded by the Diep River, revealing the fossilised sand-dunes that underpin this part of the Namib. It is a fascinating area, and these trips usually continue on to the main dune-sea, before returning to camp just after sunset.

Rates: single N$460, N$420 per person sharing, including breakfast and dinner.

Weltevrede Guest Farm (5 double rooms, 6 bungalows and campsite) PO Box 4119, Walvis Bay; tel: 063 293374; fax: 063 293375; email: aswarts@mweb.com.na.

Signposted off the east side of the C14, Weltevrede is about a 47km drive from Sesriem and just south of the Namib Restcamp, 37km from Solitaire. It has been open for three years, but retains the air of a small, friendly farm.

Next to the farm's main buildings are six square purpose-built bungalows. These are sparsely furnished, but clean and spacious with en-suite bathrooms. Adjacent is a converted farmhouse with 5 more rooms, and a basic kitchen retaining a small stock of crockery – ideal if you bring your own food and want to self-cater. This building is older, with thicker walls, so the rooms here tend to be cooler.

Weltevrede also has four pitches for tents, under shady trees, which have water but no electricity (in the bungalows, electricity is on 19.00–22.00). These have showers and toilets for men and women, and are best booked in advance. For campers or farm guests, there's a 'reservoir' (a round tank used for water storage) nearby that can be used for swimming. This is more of a farm than a lodge for visitors.

Between April and August, Weltevrede runs several scheduled special photographers' trips, for black-and-white photography, with a darkroom on site.

Rates: single N$440, N$385 per person sharing, including breakfast and dinner.

Rooisand Guest Farm (5 rooms) PO Box 2106, Windhoek; tel: 062 572119 or 061 253542; fax: 061 259247

Rooisand is situated at the foot of the Gamsberg Pass on the C26 – about 30km from the junction of the C14 and C26. A traditional guest farm, it makes a good base for hiking around Gamsberg's mountains. All five rooms have air conditioning; other luxuries include satellite TV and a large farm swimming pool.

There are Bushman paintings on various rocks around Rooisand, as well as an old Schutztruppe camp, and a quarry that occasionally throws up some interesting semi-precious stones. As a special excursion, you can be taken to the Kuiseb canyon, to where Hermann Korn and Henno Martin (author of *The Sheltering Desert*, see *Further Reading*) hid for years during World War II.

Rates: single N$550, N$420 per person sharing, including all meals.

Swartfontein Mountain and Desert Guest Lodge (8 rooms) PO Box 32042, Windhoek; tel/fax: 062 572004/572044; email: info@swartfontein.com. Reservations tel: 061 226979; fax: 061 226999; email: logufa@mweb.com.na; web: www.natron.net/tour/logufa

Run by Silvia and Roberto Scarafia, Swartfontein Lodge is at the top of the steep Spreetshoogte Pass, off the D1261, north of the D1274, and south of the D1275. It is conveniently located about mid-way on a scenic route between Windhoek and Sesriem (C26–D1265–C24, then along the D1275).

The elegant farmhouse has Italian furnishings, the odd antique painting, comfortable sofas and an interesting collection of Africana. A curio shop is to be added shortly.

A small lodge with Italian owners, its new, well-kept guest rooms are in a separate wing with good en-suite facilities. Living rooms and dining room are very comfortable, and the food is excellent, with homemade bread, pasta and ice-cream. What is more, the vistas from the nearby Spreetshoogte Pass, particularly at sunrise and sunset, are spectacular.

Swartfontein, in the Namib Spreetshoogte Nature Reserve, covers about 81km² of rolling mountains, with game and no domestic stock. They offer early morning birding walks, day and night game drives and private flights (if booked in advance). If you're staying for a while then they will also arrange trips to the Naukluft Mountains and even to Sossusvlei. This excellent lodge deserves to be better known.

Rates: single N$760, N$680 sharing, dinner, bed and breakfast.

Rostock Ritz (22 'igloos') PO Box 536, Swakopmund; tel: 064 403622, cell: 081 1292408; fax: 064 403623; email: kuecki@mweb.com.na; web: www.natron.net/rostock-ritz
Run by Kücki, of Kücki's in Swakopmund, this relatively new lodge is about 5km off the C14, a few minutes' drive south of the C26. Individual 'igloos' with en-suite facilities sleep two people, and each has magnificent view of the surrounding desert. Two units are suitable for wheelchairs.

Day visitors are welcome to take advantage of the lodge's restaurant, which serves lunch from 12.00 to 14.30. Attractions include 40km of marked hiking rails to the natural springs of the Gaub canyon, while for the less energetic there are dune drives or a three-hour trip to see the rock art of the Oase cave.

Rates: single N$713, double N$540, including breakfast.

THE PARK'S NORTHERN SECTION

Between the normally dry beds of the Swakop and Kuiseb rivers, the desert is largely rock and stone. Though the area has few classic desert scenes of shifting dunes, the landscapes are still striking and certainly no less memorable. They range from the deeply incised canyons of the Swakop River valley to the open plains around Ganab, flat and featureless but for the occasional isolated inselberg.

When to visit

The best time to visit this section of the park is towards the end of the rains, when the vegetation is at its best and, if you are lucky, you'll find scattered herds of gemsbok, springbok and zebra. During this time the best sites to go to are the more open ones, like Ganab, on the plains.

For the rest of the year it is still spectacular, but you'll find fewer animals around. Then perhaps it's better to visit Homeb, or one of the inselbergs, as the flora and fauna there remain a little more constant than those on the plains – not shrivelling up so much in the dryness of winter.

Getting organised

To venture off the main roads in this area (that is anywhere *except* the C14, C28, D1982 and D198), you need a permit from the NWR. These cost N$90 per site per night, plus park fees. They are easily obtained from the NWR in Windhoek; the park office at Sesriem; Swakopmund's Namib i information centre or the Hans Kries Service Station on Sam Nujoma Avenue; or in Walvis Bay from Suidwes Diensstasie (13th Road and 10th Street/Nangolo Mbumba Drive) or CWB Service Station at 124 Sam Nujoma Avenue. These permits allow you to venture on to the park's smaller roads and to camp in any of the area's sites. Most of the roads are navigable by 2WD, while only a few around Gemsbokwater and Groot Tinkas are classed as 4WD.

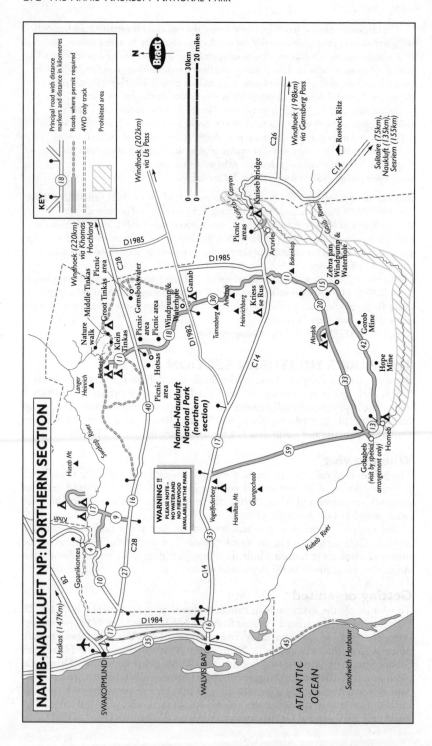

NAMIB-NAUKLUFT NP: NORTHERN SECTION

KEY

Principal road with distance markers and distance in kilometres

Roads where permit required

4WD only track

Prohibited area

N

Brandt

30km

20 miles

0

0

Windhoek (202km) via Us Pass

Windhoek (198km) via Gamsberg Pass

Rostock Ritz

Solitaire (75km), Naukluft (135km), Sesriem (155km)

C26

C14

Kuiseb bridge

Gaub River

D1985

D1985

Kuiseb Canyon

Picnic areas

Aruvlei

Bodenkop

Zebra pan Windpump & Waterhole

Windhoek (220km) via Khomas Hochland

C28

Picnic area

Nature walk

Middle Tinkas

Groot Tinkas

Picnic Gemsbokwater area

Picnic area

Ganab

Windpump & Waterhole

Arnaub

Tumasberg

Heinrichberg

Kriess se Rus

Mirabib

Gorob Mine

Hope Mine

Klein Tinkas

Blutkoppie

Langer Heinrich

Hotsas

Picnic area

D1982

C14

33

42

20

15

11

59

13

Homeb

Gobabeb (visit by special arrangement only)

Namib-Naukluft National Park (northern section)

Husab Mt

Swakop River

Khan River

Goanikontes

Usakos (147km)

B2

SWAKOPMUND

WALVIS BAY

Vogelfederberg

Hamilton Mt

Ghungochoob

Kuiseb River

WARNING !! PLEASE NOTE – NO WATER AND NO FIREWOOD AVAILABLE IN THE PARK

ATLANTIC OCEAN

Sandwich Harbour

C28

C14

D1984

40

17

35

16

11

9

4

10

27

17

16

35

45

18

Even these are probably negotiable with a high-clearance 2WD and a skilled driver, though you'd be waiting a very long time indeed for anyone to pass by if you became stuck.

Where to camp

Sites in the area have no facilities to speak of, but there is plenty of variety for you to choose from. To spend a night or two camping here – which is the only way do this part of the desert justice – you must be fully independent in terms of fuel, food, water and firewood.

Bloedkoppie (or Blutkopje) Literally 'blood hill', for its colour in the red light of sunset, this large, smooth granite inselberg rises out of the Tinkas Flats, near the Swakop River. It can provide some challenging scrambles if the heat has not drained your energies. Be careful not to approach any birds' nests, as some of the raptors in the park are very sensitive to disturbances. They may even abandon them if you go too close. Look out for the temporary pools after the rains, filled with life.

Ganab Immediately next to a dry watercourse, which winds like a thin green snake through the middle of a large gravel plain, this open site has a wind-powered water pump nearby. Around March, if the rains have been good, then it can be an excellent spot for herds of springbok and gemsbok – and you can see for miles.

Groot Tinkas Hidden away in a valley amidst a maze of small kopjes, there is a small dam with sheer walls of rock and some fairly challenging rough driving too. Look out for frogs in the pool, and turn over a few stones to find scorpions and their harmless mimics, pseudo-scorpions.

Homeb This excellent site is in the Kuiseb River valley where the perennial vegetation includes camelthorn (*Acacia erioloba*), false ebony (*Euclea pseudebenus*), wild tamarisk (*Tamarix usneoides*), and several species of wild figs. The Kuiseb forms the northern boundary of the great southern dune-field, so observe the dunes on the south side of the river as they creep northwards. Soon you realise that it's only the periodic floods of the river which prevent the park to the north from being covered in shifting sands.

Homeb's well-placed location leaves you with the opportunity to cross the riverbed and climb amongst the dunes, as well as to explore the river valley itself. The proximity of three different environments is why Namibia's Desert Research Centre is located at Gobabeb, on the Kuiseb to the west of Homeb.

Kriess-se-Rus Again found in a dry riverbed, Kriess-se-Rus lies just below a bank of exposed schist – with the layers of rock clearly seen, providing an interesting contrast to the flat calcrete plains nearby. Around you'll find quivertrees (*Aloe dichotoma*), many camelthorns, and some *Euphorbia* and *Commiphora* bushes.

Kuiseb Bridge Just off the main C14 route, west of the Gamsberg Pass, the river is said to have less underground water stored here than further down its course, though it is more prone to flash floods. This can be very bare during the dry season, but is really pleasant after the rains. Make it your lunchtime picnic stop if you are travelling between the Swakopmund and Sesriem areas (take your rubbish away with you).

Mirabib Yet another great grey inselberg, but one that is even quieter than the others. It has great views from the top. Around it, where any rainwater runs off, are small trees and bushes. There are always a few lizards to be found around here, and even the odd snake.

Swakop River Being also beacon number 10 on the Welwitschia Drive (see below) means that this beautiful dry riverbed can get rather busy at times with day-trippers from Swakopmund.

Vogelfederberg This rounded granite outcrop is the closest of the sites to the ocean, and as such it gets more moisture from the fog than the others. Its gentle shape helps form a number of fascinating temporary pools. Polaroid glasses will help you to see past the reflections and into these pools; if you've a pair, take them.

Welwitschia Drive

In the northern corner of the Namib-Naukluft National Park, the Welwitschia Drive is perhaps best treated as a short excursion from Swakopmund. Don't forget to get a permit first.

This is a route through the desert along which are 13 numbered stone beacons at points of particular interest. It takes about four hours to drive, stopping at each place to get out and explore, and culminates at one of the country's largest, and hence oldest, welwitschia plants.

An excellent, detailed booklet – well worth getting – is available from the NWR to cover this route. However as it is often difficult to obtain here's a brief outline of the different points of interest at the beacons:

1 **Lichen field** Look carefully at the ground to see these small 'plants', which are in fact the result of a symbiotic relationship (ie: a mutually beneficial relationship between two organisms, each depending on the other for its survival) between an alga, producing food by photosynthesis, and a fungus, providing a physical structure. If you look closely, you'll see many different types of lichen. Some are thought to be hundreds of years old, and all are exceedingly fragile and vulnerable.

2 **Drought-resistant bushes** Two types of bush found all over the Namib are the dollar bush, so called because its leaves are the size of a dollar coin, and the ink bush. Both can survive without rain for years.

3 **Tracks of ox-wagons** Although made decades ago, these are still visible here, showing clearly the damage that can so easily be done to the lichen fields by driving over them.

4 **The moonscape** This is an unusual and spectacular view, usually called the moonscape, looking over a landscape formed by the valleys of the Swakop River. It is best seen in the slanting light of early morning or late afternoon.

5 **More lichen fields** These remarkable plants can extract all their moisture requirements from the air. To simulate the dramatic effect that a morning fog can have, simply sprinkle a little water on one and watch carefully for a few minutes.

6 This is another impressive view of the endless moonscape.

7 **Old South African camp** This is the site of an old military camp, occupied for just a few days during World War I.

8 Turn left at this marker to visit the next few beacons.

9 **A dolorite dyke** These dark strips of rock, which are a common feature of this part of the Namib, were formed when molten lava welled up through cracks in the existing grey granite. After cooling it formed dark, hard bands of rock which resisted erosion more than the granite – and thus has formed the spine of many ridges in the area.

Above Clay castles of the Hoarusib River, Skeleton Coast National Park (CM)

Left Lithops, or living stones – one of the Namib's many unique species (CM)

Below Huge agate embedded in a hill on the Skeleton Coast (CM)

Above Cape fur seal at Cape Cross on the Skeleton Coast (CM)

Right One of the few wrecks left to be seen on the Skeleton Coast (CM)

Below Cape Cross in June, when the colony is quiet (CM)

10 **The Swakop River valley** Picnicking in the riverbed, with a profusion of tall trees around, you might find it difficult to believe that you are in a desert. It could be said that you're not – after all, this rich vegetation is not made up of desert adapted species. It includes wild tamarisk (*Tamarix usurious*), and anaboom (*Acacia albida*), better known for its occurrence in the humid Zambezi valley almost 1,000 miles east – sustained by underground water percolating through the sands beneath your feet.

11 **Welwitschia Flats** This barren, open expanse of gravel and sand is home to the Namib's most celebrated plant, the endemic *Welwitschia mirabilis*. These plants are found only in the Namib, and at just a few locations which suit their highly adapted biology.

12 **The big welwitschia** This beacon marks the end of the trail, and one of the largest *Welwitschia mirabilis* known – estimated at over 1,500 years old.

13 **Old mine workings** On the way back to Swakopmund, continue straight past beacon 8, without turning right. Where the road joins route C28 to Swakopmund, marked by this final beacon, is one of the desert's old mine workings. In the 1950s iron ore was mined by hand here. Now it is just another reminder of the park's chequered past.

Swakopmund and Walvis Bay Area

Flying low over Namibia's coastline is probably the best way to get a sense of perspective about it. You see how it divides the South Atlantic Ocean from the baking desert. Both seem harsh and unforgiving.

Clinging to the boundary, often under a blanket of morning fog, are Swakopmund and Walvis Bay. Politically, Walvis Bay has always been vital. It has the only deepwater harbour between Lüderitz and Angola. Historically, Swakopmund is probably the more interesting, with old German architecture to rival that in Lüderitz.

Most visitors stay in Swakopmund, which tends to be the livelier of the two, though birdwatchers may prefer Walvis Bay. Both have a good choice of small hotels and restaurants, making them obvious stops when driving between the Namib-Naukluft Park and the Skeleton Coast or Damaraland.

HISTORY

In 1884, the whole of present-day Namibia was declared a protectorate of Germany – except the region's only large natural harbour, Walvis Bay, which remained under British control. Thus, in order to develop their interests in the area, the German authorities decided to make their own harbour on the northern banks of the Swakop River, and beacons were planted in 1892 to mark the spot, where the Mole is today (see pages 297–8).

Following this, the German authorities made several (largely unsuccessful) attempts to develop landing facilities. A quay was built, although it subsequently silted up, followed by a wooden, and later an iron, jetty. Finally in 1915, when Germany's control of the country was surrendered to South Africa, all maritime trade reverted to Walvis Bay.

During the South African administration of Namibia, before Independence, there was a deliberate policy of developing no other ports to compete with Walvis Bay – as South Africa anticipated keeping hold of the Walvis Bay enclave, even if it were forced into giving most of Namibia independence.

As planned, South Africa kept the Walvis Bay enclave as part of the Cape Colony even after Namibian Independence in 1990, though it agreed to a joint administration in 1992, and finally relented in February 1994, when Walvis Bay officially became part of Namibia.

SWAKOPMUND

Considered by most Namibians to be the country's only real holiday resort, this old German town spreads from the mouth of the Swakop River out into the surrounding desert plain. Climatically more temperate than the interior, the palm-lined streets, immaculate old buildings and well-kept gardens give Swakop (as the locals call it) a

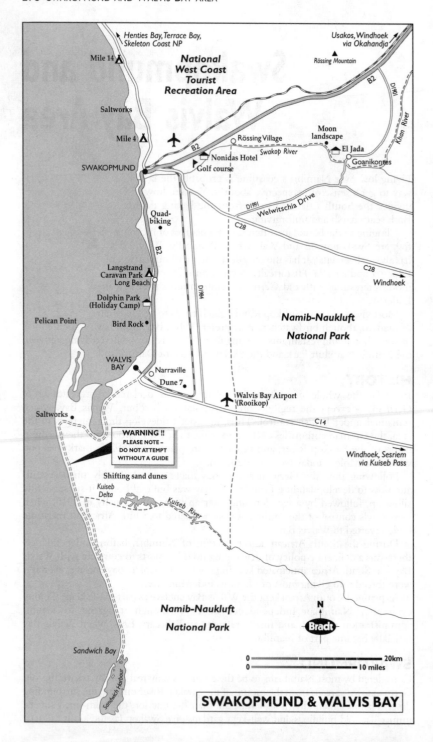

unique atmosphere, and make it a pleasant oasis in which to spend a few days.

Unlike much of Namibia, Swakopmund is used to tourists and has a wide choice of places to stay and eat, and many things to do. With numerous new and highly original options, from free-fall parachuting to dune-bike riding and sand-boarding, Swakopmund is increasingly making a name for itself as a centre for adventure travel, and attracting adventurous visitors seeking 'adrenaline' trips.

This is still too small a trickle to change the town's delightful character, but is enough to ensure that you'll never be bored. On the other hand, visit on a Monday during one of the quieter months, and you could be forgiven for thinking that the town had partially closed down!

Orientation

Viewed from above the Atlantic, Swakopmund has a simple layout. One tar road, Sam Nujoma Avenue (the B2), enters the town from the interior; another heads off left, northwards, to Henties Bay (C34). A third crosses the mouth of the Swakop, southwards towards Walvis Bay. Where they meet is the centre of town, a raised area about four blocks from the Arnold Schad Promenade – the palm-lined road which skirts the seashore.

Most of the hotels are near the compact centre, as are the shops and restaurants – so it's an easy town to walk around.

Street name changes

A number of street-name changes have recently been introduced in Swakopmund, replacing the familiar German names with others to honour local and national dignitaries. Inevitably, many of the former names are still used, as follows:

Sam Nujoma Avenue	*was*	Kaiser Wilhelm Street
Moses Garoeb Street	*was*	Nordring/Sudring
Nathaniel Maxuilili Street	*was*	Breite Street
Daniel Tjongarero Avenue	*was*	Post Street

There are yet more changes in the pipeline, with roads to be affected including the Strand, Fischreier and 1st Street, but final decisions have yet to be taken on these.

Getting there
By air

Swakopmund has regular flights to/from Windhoek (N\$385). For flights to Walvis Bay, see page 300. Expect to pay around N\$50 for a taxi from the airport into town.

By train

Swakopmund is linked to Windhoek and Tsumeb by the normal, slow TransNamib train services. These run from and to Windhoek every day except Saturday, arriving Swakopmund at 05.30 and departing at 20.35. Trains to Tsumeb depart on Mon, Wed and Fri at 18.05, and those to Walvis Bay depart at 02.35 on Tues, Thur, and Sat. See *Chapter 6*, pages 94–5, for details, or call the station in Swakopmund on tel: 064 463538.

The *Desert Express* is a completely different service, aimed primarily at visitors on holiday. It departs on Mon, Wed and Sat at 13.00 (14.00 in summer), arriving in Windhoek at about 10.00 the next day. All the cabins have air conditioning and en-suite facilities. It costs N\$1,080 per person sharing a twin cabin, including excursions, dinner and breakfast. See pages 95–6 for details, or call in at its office in the Swakopmund Hotel and Entertainment Centre.

By bus

Intercape Mainliner run a good service linking Windhoek and Walvis Bay, which stops at Swakopmund, at the Talk Shop on Roon Street. It departs for Walvis Bay at 10.35 on Mon, Wed, Fri and Sat. Then it returns to Windhoek on Mon, Wed, Fri and Sun at 12.10. It costs N$70 to Walvis Bay, and N$110 to Windhoek, and must be booked in advance. To book, contact Ritz Reise on 064 405151, or call Intercape direct on 061 227847, web: www.intercape.co.za. For more details, see *Chapter 6*, pages 96–9.

There is also a weekly bus service from Cape Town to Walvis Bay, via Swakopmund, run by Ekonolux. It leaves Swakopmund every Friday at 11.45, returning on Monday at 05.15. Fares are N$490 single, or N$880 return. For details, contact Talk Shop (see *Internet cafés* page 295), or tel: 064 205935; fax: 064 205978.

By car

For comments on the choice of roads from Swakopmund to Windhoek, see *Chapter 9*'s section *From Windhoek to the coast,* page 165. If you're taking the C28 or C26 then also see comments on the northern section of the Namib-Naukluft National Park, pages 271, 273. The long coastal road to the north is covered in the next chapter, *The Skeleton Coast.*

Getting around

Swakopmund's centre is so small that most visitors walk around it, though obviously you'll need a car to get out of the centre. Alternatively, the **Cycle Clinic** (tel: 402530), at 10 Roon Street, between the Hansa Hotel and Sam Nujoma Avenue, hires out bicycles for N$16.50 per hour, N$66 a day, or N$55 per day for 7 days or more. These range from mountain bikes to touring models. A deposit of N$200 is required.

If you're hiring a car on arrival, then all of the local **car-hire** companies will meet you at the airport. Their contact details are:

Avis at the Swakopmund Hotel and Entertainments Centre, PO Box 1403, Swakopmund; tel: 064 405792 or 402527; fax: 064 405881
Budget at Woerman and Brock supermarket, Moltke St; tel: 064 463380; fax: 064 404117
Into Namibia 1 Moltke St; tel: 064 464157; fax: 064 464158
Namib 4x4 Sam Nujoma Av; tel: 064 404100, cell: 081 124 2504; fax: 064 405277; pager: 405544
Odyssey Car Hire Sam Nujoma Av and Roon St; tel: 064 400871; fax: 064 403571
Triple Three Rentals Sam Nujoma Av; tel: 064 403190, cell: 081 1273331 or 081 127 8878; fax: 064 403191; email: oliver@iafrica.com.na; web: www.333.com.na

A word of warning for drivers It is not advisable to drive between Swakopmund and Walvis Bay late in the evening. Although the distance is short and the road good, it tends to be used as a race track by drink drivers, and there are frequent accidents.

Where to stay

When thinking about visiting Swakopmund, note that from about mid-December to mid-January, the whole population of Windhoek seems to decamp to the relative cool of Swakopmund for their 'summer break'. This means that the hotels and guesthouses are fully booked, and the town is filled to bursting. Reservations are essential. At other times, Swakopmund is not so frantic, though the better (and better value) hotels usually need reserving before you arrive.

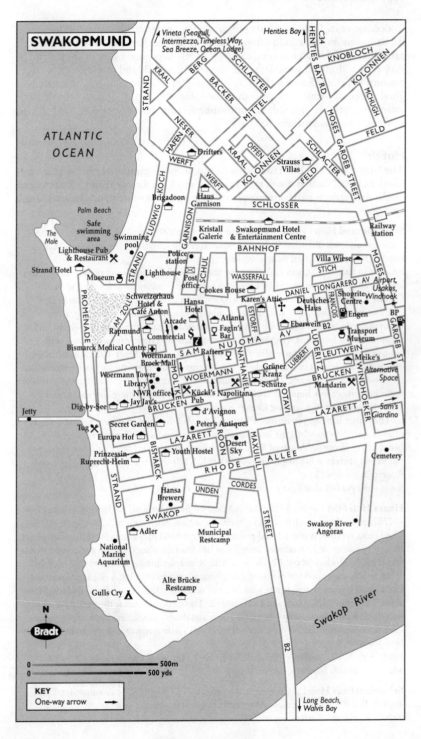

SWAKOPMUND

ATLANTIC OCEAN

↑ Vineta (Seagull, Intermezzo, Timeless Way, Sea Breeze, Ocean Lodge)

Henties Bay ↑

KNOBLOCH

HENTIES BAY RD
C34

KOLONNEN

MCHUGH

KRAAL

BERG

BACKER

SCHLACTER

MITTEL

NESER

OFFEN

MOSES GAROEB STREET

FELD

Drifters

KRAAL

KOLONNEN

Strauss Villas

WERFT

HAFEN

WERFT

SCHLACTER

FELD

Brigadoon

Haus Garnison

SCHLOSSER

LUDWIG

GARNISON

Kristall Galerie

Swakopmund Hotel & Entertainment Centre

Railway station

Palm Beach

The Mole

Safe swimming area

Swimming pool

BAHNHOF

Lighthouse Pub & Restaurant

Police station

Villa Wiese

STICH

MOSES

Strand Hotel

Museum

STRAND

Lighthouse

Post office

WASSERFALL

Airport, Usakos, Windhoek

Cookes House

SCHUL

DANIEL TJONGARERO AV

FRANCOIS

Shoprite Centre

BP

Karen's Attic

Deutsches Haus

AM ZOLL

Schweizerhaus Hotel & Café Anton

Hansa Hotel

Engen

PROMENADE

Arcade

Atlanta

ESTORFF

Eberwein

B2

Transport Museum

GAROEB ST

Rapmund

Commercial

Fagin's Bar

NUJOMA

AV

LUDERITZ

Bismarck Medical Centre

SAM

Rafters

NATHANIEL

LUBBERT

Meike's

LEUTWEIN

Woermann Brock Mall

WOERMANN

Grüner Kranz

BRUCKEN

Alternative Space

Woermann Tower

MOLTKE

Schütze

Mandarin

WINDHOEKER

Library

NWR office

Kücki's Pub

Napolitana

OTAVI

Sam's Giardino

Dig-by-See

Jay Jay's

BRUCKEN

d'Avignon

LAZARETT

Jetty

Tug

Secret Garden

Peter's Antiques

Desert Sky

Cemetery

Europa Hof

BISMARCK

LAZARETT

ROOD

Prinzessin-Ruprecht-Heim

Youth Hostel

RHODE

MAXUILILI

ALLEE

UNDEN

CORDES

STREET

Hansa Brewery

SWAKOP

Adler

Municipal Restcamp

Swakop River Angoras

National Marine Aquarium

Gulls Cry

Alte Brücke Restcamp

Swakop River

B2

N

Bradt

0 ————— 500m
0 ————— 500 yds

KEY
One-way arrow →

↓ Long Beach,
↓ Walvis Bay

Because of its cooling morning fogs, and the moderating maritime influence on its temperatures, air conditioning is seldom needed here and few of the hotels provide it. For the same reason, camping on the large, open sites by the sea can be very cold and uncomfortable, while the cheaper B&Bs and guesthouses are very reasonably priced. So even if you're camping for most of your trip, this may be a good place to treat yourself to a bed for the night. Below, the various establishments are divided, by atmosphere, into hotels, pensions and B&Bs, restcamps and backpackers' lodges.

Hotels

The large Hotel and Entertainments Centre is Swakopmund's only international-standard hotel, though if you're in search of any local flavour then look elsewhere. You'll find various basic, budget places, many small hotels full of character, and a few gems.

Swakopmund Hotel and Entertainments Centre (90 rooms) PO Box 616, Swakopmund; tel: 064 400800; fax: 064 400801; email: hrswakop@legacyhotels.co.za, hotels@legacyhotels.co.za; web: www.legacyhotels.co.za
Situated in Bahnhof St, and built from the shell of Swakopmund's old railway station, this leisure complex is now owned by Legacy Hotels. The complex includes the Mermaid Casino, a gymnasium, a hair salon and a reflexologist. Avis car hire is also situated here.
   Entering the huge lobby and passing reception, you emerge into a central grassy quadrangle, dominated by a pool. This is surrounded by palm trees and easy chairs, and surmounted by fountains. Overlooking the courtyard are brightly furnished and well-equipped rooms, which come with a tea/coffee maker, phone, Mnet TV, minibar/fridge, AC, and a safe deposit box as standard. The box may come in useful for your winnings at the casino, which has some 250 slot machines and 10 gaming tables. Fortunately, as this is often busy, it is a few hundred yards away – the hotel is having more success attracting local clientele than high-rolling foreign gamblers.
   The centre has two restaurants, Platform One and the Captain's Tavern. The former offers a varied menu while the latter specialises in seafood – the Captain's Platter (N$170) being a firm favourite. A special Sunday lunch is good value at N$55. At other times, you can expect starters at N$30–60, grills N$50, fish N$40–70 (grilled crayfish N$160), and desserts around N$20.
Rates: single N$740, double per person sharing N$590, including breakfast.

Hansa Hotel (58 rooms) 3 Roon St, PO Box 44, Swakopmund; tel: 064 400311; fax: 064 402732; email: hansa@iafrica.com.na; web: www.hansahotel.com.na
The Hansa is privately owned, and probably the best hotel in Swakopmund. It is fairly large, though has an intimate residents' lounge and bar, with fireplace for the winter, and a terrace area for light lunches (about N$45), as well as an award-winning restaurant (see page 291).
   Its rooms are a good size with solid furnishings, and feel old but well maintained and cared for. They are heated (there's no AC, nor need for it), and have direct-dial telephones, also a TV with CNN, Mnet and local stations. The garden rooms at the back have small fridges, and a few have ramps for easier access and disabled facilities. Eight of the rooms have balconies overlooking the garden. The Hansa's management is sharp, and the service here good.
Rates: single N$675, double N$895, suite N$1,150–1,540, special rates for children sharing with adults; all including breakfast.

Schweizerhaus Hotel (34 rooms) 1 Bismarck St, PO Box 445, Swakopmund; tel: 064 402419; fax: 064 405850; email: schweizerhaus@mweb.com.na; web: www.schweizerhaus.net

Above the genteel Café Anton, the Schweizerhaus has character and perhaps the best location of any of Swakopmund's hotels – overlooking the ocean and yet near to town. Its rooms are simple and German in style, with en-suite toilet, bath and shower, TV and direct-dial telephone. Most also have a balcony, including all of the luxury rooms which face the sea. Others overlook a courtyard at the back, home to free-flying parrots and various tropical birds.

The café below (see page 293) opens for extensive breakfasts and stays open until the mid-evening, and there's a night porter on duty if you arrive late. The staff are normally very friendly here, making the Schweizerhaus a good-value hotel option.
Rates: from single N$360, double N$560, including breakfast.

Strand Hotel (45 rooms) Beach Front, PO Box 20, Swakopmund; tel: 064 400315; fax: 064 404942; email: strandhotel@namibnet.com
Beside the Mole (see page 297) and the ocean, the Strand – now part of the Namib Sun Hotels group – is a large and ostentatious hotel, and the only one in Swakopmund so close to the sea. Its rooms all have Mnet TV, direct-dial phone, tea/coffee makers, ceiling fans, and baths with overhead showers. The larger ones have couches that will take two children, and interconnect as family rooms. Half face the sea, and half of those have balconies.

Downstairs is a lounge and bar, and the **Commodore Room**, which now caters for conferences. The adjacent **Werner's Restaurant** provides a varied menu which can be eaten on the terrace overlooking the Mole. Outside, the cheap-and-cheerful Strand Café is a busy open-air café serving burgers and snacks under parasols, and ice-creams to those on the adjacent beach.
Rates: single N$445, double N$590, suite N$780, including breakfast. Supplement for sea view N$50 per night.

Europa Hof Hotel (35 rooms) 39 Bismarck St (corner of Lazarett St), PO Box 1333, Swakopmund; tel: 064 405898, 405061 or 405061; fax: 064 402391; email: europa@iml-net.com.na
Built in the striking *fachwerk* style of German architecture – best described as 'Bavarian Tudor' – the Europa Hof is a very solid, imposing place. Its rooms are comfortable and carpeted, and furnished in quite an old, heavy style. All have twin beds, en-suite toilets and showers or baths, TV with Mnet, and direct-dial phone.

Behind the hotel is a large central courtyard, used for parking as well as open-air dining, under palm trees, at the hotel's restaurant (which closes at 22.00 on weekdays, and 21.30 at weekends). The menu follows traditional German lines, mainly offering game and fish> You can expect starters around N$30, and mains N$45–65 (crayfish N$170); there is also a children's menu. The Europa Hof is one of Swakopmund's more traditional, German-style hotels.
Rates: single N$391.30, double N$521.74, triple N$ 608.70, including breakfast. Children under 6 sharing are free.

Atlanta Hotel (16 rooms) 6 Roon St, PO Box 456; tel: 064 402360; fax: 064 405649
Between Sam Nujoma Av and Post St, the Atlanta Hotel is perhaps most noted for **Fagin's Bar** beneath it. It's simple and very central, with all its rooms having en-suite bathrooms, direct-dial phones, TVs and a tea/coffee tray.

The Atlanta does not have its own restaurant but the Blue Whale (see page 292) is conveniently situated next door and serves breakfast, lunch and dinner. If you're looking for somewhere inexpensive and central, perfect for forays into Swakopmund's nightlife, perhaps this is the place.
Rates: single N$280, double N$380, 3–5-bed N$420–620, excluding breakfast.

Dig By See Hotel (12 rooms) 4 Brücken St, PO Box 1530; tel: 064 404130; fax: 064 404170; email: stelgodl@iafrica.com.na
This small, inexpensive hotel is run by Stella and Manfred Godl and has been here for

years, near the promenade. Its rooms are basic but all have a bath, shower and TV, and the restaurant downstairs serves breakfasts, snacks and dinner on request. Lunch packets are also available for N$25. It's popular with a backpacking crowd treating themselves to a night that's not under canvas.
Rates: single N$180, double N$250, N$110 per person sharing a larger room, all including full breakfast.

Jay Jay's Hotel (12 rooms) 8 Brücken St, PO Box 835, Swakopmund; tel: 064 402909
Almost beside the Dig-By-Sea, Jay Jay's is another inexpensive old favourite, where the bar and pool table are seldom empty, and the atmosphere is always at least a little seedy. The rooms are very basic, though clean, and only some have private facilities. Again, this is very popular with backpackers and always a lively spot.
Rates: single (en-suite) N$65, single (shared bathroom) N$32 per person, double (en-suite) N$110, double (shared bathroom) N$65, family room (2 double bedrooms) N$240, N$25 per extra person. Breakfast N$16–23.

Hotel Grüner Kranz (21 twin rooms, 7 dorms) Nathaniel Maxuilili Av, PO Box 438, Swakopmund; tel: 064 402039; fax: 064 405016; email: swakoplodge@yahoo.com
In the centre of town, on the corner of Nathaniel Maxuilili Av and Woermann St, the Grüner Kranz is a very basic hotel despite the claims of its promising publicity leaflet. However, its rooms are relatively spacious and they have twin beds (with foam mattresses), TVs, telephones, and en-suite bathrooms with showers. There are also dormitories with 4–6 beds. The public areas, including the bar, are basic, though the place has a lively atmosphere. If you do stay here, then ask for a room far from the noisy generator. The Cape to Cairo restaurant (see page 292) is situated to the side of the hotel.
Rates: single N$200, double N$240, dorm bed N$40. Breakfast can be bought at the Crazy Corner Café next door for around N$25.

Hotel Eberwein (17 rooms), Sam Nujoma Av (corner of Otavi St), PO Box 2594, Swakopmund; tel: 064 463355; fax: 064 463354; email: eberwein@iafrica.com.na; web: www.eberwein.com.na
This former family house close to the centre of town was transformed into a privately owned hotel in December 1999. Its 16 double rooms and one single all have en-suite shower, TV, minibar, telephone and underfloor heating. They are clean and bright, with pastel pink a dominant theme, though some are Victorian in style. It is German in character, efficiently run and with friendly staff. Although the restaurant does not normally serve evening meals, these can be arranged in advance for groups of more than ten people.
Rates: single N$455, double N$665, triple N$765, Victorian rooms N$520–800, all including breakfast. Special rates for children.

Pensions and B&Bs
If you don't need the facilities of a larger hotel, then several of these smaller pensions and B&Bs are both delightful and superb value.

Meike's Guesthouse (4 rooms) Windhuker St, PO Box 2858, Swakopmund; tel: 064 405863; fax: 064 405862; email: meike@natron.net; web: www.natron.net/meikesguesthouse/
This new guesthouse opened in August 2001 in a bright, modern building, about five minutes' walk from the centre of town. You can be guaranteed a warm welcome from Meike, who used to run Ababis Guest Farm in the Naukluft Mountains, but has now opened up her family home for the use of guests.
   The rooms are simple and tastefully decorated, all with en-suite shower, TV, telephone, fridge and a small terrace in front. One room comprises a family unit of 3 beds. This is very much a personal B&B run on traditional lines.
Rates: N$180 per person, including breakfast.

Hotel Adler (14 rooms) 3 Strand St, PO Box 1497; tel: 064 405045/6/7; fax: 064 404206; email: adler@iafrica.com.na; web: www.natron.net/tour/adler/hoteld.htm
Opposite the aquarium, and just 50m from the sea, Hotel Adler is a modern, stylish pension designed with space, taste and good facilities. All the recently redecorated rooms are slightly different, but expect en-suite toilet and bath with hand-held shower, remote-control satellite TV, phone, clock/radio, and hairdryer.
    Breakfast is taken in a simple breakfast area, or outside in the airy courtyard, while above is a rooftop sun-terrace. Parking is secure, and garages are available at N$30 per day. A highlight here is the heated indoor pool, and a sauna (booked on a private basis for N$40 per person), plus a couple of exercise machines. Massages are available from N$125.
Rates: single N$375, double N$560, including breakfast.

Pension Rapmund (25 rooms) 6–8 Bismarck St, PO Box 425, Swakopmund; tel: 064 402035; fax: 064 404524; email: rapmund@iafrica.com.na
Standing beside the Schweizerhaus (Café Anton) on Bismarck St, overlooking the promenade, the old-style Rapmund has clean and simple twin rooms, four of which overlook the sea, and each with en-suite shower. Furnishing is a little stark, but Sonja Muller, who has just taken over the reins from her family, has plans to refurbish. Meanwhile, the Rapmund is friendly, central and relatively cheap, so good value for money.
Rates: single N$195.50–218.50, double N$310.50–333.50, triple N$402.50, including breakfast. No credit cards.

Pension Prinzessin-Ruprecht-Heim (21 rooms) 15 Lazarett St, PO Box 124, Swakopmund; tel: 064 402231; fax: 064 402019; email: reservation@prinzrupp.com.na, info@prinzrupp.com.na; web: www.prinzrupp.com.na
On Lazarett St, just west of Bismarck St, this was originally a German military hospital. The oldest of its buildings, at the front, has enormous rooms with high ceilings, accessed via wide old doors. Most have showers and toilets en suite. The pension's newer rooms at the back have a bath/shower instead of just a shower, but are of more normal dimensions and so lack the character of the older rooms.
    In the pension's centre is a large courtyard, dotted with palm trees and places to sit. You may have to seek out the manager here by going around the right-hand side of the pension when you arrive.
Rates: single N$180, double N$165–175; a small single room (sharing bathroom) is only N$110, including breakfast.

Sam's Giardino (9 rooms) 89 Lazarett St, Kramersdorf, PO Box 1401, Swakopmund; tel: 064 403210; fax: 064 403500; email: samsart@iafrica.com.na: web: www.giardino.com.na or www.samsgiardino.com
This charming Swiss-run B&B on the outskirts of Swakopmund is in a quiet residential area, just 10–15 minutes' walk to the centre of town. The emphasis here is very much on individual attention. High-ceilinged rooms are simple and airy, with pine-clad ceilings and furniture to match, plus en-suite shower, telephone and hairdryer. There is also a deluxe suite, with bath and shower and views over the dunes as well as the garden. Almost all the other rooms overlook the well-kept garden that gives the pension its name. It is here that Sam Eggar's canine aide-de-camp, formally known as Mr Einstein, holds court, posing regally for photographers on the bridge over the fishpond. There is secure parking and a security guard on duty at night.
    Indoors, expect candles and Wagner for breakfast, with real Swiss muesli and the warmth of an open fire to offset Swakopmund's famed morning mists. There are books aplenty, and a TV lounge with a selection of natural history videos. In the evenings, Sam will lay on a five-course meal (N$115 per person) with the help of local staff whom he has trained in European cuisine and service. But his real passion is for wine. Ask to take

part in a wine tasting and you'll find yourself surrounded by South African wines of every style in a small, purpose-built *enoteca*, or 'wine restaurant'. With a selection of 70 reds and 40 whites on offer, there's plenty of choice – and the relaxed atmosphere that makes wine tasting so pleasurable. And to round off the occasion, ask Sam about his cigars. This is a highly individual pension that would appeal to anyone seeking an oasis of calm and relaxation.

Rates: single N$540; double N$640, suite N$740, all including Swiss breakfast.

Brigadoon (4 cottages) 16 Ludwig Koch St, Swakopmund; tel: 064 406064; fax: 064 464195; email: brigadon@iafrica.com.na; web: www.wheretostay.co.za/brigadoon.htm
Quite close to the town centre, near the swimming pool and the Entertainment Centre, Brigadoon is run by the welcoming Bruce and Bubble Burns – of Scottish descent, if you haven't guessed. It has just four Victorian-style cottages, individually furnished with traditional wooden chests and wardrobes, and fronted by small gardens. Each cottage has a shower/toilet, a fully equipped kitchen and TV, and is serviced daily (laundry service is possible). There are also a further three en-suite rooms in the main house, but these lack the kitchen, though they do have a toaster and kettle. There is secure parking, too, for extra peace of mind. With the emphasis on privacy and a central location, this makes an excellent place to stay.

Rates: single N$360, double N$420, including breakfast.

Haus Garnison (4 apartments, 7 rooms) 4 Garnison St, PO Box 2188, Swakopmund; tel/fax: 064 403340; cell: 081 124 3340; email: garni@iafrica.com.na
Inland from Brigadoon, and north of the centre, Garnison is on the right of the main road towards Henties Bay. It boasts luxury apartments that cater more towards long-term, self-catering visitors than casual 'drop-ins'. Garage facilities are available for some apartments. When last visited, the reception was abrupt and unhelpful.

Rates: single N$195, per person sharing N$175, triple N$400, family room N$450. Breakfast N$25.

Hotel Schütze (7 rooms) Breite St, PO Box 634, Swakopmund; tel/fax: 064 402718
Next to Grüner Kranz, this is a very traditional hotel (all rooms with en-suite shower), with an uninviting bar that seems to attract some of the less liberal members of Swakopmund's white community. It can't be recommended for anything apart from curiosity value.

Rates: N$130 single, N$250 double. No breakfast.

Hotel-Pension d'Avignon (10 rooms) 25 Brücken St, PO Box 1222, Swakopmund; tel: 064 405821; fax: 064 405542; email: hotel.davignon@iafrica.com.na
Between Moltke and Roon streets, Hotel-Pension d'Avignon focuses so clearly on German visitors that others may find the welcome here much less than warm. For those who do stay here, there's a small pool at the back, and a TV lounge with tea and coffee. Its rooms are clean but unremarkable, with en-suite showers.

Rates: single N$190, double N$295, triple N$395, including breakfast.

Sea Breeze (5 rooms, 4 self-catering flats) Turmalin St, PO Box 2601, Swakopmund; tel: 064 463348; fax: 064 463349; email: seabre@iafrica.com.na; web: www.seabreeze.com.na
Overlooking the beach, this new pension reflects the pride of its Italian owners, Oscar Malaman and Giancarlo Ladurini. To get here, follow the beach road north towards Veneta along the Strand. The road becomes 1st Av, then eventually Fischreier; turn left into Turmalin St, and Sea Breeze is on the left by the beach. It's about 4.5km from the centre of town, which represents a 30-minute stroll along the beach, or a N$10 taxi ride.

Individual rooms are simple and tastefully decorated, with en-suite shower and/or bath. The permutations here are seemingly endless. Four of the rooms have sea view at no extra charge, so it's well worth checking what's available. Two others are in the owners' house next door, with softer décor and a shaded patio area overlooking the garden. Flats have a bedroom, lounge/kitchenette with TV, bathroom and balcony over the beach; some have up to five beds, and two have heating. The family room has no view, but four beds and a kitchenette. There's even a honeymoon suite with two bathrooms and sea view.

Outside, there is secure parking, and garage spaces for up to five vehicles at no extra charge. *Rates: single N$220, double N$400, including breakfast; family room N$250–350, without breakfast. English breakfast N$40 per person.*

Beach Lodge (16 rooms) Stint St, PO Box 79, Swakopmund; tel: 064 400933; fax: 064 400934; email: beach@iafrica.com.na; web: www.natron.net/tour/belo/main/html
The architects have excelled themselves here! Each room forms part of a boat-shaped building that occupies a stunning site right on the beach. Located 5km from town, Beach Lodge is just beyond Sea Breeze (see above). Continue past Sea Breeze and follow the road to the yellow house, then turn left into Rosequartz St, left into Plover St and left again into Stint St.

Light, airy and stylish, rooms all have en-suite shower and/or bath, with sliding doors on to a patio or a private balcony area, TV and direct-dial phone. The breakfast room follows the nautical theme with large porthole windows looking out to sea, and African music plays softly in the background. The atmosphere is one of shipshape efficiency rather than personal care, so it's well suited to those seeking absolute privacy and relaxation. *Rates: single N$350, double N$450, triple N$600, quadruple N$700. Breakfast N$25.*

Seagull B&B (5 rooms) 60 Strand St North, Swakopmund; tel: 064 405278; fax: 064 407141; email: seagullbandb@iafrica.com.na; web: www.seagullbandb.com.na
Very much a home from home, this rather idiosyncratic guesthouse just a few minutes' walk from the town centre is run by Cumbrian-born owner, Keith. It's easy to find – just follow the Strand north out of Swakopmund and it's the first bed-and-breakfast accommodation you come to on the right.

The aim here is quite straightforward: every guest has different needs, and Keith aims to cater for them all. From the grandeur of a king-size bed, with opulent décor to match, to English country chintz and primary colours for the kids, each room is totally individual. Smaller, economy rooms have two or four beds; another has its own garden shared with three tortoises. Each, however, has an en-suite shower and/or hip bath, and most have a private entrance on to a central courtyard area. 24-hour security adds to the sense of privacy. *Rates: single N$140–220, double N$200–340; breakfast N$20–30. Single night surcharge N$25 per room.*

Secret Garden Guesthouse (7 rooms) 36 Bismarck St, PO Box 2609, Swakopmund; tel/fax: 064 404037; email: secretgarden@iway.na; web: http://natron.net/tour/secretgarden
Just 500m from the beach, and close to the centre of town, this attractive, terracotta-painted guesthouse is just opposite the Europa Hof. Each of the en-suite rooms looks over the palm-shaded garden courtyard that gives the guesthouse its name. In addition to a TV lounge, there's a licensed bar and, for independent visitors, self-catering facilities and a barbecue are provided. Secure parking is available, as well as lock-up garages. Transfers to and from the airport and station are offered free of charge. *Rates: single N$260, double N$360, triple N$460, including breakfast.*

Timeless Way (3 rooms) 5 Harder St, PO Box 1140, Swakopmund; tel: 064 400126, cell: 081 242 6882; fax: 064 400138; email: 1timeless@iway.na
Although well advertised, the Timeless Way was not terribly welcoming when we visited. About 4km from town along the Strand, turn right into Harder St just off Fischreier.

Rooms are dark and cramped, if reasonably well appointed; each has en-suite shower, TV, phone and kitchenette, as well as a terrace with barbecue.
Rates: single N$200, double N$300.

Strauss Holiday Villas (6 flats) 10 Feld St; tel: 081 127 5399, 081 124 4937; fax: 064 463699; email: straussholidays@iway.na
This bright pink complex at the eastern end of Feld St is clearly signposted from Moses Garoeb St. Each of the flats has one or two bedrooms, plus a lounge, kitchen and bath or shower.

Italianate in design, the tree-shaded garden has small statues, and stone benches and tables are placed outside each room. Dinner is available on request, and there is off-street parking. The formality stretches to the welcome, which could be termed offhand.
Rates: single N$200–220, double N$280–340, extra person N$95. Breakfast N$30.

Deutches Haus (20 rooms), 13 Lüderitz St, PO Box 13, Swakopmund; tel: 064 404896; fax: 064 404861; email: deuhaus@meb.com.na; web: www.deutches-haus-swakopmund.com
This privately run hotel is in a quieter part of town and includes a sauna and a solar-heated swimming pool. The rooms are simply decorated but all have telephone, TV and en-suite bathroom or shower. Lunches are available in the small but functional dining room at N$17.50–30. The staff here are polite and efficient.
Rates: single N$275, double N$395, inclusive of breakfast.

Intermezzo (6 rooms) 9 Dolphin St, PO Box 2782, Swakopmund; tel: 064 464114, cell: 081 129 8297; fax: 064 407099; email: intermezzo@iway.na; web: http://swakop.com/intermezzo
About 15 minutes' walk from the town centre, or two minutes by car, this ultra-modern pension is run by Christa Bertram. To get here, follow the Strand north from town, go over the roundabout, and take the second on the right.

Echoing marble floors in passages and bathrooms are offset by carpet in some rooms, with rather incongruous touches provided by artificial flowers and prints of Old Masters. Simple en-suite rooms feature white bedding and light wooden furniture; facilities include TV, phone, and kettle with coffee/tea, while some also have a small balcony. There is also a big family suite with two bedrooms and a lounge area. For a sea view, though, you'll need to adjourn to the light, airy, breakfast area.
Rates: single N$230, double N$380, including breakfast.

Hotel Burg Nonidas PO Box 1423, Swakopmund; tel/fax: 064 400384; email: nonidas@namibnet.com
11km from Swakopmund on the B6, Nonidas Castle used to be a German police station, and remains something of a landmark when seen from the road. Now a German-run hotel, it has suffered from frequent changes of management, though its desert setting makes it popular for local weddings.
Rates: single N$130, double N$250, honeymoon suite/family room N$350, including breakfast..

Additional places that may be worth considering are as follows:

Charlotte's Guest Home (5 rooms) 121 Brücken St, PO Box 943, Swakopmund; tel/fax: 064 405454; email: noltesaf@iafrica.com.na
Haus Kölner Hof (10 rooms) 7 Dünen St, PO Box 2418, Swakopmund; tel: 064 404350; fax: 407240; email: worms@iafric;com.na

Smaller guesthouses

Cooke's House (3 rooms) 32 Daniel Tjongarero Av, PO Box 2628; tel: 064 462837, cell: 081 240 2088; fax: 064 462839; email: cooksb.b@mweb.com.na
Visitors to this comfortable, well-furnished bed and breakfast are very much house guests

of owners Darrell and Hannelore. Two of the pretty bedrooms share a bathroom; the third is en suite. There is secure parking, and guests have use of the garden.
Rates: from single N$160, double N$240, including German breakfast.

Restcamps

If you want your own self-catering facilities then there are three restcamps around Swakopmund, all very different. See also those which are south of here, around Walvis Bay, page 301.

El Jada Restcamp (5 apartments) PO Box 1155, Swakopmund; tel/fax: 064 400348; email: seagull@iafrica.com.na
About 12km from Swakopmund, on the D1901 (just south of the B2), El Jada is beside the Swakop River and the northern boundary of the Namib-Naukluft National Park. It promises 'German hospitality' and has serviced self-catering apartments, with en-suite toilets and showers, supplied with crockery and cutlery. Breakfast is available. The place is quiet and quite isolated, despite its proximity to Swakopmund, and birdwatching hikes along the Swakop River Valley are an attraction.
Rates: single N$150, double N$220, triple N$300.

Swakopmund Municipal Restcamp (200 chalets) Head of Tourism, Municipality of Swakopmund, P Bag 5017; tel: 064 402807/8; fax: 064 404212; email: swkmun@swk.namib.com; web: www.swakopmund-restcamp.com
On the north side of the road that crosses the Swakop River to Walvis Bay, this huge old restcamp is quite an institution. Within a large electric fence lie some 200 chalets and bungalows, all packed closely together. These vary from tiny fisherman's cabins, whose cramped beds in minute rooms have changed little in the last decade, to luxury VIP flats with modern décor and bright pastel colours. Each chalet has a telephone.

There's a rolling programme of modernising the restcamp, which at present supplies linen but not towels. The flats are fine and simple, with the luxury flats being larger, but otherwise similar. The A-frame chalets have a much more interesting design, and their wooden construction is warmer in the winter than the others – though all the beds in these are singles. All are good value, provided you don't mind getting lost in the maze of other identical chalets whilst you search for your own. When arriving, note that the office is open Mon–Fri 07.30-16.00, and Sat/Sun 07.30–11.00.
Rates: Working out the costs for these is an art, but in general the following applies: 2-bed N$110; 4-bed N$185–215; 'A' frame to VIP resthouses N$320–435. Key deposit N$100–200.

Alte Brücke Restcamp (23 chalets, 8 camping pitches) PO Box 3360, Vineta; tel: 064 404918; fax: 064 400153; email: accomod@iml-net.com.na; web: www.geocities.com/altebrucke
At the southern end of the Strand, by the Swakop River's mouth, Alte Brücke has been open since around 1992 – an upmarket version of the nearby municipal restcamp, which is also surrounded by a vicious electric fence.

The chalets here are all large, the majority with two bedrooms (two beds in each) and a bed-settee, which will take two small children. Thus they could sleep a family in each. Each has a bath/shower room, a separate toilet, and a large open-plan lounge/kitchen with Mnet TV, telephone, linen and towels.

The kitchen has cutlery, crockery and glassware, ironing board, iron, toaster, kettle, microwave, electric stove, fridge/freezer and a separate minibar – making these into comprehensively equipped little holiday homes.

There is also a spacious camping area with adequate facilities, including electricity. Maximum 6 people per site.
Rates: single N$285, two sharing N$210 per person, 3/4 adults N$169–189 per person. Children (aged 2–16) sharing N$95 each. Camping: N$150 per night (1-2 persons); additional N$50 for 3 or more people; N$25 extra for children 5-12.

Backpackers' lodges

With good transport connections, and an exploding line in adventure sports, Swakopmund is well positioned to become Namibia's backpacking capital. However, a wide choice of B&Bs and cheap hotels means few dedicated backpackers' places, a situation not helped by the municipality's strict rules on licensing. Those currently around include:

Desert Sky (13 dorm beds, 3 double rooms, camping) 35 Lazarett St, PO Box 2830, Swakopmund; tel: 064 402339, cell: 081 248 7771; email: dsbackpackers@swakop.com; web: www.swakop.com/dsb
Opened in 2001, this centrally located backpackers' hostel not far from the beach is already one of the most popular venues in town, and it's easy to see why. Manager Lofty is welcoming and helpful, the atmosphere is friendly, and facilities are good. In addition to clean, cheerful dormitories and private rooms, there is a fully equipped kitchen, storage lockers, safe, plus central coffee and tea area, pool room, TV lounge, bar and a small balcony. Internet facilities cost N$15 for ½ hour, and a laundry service is available. Outside is safe parking and a grassed area for tents. If you're after action, Lofty is the last word in the best activities around and the best people to contact.
Rates: dorm bed N$50, double (3 beds) N$120–140, camping N$40 per person.

Villa Wiese (32 dorm beds, 10 double rooms) corner of Bahnhof and Windhoeker streets, PO Box 2460, Swakopmund; tel/fax: 064 407105; email: villawiese@compuscan.co.za
This colourful old building on the outskirts of town is named after the German who built it in 1905. Now owned by Tinkie and Johan, the place was completely renovated in 2002 to give a roomy and friendly backpackers' lodge with self-catering kitchen, large upstairs bar area, internet facilities and a safe for valuables. Each dormitory has 8 beds on two levels, and its own shower and separate toilet, while double rooms are all en suite. Outside there's a barbecue in a pleasant courtyard, and secure parking.
Rates: dorm bed N$45, double N$120; breakfast extra.

Youth Hostel (60 beds) Lazarett St, P Bag 5023, Swakopmund; tel: 064 404164; fax: 064 405373
Situated diagonally opposite the Europa Hof, the government-run youth hostel is very basic and is limited to travellers aged between 15 and 30, who are housed in separate male and female dormitories in a grand old barracks building. No food is served. The office opens Mon–Fri 07.00–13.00 and 14.00–18.00, Sat 07.00–13.00, 15.00–17.00, Sundays and holidays 07.00–13.00.
Rates: N$15 per person camping, dorms N$20 per person under 18, N$30 over 18, double room (en suite) N$80 per room.

Karen's Attic (36 dorm beds) 37 Daniel Tjongarero Av (corner of Otavi St); tel: 064 402707; email: kattic@iafrica.com.na
This relatively new backpackers' place, although central, is in a quieter part of town, and comes with a good reputation; unfortunately, we weren't allowed in to have a look. The response to a phone call was friendly enough, though. Two kitchens are available with usual facilities.
Rates: dorm bed N$55 per person.

Drifter's Inn (12 rooms) 6 Werft St (corner of Mittel), PO Box 2612; tel/fax: 064 462386; cell: 081 2487751; web: www.drifters.com.za
The central location of this place makes it an attractive accommodation option, but at weekends it's occupied by group tours from South Africa. Individuals may stay during the week, though it doesn't seem particularly welcoming. Facilities include kitchen, laundry and barbecue.
Rates: single N$250, double N$360, including breakfast.

The (Alternative) Space (15 beds) 67 Lazarett St (corner of Alfons Weber St), PO Box 1388, Swakopmund; tel: 064 402713; email: nam00352@mweb.com.na
The Space is found by following Lazarett St beyond Aukas, about 15 minutes' walk due east of the centre of town. Strictly speaking, because of the municipality's business rules, Alternative Space is not officially a guesthouse. However, for the last six years, its easy-going owner, Frenus, has been happy to have friends to stay in his distinctly offbeat family home, with use of ingeniously created accommodation that includes double and triple rooms, inside and outside kitchens, a laundry – and an open-air, candlelit shower that resembles the best of 'Heath Robinson'.

The place has a great, relaxed atmosphere, with music, a bar and access to a wide-ranging music collection. Frenus will happily run you into and out of town (free) if you ask.

Rates: dorm bed N$40, double N$150, triple N$200, including breakfast.

Camping
Gull's Cry (40 pitches, max 5 people per site) The Strand, PO Box 1496, Swakopmund; cell: 081 244 0037, 081 246 6774; email: rdowning@iafrica.com.na
Swakopmund's recently opened campsite has a prime position close to the sea at the southern end of town, near the aquarium, and boasts a bird lagoon with over 60 different species. Owned by brother and sister Richard and Nadine, the site is protected by a discreet electric fence and has 24-hour surveillance, ensuring the safety of visitors. There are ambitious plans for the construction of a boardwalk and a tented camp among the trees. At the moment, though, this spacious site offers a pretty rustic setting, with limited and very basic washing and toilet facilities.

The simple, rustic restaurant on site is completely al fresco, so bring a warm jacket in the winter months. The emphasis is on seafood, all cooked to order on open fires with fresh-baked bread, and meat and vegetables also available. Prices are around N$80 per person (minimum ten diners), and there is a licensed bar. Booking is essential.

Rates: N$80 per person + N$10 entry permit; electricity N$15 per visit. Special rates for groups over 15 people.

Where to eat and drink
Restaurants
Hansa Hotel 3 Roon St, Swakopmund; tel: 064 400311; fax: 064 402732
The Hansa Hotel (see page 282) has an award-winning European restaurant serving stylish, elaborate and quite heavy cuisine – using of lots of sauces – in quite formal surroundings. It majors on seafood, though has a good range of steaks and one or two vegetarian dishes. Expect starters at about N$30–55, main courses for N$55–90, and desserts for N$20–30. Its selection of South African wines is also impressive, with bottles averaging around N$80–100 each, and some good vineyards.

Strand Hotel Beach Front, Swakopmund; tel: 064 400315; fax: 064 404942
Beside the sea, the Strand's Werner Restaurant serves à la carte seafood in season, with the choice of eating on the terrace or inside. There is a special lunch menu at about N$30. Otherwise, expect starters to be around N$25–30, mains N$30–75, and desserts N$15–20. To the side is the much less stuffy Strand Café, which offers ice-creams and burgers by the beach.

The Tug The Strand, Swakopmund; tel: 064 402356; fax: 064 402356
Perhaps the most interesting place to eat in town, The Tug is just that – an old tug raised up above the seafront next to the old jetty. Inside, the tabletops have been individually painted by different artists, and underneath is a very arty gift/curio shop (though much of its stock is imported, it is an outlet for crafts from the Nyae Nyae Development Project). The terrace is a great place to watch the surf as the sun goes down.

The food is amongst the best in town and majors on seafood, in a style that's lighter and less traditional than the restaurants of the Hansa or Strand. The wines here are undistinguished and a little expensive, at up to N$60, but the place is always full and bookings are essential. It's open every evening, but at weekends only for lunch. *Costs: starters N$12–29, large salad N$18, mains N$40–66 (seafood up to N$150).*

Diggers Restaurant Woermann Brock complex, Sam Nujoma Av
Boasts the 'best pizzas in town', but also serves pasta, burgers and steaks.

Western Saloon 8 Moltke St; tel: 064 405395
Lively and popular, this small, crowded restaurant is not a place for a quiet evening *à deux*. The menu offers plenty of fish and game, with prices on a par with similar establishments in the town.

Kücki's 22 Moltke St; tel: 064 402407, cell: 081 128 2407; email: kuecki@mweb.com.na
One of the best places in town, Kücki's has a lively atmosphere and serves very good food. It is German in character, though there are always visitors around. Kücki's shellfish is excellent, and its service is friendly. Renovated in 2001, the restaurant is now completely enclosed, with tables situated on the ground floor and on a surrounding balcony area. Expect starters to be around N$30, main courses N$40–50 and desserts N$20. Do book in advance, as it's often full.

Lighthouse Pub & Restaurant Pool Terrace, Main Beach; tel: 064 400894
Good for sundowners overlooking the sea, the large restaurant here adjoins an equally large bar. The pub is open all day, while the restaurant serves lunch 11.30–14.30 and dinner 18.30–22.30. You can eat outside on the wooden terrace with magnificent seaviews, or there are tables inside for cooler periods. You can pay from as little as N$25 to N$170 for the much-vaunted seafood platter. Charcoal grills and burgers are also available.

Napolitana 33 Nathaniel Maxuilili St; tel: 064 402773
Opposite the Grüner Kranz, this small, quiet restaurant serves a variety of simple Italian dishes, including pizza, for around N$30–50 each. It's neither as trendy nor as busy as many of the places around, but the service is friendly.

Cape to Cairo Nathaniel Maxuilili St; tel: 064 463160
As the name suggests, the restaurant upstairs at the Grüner Kranz serves traditional African food – although with a Western twist – from an assortment of countries. Very popular with backpackers. Open daily 18.00–22.30.

Blue Whale Street Café 3 Roon St; tel: 064 405777; email: bluewhale@iway.na
Formerly part of the Atlanta Hotel, and located next to it, this café is now privately run and opens 07.30–14.30 and 18.00–23.00 for breakfast and evening meals. The menu is simple with plenty of seafood and 'blackboard' specials on most days. *Costs: starters N$15–25, mains N$40–50.*

Mandarin Garden Chinese 27 Brücken St, PO Box 258; tel: 064 402081, 405257
Reputedly good Chinese food, at least by Namibian standards, but rather expensive with meals around N$100 per person. Takeaway service available.

Erich's Restaurant 21 Daniel Tjongarero Av; tel: 064 405141
Rather dull décor and a stone-flagged floor contrast with the formal service at this centrally located restaurant. The menu, though, is generally innovative, and there is a good selection of vegetarian dishes. Regarded as *the* place for well-presented fish in Swakopmund (crayfish N$195), provided you're not put off by the piped music. Closed Sunday. *Costs: starters N$12–25, main dishes around N$40–60.*

De Kelder Klimas Shopping Arcade, 10 Moltke St; tel: 064 402433
In a very uninspiring setting, hidden at the back of a concrete shopping arcade, De Kelder serves some of the best food around, including interesting options such as boboti, some innovative vegetarian dishes, and that rarity, properly cooked vegetables. The atmosphere is almost traditional Afrikaans, quite formal but with no frills.
Costs: starters N$20–30, vegetarian dishes N$25–35, mains N$30–65 (crayfish N$110).

Zur Kupferpfanne 13 Garnison St; tel: 064 405405
This relatively new restaurant, with plain wooden tables set out close together, started with a bang, but its reputation since has been patchy and prices are on the high side. The German-style menu is extensive, with numerous daily specials, so there's plenty of choice. Closed Mondays.
Costs: expect about N$70 for a main course.

Brauhaus
Tucked into The Arcade in the centre of town, this easy-going restaurant is very popular for both lunch and dinner. Although it's reputed to serve good seafood, the meat here is generally a better bet.
Costs: starters N$15–25, mains about N$40–60.

Tiffany Café Brücken St; tel: 064 463655
Despite the name, and the cottage-garden décor, this is actually a fully fledged German restaurant, with separate bar. Tiffany's specialises in fresh fish, including a fish fondue at N$94. Closed Monday.
Costs: starters N$15–38, mains N$32–55 (more for crayfish and oysters).

Papa's Pizzeria Shoprite Centre, Sam Nujoma Av; tel: 064 404747
Well off the beaten track, Papa's is Swiss owned, simple and friendly, with good pizzas as well as salads and burgers. There's a takeaway and delivery service as well. Closed Monday.

Zur Weinmaus Bahnhof St; tel: 064 400098
Just along the road from the Schweizerhaus, this German restaurant with its small, dark bar is open evenings only, with a limited menu.
Costs: starter N$16–36, main N$30–54.

Cafés and lights meals

Café Anton (at the Schweizerhaus Hotel) 1 Bismarck St; tel: 064 402419
Overlooking the Mole and the ocean, the café opens for extensive breakfasts, and stays open until the mid-evening – though it's really more of a place for morning coffee or afternoon tea. There are tables outside, under the palm trees, and often a small curio market just below. Inside the atmosphere is genteel – perfect for reading a book or relaxing, with an excellent range of cakes and pastries, and very good coffee.

Café Treffpunkt Sam Nujoma; tel: 064 461782
Opposite the Commercial Bank, this bakery and cake shop is also open at lunchtimes for sandwiches and light meals; it has a good selection of ice-creams, too.

La Marquise The Arcade; tel: 064 463454
This brightly painted French crêperie with pavement tables adjoins a small art gallery. The menu offers some interesting twists on traditional pancakes. Crêpes around N$20 each; beer N$5.

Palm's Way Near Café Anton, and overlooking the lighthouse and craft area, this is a small café serving light snacks.

Pandora's Box Sam Nujoma Av; tel: 064 403545
This small gift shop in the attractive new Ankerplatz centre off Sam Nujoma Av also serves snacks and light meals, including potato pancakes every Friday from 12.00.

Fast food

In addition to the ubiquitous **KFC**, there are a couple of branches of **Wurstbude** in town. The one next to the Municipal Restcamp (tel: 064 405562) has a broader menu than might at first appear, serving everything from pizzas at N$30 to steaks and fish. There's even a restaurant and beer garden which can be accessed from the restcamp itself. The second branch, at Vineta (tel: 064 405345) is just a takeaway. For pizzas, try the **Pizzeria** on 8 Moltke St (tel: 064 405395), which is open evenings only, to eat in or takeaway, or Papa's (see above).

Entertainment and nightlife

Swakopmund has surprisingly lively nightlife, especially in the summer holiday season, although many travellers just have a few drinks in their hotel bar before retiring to bed. Then, around Christmas and New Year, many of Windhoek's more affluent residents arrive at their cool seaside cottages, intent on fishing by day and partying by night. If you're just looking for somewhere for a sundowner, try the bar at The Tug, or the Lighthouse. The 'in' places for evenings out change with the tides, so ask around for what's in fashion, but meanwhile a few favourites are:

Rafters Action Pub (formerly **Frontiers** Restaurant) 18 Moltke St; tel: 064 404171
Next to the First National Bank, on the corner of Moltke and Woermann streets, Rafters is a lively venue, popular with tour groups. The pub is open from 16.00 till late and you can buy oysters over the bar for N$40.

Fagin's Bar 6 Roon St, tel: 064 402360; fax: 064 405649
A favourite watering hole for travellers and locals alike, Fagin's does not serve food, though it can be ordered from the Blue Whale Café. Most people just come to drink in its friendly, cosmopolitan atmosphere. It's a firm fixture on the itinerary of most overlanders. Fagin's main nights are Thursday, Friday and Saturday, when it will stay open until around 02.00. Like the rest of town, it can be very, very quiet on Sundays and Mondays.

O'Kelly's Pub Roon St, near the post office
Next to Fagin's, and downstairs in the basement, this poorly signposted bar has no food but a good dancefloor. Many Fagin's customers move here when it closes, as O'Kelly's stays open after 02.00.

Night Fever If you've survived Fagin's, outlasted O'Kelly's, and want to dance through to the morning, then try the upstairs bar/pool and disco at Grüner Kranz. This will often stay open until 04.30, though the average age of its clientele has earned it a local nickname of 'Kiddie Kranz'.

Away from the centre of town, there are a few other possibilities, though you'd be well advised to go by taxi with someone who knows the area. **Club Oxygen** is at the junction of Louis Botha and Henties Bay roads, as you head north out of Swakopmund. Nearby, on Moses Garoeb St, and close to Villa Wiese, is the **African Café & Bar** – a no-frills establishment that's open Wednesday, Friday and Saturday evenings. **Café Mocca 2000** next door looks as if it's been cloned from the same place, and offers regular live entertainment.

There's also a **cinema** in The Arcade off Sam Nujoma Avenue, with tickets at approximately N$20 (before 19.00, under 10s and over 60s are N$15). In the foyer is the Caturra bar (tel: 064 488710, open 09.00–19.00, Mon–Sat) where lunchtime specials cost around N$25.

If you're in Swakopmund over a holiday weekend, you may be lucky enough to get an impromptu concert from local schoolchildren in one of the shopping areas such as Ankerplatz. For a musical evening, check to see if there's anything happening at the **Hotel and Entertainments Centre** (page 282), or at one of the other two venues which regularly present concerts:

Namib Primary School PO Box 5012, Swakopmund; tel: 064 405028; fax: 064 405029
Haus der Jugend – Deutsche Evangelisches Luthern Gemeinde c/o Mr Schier, PO Box 9, Swakopmund; tel: 064 402874

Getting organised
In an emergency, the police are reached on tel: 064 10111, whilst the ambulance and hospital are on 064 405731, the fire service is on 064 402411/205544/405613(a/h)/404230(a/h), and if you need any sea rescue services then call 064 462041 or 405544 or the police – which is also the emergency number to use if you can't get through anywhere else. For less serious illness, there's the Bismarck Medical Centre at 17 Sam Nujoma Avenue, tel: 064 405000/405001.

There are plenty of **banks** in the centre of town. The bureau de change at the Commercial Bank on Sam Nujoma Avenue is open from 07.00 to 19.00 every day, which is a real boon if you arrive at a weekend. Note that, even if you're just changing currency, you'll need to take your passport.

If you want to organise your return flights home, or a trip around the rest of Namibia, then useful addresses include:

Air Namibia Sam Nujoma; tel: 064 405123. This is a useful office for re-confirming onward flights and other airline business.
Namib i PO Box 829; tel: 064 404827/403129; fax: 064 405101; email: swainfo@iafrica.com.na; web: www.swakop.com. The tourist information centre, on the corner of Sam Nujoma Avenue and Roon Street, has a most extensive selection of pamphlets and information on Namibia, with a special emphasis on the local area – don't miss it. Open Mon–Fri 08.00–13.00, 14.00–17.00, Sat 09.00–12.00.
Namibia Wildlife Resorts Old Woermann Haus, Bismarck St; tel: 064 402172; fax: 064 402796. This is where you can obtain permits for entry to national parks and make reservations for accommodation.
See Africa Safari Shop PO Box 1428; tel: 064 404054; fax: 064 404072. Next to the Hansa Hotel, on Roon St, Heinz Heuschneider has run this for some years. He knows what the area has to offer, and acts as agent for Desert Adventure Safaris, amongst others.

For details of local tour operators, see *Activities*, pages 314–15.

Internet cafés
There are a few internet cafés in town, as well as facilities in many backpackers' hostels and pensions:

Compucare 12 Roon St (near Namib i); tel: 064 463775; fax: 064 461063; email: compucare@compucare.com.na. Costs N$10 for ½ hour. Open Mon–Fri 08.30–18.00, Sat 08.30–16.00.
I Zone Woermann Brock complex, Sam Nujoma Av; web: www.iway.com. N$10 for ½ hour. Open Mon–Sat 07.00–22.00, Sun 10.00–22.00. Small coffee shop.
Talk Shop Roon St (corner of Woerman St); tel: 064 461333; email: talkshop51@hotmail.com. Costs N$12 for ½ hour, then N$3 for every 7½ minutes. There's also a coffee bar and light snacks. Open Mon–Fri 09.30–19.00; Sat/Sun 10.00–15.00.
Cellular phones may be hired for N$9.95 a day from Schoemans in the Klimas Building at 11 Moltke St; tel: 064 405728; fax: 064 405729.

Shopping
Supplies
Swakopmund's compact shopping centre offers plenty of choice, both for practical items and for souvenirs and curios.

On the main B2 road out of Swakopmund, at its intersection with Windhoeker St, is a 24-hour Engen fuel station. Facing that is the Shoprite Arcade which houses a First National Bank cash machine, furniture shops, a good pizzeria (see page 293) and a large **Shoprite supermarket** – which is one of the best places to stock up on food and drink before you leave Swakopmund. More central are the **Model supermarket** on Sam Nujoma Av, opposite the tourist information office, and the **Woermann Brock** supermarket in the complex of the same name on Sam Nujoma Av, near Bismarck St.

For **camping** gear, **car spares** and **cycling** gear, try Cymot at 43 Sam Nujoma Av (tel: 064 400318; fax: 064 402440; web: www.cymot.com.na), or Time Out on 32 Breite St (tel: 064 405920; fax: 064 405921; email: timeout@iafrica.com.na), who also have **angling** gear and fresh bait. There is also a Land Rover Parts Centre on Bahnhof St, tel: 064 403713; fax: 064 403717.

For **photographic equipment**, try Photographic Enterprises in the Commercial Bank Arcade, on Sam Nujoma Av, tel: 064 463980. This has film (including Fuji Velvia) and some camera equipment, though you will find a more comprehensive range in Windhoek. Another good option for camera equipment is the efficient Photo Studio Behrens at 7 Moltke St (tel: 064 404711), who will also carry out minor repairs. Both offer a one-hour developing service.

The most central of the town's three **pharmacies** is Swakopmund Apotheke, just down from Namibi i on Sam Nujoma Av (tel: 064 402825, or 463610 after hours); it is open every day, including Sundays, 10.00–12.00.

Safari clothes and equipment – including wide-brimmed hats – may be obtained from Namib Safari Shop in The Arcade (tel: 064 463214), or Safariland at 21 Sam Nujoma Av (tel: 064 462387), which is also open 10.00–12.00 on Sunday mornings.

Swakopmund Buchhandlung on Sam Nujoma Av, next to the Standard Bank, has a reasonable selection of English-language **books** on Namibia, and some novels too. The more mainstream CNA is on Roon St, next to Namib i. For secondhand novels, try Cobwebs in The Arcade.

Arts, crafts and souvenirs
Swakopmund is filled with commercial **art galleries** and **curio shops**, particularly in the centre of town around The Arcade, and in the attractive new Ankerplatz further down Sam Nujoma Av near the sea. Some of the best of these include Cobwebs in The Arcade, Rogl Souvenirs and African Art Gallery on Sam Nujoma Av (also open on Sundays), the Hobby Horse Art Gallery (tel: 064 402875) in The Arcade, which specialises in Namibian (as against African) art, and Die Muschel at 10 Roon St, next to the Cycle Clinic. Slightly further out, at 55 Sam Nujoma Av (tel: 064 404606; email: engel@mweb.com.na), the modern Engelhard Design features contemporary Namibian art and jewellery, with exhibitions changing every six weeks or so.

There is also a small street-market around the lighthouse area in front of the Schweizerhaus Hotel, with a range of crafts available for sale.

For **leather** goods, try Leder Chic in The Arcade, or Deon Sibold (tel: 064 464182), who specialise in kudu and seal boots and shoes.

A few rather more original places are worth taking a look at:

Karakulia NDC Craft Centre, Knobloch St, off Moses Garoeb St, PO Box 1258, Swakopmund; tel: 064 461415; fax: 064 461041; email: kararugs@iafrica.com.na; web: www.karakulia.com.na

Karakulia has a shop in The Arcade, where you may be able to see weavers at work, but its workshop is just off the main road as you head north from Swakopmund, about 500m from Sam Nujoma Av, on the right-hand side. It's a very long walk, so transport would be useful! Here you can watch the whole art of spinning and weaving of karakul wool into carpets and wall hangings, as well as buying the finished products. You can even have designs made to order, and then reliably shipped home for you. There is also a Save the Rhino shop, which sells original crafts from the Save the Rhino HQ in Khorixas.

Swakop River Angoras off Windhoeker St, tel: 064 405442

If you've ever wondered where the soft angora wool comes from, look no further. Mrs Tirronen's rabbits are the answer, and you can watch the wool harvested from the bunnies and spun – before (inevitably) you buy the produce. To get here, drive out of town on Windhoeker St, and when the road runs out: ask someone. It's right there!
Opens: Mon–Sat: 10.00–17.00.

Swakopmund Tannery 7 Leutwein St, Swakopmund; tel: 064 402633; fax: 064 404205

Watch how hides are transformed into leather goods, and have the chance to buy the finished items, including kudu shoes and boots.
Open: Mon–Fri 08.00–13.00, 14.00–17.30, Sat 08.00–12.30. Admission free.

The shop at the **Kristall Galerie** (see *What to see*, below) is worth a visit for those interested in semi-precious stones.

Antiques

For antique books and old African artefacts, **Peter's Antiques** (24 Moltke St, PO Box 920, Swakopmund; tel/fax: 064 405624) is perhaps the best shop in Africa, with a most comprehensive and eclectic collection. Peter is a small, intense Namibian of German origin. He started the shop nearly 20 years ago as an extension of his hobby, and since then his collection, his reputation, and the shop have gradually grown. Now he has a network of collectors all over sub-Saharan Africa, who buy and ship old African artefacts to Swakopmund. (Purchasers should carefully consider the ethics of such a collection before even considering buying.) He also sells some new, cheaper arts and crafts that are produced specifically for tourists.

The shop is now quite large, and densely packed with all sorts of things. The smells of wood, skins and dyes that go to make the pieces pervade the place, making it instantly fascinating and slightly revolting. As well as tribal artefacts, Peter's has an extensive collection of antique books, many in German, concerned with Namibia's history. In recent years he has been involved with commissioning and distributing facsimile reprints of old books and maps, reproducing these manuscripts for future generations. Open: Mon–Fri 09.00–13.00, 15.00–18.00; Sat 09.00–13.00, 17.00–18.00, Sun 17.00–18.00.

What to see and do

Unlike most Namibian towns, there's plenty to do in Swakopmund. Below are a few attractions in town, but see also *Around the towns,* from page 310, for ideas in the areas surrounding Swakopmund and Walvis Bay.

The Mole

If you only have a little time to spare, then wander down to the Mole, by the Strand Hotel. This was to be a harbour wall when first built, but the ocean currents continually shifted the sandbanks and effectively blocked the harbour before it was even completed. A similar 'longshore drift' effect can be seen all along the coast, at inlets like Sandwich Harbour. Partially because of this sandbank's protection, the beach by the Mole is pleasant (though watch out for jellyfish) and safe to swim from, if small and surprisingly busy at times.

Museums and libraries
Opening times given here are the official times, but aside from the Swakopmund Museum itself, you can expect a rather more erratic service than is indicated.

Swakopmund Museum
Situated next to the municipal swimming pool, by the Strand Hotel, the main Swakopmund Museum (PO Box 361, Swakopmund; tel/fax: 064 402695) was founded by Dr Alfons Weber in 1951. It now has exhibits on life in the Namib Desert and the South Atlantic, huge collections of insects and birds' eggs, an excellent section on rocks and minerals, and lots of information on the colonial German history in the region. There's also a re-creation of what old doctors' and dentists' surgeries must have been like. Frightening stuff.

In the museum's new wing is a recently opened ethnic exhibition, People of Namibia, covering Namibia's indigenous cultures.

Open: daily 10.00–13.00, 14.00–17.00, including Sundays and holidays. Costs: adults N$14, children N$5, students N$9.

Swakopmund Transport Museum
Housed in the newly restored Otavi Bahnhof, on the corner of Sam Nujoma (main B2) and Windhoeker Street, is the new Transport Museum. This was once the west coast terminal of the narrow-gauge railway line, which linked Swakopmund to a copper mine at Tsumeb.

It contains a photographic history of the building, the railway, the Mole and even aviation in the area, but a recent fire has destroyed some of the exhibits. Occasionally there is craftwork on sale outside the museum, but this is by no means a regular occurrence.

Open: daily from 10.00. Admission is free.

Sam Cohen Library
Next to the Transport Museum, the impressive collection of Africana books at the Sam Cohen Library (tel: 064 402695) contains about 10,000 volumes, encompassing most of the literature on Swakopmund, and a huge archive of newspapers from 1898 to the present day. (Some in German, some in English.) There's also a collection of old photographs and maps.

Open: Mon–Fri 09.00–13.00, 15.00–17.00, Sat 10.00–12.30. Admission is free.

Snake Park
Next door to the Transport Museum (see above), the snake park (tel: 064 405100) boasts more than 20 types of Namibian snakes, lizards, chameleons, scorpions and other creatures, which is enough to satisfy even the most inquisitive child – or adult. Snake feeding takes place on Saturdays from 10.00 to 12.30. That said, the place was looking very neglected when we visited, and change is almost certainly in the offing.

Open: Mon–Fri 09.30–13.00, 14.30–17.00, Sat 09.00–13.00. Admission N$10.

National Marine Aquarium
This relatively new aquarium at the southern end of town (tel: 064 410 1000) is worth a visit for its impressive displays of local marine life. It has a total of about

20 tanks, including a huge main tank containing 320m³ of water, and is crossed by an underwater walkway. Coastal angling species dominate, with plenty of kob, blacktail, steenbras, spotted grunters, sharks, skates and rays. Note that at 15.00 on Tues, Sat and Sun the larger fish are hand-fed by divers – an excellent time to visit.

Opens: 10.00–16.00 Tues–Sun and public holidays, closed Mon. Admission: N$6 adults, N$3 children, students and pensioners.

Kristall Galerie

This ultra-modern building on the corner of Garnison and Bahnhof Streets (tel: 064 406080; email: gems@kristallgalerie.com; web: www.kristallgalerie.com) houses what is claimed to be the largest-known crystal cluster in the world, estimated to be around 520 million years old. Displays include a scratch pit where visitors can search for semi-precious stones, a replica of the original Otjua tourmaline mine, and a craft area. There's a shop, of course, with semi-precious stones available in many guises, and a café area with videos about crystals. It's well worth a visit by anyone fascinated by geology.

Hansa Brewery

Tours around the brewery at 9 Rhode Allee are easy to arrange on Tuesdays and Thursdays by phoning them on 064 405021, with as much advance notice as possible. The beer is brewed, we're told, according to rigorous German standards. Tours, which are free, last around two hours.

Historical buildings

As you might expect, the town is full of amazing old German architecture in perfect condition. If you want a guide to the individual buildings then get in touch with Frau Angelika Flamm-Schneeweiss at the Sam Cohen Library (tel: 064 402695), who can arrange one-off guided walking tours. For a more general overview, contact Mr Heuschneider at Namib Tours (tel: 064 404072, or see page 315), who run a one-hour tour of the town for N$95 per person, or Charly's Desert Tours (tel: 064 404341).

Alternatively, the handout from the municipality itself, or the short book entitled *Swakopmund – A Chronicle of the Town's People, Places and Progress*, available at the museum, both give descriptions and brief histories for some of the buildings.

For an overview of the town and its setting, you could do worse than climb the **Woermann Tower** just behind the Ankerplatz complex on Sam Nujoma, near Bismarck St. Adults N$10, under 16s N$5, under 10s free.

Sporting facilities

Swimming

Opposite the main museum, by the Strand, there's an indoor Olympic-size swimming pool, entry N$4.60. Saunas must be booked at least an hour in advance, and cost N$23 per hour. Masochists shouldn't miss the opportunity to use these, and then run straight into the cold surf on the nearby beach by the Mole. Swimming elsewhere in the sea is generally not safe, for rip tides are common, so it's important to seek local advice.

Golf

About 8km west of Swakopmund, on the main B2 road from Windhoek, is Rossmund Golf Course (PO Box 348, Swakopmund; tel/fax: 064 405644). The par 72 course is open to day members, who occasionally find themselves playing alongside the local springboks. The club has its own restaurant overlooking the greens.

For Walvis Bay golf club, see page 309.

WALVIS BAY

Walvis Bay seems larger and more spaced out than Swakopmund, though also quieter and slightly lacking in character. Perhaps Afrikaans was the dominant influence here, whereas German was clearly the driving force in shaping Swakopmund's architecture and style.

Most visitors stay in Swakopmund, where they eat and relax, and venture down to Walvis Bay to go birdwatching, as there are a number of sites attracting huge flocks of seabirds and migrant waders, including the famous flamingos and pelicans. Even if you haven't much time, the drive on the Trans-Kalahari Highway between the two towns is an excursion in itself, for here is nature at her most elemental, as white rollers from the sea crash right into the sand-dunes from the Namib Desert.

In recent months, Walvis Bay has begun to change fast, reflecting the town's expanding population. Currently standing at around 62,000, it is likely to lead to a change to city status during 2002, though a small-town feel still prevails. There's lots of new development, both industrial and commercial. Many new shops are also springing up, like a big new shopping centre, including Shoprite, which is being built on Sam Nujoma Avenue (7th Street).

There's also a concerted effort to promote tourism here, though some comment that the municipality's campaigns foolishly target South African fishermen to the exclusion of others. Given the marvels of the desert around the town, it's a shame.

History

From 1990 until 1994 the port of Walvis Bay, and the enclave that surrounds it, remained part of South Africa – despite being surrounded by the newly independent country of Namibia. However, at midnight on February 28 1994 the South African flag was taken down, and five minutes later the Namibian flag was raised here. This transferred the enclave to Namibian control and ended a point of contention between the two countries. Walvis Bay is strategically important as the coast's only deepwater port, and ceding control of it to Windhoek was a very significant step for South African politicians to make.

Now the port could be poised to expand, as the tar road linking it to South Africa's heartland – the Trans-Kalahari Highway – is completed, and the promise of landing freight and then trucking it to Jo'burg becomes a reality.

Getting there
By air

Walvis Bay has regular flights from Oranjemund (N$948) and Windhoek (N$385), whilst Swakopmund only has good flight links with Windhoek. The airport is located 11km to the east of town on the northern edge of the desert. A shuttle from the airport into the centre of Walvis Bay can be pre-booked through the tourist information office for around N$50 per person.

By train

Walvis Bay is linked to Windhoek and Tsumeb, via Swakopmund, by the normal, slow train services. These run to and from Windhoek every day except Saturday, arriving Walvis Bay at 07.00 and departing at 19.00. Trains to Tsumeb depart on Mon, Wed and Fri at 16.15. See *Chapter 6*, pages 94–5, for details, or call the TransNamib in Walvis Bay on tel: 064 208504/5.

By bus

Intercape Mainliner run a good service linking Windhoek and Walvis Bay, which stops at the Omega Service on the corner of 7th Street and 15th Road. This arrives from Windhoek at 11.10 on Mon, Wed, Fri and Sat, and returns Mon, Wed, Fri and Sun at 11.30. It costs N$70 to Swakopmund, and N$110 to Windhoek, and must be booked in advance. Contact Flamingo Travel (tel: 064 203011) or Ultra Travel (tel: 064 207997) to book, and see *Chapter 6*, pages 96–9, for more details.

There is also a weekly bus service from Cape Town to Walvis Bay run by Ekonolux. It leaves Walvis Bay every Friday at 11.00, returning on Monday at 06.00. Fares are N$490 single, or N$880 return. For details, contact Talk Shop (see *Internet cafés* page 295), or tel: 064 205935; fax: 064 205978.

Orientation

Walvis Bay is built for its harbour, and its streets number from there: 1st Street is nearest the harbour, parallel to the sea, and 16th Street is furthest from it. Similarly its roads are perpendicular to the harbour, starting with 1st Road in the south and continuing to 18th Road in the north.

These somewhat unexciting thoroughfares form a grid that is the city, and are easily navigable. Or at least would have been easily navigable if the planners had had a little imagination. Instead they zealously stuck to numerical names and, where roads were split, they coined names like 3rd Street North, 3rd Street West and 3rd Street East for completely separate roads. So, whilst most things are easily found, if you see north, south, east or west in a street name – consult a map immediately.

Without Swakopmund's beautiful architecture or its buzz, Walvis Bay seems to have no real focus or centre for visitors. However, if you're a keen birdwatcher you'll probably base yourself here just for the lagoon.

Street name changes

Over the last few years, various street names in Walvis Bay have been changed. Although in theory these are all now in place, many people still refer to the original names, so the following may be useful:

Sam Nujoma Avenue	*was*	7th Street
Hage G Geingob Street	*was*	8th Street
Theo Ben Gurirab Street	*was*	9th Street
Nangolo Mbumba Drive	*was*	10th Street
Hidipo Hamutenya Avenue	*was*	14th & 13th streets
Nathaniel Maxuilili Avenue	*was*	Kuiseb Street
Ben Amathila Drive	*was*	Oceana Street

Getting around

Most visitors to Walvis Bay have their own transport, as the city's quite spread out and there's little in the way of local public transport. If you've no vehicle then walking is usually pleasant, and hitching is occasionally successful, even in town.

If you're hiring a car on arrival, or dropping one here, Avis have an office at the airport, tel: 064 207527. Alternatively, Budget are at the Protea Lodge (tel: 064 204624; fax: 064 202931) and there's also Triple Three Rentals (tel: 064 200333/206686, cell: 081 1273331 or 081 128 3138; email: oliver@iafrica.com.na; web: www.333.com.na).

Where to stay

Walvis Bay doesn't have the variety of places to stay, or to eat, found in Swakopmund. However, there is the odd gem, and if you're looking for large, family self-catering units for a longer stay, then something here may be perfect for you.

Protea Lodge (26 rooms) Corner of Sam Nujoma Av and 10th Road, PO Box 30, Walvis Bay; tel: 064 209560; fax: 064 209565; email: bay@iafrica.com.na; web: www.proteahotels.com.
Owned by the large Protea chain, and on the site of the old Flamingo Hotel, the Protea caters more to business people than tourists. It follows the standard Protea formula of having modern, carpeted twin-bed rooms with Mnet TV, facilities to make tea and coffee, direct-dial phones, air conditioning, and en-suite toilet and bath with a powerful overhead shower. There is a wheelchair-adapted room, a restaurant, and a lounge. In short, this is an efficient and comfortable but rather soulless hotel in the middle of Walvis Bay.
Rates: single N$389, double N$462, superior rooms (more space) N$511, including breakfast.

The Courtyard (11 twin, 2 family suites, 4 single rooms) 16 3rd Road (corner of 2nd St), PO Box 3493, Walvis Bay; tel: 064 206252; fax: 064 207271; email: courtyard@iafrica.com.na; web: www.courtyardhotel.com
Close to the Esplanade in a residential road, and just a few blocks from the harbour, the Courtyard is now owned by Charmaine Stewart of the nearby Langholm Hotel, and managed by her daughter-in-law, Sandi.
   Everything is set around two grassy courtyards, shaded by a couple of sturdy palm trees. The rooms all have direct-dial telephone, TV with satellite channels, and a radio/alarm clock, as well as a microwave, coffee machine, kettle, a little cutlery, washing bowl, and a small minibar/fridge (stocked if you wish). All rooms have en-suite facilities, some with bath and shower, others just with bath. The furniture is sturdy and stylish, but kept to a minimum. Downstairs is a large, cool reception/lounge/dining room, while across the courtyard is a small heated, indoor swimming pool and sauna (not always working), and secure parking. It is certainly one of the better places in Walvis Bay, good value for money and very near to the Raft Restaurant – though it is a distance from the nightlife of Swakopmund.
Rates: single N$330, double N$385, family suite (2–3 people) N$440–475, including breakfast.

Langholm Hotel (11 rooms, 1 suite) 24 2nd St West, PO Box 2631, Walvis Bay; tel: 064 209230/1/2, cell: 081 129 9230; fax: 064 209430; email: langholm@africa.com.na; web: www.langholmhotel.com.na
This friendly, green-and-white painted small hotel, owned by the welcoming Charmaine and Bruce Stewart, is very near to the Courtyard and the lagoon. Eleven of the rooms are comfortable twins, with en-suite bathrooms, direct-dial telephones and TVs. One is a self-catering suite, big enough for five. There's a relaxing lounge with a bar (open every evening until 22.00), the ceiling of which is festooned with a huge assortment of hats left by visitors, but don't sleep in so late that you miss the extensive breakfast.
Rates: single N$400, double N$450, suite N$500, including breakfast.

Lagoon Lodge (6 rooms) 2 Nangolo Mbumba Drive, PO Box 3964, Walvis Bay; tel: 064 200850, cell 081 129 7953; fax: 064 200851; email: french@lagoonlodge.com.na; web: www.lagoonlodge.com.na
This distinctive yellow building decked with flowers was opened by a French couple, Helen and Wilfred Meiller, in December 2000 and is a must for bird lovers: it is situated right opposite the lagoon with daily entertainment provided by flocks of flamingos and other waterbirds.
   Wilfred's skills as a woodturner are evident in the individually decorated rooms, each with a totally different theme – if birds are your passion, ask for their bird room! All are en-suite, with TV, telephone, and a balcony or terrace facing the lagoon. Facilities also include a small swimming pool in the rear garden.
Rates: single N$450, double N$720, family room (2 children max) N$760, including breakfast.

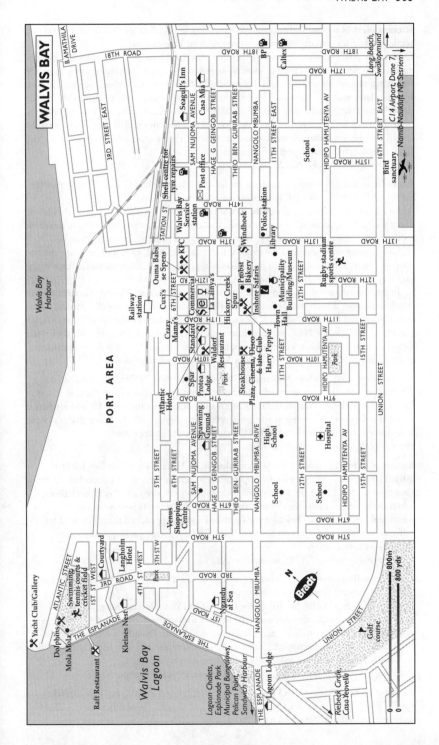

Kleines Nest (4 rooms) 76 Esplanade, PO Box 730, Walvis Bay; tel: 064 203203; email: wmlcoast@iafrica.com.na; web: www.natron.net/tour/kleines-nest/
Opened in 2001, this small, modern pension that shares its premises with the owners' engineering firm has an enviable location opposite the lagoon. Upstairs, away from the functional office-style entrance, all is light and airy. Well-appointed rooms, each with its own balcony, have en-suite shower, TV, fridge/minibar (the first couple of drinks are on the house!) and a small kitchenette area. Minimalist design is offset by pine and cane furnishings, with all rooms looking out over the water. Johann and Melani van den Berg offer guests the use of bicycles, a windsurfer and a canoe, and there's even a quad bike available for a small fee. Collection from the airport is free of charge.
Rates: single N$300, double N$420, including breakfast.

Ngandu at Sea (15 rooms) Corner of 1st Rd and 9th St West, PO Box 3192, Walvis Bay; tel: 064 207327/8; fax: 064 207350; email: theart@mweb.com.na
Although Oswald Theart is normally in residence at Ngandu Safari Lodge at Rundu, he views the 'new Ngandu' as his seaside home. Just a stone's throw from the lagoon, it takes as its theme the coastal location, with colourful murals and paintings by local artists.

Eight rooms were added to the original seven during 2002, each with en-suite shower. Double rooms with have TV with three channels, phone, tea/coffee-making facilities, fridge and fan. Several rooms are also self-catering.

In the large, angular dining area it's difficult to shake off the sense of being in a café, although lunch and dinner are served here, and there's a bar area and pool table as well. Outside, there's a tea garden, and barbecue, while on the lagoon there are canoes for the use of guests. Garage parking is available for N$25 per day. Run with Germanic efficiency, and with conference facilities for up to 40, this is a place that would suit business people as well as holidaymakers.
Rates: single N$250, double NS$400, children 5–14 N$100, including breakfast.

Seagull (8 rooms) 215 Sam Nujoma Av, Walvis Bay; tel: 064 202775; fax: 064 202455
The lack of security here, coupled with the unkempt appearance of the place, is less than inviting. Nevertheless, accommodation in en-suite double rooms with TV and kitchen is reasonable value, so it may be worth considering if money is tight. And note that it's not to be confused with the excellent B&B of the same name at Swakopmund.
Rates: N$150 per person, including breakfast.

Lagoon Chalets (27 chalets) 8th St West, Meersig, PO Box 2318, Walvis Bay; tel: 064 207151; fax: 064 207469; email: info@lagoonchalets.com.na; web: www.lagoonchalets.com.na
One style of chalet has only one separate bedroom, but can sleep six people throughout, whereas the better chalets are a similar size but with two separate bedrooms and an additional loft bedroom. They are fully furnished and equipped, and really designed for self-catering families coming on long-stay trips. There is secure parking, and garage facilities are also available.
Rates: one-bedroom chalet N$240, two-bedroom N$260.

Casa Yeovella (7 rooms) 15 Riebeeck Circle, Meersig, PO Box 1880, Walvis Bay; tel/fax: 064 200502; email: yeovella@namibnet.com
Rather hidden away to the left before the lagoon, Casa Yeovella has a range of accommodation, much of which would be suitable for families – particularly as they can provide prams, camp cots, high chairs and other equipment. En-suite rooms are kitted out like home, too, with a microwave, fridge, kettle, crockery, cutlery, iron and hairdryer – as well as a TV. This is a good-value option for those on a tight budget.
Rates: single N$120, double N$200, triple N$270, 4 people N$320, 5 people N$350.

Atlantic Hotel (18 rooms) PO Box 46, Walvis Bay; tel: 064 202811; fax: 064 205063; email: lantic@namibnet.com. Owned by Namib Sun Hotels – head office tel: 061 233145; web: www.namibsunhotels.com.na

On 7th St near 13th Road Standard Bank, the Atlantic is a rather down-at-heel town hotel, with rooms that are OK (with Mnet TV and en-suite facilities), but little to really distinguish it. Being in the centre of town makes it popular for local business-people, but less interesting for visitors. On the plus side, it has its own restaurant for lunch and dinner. *Rates: N$260 single, N$365 double, including breakfast.*

Casa Mia Hotel (23 twin rooms) 7th St, between 17th and 18th roads, PO Box 1786, Walvis Bay; tel: 064 205975; fax: 064 206596; email: casancor@iafrica.com.na
This old-style hotel remains dark and unwelcoming, in spite of a refurbishment programme that has brightened up its rooms no end. Facilities are reasonable, though; all rooms have Mnet TV, phone, tea/coffee maker, and en-suite shower or bath. The adjacent restaurant has rested on a good reputation for years, but don't come here expecting any trendy modern cuisine. There's also a rather dingy bar, Captain Solomon's, that is open 12.00–14.00 lunchtime, and 17.00–24.00 in the evening. Overall, the Casa Mia is still rather expensive for what it's offering.
Rates: single N$418, double N$569, including breakfast.

The Spawning Ground (8 dorm beds, 3 double rooms) 84 Hage St, PO Box 1575, Walvis Bay; tel: 081 1277636; email: spawning@iafrica.com or dawayner@hotmail.com
Undoubtedly the best backpackers' place in Walvis Bay, the Spawning Ground moved to new premises in 2002, just after we visited. There are now three double rooms, and just one eight-bedded dorm. There's also a self-catering kitchen and a braai area, and the place has its own campsite. Rooms at the previous address were bright, cheerful and well decorated, and there's every reason to suppose that these standards will be maintained. Because Walvis Bay is quieter than Swakopmund, the Spawning Ground tends to attract travellers who stay for several days just to relax, lending it a very laid-back air.
Rates: N$60 per person, N$150 per double room, N$30 for campers.

Esplanade Park Municipal Bungalows (27 bungalows) P Bag 5017, Walvis Bay; tel: 064 206145; fax: 064 204528
Situated on the Esplanade past 8th road on the left, on the way south towards Sandwich Harbour, this is a complex of quite smart, well-equipped bungalows facing the lagoon. All the one- and two-bedroom bungalows, each with their own living room, have proper kitchens with a stove, fridge/freezer, kettle, toaster, cutlery, crockery, and glasses. Some claim to sleep five people, others seven – though three and four people, respectively, would be about right for comfort.
They also have outside braais for barbecues, a garage for the car, and their own inside toilets and separate bathroom. Bedding is provided, but towels and soap are not. Good-value accommodation, though it feels like a restcamp and is not at all cosy. The office hours here are 08.00–13.00, 14.00–17.00, 19.00–22.00 during the week, and 08.00–13.00, 15.00–18.00 at the weekend.
Rates: five-bed bungalow N$265, seven-bed N$310.

In addition to the above, it may be worth checking out the following individual cottages:

Seashell Cottage 28 1st St West, Walvis Bay; tel: 064 207187, cell: 081 124 2022
The Whaler's Cottage 46 Sam Nujoma Av, PO Box 532, Walvis Bay; tel/fax: 064 204947/206350

At Long Beach (Langstrand)
Some 10km before Walvis Bay, on the road from Swakopmund, is the area known as Long Beach, or Langstrand. A few houses have sprung up here, alongside a couple of caravan sites. Unless you're coming for the Dolphin Resort up the road,

peace and quiet is the order of the day – there's only you and the sea to share the area, plus a small oyster bar selling just that – oysters (though they *are* good!). It's unlikely to be long, though, before a restaurant or two sees the potential and moves in to the vicinity.

Burning Shore Beach Lodge (7 luxury suites) 152 4th St, PO Box 3357, Walvis Bay; tel: 064 207568; fax: 064 209836; email: burningshore@namibnet.com (reservations tel: 061 248741; fax: 061 226535; email: intu@iafrica.com.na)
The unassuming exterior of this new beachfront lodge at Long Beach, on the coast between Swakopmund and Walvis Bay, gives no hint of the luxurious interior beyond the gate. But step inside and the atmosphere is one of discretion and taste. Traditional furnishing in each of the opulent suites is set off by elaborate drapes and numerous personal touches. En-suite bathrooms all have shower and bath (and one has its own jacuzzi), and five suites have an uninterrupted sea view.
    Downstairs, the lounge oozes colonial-style elegance, overlooking an expanse of lawn and beyond to the sandy beach. Guests stay at Burning Shore on a full-board basis, either with or without activities, as preferred. Although this is a seriously upmarket establishment, its location so far from any of the facilities of Swakopmund or Walvis Bay is likely to prove a drawback for many visitors, and most would consider a vehicle to be essential.
Rates per person, full board: luxury rooms N$675–840, suites N$760–995, suite with jacuzzi N$960–1,195. Single supplement N$250–350. Prices are also available to include activities.

Dolphin (Dolfyn) Park Recreational Resort (20 bungalows) PO Box 86, Walvis Bay; tel: 064 204343; fax: 064 209714
About 10km out of Walvis Bay, beside the road to Swakopmund and close to Long Beach, this purpose-built resort, with self-catering bungalows that look like railway carriages, is reminiscent of the UK's Butlins chain of resorts. It is on its own in the desert, by the sea, dominated by a large water-slide leading into a swimming pool. The atmosphere here is one of a holiday camp, aiming for families with children. Used mainly by Namibians and South Africans, it is very busy during the summer school holidays, but can be almost deserted during the quieter seasons. Bedding is provided, but bring your own towels.
Rates: from N$253 per 2-person bungalow.

Long Beach Resort (2 flats, 117 camping sites) P Bag 5017, Walvis Bay; tel: 064 2013267; fax: 064 204528; email: gkruger@walvisbaycc.org.na
Long Beach Resort is predominantly a municipal campsite with spaces for both caravans and tents. There are also two flats, one sleeping two people, and one for four.
Rates: N$212.75 for 2 double beds, N$161 for a small room for two. Camping N$57.50 per site plus N$6.90 per person.

Levo Chalets (3 chalets) Long Beach, PO Box 1860, Walvis Bay; tel/fax: 064 207555; email: levo@namibnet.com; web: www.levotours.com
Three self-catering chalets, just a few minutes' walk from the beach, each have three double rooms and sleep up to six people. In addition to a fully equipped kitchen, chalets have a balcony with sea view, satellite TV and a lock-up garage. These are really only suitable for long stays; no meals are available.
Rates: single N$250, double N$350, triple N£350, quadruple N$500, 5–6 people N$600.

Where to eat
Gallery Restaurant The restaurant that's adjacent to Walvis Bay Yacht Club serves a varied seafood menu that comes with a good recommendation, though the venue is less attractive than the Raft. Officially it's open Mon and Thu 11.00 – 15.00, 17.00 – 24.00 and Wed 17.00–24.00, but the actual hours seem rather erratic.

Probst Bakery & Café 148 9th St (near 12th Road); tel: 064 202744
This popular café and bakery has a reasonably priced menu for breakfast and lunch, as well as being a good place for snacks and takeaway fare. It's open 06.15–18.00. Breakfast is N$4.50–10.50; set lunches N$20–25.

Dolphins Close to the yacht club, this small, pleasant 'coffee shoppe' is open 08.00–16.00 (or 14.00 Fridays and weekends) for breakfast, cakes and sandwiches or salads.

Lagoon Restaurant 8th Rd West; tel: 209412
On the same site as Lagoon Chalets, but privately run, the Lagoon Restaurant is open for breakfast, lunch and dinner. Specialising in seafood and venison, it is rather drab inside, with dark, rustic décor. Prices average N$20 for starters, or N$40 for main courses. Upstairs, the bar stays open 'till the last man falls'. Pool tables and gambling machines enliven the place, as well as live music on occasion.

Waldorf Restaurant 10th Road, between 7th and 8th streets (opposite Proteas Hotel); tel: 064 205744
Simple, good-value menu, with lunch specials at N$15–30. There's a takeaway service, too. Breakfast: N$25; grills: N$20–45.

Raft Tel: 064 204877; fax: 064 202220
Owned by the team that also owns the Tug in Swakopmund (see page 291), this is an even more adventurous construction. It is a raft built on stilts in the middle of Walvis Bay lagoon, off the Esplanade (the seafront road), near to the yacht club. It is very good, but relatively expensive, especially in the evening – when the bar is by far the most stylish place in town.
It opens for lunch from about 12.00 to 15.00, with a setting that is more formal than you might expect. Bring your binoculars and ask for a window table – the opportunities for birdwatching here are such that you may just forget about your meal. The menu is the same for lunch and dinner; if the house steenbras speciality is on the menu when you visit, it's strongly recommended. Vegetarian options are well worth trying, too.
Later on the bar opens at 17.00, making this a great place to watch the sun sink into the waves. Dinner is served from 18.00 to 22.00, but the restaurant closes on Sunday.
Costs: starters N$18–25, vegetarian meals N$27–38, mains N$40–60 (with crayfish from N$140)

Crazy Mama's 133 7th St, between 10th and 11th roads; tel: 064 207364
Opposite the Atlantic Hotel, Crazy Mama's has an enthusiastic fan-club of locals and travellers. It serves what some claim are the best pizza and pasta dishes in Namibia, and does a reasonable line in seafood, too. It's also fairly cheap at around N$80 for a two-course meal with a beer or a glass of wine. It's second only to the Raft, and much lighter and less serious.
Costs: starters N$18–27, main courses N$25–60.

Atlantic Hotel 7th St near 13th Road; tel: 064 202811; fax: 064 205063
The Atlantic's restaurant serves reasonable German/European fare at fairly high prices, though may be useful in an emergency.
Costs: starters N$20–35, main courses N$40–60.

Hickory Creek Spur on 9th St, close to 12th Road; tel: 064 207990/1
This chain outlet serves good American burgers, steaks, and a host of side orders together with a good salad bar and children's menu. It is lively and opens every day.
Costs: starters N$10–20, light meals during day N$15–30, main courses N$40–60.

Casa Mia 7th St; tel: 064 205975
The Casa Mia Hotel's restaurant has an old-fashioned feel to it, with heavy furnishings. The menu is varied but on the pricey side, with starters at N$30–70, and mains N$40–80. It's open 12.00–14.00 and 19.00–21.00.

Cuxi's Sam Nujoma Av; tel: 206208
This air-conditioned coffee shop opposite the Computerland internet café has daily homemade specials for around N$25, plus sandwiches, burgers and ice-creams. Open Mon–Fri 07.00–19.00, weekends 07.00–14.00.

Ouma Babs se Spens Sam Nujoma; tel: 207916
A simple breakfast and burger place serving soft drinks. Closed Sundays.

Steve's Takeaway on Hage St has a surprisingly varied menu, from pies to T-bone steak. Closed Sundays.

Harry Peppar corner of Nangolo Mbumba Av and 11th Rd; tel: 064 203131/209977
An unexpected small pizza restaurant with cosy décor and wooden furnishing, where every pizza is a flat N$34. Open daily, 10.00 till late; free delivery.

Nightlife and entertainment

Like Swakopmund, Walvis Bay usually has several **nightclubs** which operate all year. More spring up during the peak holiday period for the local market around December/January. These can be great fun, but go in and out of fashion swiftly – probably rendering obsolete anything written here. Ask local advice as to what's good, and take care if you're thinking of a club in one of the townships. Currently the best venues are:

The Plaza Above the Plaza Cinema on 10th St, this late-night club opens every night from midnight onwards. Racially it's very mixed and its best nights are Friday and Saturday. There is usually a cover charge of N$5–10.

Club 9-5 This is in Naraville township, so less racially mixed, but it's still fairly safe and hassle-free – though do go with a local guide if possible, or by taxi.

There's not much choice of late-night bars, though it may be worth checking out the upstairs venue at the Lagoon Restaurant or the bar at the Casa Mia Hotel (see page 305). **La Lainya's Bar** on Sam Nujoma Avenue is all that is left of La Lainya restaurant, which closed in 2000. Open 10.00–14.00, is rather unprepossessing, with slot machines and a drab interior.

The only major concert venue in Walvis Bay is the **Municipal Hall** (10th Street, PO Box 5017; tel: 064 205981; fax: 064 204528). Any touring show will perform either here or at one of Swakopmund's main venues (see pages 294–5). There's also a cinema on 10th Street, opposite the Municipal Hall.

Getting organised

In an emergency, the police are reached on tel: 064 10111, whilst the ambulance is 064 205443, the hospital is 064 203441, and the fire service is 064 203117. If you need any sea rescue services then tel: 064 203202, 203581 or 202064 or 208317 or the police – which is also the emergency number to use if you can't get through anywhere else. For less serious illness, there's the NMA Health Care Centre on 14th Street, tel: 064 206098 or 206118, or the EPHS Centre at 203 2nd Street, tel: 064 207063.

The **tourist information centre** (tel: 064 209170; email: walvisinfo@ iml.com.na), on the right as you enter the civic centre on 10th Street (by 12th Road), ought to be your first stop for information. The manager is very helpful, and knows the area in detail. It's open Mon–Fri 08.00–17.00, and Sat 09.00–12.00.

There's a Computerland **internet café** on Sam Nujoma Av; web: www.namibnet.com. It's open Mon–Fri 08.00–late, Sat 09.00–late, Sun/holidays 10.00–late, and charges N$10 for half an hour.

Shopping

With your own car, you are close enough to drive easily to Swakopmund, where the choice of shops is usually greater. However, there are a number of shops and services within Walvis itself. If you need **food and provisions**, then the best places are **Model** and **Multisave**, both on Hage Street, or **Shoprite** on Sam Nujoma Avenue, the super Spar at 230 12th Street, the Portuguese Market Garden at 112 Sam Nujoma Avenue Street, or the Walvis Bay Service Station on the corner of 8th Street and 14th Road.

There are plenty of 24-hour **fuel stations** around town. Garages for **vehicle repairs** include Kwik-Fit Exhaust Systems on 18th Road (tel: 064 202409), Autowagen Repairs at 271 9th Street (tel: 064 206949), and Hans Kriess Motors on 8th Street (tel: 064 202653; fax: 064 206748), who specialise in VW and Audi models, but will also repair others.

For **camping equipment**, car spares and cycling gear, try Cymot at 136 8th Street (tel: 064 202241; fax: 064 205745; web: www.cymot.com.na). **Anglers** will appreciate Anglers Kiosk behind Caltex Petrol Station on Hage/13th.

For **photographic** needs try Photo Krause at 153 Sam Nujoma Avenue, tel: 064 203015; fax: 064 206439. They have film and some camera equipment, and can process print film in under 24 hours.

On the main street, Sam Nujoma Avenue, there are a couple of shops catering for the tourist market. **Desert Jeweller & Curios** has an upmarket range of gifts and souvenirs, including wood carvings, while if modern art is more your style, take a look at **Die Galerie** opposite.

What to see and do

Turning right after leaving the tourist information office takes you to the office of the Municipality of Walvis Bay, where local people make their water and electricity payments. The walls are covered in an intricate **bas-relief** of wooden carvings, showing, amongst other things, the mating dance of flamingos, desert life, sea life and human fishing. Impressive, and all done by the local artist Peter Downing. Otherwise, there is little to see in the town itself.

Most of the town's activities centre around the **lagoon**. There are some superb birdwatching opportunities both here and in the surrounding area (see page 317), and a couple of highly recommended kayak trips in the lagoon and out to Pelican Point (see page 310). Boat trips from the yacht club take visitors out to see dolphins in the lagoon and beyond (see below). Alternatively, you can also drive out towards Pelican Point around the lagoon, past the saltworks: a desolate track lined with salt ponds that have been reclaimed from the sea, inhabited only by seabirds and just the occasional brown hyena.

There is a **golf** course on the left of 18th Street before the lagoon. For details of fees for visitors, tel: 064 206506.

Boat trips

There are a few companies running excellent boat trips from the harbour around the lagoon and out to Pelican Point and Bird Island. Trips usually start from the yacht club, and vary from short cruises in the lagoon to longer cruises round the harbour and out to Pelican Point, or birdwatching trips further out to sea. In October and November, whales frequent these waters, with possible sightings of humpback, southern right, Minke and even killer whales, while from then until April there is the chance of seeing the leatherback turtle. Dolphins – both the bottlenose and the endemic Benguela (heavysides) – are present all year round, as are Cape fur seals, which may often cavort around the boats. To find out more, pick up a copy of *Namibia Marine Life*.

Aquanaut Tours PO Box 492, Swakopmund; tel: 064 405969, cell: 081 128 0374; email: fishark@iafrica.com.na; web: www.tauchferien.com/namibia/

Charter Dynamix Tel: 064 209219, cell: 081 124 9443/081 129 9451

Levo PO Box 1860, Walvis Bay; tel/fax: 064 207555; email: levo@namibnet.com; web: www.levotours.com. Ottmar and Merrilyn started up Levo seal and dolphin cruises from Walvis Bay 15 years ago. Trips depart from the yacht club in ski-boats at 08.30 and last about four hours, covering around 50km in that time. Prices, including a luxury lunch and champagne, are N$300 per person. They also offer fishing trips (see page 314).

Mola Mola Corner of Esplanade and Atlantic St, PO Box 980, Walvis Bay; tel: 064 205511, cell: 081 127 2522; fax: 064 207593; email: megan@mola-namibia.com; web: www.mola-namibia.com. The well-respected Mola Mola organises bird- and dolphin-watching cruises, as well as angling trips (day and overnight), and boat trips on the lagoon. These cost about N$350 for a dolphin cruise lasting about four hours.

Sunrise Tours & Safaris 8 Roon St, Swakopmund; tel/fax: 064 404561; email: sunrisetours@ iafrica.com.na' web: www.sunrisetours.com.na. Boat trips, fishing excursions and desert tours.

Kayak trips

Jeanne Meintjes runs Eco Marine Kayak Tours (PO Box 225, Walvis Bay; tel/fax: 064 203144). There is a choice of two guided excursions. The first takes birdwatchers on to the lagoon for two hours (cost N$110), while the second involves a Land Rover trip to Pelican Point, where visitors kayak around Pelican Point and out to the seal colonies (cost N$260 for a five-hour trip). Trips are run in the mornings only, when winds are light and the sea is generally calm.

For details of fishing trips, see page 314.

AROUND THE TOWNS

Because the towns of Swakopmund and Walvis Bay are just 30km apart (about 25 minutes' drive, on a super tar road), this section covers attractions in the areas outside both of the towns.

Activities

Swakopmund has become a lively centre for adventure-sports, attracting those in search of action and extra adrenaline. It is already a stop on the route of the overland companies, which supply a constant flow of people in search of thrills.

Many of the adventure companies are specialists in a particular field, so are listed under that activity, but for a one-stop shop before you start, try **NamibFun** at the Swakopmund tourist office (tel: 064 463921; fax: 064 463917; email: namibfun@mweb.com.na; web: www.namibfun.na), or:

Desert Explorers Adventure Centre 2 Woerman St; PO Box 456, Swakopmund; tel: 064 406096; fax: 064 405649; email: desertex@iafrica.com.na

Formerly Swakopmund Adventure Centre, this is the booking office for the Desert Explorers quad-bike trips. It also acts as agent for most, but not all, of Swakopmund's small adventure operators, with activities like dune-boarding, skydiving, kayaking, abseiling etc. There are internet facilities here, too, at N$10 for 20 minutes. Open 08.00–19.00, Sat/Sun 08.00–18.00.

Action in the dunes

New activities in the dunes are constantly being dreamed up to add to the existing range. Current options, many of which can be organised through Desert Explorers, include:

WALVIS BAY LAGOON: A BLEAK FUTURE

Walvis Bay lagoon dates back some 5,000 years, making it the oldest lagoon on the Namibian coast. A safe haven for up to 160,000 birds, it also acts as a feeding station for a further 200,000 shorebirds and terns on their bi-annual migration to and from the Arctic. Up to 90% of all South African flamingos spend the winter here, while 70% of the world's chestnut-banded plovers depend on the lagoon for their survival.

Pressure on the lagoon in recent years has built up from a number of areas: construction of housing to the southeast, salt pans to the south and west, and a road dyke to the east and south. All these factors have served to reduce flooding, which would naturally keep up the water levels. Added to this is the knock-on effect of the diversion of the Kuiseb River in 1967, since when the dunes have effectively 'marched round' and headed straight for Walvis Bay. The sand blown from the desert contributes significantly to the silting up of the lagoon.

The saltworks that surround the edge of the lagoon in Walvis Bay are South African owned; salt is exported raw from Namibia, then processed in South Africa for industrial use (as against that from Swakopmund which is for human consumption). The salt pans in Walvis Bay are entirely manmade, with the company now owning up to Pelican Point. As salt extraction increases, it is forecast that the entrance to the lagoon will eventually close up and the lagoon itself will dry up. Initiatives to re-establish the natural flow of water include the construction of culverts under the road leading to the saltworks.

On the basis of current estimates, the lagoon is likely to disappear completely within just five to ten years. The Coastal Environmental Trust of Namibia, PO Box 786 Walvis Bay; tel: 064 205057; fax: 064 200728; email: cetn@iafrica.com.na) is working hard to protect the lagoon, which since June 1995 has been a wetland of international importance under the Ramsar Convention. Protection of the lagoon is also part of the Walvis Bay Local Agenda 21 Project, based at the municipality.

Sand-boarding in the dunes, organised by Chris and Beth of Alter-Action Ltd (PO Box 1388; tel/fax: 064 402737; cell: 081 128 2737; email: alteraxn@iafrica.com.na). Their trips leave from Swakopmund at 09.30, collecting you from where you are staying. Adventurers are supplied with a large flat piece of masonite/hardboard, also safety hats, elbow guards and gloves. The idea is to push off the top of a dune, and lie on the board as it slides down. Speeds easily reach 70km/h, though first you'll do a few training rides on lower dunes, where you won't go much faster than 40km/h. Finally, they take you to a couple of the larger dunes, for longer, faster runs, before lunch in the desert, and the return drive to Swakopmund. Trips costs about US$20 for half a day.

Dune-boarding is different. It may have more finesse, and certainly requires more skill. Here adventurers stand up on a small surfboard, which shoots down the side of dunes – rather like skiing, only on sand. The major operator is Alter-Action (see above), whose trips start at 09.30, include lunch and drinks, and cost US$30. Dune-boarding is also offered by Dare Devil Adventures (see Quad-biking, below).

DESERTS – BY DEFINITION

'Desert' is an arbitrary term whose meaning is widely disputed, even amongst experts. Some refer to Noy-Meir's definition of a 'water-controlled ecosystem with infrequent, discrete and largely unpredictable water inputs'. Others are quantitative, defining a desert as receiving an average of less than 100mm of rain per annum. In practice, any arid habitat can be called a desert – and the Namib is certainly very arid.

Antarctica has close to zero precipitation, and most of the water there is frozen, so, strictly speaking, the whole continent is a desert. However the normal usage of 'desert' refers to dry places which are also hot. These cover 5% of the land on Earth, and are to be found in two neat rings around the globe, straddling the lines of the tropics of Capricorn and Cancer.

The uniform distribution of deserts is due to the pattern of sunlight landing on the planet. Sunlight intensity is highest at the Equator, which is directly underneath the sun for most of the year. With all this light energy, water evaporates more vigorously at this latitude. As the water rises in the atmosphere, it condenses and falls on to the equatorial rainforests. The dry air remaining in the upper atmosphere journeys away from the Equator towards the tropics. Here it descends to ground level, waterless. What water there is at ground level is then picked up and exported by low-altitude winds travelling back towards the Equator to complete the cycle – hence the desert.

This desiccating climate creates a habitat that challenges life. Levels of solar radiation are enormous; air temperatures can soar during the day and, without insulating cloud cover, plunge below freezing at night; the ground is almost too hot to touch; strong winds are common and, where there is sand, sandstorms scour the land. Worst of all, water becomes a luxury. Since all living things are built from water-packed cells, there could hardly be a more uninhabitable environment on Earth. It is a credit to evolution that deserts are often inhabited by a wealth of organisms with sophisticated adaptations to survive in these conditions.

With a wide variety of fascinating species and unique adaptations, the Namib's community of animals and plants may not be as obviously appealing as those on Africa's grasslands, but it is equally impressive to the informed and observant visitor.

Dune thunderball is the latest activity to hit town, and it's certainly not for the intrepid. For N$200, participants have three rides inside an oversized ball and hurtle down the dunes. For details, contact NamibFun, page 310.

Quad-biking involves riding four-wheel motorcycles through the dunes, and is organised by a number of companies, of which the best known is Desert Explorers (see above for contact details). Trips cost US$50 per person for 2 hours, although longer and shorter trips are available as well. Other operators include:

Dare Devil Adventure Tel: 064 209532, cell: 081 127 5701
Kuiseb Delta Adventures Tel: 064 202550, cell: 081 128 2580; email: fanie@kuisebonline.com. web: www.kuisebonline.com
Outback Orange Tel: 064 400968, cell: 081 129 2877/081 128 1778; email: outbackorange@yahoo.com. They offer a free video of your trip.
Swakopmund Quad Biking Tel: 064 405455/405256; email: bpwcsc@mweb.com.na
Total Tel: 081 127 6005; email: swktotal@iway.na

Normal trips with Desert Explorers depart at 09.30, 11.30, 14.00 and 16.00. First they follow an easy track down the Swakop River valley, before a stop for refreshments and a foray into the Namib's main dune-sea. It all takes about 2½–3 hours. Petrol, soft drinks, and transport are included for N$500 per person. Manual, semi-automatic, and automatic bikes are available. Helmets, goggles and gloves are provided. If you're setting off on your own, please consider the harmful effect on the environment (see box below). Note that bikes are not allowed into the Namib-Naukluft National Park.

Action in the air

With clear air and a starkly beautiful coastline, Swakopmund is a natural space to learn to fly, parachute or even skydive. All take a while, although the Swakopmund Skydiving Club runs tandem free-fall jumps for novices, which are increasingly popular. After a little basic safety chat and a scenic flight over Swakopmund and the surrounding area, you can be strapped to an experienced instructor to throw yourselves out of a plane at 10,000ft. Your free-fall lasts for about half a minute before, hopefully, your parachute opens. This costs US$150 per jump, and includes a free video of your trip. Trips are run by Ground Rush, tel: 081 124 5167; email: freefall@iafrica.com.na; web: www.skydiveswakop.com.na), or Tandem Adventure (tel: 081 124 2588, email: tandemadventure@iway.na). For safety reasons, participants may be limited to those over 16, and within a weight range of 105–220kg.

For a more leisurely aerial experience, African Adventure Balloons (tel/fax: 064 403455, cell: 081 242 9481; email: flylo@iway.na) organise champagne breakfast flights over the desert (US$160), while the more intrepid can try their hand at parasailing over the dunes (US$35). If it's an adrenalin rush you're after, you could consider taking on the 1,100m flying fox at Rössing Mountain for US$50; trips include a 4WD journey to the top through spectacular mountain scenery.

PROTECTION OF THE DESERT

Many companies in the Swakopmund area have taken advantage of the unique environment to bring adventure sports to the area. Quad biking, sandboarding, sand skiing and other such activities are growing in popularity, but their proliferation could have serious consequences for the sand-dunes and other desert areas on which they depend.

While most operators take this issue seriously, confining their sports to a specific area and spelling out to participants the harm that can be caused by thoughtless manoeuvres, individuals may not be so careful. Even then, sandboarding and sandskiing have a weight-to-surface relationship that is unlikely to cause significant damage. Sadly, though, serious harm is being caused by individuals on privately owned bikes setting off across the dunes and gravel plains without any understanding of the nature of the area.

Broadly, the low-impact part of the dunes is the area on the top, with the greatest potential for danger to the habitat being on the lee side. Since most of the life in the dunes is found in the top 10cm, a thoughtless biker can cause untold damage in just a few seconds of 'fun'. Beyond the dunes, slow-growing lichens form an integral part of the region's ecology, but they are extremely fragile. Trample them underfoot, or ride over them, and they are unlikely to survive, depriving many forms of wildlife of food and even shelter. And then there is the Damara tern. The gravel plains of the Namib Desert are the nesting area of this endemic bird, one of the rarest terns in the world, yet – with a quick twist of the handlebars – a nest can be crushed in seconds.

Pleasure flights can also be organised through Pleasure Flights & Safaris (tel/fax: 064 404500; email: redbaron@iafrica.com.na; web: www.pleasureflights.com.na), Atlantic Aviation (tel: 064 404749; fax: 064 405832; email: info@flyinnamibia.com), or Desert Explorers (see above) to a number of places, including Sossusvlei or the Skeleton Coast. Prices with Desert Explorers are from N$970 and N$1,260 respectively, depending on seat availability.

Riding

Okakambe Trails (PO Box 1668, Swakopmund; tel: 064 402799, 405258, cell: 081 124 6626; email: okakambe@mweb.com.na) have well-trained **horses** available for both novices and experienced riders to take accompanied rides into the moon landscape and the Swakop River valley. At N$287 for 1½ hours, it's not cheap though. The farm is reached along the D1901, south of the B2 just east of town. Riding hats are available.

Alternatively, for a more Arabian experience, **camel** riding is available between 14.00 and 17.00 each afternoon. Short excursions into the desert (Arab-style attire for hire) are offered for around N$50 per person for 15 minutes; telephone Ms Elke Erb on 064 400363 to arrange a trip.

Action at sea
Surfing
Relatively new to Swakopmund, surfing is gaining in popularity on the stretch between Long Beach and Walvis Bay. The best people to contact are Tok-Tokkie Tours (tel: 018 250 4675).

Kayaking
Kayak trips are run from Walvis Bay (see page 310).

Fishing
Fishing has long been popular all along this coastline with South African visitors. Although fishing is good all year round, the best times are October to April. The turn of the year is particularly popular, with many anglers arriving in search of big-game fish such as copper sharks and other similar species, which can weigh as much as 180kg. Other species that may be caught include kabeljou, steenbras, barber, galjoen and garrick.

The area is good for crayfish, too, though the catch is limited to a maximum of 7 per person, or 14 per vehicle. Permits are required for all types of fishing.

Local tour operators who specialise in beach fishing include Mola Mola (see page 310), who practise catch and release. Watch out for operators who may be less environmentally aware. Mola Mola rates, which include fishing permits, are approximately N$948 per person for two anglers, or N$632 per person for three or more – but note that rates do vary. All tours are taken by a professional guide using a 4WD vehicle that takes a maximum of 4–5 visitors. All equipment is provided, although clients may bring their own reels. Other operators who offer angling trips include Levo (see page 310), who also have bottom and deep-sea fishing, and Sunrise (see page 310). On average, boat fishing will cost from N$440 per person.

For boat trips around Walvis Bay Lagoon, see page 309.

Excursions
Tour operators
Several tour operators and guides specialise in land-based local excursions. Almost all operators will visit the Namib Desert, but the experience you get will depend

very much on your guide. Several operators also run speciality excursions, focusing for example on gems, or up the coast to the seal colony at Cape Cross (see pages 327–9). Prices vary according to the type of terrain, the destination, the number of people and the individual operator, but you can expect to pay around N$200–300 per person for a half-day trip, or N$350–580 per person for a full day. Operators include the following:

Africa Adventure Tours & Safaris Tel: 064 406038, cell: 081 124 6038; fax: 064 406036; email: desert@africaadventure.com.na. Half and full-day excursions in the vicinity, and three-day trips to Sossusvlei and Damaraland.

African Heritage PO Box 1185, Walvis Bay; tel: 064 207401; fax: 064 204850; email: afrherit@iafrica.com.na; web: www.african-heritage-tours.com. A variety of 4WD tours, including tuition for self-drive visitors, plus mini dune-jeep tours, all with an emphasis on conservation.

Charly's Desert Tours PO Box 1400, Swakopmund; tel: 064 404341; fax: 064 404821; email: charlydt@mweb.com.na. Half-day trips include sightseeing tours of Swakopmund and Walvis Bay, plus trips into the desert and to Cape Cross, while full days go further into the desert or down to the Kuiseb Delta.

Desert Adventure Safaris PO Box 339, Swakopmund; tel: 064 404459; fax: 064 404664; email: dassaf@iafrica.com.na. Day trips around Swakopmund to Cape Cross, Spitzkoppe or the Namib Desert, plus longer trips and camping safaris into Damaraland and Kaokoland.

Inshore Safaris PO Box 2444, Walvis Bay; tel: 064 202609; fax: 064 202198; email: info@inshore.com.na; web: www.inshore.com.na. Full-day Welsitschia Desert Tour, as well as other trips on request.

Namib Tours PO Box 1428, Swakopmund; tel: 064 404072, 404054, cell: 081 128 6111; fax: 064 404072. A range of tours, from a one-hour Historical Swakopmund trip to a two-day camping trip into the Erongo Mountains.

Swakop Tour Company PO Box 1725, Swakopmund; tel: 064 405128, cell: 081 124 2906; email: proverb@mweb.com.na. Set tours for small groups include a five-hour klipspringer tour into the desert, and a shorter 'dunes of the Namib' tour around sunset.

Tommy's Tours and Safaris PO Box 3599, Swakopmund; tel/fax: 064 461038; email: tommystours@yahoo.com. A wide choice of options covering almost every aspect of this area.

Turnstone Tours PO Box 307, Swakopmund; tel: 064 403123; fax: 064 403290; email: turn@iafrica.com.na; web: www.turnstone-tours.com

If you're interested in a really informative day in the desert with a first-rate guide who is also excellent company, try Bruno Nebe at Turnstone Tours. You'll pay a bit more than you will for a normal tour, but he takes a maximum of four passengers, and you often get the Land Rover and Bruno to yourselves. Turnstone's trips come with a delicious picnic hamper full of food and drink (instead of just a lunch pack) and visit destinations like Sandwich Harbour and the Namib Desert (half-day tours are also available for a minimum of four people at N$460 per head), as well as others on request. For those with more time, there are short camping tours into Damaraland, the Erongo Mountains and the Namib Desert. Day-trips cost N$750 per person (including VAT, lunch, soft drinks and park permits), with a minimum of two people – a bargain for one of Namibia's best guides.

Welwitschia Drive

In the northern corner of the Namib-Naukluft National Park, an afternoon's excursion from Swakopmund or Walvis Bay, the Welwitschia Drive is a route through the desert with numbered beacons at points of interest, culminating in one of the country's oldest welwitschia plants.

An excellent, detailed booklet is available from the Swakopmund tourist office, from where you must buy a permit for the park before you enter (permits are N$20 per person, and N$20 per vehicle). See *Chapter 12,* pages 274–5, for a full description of the route.

Part of the Welwitschia Drive is the 'moon landscape', or 'moonscape' – a rolling, barren area of rocky desert formed by the valleys around the course of the Swakop River. It's a spectacular sight, often spoken of, and best viewed by the slanting light of mid-morning or late afternoon.

Dune 7

Past the Bird Sanctuary, just off the C14 on the way to the airport and Sesriem, this is one of the highest dunes in the area and has a small picnic site near its base, amongst a few shady palms. It's a popular spot for both energetic dune-climbers and sundowner drinks.

Other desert tours

While many local companies offer half-day or even full-day tours covering a relatively well-beaten trail that includes the Welwitschia Drive, a really attractive alternative is to discover less well-known areas of the desert in the company of a specialist, such as Turnstone Tours. One such trip might take you inland near the old railway, then over rolling dune fields towards the moonscape, from where you can see Rössing Mountain in the distance. Down below, mining claims have been staked out here and there on the gravel plains. While most of the material mined is granite, many other minerals are to be found, including small quantities of yellowish-green uranium oxide, or purpurite; this is the raw material that is processed into yellowcake, and eventually refined into plutonium and other substances. Look out, too, for the cellophane-like hornblend, or the pinky-orange of titanium.

There's a lot more to this apparently barren plain than minerals, though. Individual welwitschia plants and quivertrees form an integral part of the landscape, as do the tiny stone plants, *Lithops karasmontana,* that may be encountered hidden beneath an outcrop of quartz. Lichens cling to the rocks, small holes tell of hairy-footed gerbils and day geckos scurry past. Across the plain is the linear oasis of Goanikontes on the Khan River. Built by the Germans, Goanikontes was originally used as a staging post for horsecarts from Swakopmund, since food for horses and cattle could be grown. Here, and along the huge plain of the Swakop River, numerous plants can be identified clinging to life in this harsh landscape, and klipspringers eke out a precarious existence along the rocks.

Rössing

Rössing is remarkable, particularly if you're interested in engineering, mining or geology. It's an enormous, open-cast uranium mine. For children (especially the sort that never grow up) there are the biggest lorries in the world and some enormous vehicles.

The open-cast mine is awesome, so deep that the same vehicles working at the bottom of the pit look like Dinky toys. You certainly get an alternative view of the desert, and the viewpoints Rössing has set up (with information plaques) provide interesting photo opportunities. There's a video charting the mines and the uranium production process, with the requisite emphasis on safety, and a tour of the whole site.

Visiting Rössing is probably the sort of thing that I would have done when I was a child, on holiday with my family, to fill in a rainy day. Then I'd look back on it, and be glad that I'd done it. It certainly appeals to those already interested, but many will feel only too glad to leave this kind of suspect industrial 'development' behind them in Europe. Trips are run every Friday, leaving Swakopmund Museum at 10.00. Reservations should be made at the museum.

Swakopmund Asparagus

To see how asparagus is grown in the desert, look no further than the asparagus farm just to the west of Swakopmund (tel: 064 405134). To get there, follow the main B2 towards Windhoek for 11km, then take the El Jada turning to the right and continue on this road for a further 4km.

Birdwatching and other wildlife

There is some excellent birdlife in the vicinity. Just take a walk on the southwest side of Walvis Bay, around the lagoon. The flock of feeding flamingos and pelicans that I often find there usually allows me to get much closer than others that I come across in the area. Birdwatchers might also look into the bird sanctuary at the end of 13th Street, as well as stopping at one of the guano platforms in the sea between Walvis and Swakopmund.

Bird sanctuary

If you follow an extension of 18th Road (the C14 towards Sesriem and the airport) inland from Walvis Bay and over the roundabout, heading for Dune 7, then on your right you will shortly see a series of freshwater pools. Alternatively, following 13th Road inland and taking a left will lead you, over a few dunes, to a small wooden hide overlooking some of these.

Sit here with binoculars for a few minutes and you'll often be able to spot some of the pelicans, flamingos, avocets, and assorted waders that attract birdwatchers to flock to Walvis Bay. Enthusiasts may wish to check what's here as well as scanning the main lagoon itself.

Swakop River Delta

Here small tidal lagoons surrounded by reeds are very good for birding. Expect whimbrils, curlews, the odd flamingo and pelican, white-breasted cormorants, Cape cormorants, black-winged stilts, avocets, and more.

The remains of the old railway bridge lie here, washed down in 1934 when the Swakop River performed its flood-of-the-century stunt. On the pillars there are often crowned and bank cormorants, while along the riverbed, between the tamarisk trees, kestrels swoop around catching mice.

The local Wildlife Society has laid out a pleasant, well-marked 4km trail starting next to the cemetery. This takes you downstream into the river mouth, and back to the beach. Walkers should beware of quad-bikes that move pretty fast through this area.

Kuiseb Delta

This fascinating area is criss-crossed by a labyrinth of tracks in which even experienced guides sometimes get lost. Various unmarked archaeological sites dot the area, where pottery shards, beads, shell middens and stone tools can be seen. The wildlife found here includes springbok, ostrich, jackal and brown hyena, and many birds including the endemic dune lark.

Look out for the nara bushes, *Acanthosicyos horrida* – their spiky green (and hence photosynthesising) stems have allowed them to dispense with leaves completely. This is an advantage given the propensity of leaves to lose water. Naras are perhaps not truly desert plants for their roots go down many metres to reach underground water, which they need in order to survive. From February to April and August to September the local Topnaar people harvest nara melons here.

The whole area is only accessible by 4WD and you'll only appreciate it with a good guide. To approach on your own, take the Esplanade by the lagoon southwest from Walvis Bay, and after about 4km ignore the sign to Paaltjies (where the road divides) and keep left. The tracks then splits and you take the left fork marked Rooibank via Wortels.

Sandwich Harbour

This small area about 45km south of Walvis Bay contains a large saltwater lagoon, extensive tidal mudflats, and a band of reed-lined pools fed by freshwater springs – which together form one of the most important refuges for birdlife in southern Africa. Typically you'll find about 30 species of birds at Sandwich at any given time. It offers food and shelter to countless thousands of migrants every year and some of the most spectacular scenery in the country – for those visitors lucky enough to see it. Where else can you walk alone along a pelican-covered beach while pink flamingos glide above the sand-dunes?

Regulations and warning

Getting to Sandwich Harbour requires a high-clearance 4WD and an experienced driver. As several vehicles have been lost to the sea in recent years, many of the area's guides have stopped coming here. Despite this difficulty of accessing it, Sandwich Harbour is still the best place for birding in the area. So don't believe convenient rumours that it's silted up, or devoid of birdlife. It isn't – it's superb.

The most experienced operator doing proper trips here regularly is Bruno, of *Turnstone Tours*, who runs full-day trips for a maximum of four people at a time. These are best booked far in advance, and are highly recommended (see page 315). Other tour operators are Mola-Mola Tours (N$700 per person, including lunch and drinks), Levo, African Heritage and Inshore Safaris.

The reluctance of most guides to come here should be a warning to you: even experienced desert drivers get stuck here regularly if they don't know the place, so it's dangerous to go without a local expert. If you do try to drive yourself, then check the fine print of your vehicle's insurance and buy an NWR permit in advance from the NWR office in Swakopmund, or the Omega or other filling stations in Walvis Bay. These cost N$20 per adult, and N$20 for the vehicle.

Getting there

Take the Esplanade by the lagoon southwest out of Walvis Bay. After about 4km ignore the sign to Paaltjies (where the road divides) and keep to your left. The tracks then splits and you take the right fork, ignoring the road marked Rooibank via Wortels. Cross the salt flats and continue until you reach a fence which marks the boundary of the Namib-Naukluft National Park. Turn right and drive along the fence towards the beach, crossing into the park where the fence stops. You'll be turned away if you don't have a permit.

From this checkpoint it's about 20km of sandy terrain to Sandwich Harbour. You can drive all the way on the beach if you wish, following in the tyre-tracks of the fishermen, although the going can get rough. Beware: if the tide is high and catches you, expect serious problems.

It's better to take an immediate left after passing the control post, and follow these tracks. After some 200m, they turn parallel to the sea and are considerably firmer than the ones on the beach. Leaving these tracks to cross the apparently dry pans, where there are none, is foolhardy.

FLAMINGOS

Of the world's half-dozen or so species of flamingo, two are found within southern Africa: the greater, *Phoenicopterus ruber*, and the lesser, *Phoenicopterus minor*. Both species have wide distributions – from southern Africa north into East Africa and the Red Sea – and are highly nomadic in their habits.

Flamingos are usually found wading in large areas of shallow saline water, where they filter-feed by holding their specially adapted beaks upside down in the water. The lesser flamingo will walk or swim whilst swinging its head from side to side, mainly taking blue-green algae from the surface of the water. The larger greater flamingo will hold its head submerged while filtering out small organisms (detritus and algae), even stirring the mud with its feet to help the process. Both species are gregarious; flocks can number millions of birds, although hundreds are more common.

Only occasionally do flamingos breed in southern Africa, choosing Etosha Pan or perhaps Botswana's Makgadikgadi Pans. When the conditions are right (usually March to June, following heavy rains) both species build low mud cones in the water and lay one (or rarely two) eggs in a small hollow on the top. These are then incubated by both parents for about a month until they hatch, and after a further week the young birds flock together and start to forage with their parents. Some ten weeks later the young can fly and fend for themselves.

During their first few months, the young are very susceptible to the shallow water drying out. In 1969, a rescue operation was mounted when Etosha Pan dried out. Thousands of chicks were moved to nearby Fischer's Pan, which was still covered in water.

The best way to tell the two species apart is by their beaks: that of the greater flamingo is almost white, whilst the lesser flamingo has a uniformly dark beak. Looking from further away, the body of the greater flamingo appears white, whilst that of the lesser looks smaller and more pink.

Namibia's best places for flamingos are usually the lagoons at Walvis Bay and Sandwich Harbour – unless you hear that Etosha or Nyae Nyae are full of water. Then, by the time you arrive, the flamingos will probably have beaten you there.

What to see and do

Once you reach the bird sanctuary, vehicles must be left and you have to proceed on foot. The northern part consists of a number of almost enclosed reed-lined pools at the top of the beach, which back directly on to huge dunes. These are fed partly by the sea via narrow channels which fill at high tide, and partly with fresh water which seeps from a subterranean watercourse under the dunes and enables reeds (albeit salt-tolerant ones) to grow. These in turn provide food and nesting sites for a number of the resident waterbirds found here. On my last visit I managed to spot dabchicks, moorhens, shelducks, common and marsh sandpipers, several species of tern (Caspian, swift, white-winged and whiskered all visit) and even avocets and African spoonbills – as well as the pelicans and flamingos.

As you continue along the beach, the 'harbour' itself comes into view. During the early 18th century it was used by whalers for its deep, sheltered anchorage and ready supply of fresh water. Subsequently a small station was established there to trade in seal pelts, fish and guano. Later, in the early part of this century, it was used as a source of guano but, after the mouth of the harbour silted up, this ground to a halt in 1947, leaving only a few bits of rusting machinery to be seen today.

It's worth climbing up one of the dunes, as from there you can see the deep lagoon, protected from the ocean's pounding by a sand spit, and the extensive mudflats to the south – which are often covered by the tide.

This is definitely a trip to make a whole day of, so, when you start walking from your vehicle, bring some windproof clothes and a little to eat and drink, as well as your binoculars, camera and lots of film. Even if you're not an avid ornithologist, the scenery is so spectacular that you're bound to take endless photos.

The Skeleton Coast

By the end of the 17th century, the long stretch of coast north of Swakopmund had attracted the attention of the Dutch East India Company. They sent several exploratory missions, but after finding only barren shores and impenetrable fogs, their journeys ceased. Later, in the 19th century, British and American whalers operated out of Lüderitz, but they gave this northern coast a wide berth – it was gaining a formidable reputation.

Today, driving north from Swakopmund, it's easy to see how this coast earned its names of the *Coast of Skulls* or the *Skeleton Coast*. Treacherous fogs and strong currents forced many ships on to the uncharted sandbanks that shift underwater like the desert's sands. Even if the sailors survived the shipwreck, their problems had only just begun. The coast here is but a barren line between an icy, pounding ocean and the stark desert interior. The present road (C34) runs more or less parallel to the ocean, and often feels like a drive along an enormous beach – with the sea on one side, and the sand continuing forever on the other.

For the first 250km or so, from Swakopmund to about Torra Bay, there are almost no dunes. This is desert of gravel and rock. Then, around Torra Bay, the northern dune-sea of the Namib starts, with an increasingly wide belt of coastal dunes stretching north to the Kunene River. But nowhere are these as tall, or continuous, as the Namib's great southern dune-sea, south of the Kuiseb River.

At first sight it all seems very barren, but watch the amazing wildlife documentaries made by the famous film-makers of the Skeleton Coast, Des and Jen Bartlett, to realise that some of the most remarkable wildlife on earth has evolved here. Better still, drive yourself up the coast road, through this fascinating stretch of the world's oldest desert. You won't see a fraction of the action that they have filmed, but with careful observation you will spot plenty to captivate you.

FLORA AND FAUNA
Sand-rivers
A shipwrecked sailor's only hope on this coast would have been to find one of the desert's linear oases – sand-rivers that wind through the desert to reach the coast. The Omaruru, the Ugab, the Huab, the Koichab, the Uniab and the Hoanib are the main ones. They are few and far between. Each starts in the highlands, far inland, and, although normally dry, they flood briefly in years of good rains. For most of the time their waters filter westwards to the sea through their sandy beds. Shrubs and trees thrive, supporting whole ecosystems: green ribbons which snake across seemingly lifeless plains.

Even in the driest times, if an impervious layer of rock forces the water to surface, then the river will flow overland for a few hundred metres, only to vanish into the

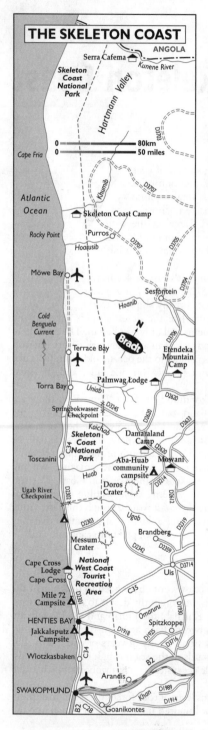

THE SKELETON COAST

ANGOLA

Serra Cafema
Kunene River

Skeleton
Coast
National
Park

Hartmann Valley

0   80km
0   50 miles

Cape Fria

D3703

Khumib

D3707

*Atlantic
Ocean*

Skeleton Coast Camp

Rocky Point   Purros
Hoatusib   D3707   D705

Möwe Bay

Sesfontein   D3704

Hoanib

*Cold
Benguela
Current*

N
Bradt

Terrace Bay   Etendeka
Mountain
Camp

D2620

Palmwag Lodge

Torra Bay   Uniab   D2620

Springbokwasser   D3245
Checkpoint

D1633

Koichab
Skeleton   Damaraland
Coast   Camp   D2620
National
Park   Aba-Huab   Mowani
Toscanini   community
campsite   D3714
Huab   Doros
Crater   D3612

Ugab River
Checkpoint   D2303   Ugab

D2303   Brandberg   D2319

Messum   D2342   D2359
Crater

Cape Cross   National   D3714
Lodge   West Coast   Uis
Cape Cross   Tourist
Recreation   C35
Mile 72   Area
Campsite

Omaruru   D1990

HENTIES BAY   Spitzkoppe
Jakkalsputz   D1918   D1925   D3716
Campsite

Wlotzkasbaken   C34   B2

Arandis

SWAKOPMUND   Khan   D1989
B2   C28   D1914
Goanikontes

sand again as swiftly as it appeared. Such watering places are rare, but of vital importance to the inhabitants of the area. They have allowed isolated groups of Himba people to stay in these parts, whilst also sustaining the famous desert populations of elephant and black rhino.

In many of these river valleys there are thriving populations of gemsbok, kudu, springbok, steenbok, jackals, genets and small wild cats. The shy and secretive brown hyena is common, though seldom seen. Giraffe and zebra are scarce residents, and even lion or cheetah will sometimes appear, using the sand-rivers as alleys for hunting forays. Lion used to penetrate the desert right to the coast to prey on seals. Although it is many years since the last such coastal lion was seen, rising game populations in the interior are encouraging a greater population of lion in the region, so perhaps we'll see individuals on the beaches again before too long.

Beside the sea

Outside the river valleys, the scenery changes dramatically, with an outstanding variety of colours and forms. The gravel plains – in all hues of brown and red – are bases for occasional coloured mountains, and belts of shifting barchan sand-dunes.

Yet despite their barren appearance, even the flattest of the gravel plains here are full of life. Immediately next to the sea, high levels of humidity sustain highly specialised vegetation, succulents like lithops, and the famous lichens – which are, in fact, not plants at all but a symbiotic partnership of algae and fungi, the fungi providing the physical structure, while the algae photosynthesise to produce the food. They use the moisture in humid air, without needing either rain or even fog. That said, frequent coastal fogs and relatively undisturbed plains account for their conspicuous success here.

In some places lichens carpet the gravel desert. Take a close look at one of these

Previous page Brown hyena in Skeleton Coast National Park (CM)

Above Spotted hyena relaxing on Etosha pan (CM)

Left Male lion (AZ)

Below Wild dog in the northern Kalahari (CM)

gardens of lichen, and you'll find many different species, varying in colour from bright reds and oranges, through vivid greens to darker browns, greys and black. Most cling to the rocks or the crust of the gypsum soil, but a few species stand up like the skeletons of small leafless bushes, and one species, *Xanthomaculina convoluta*, is even windblown, a minute version of the tumbleweed famous in old Western films.

All come alive, looking their best, early on damp, foggy mornings. Sections appear like green fields of wispy vegetation. But if you pass on a hot, dry afternoon, they will seem less interesting. Then stop and leave your car. Walk to the edge of a field with a bottle of water, pour a little on to a small patch of lichens, and stay to watch. Within just a few minutes you'll see them brighten and unfurl.

Less obvious is their age: lichens grow exceedingly slowly. Once disturbed, they take decades and even centuries to regenerate. On some lichen fields you will see vehicle tracks. These are sometimes 40 or 50 years old – and still the lichens briefly crushed by one set of wheels have not re-grown. This is one of the main reasons why you should *never* drive off the roads on the Skeleton Coast.

Further inland

East of the coastal strip, between about 30 and 60km inland, the nights are very cold, and many mornings are cool and foggy. However, after about midday the temperatures rocket and the humidity disappears. This is the harshest of the Namib's climatic zones, but even here an ecosystem has evolved, relying on occasional early-morning fogs for moisture.

This is home to various scorpions, lizards, and tenebrionid beetles, living from wind-blown detritus and vegetation including dune-creating dollar bushes, *Zygophyllum stapffii*, and perhaps the Namib's most fascinating plant, the remarkable *Welwitschia mirabilis*.

NATIONAL WEST COAST RECREATIONAL AREA

The coast is divided into three areas. North of Swakopmund up to the Ugab River, covering about 200km of coast, is the National West Coast Tourist Recreational Area. No permits are needed to drive through here and there are a few small towns and several campsites for fishing parties.

Getting there

It is even more vital here than in the rest of Namibia: you need a vehicle to see this part of the Skeleton Coast. Hitchhiking is not restricted, but with bitterly cold mornings and desiccating afternoons it won't be pleasant – heat exhaustion would be a real danger. A few tour companies in Swakopmund run excursions to Cape Cross, about 120km or 1½ hours' drive from Swakopmund (see page 315), which stop at one of the lichen fields, and some of the more obvious sites of interest on the way.

By far the best method is to drive yourself, equipped with plenty of water and a picnic lunch, and stop where and when you wish to explore. Set off north as early as possible, catching the southern sections of the road in the fog, and pre-book to stay at Terrace Bay for the night. The drive alone will take about five hours, though most people stop to explore and have refreshments, and so make a whole day of it.

The main C34 is tarred up until the C35 turn-off, just north of Henties Bay. After that it becomes what is known locally as a *salt road*, made of salt, gypsum and gravel compacted hard over the years. It has no loose surface, and so is almost as solid and safe as tar. You can drive faster on this than you would on normal gravel, though it sometimes twists around and gets bumpy – so there's no leeway for a lack of concentration.

Swakopmund to Henties Bay
The sea ponds
About 7km north of Swakopmund lie a number of large shallow ponds. These are mostly natural ponds used for salt production by the Salt Company. Some are filled with seawater, which is then left to evaporate, whilst others are used for farming oysters. Sometimes you'll see one coloured bright red or green by algae, or pink by a flock of feeding flamingos!

Nobody lives here, but workers from Swakopmund manage the site. Both the salt and the oysters are sold within Namibia, and most restaurants in Swakopmund will offer you both.

Wlotzkas Baken
This small settlement, about 31km north of Swakopmund, looks like a colony on the moon. Its houses spread out along the desert coast, each overshadowed by its own long-legged water tower (which rely on tankers driving the water from inland.) It was named after Paul Wlotzke, a keen Swakopmund fisherman who first built a hut here, and guided visitors to this rich area for fishing.

Like the ghost towns near Lüderitz, nobody lives here permanently. Wlotzkasbaken is simply a collection of holiday homes, used mainly by those Namibians who love sea fishing and come here for their annual summer breaks around December and January.

East of here are a few apparently barren hills and boulders. Get out of the car to take a closer look, and you'll find many small plants and shrubs there. The Namib's fogs are densest (and so deliver the more moisture) at higher elevations, so even these relatively small hills catch much more water from the fog than the flat plains.

Amongst the boulders are also small land snails, beetles and small vertebrates. These include what is thought to be the world's only lizard that actually mimics an invertebrate for protection. The juveniles of the *Eremias lugubris* species have the same coloration and style of movement as a beetle known locally as the 'oogpister' – which protects itself like a skunk by expelling a foul-smelling liquid.

Where to stay
Mile 14 Campsite book via the NWR in Windhoek, see page 118.
This is the first coastal campsite north of Swakopmund, used mainly by families in the high season on fishing trips to the coast. It is massive, stretching some 3–4km along the beach, with sites marked by wooden pegs, and ablution blocks built regularly every 100m. (Showers and water are free here.)

Expect this to be totally empty except for high summer, when you will find it busy with plenty of Namibians and South Africans. During Namibian school holidays there is even a basic shop that opens here – though this is hard to believe if you pass in the quiet season.
Rates: N$110 per site, for up to 4 people, plus N$10 per extra person (to a maximum of 8 people).

Jakkalsputz Campsite Book via the NWR in Windhoek, see page 118.
This is a few kilometres south of Henties Bay, and similar to Mile 14 – small plots of desert beside the beach, with pitches marked off as campsites.
Rates: N$110 per site, for up to 4 people, plus N$10 per extra person (to a maximum of 8 people).

Henties Bay
About 76km from Swakopmund, this windswept town is set immediately above the shore and around one stream (normally just sandy) of the River Omaruru. Overseas visitors will find little to do here, though in December and January

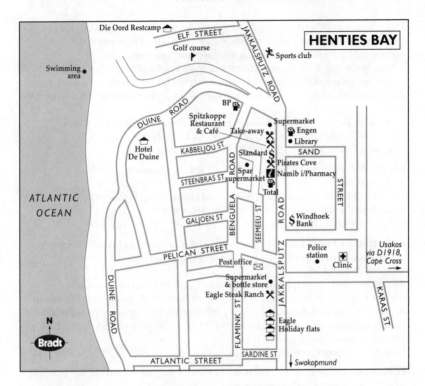

Namibians flock here on their annual holidays, to escape the interior's heat and go fishing. If you'd like to join them, try contacting West Coast Angling Tours (tel: 064 500675) Non-fishing visitors might like to take a short wander up the Omaruru's course, though most will simply refuel here before leaving as quickly as they arrived.

While keen fishermen delight in the pronunciation of their catches – galjeon, kabeljou, steenbras and stompneus – ardent golfers can have a game at the Henties Bay Golf Course. This resides in a section of the riverbed, just near to De Duine Hotel, and doesn't suffer from a shortage of sandy bunkers. And for fit, acclimatised hikers, a new circular hiking trail of 35–40km has just been designated, taking in some of the desert scenery around the town.

Do fill up with fuel in Henties Bay if you're heading north. Fuel stations are rare further north, but there are several here: one on the main road which slightly bypasses town, and two in town itself.

If you haven't been able to stock up on food and drinks in Swakopmund, then Henties Bay does have a reasonable supermarket and a few general shops, including a couple of bottle stores, and a paint and hardware store that will rent out basic camping gear and fishing equipment. Some are centred on the Eagle Complex (location of the holiday flats), in the middle of town, but carry on up the road and you'll come to the supermarket, a couple of restaurants, and the fuel stations.

Where to stay

Hotel De Duine (20 rooms) 34 Duine Rd, PO Box 1, Henties Bay; tel: 064 500001; fax: 064 500724; email: afrideca@mweb.com.na; web: www.namibialodges.com. (Not to be confused with *Die* Duine, in the NamibRand Reserve.)

This reliable hotel is across the road from a steep beach and the ocean. Its owners are friendly and helpful, and if you stay a while they will go out of their way to help you organise fishing trips – especially if you don't arrive in their busy season.

The rooms have recently been refitted, and all are comfortable with direct-dial telephones and en-suite bathrooms. The restaurant is à la carte, simple but good. Some claim that Henties Bay has the world's best crayfish, so perhaps this is the place to try them out.

If you are just passing through and want a break, then breakfast is served about 8.00–10.00, lunch 12.30–14.00, and dinner usually 19.00–21.00.

Rates: single N$295, double N$430, including breakfast. Dinner N$75.

Die Oord Restcamp (15 chalets) PO Box 82, Rob St, Henties Bay; tel: 064 500239/500165

This small, pleasant restcamp has fully equipped chalets for up to four or five people. Don't expect luxury, but if you want a place to sleep then it is fine.

Rates: 2-bed bungalow N$210, 3-bed N$240, 5-bed N$350.

Eagle Holiday Flats (2 chalets, 13 rooms) 175 Jakkalsputz Rd, PO Box 20, Henties Bay; tel: 064 500032; fax: 064 500299; email: eaglesc@iafrica.com.na; web: www.eagleholiday.com

Basic twin rooms and simple self-catering chalets, each with two bedrooms, are conveniently situated in the centre of town, part of the main shopping centre. Rooms have en-suite facilities; flats are clean, cool and a little spartan. The kitchens have microwaves, toasters and even a second freezer specifically for fish – and yet no dishcloths. Each has a TV, and bathroom with a shower.

Rates: N$90 per person per night.

Fisherman's Lodge (9 rooms) PO Box 200, Henties Bay; tel: 064 501111; fax: 064 501177; email: fishermanslodge@iway.na

The bright yellow building that is Fisherman's Lodge (formerly Henties Bay Guesthouse) lies just 200m from the beach. Popular with anglers, it has a lounge, bar and restaurant where breakfast, lunch and dinner are available (the latter on request). Double rooms are all en suite, with minibar, TV and telephone. Public rooms and three of the bedrooms are accessible by wheelchair. Outside, secure parking is available. Deep-sea fishing, guided rock and surf angling, and dolphin- and seal-viewing trips can all be organised, along with other shore-based activities. Meals are available by arrangement.

Rates: single N$350, double N$450 per person sharing.

Haus Estnic (3 rooms) Omatako St; tel: 064 500992; fax: 064 501143; email: hausestnic@yahoo.com

This small B&B offers well-appointed double rooms around a small courtyard with braai facilities. Each en-suite room has a fridge, hairdryer, kettle and cafetiere.

Rates: single N$200, double N$300, including breakfast.

Where to eat

Close to the supermarket and petrol stations are a couple of simple restaurants. There's the **Desert Sands** Restaurant and Pub (tel: 064 500008), and the nearby **Pirates Cove** (tel: 064 500960), a sports bar serving steak and pizza that also offers accommodation. Behind the bank (which has a useful ATM) is the Spitzkoppe café.

North from Henties Bay

Two roads break away from the main coastal road near Henties Bay. The D1918 heads almost due east for about 121km, passing within 30km of Spitzkoppe (see page 345) before joining the main tarred B2 about 23km west of Usakos. The more popular C35 heads northeast across an amazingly flat, barren plain: certainly one of the country's most desolate roads. This is the way to Uis Mine, Khorixas, and southern Damaraland, unless you are planning to stop for the night somewhere like Terrace Bay.

Ignoring both these right-turns, and continuing northwest along the C35 coast road, you soon reach…

Mile 72 Campsite Book via the NWR in Windhoek; see page 118.
Yet another desolate row of ablution blocks – unless you're here in the summer. In season, this has a useful fuel station. By the time you are this far up the coast, fresh water costs 10c per litre, and hot showers are N$1 each.
Rates: N$110 per site, for up to 4 people, plus N$10 per extra person (to a maximum of 8 people)

The Omaruru River

Driving north past Henties Bay, note all the vegetated depressions (indicating watercourses) that you pass through, spread out along 10–15km around the town. These are all part of the Omaruru River Delta. Because of the high rainfall in its catchment area, in the mountains around Omaruru, this flows regularly and the sandy riverbed usually supports quite a luxurious growth of vegetation.

The vegetation includes a variety of desert flora, native to the Namib's many riverbeds, as well as some exotics like wild tobacco (*Nicotiana glauca)*, jimson weed (*Datura stramonium),* and the castor oil plant (*Ricinus communis)*. These are found from here northwards, in many of the other river valleys also, and Dr Mary Seely, in her excellent book *The Namib* (see *Further Reading*), suggests that the seeds for the first such plants might have been imported with fodder for horses during the South African War. As they are hardy plants, eaten by few animals, they have been very successful.

Gemstones

With so little precipitation, even unobservant visitors notice that the basic geology of the Namib often lies right on its surface, just waiting to be discovered. Don't miss the chance to stop somewhere on the C34 or C35 around here. Wander a few hundred metres from it, and do some gem hunting. Even if you're not an expert, you will find some beautiful crystals.

It was whilst staying at Mile 72 in 1972 that a Namibian mineralogist, Sid Peters (owner of the *House of Gems* in Windhoek, see page 148), went hunting for minerals. He found several aquamarines and then a long light-blue crystal that he couldn't identify. Eventually the Smithsonian Institute in Washington DC confirmed that this was *jeremejebite*, a very rare, hard mineral containing boron, first discovered in its white form over 80 years ago in Siberia.

Cape Cross Seal Reserve

Open: daily 10.00–1700 every day. No motorcycles.
Costs: N$20 per adult, N$2 per child, plus N$20 per car.
Here, in 1485, the Portuguese captain and navigator Diego Cão landed. He was the first European of his time to reach this far south down the coast of Africa, and to mark the achievement he erected a stone cross on the bleak headland, inscribed in Latin and Portuguese with:

> Since the creation of the world 6684 years have passed and since the birth
> of Christ 1484 years and so the illustrious Don John has ordered this
> pillar to be erected here by Diego Cão, his knight.

THE SEALS

In mid- to late-October the large males, or bulls, arrive, their massive body weight of around 360kg far exceeding that of the 75kg females. They stake their territorial claims and try to defend them from other males. Shortly afterwards, in late November or early December, each of the pregnant females gives birth to a single pup. These will remain in and around the colony, and continue suckling for the next ten or eleven months.

Shortly after giving birth, the females mate with the males who control their harems, and the cycle continues, with the pups born about a year later. When the females have all given birth, and mated, most of the males will leave to break their fast and replenish the enormous amounts of body-fat burned whilst defending their territories. In the last few months of the year, the scene can be quite disturbing, with many pups squashed by the weighty adults, or killed by the area's resident populations of jackal and brown hyena.

Diego Cão died for his daring, and was buried on a rock outcrop nearby, which they called *Serra Parda*. His cross remained in place until the 1890s, when it was taken to the oceanographical Museum in Berlin, and in 1974 the whole area was landscaped and a replica cross erected, which stands there today.

David Coulson, in his book *Namib* (see *Further Reading*), relates that an old slate was found half-buried in the sand around here, with a message dated 1860 reading:

> I am proceeding to a river sixty miles north, and should anyone find this
> and follow me, God will help him.

It is not known who wrote the message, or what became of them.

All along the Namibian coast there are seal colonies, though the one at Cape Cross is one of the easiest to access. It is a colony of the Cape fur seal, *Arctocephalus pusillus pusillus*, numbers up to 100,000 animals, and is occupied all year round.

At any time of year, the amazing sight of tens of thousands of heads bobbing on land and in the water is only matched by the overpowering stench of the colony that greets you. The noise, too, is unexpected – a positive cacophony of sound that resembles an entire farmyard of animals at full volume.

Where to stay

Cape Cross Lodge (14 rooms) PO Box 259, Henties Bay; tel: 064 694012; fax: 064 694013; email: capecross@africaonline.com.na; central reservations tel: 061 255488; fax: 061 251400; email: reservations@africansolutions.org or info@africansolutions.org
Opened in 2001, just 4km from the seal colony, this brand new lodge is a beacon for visitors to this area, with accommodation that puts Cape Cross firmly on the map. This is where the desert meets the sea, and the large, airy rooms of this well-appointed lodge reflect the vast open spaces all around.

En-suite rooms are modern and spacious, with rooms at the front having panoramic views out to sea from individual balconies. There is a real sense of taste here, with solid, limed-wood furniture, stone floors and soft blue-and-white décor that compliment the nautical setting. Two of the rooms are linked by an adjoining door, making a family suite possible.

Downstairs is a huge lounge and dining area with a central barbecue and a bar at one end. The restaurant is open to day visitors as well as residents, with both snacks and main meals available. Plans are in hand to increase privacy for residents by opening a cellar bar in mid 2002, and introducing a more private dining area. In the evenings, though, the place is open only to residents, with occasional candlelit dinners on the beach, and a good selection of wines on offer. Lunch for residents is N$65 per person, and dinner N$110.

Aside from the seal colony itself, visitors here are attracted by the sheer beauty of the setting. Just to sit on the outside terrace and watch baby seals cavorting in the waves can occupy half the afternoon, though for the more energetic there are plenty of walks and opportunities for birdwatching. There are as yet no formal facilities for watersports, so those planning to kayak, or to discover 'some of the best surfing in Namibia', should bring their own equipment and discuss plans with the staff, some of whom are enthusiasts themselves. A word of warning: don't even think of swimming without taking local advice; the water is cold, currents are very strong and rip-tides can be extremely dangerous. Traditionally, fishing has been the main attraction for visitors to the area, and tours can be arranged. It is also possible to organise a visit to Messum Crater.

Rates: single N$775–920, double N$980–1,150, family (4) N$1,380–1,610, depending on season (high season March, April, July and October). All rates include breakfast.

Mile 108 Book via the NWR in Windhoek; see page 118.

Could this be even more desolate than Mile 72? Again, in season Mile 108 has a useful fuel station and a small kiosk. Water costs 10c per litre (bring your own container), and hot showers N$1 each.

Rates: N$110 per site, for up to 4 people, plus N$10 per extra person (to a maximum of 8 people).

Wreck of the *Winston*

Just before the entrance to the Skeleton Coast Park is a signpost west to the first of the coast's wrecks: the *Winston*, a fishing boat that grounded here in 1970.

Note Beware of driving on the salt pans here (or anywhere else on this coast), as they can be very treacherous.

SKELETON COAST PARK

Costs: N$20 per adult, N$1 per child, plus N$20 per car.

From the Ugab to the Kunene, the Skeleton Coast Park and Wilderness Areas protect about one-third of the country's coastline. The southern half of this, the Skeleton Coast Park, is easily accessible to anyone with a car and some forward planning. It's a fascinating area and, surprisingly, is often omitted from scheduled tours and safaris. This is a shame, though it does mean that from July to September – when some of the rest of the country is busy with overseas visitors – this is still a blissfully quiet area.

Getting there

Because the climate here is harsh, and the area quite remote, the Ministry of Environment and Tourism have fairly strict regulations about entry permits – which must be followed.

If you are just passing through, then you can buy your entry permit at either gate: the Ugab River gate on the C34, or the Springbokwasser gate on the D3245. You *must* reach your gate of entry before 15.00 to be allowed into the park – otherwise you will simply be turned away.

If you plan to stay at either Torra or Terrace Bay, then you must have a booking confirmation slip, issued by the main NWR office in Windhoek. You cannot just turn up at the gate, or one of the camps, to see if they have any space. You *must* pre-book these camps in Windhoek. In that case, if you arrive from Swakopmund along the C34, you must pass the Ugab River no later than 15.00. Similarly, if

SURVIVING IN THE NAMIB: WHERE TO FIND LIFE?

Jonathan Hughes

The Namib Desert receives its stingy allotment of water in two ways. Its eastern edges, near the escarpment, get rare showers of rain. There you will find inselbergs (see page 253) which can store the water for a time and support permanent communities of perennial plants and resident animals. At the coast, the desert's western edge, the annual rainfall is even lower (less than 5mm at Walvis Bay), and there most organisms rely on the fogs which regularly roll in from the sea. However, in the middle of the desert where neither the rain nor fog reach, there is very little life indeed.

coming from Damaraland, on the D3245, you must pass the Springbokwasser gate by 17.00.

In the Skeleton Coast Park, the road is mostly just normal gravel, so keep your speed below 80km/h to be safe.

The Ugab River

Its catchment area stretches as far as Otavi, so the Ugab is a long and important river for the Namib. It flows at least once most years, and you drive across its bed just after the gate into the park. Although much of the visible vegetation is the exotic wild tobacco, *Nicotiana glauca*, there are still some stunted acacia trees and other indigenous plants, like the nara bushes, *Acanthosicyos horridus*, with their (almost leafless) spiky green stems, and improbably large melons.

Shortly after passing the Ugab, look east to see the view becoming more majestic, as the escarpment looms into view above the mirages, which play on the gravel plains. Near the mouth of the Ugab is the wreck of the *Girdleness*, though it is difficult to see.

Ugab River hiking trails

For keen, self-sufficient hikers there is a two-night, three-day hiking trail, guided by one of the Nature Conservation rangers, which explores the Ugab River in much more depth. Trails run throughout the cooler months, from April to October, starting on the 2nd and 4th Tuesdays of each month, and ending on the Thursday afternoon. Most people camp at Mile 108 for the previous night.

This covers a total of about 50km, reaching as far inland as the foothills of the escarpment where there are some natural springs. Groups are limited to between six and eight people, and the guiding costs N$200 per person. You need to bring a sturdy rucksack with all your own camping equipment and food, and make a booking for the trail with the Nature Conservation office in Windhoek as far in advance as possible (ideally 18 months or so). Then all the participants will need a medical certificate of fitness issued a maximum of 40 days before the hike commences. Having gone to all this trouble, you won't regret it – participants confirm that it is fascinating.

Wreck of the *South West Sea*

Near the road, just north of the Ugab River, this is clearly signposted and very easy to visit. It is one of the coast's most convenient wrecks (for the visitors, not the sailors), so if you're looking for a picnic stop, it is ideal. The ship itself was a small vessel that ran aground in 1976.

Imagining the Skeleton Coast, most people think that it's littered with dozens of picturesque wrecks – but that's really no longer the case. Shipwrecks do gradually disintegrate. They're pounded by the waves, corroded by the salt water, and eventually what's left of them washes out to sea or vanishes into the sands. Further, modern navigation techniques, using accurate charts and, most recently, GPS receivers have greatly reduced the accident rate on this coast. Thus whilst a few decades ago the coast probably was littered with wrecks, now they're few and far between – so take advantage to wander down to this one whilst you can!

The Huab River

North of the Ugab, the next river crossed is the important Huab River. This rises in the escarpment around Kamanjab, and is one of the coast's most important corridors for desert-adapted elephants and rhinos – though you're most unlikely to see either so far from the mountains.

Immediately north of the river, if you look to the east of the road, you can see the beginnings of barchan dunes standing on the gravel plains. Here sand is blowing out of the bed of the Huab, and actually forming a dune-field (see page 35 for the origins of barchan dunes).

It's much easier to spot the rusting hulk of an old oil rig, circa 1960, with a turn-off to a small parking area adjacent. This was originally part of a grand scheme to extract oil from the coast, organised by Ben du Preez, which ran up huge debts before his banks foreclosed. Amy Schoeman's superb coffee-table book, *The Skeleton Coast* (see *Further Reading*), relates this story in detail. As a postscript, she notes that some of Terrace Bay was originally built by du Preez as his base.

Now the old framework provides a perfect breeding spot for Cape cormorants, and so be careful not to disturb the birds by getting out of your car between around September and March.

Toscanini

For such a significant dot on the map, this minute outpost will seem a great disappointment, especially if you miss it! Despite sounding like another campsite, it is in fact the site of a disused old diamond mine. More rusting hulks and decaying buildings.

Elsewhere this kind of dereliction would be bulldozed, landscaped and erased in the name of conserving the scenery, but here it's preserved for posterity, and the visiting seabirds.

The Koichab River

Squeezed between the larger Huab and Uniab rivers, the Koichab (not to be confused with the *Koichab Pan* near Lüderitz) has quite a small catchment area and floods relatively rarely. Thus it seems more of a depression than a major riverbed. For fishing visitors, the Koichab is the southern boundary of the Torra Bay fishing area.

Meanwhile south of this river, but north of Toscanini, you do pass the wrecks of the *Atlantic Pride*, the *Luanda* (1969), and the *Montrose* (1973), though they're not easy to spot, and often the road is far enough from the sea for what's left of these wrecks to be obscured.

Torra Bay

Shortly before Torra Bay, the D3245 splits off from the main coastal C34 and heads east, leaving the park (39km later) at the Springbokwasser gate and proceeding into Damaraland. This beautiful road passes the distinctive Sugar Loaf

SURVIVING IN THE NAMIB: BY ESCAPING
Jonathan Hughes

Many of the Namib's species can only survive at all if they either escape or retreat from the extremes. An 'escape' is an extended period of absence from the desert community, such as a suspension of the life cycle, aestivation (the desert equivalent of hibernation), or by actually migrating out of the desert.

Many of the Namib's plants stop their life cycle for particularly harsh periods, leaving behind dormant seeds able to withstand temperatures of up to 100°C and remain viable for years. Growth is eventually triggered by a threshold amount of rainfall, leading to the phenomenon of the 'desert bloom', where a carpet of flowers covers the ground. These plants, called ephemerals, must then complete their life cycles in a matter of days before the water disappears. A blooming desert obviously requires its pollinators, so various insect species also conduct ephemeral life cycles, switching them on and off as rainfall dictates.

On the great plains of the Namib, a different community waits for rain in any slight depression. When it arrives, and the depression fills, an explosion of activity occurs and pond life comes to the desert. Algae, shrimps and tadpoles fill the ponds for their short lives, employing rapid development techniques to swiftly mature to adulthood.

Large-scale migrations are not common in the Namib, but springbok do trek between arid regions, following any rain, and the Namib's largest mammal, the gemsbok, also moves in a predictable pattern. They move into the Namib's dune-sea after rainfall, looking for the ephemeral grasses. When these vanish, they travel to the dry Kuiseb River bed to compete with the resident baboons for acacia pods and water. Here they excavate waterholes, which they maintain from year to year.

Hill on the right and some large *welwitschia* colonies, which spread either side of the road, before gradually climbing into the foothills of the Kaokoveld. Watch the vegetation change quite quickly on this route, as the road passes through ecosystems that are increasingly less arid, before finally entering Damaraland's distinctive mountains dominated by huge *Euphorbia damarana* bushes.

Just north of this C34/D3245 junction is a section of road standing in the path of barchan dunes that march *across* it. Stop here to take a close look at how these dunes gradually move, grain by grain, in the prevailing southwest wind. Then turn your attention to the build-up of detritus on the leeward side of the dunes, and you may be lucky enough to spot some of the area's residents. Look carefully for the famous white beetles, *Onymacris bicolor*, which are endemic to the area and have been the subject of much study. White beetles are very uncommon, and here it is thought they have evolved their colouration to keep cool, enabling them to forage for longer in the heat.

Many of the plants on this gravel plain around the barchan dunes build up their own small sand-dunes. The dollar bushes, *Zygophyllum stapffii*, with their succulent dollar-shaped leaves, and the coastal ganna, *Salsola aphylla*, are obvious examples. Big enough to act as small wind-breaks, these bushes tend to collect windblown sand. These small mounds of sand, being raised a little off the desert's floor, tend to have more fog condense on them than the surrounding ground. Thus the plant gets a little more moisture. You will normally see a few beetles also, which survive on the detritus that collects, and add their own faeces to fertilise the plant.

The campsite at Torra Bay will be another disappointment unless you arrive in December or January. Then this coastal site opens for the summer. It has ten ablution blocks, a shop and a filling station. The small, square pitches are marked out by rows of stone. Expect a plethora of fishing parties, and a charge for taking a shower or buying water.

Just inland from Torra Bay is a fascinating area of grey-white rocks, sculpted into interesting curves by the wind and the sand-grains.

Rates: N$100 per site, for up to 4 people, N$10 per extra person (to a maximum of 8 people). Open: December 1 to January 31 only.

The Uniab River

Perhaps the most accessible river for the passing visitor is the Uniab River valley, between Torra Bay and Terrace Bay. If you only stop in one river for a good look around, stop here in the Uniab. Not only is it quite scenic, but its headwaters come from around the huge Palmwag concession, home to many of the region's larger mammals. So the Uniab offers your best chance of spotting the park's scarce bigger game.

In ancient times, the river formed a wide delta by the sea, but that has been raised up, and cut into by about five different channels of water. When the river floods now, the water comes down the fourth channel reached from the south, though the old channels still support much vegetation.

At one point whilst crossing the delta, there's a sign to a waterfall about 1.5km west of the road. Here a gentle trickle of water (supplemented by an occasional rainy-season torrent) has eroded a narrow canyon into the sandstone and calcrete layers of the riverbed, before trickling to the sea. If you go down as far as the beach, then look out for the wreck of the *Atlantic*, which grounded here in 1977.

All throughout this delta you'll find dense thickets of reeds and sedges and small streams flowing over the ground towards the sea. Sometimes these will attract large numbers of birds – plovers, turnstones and various sandpipers are very common. Palaearctic migrants make up the bulk of the species.

SURVIVING IN THE NAMIB: BY RETREATING

Jonathan Hughes

A 'retreat' is a short term escape, typically a matter of hours. This has a serious disadvantage: it results in what ecologists call a 'time crunch', where time for foraging and social activity is greatly reduced. It follows that retreating animals must be very efficient at foraging.

Most species retreat to some extent. The Namib's beetles, reptiles, birds and mammals disappear into burrows and nests during the hottest periods of the day. One of the most visible is the social weaver bird, which builds enormous communal nests which insulate the birds during cold nights, and provide a handy retreat during the heat of the day.

In order to extend the time spent on the surface, and minimise this time crunch, one Namib resident, the sand-diving lizard, has developed the remarkable behaviour of 'dancing' on the surface. By lifting its legs at intervals, (never all at once!), it manages to reduce its body temperature and stay out for a few extra minutes of activity.

Although some form of escape or retreat is practical for most animal species, plants do not have the same luxury. They cannot move quickly and therefore have to become tolerant.

As well as the waterfall walk, there's a shorter walk to a small hide overlooking an open stretch of water that attracts birds. Keep quiet whilst you are walking and you should also manage to spot at least some springbok, gemsbok and jackal, which are all common here.

Elephant, lion and cheetah have also been spotted here, but very rarely. Slightly elusive are the brown hyena, whose presence can be confirmed by the existence of their distinctive white droppings (coloured white as they will crunch and eat bones). Their local name, *strandwolf*, is an indication that they are often to be seen scavenging on the beaches for carrion (especially near seal colonies). Whilst these animals look fearsome with powerful forequarters and a thick, shaggy coat, they are solitary scavengers posing no danger to walkers unless cornered or deliberately harassed.

Terrace Bay

About 287km from Henties Bay, the restcamp at Terrace Bay is the furthest north that visitors can drive on the coast. It's a real outpost, appearing just a few kilometres after a sign points off to Dekka Bay. It was built originally for a mining venture, and inherited by the government when that failed. Now there's nothing here apart from the small camp for visitors, run by the NWR, and its staff accommodation.

Fishermen come here all year, and even the President, Sam Nujoma, often takes his holidays here. His phalanx of bodyguards used to make fun company for the unsuspecting visitors he met there. Now, sadly, it seems that he books the whole place for himself and his entourage.

Terrace Bay's facilities are mostly old and basic, but all the bungalows have a fridge, a shower and a toilet. Bedding and towels are provided. Though not luxurious, the accommodation is adequate and Terrace Bay feels so isolated and remote that it can be a lot of fun for a day or two.

All your meals are provided whilst staying here, but there is also a small food shop by the office stocking alcohol, basic frozen braai meats and a few basic supplies, and a vital petrol station/garage.

If your time allows then one of the staff members (ask for Hans) might be persuaded to take you fishing. He can provide the tackle, bait, and know-how, making this a lot of fun even for the uninitiated. A typical trip would take from 14.00 to 17.00. Note that because the staff at Terrace Bay are government employees, they are forbidden from charging for such fishing expeditions, but do appreciate a reasonable 'tip' for their time and help.

Before you dine here, go and take a look at the big shed behind the office. On it you'll see (and smell) hundreds of cormorants which roost there every night – attracted by the warmth from the generator within. Check with the staff, but it may also be worth returning around 22.00 as a brown hyena is said to often stroll by then, looking for hapless cormorants that have fallen from the roof. Check also by the waterfront, where the day's catch is gutted.

Terrace Bay makes an excellent short stop between Swakopmund and Damaraland, and offers the opportunity for you to know the desert better. I normally recommend visitors who don't fish to stay here for a maximum of one night.

Rates: Basic two-bed bungalows: single N$500, double N$3500 per person sharing, including breakfast, dinner, and the use of freezer space. The luxury suite sleeps four and costs N$2,200 – complete with TV and hi-fi!

Möwe Bay

Around 80km north of Terrace Bay, this is the administrative centre of the Wilderness Area, and is not open to visitors. This acts as a base for the few researchers who are allowed to work here.

SKELETON COAST WILDERNESS AREA

To understand the current situation in the Wilderness Area, you need to know the recent history of the park, as well as some politics.

History

The Skeleton Coast Park was initially part of the Etosha National Park, proclaimed in 1906. Then in 1967, South Africa's Odendal Commission cut it down to 25% of its original size, making in the process several 'homelands' for the existing communities. Included amongst these were parts of what is now known as Damaraland and Kaokoland, and also the Skeleton Coast.

During the late '50s and '60s permission was granted to private companies, including one called Sarusas Mining Corporation, for mining and fishing rights on the Skeleton Coast. During the late 1960s, they assembled a project team to build a brand new harbour at Cape Frio. They did all the research and got backing from investors, but at the last moment the South African government pulled the plug on the project. After all, a new Namibian port would reduce the stranglehold that Walvis Bay had on the country – and that had historically belonged to South Africa even before it took over the administration of German South West Africa (Namibia).

The Sarusas Mining Corporation were not happy and took the case to court. Instrumental in this was the young lawyer on their team, Louw Schoemann. As part of the out-of-court settlement, the South African government agreed to allow the area to be re-proclaimed as a national park – and hence the Skeleton Coast was proclaimed as a park in 1971.

However, during the course of all this research, Louw had fallen in love with the amazing scenery and solitude of the area. He had already started to bring friends up to the area for short exploratory safaris. As word spread of these trips, he started taking paying passengers there as well.

In order to preserve part of the area in totally pristine condition, the northern part was designated as a 'Wilderness Area' – to be conserved and remain largely untouched. Strictly controlled rights to bring tourists into one part of this area were given to just one operator. Rules were laid down to minimise the operator's impact, including a complete ban on any permanent structures, a maximum number of visitors per year, and the stipulation that *all* rubbish must be removed (no easy task) and that visitors must be flown in.

Louw won the tender for this concession, giving him the sole right to operate in one section of the wilderness area. So he started to put his new company, Skeleton Coast Fly-in Safaris, on a more commercial footing. The logistics of such a remote operation were difficult and it remained a small and very exclusive operation. Its camps took a maximum of twelve visitors, and much of the travel was by light aircraft. The whole operation was 'minimum impact' by any standard. Louw was one of the first operators to support the pioneering community game-guard schemes in Namibia (see page 45), and he maintained a very ecologically sensitive approach long before it was fashionable.

I travelled to the coast with Louw in 1990. It was spellbinding; one of the most fascinating four days that I've spent anywhere. Partly this was the area's magic, but much was down to the enthusiasm of Louw, and the sheer professionalism of his operation.

Gradually, Skeleton Coast Fly-in Safaris had become a textbook example of an environmentally friendly operation, as well as one of the best safari operations in Africa. Louw's wife, Amy, added to this with the stunning photographs in her book, *The Skeleton Coast*. The latest edition of this (see *Further Reading*) is still the

SURVIVING IN THE NAMIB: SPECIALISED PLANTS
Jonathan Hughes

Most of the Namib's plants have very deep root systems, to acquire what little ground water is available, and adaptations to reduce water loss. Their leaves are usually small and often covered in hairs or a waxy coating. These designs all reduce water loss by evaporation. Smaller leaves mean less surface area, hairs trap still air adjacent to the leaf and waxy coatings don't allow moisture to pass through. The swollen, waxy leaves of succulents are filled with water, and hence must be protected from thirsty grazers. They usually employ toxins, or spines, but in the Namib there are also the extraordinary *geophytes*, plants which camouflage themselves as stones. Add to the problem of desiccation that of overheating. Most desert plants are orientated to minimise heating, by having their narrowest edge facing the sun. Some geophytes go one better by growing almost entirely underground.

definitive work on the area. His sons, André and Bertus, joined as pilot/guides, making it a family operation. In many ways, Louw's operation put the area, and even the country, on the map as a top-class destination for visitors. Fly-in safaris to the Skeleton Coast had become one of Africa's ultimate trips – and largely due to Louw's passion for the area.

Politics in the 1990s

In 1992, the new government put the concession for the Skeleton Coast Wilderness Area up for tender, to maximise its revenue from the area. No local operator in Namibia bid against Louw; it was clear that he was operating an excellent, efficient safari operation in a very difficult area – and such was the operation's reputation, no local company would even try to bid against them.

However, a competing bid was entered by a German company, Olympia Reisen, headed by the powerful Kurt Steinhausen, who have extensive political connections in Namibia and Germany. They offered significantly more money, and won the concession. (They subsequently built the enigmatic Oropoko Lodge, near Okahandja. See page 172.)

Local operators were uniformly aghast. Suddenly a foreign firm had usurped Namibia's flagship safari operation. Negative rumours of Olympia Reisen's other operations did nothing to allay people's fears.

Inevitably given his legal background, Louw started legal proceedings to challenge the bid. However, the stress of the situation took its toll and tragically he died of a heart attack before the case was heard. The challenge succeeded, but Olympia Reisen appealed to the High Court, who referred the matter to the cabinet. The cabinet set aside the ruling, and awarded the concession to Olympia Reisen for an unprecedented ten years. Olympia Reisen's political connections had won through.

The rules of the game had clearly changed. The monthly 'rent' for the concession that Skeleton Coast Safaris used to pay has been abolished. In its place, Olympia Reisen pays the government N$1,000 for every visitor taken into the concession. However, with no 'rent' and no minimum number of visitors, the government's income from the area dropped drastically. In the first four years of Olympia Reisen's operation they carried fewer than 400 people into the concession – less than half the number of visitors taken in *annually* by Skeleton Coast Safaris.

Olympia Reisen is widely viewed with suspicion in Namibia, and conspiracy theories abounded about what they were doing up on such a remote stretch of coast where nobody could watch their operations. Their negative attitude to journalists, including myself, did nothing to help counter the rumours.

The current situation

By the mid-1990s it was becoming clear that Olympia Reisen were never going to make a commercial success of safaris to the area, and whilst they were there, nobody else could see the area. Finally in 1999, Wilderness Safaris – a major player in southern Africa with a good reputation for sensitive development and responsible operations – became involved. They made a deal with Olympia Reisen to take control of tourism in the area.

They ripped down the poor structures that Olympia Reisen had erected, removed from the area numerous truckloads of accumulated rubbish, and set about a series of ecological impact assessments prior to opening a totally new Skeleton Coast Camp in April 2000. They also took control of all the ecological monitoring in the area, effectively putting an end to the many rumours about what had been happening in the wilderness area – and ultimately providing a base for a number of wildlife researchers who now have projects in the area. The tender for this area is again due to be up for bidding at the end of 2003. Given the excellent track record of the current operation, and the difficulty of working in this area at all, Wilderness Safaris is widely expected to retain the concession.

Meanwhile, after losing the rights to use the Skeleton Coast Wilderness area to Olympia Reisen in 1992, the Schoeman family continued to operate their own fly-in safaris. They did this using remote areas of the Skeleton Coast just south of the wilderness area, and parts of the western Kaokoveld and Damaraland just east of the park's boundary. Although they were slightly different areas of the coast and its hinterland, their style and guiding skills remained as strong as ever – and their trips remained superb. On several occasions I've spoken with travellers that I've sent on these trips who have been full of praise and described them as 'life-changing experiences'.

Fly-in safaris: the two options

Thus the visitor looking to see this remarkable area has two choices. Both are fairly costly and packed full of activities, but they're very different in style. Both rank amongst the best trips on the subcontinent.

The only caveat to this eulogy is that whilst this region appears harsh and 'in your face', it actually offers some of Africa's most subtle attractions. Endless savannah covered with wildebeest is enthralling; gravel plains dotted with *welwitschia* may seem less so. Most appreciate leopards, but the lichens' appeal is less obvious. Hence in some ways both of these trips are better suited to visitors who have been on safari to Africa before. Often it seems that the trips are praised most highly by the most experienced safari-goers. Much of the credit here is due to the calibre of the guides: the area's subtle attractions require top guiding skills to bring them to life – and both operations have this.

Skeleton Coast Fly-in Safaris

Visitors imagine that the original fly-in safaris to the Skeleton Coast went only into the narrow concession area, by the ocean's edge. But they are wrong. Even in 1990, when I first visited with Louw Schoeman, we spent much time outside the concession – in the adjacent Kaokoveld, for example, and visiting Purros and the Kunene – as well as time in it. Thus although being excluded from the concession

SURVIVING IN THE NAMIB: ANIMAL ADAPTATIONS
Jonathan Hughes

Water, the ultimate limitation of the desert, is of key importance to the Namib's animals. Without exception, all of the animal species here tolerate extreme levels of desiccation, and some employ interesting techniques. The male namaqua sandgrouse travels miles to find water each day. When successful, he paddles in it, allowing his breast feathers to absorb water like a sponge. Laden with this cargo he travels back to the nest to feed the thirsty young and his partner. Springboks and gemsbok have kidneys that are so efficient at absorbing water that a pellet form of urine is produced.

The African ground squirrel faces away from the sun at all times, and uses its tail as a parasol while it forages. Perhaps most peculiar to the Namib are the dune beetles, which inhabit the crests of the desert's taller sand-dunes. They are early risers when there is fog about, and sit motionless for hours in order to allow it to condense on their bodies. Periodically they perform a spectacular dance to move the precious water along their bodies and into their mouths.

in 1992 was a blow, they were able to adapt their trips to use similar, adjacent areas and offer trips which were just as good, if not better, than the original ones. The flying and guiding ability of the Schoemans is such that they could organise a fly-in safari to an industrial wasteland ... and end up making it one of the most fascinating places you've ever been.

Skeleton Coast Safaris use light aircraft (typically 6-seater Cessnas) like most safaris use Land Rovers; exploring areas from the sky, flying low-level over dunefields, and periodically turning back for better views. So there's a lot of flying in small aircraft – generally short 30–40 minute hops which most people find fascinating. Currently they concentrate on four main trips, Safaris A, B, C and D respectively, though these are really just variations around the main theme of their most popular trip:

Safari A

This starts at 10.00 at Eros Airport in Windhoek, before flying west over the escarpment to Conception Bay, south of Sandwich Harbour, and north to refuel at Swakopmund. It stops again at Cape Cross, for lunch and a visit to the seal colony, before flying north and inland to the first of their three main camps, **Kuidas Camp.** This is in the Huab River Valley, west of Damaraland Camp and east of the park's boundary. It's positioned in a dry, rocky landscape that's typical of western Damaraland, and there are some rock engravings within walking distance of the camp. Like all of these camps, Kuidas has small but comfortable igloo tents containing twin beds separated by a bedside table, an en-suite bucket shower, and a chemical loo (so you don't need to go outside of your tent to use the toilet at night). There's also one main flush toilet in the camp. Kuidas Camp is the base for the next morning's exploration of the Huab River Valley and huge gravel plains dotted with *Welwitschia mirabilis.*

After lunch you'll hop to Terrace Bay for a short Land Rover trip to explore the beach and nearby roaring dunes (one of the highlights of the trip for me; totally surreal), before flying out to **Purros Camp**, in the heart of the Kaokoveld near the Himba community at Purros. Camp is under a broken canopy of camelthorns (*Acacia erioloba*) and makalani palms (*Hyphaene petersiana*), near the (invariably dry) Hoarusib River. From here the early morning is spent exploring the river valley, which has a thriving population of desert-adapted elephants, amongst other game, and visiting some of the local Himba people.

Continuing up the coast there are the remains of the Kaiu Maru shipwreck to be seen before the northwestern corner of Namibia is reached: the mouth of the Kunene River. Further inland, east of the dunes (which cover most of the park in this northern area), you'll land at the north end of Hartmann's Valley. The afternoon is spend exploring this beautiful and very remote area, before finally reaching the last camp, **Kunene Camp**, which overlooks the river at the north end of Hartmann's Valley. The last morning of the trip is usually spent on a boat trip on the Kunene, before lunch and a long scenic flight to arrive back at Eros Airport, in Windhoek, in the late afternoon.

Rates: Safari A lasts four days and three nights and costs US$2,585 per person, including all meals, drinks and activities.

Safari B

This starts earlier, and includes a stop at Sesriem, a drive into Sossusvlei, and a scenic flight over the vlei before flying on to Conception Bay, and continuing with the normal plan for Safari A.

Rates: Safari B lasts four days and three nights and costs US$2,770 per person, including all meals, drinks and activities.

Safari C

Starts off like Safari B, but then after Kunene Camp includes a final night beside Etosha National Park, at one of the lodges on the Eastern side (normally Etosha Aoba or Mushara), and time spent exploring the park by private 4WD.

Rates: Safari C lasts five days and four nights and costs US$3,040 per person, including all meals, drinks and activities.

Safari D

Starts off at 07.00, with a flight to Sesriem and a trip into Sossusvlei, before flying on to Wolwedans Dune Lodge (see page 255), your base for two nights. An afternoon exploring the NamibRand Reserve is followed the next day by a flying day-trip south, to Lüderitz, for a 4WD excursion into the Sperrgebiet, ending up at Elizabeth Bay (see page 244). This has big advantages over doing the same excursion on your own from Lüderitz, as you'll have one of Skeleton Coast's excellent guides with you, who will bring this amazing area to life. After your second night at Wolwedans, this trip continues as Safari A.

Rates: Safari D lasts six days and five nights and costs US$3,575 per person, including all meals, drinks and activities.

Bookings

Skeleton Coast Fly-in Safaris can be contacted at PO Box 2195, Windhoek; tel: 061 224248; fax: 061 225713; email: sksafari@mweb.com.na; web: www.orusovo.com/sksafari/default.htm

They operate all year, and normally require a minimum of two people to confirm a safari on any given date. As with most upmarket options in Africa, you should find it slightly cheaper to book this through an overseas tour operator who specialises in the region.

Skeleton Coast Camp

With just 12 beds, the Skeleton Coast Camp is one of the flagships of Wilderness Safaris camps in the subcontinent. In contrast to the Schoeman's operation, this one fairly luxurious camp is the base for your safari here which usually lasts three, four or seven days.

The camp itself stands in a sheltered corner of the Hoarusib River. All of the six tented rooms are raised on wooden decks, and have en-suite bathrooms with flush toilets, a hand basin and a hot shower. These substantial rooms are very comfortable, complete with fans and 12v lighting systems – although given the cold nights here, it's the thick duvets and warm comfy beds that often prove more essential. Artistic arrangements of local materials, and welcome hot-water bottles that magically appear in your bed, help make the rooms a real pleasure.

The main dining area is also raised up, and includes a dining room and comfy lounge/bar area, surrounded by plenty of glass which, when there's no fog around, allows good views of the desert. After-dinner drinks, and sometimes dinner, are often taken around a campfire outside, under an old leadwood tree. The food, as you'd expect, is of a high standard.

The sights

So here you'll have dinner, sleep and have breakfast at camp – but you'll usually spend each of your days out on a whole-day 4WD safari exploring some of the area's many attractions. These can be long days, but are always varied – and punctuated by stops for regular drinks and picnics. Although this area has some specific 'sights' to see, these are almost incidental in comparison with simply experiencing the solitude and singular beauty of the area. Visiting this whole region is about experiencing a variety of beautiful landscapes, each with its own fragile ecosystem, existing side by side. Whilst on safari, you'll frequently stop to study the plants and smaller animals, or perhaps to capture landscapes on film. A few of the better-known places in the area include:

Rocky Point is a rocky pinnacle that juts out from a long, open stretch of sand, and in times past was an important landmark on the coast for passing ships. Now it's a good spot for a little gentle surf fishing, birdwatching, or simply watching the odd Cape fur seal bob crawl out onto the rocks for some sun.

Cape Frio is another, smaller rocky outcrop on the coast, but this one is home to a colony of up to 20,000 Cape fur seals. With patience and care, you can approach close enough to get a good portrait photograph whilst still not disturbing them. Keep an eye out for jackals, and if you watch for prints in the sand you'll usually find brown hyena have also been here.

Strandloper rock circles are found in several places on the coast. Probably made by Khoisan people, some of these are simply circles, the remains of shelters used by hunter/gatherers who lived near the shore (Strandlopers). Others are more elaborate, covering larger areas and laid out in lines, and it's speculated that perhaps they were hunting blinds – which suggests that the area had a denser population of game in relatively recent (in geological terms) times.

Lichen fields and welwitschia plants are widespread on gravel plains throughout the Namib. However, here they are at their most extensive and usually in pristine condition. In several places there are clearly visible vehicle tracks which have left a lasting impression on the lichens. These can be precisely dated by historical records. They're the subject of much scientific interest, including a project by an Oxford University researcher who is based at the camp.

The Clay Temples of the Hoarusib Canyon are tall structures made of soft sand which line the sides of the Hoarusib's steep canyon, resembling some of the ancient Egyptian temples. When I first visited the area many years ago, our driving on the dry river's sand here was instantly halted by a patch of quicksand.

The beaches Throughout the coast's misty, desolate beaches there is always something of interest to take a closer look at, or to photograph. Ghost crabs scuttle amongst the flotsam and jetsam of the centuries, while rare Damara terns fly overhead.

The Roaring Dunes are one of the most amazing experiences on the coast. If you slide down one of the steep lee sides, these large sand-dunes make an amazing and unexpected loud noise which reverberates through the whole dune. It really has to be felt to be believed, and gets even louder when you slide a whole vehicle down the dune! One theory links the 'roar' with electrostatic discharges between the individual grains of sand when they are caused to rub against each other. Why some dunes 'roar' and others don't remains a mystery – but there are other roaring dunes: there are also some in the Namib south of the Hoanib River, and in Witsand Nature Reserve in South Africa's northern Cape.

Himba village One of the camp's first guides, the excellent Chris Baccus, worked with the Himba communities for years before helping to set up and start off the Skeleton Coast Camp. He's a very good relationship with the communities in the area, and now the camp's guides will take visitors (who approach with some cultural sensitivity) to one of the area's Himba villages, and introduce them to the people there. As with all such meetings, it can be a fascinating and humbling experience. Also, importantly, the villages are deriving a good income from these visits, both directly and by making and selling traditional crafts.

Bookings
The Skeleton Coast Camp is booked via Wilderness Safaris who can be contacted at PO Box 6850, Windhoek, Namibia; tel: 061 274500; fax: 061 239455. However, their website (www.wilderness-safaris.com) advises that they prefer travellers to make arrangements through a good overseas tour operator (see pages 50–1) in their own country, rather than directly with them in Namibia.

Trips lasting four nights and five days usually start on a Saturday morning from Eros Airport, and return on Wednesday afternoon. Flights up to the camp, and back, are usually in a comfortable twin-engined 13-seater 'caravan' (a type that's increasingly common in southern Africa). From July to October, these trips cost US$3,082/3,582 per person sharing/single, and include all meals, drinks and activities; the rest of the year, they are US$2,568/3,068. A shorter trip, lasting three nights and four days, usually starts on a Wednesday morning and costs US$2,733/3,133 per person sharing/single in high season, or US$2,432/2,832 during the rest of the year. Opt for the longer trip if funds allow – you'll still leave feeling that you've only scratched the surface – or consider combining a trip here with the new Serra Cafema Camp (see page 368), on the northern edge of Hartmann's Valley, northeast of the Skeleton Coast Camp.

The Kaokoveld

The Kaokoveld is one of Africa's last wildernesses. Namibia's least inhabited area, it stretches from the coastal desert plain and rises slowly into a wild and rugged landscape. Here slow-growing trees cling to rocky mountains, whilst wild grass seeds wait dormant on the dust plains for showers of rain.

Because of the low population in the northern parts of the Kaokoveld, and the spectacularly successful Community Game Guard scheme (see *Chapter 3*, page 45), there are thriving populations of game here, living beyond the boundaries of any national park. This is one of the last refuges for the black rhino, which still survive (and thrive) here by ranging wide, and knowing where the seasonal plants grow.

It is also home to the famous desert elephants. Some naturalists have cited their apparently long legs, and proven ability to withstand drought, as evidence that they are actually a subspecies of the African elephant. Though this is not now thought to be the case, these remarkable animals are certainly adept at surviving in the driest of areas, using their amazing knowledge of the few water sources that do exist.

Historically the Kaokoveld has been split into two areas: Damaraland in the south, and Kaokoland in the north. Though it is all now officially known as the Kunene region, this book has retained the old names as they are still widely in use. Further, this chapter subdivides Damaraland because, for the visitor, its north is very different from its south.

Southern Damaraland's most interesting places are easily accessible in your own 2WD vehicle. It is an area to explore for yourself, based at one of the camps or lodges. Its main attractions are the mountains of Spitzkoppe and Brandberg, the wealth of Bushman rock art at Twyfelfontein, the Petrified Forest, and various rock formations.

Northern Damaraland attracts people to its scenery, landscapes and populations of game – and is best visited by driving yourself to one of the four huge private concession areas: Hobatere, Palmwag, Etendeka and the Damaraland Camp. From there you can join the guided 4WD trips run by these lodges, which is the best way to appreciate the area.

Kaokoland is different. North of Sesfontein, there are no lodges and few campsites. This is the land of the Himba (see *Chapter 2*, page 23), a traditional, pastoral people, relying upon herds of drought-resistant cattle for their livelihood. Their villages are situated by springs that gush out from dry riverbeds. Kaokoland's remote 'roads' need high-clearance 4WD vehicles and are dangerous for the unprepared. The best way to visit is by air, or using one of the more experienced local operators who know the area and understand the dangers. To visit independently you need your own expedition: two or more equipped 4WDs, with

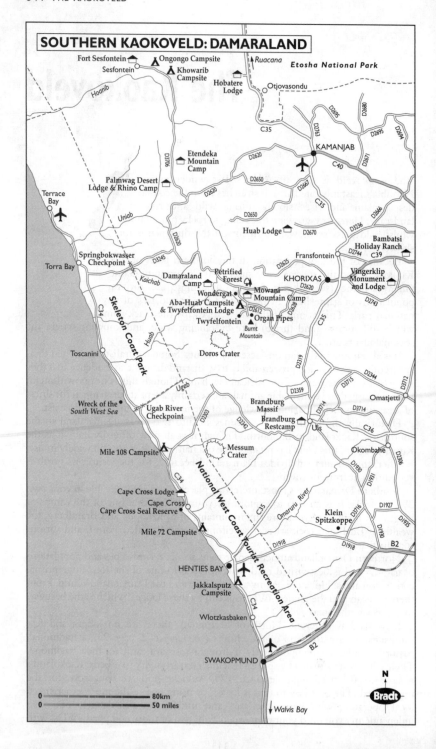

SOUTHERN KAOKOVELD: DAMARALAND

Fort Sesfontein
Ongongo Campsite
Sesfontein
Khowarib Campsite
Ruacana
Etosha National Park
Hobatere Lodge
Otjovasondu
Hoanib
C35
D3695
D2680
D3694
D3695
D2763
Etendeka Mountain Camp
D2620
KAMANJAB
C40
D3706
D2650
D371
Palmwag Desert Lodge & Rhino Camp
D2650
D2467
Terrace Bay
D2630
C35
Uniab
D2650
D3236
Huab Lodge
D2670
Bambatsi Holiday Ranch
Springbokwasser Checkpoint
D620
Fransfontein
D2744
C39
Torra Bay
D3245
D2625
Vingerklip Monument and Lodge
Koichab
Damaraland Camp
Petrified Forest
KHORIXAS
D2620
Wondergat
Mowani Mountain Camp
D2743
Aba-Huab Campsite & Twyfelfontein Lodge
D2612
D2608
Organ Pipes
Twyfelfontein
C35
Burnt Mountain
Huab
Doros Crater
Toscanini
D2319
D2344
Ugab
D2359
D3715
D3712
Wreck of the South West Sea
Brandburg Massif
Omatjetti
Ugab River Checkpoint
D2303
Brandburg Restcamp
D3714
D3714
C36
Uis
Mile 108 Campsite
C34
Messum Crater
Okombahe
D1930
D3396
D1931
D1927
Cape Cross Lodge
C35
Omaruru River
Cape Cross
Klein Spitzkoppe
D3716
D1935
Cape Cross Seal Reserve
Mile 72 Campsite
D1930
D1918
D1918
B2
HENTIES BAY
Jakkalsputz Campsite
C34
Wlotzkasbaken
SWAKOPMUND
B2
N

Bradt

0 ————— 80km
0 ————— 50 miles

Skeleton Coast Park

National West Coast Tourist Recreation Area

↓ Walvis Bay

experienced drivers and enough fuel and supplies for a week or more. This isn't a place for the casual or inexperienced visitor.

SOUTHERN DAMARALAND

With several very accessible attractions, this is an easy area to visit yourself. Because of the region's sparse population, it's wise to travel here with at least basic supplies of food and water, and if you come fully equipped to camp and fend for yourself, then you will be more flexible in visiting the area's great mountains: Brandberg and Spitzkoppe.

If you see local people hitching, bear in mind that there is no public transport here. In such a rural area, Namibians will stop to help if there is a hope of cramming a further person into their car. Seeing foreign tourists pass by with a half-empty vehicle will leave behind very negative feelings. (Although, as anywhere, single women drivers might justifiably pause for thought before offering lifts.)

Spitzkoppe

At the far southern end of the Kaokoveld lies a small cluster of mountains, rising from the flat gravel plains that make up the desert floor. These include Spitzkoppe, Klein Spitzkoppe and the Pondok Mountains. Of these the highest is Spitzkoppe which towers 600m above the surrounding plains: a demanding technical climb. Its resemblance to the famous Swiss mountain earned it the name of the Matterhorn of Africa while the extreme conditions found on its faces ensured that it remained unclimbed until 1946.

Getting there

Spitzkoppe is reached on the D3716. Approaching from Henties Bay take the D1918 westwards for 103km, then turn left on to the D3716. Coming from Usakos, take the Henties Bay turn-off after 23km on the B2 and follow it for about 18km before taking a right turn on to the D3716. From Uis Mine, leave on the C36 to Omaruru, but turn right on to the D1930 after only 1km. From there it's about 75km to the right turn on to the D3716.

What to see and do

Currently there are no facilities here, though for the self-sufficient it's yet another spectacular place to camp, and its lower slopes provide some difficult scrambles. At the extreme eastern end of this group of hills is a verdant valley known as Bushman's Paradise, which you can reach with the help of a fixed steel cable. Sadly the rock paintings under the overhang have been vandalised (even here!) and little is left of them, but the valley is still worth a visit. If you have an hour to spare, then an alternative descent is to continue to follow the gully out of the valley – though this route is not an easy option.

Because of their height and proximity to the ocean, these mountains receive more fog and precipitation than most, much of which runs off their smooth granite sides to form small pools. These are ideal places to search for the shrimps and invertebrates, which have adapted to the environment's extremes by laying drought-resistant eggs.

Uis

Once known as Uis Mine, this small town was almost an extension of the tin mine which dominated it. Sadly this closed, and much of the town's population left as a result. Those who remained are fighting to survive, and tourism is an important source of income to them. There is still a useful fuel station here, open 07.00–19.00 Mon-Sat and 10.30–16.30 on Sunday. Nearby the Brandberg Supermarket sells basic foods. It opens 08.30–14.00 and 17.00–19.30 Mon-Sat, and 11.00–14.00 and 17.00–19.30 on Sundays.

Brandberg

Measuring about 30km by 23km at its base, and 2,573m at its highest point, this ravine-split massif of granite totally dominates the surrounding desert plains.

Getting there

Though you cannot miss seeing it whilst driving in the vicinity, getting to Brandberg without driving over the fragile lichen plains needs thought. Its eastern side, around the Tsisab Ravine, is easily reached using a 2WD car via the D2359, which turns west off the C35 about 14km after Uis Mine on the way to Khorixas. It is signposted to the White Lady (Witvrou in Afrikaans), the famous rock painting.

Those with 4WD vehicles can also use the extensive network of rough tracks which turn towards the massif from the north, west and south, off the D2342, starting some 14km southwest of Uis Mine on the Henties Bay road.

If you are heading out to the coast, then the D2342 and D2303 are passable in a 2WD. The second is in better repair than the first, as it gets much less traffic. The D2342 is often used by small-scale miners, and it has patches of bad corrugations with sharp turns, though the spectacular scenery and profusion of *welwitschia* plants make it worth the journey. Note that the most northerly 5km of the D2303, where it approaches the Ugab River, is in very poor shape and should not be attempted. In case of emergency, Save the Rhino Trust usually staff a base at the end of this stretch. If taking either road, phone ahead to your destination so that someone expects you, and will know where to look for you if you don't arrive.

Where to stay

There's only one place to stay, and that's the restcamp, which makes a good base for exploring Brandberg:

Brandberg Restcamp (11 flats, campsite) PO Box 35, Uis; tel/fax: 064 504038
This small restcamp has five 2-bedroom flats and several 3–4-bedroom houses The flats each have four beds, two baths, two toilets, and a kitchen. The houses each take 6–8 people. There's also a camping site, a 25m swimming pool, tennis courts, a full-size snooker table and a badminton court here – at a restcamp that's trying very hard to survive and thrive even after the closure of the mine. The restaurant serves breakfast for N$31, and lunch and dinner à la carte.

Although the erstwhile gem-cutting school has now closed, there is still a souvenir shop selling some stones.
Rates: single N$120, twin room N$200, N$300 for a 3–4 person flat or a 6-bed house, and N$400 for an 8-bed house.

What to see and do

Two attractions are drawing increasing numbers of visitors:

Climbing

With the highest point in Namibia and some good technical routes in a very demanding environment, the massif attracts serious mountaineers as well as those in search of a few days' interesting scrambling. It's very important to remember to

WELWITSCHIA MIRABILIS

Welwitschia, perhaps Namibia's most famous species of plant, are usually found growing in groups on the harsh gravel plains of the central Namib and western Kaokoveld. Each plant has only two, long, shredded leaves and is separated from the other *welwitschia* plants by some distance. They appear as a tangle of foliage (some green, but mostly desiccated grey) which emerges from a stubby wooden base.

They were first described in the west by Friedrich Welwitsch, an Austrian botanist who found them in 1859. Since then scientists have been fascinated by *welwitschia*, earning the plant the scientific name of *mirabilis* – Latin for marvellous!

Research suggest that *welwitschia* can live for over 1,000 years and are members of the conifer family (some sources still class them with the succulents). Though their leaves can spread for several metres across and their roots over a metre down, it is still a mystery how they obtain water. One theory suggests that dew condenses on the leaves, and drips to be absorbed by fine roots near the surface of the ground.

Welwitschia rely on the wind to distribute their seeds, but young plants are rare. They germinate only when the conditions are perfect, in years of exceptional rain. I was shown one on the Skeleton Coast that was eight years old. It was minute: consisting of just two seedling leaves and no more than two centimetres tall.

Their ability to thrive in such a harsh environment is amazing, and their adaptations are still being studied. There has even been a recent suggestion that the older *welwitschia* plants may change the chemical constitution of the soil around them, making it harder for young plants to nearby and compete for water and space.

take adequate safety precautions though, as the temperatures can be extreme and the mountain is very isolated. Unless you are used to such conditions, stick to short trips in the early morning or late afternoon, and take a long siesta in the scorching midday heat.

Serious climbers should seek advice from the Mountain Club of Namibia, in Windhoek, well before they arrive or contact Joe Walter, at Damaraland Trails and Tours (tel: 061 234610; fax: 061 239616). He knows the area well, and organises small backpacking groups.

Paintings

This area has been occupied by Bushmen for several thousands of years and still holds a wealth of their artefacts and rock paintings, of which only a fraction have been studied in detail, and some are undoubtedly still to be found. The richest section for art has so far been the Tsisab Ravine, on the northeastern side of the massif. Here one painting in particular has been the subject of much scientific debate, ever since its discovery by the outside world in 1918: the famous White Lady of Brandberg.

The figure of the white lady stands about 40cm tall, and is central to a large frieze which apparently depicts some sort of procession – in which one or two of the figures have animal features. In her right hand is a flower, or perhaps an ostrich egg-cup, whilst in her left she holds a bow and some arrows. Unlike the other figures, she has been painted white from below the chest. The coloration and form of the figure is very reminiscent of some early Mediterranean styles and, together with points gleaned from a more detailed analysis of the pictures, this led early scholars to credit the painters as having links with Europe. Among the site's first visitors was the Abbé Henri Breuil, a world authority on rock art who studied these paintings and others nearby in the late 1940s, and subsequently published four classic volumes entitled *The Rock Paintings of Southern Africa* (see *Further Reading*). He concluded that the lady had elements of ancient Mediterranean origin.

More recent scholars seem to think that the people represented are indigenous, with no European links, and they regard the white lady as being a boy, covered with white clay whilst undergoing an initiation ceremony. Whichever school of thought you prefer, the white lady is well signposted and worth the scramble needed to reach it.

Further up the Tsisab Ravine there are many other sites, including the friezes within the Girl's School, Pyramid and Ostrich shelters. If you wish to get more out of the rock art, then Breuil's books cannot be recommended too highly – though as beautifully illustrated antique Africana they are difficult to find, and expensive to buy.

Two craters

In the remote west of southern Damaraland, these two craters are close to accessible areas, and yet themselves very remote. The only practical way to get in here is with a guide who knows the area – as for safety's sake you need back-up in case of problems.

Messum Crater

Southwest of Brandberg, straddling the boundary of the West Coast Recreational Area, Messum Crater is an amphitheatre of desert where once there was an ancient volcano, over 22km across. Now two concentric circles of mountains ring the gravel plains here.

Messum is named after Captain W Messum, who explored the coast of southwest Africa from the sea, around 1846-8, venturing as far inland as Brandberg – which he modestly named after himself. Only later did it become known as Brandberg.

Doros Crater

Just south of Twyfelfontein, northwest of Brandberg, is the Doros Crater (or Doros Craters, as it is sometimes called). A permit from the NWR, and a full 4WD expedition, is needed to get into this remote concession area in southern Damaraland. The geology's interesting here, and there's evidence of early human habitation.

Khorixas

Khorixas used to be the administrative capital of the old 'homeland' of Damaraland. Now it is not so important – and certainly isn't excessively tidy or even pretty, but it is conveniently placed for the visitor between Swakopmund and Etosha. Because of this, and its accessibility by tarred road from the east, it makes a good base for visiting southern Damaraland's attractions. On a practical note, there is a reliable fuel station here, and several shops, so many people come by just to replenish their supplies.

Where to stay

There are several options in the Khorixas area, all with their advantages:

Khorixas Lodge/Restcamp (38 bungalows & campsites) PO Box 2, Khorixas; tel: 065 331111; fax: 065 712388

In a convenient position, just to the west of town, this is sometimes signposted simply as 'ruskamp'. Now privately run, the restcamp has been here for years. The camp is quite large, and the bungalows come as standard, semi-luxury or luxury – although none is luxurious. (If four plan to share one bungalow, then it's worth going for 'luxury'.) Expect clean towels and linen to be supplied, and each bungalow to have basic kitchen facilities and an en-suite shower/toilet.

The restcamp has a large swimming pool, a relaxed, almost café-style, small restaurant with an à la carte menu, and a curio shop. It's a clean, well-run and unpretentious place, and good value.

Rates: Standard single N$325, double N$550; semi-luxury single N$400, double N$700, triple N$900; luxury (max 4 persons) single N$450, double N$800, triple N$1,050, 4 people N$1,300, including breakfast. Camping adult N$40, children N$20.

Bambatsi Holiday Ranch (8 bungalows) PO Box 120, Outjo; tel: 067 313897; fax: 067 313331; email:bambatsi@iway.na; bamabatsi@natron.net

About 58km east of Khorixas, and 75km from Outjo, on the C39, towards Khorixas, Bambatsi is situated on a plateau overlooking mopane woodlands. Bambatsi is a guest farm, not a restcamp. Bambatsi has just 8 bungalows, each of which has an en-suite shower and toilet. It serves good food and offers 'German hospitality', though parts of it could do with smartening up and repairing.

Facilities here include a tennis court and swimming pool, and the owner-manager, Rudi Zahn, has two tamed cheetah, Shaka and Shiri, which he found as orphaned puppies in May 1996.

Rates: single N$535, N$450 per person sharing, including dinner, bed and breakfast.

Vingerklip Lodge PO Box 443, Outjo. Reservations: PO Box 11550, Windhoek; tel/fax: 061 255344; email: vingerkl@mweb.com.na; web: www.vingerklip.com.na

Immediately next to the Vingerklip itself, on the D2743 southeast of Khorixas, this lodge has been designed to take advantage of the scenery. Its thatched bar is more of an observation deck, standing on its own small hilltop, with 360° views around it. Below the deck, its plunge-pool, normally surrounded by shady umbrellas and sun-loungers, has equally breathtaking views.

Vingerklip's main lounge-dining area is large, and the food is good – though usually a buffet rather than à la carte (so don't leave dinner too late, or you may find little left). Its bungalows are spread out along an adjacent hillside. Each has adjacent twin beds and en-suite facilities, more than basic, but slightly less than luxurious. Their strongest point is a stunning view.

Rates: single N$747.50, N$626 per person sharing, for dinner, bed and breakfast.

Aba-Huab Community Campsite c/o Elias Aro Xoagub, PO Box 131, Twyfelfontein via Khorixas

This was the first of several camps in Damaraland to be set up with the help of Namibia's Save the Rhino Trust, and run by local people. Aba-Huab camp is now effectively owned and managed by the entrepreneurial Elias, and is well signposted about 11km before Twyfelfontein, on the D3254. It stands beside a (usually) dry riverbed, and provides campers with solar-heated showers, toilets, a communal fire pit, shady campsites and a bar for cool drinks. As an alternative to camping, there are simple A-frame shelters for sleeping which raise you off the ground – though you need at least a sleeping bag, and preferably a foam mattress. Heading towards Twyfelfontein, the main camp is on the right. However, if you don't mind walking a little to the toilets, then you can camp on the left, which is much quieter. Note that you can't easily book this in advance, but they'll always have camping space.

Rates: N$25 per person for the sites.

Mowani Mountain Camp (24 beds) PO Box 40788, Windhoek; tel: 061 232009; fax: 061 222574; email: mowani@namibianet.com; web: www.mowani.com
Well-signposted on the D2612, about 6km south of its junction with the D3214, Mowani is owned by Andre Louw and his team, who also run Villa Verdi in Windhoek. Their keen eye for innovative design shines through, and the round, thatched domes of Mowani's main buildings give the impression of a grand African village, whilst blending beautifully with the granite boulders that surround them.

Away from these, and dotted around the surrounding kopjie, are 12 large and fairly luxurious tents. These are all raised up on platforms, and most have great views across the surrounding countryside. All are fairly stylish with double or twin beds, and en-suite showers and toilets.

Activities here include nature drives and excursions to the local attractions around Twyfelfontein although, like Twyfelfontein Country Lodge, many people use this as a base for driving themselves around the area. Mowani isn't cheap, but you do get a lot of good design for your money!
Rates: single N$1,335, double N$1,090, including all meals. Open all year.

Twyfelfontein Country Lodge (52 twin and 4 double rooms) PO Box 6597, Ausspannplatz; tel: 061 240375; fax: 061 256598; email: afrideca@mweb.com.na; web: www.namibialodges.com.
Owned by Namibia Country Lodges, this three-star lodge was opened in July 2000. Its en-suite thatched units are set in a rock-strewn valley near the Aba-Huab River, 10km from the world-renowned rock-art site of Twyfelfontein along the D3214. These are all built in rows of four rooms, which feel quite small inside. Expect twin beds, a bathroom with a shower and flush toilet, and fairly traditional, even heavy, décor with dark wood and African-print fabrics. A very large thatched open-plan central area, built in two tiers with open sides, backs onto a rocky hillside. This has a dining room and bar upstairs, with toilets, offices and a curio shop below. It all overlooks quite a large, curved swimming pool. Walks can be arranged from here, as can nature drives (in quite large, truck-like 4WDs) down the Huab River in search of elephants and other wildlife. There's an airstrip at the lodge, and scenic flights are possible, although there's not currently a plane based there. That said, most people will use this simply as a base to drive themselves around the area, or as a stopover that's conveniently close to Twyfelfontein.
Rates: single N$715, double N$1,000, including breakfast. Lunch N$66, dinner N$105. Open all year.

What to see and what to do
There's a lot to see and do in Southern Damaraland, and virtually all of it is easily accessible with your own vehicle.

Vingerklip – the rock finger
For years now the Vingerklip, or rock finger, has been a well-known landmark in this area. Around it are flat-topped mountains, reminiscent of Monument Valley (in Arizona), which are so typical of much of Damaraland. They are the remains of an ancient lava flow which has largely now been eroded way.

Amidst this beautiful scenery, Vingerklip is a striking pinnacle of rock, a natural obelisk balancing vertically on its own. It's an impressive sight, and similar to the (now collapsed) Finger of God near Asab.

Twyfelfontein rock art
Twyfelfontein was named 'doubtful spring' by the first European farmer to occupy the land – a reference to the failings of a perennial spring of water which wells up near the base of the valley.

Formerly the valley was known as Uri-Ais, and seems to have been occupied for thousands of years. Then its spring, on the desert's margins, would have attracted huge herds of game from the sparse plains around, making this uninviting valley an excellent base for early hunters.

This probably explains why the slopes of Twyfelfontein, amid flat-topped mountains typical of Damaraland, conceal one of the continent's greatest concentrations of rock art. This is not obvious when you first arrive. They seem like any other hillsides strewn with rocks. But the boulders that litter these slopes are dotted with thousands of paintings and ancient engravings, only a fraction of which have been recorded.

Amongst African rock-art sites, Twyfelfontein is unusual in having both engravings and paintings. Many are of animals and their spoor, or geometric motifs – which have been suggested as maps to water sources. Why they were made, nobody knows. Perhaps they were part of the people's spiritual ceremonies, perhaps it was an ancient nursery to teach their children, or perhaps they were simply doodling...

Even with a knowledgeable local guide, you need several hours to start to discover the area's treasures. Begin early and beware of the midday heat. Take some water up with you, also stout shoes and a hat!

To reach the valley, which is well signposted, take the C39 for 73km west from Khorixas, then left on to the D3254 for 15km, then right for about 11km (ignoring a left fork after 6km) on the D3214. Entrance to the valley costs N$5 per person and N$5 for a vehicle, and a (compulsory) local guide is N$20. (Small extra tips are greatly appreciated.)

Organ pipes

Retracing your tracks from Twyfelfontein, take the left fork which you ignored earlier (see directions above), on to the D3254. After about 3km there's a small gorge to your left, and above it a flat area used for parking. Leave your vehicle and take one of the paths down where you'll find hundreds of tall angular columns of dolorite in a most unusual formation. These were thought to have formed about 120 million years ago when the dolorite shrank as it cooled, forming these marvellous angular columns up to 5m high in the process.

Burnt Mountain

Continuing just past the Organ Pipes, on the D3254, you'll see what is known locally as the 'Burnt Mountain'. Seen in the midday sun this can be a real disappointment, but when the red-orange shales catch the early morning or late afternoon light, the mountainside glows with a startling rainbow of colours, as if it's on fire.

Petrified Forest

Signposted beside the C39, about 42km west of Khorixas, lie a number of petrified trees on a bed of sandstone. Some are partially buried, while others lie completely exposed because the sandstone surrounding them has eroded away. It is thought that they were carried here as logs by a river, some 250 million years ago, and became stranded on a sandbank. Subsequently sand was deposited around them, creating ideal conditions for the cells of the wood to be replaced by silica, and thus become petrified.

Now there is a small office here, a car park, and demarcated paths around the site. A small entrance fee is charged (about N$10), and there are helpful guides who will show you some of the highlights of the forest in about an hour.

Wondergat

Off the D3254, about 4km north of its junction with the D3214, a track heads west from the road. After about 500m this comes to a huge hole in the ground – thought to be the remnants of a subterranean cave whose roof collapsed long ago. There are no signposts or safety barriers, so be careful near the edge.

Ballooning

Francolino Fly-ins Tel: 067 697041; fax: 067 697042; email: francolino-flyins@iway.na
Set up around 2001, and run by Francesca Mattei and Wolfgang Rapp, Francolino offer ballooning, micro-lighting and scenic flights in a light aircraft. They are located at Rag Rock, which is signposted from the D2612. It's very close to Mowani, and about 4km from Aba-Huab Campsite. Last time I was in the area they were not around, and thus trips were not possible... so pre-booking these activities would be very wise.
Rates: N$2,500 for about an hour's balloon trip, including breakfast on landing; N$865 per person for about 30 minutes' micro-light flight; N$2,760 per hour for a plane taking five passengers. Open all year, and best pre-booked.

NORTHERN DAMARALAND
The concession areas

North of the Huab River lie a number of large areas known as concession areas, which are set aside for tourism. These are chunks of land that the government has allocated to one operator, who has the sole use of the land for tourism purposes. Local people can live and even keep animals within some of these tourism concessions, but development is limited.

Currently four such concessions are being used by operators to give visitors an insight into the area's ecosystems: Palmwag, Etendeka, Damaraland Camp, and Hobatere Lodge. Each is different, but all require time to do them justice. These aren't places that you can drop into for a day and expect to fully appreciate, and a visit to any is best arranged in advance. (Huab Lodge's private reserve isn't technically a concession area, but is similar in style and so included here.)

Landscapes and vegetation

Approaching from the coast, along the D3245, is perhaps the most interesting way to enter this area. After the flat coast, you soon find the gravel plains dotted first with inselbergs, then with low chains of weathered hills. The land begins to rise rapidly: you are coming on to the escarpment, around 50km from the coast, which is the edge of one of the largest sheets of ancient lava in the world. Sheets of molten lava poured over the land here in successive layers, about 300 million years ago. Now these Etendeka lavas dominate the scenery, with huge flat-topped mountains of a characteristic red-brown-purplish colour.

The rainfall here is still low, and the sparse covering of grasses is dotted with large *Euphorbia damarana* bushes. These grow into spiky, round clumps, perhaps three metres in diameter and over a metre tall, and are endemic to this region. Break a stem to reveal poisonous milky-white latex, which protects the bushes from most herbivores, except black rhino and kudu, which are both said to eat them. (A tale is told of a group of local people who roasted meat over a fire of dead *Euphorbia* stems – only to die as the result.)

If you could continue as a bird, flying northeast towards Etosha, then the land below you would become progressively less dry. Flying over the Hobatere area, you'd notice that the higher rainfall promotes richer vegetation. In the northern areas of that concession you would see an undulating patchwork of mopane scrub and open grassy plains, dotted with various trees, including the distinctive flat-topped umbrella thorn, *Acacia tortilis*. You would have left the desert.

Fauna

Generally the amount of game increases as the vegetation becomes more lush in the east. In the mountains around Palmwag, Etendeka and Damaraland Camp, there are resident steenbok, baboon, kudu, porcupine and the occasional klipspringer and warthog, joined by wide-ranging herds of Hartmann's mountain zebra, gemsbok and springbok. Equally nomadic but less common are the giraffe and desert-adapted elephant.

An enduring memory from here is the sight of a herd of giraffe. We watched them for almost an hour, as they skittishly grazed their way across a rocky hillside beside the main D3706 road. Their height seemed so out of place in the landscape of rocks and low trees.

Black rhino are present throughout the region, but spend most of their days sleeping under shady bushes, and so are rarely seen, even by those who live here. (Both Etendeka and Palmwag occasionally run strenuous rhino-tracking trips, the former more on foot, the latter making more use of vehicles. These expensive but fascinating trips are specially arranged on request.)

Leopard occur, and both cheetah and lion have been seen – but it is thought that only small numbers of big cats are left in the region, and they range over huge areas in search of suitable prey.

The birdlife is interesting, as several of the Kaokoveld's ten endemic species are found here. Perhaps the most obvious, and certainly the most vocal, are Rüppell's korhaan – whose early-morning duets will wake the soundest sleeper. The ground-feeding Monteiro's hornbill is another endemic, though not to be confused with the local red-billed hornbills. There is also an endemic chat, the Herero chat, which occurs along with its more common cousins, the ant-eating tractrac and familiar chats. Though not endemic, black eagles are often seen around the rockier hillsides: surely one of Africa's most majestic raptors.

Looking further east, to Hobatere and Huab, there is more vegetation, making a classic environment for big game animals. These areas can support more game, and it shows. Elephants are certainly more common, and more easily spotted. The desert-adapted species seen to the west are joined in Hobatere by eland, black-faced impala and Damara dik-dik – both of the latter are subspecies endemic to the region. Similarly, the variety of birds becomes wider as you move east, with species that occur in Etosha often overlapping into Hobatere.

Where to stay

Each of these concessions is totally different, though Palmwag, Etendeka and Damaraland Camp occupy broadly similar environments, as do Hobatere and Huab Lodge.

Hobatere (12 rooms) PO Box 110, Kamanjab; tel: 067 330261; email: hobatere@mweb.com.na, res@discover-africa.com.na, hobatere@mweb.com.na; web: www.resafrica.net

About 80km north of Kamanjab, Hobatere is easily found on the banks of the small Otjivasondu River. Take the main C35 road northwest from Kamanjab towards Ruacana. After about 65km, just past the entrance to western Etosha, Hobatere is signposted to the left through imposing gates. A clear bush road then leads through several riverbeds before reaching the lodge after about 16km. A 2WD is usually fine for this but, if attempting the road during the rains, ring the lodge as you pass through Kamanjab – so that they know of your arrival, and will search for you in those riverbeds if you get stuck.

Steve and Louise Braine have run Hobatere for 18 years now. Accommodation is in comfortable twin-bedded, thatched brick cottages, each with en-suite shower and toilet (the internal doors are decorative, not functional, so you will be on intimate terms with your companion). These are set in plenty of space, spread around the main lodge allowing you a feeling of independence: to join in if you wish to, or just to relax if you don't.

In the lodge's main building there is a bar, lounge and separate dining area, where good food is served from the house menu. Guests dine separately, as at a restaurant, rather than automatically joining in on one big table with the hosts. For cooling afternoon dips there's a clear pool, which was recently fortified to be elephant-proof, after a baby elephant fell in and its mother smashed up the whole area in her frantic (and eventually successful) attempts to help it out. Approximately 300m from the lodge there is a hide overlooking a waterhole, which is especially interesting in the dry season.

Hobatere's game is established and relaxed and its standard of guiding is good (with Steve himself being a birder of note). It is normal to book here on a full-board basis, and then pay the lodge for your activities. Normally, game drives (day and night) are charged at N$120 per person, and they take a maximum of 9 passengers. Walks are N$70 per hour, for a maximum of 8 people.

Rates: single N$690, double N$1,260, including full board. Note that Hobatere accepts MasterCard, Visa, Diner's and American Express. Open: all year.

Palmwag Lodge (7 bungalows) contact via Palmwag Travel Shop, PO Box 339, Swakopmund; tel: 064 404459; fax: 064 404664
On the edge of a huge concession, Palmwag is beautifully situated next to a palm-lined tributary of the Uniab River, which often flows over-ground here. As water is very scarce in this area, its presence regularly draws elephants close to camp.

Reaching Palmwag is easy; it is just a few kilometres north of the junction of the D3706 and the D2620. Heading north, it is on the left, immediately after the veterinary fence, and its concession stretches off to the west, as far as the Skeleton Coast. On the opposite side of that same road (D3706) is the Etendeka concession.

Palmwag is the oldest lodge in the area, and was run for years by DAS (Desert Adventure Safaris), an old Namibian company based in Swakopmund. In late 2002, this changed, and there are more developments in the pipeline here. So expect Palmwag to be gradually changing over the next few years, although it will probably remain slightly offbeat and idiosyncratic whatever happens.

Currently Palmwag has campsites as well as a variety of rooms here, and its facilities attract an assortment of visitors, ensuring that Palmwag remains a crossroads for travellers in the area. You meet all sorts here, from shady mineral prospectors to South African families camping, and from upmarket visitors on fly-in safaris to local game guards back from the bush, who are staying at the adjacent base of the excellent Save the Rhino Trust.

Palmwag's shop is poorly stocked, though still the best in the area. It opens 08.00–12.30 and 14.00–17.30 during the week, and 08.00–12.30 at the weekend. Fuel is available from the station next to the veterinary fence from 07.00 to 19.00 every day (with a N$5 levy on Sundays). Everybody seems to fill up here.

There is a variety of accommodation here. At the centre of the camp are 12 simple thatched, reed bungalows, with en-suite facilities. One of these is a family unit, and all are being gradually upgraded. These are now all clean, bright and functional, but not overly large or luxurious, and clustered around the 'Uniab Inn' bar, where guests can relax and have dinner.

On the north side of the camp, the extreme right-hand side as you enter it, are four large and really very beautiful tents, all raised on decking and overlooking the reedbeds and palm trees of the Uniab River. These have large, beautifully designed en-suite bathrooms, with plenty of lovely luxurious touches. (Note that both the bungalows and the tents have

220V electricity from a generator. This is switched off at night, and 14.00–16.00, when battery-powered lights are used.)

To the south, on the other side of the lodge (in more ways than one) a large lawn is set down in the green and well-watered channel of the Uniab River. There's a small swimming pool here and a pool bar which serves snacks, and six nearby campsites. Any number of people are allowed on each site, but Palmwag won't accept more than six groups, and will turn away people who haven't booked. If camping you can book into the restaurant (if there's space), or eat down at the pool bar where a good evening meal costs around N$80.

Experienced 4WD enthusiasts, who are used to the terrain, and have good navigational skills (and preferably a GPS), can buy a permit to drive around the Palmwag concession. However, for most visitors this is not practical. (One trainee guide based at Palmwag recently got lost in his vehicle, became disoriented, and was found severely dehydrated in the Skeleton Coast Park. It is a difficult area.) However, there are plans to build a few designated private campsites and allow such visitors to camp at these on a trail through the concession – a practice that's not currently allowed.

Regardless of this, the best way to see the area is still to leave your car at the lodge and take one of the guided game drives. The area's ecosystem is too fragile to withstand the impact of many vehicles, and the animals are still wary of people. They have enough problems without being frightened from waterholes by tourists seeking pictures.

These guided drives cost N$175 per hour per vehicle, taking a maximum of five people for 2–3 hours. This can become costly if you are here on your own in the quiet season. Short self-guided walks are also possible – ask at reception.

SAVE THE RHINO TRUST

This excellent local charity, founded by Blythe and Rudi Loutit, grew out of the slaughter of the region's wildlife that was taking place in the early 1980s. As the rhino numbers shrank to near extinction, Blythe and Rudi started a pressure group to stop the indiscriminate hunting in the area. (This was mainly perpetrated by military staff of the South African Defence Force, who were shooting black rhino and elephant from vehicles and even helicopters.)

Once the worst of the hunting was stopped, SRT continued and pioneered conservation and protection in the area, even employing convicted poachers as game scouts. Who would know better the habits of rhino, and the tricks of the hunters? Eventually, they were able to reverse the extermination of the rhino from the communal areas of the Kaokoveld – a process that's has been enthusiastically supported by the chiefs and headmen, as well as the neighbouring farming community. In many ways it's work like this so long ago that laid the foundations for the successful community conservation programmes that now operate in the region.

Working with the government and many local communities has gradually brought more benefits to these communities, through revenues generated by tourism, as well as providing security for the rhino. Even today, SRT operates many daily rhino patrols, monitoring and protecting the rhino. These include patrols from Palmwag (N$1,208 per person per day) and the Palmwag Rhino Camp, which guests can join. The income from these trips funds some of the trust's patrols and rhino-monitoring programmes.

For further details, check out their website, www.rhino-trust.org.na (currently only in German); or email them at srt@rhino-trust.org.na.

Rates: bungalows from N$760 single and N$550 per person sharing, which includes dinner, bed and breakfast and concession fee. Luxury tents are N$870 per person sharing. Camping is N$60 per person; morning or evening game drives are N$140 per person. Open: all year.

Palmwag Rhino Camp (8 twin-bed tents) contact via Namib Wilderness Safaris, PO Box 5048, Windhoek; tel: 061 225178/234793; fax: 061 239455
This small, tented camp stands in the Palmwag Concession and usually takes a maximum of just twelve guests. Although the tents are large, walk-in Meru-style tents, and each has an en-suite flush toilet and simple bucket shower (hot water available on request, by the bucket!), the camp's location can be fairly easily moved.

Activities will major on rhino-tracking excursions – usually with one of the Save the Rhino Trust team guiding the party. These usually involve driving around while tracking from the vehicle, and then following a set of tracks on foot when an animal is located. It's an excellent option if you are moderately fit and want to do some serious rhino-tracking.

However, note that the dangers inherent in approaching big game at close quarters can be thrown into sharp contrast on rhino-tracking trips. No trip to Africa (or indeed anywhere) can be guaranteed as totally safe, and this is no different. If you don't follow your guide's instructions precisely, then you're quite likely to have 1,000kg of nimble-footed, sharp-horned rhino heading at you very rapidly. These activities are not for the faint-hearted, so don't book in here unless you fully accept that you may be placing yourself far out of your comfort zone – and potentially in some danger.
Rates: Nov–June: N$2,675 single, N1,895 per person sharing, including all meals, game drives and rhino-tracking; July–Oct: N$3,175 single, N$ N2,395 per person sharing. Open all year. Pre-booking is essential.

Etendeka Mountain Camp (8 twin-bed tents) PO Box 21783, Windhoek; tel: 061 226979; fax: 061 226999; email: logufa@mweb.com.na
Etendeka is an excellent tented camp about 18km east of Palmwag, on the open, rolling Etendeka lava plains. It is owned and run by Dennis Liebenberg, who takes a no-frills approach to giving his guests a real experience of the Kaokoveld.

Numbers are limited to 16 guests, accommodated in large tents. Each of the walk-in tents is provided with two beds, linen, towels, washbasin, a bush shower with hot and cold water, a flush toilet and electric light. Etendeka doesn't aim at luxury; but what it does, it does very well. The main dining and bar area are under canvas, and meals are a social occasion when everybody, including Dennis and the guides, normally eat together around the fire (it gets very chilly in winter), upon which much of the food is cooked. Such bush-cooking has been refined to an art form, so the cuisine from the embers is impressive.

Activities – guided walks and scenic and game drives – are all included, and tailored to guests' interests and abilities. After an early breakfast, a normal day might include a 2–4-hour walk, lunch, a few hours to relax, and perhaps a long afternoon game drive, incorporating a short hike on to one of the area's mountains for a sundown drink. If you're fit and active, then this is a great place to come walking.

The concession's game includes good populations of Hartmann's mountain zebra, oryx and springbok, as well as occasional giraffe and desert-adapted elephant, and very occasionally black rhino. The striking *Euphorbia damarana* are the predominant shrubs all around this area, and Etendeka's guides are excellent on their plants and birds, as well as animal identification.

Etendeka is remote and you cannot 'drop in' as you can at Palmwag. It must be booked in advance. Visitors normally drive themselves to a rendezvous by the veterinary fence (normally 16.00 in summer, 15.30 in winter – but check when you book), where Etendeka has covered parking places. From there the camp's 4WD will transfer them to the camp. It is especially good to note that Etendeka is closely involved with the region's Community Game Guard scheme, and that it gives a proportion of its revenue to the local communities, so that they benefit from the income generated by visitors, and have an incentive to help preserve Kaokoveld's wild game.

Rates: single N$1,750, per person sharing N$1,350, including dinner, continental breakfast, lunch, afternoon tea, a full bar, transfer to the camp, guided nature walk and scenic drive. Open: all year, except January. Pre-booking essential

Damaraland Camp (8 twin-bed tents) contact via Namib Wilderness Safaris, PO Box 5048, Windhoek; tel: 061 225178/234793; fax: 061 239455

Damaraland Camp was originally modelled on Etendeka, and initially they seemed very similar. It was another remote tented camp on a rocky hill, amidst the stunning red-purple mountain scenery that is typical of the Etendeka lava flows. Its facilities have always been a little more luxurious than Etendeka's, as each tent had a flush toilet and shower en suite from the start. However, Damaraland Camp had a much stronger community involvement from the beginning, and now that's what shines out when you visit the camp.

Physically, the camp is about 11km from the D2620 road, signposted to the west – just north of the point where the Huab River crosses the road, next to a smallholding. The area around the camp is dry and hence vegetation is sparse – even *Euphorbia damarana* are not present to any great extent. However, there are some good examples of *welwitschia* nearby, on the way to the Huab Valley. This river valley makes a good venue for expeditions in search of desert elephant, and other game, so many drives head in that direction.

Activities here are based on walks and drives, with the emphasis on the driving – usually into the Huab River Valley in search of wildlife, where elephants are fairly frequently seen. It's not a camp that you can just drop into; your stay must be arranged in advance. Normally a rendezvous is arranged just off the main D2620 road – where cars are parked, under the watchful eyes of a local family. Then you'll be met and taken to the camp by a 4WD, although an experienced driver going slowly could negotiate the 11km to camp in a normal 2WD vehicle that's not overloaded. Check the rendezvous time when you book.

Damaraland Camp's own brand of community involvement is especially interesting, meriting a high commendation from the British Guild of Travel Writers (see box on next page), and numerous subsequent accolades. These aside, this is one of Namibia's best camps, and it is also owned and now largely run by the local community. Visitors often return commenting on just how positive and happy the atmosphere there is, so is well worth stopping at for two or three nights. (Don't stop for just one night; it's too short.)

Rates: Nov–June: N$3,010 single, N1,895 per person sharing, including all meals, game drives and walks; July–Oct: N$3,515 single, N$2,395 per person sharing. Open all year. Pre-booking is essential.

Huab Lodge (8 bungalows) PO Box 103, Kamanjab; tel: 067 697016; fax: 067 697017; email: huab@iway.na.

Though frequently listed as a guest farm near Kamanjab, or even Outjo, Huab is a private concession area in spirit. It was founded by two well-known couples, Jan and Suzi and Dot and Udo. Both couples are well connected in Namibia, and have worked in tourism for years.

They came together to buy up a number of adjacent farms in a hilly area, around the headwaters of the Huab River. This land was previously farmed, but is of more significance as a refuge for some of the Huab River's desert-adapted elephants. The farmers had been fencing the land, and didn't enjoy the elephant's feeding forays on to their farms, causing much tension for both men and beasts. Now the internal fences are down over a large area, and antelope have been reintroduced to boost the existing populations. As the ecosystem reverts to its natural state, elephants are gradually being seen around the lodge more. This lodge is a textbook demonstration of how tourism can be used to finance conservation initiatives, and is a compelling argument for encouraging eco-tourism to Namibia.

FRANZ AND THE SILVER OTTER

From an article by the author in Wanderlust, February 1998

'I applied for a job as guide, but I was good at entertaining guests – and so trained for the bar. But I still want to be a guide, so I've built a small water-bowl near my tent. I watch the birds, and learn to identify them from a book.'

Franz Coetzee's bird-bowl seemed a long way from the Savoy, where a waiter filled our glasses as we listened for the British Guild of Travel Writers' Silver Otter award to be announced. I wondered if all this pomp would make any difference to Damaraland Camp, or Franz's rural community there that ekes out its living on the fringes of the Namib Desert.

The trip to London had certainly affected Franz, who had seldom stopped smiling. Until now, his longest journey had been as a child, when his parents' community had been displaced from South Africa and trekked into Namibia. They settled in the arid, semi-desert region of Damaraland. 'It was good that we came to Damaraland,' he assured me. Despite entering an area already occupied with Damara people, 'We mixed with those people, and we accept each other.' So Franz and his family stayed on, when most returned to South Africa, two years ago. 'We won our land back, but my parents wanted to stay in Namibia. I don't know anything more. So I stayed also.'

After finishing school, he searched for a job. 'I went to town, with no luck. To Walvis Bay, as my sister was there. There is a really big problem with jobs – unemployment. I decided to go back to Damaraland to concentrate on farming.'

Hence, like most of his community, Franz lived by tending cattle, sheep and goats. Damaraland may be spectacularly beautiful, but its land is poor for farming. Rocky hills and minimal rainfall mean a difficult life. There is game around, and sometimes he would hunt springbok, or even zebra, kudu or oryx. Occasionally he would glimpse the area's desert-adapted black rhinos – but elephants were a different story. 'They visited the water-points during the night and our vegetable gardens on the farm. I remember once, a month before the harvest, a lot of elephants came, damaging the farm. The dogs barked, and we became nervous. We just... stood. You can do nothing to an elephant. You can't even chase him away. You just clap your hands, but stay out of the way.' Though rare, these desert elephants meant nothing to Franz when compared to his vegetables.

The lodge itself is situated between the Huab and one of its tributaries, at their confluence. (Beware: if the rivers are in flood, reaching here can be difficult.) It is well signposted, and easy to find off the C35 between Kamanjab and Khorixas. Once you turn off the C35 the D2670 is some 30km long; it, has two farm gates on it, and becomes increasingly scenic, so don't expect a quick arrival.

Huab has been voted Namibia's best lodge every year since 1994. It shows: stunning thatch-on-brick design, tasteful décor, a little landscaping, and lots of quality. The huge bungalows all have two queen-sized beds and separate en-suite rooms for the toilet, and bath and shower. Electricity and hot water are mostly solar.

The guiding is top class. Jan is renowned as founder of Etosha Fly-in Safaris, and one of the country's best guides, so even if there's no game around, you'll still find the drives and walks fascinating. Similarly, Huab's hospitality is faultless, with delicious meals served for everyone together – relaxed, very social occasions. This could become pure eulogy, but Huab has two minor weak points. Firstly, its game density is increasing but still relatively

Then things started to change. A government survey visited farms, explaining how they could benefit directly from the wildlife and tourism. Eventually the 70 households in Franz's community established themselves as custodians of the land, forming the Ward 11 Residents' Association – with its own constitution and membership. They then sought investors, and after two years of tortuous negotiations, involving the whole community, they settled on an agreement with Wilderness Safaris, who would build Damaraland Camp, and train local people to run it. The community getsthe jobs, and 10% of the profits. After ten years, ownership of the camp will revert to the community.

Franz is enthusiastic about the benefits, and to date the community has N$57,000 in the bank. 'We will try to renovate our local clinic, and have donated N$2,000 to the school for a photocopier. At first it was just a loan, but later we said "Just donate it. It's for our children."' But he recognises that the next challenge is to decide how to use the increasing revenues. 'Farms which have had windmills damaged [by elephants seeking water] will be the first to get help. And there are other problems – predators like jackal catch goats and sheep.'

Gradually attitudes to wildlife have changed. Now Franz tells stories about elephants over breakfast, before guests go out on safari. The community knows how to deal with them, and nobody kills wild animals to eat – they're worth more alive, as attractions.

Almost two years since it started, Damaraland Camp is now one of the most popular camps in Namibia. Except for two managers from Wilderness, all the staff are from the community – and next year two will start training to replace the existing managers. Franz explained that his work of 'entertaining guests' meant 'telling them about yourself – visitors usually want to know about our traditions.' With a ready smile, and a disarming line in chat, it's clear why he was perfect for this.

Later that evening, the winner was announced: the city of Dubrovnik, for its restoration work. Damaraland Camp was highly commended, followed by Madikwe Game Reserve, in South Africa, which had a similar approach to conservation.

Franz's smile never wavered – clearly the award would make no difference to that. But why was this project so special? Surely all camps should be run like this?

low, especially when compared with, say, the long-established Hobatere. At Huab you may not actually see many of the larger animals. Secondly, it is one of Namibia's more expensive lodges – though I've yet to hear a visitor say that the lodge was poor value, and it costs a fraction of the price that similar quality commands in the rest of Africa.
Rates: N$1,260 per person, including all meals, wine, game drives and walks.
Open all year. Pre-booking is essential.

Warmquelle

About 87km north of Palmwag Lodge, on the way to Sesfontein lies Warmquelle, a small settlement situated on the site of a spring. In the early years of this century the spring was used in an irrigation project, for which an aqueduct was constructed. Now only a few parts of the old aqueduct remain, together with a small Damara settlement and quite a large school.

Near here there are two locally run campsites, both just off the D3706.

Khowarib and Ongongo were set up with the help of the Save the Rhino Trust and the Endangered Wildlife Society, and both aim to channel most of their income back into their local communities.

Where to stay

Khowarib Camp web: www.nacobta.com.na
The turn-off for the Khowarib campsite is signposted about 75km north of Palmwag, 32km south of Sesfontein, on the D7306. The track to the camp is suitable for 2WD vehicles and runs for about 3km east from the main road along the Khowarib Gorge.

The campsite sits on the banks of the Khowarib River and consists of seven basic huts, built by the local villagers using local materials to traditional designs. Some are rounded and mud-clad, Himba-style, and others are thatched. There are also five campsites for pitching tents. Bucket showers and bush toilets are provided and, with notice, simple local meals can be arranged.

The local community runs the camp. Guides can sometimes be arranged for walks around the area. (Note that a Save the Rhino base camp, sited just next to this visitor's camp, has long been one of the bases for their camel-mounted anti-poaching patrols around the region.)
Rates: N$15–20 per person camping.

Ongongo Campsite web: www.nacobta.com.na
About 11km further along the (D3706) road is the turn-off northeast for the Ongongo campsite. To reach this, turn at Warmquelle and watch for the signs (if there are any left). You will follow a water pipeline for about 6km, heading roughly northwards. The road is rough and very rocky in parts, sandy in others, and at one point you cross the dry bed of the river, before turning right to reach the site's office hut. A 2WD will usually just make it – depending on its ground clearance.

The main attraction here is the Ongongo waterfall, where a deep, clear pool is sheltered by an overhang of rock. Few resist the temptation to strip off and swim here, which isn't surprising given the temperature. The Ongongo community now administers the camp and several shaded huts are available to camp under, but bring all your food and equipment as nothing else is available.
Rates: a visit for the day is N$10 per person; camping is N$20 per person.

Sesfontein

Sesfontein was named after the 'six springs' that surface nearby. It stands in the Hoanib Valley and marks the northern edge of Damaraland. The road from Palmwag, the D3706, makes an interesting drive in a normal 2WD vehicle, and passes through a narrow gap in the mountains just before this small town. North of town, the going gets much tougher.

Sesfontein is a dusty but photogenic spot, set between mountains in the Hoanib Valley. The local vegetation is dominated by umbrella thorns (*Acacia tortilis*), the adaptable mopane (*Colophospermum mopane*, recognised by its butterfly-shaped leaves), and the beautiful, feathery real fan palms (*Hyphaene petersiana*). You will often be offered the 'vegetable ivory' seeds of these palms, carved into various designs, as souvenirs by the local people – which are highly recommended, as often the sellers are the carvers, and it is far less destructive than buying carvings of wood.

In the earlier part of this century, the German administrators made Sesfontein into an important military outpost. They wanted to control movement of stock around the country, after the severe rinderpest epidemic in 1896. So in 1901 they built a fort here, complete with running water and extensive gardens to grow their own supplies. However, by the start of World War I this had been abandoned, and it is only in the last few years that this has been renovated into a picturesque new lodge.

Sesfontein still feels like an outpost in many ways, despite being an important centre for the local people, who live by farming goats and the occasional field of maize. The efficiency of the foraging goats is witnessed by the lack of vegetation lower than the trees, and hence the clouds of fine dust which often hang in the valley's air.

Sesfontein offers the adventurous an interesting view of a real town, not sanitised by the colonial designs of townships. It is spread out, and very relaxed. If you're staying here, then try to rise early to watch the village come to life. On most days the national anthem will drift across the cool air, beautifully sung by the school within earshot of the fort. Watch as the farmers drive their cattle to water, and smartly dressed workers head for town.

In the afternoon there are always a few people about, and there's no better way to watch village life than sitting with a cold drink on the steps of one of the shops – though you may attract a crowd of playful children. If you are just passing through then you'll find the supplies in these shops useful, and there is a convenient petrol station here. There is little other fuel available between Sesfontein and the Kunene, except at Opuwo.

Where to stay

If you've passed the Khowarib and Ongongo campsites, mentioned above, then Fort Sesfontein is the area's only other place to stay.

Fort Sesfontein (13 double rooms, camping sites) PO Box 22114, Windhoek; tel: 065 275534/5; fax: 065 275533; email: fort.sesfontein@mweb.com.na; web: www.natron.net/tour/sesfontein/lodged.htm

Opened in 1995, Fort Sesfontein is one of the most original and imaginative places to appear since independence. The fort has been rebuilt more or less to its old plans, set around a lush central courtyard full of palm trees and fountains. The rooms are spacious and rustically decorated, with en-suite facilities and fans – which are as essential as the swimming pool: Sesfontein can get very hot. The old officers' mess is now a large bar/lounge with sitting and dining areas. Given its remote location, the standards of food and service in the lodge are superb.

Electricity is from a generator, which runs for most of the day, but if you need a TV, or contact with the outside world, then you are in the wrong place. There is no direct phone or fax here. The difficult radio-telephone, via Walvis Bay, is the swiftest way to communicate in an emergency.

If you don't have your own 4WD then the lodge can organise full-day (N$1,100 per vehicle) or half-day (N$600 per vehicle) tours to local Himba villages, with a guide. Judge the sensitivity of these yourself, but it is a good sign that the lodge insists that you also pay for a package of food for the village that you visit. A full-day tour down the Hoanib River Valley also costs N$1,100 per vehicle, and includes lunch. If you haven't got a vehicle at all, then there is a 2km landing strip at Sesfontein, from which the lodge will collect you.

Rates: single N$640, N$490 per person sharing, including breakfast. Dinner N$95, and lunch N$30, are best booked in advance. Camping N$55 per person.

What to see and do

Aside from relaxing in town, to explore further into Kaokoland is difficult (see below). For most people, the best way to see the area is on an organised trip: either one pre-arranged with a specialist before you arrive, or a day-trip arranged by Fort Sesfontein.

KAOKOLAND

This vast tract of land is Namibia at its most enticing – and yet most inhospitable. Kaokoland appeals to the adventurer and explorer in us, keeping quiet about the dangers involved. On the eastern side, hilly tracks become mudslides as they get washed away by the rains, whilst the baking desert in the west affords no comfort for those who get stranded. Even dry riverbeds hide soft traps of deep sand, whilst the few which seem damp and hard may turn to quicksand within metres. Having struggled to free a Land Rover with just one wheel stuck in quicksand, it is easy to believe tales of vehicles vanishing within an hour.

One road on the eastern side was particularly memorable for me – it started favourably as a good gravel track. After 20km, it had deteriorated into a series of rocky ruts, shaking us to our bones and forcing us to slow down to 10km/h. After a while, when we'd come too far to think of returning, the track descended into a sandy riverbed, strewn with boulders and enclosed by walls of rock. The only way was for passengers to walk and guide the driver, watching as the tyres lurched from boulder to boulder.

Hours later we emerged – on to another difficult track. Gradually it flattened and the driving eased: we were happy to be travelling faster. Then the pace was interrupted. Streams crossed the road. Someone would wade across to check the depth, and then the 4WD would swiftly follow, its momentum carrying it across the muddy bed. The third stream stopped us: more than thigh-high, fast flowing – a river in flood. We slept dry in our tents, thankful that the floods hadn't reached that first rocky riverbed whilst we were there.

To come to Kaokoland independently, you should have a two-vehicle 4WD expedition, all your supplies, an experienced navigator, detailed maps and good local advice on routes. Even then you'll probably get lost a few times. This is not a trip to undertake lightly: if things go wrong you will be hundreds of kilometres from help, and days from a hospital.

OWAMBO–HIMBA POLITICS IN THE KAOKOVELD

For many years now, conservationists have argued that Kaokoland ought to revert to its previous status as a national park. They cite as a model the Masai Mara, in East Africa, where the Masai people live in the park, their cattle coexisting with the game. The Himba people of Kaokoland (see page 23) have a similar culture, and could similarly coexist. This type of protection would stem the worst aspects of development in the region, and go some way to protecting both the Himba culture and the wildlife.

However, this view has not found favour within the SWAPO government. They are keen to present Namibia to the world as a modern, forward-looking country, and seem to feel that cattle-herding tribesmen in ochre and animal skins will damage this image. One government minister, Hidepo Hamutenya, is on record as suggesting that the Himba 'should be in ties and suits, rather than being half-naked and half dressed'.

Cynics point out that the Owambo (Namibia's dominant tribe, and SWAPO's power-base, see page 24) and the Himba did not fight side-by-side in the liberation struggle, so SWAPO's will to act in the best interests of the Himba is very limited. These issues are coming to a focus in controversial plans for a hydro-electric dam at Epupa. (See pages 365, 366 and 367 for comments on the Epupa Dam project.)

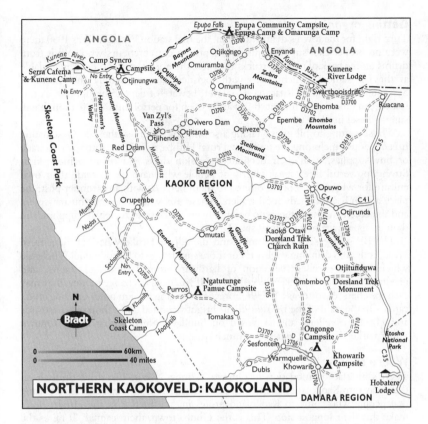

NORTHERN KAOKOVELD: KAOKOLAND

If you can get an expedition together, then in contrast to Damaraland's regulated concession areas, Kaokoland has yet to adopt any formal system of control. You are free to travel where you can. However, this freedom is causing lasting damage to the area. The Kaokoveld's drier areas, especially to the west, have a very fragile ecosystem: simply driving a vehicle off the tracks and 'across country' can cause permanent damage – killing plants and animals, and leaving marks that last for centuries. Vehicle trails made 40 years ago can still be seen as the crushed plants and lichens haven't recovered yet. Here, you must be responsible and treat the environment with care. Never drive off the tracks.

Opuwo

This rough and ready, frontier town is the hub of Kaokoland. It has shops, a good bakery, several garages, a large school, and even a short stretch of tarred road in the centre of town, despite being over a hundred kilometres from the nearest other tar (south of Kamanjab, or east of Ruacana).

Getting there

Opuwo is 54km of mediocre gravel from the main Kamanjab-Ruacana road and greets you with large, irrigated maize fields on the right, and probably a couple of stray cattle in front. Soon the dry, dusty town appears, sprawling over a low hillside with no apparent centre: its buildings are functional rather than attractive, and the outskirts fade into groups of round Himba huts.

Getting organised

Turn right for the town's main attraction, the fuel station. As recently as 1990 there were no proper fuel supplies, just a few private entrepreneurs who sold it from drums on the back of pick-up trucks for twice the normal price. Now it is available at the BP station, which helps with logistics, being the only fuel north of Sesfontein and west of Ruacana. However, beware of depending upon it, as this station can (and does) run out. It is usually open for petrol until 17.00, though will supply diesel until 19.00.

Whilst waiting to fill up, or taking a stroll, look around – there is a fascinating mix of people, including the traditional rural Himba, who come into town to trade or buy supplies, with their decorated goatskin dress and ochre-stained skins. Strong, powerful faces speak clearly of people who have yet to trade their own culture for what little is being offered to them here. As with any frontier post, the place abounds with shady local traders. These mix with occasional businessmen, and the eccentric characters who emerge from the bush to replenish supplies, and then disappear again with equal speed.

The BP garage sells cool drinks, and the adjacent bakery has excellent fresh bread, rolls, and drinking yoghurt. For more supplies go to Groothandel Wholesale which has an excellent selection of hardware, tinned food and staples, and produces large blocks of ice for cool-boxes. If you need to change money, they may cash travellers' cheques as a favour. Forget exchanging foreign notes or using credit cards. On the right of the BP station, the brightly painted curio shop sells postcards and Himba jewellery, and is closed on Sundays. Next to that is the Opuwo Supermarket, but don't expect too much from it.

Where to stay

There's little accommodation in Opuwo, as most visitors just drive through on their way into Kaokoland, or back towards Etosha. This is a shame. It is surprising that people who come to Kaokoland professing an interest in the Himba don't make this their longest stop. This is the Himba town, their 'capital'. It raises the question of what those travellers are really seeking: is it the Himba – or is it simply photographs to match their image of 'primitive tribespeople', regardless of the reality?

If you do stop here, then ignore the ill-informed advice of guidebooks that mention asking for help from the town's missions. They have more pressing calls from local people, and little time for scrounging travellers. Instead head for the:

Ohakane Guest House (10 rooms) Tel: 065 273031; fax: 067 273025; email: ohakane@iafrica.com.na
This small lodge, named after the local word for 'wild dog', opened in 1995 and is well signposted just after the petrol station. Its rooms all have air conditioning and en-suite facilities, and there's even a swimming pool outside. It serves lunch and dinner, and has a small selection of curios for sale. There is also a private plane if you want to organise fly-in trips.
Rates: single N$360, double N$260 per person, including breakfast. Lunch N$40; dinner N$90.

Kunene Village Restcamp Tel 065 273043; web: www.nacobta.com.na
This fairly new community-run campsite is about 2km west of Opuwo, on the road to Etanga (D3703), and it is well signposted. It has two stone bungalows with twin beds (though no linen), and a number of grassy campsites. There's also an ablution block with flush toilets and hot showers, and a bar for cool drinks.
Rates: camping N$40 per person; bungalows are N$170 per twin, N$140 single. Firewood is available for N$10 per bundle.

EPUPA DAM PROJECT: THE CONTROVERSY

For several years the Namibian and Angolan governments have been cooperating in studies to build a hydro-electric dam across the Kunene. Two sites have been mooted: one in the Baynes Mountains, and one at Epupa. Advocates of the scheme have pointed to Namibia's rising power consumption, and the apparent 'waste' of the Kunene's huge potential. They also cite the project as a source of work in the northern Kaokoveld – an area that lacks virtually any formal employment opportunities.

Critics regard this as a 'prestige project' for the government, which is both superfluous and damaging. They claim that its power will be expensive and unnecessary, and it will do immense damage to the Kunene's ecosystems and the culture of the Himba people who live near the river.

Cynics suggest that part of the SWAPO government's enthusiasm for the project is due to the work that it would generate for migrant workers from outside the Kaokoveld. Most would come from the densely populated areas to the east, the Owambo heartlands, which are SWAPO's constituency. They also observe that the Himba generally did not side with SWAPO during the liberation struggle, and suggest that the government is now trying to marginalise them and destroy their traditional lands and culture.

Several organisations have helped the Himba communities to put their point forward, and campaign against the dam. These include, in Namibia, the non-profit law firm Legal Assistance Centre (LAC), and, abroad, the London-based Survival.

Despite Namibia's constitution, the president, Sam Nujoma, was reported as becoming exasperated by the extended opposition to the project, which he seems to believe is fermented by foreign groups rather than local people. In June 1998 *The Namibian* described one of his speeches as being 'laced with hostile references to people who did not fall in line with government thinking'. The debate continues.

Survival is a worldwide organisation supporting tribal peoples. It stands for their right to decide their own future and helps them protect their lives, lands and human rights. You can join Survival by contacting them at 11–15 Emerald St, London WC1 3QL, UK; tel: 020 7242 1441; fax: 020 7242 1771; email: survival@gn.apc.org.

Epupa Falls

Though visitors go to Kaokoland more for the whole experience than any individual sight, Epupa is one of its highlights.

About 145km west of Ruacana, the Kunene River is already threading its way through the Baynes Mountains, en route to the Atlantic. It winds between arid hills and wild, rough-looking mountains on both sides. Angola lies to its north, Namibia to its south: both look identical. As it meanders east, a thin strip of verdant palm-forest lines its path. Photogenic, feathery fronds of green Makalani palms extend for perhaps only 30m from the river itself. Further from the water than that, the land reverts to its parched, dry state: the preserve of the Kaokoveld's semi-desert flora and fauna.

Here at Epupa the river widens to accommodate a few small islands, before plunging into a geological fault. This is 35m deep in places and, as the river is sizeable, it makes a lot of noise and some spray. The Epupa Falls don't compare with Victoria Falls in scale, but they are all the more beautiful for occurring in such an arid region. Add to the scene a phalanx of watchful baobabs, many balancing improbably on precarious rocks above the chasms, or standing forlornly on the small islands in the stream. It's a magical spot.

Flora and fauna

Epupa's flora and fauna are representative of the ecosystem found in the palm-forest which lines the river for most of its length.

Hippos have been exterminated from this section of the river, though crocodiles are still common (bathing is only safe immediately beside the Falls) and small mammals are common in the palm-forest. There are no large wild mammals commonly seen around here

Ornithologists will find a fascinating variety of birds, including the inevitable fish eagles, various bee-eaters, kingfishers ranging from the giant to the tiny malachite kingfisher, louries, bulbuls and hornbills, as well as rollers (purple, lilac breasted and European), golden and lesser masked weavers, scarlet-breasted sunbirds, and perhaps the odd, lost, great white eagret. The rufus-faced palm thrush also occurs, though is very rare: this riverine palm-forest is typical of its highly restricted habitat.

Easier to see is a breeding colony of rosy-faced lovebirds, living amongst the trees in a nearby valley, and the fearless pair of paradise flycatchers that were nesting at eye-level just above my tent.

Other attractions

Gemmologists should seek out the same valley as the lovebirds, but keep their eyes on the ground for the rose quartz crystals that abound. You may also find the chipped stone implements of past inhabitants.

EPUPA DAM PROJECT: THE FEASIBILITY STUDY

To dispel the controversy over the project, a full feasibility study was commissioned by the government for the Epupa Dam project. This US$7million study was awarded in 1995 to NAMANG, a consortium composed of Norconsult (from Norway), Swedpower (Sweden), Saopro (Angola) and Burmeister van Niekerk (Namibia). The pre-feasibility study, completed in 1993, was drafted by almost the same team.

Even before the study was published, Namibian government officials were on record as saying that the decision on the project had already been taken. Nobody was surprised when, at the start of 1998, the official report backed the dam, claiming that its few negative impacts would be greatly outweighed by the positive ones.

However, a panel of seven international experts swiftly discredited this feasibility report. These included internationally renowned specialists in ecology, water-management, economics, alternative energy and Namibian law. They scrutinised it at the request of several non-governmental organisations, including the California-based International Rivers Network. These independent experts concluded that the report was 'riddled with incorrect conclusions, false assumptions and missing data so that it cannot be used as a basis for a well-informed decision on the project'.

EPUPA DAM PROJECT: THE VIEW OF THE HIMBA PEOPLE

Most Himba people don't want a dam. In February 1998, 26 out of the 32 traditional leaders in the Kunene Region submitted a detailed document to the government explaining why. It noted eleven major objections to the dam:

- *Loss of land* The dam would inundate about 190km^2 on the Namibian side of the river, including 110 permanent dwellings.
- *Loss of riverine resources* The narrow palm-forest beside the river is a vital source of food for both people and livestock.
- *Loss of gardens* Many of the Himba people cultivate small gardens on the alluvial soils.
- *Disappearance of wildlife* Without the river much wildlife would be lost.
- *Inundation of ancestral gravesites* These are very important in Himba culture in defining to whom the land belongs.
- *Barrier effect of the dam* Himba communities live on both sides of the river, and regularly cross it. A large dam would make this difficult or impossible.
- *Health threats* A large lake would introduce more malaria and bilharzia, and the influx of a mobile labour force would probably bring with it carriers of HIV infection, and other sexually transmitted diseases.
- *Overcrowding* The dam would require about 1,000 workers, and a construction town would probably have a population of about 5,000. When the dam is finished the area would go 'from boom to bust'.
- *Increased crime* The influx of construction workers would probably increase the crime rate, which is currently very low.
- *Loss of control* The Himba people fear the loss of their lands to outsiders.
- *Loss of eco-tourism potential* Without the dam, Epupa could be a major attraction for tourists, which would benefit the local community.

Sunrise bathes the nearby hills in clear red light, and this is a good time to explore. The hills have an uneven surface of loose rock so wear a stout pair of shoes and watch out for snakes. Temperatures are cold at first, but it warms up very rapidly so take water, a sunhat and suncream. As with exploring anywhere near this border, seek local advice. Some areas were mined during the liberation struggle, and injuries still occur.

Because Epupa is situated in a traditional Himba area, you may get the opportunity to visit a typical local family. Go with a guide who speaks the local language, and make sure that the village receives some real benefit from your visit. Buying craftwork made by the villagers is one very good way of doing this, but simply taking along some mealie-meal would also be a positive gesture. With patience, your interpreter should help you to glimpse a little of their lifestyle.

Of all the Namibians that you encounter, the Himba require some of the greatest cultural sensitivity. Their culture is adapting to centuries of changes within a matter of years. Until the late 1980s there were people living in the area who relied entirely on a hunter-gatherer existence, using only stone implements – a reminder of how remote this area was until very recently.

The western valleys

In the west, Hartmann's Valley and the Marienfluss are often visited by the Kaokoveld's specialists. Both valleys run north–south, bounded in the north by the Kunene, which flows all year.

Hartmann's Valley

As you enter the valley, there is a small sign covered with weatherworn glass. It stresses the ecologically important things you must do, and includes a diagram of how to turn a vehicle around to minimise damage to the environment. Take time to read it and remember.

Hartmann's Valley itself is very arid, though its weather can vary dramatically. As well as searing heat, the valley receives sea mists, which creep up from the coast, making it an eerie place to visit.

It is 70km from end to end, a minimum of 2½ hours' drive one way, and the condition of the track along it varies. In the south, the road starts by crossing a number of steep-sided river valleys. It soon changes to compacted corrugated sand, which shakes your vehicle violently. Finally, this becomes soft before high dunes prevent you reaching the Kunene by vehicle. Despite the harsh conditions, it is very beautiful. Drive through at sunrise if possible; then it's cooler than later and shows off the surrounding hills at their finest.

Where to stay

There are two private camps at the end of the valley:

Serra Cafema Camp Tel: 061 274500; fax: 061 239455; email: info@nts.com.na (Wilderness Safaris)

Recently taken over by Namib Wilderness Safaris (see page 341), this has been long been a very basic camp owned by the owners of Palmwag (pages 354–6). As I write, it is being rebuilt, and is due to open in mid to late 2003 as a very upmarket, luxurious camp. It's planned to have six large canvas and thatch chalets, built like the rest of the camp on substantial elevated wooden decks, beside the edge of the Kunene. These will have the high quality and space that's become a trademark of Wilderness's properties, and guests will fly in here – not drive.

The intention is to create a camp to which visitors can come after a trip to the Skeleton Coast Camp. Because the Skeleton Coast is quite a harsh environment, and the long excursions there can be tiring, Serra Cafema is envisaged as a more laid-back, relaxed spot. Having spent time here recently at the old camp, and enjoyed both floating down the river and exploring the outlying areas with a super guide, it's easy to see how it makes sense. Because of the difficult logistics of getting here, and the high comfort levels of the camp itself, it's not a cheap camp – however it can offer some of the experience of the Skeleton Coast Camp at a substantially lower cost. (That said, it also works well for a few days relaxing by the river after a Skeleton Coast trip.)

Kunene Camp

Run by Skeleton Coast Safaris, this very small and simple camp is usually used for a final night as part of their fly-in trips to the Skeleton Coast and the Kaokoveld. See pages 337–9 for more details on this operation, and note that this is always pre-booked as part of a fly-in trip. They cannot accept people who try to just drop in.

The Marienfluss

The next valley inland from Hartmann's is the Marienfluss. If you are driving, this is reached via Red Drum – a crossroads marked by a red oil can. There is a fairly new-looking Himba settlement at Red Drum.

The Marienfluss has more soft sand and is greener than Hartmann's Valley. It is covered with light scrub and the odd tree marks an underground river. A most noticeable feature of the Marienfluss is its 'fairy circles', although they are also found, to a lesser extent, in Hartmann's Valley. These are circular patches without any vegetation. Studies by Professors G Theron and E Moll, from the universities of Pretoria and Cape Town, put forward three possible theories for their origin.

One theory suggests that *Euphorbia* bushes once grew here. It's thought that when they died, they may have left poisonous chemicals in the soil, which prohibit grass from growing. Another idea is that tropical termites may be blown into the Pro-Namib during wet cycles, starting colonies that kill the grasses. During the dry cycles, these die off leaving the bare circles that we see. A third theory suggests that there are 'hardpans' in these patches. That is, layers of soil through which water cannot penetrate, making plant life impossible. Of course, one other common explanation is that they were, indeed, made by fairies...

Where to stay

At the northern end of the Marienfluss, there is a public and also a private campsite. Both are set on the banks of the Kunene mainly under the shade of camelthorn trees, *Acacia erioloba*.

On the track that goes past these camps there is a sign saying 'no photographs'. (The logic of this isn't obvious, except for the proximity of the Angolan border.) After a further 3km the road divides into three. The left fork goes to an excellent viewing point, over some rapids in the river. The centre and right turns are both blocked. If you walk up the middle track, you'll find a small beach on the Kunene. The right track leads off to some trees, which may have been a campsite once.

In morning and evening you'll see many Himba people going about their business, often with their cattle. There is also some wildlife around, including springbok, ostrich, bat-eared fox, bustards, korhanns, and many other birds.

Okarohombo Campsite Web: www.nacobta.com.na
On the banks of the Kunene, at the northern end of the Marienfluss, is a simple signposted campsite under ana trees, run by the local Himba community (who speak little English). Facilities at the five pitches are limited to a few flush toilets and fireplaces. Cold showers are sometimes available but could be washed away as the camp is at floodwater level. As this is one of the more remote areas where Himba people live, it is less commercialised than other places, and is a good location to experience their lifestyle. Like most community campsites, this is worth your support.
Rates: N$25 per person camping.

Camp Syncro See *Kaokohimba Safaris*, page 372, for more details.
This small, simple camp occupies a lovely spot overlooking the Kunene, from the end of the Marienfluss. It has just four simple thatched houses constructed from stones from the river and standing in the shade of ana trees. Each has water for drinking and twin beds. Two showers and long-drop toilets are shared between the houses. But then you don't come here for the camp; you come to explore the area with Koos, and to meet the local people.

How to visit Kaokoland

Because Kaokoland is remote, the few camps here tend to be either very basic or very organised. The basic ones are a couple of simple campsites, often run by the local communities with the backing of one of the conservation/development organisations. The organised camps are a few expensive camps linked with small specialist fly-in operators.

MINIMUM IMPACT IN KAOKOLAND
Read the camping advice in *Chapter 7*, and remember the following:

- Never camp in a riverbed; flash floods often claim lives.
- Never camp close to a water point. Desert-adapted animals will often travel for days to get to one of these. They may die of thirst if you keep them from the water with your presence.
- Gather any firewood you will need in the highlands before you get to this area, and keep its use to a minimum.
- In such a dry landscape be very careful not to cause bush-fires.
- Take home everything that you bring in. No rubbish should be buried: it may take centuries to decay, and will almost certainly be dug up before then by scavengers.
- Water is very limited, so bring in all you need. Use sparingly any that you find.
- The few streams and springs in the area are used for drinking by animals and people. Do not contaminate them, and be sure to wash well away from them.

Simple camps

If you are planning an expedition, then in most places you must camp. There are demarcated camping sites at Purros and Epupa Falls, which are run by the local people, and for the local people. These are like Ongongo (page 360) and Khowarib (page 360), catering for self-sufficient expeditions in 4WDs. Such travellers are urged to support these.

In the very north, at the end of the Marienfluss Valley, there is a public campsite, with no facilities. Anywhere else in the region you can choose your own site, provided that you obtain permission from the head of the local village, and show due respect to the area's inhabitants (see *Where you can camp*, pages 101–2). Here, more than anywhere else, there is a need to be responsible. The three organised campsites north of Sesfontein are:

Purros Campsite aka **Ngatutunge Pamue Campsite** (5 sites) c/o IRDNC, PO Box 1715, Swakopmund; web: www.nacobta.com.na
Ngatutunge Pamue means 'we build together', and this is a super site, about 100km northwest of Sesfontein, near the Purros village. It is run by Peter Uaraavi and his family. The pitches are on the wooded bank of the Hoarusib River, 3km north of Purros. Each has a flush toilet (surrounded by reeds), shower and fireplace (no grid) with tap and bin. Nearby is a section of the river that is normally forced over-ground by a rock barrier.

One main purpose of the camp is to provide employment for the local Himba from Purros village, so you are strongly encouraged to hire guides for your own game drives and to take guided walks looking for plants used in traditional medicine, as well as escorted trips to Himba villages. Costs are very reasonable, about N$25 for a few hours, and this is an effective way to put some money directly into the local economy.

Peter encourages visitors to spend time at the village of Purros, and will introduce you as a guest, rather than just some foreigner who gawps. So greet the villagers, and spend time talking with them, and learning a little of how they live. Many now are helped by the income made from selling jewellery, or guiding visitors around their local area – they deserve your support. Ask your guide to include a few walks. It makes a pleasant break from driving over poor surfaces and allows time to take in your surroundings. Around Purros it is usually possible to visit Himba villages on foot, which is a more leisurely and satisfying way to meet these pastoral people, allowing plenty of time for an exchange of views and questions through your guide. After all, how would you like it if a group of

Previous page Damaraland, home to thriving populations of wild black rhino (CM)

Above Gemsbok fighting at Ozonjuitji m'Bari waterhole in Etosha National Park (CM)

Right Shovel-snouted lizard (RM)

Below Springbok at one of Etosha's signposts (CM)

strangers drove up to your house, came in and took pictures of your family and then departed within five or ten minutes?

Note that elephants occur frequently in the area and around the campsite and should not be harassed in any way; they are dangerous and unpredictable animals, and have killed people. *Rates: N$30 per person camping. Firewood is available for N$15 per bundle – but use sparingly as it's in very short supply.*

Epupa Community Campsite
Epupa has become such a Mecca for visitors to the Kaokoveld that people camped here long before a site existed. Eventually the community set up the site to benefit from these visitors, and in order to protect the fragile palm-forest from being ruined by visitors in search of virgin camping sites.
Rates: N$20 per person camping.

Kunene River Lodge (5 bungalows and camping) PO Box 643, Ondangwa; tel: 065 274300; fax: 065 274301; email: info@kuneneriverlodge.com; web: www.kuneneriverlodge.com.
Near Swartbooisdrift, about 50km west of Ruacana, on the D3700, is a simple, privately run lodge with some rustic bungalows, all of them en suite, and camping plots under trees by the river. By the campsite is a bar, and a shop stocking basic provisions.

Among the activities available are whitewater rafting, canoeing, fishing and mountain biking.
Rates: single N$320; double N$440; $40 per person camping.

Upmarket camps
There is just one upmarket camp in the region that isn't linked to one of the specialist operators listed below. This relies on a mixture of jaded explorers desperate for some comfort, and fly-in visitors who come just to see Epupa Falls for a day or two:

Epupa Camp (12 tents) PO Box 90466, 5 Robert Mugabe Av, Windhoek; tel: 061 246427; fax: 061 246428/225084
On the palm-fringed banks of the Kunene, 700m east of the main falls, the tents here have solar-powered lights, mosquito-netted doors and windows, and they share toilets and showers.

Activities include walks around the local area and guided visits to a local Himba village. The camp makes much of its 'sound ecological policy', and works closely with the local community. To reach it a charter aircraft or fully equipped 4WD is needed. Flying is the best way to arrive, but if you drive then the easiest route is from Opuwo via Okongwati (about 200km, of which the last 80km are the worst). Note there is no help on this route if an emergency occurs. As with anywhere in this area, you ought to be in a party of at least two 4WDs with experienced drivers.
Rates: N$655 single, N$540 per person sharing, including activities, meals and drinks

Specialist Kaokoveld operators
When planning a visit to this area, you should consider who is taking you, rather than exactly where you're staying. Choose the most knowledgeable operator with whom you feel comfortable, and then go with them.

Kaokoland is rugged and remote. Trusting your arrangements to anyone who does not know it intimately is foolish. Don't visit here accompanied by someone who runs general trips all over the country. Instead choose one of the specialists who concentrate on this area. Finally, do satisfy yourself that your operator values the fragility of the area and its culture. Amongst other things, consider:

- How (if at all) your operator ensures that the local people benefit from your visit. Is there an automatic bed-night levy paid into local community funds?
- How sensitive the operator is to the local cultures. Do their staff speak the local languages?
- Do they use local people for staff, creating local employment prospects?

Such operations may use their own fixed camps, or mobile camps, which can be moved when necessary. This is the most comfortable way to see Kaokoland, and also the best way. You need a good guide here. Amongst many that run occasional trips, two excellent specialists stand out:

Kaokohimba Safaris PO Box 11580, Windhoek; tel/fax: 061 222378; email: kaokohimba@natron.net
Kaokohimba Safaris started up in 1990 and are certainly a contender for the area's best operation. They don't organise tours anywhere else, and the company's founder, Koos Verwey, conducts all the tours himself. Importantly, they are also involved in positive local community projects, and you probably won't find anyone who knows this area better. In fact, Koos is often said to care more for the Himba people than he does for the difficult guests on his safaris.

Kaokohimba's base is their Camp Syncro, at the northern end of the Marienfluss, east of the Hartmann Mountains. Their trips are active, though not necessarily strenuous. If you want to sit back passively and just watch, then these are not for you. They are all fly-in trips, and vary from two nights exploring the Marienfluss and Epupa, to six nights covering the Namib in the western Kaokoveld, Marienfluss, Hartmann Valley and the Kunene. There are also trips lasting 12 days, which include donkey-treks led by Himba guides into the most remote corners of the Kaokoveld.

Skeleton Coast Fly-in Safaris PO Box 2195, Windhoek; tel: 061 224248; fax: 061 225713. See pages 337–9 for further information.
Though you might not immediately associate the experts on the Skeleton Coast with the Kaokoveld, most of a trip to the Skeleton Coast is, in fact, spent just inland in the Kaokoveld. They normally visit the Purros area, and the region around the Kunene River, at the north end of the Hartmann's Mountains. The experience offered by Skeleton Coast Safaris is just as much about the Kaokoveld as it is about the coast – and that's how these trips have always been. Their founder, the late Louw Schoeman, was also an early supporter of the Auxiliary Game Guard scheme (now called the Community Game Guard scheme) that has done so much good in the region. Their eco-credentials are amongst the best in the business, and it remains a superb operation.

Etosha National Park

Translated as the 'Place of Mirages', 'Land of Dry Water'
or the 'Great White Place', Etosha is an apparently endless
pan of silvery-white sand, upon which dust devils play and
mirages blur the horizon. As a game park, it excels during
the dry season when huge herds of animals can be seen
amidst some of the most startling and photogenic scenery in
Africa.

The roads are all navigable in a normal 2WD car, and the park
was designed for visitors to drive themselves around. If you insist
on guided trips then look to one of the private lodges just outside
the park or, better, to the concession areas in Damaraland. Etosha
is a park to explore by yourself. Put a few drinks, a camera, lots of
film and a pair of binoculars in your own car and go for a slow drive, stopping at
the waterholes – it's amazing.

There are three restcamps within the park, and several lodges outside its
boundaries, and yet the park is never busy in comparison with equally good
reserves elsewhere in Africa.

BACKGROUND INFORMATION
History
Europeans first knew Etosha in the early 1850s when Charles Andersson and
Francis Galton visited it. They recorded their early impressions:

> ...we traversed an immense hollow, called Etosha, covered with saline
> encrustations, and having wooded and well-defined borders. Such places
> are in Africa designated 'salt pans'... In some rainy seasons, the Ovambo
> informed us, the locality was flooded and had all the appearance of a lake;
> but now it was quite dry, and the soil strongly impregnated with salt.
> Indeed, close in shore, the commodity was to be had of a very pure
> quality.

They were amongst the first explorers and traders who relentlessly hunted the
area's huge herds of game. In 1876 an American trader, McKiernan, came through
the area and wrote of a visit to Etosha:

> All the menageries in the world turned loose would not compare to the
> sight that I saw that day.

The slaughter became worse as time progressed and more Europeans came until,
in 1907, Dr F von Lindequist, the governor of German South West Africa (as
Namibia was then), proclaimed three reserves. These covered all of the current
park, and most of Kaokoland – between the Kunene and Hoarusib rivers. The aim
was to stem the rapid depletion of the animals in the area, and protect all of the land

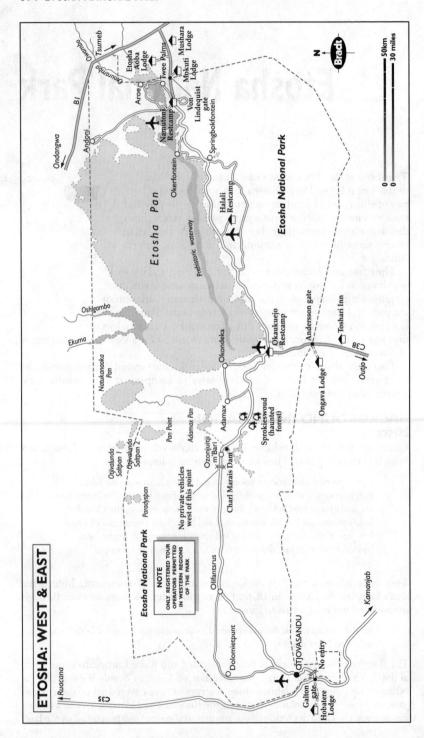

ETOSHA: WEST & EAST

Etosha National Park

NOTE
ONLY REGISTERED TOUR
OPERATORS PERMITTED
IN WESTERN REGIONS
OF THE PARK

No private vehicles
west of this point

Etosha National Park

Etosha Pan

Prehistoric waterway

Natukanaoka Pan

Oshigambo

Ekuma

Natukanoka Pan

Adamax Pan

Pan Point

Ojivalunda Saltpan 1

Ojivalunda Saltpan 2

Paradyspan

Ozonjuitji m'Bari

Charl Marais Dam

Sprokieswoud (haunted forest)

Adamax

Okondeka

Okaukuejo Restcamp

Andersson gate

Toshari Inn

Ongava Lodge

Otjjo

C38

Olifantsrus

Dolomietpunt

OTJOVASANDU

No entry

Galton gate

Hobatere Lodge

Kamanjab

Ruacana

C35

Okerfontein

Okerfontein

Halali Restcamp

Springbokfontein

Von Lindequist gate

Namutoni Restcamp

Andoni

Aroe

Etosha Aoba Lodge

Twee Palms

Mokuti Lodge

Mushara Lodge

Tsumeb

Omuramba

Omuramba

B1

Ondangwa

Ondangwa

N

Bradt

50km
30 miles

through which the seasonal migrations passed. It was an excellent plan for conserving the wildlife – though perhaps not so perfect for the people who lived in these areas.

This protected area remained largely intact until the 1950s and 60s. Then, just as a nature conservation unit and several tourist camps were set up, the reserves were redefined and Etosha shrank to its present size.

Geography, landscape and flora

The defining feature of the national park is the huge Etosha Pan, which appears to be the remnant of a large inland lake that was fed by rivers from the north and east. One of these was probably the Kunene, which flowed southeast from the Angolan highlands and into the pan. However, some 12 million years ago continental uplift changed the slope of the land and the course of these tributaries. The Kunene now flows west from the Ruacana Falls and into the Atlantic. Thus deprived, the lake slowly vanished in the scorching sun, leaving behind only a salty residue. Few plants can grow on this and so erosion by the wind is easy, allowing the pan to be gradually hollowed out.

The pan has probably changed little over time. It is roughly 110km from east to west and 60km from north to south, covering an area of 6,133km² (around a quarter of the park's surface) with flat, silvery sand and shimmering heat. If the rains to the north and east have been good, then the pan will hold water for a few months at the start of the year, thanks mainly to the Ekuma River and Omuramba Owambo. Only very rarely does it fill completely.

In the rest of the park, beyond the sides of the pan, the terrain is generally flat with a variety of habitats ranging from mopane woodland to wide, open, virtually treeless, plains. In the east of the park, around Namutoni, the attractive makalani palms, *Hyphaene ventricosa*, are found, often in picturesque groups around waterholes. The small, round fruit of these palms, a favourite food of elephants, is sometimes called vegetable ivory because of its hard white kernel. In the west, one of the more unusual areas is the Haunted Forest, *Sprokieswoud* in Afrikaans, where the contorted forms of strange moringa trees, *Moringa ovalifolia*, form a weird woodland scene.

Etosha is so special because of the concentration of waterholes that occur around the southern edges of the pan. As the dry season progresses, these increasingly draw the game. In fact, the best way to watch animals in Etosha is often just to sit in your vehicle by a waterhole and wait.

Three types of spring create these waterholes, which differ in both appearance and geology:

Contact springs

These occur in situations where two adjacent layers of rock have very different permeabilities. There are many to be seen just on the edge of the pan. Here the water-bearing calcrete comes to an end and the water flows out on to the surface because the underlying layers of clay are impermeable. Okerfontein is the best example of this type of spring, which is generally weak in water supply.

Water-level springs

Found in hollows where the surface of the ground actually cuts below the level of the water table, often in large depressions in the limestone formations. These are inevitably dependent on the level of the water table, and hence vary greatly from year to year. Typical of this type are Ngobib, Groot Okevi and Klein Okevi.

Artesian springs

Formed when pressure from overlying rocks forces water up to the surface from deeper aquifers (water-bearing rocks). Here they normally occur on limestone hillocks, forming deep pools, which will often have clumps of reeds in their centre. These springs are usually very reliable and include Namutoni, Klein Namutoni, Chudob and Aus.

Mammals

The game and birds found here are typical of the savannah plains of southern Africa, but include several species endemic to this western side of the continent, adjacent to the Namib Desert.

The more common herbivores include elephant, giraffe, eland, blue wildebeest, kudu, gemsbok, springbok, impala, steenbok, and zebra. The most numerous of these are the springbok which can often be seen in herds numbering thousands, spread out over the most barren of plains. These finely marked antelope have a marvellous habit of pronking, either (it appears) for fun or to avoid predators. It has been suggested that pronking is intended to put predators off in the first place by showing the animal's strength and stamina; the weakest pronkers are the ones predators are seen to go for. The early explorer Andersson described these elegant leaps:

> This animal bounds without an effort to a height of 10 or 12 feet at one
> spring, clearing from 12 to 14 feet of ground. It appears to soar, to be
> suspended for a moment in the air, then, touching the ground, to make
> another dart, or another flight, aloft, without the aid of wings, by the
> elastic springiness of its legs.

Elephant are very common, though digging for water below the sand wears down their tusks and so big tuskers are very rare. Often large family groups are seen trooping down to waterholes to drink, wallow and bathe. The park's population has been under scientific scrutiny for the infrasonic noises (below the range of human hearing) which they make. It is thought that groups communicate over long distances in this way.

Among the rarer species, black rhino continue to thrive here, and the floodlit waterholes at Okaukuejo and Halali provide two of the continent's best chances to observe this aggressive and secretive species. On one visit here, I watched as a herd of 20 or so elephants, silently drinking in the cool of the night, were frightened away from the water, and kept at bay, by the arrival of a single black rhino. It returned several times in the space of an hour or so, each time causing the larger elephants to flee, before settling down to enjoy a drink from the pool on its own.

In the last few years, about a dozen white rhino have been introduced. Your best chance of seeing these is in the east of the park, around Aus, Springbokfontein, Batia or Okerfontein, either early or late in the day.

Black-faced impala are restricted to Namibia and southern Angola, occurring here as well as in parts of the Kaokoveld. With only isolated populations, numbering under a thousand or so, they are one of the rarest animals in the region. The Damara dik-dik is the park's smallest antelope. Endemic to Namibia, it is common here in areas of dense bush.

Roan antelope and red hartebeest occur all over the subcontinent, though they are common nowhere. This is definitely one of the better parks in which to look for roan, especially in the mopane areas around Aus and Olifantsbad.

All of the larger felines are found here, with good numbers of lion, leopard, cheetah and caracal. The lion tend to prey mainly upon zebra and wildebeest, whilst the cheetah rely largely upon springbok. The seldom-seen leopard take a varied diet, including antelope and small mammals, whilst the equally elusive caracal go for similar but smaller prey.

There have been several attempts to introduce wild dog here, but so far no success. The usual problem has been that the dogs don't know to avoid lion, which have subsequently killed them for no apparent reason.

Also found in the park are both spotted and brown hyenas, together with silver jackal (or cape fox), and the more common black-backed jackal – many of which can be seen in the late evening, skulking around the camps in search of scraps of food.

Birds

For ornithologists, some 340 species of birds have been recorded, including many uncommon members of the hawk and vulture families.

Amongst the birds of prey, bateleur, martial, tawny and Wahlberg's eagles are fairly common, as are black-breasted and brown snake eagles. Pale-chanting goshawks are more often seen than the similar Gabar or the smaller little banded goshawk. The list of harriers, falcons and kestrels occurring here is even longer, and worthy of a special mention are the very common rock kestrels, which are everywhere, and the unusual red-necked and particularly cute pygmy falcons, which are less readily seen. The impressive peregrine falcon and Montagu's harrier are two of the rarer summer migrants.

Lappet-faced and white-backed vultures are common here, outnumbering the odd pair of white-headed or hooded vultures. Palmnut vultures are occasionally seen in the east of the park.

The number of large birds stalking around the plains can strike visitors as unusual: invariably during the day you will see groups of ostriches or pairs of secretary birds. Equally, it is easy to drive within metres of many kori bustards and black korhaans, which will just sit by the roadside and watch the vehicles pass.

Blue cranes, both beautiful and endangered, are common here in the wet season. Etosha is worth visiting in January and February for them alone. Other specialities of the park include violet woodhoopoe, white-tailed shrike, bare-cheeked and black-faced babblers, short-toed rock thrush, and a pale race of the pink-bellied lark.

PRACTICAL INFORMATION

To see Etosha you need to drive around the park. There is no way to walk within it, or to fly just above it. If you do not have your own vehicle then you must either hire one, or book an organised trip.

Hiring your own vehicle is best done in Windhoek. See *Driving in Namibia,* pages 79–83. However, if you are just travelling though, and hiring a car just for Etosha, then consider doing so from Tsumeb. This is normally best organised in advance, through a tour operator (pages 50–1) or the car-hire companies in Windhoek (see page 83), some of which will let you pick up and drop off cars at Mokuti or Ongava.

Organised trips to the park emanate from the private lodges around the park. See *Lodges outside Etosha*, page 383, for ideas about what is possible from each. Other than these, many operators organise guided trips around Namibia including a few days in Etosha, often staying in the National Park's accommodation. However, you only need to see one air-conditioned 75-seater coach driving through the park to convince you that this is not the best way to visit either Etosha or Namibia. Most have their bases in Windhoek; see page 119 for details.

When to visit

To decide when to visit, think about the weather, consider the number of other visitors around, and work out if your main reason for coming is to see the animals or the birds.

Weather

Etosha's weather is typical of Namibia, so see *Chapter 3*'s section on *Weather* for a general overview. At the beginning of the year, it's hot and fairly damp with average temperatures around 27°C and cloud cover for some of the time. If the rains have been good, then the pan will have some standing water in it.

The clouds gradually disperse as the rains cease, around March–April. Many of Etosha's plants are bright green during this time, but with some cloud cover the park's stark beauty isn't at its most photogenic.

From April to July the park dries out, and nights become cooler. Nights in August are normally above freezing, and by the end of September they are warm again. October is hot, and it gets hotter as the month progresses, but the humidity remains very low.

Even the game seems to await the coming of the rains in late November, or perhaps December. When these do arrive, the tropical downpours last only for a few hours each afternoon, but they clear the air, revive the vegetation, and give everything a new lease of life.

Photography

From a photographic point of view, Etosha can be stunning in any month. A personal favourite is late-April to June: when the vegetation is green, yet the skies are clear blue and there's little dust in the rain-washed air.

Other visitors

Etosha is never crowded. Compared with the hordes of tourists that fill Kruger or the game parks of East Africa. Etosha always seems deserted, even when its lodges and restcamps are full. It becomes busier around Easter and from late-July to September. Then advanced bookings are *essential*; you may not even get a camping site without a prior reservation. The accommodation inside the park during August can be full as early as the end of April.

The dates of the South African school holidays seem to be less relevant than they used to be, as Namibia is no longer the only foreign country where South African passport holders are welcomed. However, ideally try to avoid Namibian school holidays. February to mid-April, late-May to July and November are probably the quietest months.

Game viewing

Etosha's dry season is certainly the best time to see big game. Then, as the small bush pools dry up and the green vegetation shrivels, the animals move closer to the springs on the pan's edge. Before the game fences were erected (these now surround the park completely) many of the larger animals would have migrated between Etosha and the Kaokoveld – returning here during the dry season to the region's best permanent waterholes. Now most are forced to stay within the park and only bull elephants commonly break out of their confines to cause problems for the surrounding farmers.

Hence the months between July and late October are ideal for game. Though the idea of sitting in a car at 40°C may seem unpleasant, October is the best month for game and the heat is very dry. Park under a shady tree and be grateful that the humidity is so low.

During and after the rains, you won't see much game, partly because the lush vegetation hides the animals, and partly because most of them will have moved away from the waterholes (where most of the roads are) and gone deeper into the bush. However, often the animals you will see will have young, as food (animal or vegetable) is at its most plentiful then.

Birdwatching

The start of the rainy season witnesses the arrival of the summer migrants and, if the rains have been good, the aquatic species that come for the water in the pan itself. In exceptional years thousands of flamingos will come to breed, building their nests on the eastern side of the main Etosha Pan, or in Fischer's Pan. This is an amazing spectacle (see box on *Flamingos*, page 319). However, bear in mind that Etosha's ordinary feathered residents can be seen more easily during the dry season, when there is less vegetation to hide them.

Getting there

All of Etosha's roads are accessible with a normal 2WD vehicle, and an excellent map of the park is available from the restcamps. A more colourful 'Honeyguide' publication also has a few pages of colour sketches of most of the common birds and animals. Both are normally for sale at a reasonable price in the restcamp shops, and the maps are also available from the restcamps' fuel stations.

By road

You can enter the park via either the Von Lindequist Gate, near Namutoni, which is 106km from Tsumeb, or the Andersson Gate, south of Okaukuejo, 120km from Outjo. There is a road through to the western end of the park, and a gate on the park boundary. Until the long-planned fourth camp, Otjovasandu, opens, this whole region is closed to private visitors.

Entry permits to the park are issued at both gates. Then you must proceed to the nearest camp office and settle the costs of your accommodation and permits. Accommodation costs include entrance fees to the park, so the only extra that you will have to pay if you are staying overnight is the charge for the entry of your vehicle (N$10 for most small vehicles).

If you are just visiting the park for the day, then you will have to pay 'day visitor' park fees of N$30 per person per day, plus N$10 for the car. If you go out of the park for lunch, then strictly you should pay two park entry fees, but this rule *may* be relaxed if you politely tell the gatekeeper that you intend to return later in the day.

The gates open around sunrise and close about 20 minutes before sunset. For the precise times on any given day, see the notice next to the entry gates of each camp. Driving through the park in the dark is not allowed, and the gates do close on time. Neither hitchhiking nor bicycles (push or motor) are allowed in the park.

By air

Mokuti Lodge is on the regular scheduled flight between Windhoek and Victoria Falls, which also calls at Katima Mulilo (N$1,140). The Windhoek flights are N$700 to Mokuti. The occasional links to Ondangwa are also available; allow around NS$700 per leg for these.

Ongava has a good airstrip, which sometimes receives internal flights, though none are currently scheduled.

Organised tour

Etosha has always been designed for visitors to drive themselves around. The roads are good; a normal 2WD car is fine for all of them. The landscapes are generally open, as the vegetation is sparse, so you don't need eyes like a hawk to spot most of the larger animals. Thus very few people use organised tours to visit the park. However, if you really don't want to drive yourself around, then the alternatives are:

Ongava Lodge PO Box 6850, Windhoek; tel: 061 274500; fax: 061 239455; email: info@nts.com.na; web: www.ongavalodhge.com or www.ongavatentedcamp.com
See pages 383–4 for full details, but Ongava's normal activities include half-day drives in the Okaukuejo area of the park. These are usually included in Ongava's all-inclusive rates.

Mokuti and Etosha Aoba Lodges
On the eastern side of the park, Mokuti Lodge has its own vehicles and drivers, and runs several drives into the park daily. Etosha Aoba has equivalent arrangements to provide trips for guests.

Etosha Fly-in Safaris PO Box 1830, 447 Fifth Av, Tsumeb; tel: 067 220574; fax: 067 220832
Based in Tsumeb, and operating from the new Mushara Lodge, Etosha Fly-in Safaris is probably the only operator specialising in guided trips around the park. They have their own four-seater aircraft (or charter larger ones) for collections, and use VW Combi Minibuses or Mercedes buses for driving around the park.

Some of their business is fly-in safaris around the country, including Etosha. On the ground, they cater for groups staying in Mushara or the other nearby lodges. Expect a morning game drive to cost around N$340 per person, including lunch, while an afternoon game drive only would be about N$250 per person, for a minimum of two people.

Restcamps inside Etosha

There are three national parks restcamps inside Etosha, all of them very similar – offering good simple facilities at reasonable prices. Each has a range of accommodation, including bungalows and a campsite, swimming pool, shop, fuel station and a restaurant.

Aim to spend a minimum of two nights at any camp you visit. Remember that with a speed limit of 60km/h, it will take you at least two hours to drive between Namutoni and Halali, or Halali and Okaukuejo.

Bookings

Booking accommodation in advance at the NWR (email: reservations@mweb.com.na; web: www.namibiawildliferesorts.com) in Windhoek (page 118) is wise, but you need to be organised and stick to your itinerary. The alternative is to plan on camping, whilst hoping for spaces or cancellations in the chalets and bungalows. For this you'll need to ask at the camp office just before it closes at sunset. This is often successful outside the main holiday months, but you need a tent in case it is not.

Note that during the main holiday seasons, around Easter and August, even Etosha's campsites are fully booked in advance. If you haven't a reservation, you must stay outside the park and drive in for day-trips.

Accommodation: styles and costs

All the camps have roughly similar rooms and bungalows – see the NWR's current *Accommodation Guide for Tourists* for the fine details of the facilities at each.

Generally, all the rooms have private toilet and baths or showers, a fridge and a kettle. Towels and bed linen are always supplied. Most are air conditioned, and the VIP units even have cutlery and utensils. Bungalows also have hotplates and kitchen facilities, whilst rooms (which used to be called 'bus quarters', and are now usually referred to as 'de luxe rooms') generally do not. All are normally clean and well kept, though functional rather than luxurious

Accommodation prices vary slightly between camps, though a camping pitch is always N$160, for up to eight people and two vehicles. This makes camping cheap for large parties.

Getting organised

The reception office at each restcamp opens from dawn to dusk, and there you pay for your stay, as well as any park fees due. Don't forget to pay *all* your park fees before you try to leave the park. You can't pay them at the gate.

Each camp has a shop, which usually sells a remarkable assortment of foodstuffs: frozen meat, sausages and firewood (with braais in mind), as well as tinned and packet foods and often bread, eggs, and cheese. Beer, lots of cold drinks, and a limited selection of wine (but no wine can be sold on a Sunday) are also found here. Take your own cooking equipment.

Aside from food, these have the usual mix of tourist needs from curios, T-shirts, print film (occasionally slide, but nothing too unusual) and wildlife books to postcards and even stamps. These shops open 07.30–09.30, 11.30–14.00 and 17.00–20.00. Nearby is a payphone; you can normally buy phonecards at the shop. Those at Namutoni and Okaukuejo seem to have a little more stock than the one at Halali.

Where to eat

Each restcamp has a restaurant where most visitors eat at least one of their meals. In recent years these have been privatised, introducing buffet meals rather than silver-service à la carte menus. However, they have all carefully retained some of the old feeling of school dining halls.

Breakfast is served 07.00–09.00, lunch 12.00–14.00 and dinner 18.00–21.00, though if you arrive after 08.30, 13.30 or 20.30 respectively, the staff may refuse to serve you. In any case, buffet meals mean that it is *much* wiser to arrive earlier rather than later if you want a good choice of hot food.

Expect dinner to cost about N$60 for three courses, plus N$35 for a bottle of wine. It's not haute cuisine, but is varied, good value, and generally has a good choice of vegetables for vegetarians.

Outside of the prescribed meal times, there's normally a kiosk that sells drinks and snacks. These open between meals, 08.30–12.00 and 13.30–18.00. After dinner, the bar normally stays open until about 21.30.

Okaukuejo Restcamp (90 bungalows and 26 tent pitches) PO Box 36, Okaukuejo; tel: 067 229800; fax: 067 229852

This was the first restcamp to open, and is the administrative hub of the park and the centre of the Etosha Ecological Institute. It is situated at the western end of the pan, about 120km north of Outjo.

One big attraction of this camp is that it overlooks a permanent waterhole which is floodlit at night, giving you a chance to see some of the shy, nocturnal wildlife. The animals that come appear oblivious to the noises from the camp, not noticing the bright lights or the people sitting on benches just behind the low stone wall. The light doesn't penetrate into the dark surrounding bush, but it illuminates the waterhole like a stage – focusing all attention on the animals that come to drink.

During the dry season you would be unlucky not to spot something of interest by just sitting here for a few hours in the evening, so bring a couple of drinks, binoculars, and some warm clothes to settle down and watch. You are virtually guaranteed to see elephant and jackal, while lion and black rhino are very regular visitors. The main annoyance is noise from the bungalows beside the waterhole, or from the many people sitting around.

Accomodation is in luxury and standard bungalows. The camp sites have barbecue facilities and power points, and the rebuilt restaurant serves adequate buffet fare at reasonable prices. Sweets and drinks are available from the kiosk by the swimming pool.

Okaukuejo's shop is well stocked, and opposite reception is the park's only post office, open Mon–Fri 08.30–13.00 and 14.00–16.30, and 08.00–11.00 on Saturday. Nearby is a small round tower, which can be climbed, by a spiral staircase inside, for a good view of the surrounding area. Okaukuejo has a small museum, but this was closed when last visited.

Rates: 'luxury' four-bed bungalow N$490–800, simple three-bed bungalow N$350, basic two-bed room/bungalow N$280, camping pitch N$160.

Halali Restcamp (62 bungalows and 40 tent pitches) P Bag 2016, Tsumeb; tel: 067 229400; fax: 067 229413

The newest of the camps, opened in 1967, Halali stands between the others, 75km from Namutoni, 70km from Okaukuejo. It is just to the northwest of the landmark Tweekoppies, and there's a small dolomite kopje within the camp's boundary, accessible on a short self-guided trail signposted as 'Tsumasa'.

Halali is the smallest, and usually the quietest, of the three camps. In 1992 an artificial waterhole, the Moringa waterhole, was built on its boundary, and can be viewed from a natural rock seating area a few hundred metres beyond the campsite. This regularly attracts elephant, black rhino and other game. It isn't as busy as Okaukuejo's waterhole, but it is set apart from the camp, so has fewer disturbances and a more natural ambience.

The shop and restaurant at Halali are either side of the office and reception, on the right as you enter the camp. The kiosk is behind the restaurant, by the pool.

Rates: 'luxury' four-bed bungalow N$700, simple four-bed bungalow N$360–400, basic two-bed room N$315, camping pitch N$160.

Namutoni Restcamp (72 bungalows and 40 tent pitches) P Bag 2015, Tsumeb; tel: 067 229300; fax: 067 229306

Situated on the eastern edge of the pan, Namutoni is based around a beautiful old 'Beau Geste' type fort, in an area dotted with graceful makalani palms, *Hyphaene petersiana*. It originally dates back to a German police post, built here before the turn of the century. Later it was used as an army base and then for English prisoners during World War I, before being restored to its present state in 1957. Perhaps as a reminder of its military past, sunrise and sunset are heralded by a bugle call from the watchtower in the fort's northeastern corner – on to which you can climb for a better view of the park in the setting sun.

Some of the rooms within the fort itself share facilities and are not air conditioned. They cost from N$190 for two beds. The newer rooms have en-suite shower, toilet and bath, and usually AC, Namutoni's office and reception are on the right beyond the fuel station, as you enter camp. Its shop and restaurant are a few minutes' walk – if driving then continue past the office and turn right.

Rates: 'luxury' four-bed suite N$750, simple four-bed bungalow N$380–420, basic two-bed room N$140–310, camping pitch N$160.

Otjovasandu

For many years there has been a small base for the park's wardens and researchers at Otjovasandu, in the far western end of the park. Around there the land is hilly with much bush: very pretty but with few obvious centres for the game to congregate. At present, only organised groups, led by a licensed Namibian tour operator, are allowed into this area, and then only to transit between the western gate near Hobatere and Okaukuejo. The government is said to be seeking suitable bids to establish a camp for private safaris here – so in the next few years it is likely that something will open. When it does it would be best to combine it with a stay further east, where the more prolific areas of game occur.

Lodges outside Etosha

Several private lodges are clustered around each of Etosha's entrance gates. Mokuti, Etosha Aoba and Mushara are on the eastern side, near Namutoni, while Ongava and Toshari Inn are south of Okaukuejo. Hobatere is adjacent to the park's western boundary, but operates as a self-contained concession area, rather than an adjunct to Etosha.

All usually cost more than the public camps, but their facilities are generally more modern and comfortable. Some have their own vehicles and guides. However, all vehicles in the park are subject to the park's strict opening and closing times. None are allowed off the roads whilst inside Etosha.

Ongava Lodge and Tented Camp (10 chalets, 3 luxury suites, 6 canvas chalets) PO Box 6850, Windhoek; tel: 061 274500; fax: 061 239455; email: info@nts.com.na; web: www.ongavalodhge.com or www.ongavatentedcamp.com
South of Okaukuejo, this is Etosha's most luxurious lodge. It operates in its own private game reserve of 30,000 hectares (managed by Wilderness Safaris), abutting Etosha's southern side. The environment and wildlife are similar to those near Okaukuejo. Ongava has a greater choice of activities than is possible in the national park. However, it also seems to have a lower density of game than the park, and without the huge saltpan its scenery is less spectacular. That said, Ongava has over 20 lions and over 3,500 head of game. It is also one of the few remaining places in Africa where visitors have a fairly reliable chance of encountering both black and white rhinoceros.

You can use small aircraft, operated by Sefofane Air Charters, for costly but quick transfers, or drive yourself to Ongava. The turn-off into Ongava is now adjacent to the Andersson Gate into Etosha, and the main lodge is about 7km from this gate. There are lion around, so don't try to walk without a guide.

Two separate camps operate on the reserve. The main **Ongava Lodge** is centred around a split-level thatched boma that covers the lounge and bar, set high on a hill. Excellent food is served here, and there's plenty of space for relaxing and watching any game that comes to the small waterhole below. Alternatively there's a swimming pool for you to venture into. The large thatched chalets stand in two rows on the hillside. Each is surrounded by eco-friendly vegetation with a view over the reserve. These are large and luxurious. The en-suite bathroom contains a bath (with a view), shower and toilet. All are air conditioned and have twin queen-sized beds, 24-hour mains electricity, fridge, a kettle with tea/coffee supplied, and lots of other mod cons. Each has its own private wooden-deck veranda for sitting on to admire the view. A further three – exclusive luxury suites in a self-contained camp on the crest of the hill are expected to open in April 2003.

Ongava's **Tented Camp** has six twin-bedded Meru-style tents (under thatch shadings), erected on solid slate bases, plus a family unit with four beds. These have en-suite bathrooms, and a star-lit shower, twin beds, chairs, and mosquito nets. Meals are prepared outside and taken in the central boma area.

Activities at either camp feature escorted walks/drives on Ongava's own reserve, and longer game drives into the main park. In summer there is normally a long (around 5 hours) activity in the morning – perhaps a drive and escorted walk inside the reserve, or a longer drive into Etosha. This is followed by lunch and time at leisure before dinner, after which there is a night drive. In winter the morning activities are shorter, about 3–4 hours long, and lunch is normally followed by a late-afternoon game drive which stays out, becoming a floodlit night drive after dark.

Rates: N$1,895 (Jan–Jun), N$2,495 (Jul–Oct) per person sharing, including all meals and activities. Single supplement N$1,115.

Toshari Inn (16 rooms, camping) PO Box 164, Outjo; tel: 067 333440; fax: 067 333444; email: toshari@out.namib.com

About 71km north of Outjo, and 27km from the Andersson Gate, Toshari is owner-managed; a pleasant and affordable alternative to Okaukuejo. If you are unsure of reaching the park's gate by sunset, or the restcamps in the park are full, then this is an excellent base to sleep and eat.

Toshari's rooms are all alike. Each is carpeted and has two double beds and plenty of space. (Children sharing with parents are usually free.) The windows have mosquito-proof gauze netting, and there's a fan overhead. The bathroom has a large shower, toilet and washbasin. Clean, comfortable, and functional.

Outside is a large round water-reservoir which has been converted into a pool near the open-air braai area, and a short (1km) marked trail leads to a small waterhole in the bush, which attracts the odd steenbok, warthog or porcupine.

Rates: from N$250 per person including breakfast. Camping N$100 per site.
Open: All year though often closes for a few weeks in January.

Hobatere Lodge (12 rooms) PO Box 110, Kamanjab; tel: 067 330261; email: hobatere@mweb.com.na, res@discover-africa.com.na, hobatere@mweb.com.na; web: www.resafrica.net

This long-established private concession area is reached about 80km northwest of Kamanjab, by taking the main C35 road towards Ruacana. Its imposing gates are just past the entrance to western Etosha. The guides at Hobatere sometimes run trips in the western part of Etosha, which is closed to the general public, although Hobatere is too far west to organise trips into the most interesting areas of the park around the pan. See *The Kaokoveld*, page 353, for a comprehensive description.

Mokuti Lodge PO Box 403, Tsumeb; tel: 067 229084; fax: 067 22909; email: mokuti@mweb.com.na; web: namibsunhotels.com.na/mokutilodge

Situated on the C38, 25km west of the B1, Mokuti is set in its own small reserve, immediately next to Etosha's Von Lindequist Gate. This is the flagship of the Namib Sun Hotel group, with a number of awards for its excellent facilities. It feels like a rambling hotel – spread out, yet modern.

Mokuti's reserve has no very dangerous game, and is safe to wander around. Several short hiking trails are clearly marked, though it is equally easy to spot wandering antelope from the poolside. Look out for the bontebok, which are not indigenous, but come from the Cape. The lodge has conference facilities and a comfortable bar. A gift shop has the usual nature books, T-shirts, postcards and stamps. A fire in early 1997 burnt down much of its main building, but Mokuti has worked hard to rise from the ashes. Its normal accommodation is twin air-conditioned rooms with high thatched ceilings and en-suite facilities, which are scattered over lawns. There are a few more luxurious units, complete with double beds and separate lounges; several 'family units', which are cheaper if you are travelling with children; and two twin and two luxury units for disabled people.

Most people who stay here have their own cars, and drive themselves around eastern Etosha. However, Mokuti does run game drives into Etosha with its own vehicles and guides, which go for four hours in the morning, leaving at 07.30 winter time and 07:00 summer time, and for three hours in the afternoon, departing 15.00 until sunset. They cost N$275 per person per drive.

Rates: single N$620, double N$880, family room N$960 (2 adults + 3 children), luxury room N$1,070, all including breakfast.

Etosha Aoba Lodge (10 chalets) PO Box 469, Tsumeb; tel: 067 229100; fax: 067 229101; email: aoba@tsunamib.com; web: www.etosha-aoba-lodge.com
The entrance to Etosha Aoba is about 13km from the B1, and 10km east of Etosha's Von Lindequist entrance gate (22km from Namutoni), on the C38. The lodge itself is a further 10km of smooth but twisting road from its turning, through a dense area of woodlands dominated by tamboti, terminalia and leadwood trees.

Etosha Aoba's thatched bungalows are beautiful. A large patio window, which interchanges with a gauze screen, opens on to a small veranda with a couple of chairs. Inside are twin beds covered by a mosquito net, and above them a ceiling fan beneath the thatch. There's a tiled bathroom with toilet and shower – all spotless.

The main lodge consists of a large thatched area with bar and tables, for breakfast and dinner, and a small office which doubles as a curio shop. Beside that is a large pool surrounded by sun-loungers for the foolhardy. Arrangements can be made for those without vehicles to visit Etosha with Etosha Game Viewers open-sided vehicles, but most guests drive themselves from here.

Etosha Aoba lacks the camaraderie of an all-inclusive lodge and is about 30 minutes' drive from the park's gate. However, it is comfortable, well designed and good value. It makes an excellent base for driving around eastern Etosha.
Rates: single N$760, N$560 per person sharing, bed and breakfast. Dinner is a 3-course set menu at N$115.

Mushara Lodge (10 twin chalets, 2 single rooms, family unit) PO Box 1814, Tsumeb; tel: 067 229106; fax: 067 229107; email: mushara@iafrica.com.na; web: www.musharalodge.com
Located 8km from the eastern entrance of the national park, Mushara is close to a private airstrip. Its individual thatched bungalows have en-suite bathrooms, together with air conditioning, mosquito nets, telephones and minibar. Nature walks are available to guests, and regular game drives are run by Etosha Game Viewers.
Rates: single N$660, double N$1,080, family N$1,620.

What to see and do
If you are staying at one of the private lodges then you may have the choice of walking trips on their land. That aside, most visitors come to Etosha to explore the park for themselves by car.

Organising your own safari
The best times for spotting animals are in the early morning and the late afternoon, when they are at their most active. So, if you can, leave your camp as the gates open at sunrise, for a few hours' drive before breakfast. Before you leave, check the book of recent sightings in the park office, as animals are creatures of habit. This record may help you to choose the best areas to visit for that particular day.

Use the middle of the day for either travelling or relaxing back at camp. Dedicated enthusiasts may park beside one of the more remote waterholes. Excellent sightings are occasionally reported in the midday heat – though photographs taken in the glare of day are disappointing.

Finally, check when the gate to your camp closes, and then leave for a late afternoon drive. Aim to spend the last few hours before sunset at one of the waterholes near your restcamp, or the entrance gate if you're staying outside the park. Leave this in time for a leisurely drive back.

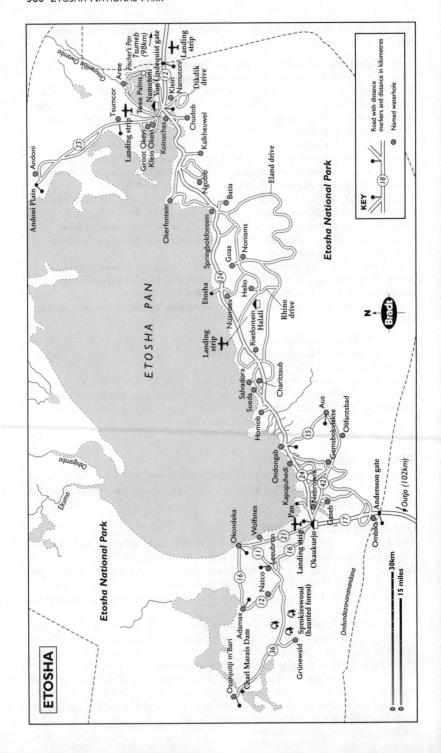

Most of the roads in Etosha are made of calcrete and gravel, which gives a good driving surface, without tar's unnatural appearance, although they can be slippery when wet. Be warned that most of the park's accidents occur near sunset, as people try to dash back to camp before the gates close.

The waterholes

The excellent map of Etosha available at the park shows the roads open to visitors, and the names of the waterholes. Obviously the game seen at each varies enormously. One day you can sit for hours watching huge herds; the next day the same place will be deserted. However, some waterholes are usually better, or at least more photogenic, than others. Here are a few brief personal notes on some of the main ones:

Adamax A dry waterhole in acacia thickets, notable more for adjacent social weaver nests than for its game.

Andoni As far north as you can go, through some elephant-damaged mopane woodlands, this isolated spot is a manmade waterhole in the middle of an open vlei. I've never seen much game up here.

Aus A natural water-level spring here is supplemented by a solar pump, in the middle of woodlands of stunted mopane. As you look from the parking area, the sun rises directly over the pan. It is said to be a good, busy spot for animals – though the author has never had much luck here.

Batia Away from the side of the pan, near Springbokfontein, the road to Batia is often better than the waterhole itself, which is a very flat and almost marsh-like collection of reeds with puddles dotted over a large area.

Charitsaub Away from the pan, Charitsaub is in the middle of a huge area of grassy plains. It has a small spring below, and close to, the parking area. Likely game includes zebra, wildebeest and springbok.

Chudop An excellent artesian waterhole, which usually hosts good concentrations of game. There's lots of open space around the water, and I've spent many hours here on several occasions. Don't miss it.

Etosha, just north of Halali, is not a waterhole, but is a most spectacular lookout place. There's a short drive across the pan, joining a circle where you can stop and admire the flatness. It is often closed when wet.

Fischer's Pan The road from Namutoni skirts the edges of this small pan, and when there's standing water in the pan it is *the* area for waterbirds. Take care of the road across the pan, between Aroe and Twee Palms, which often floods. When dry there will be less around, though the palm trees remain picturesque.

Gemsbokvlakte In the middle of a grassy plain, dotted with the odd stand of *Acacia*, *Combretum* and mopane bushveld, this permanent (with a solar-powered pump) waterhole attracts plains game species like springbok, gemsbok, zebra, giraffe and ostrich.

Goas This is a large, flat, natural waterhole and cars can view it from several sides, which is good as there's often a lot of game here. Elephants drinking here can be spectacular, and it is big enough to attract a constant buzz of bird activity.

Groot Okevi The parking area is a super vantage point, overlooking the waterhole which is about 25m away. There is some thick bush around the water. This is a known haunt of black rhino and conveniently close to Namutoni.

Helio A small, flat manmade waterhole near Halali, just a few hundred metres from one of the kopjes. Its position is marked incorrectly on the national park map, and the author has rarely seen any game there.

Homob A small spring in a deep depression, quite far from the viewing area. Just a few springbok and oryx were present when last visited. There is also a long-drop toilet here; bring your own toilet paper.

Kalkheuwel A super waterhole which often has lots of game. There's a permanently filled water trough, and usually also a good pan, which is close to the car park.

Kapupuhedi On the edge of the pan, with the parking area above it, this is often dry.

Koinachas A very picturesque artesian spring, perhaps 100m in diameter, with a large thicket of reeds in the centre. It's an excellent birding spot, but seldom seems crowded with game.

Nebrowni A small waterhole on the edge of a side-channel to the main pan. This is just 200m from the main road, but often omitted from maps. With bush to one side, and grassy plains to the other, it can attract a wide variety of game, though is often deserted.

Noniams Though it's convenient for Halali, I've never had much luck seeing any game here.

Nuamses A very deep water-level spring with a large clump of tall reeds in the centre. Quite photogenic with lots of rocks around – though the foreground is obscured by a lip of rock in front of the waterhole. Not known for its prolific game.

Okerfontein is right on the edge of the pan. The viewpoint is slightly elevated, and the nearer parts of the water are hidden from view by a lip of rocks.

Okondeka This waterhole often attracts large numbers of wildebeest, zebra, oryx, springbok and ostrich. On the edge of the pan, Okondeka often has streams of game arriving and leaving it, which stretch for miles across the surrounding grasslands. The water is a little far from the car-parking area for close-up photos, but shots taken from the road just before the parking area, with vistas of the main pan in the background, can be spectacular.

Olifantsbad Literally 'elephant's bath', this is another natural water-level spring helped by a solar pump – making two good waterholes in a large arena for wildlife. It is notable for elephant, kudu, red hartebeest and black-faced impala.

Ombika Despite its proximity to the Andersson Gate, Ombika shouldn't be underestimated as it is often a busy waterhole. Unfortunately for photographers, this water-level spring is far from the viewing area, inside a deep natural rock cavern, allowing even zebra to almost disappear from view when drinking.

Ondongab Like Kapupuhedi, this is on the edge of the pan but recently dry. Its view is spectacular.

Ozonjuitji m'Bari A small waterhole filled by a solar pump. This is the furthest point west that private visitors are allowed to drive themselves. Flat, grassy plains surround it, and the game varies greatly. Sometimes it is deserted, and on other occasions you'll find one of the park's largest gatherings of gemsbok. In the dry season, likely sights include ostrich, wildebeest, zebra, springbok, perhaps the odd giraffe and lots of dancing dust devils in the background. (One correspondent recently spotted a black rhino here during the day.)

Pan On the edge of the pan, the waterhole is not obvious, and there is often little game. This road becomes a mess of sludge in the wet season.

Rietfontein A large, busy water-level spring, with quite a large area of reeds in the water, surrounded by much open ground. There's a wide parking area with plenty of space, and at the waterhole giraffe, zebra and springbok were drinking when last visited.

Salvadora On the edge of the pan, Salvadora attracts columns of zebra, wildebeest and springbok. The viewpoint is higher than the spring, and close to it – so is perfect for photographs, with the main pan stretching off forever behind it.

Springbokfontein Shallow collection of reeds to one side of the road, which often has little game at it. However, look to your right as you drive to nearby Batia, as there is often game at a spring there.

Sueda Away from the pan, and just west of Salvadora and Charitsaub, Sueda has a large area of reeds, and rock-like clay outcrops, around a spring on the edge of the pan. Again, parking is above the level of the spring.

Wolfnes A location where you can appreciate the vast expanse of the pan. Just switch your motor off, and listen to the silence.

North-Central Namibia

While Etosha is the main attraction in the north of Namibia, the region south of it has much of interest. Large farms dominate these hilly, well-watered highlands, and many have forsaken cattle in favour of game, to become guest farms that welcome tourists. Okonjima Guest Farm has been one of the first of these, and is a major draw for visitors. Many of the others are less famous, but they still offer visitors insights into a farmer's view of the land, and opportunities to relax. On the eastern side of this area, the Waterberg Plateau is superb, though more for its hiking trails and scenery, and feeling of wilderness, than for its game viewing.

OMARURU

On the tarred C33, about 60km north of Karibib, Omaruru is a green and picturesque town astride the (usually dry) river of the same name, in a gently hilly area. Many of the farms around it have turned to tourism, so there is no shortage of lodges or guest farms in the area.

Where to stay

In town, there are just two old hotels:

Hotel Steabe (26 rooms, small campsite) Scheepers Drive, PO Box 92, Omaruru; tel: 064 570035; fax: 064 570450; email: staebe@iafrica.com.na; web: http://members.africa-adventure.org/s/staebe
To the south of the river, this is an efficient hotel with a clean, German atmosphere. In recent years it has catered for group trips who stop here for lunch at its restaurant, or to overnight. It has a swimming pool and off-street parking.
Rates: single N$275, double N$400, including breakfast.

Central Hotel (12 rooms) Wilhelm Zeraua Rd, PO Box 29, Omaruru; tel: 064 570030; fax: 064 571100; email: central@africaonline.com.na
On the main street north of the river, this smaller hotel is more traditional and less inviting. It also has a pool, and its bar, adorned with old hunting trophies, is a focus for some locals in the evening.
Rates: single N$240, double N$340, including breakfast.

Where to eat

Both hotels have restaurants, and will cook to order.
Errol's Pub and Steakhouse, on the main street, is probably the best evening venue; at least it delivers its promise of ice-cold beer. For a swifter bite try the Kwik-stop supermarkets and take-away, or the Dampf Bäckerei Café. Here the menu is in German but a reasonable schnitzel and salad costs N$15 for lunch, even

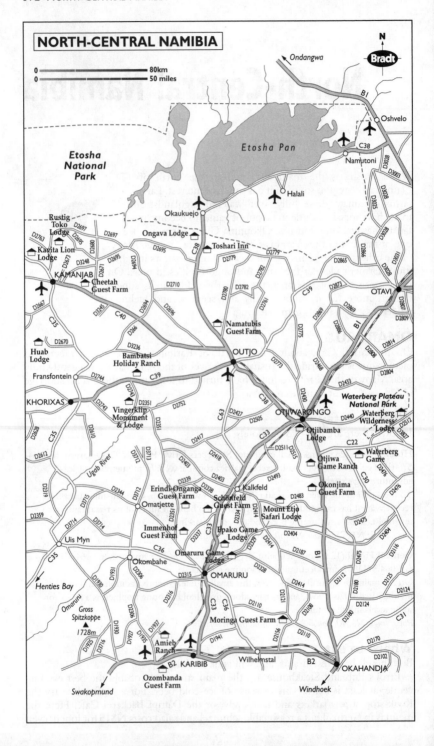

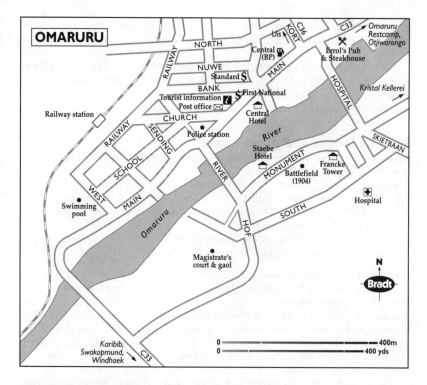

if the salad's a cross between pasta salad and coleslaw. They also offer tasty toasted sandwiches, cold drinks, and homemade cakes and biscuits.

At the Kristal Kellerei, the region's only vineyard offering wine-tasting, they also do an excellent lunch of cold meats and cheeses; book ahead for this on tel: 064 570083. Opening times Mon–Fri 09.00–18.00; Sat 09.00–13.00. The Sand Dragon coffee and gift shop and information centre in the main street is expected to open shortly for light lunches and snacks.

Getting organised

There is a First National Bank, a Standard Bank, and a post office, all on the main Wilhelm Zeraua Road, as well as several garages. There's a good **Namib i** tourist office and curio shop next to the post office, and a new brightly coloured gift shop has opened opposite the municipality.

Mineralogists shouldn't miss dropping into see Karen & Christopher Johnston, at Johnston's Gems & Minerals, who have a fascinating selection of very specialist local minerals which they even send abroad on a mail-order basis. Contact them first on PO Box 354, Omaruru; tel: 064 570303; fax: 064 570548; email: karen@johnston.com.na.

In an emergency, the police are reached on tel: 064 10111, the ambulance and hospital on 064 570037 or 570051.

What to see and do

The town's main attraction is **Franke Tower,** a monument to Captain Victor Franke who is said to have heroically relieved the garrison here, after they were besieged by the Herero in 1904. The achievement earned him Germany's highest military honour and this monument – built by grateful German settlers in 1908. It's normally locked, but to climb up it just ask at either hotel for a set of keys.

For a day of relaxation, Omburu Health Farm (tel: 081 125 0114), about 50km east of Omaruru, can be booked. Facilities include massages, jacuzzi, manicure and pedicure. You can also visit the Kristal Kellerei for a tour of their cellars and vineyards and an insight into the making of the local wine.

Nearby lodges and guest farms

Omaruru Restcamp and Caravan Park (6 rooms, camping) PO Box 400, Omaruru; tel: 064 570516; fax: 064 571017; email: jdg@iway.na
Owned by Corrie and Johan Burger, this municipal restcamp just on the north side of town has a couple of rondavels, chalets and bungalows, each with air conditioning and TV. The campsite has power and DSTV points, hot water and 24-hour security surveillance. Meals can be ordered at the sports bar.
Rates: single N$150–250; double N$240–370; triple N$300-410; four N$370–490, including breakfast. Caravans N$21–30 per person; camping N$20–35 per person.

Omaruru Game Lodge (20 bungalows, of which 5 are self-catering) PO Box 208, Omaruru; tel: 064 570044; fax: 064 570134; email:omlodge@iafrica.com.na; web: www.omaruru-game-lodge.com
Just north of Omaruru, about 15km along the D2329, Omaruru Game Lodge is owned by a Swiss architect, which explains the impressive design of its bungalows. All are beautifully built of stone, with thatch roofs that reach almost to the ground, air conditioning, heating and en-suite showers and toilets. Some are designated as 'superior' bungalows, which simply means they are bigger.

The lounge/bar/dining area is equally impressive, and overlooks a dam on one side of the lodge's 'small game park' (150ha in size), which is regularly visited by game, including giraffe, hartebeest, wildebeest, eland, sable and roan antelope to name but a few. This fenced-off small reserve is separate from the lodge's 'large game park' which covers a more respectable 3,500ha, and is home to the same range of antelope plus elephants (just four so far).

The paths around the camp, the lounge/dining area and the figure-of-eight pool all wind amongst well-watered lawns under beautiful apple-ring acacias, *Acacia albida* – which the elephants would relish if only they could get to them. Walk at night, when the paths are lit, and it's hard to escape the feeling that this is Africa at its neatest and tidiest, but not its wildest.

The lodge also has five self-catering bungalows set a few hundred metres from the rest. These are more basic. Each has a useful kitchenette (with no cutlery) and an outside fireplace. They share a separate swimming pool.
Rates: standard single N$$520, standard double N$780, superior single N$595; superior double N$944, including breakfast. Self-catering chalets cost about N$120 per person sharing.

Epako Game Lodge (24 rooms) PO Box 108, Omaruru; tel: 064 570551/2; fax: 064 570553; email: epako@iafrica.com.na
20km north of Omaruru, just off the main C33, Epako is one of Namibia's more luxurious game lodges and occupies about 110km² of the Omaruru River Valley. It has a wide variety of game, including four white rhino, several elephant, giraffe, eland, kudu, oryx, blesbok, waterbuck, ostrich, blue and black wildebeest, Hartmann's mountain and Burchell's plains zebra, black-faced and common impala, and many other buck, several of which are not native to the area. Leopard and cheetah also occur, but there are no lion.

Epako's accommodation is plush. The rooms are the style and quality of very good hotel rooms, with air conditioners which double as heaters in the cooler months, and heavy teak furniture made from railway sleepers. Their facilities include a minibar, telephone and a bath as well as a separate shower. The lodge also offers internet facilities and secretarial services.

In the main building is an upmarket curio shop with good fabrics, a bar that will open when needed, and the real focus of the lodge: the restaurant. Food is taken seriously here. The restaurant's glass sides overlook the river and a busy waterhole below. Its food is excellent, so expect extensive choices for breakfast and four- or five-course dinners of quality cuisine with a French influence.

When last visited, the lodge's accommodation and food were superb, but these were not matched by the standard of the guides.

Rates: N$667 per person sharing, including breakfast and dinner, N$777 full board. Game drive N$130 per person.

Erongo Wilderness Lodge (10 tents) PO Box 581, Omaruru; tel: 064 580537; fax: 064 570536; email: info@erongowilderness.com; web: www.erongowilderness.com
Travelling from Omaruru, take the C33 south for 2km and turn right onto D2315. You'll soon enter an area of many kopjes – huge piles of rounded rocks which make up hills that look like piles of giant pebbles. These are the Eronga Mountains, and 10km from the junction you'll find Erongo Wilderness Lodge on the south side of the road.

Accommodation here is in ten thatched, Meru-style tents that have been built on wooden platforms and dotted around the foothills. Various wooden walkways and paths connect these to the main lounge and dining room area, which has a large veranda overlooking a stunning vista of the mountains. Nearby a small swimming pool has been built into the rocks.

It's a lovely spot to spend a few days, but Erongo's real attraction is as a base for walking in the hills. The guide here lead short walks in the late afternoon as part of your stay (usually to the top of the nearby kopje for a gin and tonic whilst the sun sets) but the more energetic will enjoy heading out from the lodge for much longer walks. These can be on the flat, around the base of the hills, or steeper routes where short scrambles may be needed. They should either pay a guide to accompany them or, at the very least, take a GPS – it's easy to get disoriented or lost in these hills. The rough rock generally grips rubber soles well, and it's not difficult to find lovely routes that make easy walks.

Pause for a while wherever you are and you'll realise that there's game around, from leopards and klipspringers to dassies and brightly coloured rock agamas, but you'll have to look for it.

Rates: single N$795, double N$990 including dinner, bed and breakfast and a guided walk.

Erindi-Onganga Guest Farm (4 twin rooms, 1 single) PO Box 113, Omaruru; tel: 067 290112 or PO Box 20147, Windhoek; tel/fax: 061 232624; email: fnolte@iway.na
This traditional, working guest farm with a German atmosphere is about 64km from Omaruru. To reach it take the C36 towards Uis Myn for about 6km before branching right on to the D2344 towards Omatjette. Follow this for about 25km before turning right on to the D2351 towards Epupa (note this Epupa is closer than the one on the River Kunene!). After about 25km Erindi-Onganga is signposted off to the right, about 6km along a farm road.

This is a traditional, German-style farm. Accommodation is carpeted throughout, and rooms are clean with en-suite facilities. The main farmhouse has a dining room, a lounge area with large fire for cool evenings, and even a sauna. Outside there is a swimming pool, some marked hiking trails and the working farm which most visitors come to see. Donkey-cart rides are possible, at N$20 per person per hour.

Rates: single N$400, N$380 per person sharing, full board. This includes farm drives for guests staying two or more nights.

OTJIWARONGO

Originally a staging post on the railway from Tsumeb to Swakopmund, this small town is conveniently situated at a crossroads for both the railway and the road network, in an area dominated by commercial cattle ranching. Though pleasant enough, Otjiwarongo has few intrinsic attractions, and most visitors just pass through.

Getting there

By bus

The Intercape Mainliner service linking Windhoek with Victoria Falls drops into Otjiwarongo, stopping at Marina Toyota. Going northbound, is stops at 22.10 on Fri and Mon. Heading south it stops at 00.10 on Mon and Thu. To book contact Welwitschia Travel, tel: 0651 303437. See *Chapter 6*, pages 96–9, for more details.

By train

On Mon, Wed and Fri, trains depart from Otjiwarongo for Tsumeb at 05.35, for Walvis Bay at 16.45 and for Windhoek at 17.55. On Tue Thu and Sun there's also a 05.35 departure for Tsumeb, and a 17.45 departure for Windhoek. See pages 94–5 for more details.

Hitching

Hitching from central Otjiwarongo is difficult. First start walking out in the direction you want to go, and then hitch from there.

Getting organised

There are several fuel stations around town (some open 24 hours), and Standard, First National and the Bank of Windhoek are all in the centre. If you need food and supplies, then there are plenty of shops on the main Hage Geingob Street and St Georges, including a large Sentra.

In an emergency, the police are reached on tel: 0651 10111, the ambulance on 067 312122 or 303734/5 and the main government hospital on 067 302491. There is also an excellent private hospital, **Mediclinic Otjiwarongo**, which handles serious cases for much of northern Namibia. This should be your first call. A friend of mine needed some serious emergency surgery here, and on returning to London her private consultant told her that the operation had been performed to the highest standards. It is on Sonn Road, tel: 067 303734/5, 303323 or 303492; fax: 067 303542.

Where to stay

Most visitors in the area stay at one of the guest farms, and even business people find Otjibamba so close to town that it can be treated as a hotel. However, actually in town are:

Hotel Pension Bahnhof PO Box 100, Otjiwarongo; tel: 067 304801/2; fax 067 304803 *Rates: single N$190; double N$250.*

Bush Pillow PO Box 801, 47 Sonn Rd, Otjiwarongo; tel: 067 303 885; fax: 067 301264; email: artworks@iafrica.com.na

This good, trendy small guesthouse is reached from the Windhoek road by turning left into Sonn Road at the first Caltex fuel station; Bush Pillow is then at the corner of Sonn Rd and Hoog St.

It has safe parking and a pleasant garden (with pool) behind secure walls, where there's also space to have a braai. The rooms are clean and bright,with en-suite bathrooms and

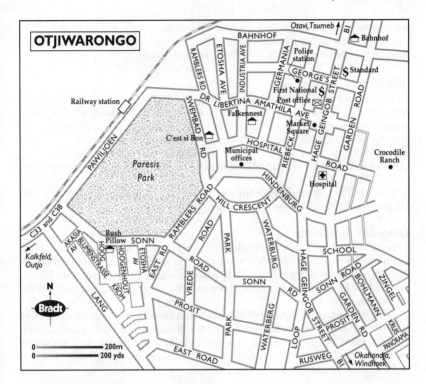

OTJIWARONGO

many have fun artistic touches. All are named after famous elephants (!) and have TVs. Bush pillow's communal areas include a bright breakfast/lunch area and a well-stocked bar. There's a satellite TV in the lounge, and both laundry and internet facilities are available. *Rates: single N$195, double N$300, including breakfast.*

C'est Si Bon Hotel (22 rooms) Swembad Rd, PO Box 2060, Otjiwarongo; tel: 067 301240/304915; fax: 067 303208; email: sibon@iafrica.com.na
Driving from Windhoek, you'll find yourself entering town on the main Hage Geingob St. Take a left turn between the church and the BP fuel station, and follow the signs to C'est Si Bon, which you'll find on Swembad Rd.

C'est Si Bon is one of a new breed of medium-sized hotels/lodges in Namibia that are situated in the provincial towns and really aim to cater for small groups that stop over for the night. This means that it's a thoroughly efficient, impressive and comfortable place, though it lacks some of the individuality (and idiosyncrasies) of the smaller establishments. That said, it's certainly the best place in town to eat and stay.

Its rooms are spread around the edges of a large lawn. Each is adequate but not huge, and has a TV, tea/coffee facilities, and an en-suite toilet, shower and washbasin. Some also have air conditioning.
Rates: single N$350, double N$600 , including breakfast.

Falkennest (10 rooms) 21 Industria Av, PO Box 107, Otjiwarongo; tel: 067 304151/302616; fax: 067 302616; email: otjbb@iafrica.com.na; web: www.natron.net/tour/falkennest/main.html
To find this small B&B, follow Dr Libertina Amathila Av west from where it crosses Hage Geingob St at the market square. About three blocks later, take a left on to Industria Rd, and number 21 is shortly on your left. Within, Karin Falk runs a small-scale operation with

ten en-suite bedrooms. All are clean, pleasant and have their own private toilets and showers. There is also safe off-street parking.

Rates: single N$140, double N$240, triple N$330, including breakfast.

What to see and do

In Otjiwarongo, the **Crocodile Ranch** (tel: 067 302121; fax: 067 302926) opens 09.00–16.00 Mon–Fri, and 11.00–14.00 at the weekend. Entry costs N$25, and a wander around takes under an hour, but is interesting. The ranch has been going now for over 13 years, and has established a small export business for crocodile skins, while the meat is sold locally. It is one of just a few captive breeding programmes for the Nile crocodile (*Crocodylus niloticus*) which has been registered with CITES.

Further afield, **Waterberg Plateau** is a destination in its own right. The only attraction suitable for an excursion from Otjiwarongo is:

Dinosaur footprints

Several fossilised animal tracks are preserved here, on the farm Otjihaenamaparero, in the area's distinctive Etjo sandstone. All date from about 150–200 million years ago. The most spectacular is a series of prints, about 25m in length, which were made by a large, three-toed, two-legged dinosaur. Just imagine yourself in Jurassic Park...

To get here take the C33 south for over 60km from Otjiwarongo until Kalkfeld is signposted left, on to the D2414. The farm with the unforgettable name (above), is 29km from there. There is a basic campsite near the footprints, with water, toilets and even simple refreshments. Entry costs N$5, camping N$30, and you must sign the visitor's book.

Nearby guest farms

There are several guest farms in the area. Okonjima is well known for its excellent work with big cats, and Otjibamba makes an excellent stop-over. Otjiwa really needs re-designing, and Mount Etjo has much good publicity material, though seems to appeal more to Afrikaans-speaking visitors than those who rely on English. Waterberg is close, and deserves a separate section to itself, following this one.

Okonjima (10 twin rooms at main camp, 8 chalets at bushcamp) PO Box 793, Otjiwarongo; tel: 067 304563/4 (emergency V-SAT numbers 067 697030 / 1); fax: 067 304565; email: okonjima@iway.na or info@okonjima.com; web: www.okonjima.com
Set in 120km² of rolling hills, Okonjima is best reached from the B1, about 130km north of Okahandja (47km south of Otjiwarongo). Take the private road that is clearly signposted 'Okonjima 24km', and follow the signs to the lodge.

Run by the Hanssen family, this relaxed place has, over the years, been one of Namibia's most popular and successful guest farms. Much of its appeal has been because this is base for the work of the Africat Foundation (see box), and thus visitors are virtually guaranteed to get close to some of the big cats. That said, its levels of hospitality have always been well above the norm, and the team here is very professional. (They are particularly adept in dealing with film crews and the media – hence their exposure in the media is second to none in southern Africa.)

The two camps here operate independently. Main Camp is the old guest farm, familiar to visitors who have been coming here since the early 1990s. This has seven comfortable double rooms, built around a central lawn, and three twin-bedded tents which are a very short walk away. All have en-suite facilities. The newer Bush Camp offers more luxurious

THE AFRICAT FOUNDATION (email: africat@natron.net)
This is a non-profit organisation, based out of Okonjima, which aims for the long-term conservation of large carnivores in Namibia. They aim to rescue, relocate and even rehabilitate problem big cats, and also to raise awareness of the issues involved. Current conservation projects focus on Namibia's large carnivores, and concentrate on environmental education programmes, trying to preserve habitat, and supporting animal welfare.

Visitors interested in the Africat Foundation generally stay at Okonjima, and learn more about the foundation's work from there. Neither the foundation nor the guest farm usually accept day-visitors dropping in.

and spacious thatched chalets with canvas panels at the front that roll down at night; each has its own birdbath within view. Each camp has its own dining facilities; meals, served plated or buffet style, are consistently good (though some quip that wine prices are high!).

The main and bush camps have separate activities, of which there's usually a choice, but they essentially offer the same ones. In the morning, after a coffee and some cereal, there's usually the option to head out on the 'Bushman Trail', where you walk with a guide through the bush and s/he explains some of the plants that the Bushmen use, and how they use them; or it's sometimes possible to go tracking cheetah on foot in one of the enclosures; or to do a nature drive around the farm, or to go on a nature walk. After that there's usually a substantial late-morning brunch, and then siesta time.

The afternoon activities start after tea, when visits are organised to the cheetah project, or there's the possibility of tracking one of the resident leopards from a 4WD, and opportunities to view animals which have been attracted to hides with food. Leopard-viewing around sunset at Okonjima's hide has yielded many superb photographs, and if you look closely, many winners of photo competitions have got their shots from Okonjima! After dinner in the evening, scraps are put out at a floodlit hide to attract the local porcupines and honey badgers; if you can drag yourself away from the bar for an hour's watching and waiting, this can be fun.

Note that Okonjima used to allow guests into much closer contact with other animals, and even to stalk the cheetahs, but they've now stopped this. However, you'll still see the occasional animal wandering around camp that has become exceedingly used to the visitors. (Don't mistake these for 'tame' animals though – they're too unpredictable to treat as harmless, even the ones that look cuddly. Keep your distance.)

Okonjima is ideal for a one- or two-night stop at the end of your trip to Namibia, and it's usually best to time your arrival here for around 16.00 (15.00 in winter), which is in time for tea and the various afternoon activities. It's expensive by Namibian standards, but there's nowhere else quite like it and a 'must-see' for some visitors.
Rates: Main Camp – single US$250, US$200 per person sharing; Bush Camp – single US$270, US$220 per person sharing, including all meals and activities.

Otjibamba Lodge (20 rooms) PO Box 510, Otjiwarongo; tel: 134, Otjiwarongo; tel: 067 303133; fax: 067 304561; email: bamba@iway.na
Situated just 1km off the main B1, a few kilometres south of Otjiwarongo, Otjibamba has become a popular overnight stop for visitors on their way from Windhoek to Etosha. It's more like a modern hotel set in the country than a guest farm, as its lounge and dining room are large and comfortable, but not very personal. The restaurant is similar, and there's a well stocked curio shop and a nice pool outside.

Otjibamba's rooms are purpose-built bungalows, set out in rows separated by lawns. They are like hotel rooms in style, and quite close together. Each has the same two double beds, carpets, and medium-sized en-suite bathroom, with separate bath and shower cubicles. Efficient but anonymous, although if you've been forced to be sociable at lots of guest farms, then a dinner from room service may be just what you need. The rooms overlook a waterhole frequented by a variety of game.

The lodge stands in its own small game park, stocked with giraffe, black and blue wildebeest, red hartebeest, blesbok, gemsbok, kudu, eland, nyala, springbok, impala, zebra, ostrich and waterbuck. There are lion here, kept in a small enclosure to themselves. *Rates: single N$380, N$275 per person sharing, including breakfast.*

Mount Etjo Safari Lodge (27 rooms in main lodge, 8 rooms in Rhino lodge, and a camping site) PO Box 81, Kalkfeld; tel: 067 290173/4; fax: 067 290172; email: mount.etjo@iafrica.com.na
About 63km south of Otjiwarongo, turn west from the main B1 on to the D2483, and Mount Etjo is 40km of gravel away. This becomes quite an interesting drive, as the road heads towards the huge, flat-topped sandstone massif of Mount Etjo – which is often a deep shade of burgundy. The gravel on the road changes from white to red in the distance, but watch how it differs from the deeper soil, made into tall termitaria. Approaching from the west, Mount Etjo is about 18km from Kalkfeld: take the D2414 then the D2483.

Mount Etjo Safari Lodge was founded as long ago as the early seventies by Jan Oelofse, a high-profile hunter now well-known in local political circles. (The 'Mount Etjo Declaration' was signed here on the way to political independence in 1989.) Jan still offers hunts on the property (web: www.janoelofsesafaris.com; email: jan.oelofse@iafrica.com.na) from February to November. I'm told that this operation is responsible for a number of record-breaking lion trophies (ie exceedingly large lions shot by hunters); however, I've not had time to verify this.

'Etjo' means 'a place of refuge.' Here Mount Etjo Safari Lodge itself offers accommodation and photographic trips around this area in open 4WD vehicles. Accommodation in the Main Lodge is luxurious, with king-size beds and en-suite bathrooms furnished with large round bathtubs, private dining and sitting rooms, and private gardens with jacuzzis. Dinners are often served around a campfire. There's also a smaller camp on the property, known as the Rhino Lodge.

Outside there are usually two activities per day, and there's no lack of game on the ranch. If photography is paramount then you can probably get very close to some of the game.
Rates: single from N$520, N$550 per person sharing, including dinner and breakfast. Game drives N$40 per person.

Otjiwa Game Ranch PO Box 1231, Otjiwarongo; tel: 067 306667; fax: 067 306670; email: nshmarket@olfitra.com.na; web: www.namibsunhotels.com.na
Otjiwa (pronounced Oh-shi-wa) is signposted 150km north of Okahandja, and stands about 1.5km from an imposing entrance gate on the western side the main B1. Rooms are all separate prefabricated bungalows, protected from the heat of the sun by corrugated metal roofs supported above the bungalows. Outside these appear flimsy; inside the partition walls are hardboard with a fake wooden pattern. This is not attractive. Otjiwa's game is excellent. Their animals number about 1,800 head of game, and include 19 white rhino and about 80 giraffe. They have re-introduced roan, sable, and lechwe (well out of its natural environment) to the area. But despite this, the management seems more concerned about quantity rather than the quality of the rooms. Otjiwa appears to be aiming for the local conference boom, and it doesn't appeal to most overseas visitor.
Rates: single N$195–265, double N$282–361, family unit (3 beds) N$352–417, family unit (4 beds) N$426–509, including breakfast.

WATERBERG PLATEAU PARK
2WD. Entrance fees for day visitors: N$20 per person and N$20 for a car.
Historically important during the war between the German forces and the Hereros, the plateau was first envisaged as a reserve for eland, Africa's largest species of antelope. In 1972 it was proclaimed a reserve and has since become a sanctuary for several rare animals, including eland and (introduced) white rhino. Now it is becoming renowned for its long guided walking safari.

Geography
The park centres on a plateau of compacted Etjo sandstone, some 250m high. This lump of rock, formed about 180–200 million years ago, is the remnant of a much larger plateau that once covered the whole area. It is highly permeable (surface water flows through it like a sieve), but the mudstones below it are impermeable. This results in the emergence of several springs at the base of the southern cliffs.

Flora and fauna
For a fairly small park, there are a large number of different environments. The top of the plateau supports a patchwork of wooded areas (mostly broad-leafed deciduous) and open grasslands, while the foothills and flats at the base of the escarpment are dominated by acacia bush, but dotted with evergreen trees and lush undergrowth where the springs well up on the southern side. This diversity gives the park its ability to support a large variety of animals.

Recently, Waterberg has become an integral part of a number of conservation projects, seeing the relocation of several endangered species (including white rhino, roan and sable antelope) in an attempt to start viable breeding herds. These have added to the game already found here, which ranges from giraffe and kudu to leopard, brown hyena, cheetah, and (reports claim) wild dogs.

The birdlife is no less impressive, with more than 200 species on record. Most memorable are the spectacular black eagles, and Namibia's only breeding colony of Cape vultures. Numbers of these imposing raptors have sharply declined in recent years due to both the changing environment, and the increasing use of farm poisons (both intentional poisons, and the chemicals in fertilisers and pesticides). One innovation encourages them to eat at a vulture restaurant (open once a week, on Wednesday morning) where carcasses are prepared and left out for them.

Getting there
Waterberg is very clearly signposted, 91km to the east of Otjiwarongo: follow the B1, the C22 and finally the D2512.

Where to stay
The park was made for animals, not visitors, and the Bernabé de la Bat Rest Camp has only been operating since June '89. Its accommodation and amenities are beautifully landscaped over the escarpment's wooded slopes, and include a restaurant, kiosk, large swimming pool and a range of accommodation.

Camping costs N$100 per site (for a maximum of eight people, two vehicles, and one caravan or tent). A two-room, five-bed 'luxury bungalow' is N$400; a one-room, three-bed bungalow is N$360; and a room for two is also N$330. These should be booked in advance at the NWR in Windhoek, or at the park office between 08.00 and sunset.

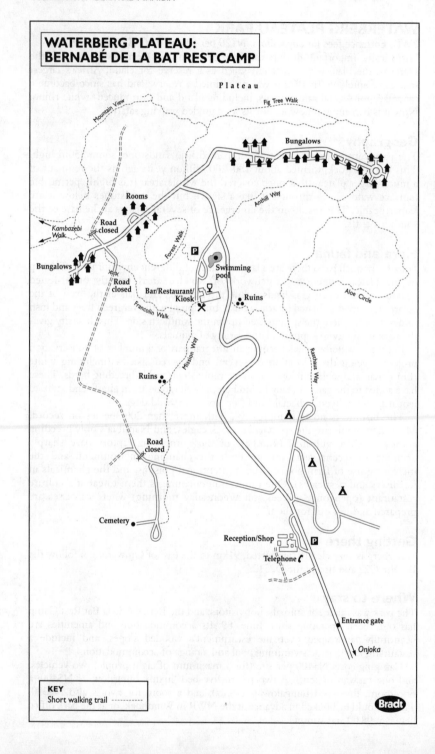

WATERBERG PLATEAU:
BERNABÉ DE LA BAT RESTCAMP

Plateau

Fig Tree Walk

Mountain View

Bungalows

Rooms

Anthill Way

Kambazebi
Walk

Road
closed

Forest Walk

P

Aloe Circle

Swimming
pool

Bungalows

Road
closed

Bar/Restaurant/
Kiosk

Ruins

Francolin Walk

Mission Way

Rashaus Way

Ruins

Road
closed

Cemetery

Reception/Shop

P

Telephone

Entrance gate

Onjoka

KEY
Short walking trail --------

Bradt

What to see and do

This park is unusual in that you can't drive yourself around. Instead you must either hike, or take one of the park's organised drives with one of their driver/guides.

Keen walkers will book in advance one of the excellent wilderness trails (see *Hiking* below). But if you haven't done this, then there are some excellent marked trails around the camp area, and even up on to a lookout point on the plateau. These are perfect if you are bored sitting in a vehicle and yearn to stretch your legs.

The park's own organised drives take about three hours; one runs in the morning, and one in the late afternoon. They cost N$90/40 per adult/child, and are best booked with the park office as soon as you get there. They tour around the plateau in search of game, visiting the permanent waterholes and some of the hides, but are generally disappointing for two reasons. Firstly, the bush is thicker and the game densities appear much lower than, say, Etosha. So although there are good chances of seeing uncommon sable and roan antelope, many visitors find the game disappointing. Secondly, the driver/guides are often very uncommunicative about the wildlife (although if you quiz them, they are knowledgeable). Thus you end up being driven through lots of apparently empty bush, with no illuminating commentary to hold your attention.

One possibility for the dedicated is to take the morning trip on to the plateau, get off at one of the hides, and spend the day there game-watching. You need to take some food and water (and perhaps a good book), but can then return to camp with the afternoon drive.

Hiking

This is the way to get the best out of Waterberg. All year round there are nine short trails that you can take around the vicinity of the camp, described in booklets from the office. These are designed to give visitors a flavour of the park, and the panorama from the end of the trail up to Mountain View is definitely worth the effort that it takes to get there. If you come to Waterberg for the walking, then you won't be disappointed.

During the dry season, from April to November, there are also two hikes organised: an accompanied one in the west of the park, and an unguided alternative in the south. There are no better ways to experience this game park, though reservations must be made months in advance.

You need to bring your own sleeping bag, food and cooking utensils. During both walks you will sleep in stone shelters, provided with simple long-drop toilets and water.

Accompanied trail – Waterberg Wilderness Trail

The three-day accompanied hiking trail begins on the second, third, and fourth weekends from April to November. It starts at 14.00 on the Thursday and continues until Sunday afternoon, taking one group of between six and eight people, for N$200 each.

This starts at Onjoka, the wildlife administration centre, from where the group is driven up on to the plateau. There is no set trail to follow; the warden leading the trail will just guide you across the plateau and go wherever looks interesting. The distance covered will depend on the fitness and particular interests of the group, but 10–15km per day would be typical. This is not an endurance test, but an excellent way to get to know more about the environment with the help of an expert guide.

Unguided trail

The four-day unguided trail runs during the same period, starting every Wednesday. Only one group of from three to ten people is allowed on the trail every week, and it costs N$90 per person.

After a short walk from the restcamp to Mountain View, on the top of the escarpment, the trail begins. From here it is a relatively short 42km. The first night is spent at the Otjozongombe shelter, and the second and third nights at the Otjomapenda shelter, allowing you to make a circular day-walk of about 8km. This all takes place around the spectacular sandstone kopjes on the southern edge of the plateau.

Nearby guestfarms

Waterberg Wilderness Lodge (Farm Otjosongombe – 7 rooms) PO Box 767, Otjiwarongo; tel: 067 306303; fax: 067 306304; email: wwl@natron.net; web: www.natron.net/tour/wwl

The lodge is situated 280 km north of Windhoek: turn off the B1 on to the C22 (28km south of Otjiwarongo), turn left onto the D2512, and drive past the Bernabé de la Bat Camp; at Otjosongombe turn left towards a small gorge in the plateau, and drive for a further 4km. Driving up into the gorge, eventually you reach the lodge in a little green oasis surrounded by cliffs, which mark the edge of the plateau. It's very picturesque.

Here Joachim and Caroline Rust have recently modernised a farm that's long been in their family. They now run this delightful small lodge, which has just seven rooms. There's one double-storey family room and the rest are twin-bedded. All rooms have en-suite facilities and are spotlessly clean, fairly spacious and designed traditionally though with an eye for touches of stylish minimalism. Expect halogen lights and some of the best showers you'll find anywhere in Namibia. The hosts are German-speaking, but the atmosphere has a very international outlook; Joachim often displays a very English sense of humour. Breakfast and lunch are usually buffets, often mixing traditional German fare with other European styles. If you arrive by 15.30 on your first afternoon then you'll also be in time for tea and cakes (also included); later dinner is served and everyone eats together.

The farm owns part of the Waterberg Plateau itself, as well as some of the flatter farmland around. Your stay here includes the option of joining guided hikes on to and around the plateau. These last 2–4 hours and are led by one of the lodge's team; usually one in the morning, and another in the afternoon. The scenery is stunning, and although getting on to the plateau can be steep at times, walking around the top is relatively flat. You'll see plenty of signs of game although, like walking safaris anywhere, the animals will usually flee before you get too close. Given that both buffalo and rhino live on the plateau, it's still wise to keep your wits about you.

The drives on the flat land below the plateau are more productive for game, and the lodge is gradually re-stocking the area, having converted it from a cattle farm to a game area. It's a good place to spot Damara dik-dik, and along with the usual antelope there's also a small group of giraffe here.

In short, Waterberg Wilderness is an excellent, and good-value spot for a little relaxed walking; it's perfect for a two- or three-night stay.

Rates: single N$760, double N$700 per person, family room N$630 per adult (half-price for children under 6). These include dinner, bed, breakfast and guided hikes onto the plateau in the morning and afternoon. Afternoon game drives are N$60 extra per person.

Waterberg Game P Bag 2208, Otjiwarongo; tel/fax: 067 302223; email: waterberg@natron.net; web: www.natron.net/tour/waterberg/main.htm

Conveniently situated on the south side of the tarred C22, just a few kilometres east from the main B1, Waterberg Game is a relatively new guest farm. It's run by the engaging Harry

CHEETAH CONSERVATION FOUNDATION

The Cheetah Conservation Foundation (PO Box 1755, Otjiwarongo, Namibia; tel: 067 306225; fax: 067 306247; email: cheeta@iafrica.com.na; web: www.cheetah.org) was started by Laurie Marker in 1990 to develop a permanent conservation research centre for cheetah. Today they are based on a 15km² farm northwest of Waterberg Plateau. In July 2000 CCF opened their field research station to the public, having developed a Visitor's Centre and a Cheetah Museum and Education Centre. Their aim is to 'secure habitats for the long term survival of cheetah and their ecosystem through multi-disciplined and integrated programs of conservation, research and education'.

The Cheetah Conservation Fund's activities include: radio-tracking research to understand more about cheetah distribution and ecology; bio-medical research to learn more about overall health, diseases and genetic make-up; habitat and ecosystem research; wildlife and livestock management to reduce predator conflicts; and non-lethal predator control methods. CCF also supports extensive environmental education programmes; staff conduct school assemblies throughout the country as well as at CCF's Centre.

Most visitors to the centre stay for a couple of nights at Waterberg game, or Waterberg Wilderness Trails, and spend half a day visiting the centre from there – for which a donation is usually in order. There is no accommodation for visitors at the CCF.

and Hannah Schneider-Waterberg, who are gradually turning the focus of the farm from hunting to photographic tourism.

The rooms are all part of the existing farm buildings, which have been converted with care and quality. The twin rooms are spacious and simply furnished; the 'family unit' consists of a linked double room and twin room, each with en-suite facilities, and a small sitting area. Outside is a small splash pool and, beside it, a thatched bar and breakfast area. For cooler days, there's an almost palatial dining room and lounge, which also houses an impressive wine collection.

The main activities here are half-day trips to the nearby Cheetah Conservation Foundation (situated north of Waterberg Game, and south of African Wilderness Trails). Waterberg Game also have, behind their farm, a mountain of very similar geology and form to the Waterberg which is good for hiking. Harry's a good birder, and knows his way around the bush very well – so is a good man to guide you around if he's there.
Rates: single N$650, double N$560 per person, including breakfast.

OUTJO

This small ranching town of about 5,000 people is some 65km from Otjiwarongo and 115km south of Etosha's Okaukuejo camp. It stands on a limestone formation in fertile grasslands, dotted with livestock ranches and the odd fruit farm. The name 'Outjo' is variously translated as 'place on the rocks' or 'little hills' – referring to the area's hilly topography. This territory had long belonged to the Herero people when the first Europeans arrived to stay. The adventurer Tom Lambert settled here with his family in 1880, and few others followed until the Schutztruppe established a control post here in 1897. The following year the first 'stand' of town land was officially given out.

In 1901 the town Water Tower was completed, and is still easily seen today. Development ground to a halt during the Herero war around 1904–5, and again

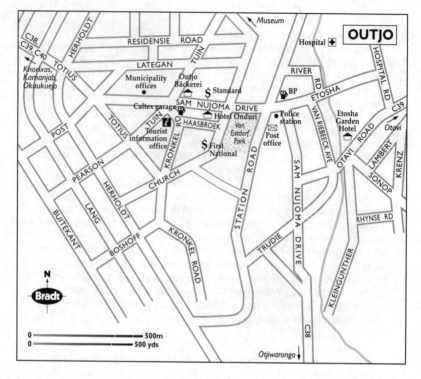

just before independence, but in the last five to six years the town seems to have had a new lease of life.

In the centre of Outjo is an open area, like a village green, with a fuel station, a couple of grocery shops, several butchers, a few take-aways and a post office. (The latter was memorable for having an old-style public phone as late as 1994, which accepted 10 or 20c pieces and needed cranking into action.)

Outjo is a useful pit-stop on the way to or from Etosha, Khorixas or the northern Kaokoveld, but not usually a destination in itself; except, perhaps, for Setenghi or the excellent Etosha Garden Hotel.

Where to stay

Hotel Onduri (29 rooms) PO Box 14, Outjo; tel: 067 313405; fax: 067 313408; email: onduri@iafrica.com.na; web: www.natron.net/tour/onduri/hotel.htm
This simple old-style town hotel has air-conditioned rooms with telephones, and en-suite rooms, but is really in need of some fresh ideas and a refurbishment.
Rates: single N\$330, double N\$510, including breakfast.

Etosha Garden (Garten) Hotel (15 twin, 3 single, 1 family unit with 2 rooms) PO Box 31, Outjo; tel: 067 313130; fax: 067 313419; email: egh@mweb.com.na
The backstreets of Outjo are the last place that you might expect to find a hotel this good, but follow the signs for a kilometre from the centre, and prepare to be surprised. This was just another basic hostelry until taken over by an enthusiastic Austrian couple a few years ago. Now it is one of the best small-town hotels outside Windhoek or Swakopmund.

The rooms are large, normally with twin beds adjacent to each other, simple wooden furniture, and rugs scattered on the cool, waxed-concrete or tiled floors. Each has tea/coffee-making facilities, and a large bathroom with shower. All are spotless, and overlook an open courtyard, shaded by jacaranda, palm trees and lush greenery. There is also a small swimming pool. Adjacent is an à la carte restaurant where you can enjoy lunch, tea or coffee with apple strudel, or dinner. The restaurant is well known for its game specialities. Starters N$16–35, game, seafood and steaks N$40–68, desserts N$20.

This is recommended for a one-night stop, or even just an extended lunch, on the way to/from Etosha.

Rates: single N$245, double N$390, triple N$520, family N$625, including breakfast.

Getting organised

Outjo's a good place to get organised, especially for **banks**. The First National Bank beside the green opens Mon–Fri 08.30–12.45 and 14.00–17.30, also 09.00–11.00 on Saturdays (except for the busy first and last Saturdays of the month, when it opens at 08.30). The Bank of Windhoek, next to the Sentra supermarket in Sam Nujoma Drive, and the Standard Bank, opposite the Hotel Onduri, operate similarly.

Outjo Bäckerei, directly opposite the Caltex garage on the north side of town, has eat-in or take-out burgers, pies and a good range of confectionery and German-style pastries: perfect for a picnic on the road. For fuel there are the BP station opposite the police station, the Engin garage (with workshop) next to the Standard Bank, and the Total station on the way north out of town. All are open 24 hours.

There is a general **tourist information office**, on the corner almost opposite the Outjo Bäckerei. This is well worth dropping into, and has facilities for visitors to buy light meals, ice and wood, as well as use telephones, faxes, and email. It opens 08.00–17.00 daily. The museum and the curio shop opposite the Caltex also have helpful local tourist information.

In an emergency, the police are reached on tel: 0654 10111, the ambulance on 0654 313044, and the hospital on 0654 313250. GSM cellphone users will be pleased that the area has recently been connected up, and their phones should work here.

What to see and do

The town's **museum** opens 10.00–12.00 and 14.00–16.00, and has displays of local history and a variety of animal horns, skins and bones, minerals and gemstones. There's also a unique sheep-shearing machine that works with a bicycle chain. It's well worth a visit, and after hours ring Mrs Karin Rudman on 0654 313444 if you can't get to it during its normal opening hours. Entrance fee is N$5 per person.

Nearby mountains

The hills of the Ugab Terrace, near the town, deserve special mention for their unusual shapes. A particularly interesting section can be found on the property of what used to be Camp Setenghi. There some of the formations have been likened to castles from the middle ages. These are made of conglomerate, and stand on the edge of a plateau that stretches for more than 80km and eventually forms the northern boundary of the Ugab River Valley. Because of differential erosion, only the harder section now remains – often sculptured rather spectacularly.

Nearby guest farms

Ombinda Country Lodge (19 chalets) PO Box 326, Outjo; tel: 067 313181; fax: 067 313478; email: discover@iafrica.com.na; web: www.discover-africa.com.na
Ombinda rose from the remnants of Outjo's old municipal restcamp in 1995, and has been thriving ever since. Like most provincial restcamps, it is just outside town, signposted off the main C38 about 1km southeast of Outjo.

Many of the old bungalows have been kept, but refurbished throughout and clad in wood to give a log-cabin feel to the restcamp. Each is clean and well-kept with twin beds and a private bathroom. Many have their toilet and shower partially open to the stars – a great improvement.

All the chalets are built around a large pool, next to which are a bar and al fresco dining area. Ombinda is a clean, safe and secure place, which suits families with children. However, its bungalows are close together so this may not be the place to get away from it all. Whatever you do, don't miss the band of tame mongooses that roam the camp, investigating anything that you leave lying around.

Rates: N$340 for a cottage for two, or N$410 for a bungalow for three. Camping is N£35 per person. Breakfast is N$30, lunch N$40 and dinner N$50.

Namatubis Guest Farm (23 chalets) PO Box 467, Outjo; tel: 0654 313061 or bookings to PO Box 21783, Windhoek; tel: 061 226979; fax: 061 226999; email: logufa@mweb.com.na Just 15km north of Outjo on the C38, Namatubis is 83km from the gate into Etosha (40 minutes' drive). It is only a few hundred metres off the main road, along a palm-lined drive. Hosting guests started as a hobby on the farm for Adri and Freddie Pretorius, and has grown into their main business. Behind an efficient reception area (adorned with work by local artists), the pastel-coloured chalets are lightly built with tin roofs. It's a particularly lush spot; lots of green lawns and walkways.

Each chalet has tiled floors spread with Namibian rugs, twin double beds under a fan, a tea/coffee maker for hot drinks, a minibar/fridge for cold ones, and an en-suite shower and toilet. Outside is a small pool and a barbecue area capable of catering for the groups that often stop here for lunch.

Adri and Freddie provide good, traditional Namibian cooking, typical of a guest farm, in a hospitable atmosphere. However, Namatubis is a little too big to be a guest farm; it feels more like a small hotel. Most visitors pass through here for a night, en route to or from Etosha.

Rates: single N$580, N$490 per person sharing, including dinner, bed and breakfast.

KAMANJAB

Just to the east of Damaraland, this town's sealed roads, fuel station and well-stocked supermarket will come as a relief to those driving south from Kaokoland. However, there are no major attractions here so most people just pass through after stocking up on fuel and cold drinks.

The road from Kamanjab to Ruacana is about 291km of good gravel. Initially it passes through ranch country, and then between the game areas of Hobatere and Etosha (note the high game fences here). About 8km north of Hobatere's entrance is a checkpoint on the veterinary cordon fence, after which the land reverts to subsistence farms – so watch for domestic animals straying on to the road. From here the bush is bare: only mopane bushes and acacia survive the relentless onslaught of the local goats.

Getting organised

Kamanjab is tiny town with a couple of small supermarkets, a police station, a mobile Bank of Windhoek (open once a month) and a post office. Notably, it also has a 24-hour petrol station, which also sells drinks, where virtually everyone stops. If you're heading north, then it's the last certain fuel stop before Rauacana.

Where to stay

There's only one place to stay in Kamanjab itself:

Oase Garni Guest House (5 rooms) PO Box 86, Kamanjab; tel: 067 330032
This is a small hotel in the very centre of the town. Its rooms are clean and comfortable, with tabletop fans and en-suite shower and toilet, but not at all large. There's a lounge area for relaxing, and the owners are friendly and helpful. This is a favourite with business people, but is fine for tourists wanting just a brief overnight stop.
Rates: N$250 per person including breakfast. Dinner available at N$35.

Nearby guest farms

There are several guest farms around Kamanjab, especially to its south, and nearby are two large private reserves: Hobatere and Huab.

Hobatere and Huab Lodges

Though both Huab and Hobatere are near Kamanjab, in style they are both most similar to the private concession areas of Southern Damaraland – so see pages 384 and 357–9 respectively for full descriptions.

Kavita Lion Lodge (3 rooms and 5 chalets) PO Box 118, Kamanjab; tel: 067 330224; fax: 067 330269; email: kavita@iway.na; web: www.kavitalion.com; central reservations: 061 226979; email: logufa@mweb.com.na
Signposted from the C35, about 35km north of Kamanjab, Kavita is run by Tammy Hoth, who is closely related to the Hanssen family running Okonjima, and her husband Uwe. It clearly aims to emulate Okonjima's success.

The rooms here are spacious, clean and well furnished, like the best guest farms. There's a large pool outside, and well-planned days for guests involve morning or evening nature/game drives, time to see how the farm works as well as spot some of the game, plus guided birding walks and walking trails. With notice they can organise trips and longer safaris into Etosha, the Kaokoveld or Owamboland.

Kavita is a pleasant place to stay, but it has attracted attention mostly for its Afri-Leo Foundation, and visits to this are one of the lodge's activities. The foundations stated aims are: 'The Afri-Leo foundation, dedicated to the protection and conservation of the lion in Namibia, supports environmental education, research and farmer-predator conflict resolution.'

In short, Tammy believes that lions will become endangered in Africa, and hence they need a charity to protect them. She aims 'to be there for the African lion when it is needed'. As a first step, the Foundation is accepting donations, however small. As a second, they found space for some lions that had been kept at Rundu zoo (which closed in 1997), and have constructed enclosures for them. Their third step, of finding places to release the rescued lions, may be more challenging.
Rates: single N$850, double N$750 per person, including all meals and activities on the game ranch.

Rustig Toko Lodge & Safaris (10 rooms and camping) PO Box 25, Kamanjab; tel: 067 330250; fax: 067 330265; email: rustig@iway.na or ondjamba@ondjamba.com.na; web: www.natron.net/rustig/ or www.ondjamba.com.na
Run by the delightful Heidi and Jürgen Göthje, Rustig is signposted along the D2763 and D2695, about 19km from the C35 north of Kamanjab. This is an excellent traditional guest farm, which covers about 60km². It isn't for those in search of the glittery or fake: you'll find no recently arranged attractions to tempt you. However, if you want a well-run, traditional guest farm, where the hospitality is warm and spontaneous, then Rustig is a good choice.

Rustig's five rooms are large, and each is carpeted and furnished with nice fabrics, twin beds, and a table and chairs. Outside each is a big veranda, and there is a small plunge-pool with a good view. Drives around the farm and around nearby game areas (N$80–100) are part of the normal activities here, while expeditions further afield to Bushman paintings around Kamanjab would be N$600 per vehicle.

Also run by Jürgen, and based out of the farm, Ondjamba Safaris organises a variety of longer trips and safaris around the region. These include two-day trips into western Etosha (around N$7,000 for four people), four-day trips up the Epupa Falls and the northern Kaokoveld (around N$14,300 for four people), and longer safaris as far as Botswana or Zimbabwe.

Rates: single N$580 single, N$500 per person, including all meals.

Rustig Camping PO Box 25, Kamanjab; tel: 065 521903; fax (Windhoek): 061 239995
For the busy periods, when the accommodation space in Etosha is often full to overflowing (like July and August), Rustig has a few good campsites in an area of mopane bush, a little way from the lodge. These are well set up with hot showers, flush toilets and a place to cook. You can then stay here and drive (about two and a half hours) across the back-roads to the gate south of Okaukuejo. If you ask when you book the site, you can usually arrange to eat in the farmhouse whilst camping.

Rates: N$25 per person.

Cheetah Guest Farm (6 rooms) PO Box 60, Kamanjab; tel/ fax: 067 330201; email: cheetahs@iway.na
Clearly named for its main attraction, Cheetah Guest Farm is found about 24km southeast of Kamanjab on the C40. Turn left on to the P2683 and 8km further you will find the reception; the lodge is another 2km from here. Elaborate chalets are faced in local stone, and nearby is a camping area. There is a bar/dining area for lodge guests, and a separate bar for campers. In the evening, atmospheric paraffin lanterns are used throughout, adding to the strange impression that this is neither a lodge nor a guest farm, but something between.

To attract visitors, the farm has five tame cheetahs, as well as 19 wild ones contained in a 250-hectare area. Game drives or walks are possible in a small plot containing both cattle and game, including giraffe, oryx, kudu, mountain zebra and some smaller buck.

Rates: N$520 per person sharing, including full board and activities. Camping N$50 per person (it is sometimes possible to arrange meals). Cheetah tours N$100 per person.

The Triangle and Bushmanland

The triangle of Otavi, Tsumeb and Grootfontein has long been one of the most prosperous areas of Namibia, rich both minerally and agriculturally. Geologists will find it particularly fascinating because of its interesting underground caverns and the famous Tsumeb mine, whilst the rolling farmland here has a lush, well-watered feel that is seldom found south of here.

To the west, Hereroland and Bushmanland extend east, sloping down from the agricultural plains of the central plateau into the endless, gently undulating Kalahari. This 'desert' is very different from the Namib, in landscape and people, although its population density is almost as low. This northeastern corner of the country is time-consuming, and even difficult, to visit, but offers a fascinating wilderness experience for those who are well prepared and make the time to reach it. It's also the home of many groups of San people; a draw for a small, but increasing, number of visitors.

OTAVI

Situated in a fertile farming area, near one of the country's biggest irrigation schemes, this small town has a 24-hour Total service station on the main road that skirts around it. As you turn into the town, Otavi seems small and quiet. Some of the streets are tar, others are gravel. There's a reasonable Sentra store and, next to the BP station, a very good Spar supermarket (open Mon–Fri 08.00–18.00 and Saturday 08.00–13.00).

Turn right after the Otavi Fruit Store to reach the restcamp and, after that, the municipal offices. You find fish and chips at the Fruit Store, and drinks at Ot-Quell Bottle Stall or Mr Liquor World. There's a small post office, and Standard and First National banks.

Near Otavi are several interesting cave systems, though visits to these need to be carefully organised in advance.

Getting there
By bus
Intercape Mainliner's services from Windhoek to Victoria Falls also stop at the Total service station: at 23.25 on Mon and Fri, and in the opposite direction at 22.50 on Mon and Thu. Trips cost N$230 to Windhoek, and N$380 to Victoria Falls. The service between Windhoek and Oshikango which used to stop here has been suspended. See *Chapter 6*, pages 96–8, for more details.

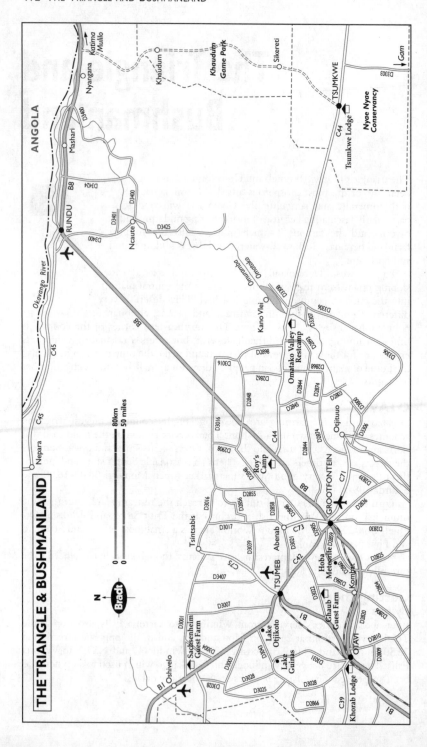

By train
Trains depart from Otavi southbound for Windhoek and Walvis Bay at 12.45 on Mon, Wed and Fri. They travel in the opposite direction, to Tsumeb, departing at 08.20, on the same days of the week. See pages 93–5 for more details.

Hitching
The main Fourways Total service station is probably the best place to hitch here, and it sells drinks and snacks whilst you are waiting. The small local minibuses (normally VW combis) which link Otavi with Tsumeb and Grootfontein will also usually stop here.

Where to stay
Otavi Garden Hotel and Grasdak Restaurant (10 rooms) PO Box 11, Otavi; tel/fax: 067 234336/234333; fax: 067 234335/234334
This basic hotel has seven rooms with en-suite facilities and a few others where they are shared. The busy bar seems also to act as reception as well as a restaurant and focal point for some of the town in the evening.
Rates: single N$95, double N$155, including breakfast.

Guest House 96 Hertzog Av, PO Box 392, Otavi; tel/fax: 067 234199
All rooms have en-suite bathrooms. There is a swimming pool.
Rates: N$185 per person, including breakfast.

Municipality Restcamp
This used to be called the Lion's Restcamp, but is now run by the municipality. It has half a dozen well-equipped, but not at all plush, bungalows.
Rates: For one person these cost N$98, including bedding, but for four people only N$200. Alternatively, you can camp here for N$21.09 per person!

What to see and do
Otavi doesn't have a wealth of big attractions, unless your passion is caves. In that case, plan to spend quite a lot of time around here, as the area has many systems to explore.

Khorab memorial
This marks the spot where the German colonial troops surrendered to the South African forces on July 9 1915. It is only 3km out of town but exceedingly well signposted.

Gaub caves
On the Gaub Farm, 35km northeast of Otavi, there are some caves famous for their stalactites and Bushman paintings. Despite being on private property, these are a National Monument so a permit to visit must be obtained from the Windhoek MET before you arrive.
They're signposted close to the junction of the D2863 and the D3022, but facilities are minimal and you'll need to inform the landowner that you're going down. After a short walk through the bush, there's a small hole in the ground into which you must squeeze. A lot of powdery sand is around, making this quite difficult, and initially it's a very steep incline to get into the caves. They aren't suitable for a casual visit, and if you do come then bring heavy-duty torches.

Aigamas caves
33km northwest of Otavi, on a tectonic fault line, this cave system is about 5km long. It has aroused particular interest recently as the home of *Clarius cavernieola*,

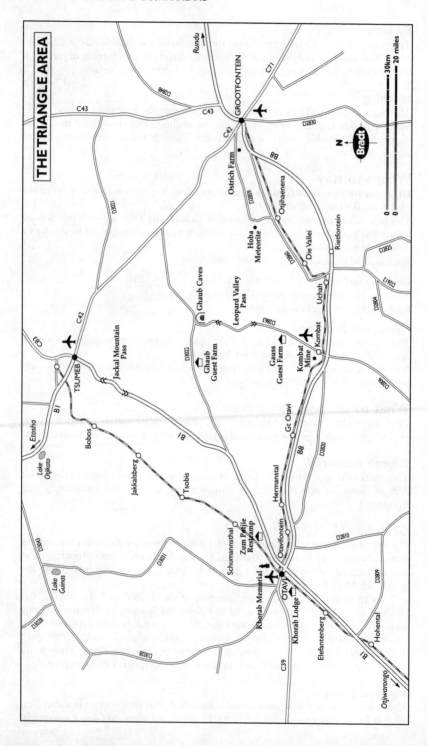

a species of fish which appears to be endemic to this cave system. These fish, members of the catfish family, are a translucent light pink in colour and totally blind, having evolved for life in the perpetual darkness of these caves. Interestingly, their breeding habits are still unknown and no young fish have ever been found.

To visit the cave, make arrangements at the municipal offices, just to the right of the restcamp. This may take several days.

Uiseb caves

More extensive than Gaub, these caves have several different chambers and passages containing some impressive stalactites and stalagmites. With no facilities at all, they are described as 'unspoilt' and arrangements to see them must be made at the municipal offices.

Nearby guest farms

Khorab Safari Lodge (10 chalets) PO Box 186, Otavi; tel: 067 234352; fax: 067 234520; email: khorab@iafrica.com.na. Reservations; PO Box 21783, Windhoek; tel: 061 226979; fax: 061 226999; email: logufa@mweb.com.na

About 3km south of Otavi, Khorab is set back just off the main B1 road to Otjiwarongo. It was built in 1996 and is a beautiful place to stop. Khorab's main building has a large, plush bar area, relaxing couches, a small curio shop and a breakfast room, all under high thatched ceilings. At the back of this, set around green lawns, herbaceous borders and even a small artificial stream, are ten chalets, six of which can be linked (if necessary) to make larger family rooms.

Each chalet has tiled floors dotted with rugs, twin beds (which can be pushed together for a double), and airy thatched ceilings. They are large and well built, using colourful fabrics, with en-suite showers and toilets, and much space and style – though they do not have telephones, fans or air conditioning. This is a stylish place to stop for a night, but lacks intrinsic reasons to encourage you to stay longer.

Rates: single N$435, N$320 per person sharing, including breakfast. Children under 12 sharing N$100. Dinner N$90, lunch N$55.

Zum Potjie Restcamp (5 twin bungalows and camping) PO Box 202, Otavi; tel: 067 234300; fax: 067 221964; email: zumpot@tsu.namib.com; web: http://resafrica.net/zumpot/ Signposted 6km north of Otavi, Zum Potjie is 2.5km off the main road to Tsumeb. Each of the bungalows is clean and simple with a basic, prefabricated design and en-suite shower and toilet. There's a small swimming pool, food is available, laundry can be arranged, and there's a camping site. If you plan to stay, then short guided trips are possible.

Rates: single N$240 single, N$190 per person sharing, including breakfast. Camping N$20.

Kombat

Kombat is memorable largely for its name. It is just off the main road, about halfway between Otavi and Grootfontein, and known in Namibia for its mine. This accounts for a thriving little centre, where you'll find Bob's Self-help Bakery and a small post office. Turn off here for the Leopard Valley Pass and Gauss Guest Farm.

Gauss Guest Farm (5 twin rooms) PO Box 6, Kombat; tel/fax: 067 231 083

To reach Gauss, turn into Kombat from the main Otavi–Grootfontein road, then turn right, left, right, and left at successive junctions, heading in the same direction as the sports fields.

The farm itself is in a beautiful open area of fields, surrounded by mountains. Accommodation is in a large bungalow a distance from the main house. Within this is a bar and lounge, as well as five twin rooms, all carpeted, with en-suite showers and toilets. Outside is a large swimming pool.

Active visitors will go walking in the hills, and your hosts can arrange food-drops in caves if you want to stay out for a while. Then there are mountain bikes available to borrow if you wish, and the farm's owner has a landing strip and a micro-light. Note that like most guest farms, you must pre-arrange your stay here.

Rates: around N$400, N$300 per person sharing, full board.

TSUMEB

The attractive town stands in the north of the central plateau, an area of rich farmland and great mineral wealth. Tsumeb's wide streets are lined with bougainvillaea and jacaranda trees. In the centre of town is a large, green park, a favourite for the townspeople during their lunch.

Economically the town was dominated by the Tsumeb Corporation which, in the early 1990s, mined a rich ore pipe here for copper, zinc, lead, silver, germanium, cadmium and the variety of unusual crystals for which Tsumeb is world famous. Tsumeb's one pipe has produced about 217 different minerals and gemstones, 40 of which have been found nowhere else on earth. However, in the late 1990s this closed – which badly affected the town. Although the mine's recently been reopened for specimen mining, this isn't on a fraction of the scale of the original operation.

Fortunately, Tsumeb still retains some light industries, and is close enough to Etosha to benefit from a steady flow of tourists. It remains a pleasant place to visit, and doesn't have any of the air of depression that you might expect given the importance of the mine that's now closed.

Getting there

Tsumeb is the largest of the triangle's towns, and generally has the best connections.

By air

Air Namibia have flights to and from Mokuti Lodge, from where any of the local travel companies can arrange transfers. Tsumeb also has its own airstrip, though this is rarely used by visitors.

By bus

Intercape Mainliner's services from Windhoek to Tsumeb leave Windhoek at 18.55. On Mon and Fri, buses leave Tsumeb for Victoria Falls at 00.15, returning to Tsumeb on Sun/Wed at 22.10, and departing for Windhoek at 22.15. See *Chapter 6*, pages 96–8, for details.

TransNamib's Starline service between Tsumeb and Rundu is no longer running.

By train

Trains depart from Tsumeb for Windhoek and Walvis Bay at 11.00 on Mon, Wed and Fri. See pages 94–5 for more details.

Hitching

Hitching from central Tsumeb is difficult, and you must first get yourself to the main junction of the B1 and the C42. Keep a look out for the small minibuses (normally VW combis) which link the triangle towns. They depart north from the Trek and Auto Clinic, on Bahnhof Street. If you're going south, then hitch on Omeg Allee, about 500m after the VW garage, and before the caravan park. Southbound local combi buses also stop there.

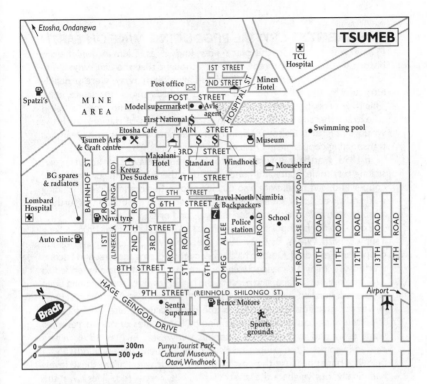

Map labels: Etosha, Ondangwa / TSUMEB / TCL Hospital / 1ST STREET / Minen Hotel / Post office / 2ND STREET / Spatzi's / MINE AREA / POST STREET / Model supermarket / Avis agent / First National / Etosha Café / MAIN STREET / Swimming pool / Tsumeb Arts & Craft centre / Museum / Makalani Hotel / 3RD STREET / Standard / Windhoek / Mousebird / BG spares & radiators / Kreuz / Des Sudens / 4TH STREET / Lombard Hospital / 5TH STREET / 6TH STREET / Travel North Namibia & Backpackers / BAHNHOF ST / Nova tyre / 7TH STREET / Police station / School / Auto clinic / 8TH STREET / OMEG ALLEE / 9TH ROAD (ILSE SCHATZ ROAD) / 10TH ROAD / 11TH ROAD / 12TH ROAD / 13TH ROAD / 14TH ROAD / 1ST ROAD (LINEKELA KALENGA RD) / 2ND ROAD / 3RD ROAD / 4TH ROAD / 5TH ROAD / 6TH ROAD / 9TH STREET (REINHOLD SHILONGO ST) / Airport / HAGE GEINGOB DRIVE / Sentra Superama / Bence Motors / Sports grounds / Bradt / 0 300m / 0 300 yds / Punyu Tourist Park, Cultural Museum, Otavi, Windhoek

Getting organised

If you are just passing through, there are several **fuel stations** around town (including several open 24 hours), and Main Street has branches of Standard, First National and the Bank of Windhoek. For those staying longer, the mine has made Tsumeb relatively rich, and its main shopping street is often bustling, with a branch of Edgar's department store, various clothes shops, take-aways and several curio shops.

For **food shopping**, you'll find the Model supermarket at one end of Post Street (opposite the Post Office), also the Sentra Superama in 9th Street, which are probably the best places in the centre. However, just off the main road from Grootfontein or Otavi, a little closer than the Punyu Restcamp, there's a new Alfa Co-op hypermarket.

In an emergency, the police are reached on tel: 067 10111, the ambulance service on 067 221911, 221912 or 221998. The hospital is on 067 221082 and the fire service on 067 221056 or 221042 (a/h) or 221004 (pager). There is also a private hospital serving the mine, tel: 067 221001, who may be able to help in an emergency.

Certainly worth stopping for is the **Etosha Café and Beer Garden**, on Main Street opposite the mine. There's a very relaxing garden café at the back, and next door is the TACC, mentioned below. Tsumeb's most useful and interesting places include:

Travel North Namibia – Tourism Centre and Backpackers Omeg Allee between 4th and 5th streets, PO Box 779, Tsumeb; tel: 067 220728, cell: 081 1246722; fax: 067 220916; email: travelnn@tsumeb.nam.lia.net

THE GREATEST CRYSTAL-PRODUCING MINE ON EARTH

Mining was started in the place now known as Tsumeb well before historical records were kept. Then it's thought that the San, who were known to have settlements at Otjikoto Lake, 24km away, were probably attracted by the hill's green colour, and perhaps mined malachite here. This they probably then traded with Ovambo people who would smelt it to extract the copper. Perhaps the earliest records of this are from the writings of Francis Galton who, in 1851, met both Bushmen and Ovambos transporting copper near Otjikoto.

In 1893, Matthew Rogers came to the Green Hill here for about a year, sinking test mine shafts and concluding that there was a major deposit of copper and lead here, with also quantities of other commodities including gold and silver. Later similar tests in 1893 and 1900 quantified this further; all suggested a very rich area for minerals and ore.

To exploit this deposit, a railway was built in 1905 and 1906, linking Tsumeb with Walvis Bay. By 1907 the mine was producing high-grade copper and lead ores. Despite halting production during the First and Second world wars, mining expanded steadily here. By 1947 the mine extended to 576m below the surface, and most of the higher levels of the mine had been exhausted. Further investigations showed the existence of further reserves.

Various changes in ownership of the mine occurred after the wars. By 1966 the mine had produced over nine million tonnes of ore; its reserves were estimated at eight million tonnes. However, in May 1996 mining ceased in some of the deeper levels (which, by then, were around 1650m below surface) because the cost of pumping out water from these levels had finally outweighed the cost of the ore recovered. This was the beginning of the end. In June one of the main shafts was flooded after its pumps were switched off, and a large strike (July/August 1996) finally stopped mining operations, and the mine closed.

As well as producing huge quantities of ore, Tsumeb was described as 'the greatest crystal-producing mine on earth' for its amazing variety of geological specimens, crystals and minerals. Numerous rare minerals had been found here, some had been completely unique to Tsumeb. Thus, in October 2000, a specialist mining company – Tsumeb Specimen Mining (Pty) Ltd – again started mining the upper levels of the complex. This time they were looking for one-off 'specimens' of minerals, rather than large quantities of ore.

For much more information on the mine and its minerals, both past and present, see the excellent www.mineralmining.com. Here you'll also find updates on what's been found most recently there, and some very technical information on the mine's geology.

Tsumeb's super tourist information centre has moved from opposite the Makalani Hotel to Omeg Allee, about 300m from the main traffic lights. Leon and Anita Pearson also offer simple accommodation (see *Where to stay*, below).

Leon has lived in Tsumeb since 1963, and knows the place very well. Here you'll find an extensive resource centre of leaflets and information from around the country, and very helpful staff.

They also act as an efficient local travel agent, so can sort out any travel problems you have, or arrange bookings for anywhere in Namibia. As official agents for Imperial Car Hire in the north, they organise car hire and transfers in the area. As representatives for Air

Previous page Himba boy (RJ)

Above The rock art at Twyfelfontein
is easily visited (CM)

Right Kgao, a Ju/'hoan man from
Dee≠ uha village, Bushmanland,
making a snare (CM)

Below Himba woman and traditional
homestead, near Purros (CM)

Namibia, and a local light aircraft charter company, they can also arrange transfers by small charter flights.

At the back of the tourism centre local curios are for sale, and there is a PC where you can send emails (N$10 for first message, N$5 each for subsequent messages), and a fax machine for visitors to use (N$4 per page received or 50c per metered telephone unit to send).

Tsumeb Aviation Services Safari Centre, Jordan St, PO Box 284, Tsumeb; tel: 067 220520; fax: 067 220821

This is on Omeg Allee, off Main Street, by the car park, and will also organise bookings and car hire arrangements; they are Tsumeb's appointed Avis representative. It has been recommended for confirming return flights if you're soon to depart. They usually charge N$10 for the service.

Where to stay

Tsumeb has several old hotels, a pension, a restcamp, and a place for backpackers – something for everyone!

Makalani Hotel (17 rooms) 4th St and 3rd Rd, PO Box 27, Tsumeb; tel: 067 221051; fax: 067 221575; email: makalani@mweb.com.na; web: www. makalanihotel.com
This hotel has been recently been upgraded. Its rooms have comfortable (hard!) twin beds, direct-dial phones, AC, and satellite TV. The Makalani's restaurant is small and friendly, with a reasonable, if not adventurous menu. Other facilities include a lapa bar, private bar, gambling house, beer garden and swimming pool.
Rates: single N$320, N$230 per person sharing, including breakfast

Minen Hotel (49 rooms) Post St, PO Box 244, Tsumeb; tel: 067 221071/2; fax: 067 221750; email: minen@mweb.com.na; web: www.minenhotel.com
The Minen has been going for years in a beautiful spot opposite the park. At its side is a very relaxing outdoor veranda with umbrella-shaded tables and chairs amidst impressively tropical gardens, served by the bar and kitchen. Inside the restaurant opens during the week from 19.00 to 21.30.

The hotel has new luxury rooms situated around a courtyard with a swimming pool and a beautiful lush garden, in addition to its standard rooms. All have double or twin beds, a television, en-suite toilet and shower and new air conditioner (luxury) and water coolers (standard).

Its older rooms are at the back, around an enclosed green courtyard protecting some tall rubber plants (now trees). Each has twin beds and flowery fabrics, a television, en-suite toilet and bath (with shower attachment) and a fan. Each also has a vintage air conditioner, but it seems unlikely that many of these still work.

Rooms are basic but clean, and almost out of earshot of the busy bar at the front, which can become quite lively at the weekends, especially at the end of the month when people are paid.
Rates: luxury single N$340.50, double N$508.50; standard single N$260, double N$393.50, including breakfast.

Kreuz Des Südens (3 rooms) 501–502 3rd St, PO Box 130, Tsumeb; tel/fax: 067 221005
This small German-run guesthouse is currently closed, but is scheduled to reopen at the end of 2003.

Travel North Namibia – Backpackers (2 rooms, 4-bed dorms) Omeg Allee between 4th and 5th streets, PO Box 779, Tsumeb; tel: 067 220728; cell: 081 124 6722; fax: 067 220916; email: travelnn@stu.namib.com
Leon and Anita Pearson have branched out to offer a couple of en-suite twin rooms, and a few 4-bed dorms for backpackers, sharing showers, toilets and a kitchen. These are on the site of the office, and there's always someone there to let you in.
Rates: single N$150, double N$230. Dorm beds N$50 per person, including bedding.

Mousebird Backpackers (4 rooms plus dorm beds) 533 4th St, PO Box 1712, Tsumeb; tel: 067 221777; fax: 067 221778; email: info@mousebird.com; web: www.mousebird.com
This lodge opened around February 2002 in the centre of town, near the museum. It's aiming squarely at backpackers, offering safaris around the region as well as accommodation.

The lodge itself has a fully equipped kitchen and dining room, with free tea and coffee, and a washing machine. The small bar area is usually busy, and for those who miss their electronic home comforts too much, there is a satellite TV, a collection of videos and a PlayStation in the lounge. Outside, the parking is secure and, if you want to cook for yourselves, you can do so in the braai area. At extra cost there's internet access and a phone/fax.
Rates: N$50 per person for a dorm bed; N$150 for a private twin/double room, and N$40 per person to camp on the lawn.

Punyu Tourist Park PO Box 319, Tsumeb; tel/fax: 067 221996
The old municipal campsite, found about halfway between the town and the main road intersection, about 1km from each, has been re-branded but little has changed. It is still a long way from the centre of town, but is a clean and quite pleasant place to stay.
Rates: N$5 entry, children N$3. Tent N$20 per day, caravan N$30 per day.

What to see and do
Museum
Facing the park, on Main Street, next to a beautiful Lutheran church, is one of Namibia's best little museums. It has an excellent section on the region's geology and exhibits many of the rare minerals collected from the mine. It also has displays on the German colonial forces, and a small section on the lifestyle of the Bushmen and the Himba people.

The 'Khorab' room contains old German weaponry, recovered from Lake Otjikoto, which was dumped there by the retreating German forces in 1915 to prevent the rapidly advancing Union troops from capturing it. Since that time, pieces have been recovered periodically, the most recent being the Sandfontein cannon on display here.

The uniform of the German Schutztruppe (stormtroopers) has recently been acquired, along with the photo album of one of them, General von Trotha, which makes fascinating reading if your German is good. Appropriately, the museum itself is located in a historic German school dating from 1915.
Open: Mon–Fri 09.00–12.00 and 15.00–18.00 in summer, 09.00–12.00 and 14.00–17.00 during winter. On Saturdays it opens 09.00–12.00. Costs: N$5 per person.

Cultural Museum
Between the Tourist Park and the centre of town is a relatively new and expensive-looking building. This has been funded by Norwegian donations and has open-air displays on all of the country's main ethnic groupings and their traditional housing.

Tsumeb Arts and Crafts Centre (TACC)
18 Main St, PO Box 1812, Tsumeb; tel/fax: 067 220257
Next to the Etosha Café, on Main Street, the TACC is a charitable trust set up to help develop the skills of Namibian artists and craftspeople. It provides them with a base, skills training, and some help in marketing their produce – including this shop selling their work. It's well worth a visit.
Open: Mon–Fri 08.30–13.00 and 14.30–17.00, Sat 08.30–13.00. After-hours visits can sometimes be arranged by phone.

Nearby guest farms

Sachsenheim Guest Farm (7 rooms and campsite) PO Box 1713, Tsumeb; tel: 067 230011; fax: 067 230072; email: sachse@iway.na (as electricity supply cannot always be guaranteed for the computer, faxes are safer)

Just north of where the C38 turns west of the B1 to go towards Namutoni, Sachsenheim is an old-style game farm (accepting hunting and photographic clients) turned restcamp, at its busiest when Namutoni, Mokuti and Etosha Aoba are all full. Reports are positive but sketchy, and the author has not visited it.

Rates: single N$250, N$220 per person sharing, including breakfast. Camping N$30 per person, N$10 per vehicle.

Excursions around Tsumeb
Lake Otjikoto

About 20km from Tsumeb, signposted next to the B1, this lake (once thought to be bottomless) was formed when the roof of a huge subterranean cave collapsed, leaving an enormous sinkhole with steep sides. Together with Lake Guinas, the lake is home to a highly coloured population of fish: the southern mouthbrooder, *Pseudocrenilabrus philander*. These have attracted much scientific interest for changes in their colour and behaviour as a result of this restricted environment. Now the lake is also home to some *Tilapia guinasana*, which are endemic to Lake Guinas but have been introduced here to aid their conservation.

Sub-aqua enthusiasts regularly dive here and have recovered much weaponry that was dumped in 1915 by the retreating German forces. Much is now on display in Tsumeb Museum, though some is still at the bottom of the lake.

Andersson and Galton passed this way in May 1851, and commented:

> After a day and a half travel, we suddenly found ourselves on the brink of Otjikoto, the most extraordinary chasm it was ever my fortune to see. It is scooped, so to say, out of the solid limestone rock... The form of Otjikoto is cylindrical; its diameter upwards of four hundred feet, and its depths, as we ascertained by the lead-line, two hundred and fifteen... To about thirty feet of the brink, it is filled with water.

After commenting that the local residents could remember no variation in its height, and musing on where its supply of water came from, Andersson described how he and Galton:

> ...standing in need of a bath, plunged head-foremost into the profound abyss. The natives were utterly astounded. Before reaching Otjikoto, they had told us, that if a man or beast was so unfortunate as to fall into the pool, he would inevitably perish.
>
> We attributed this to superstitious notions; but the mystery was now explained. The art of swimming was totally unknown in these regions. The water was very cold, and, from its great depth, the temperature is likely to be the same throughout the year.
>
> We swam into the cavern to which the allusion has just been made. The transparency of the water, which was of the deepest sea-green, was remarkable; and the effect produced in the watery mirror by the reflection of the crystallized walls and roof of the cavern, appeared very striking and beautiful...
>
> Otjikoto contained an abundance of fish, somewhat resembling perch; but those that we caught were not much larger than one's finger. We had several scores of these little creatures for dinner, and very palatable they proved.

The lake has changed little since then, except perhaps for its water level, which has lowered as a reflection of the area's water-table. The gradual diminution of the groundwater around here is a threat to the lake's future.

Now there is a kiosk by the lake which sells drinks, curios and woodcarvings from dawn until dusk, and charges a few dollars admission to see the lake.

Lake Guinas
This is reached 32km after Tsumeb by turning left off the B1 to Ondangwa, on to the D3043, and then left again after 19km on to the D3031. The lake is about 5km along, near the road. It is deeper and more attractive than Otjikoto, though there are no facilities at all here. It is home to a colourful species of cichlid fish, *Tilapia guinasana*, which is endemic here. In recent years they have been introduced into Otjikoto and several reservoirs to safeguard their future.

GROOTFONTEIN
This small, pleasant town is found at the northern end of the central plateau, amidst rich farmland. For the visitor, Grootfontein has few intrinsic attractions but is the gateway to both Bushmanland and the Caprivi Strip. If you are heading to either, then resting here for a night will allow you to tackle the long drive ahead in the cool of the morning.

Getting there
By bus
Intercape Mainliner's services between Windhoek and Victoria Falls stop at Maroela Motors. En route to Victoria Falls, these stop on Mon and Fri at 01.10. Southbound they return on Wed and Sun at 21.25. See *Chapter 6*, pages 96–8, for details.

Hitching
Hitching from Grootfontein is relatively easy, as most traffic passes through town. However, you will need a clear sign to hitch with. Alternatively, talk to drivers at the fuel stations or walk out of town to get a good lift.

Where to stay
Grootfontein does not have any really impressive hotels, but several are adequate for brief stops.

Meteor Travel Inn (24 rooms) 33 Okavango Av (corner Okavango Rd and Kaiser Wilhelm St), PO Box 346, Grootfontein; tel: 067 242078/9; fax: 067 243072; email: meteor@iway.na; web: http://resafrica.net/meteor-travel-inn
The Meteor's rooms are laid out around a courtyard at the back. Each has a direct-dial telephone, wall-mounted fan, and twin beds. It isn't luxurious, but neither is it at all dingy, as small-town hotels often are. There is another open courtyard where, beneath banana trees, lunch, dinner and drinks are served. On Friday evenings pizzas are the speciality, from purpose-built brick ovens.
Rates: N$230 single, N$368 double, including breakfast.

Guest Farm Ghaub (10 twin rooms) PO Box 786, Grootfontein; tel/fax: 067 240188; email:ghaub@iway.na. Central reservations tel: 061 233145; fax: 061 234512; email: nshmarket@olfitra.com.na; web: www.namibsunhotels.com.na
An unlikely part of the large Namib Sun Hotels group, this farm is situated in the Otavi mountains, in the heart of the triangle, some 60km from Otavi. It's on the south side of the D3022, about 3km west of its junction with the D2863.

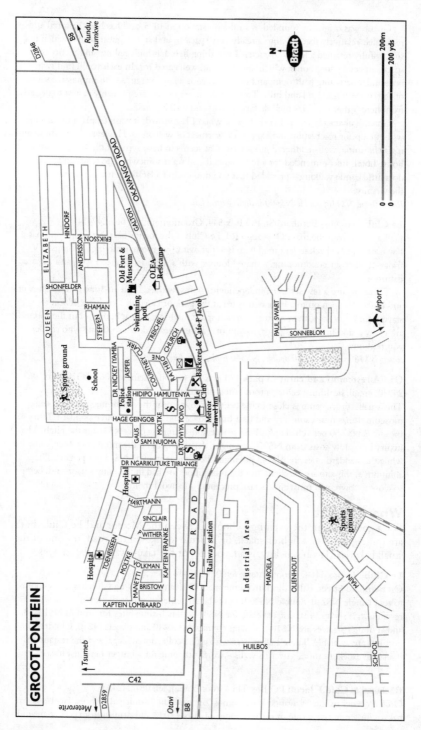

Ghaub was originally founded as a mission station in 1895, and has been restored and renovated relatively recently into a really very spacious and stylish guest farm – which has successfully retained a lot of character. Everything here has high ceilings and plenty of space, especially the rooms, which are clean and well cared for. In each you'll find twin beds and an en-suite bathroom, and outside each is a large veranda with impressive views of the surrounding land and hills. Tours of the nearby caves are probably easiest to organise from here; other activities include farm drives and walking trails.

Ghaub's character seemed fairly formal when I last visited; it wasn't a place to turn up without a prior reservation and expect the warmest of welcomes. However, book ahead and it's a charming, well-mannered guest farm that seems to have some of the air of a country house hotel. Recommended for a few nights if you want somewhere to relax, and perhaps do a little gentle walking – provided that you don't mind a lack of must-see attractions in the vicinity.
Rates: single N$410; double N$600 including breakfast.

Le Club (6 rooms) Bernhard St, PO Box 544, Grootfontein; tel: 067 242414
Half a block from the main Okavango Rd, Le Club is the town's best restaurant, and has a few rooms at the back to let out. There is a 'flat' with two rooms with high ceilings, TV, fridge-freezer, air conditioning, a shared lounge with a memorable green sofa, and a shared bathroom.

There are also a few separate, independent rooms, with AC and en-suite bath or shower and toilet. All open on to a large courtyard at the back of Le Club's kitchens. If you're staying for a few days, then having so much space might be a great bonus – but the rooms are really a side-line for this place, so you may have to track down someone who can let you rent one.
Rates: N$180 single, N$220 double, N$350 triple, including breakfast.

OLEA restcamp and caravan park PO Box 23, Grootfontein; tel: 067 243101; fax: 067 24930; email: healthinspector@grootfonteinmun.com.na.
This small, spruce camp is close to the centre of town, near the swimming pool and the museum. It has nine campsites and four bungalows: one luxury and three standard. Entry to the site is N$7.50 per vehicle plus N$5 per person. Camping costs N$21 for the pitch. The luxury bungalow costs from N$270 per night, depending upon the number of occupants, while the standard ones are N$144 per night. Bedding is an extra N$15 per person. The ablutions at this site are excellent, but the mosquitoes are bad in the rainy season and, being so close to town, you must always take precautions to avoid theft.

Where to eat
For a good meal in the evenings, choose between the Meteor and Le Club; both are quite good. For a lighter snack, or a picnic to take on the road, try one of the small bakeries (Jacob's, below, is a favourite) or the take-aways at the garages.

Le Club PO Box 1184, Grootfontein; tel: 067 242414
On Bernhard Street, half a block from the main Okavango Road, Le Club has a few rooms to rent (single N$230, double N$300) but is better remembered as the town's best restaurant. It serves breakfast à la carte for N$9–17, lunch-time bites for around N$10–15, and at dinner starters are N$10–15, main courses N$30–40 and sweets N$10. Children's portions are available. There's a bar here with a fine collection of caps, and the restaurant has some excellent murals over its walls – worth stopping for a burger here just to see those!

Bäckerei & Café F Jacob PO Box 345, Grootfontein; tel: 067 242433
On the corner of the Okavango Road, almost opposite the Municipal Offices, Jacob's is a bakery incorporating a café. It serves a range of tasty snacks and drinks, from pies at around

N$3–4, sandwiches N$3–6, and even steaks for N$20. Jacob's milkshakes, toasted sandwiches and hot dogs are especially commended.

It also sells a range of cakes and pastries – which are baked on the premises – and cold drinks. It is on the main road, so ideal for buying a picnic with which to travel. Don't miss the marvellous mobile on the café's ceiling.

Opens: Mon–Fri: 06.00–16.30, Sat: 06.00–12.30.

WARNING Beware of leaving your car unattended for even a few minutes if you're passing through Grootfontein. Tourist vehicles from Etosha, often stopping at a bakery, are regularly broken into and luggage is frequently the target. Even one person left in the car may fall victim. Typically a gang will approach a vehicle with open windows, and some will distract the driver, whilst others steal from the other side of the vehicle. (As far as I know, there has never been any violence reported.) This happens in broad daylight, despite the best efforts of many of Grootfontein's citizens – so take care when stopping here with a full vehicle.

Getting organised
Grootfontein is a good stop for supplies. There's a Standard, a First National and a Bank of Windhoek, several garages, a tyre centre, and a well-stocked Sentra supermarket all in the centre of town.

The post office is just behind the municipal centre, between the main Okavango Road and Rathbone Street. One block away, next to Le Club on Bernhard Street, Heinke Relling has a limited selection of cameras and film.

In an emergency, the police are reached on tel: 067 10111, the ambulance on 067 242141, the hospital on 067 242041/ 242141, and the fire service on 067 243101 or 242321.

Changes of road names
In the last few years, the local council have changed many of Grootfontein's street names, though many of the old names are still found on maps. The main changes are:

Kaiser Wilhelm St	has become	Hage Geingob St
Goethe St	has become	Sam Nujoma Drive
Schiller St	has become	Dr Ngarikutuke Tjiriange St
Bernhardt St	has become	Hidipo Hamutenya St
Upingtonia St	has become	Dr Nickey Iyamba St
Bismarck St	has become	Dr Toivi Ya Toivo St

Tourist information office
If you have the time, then the small but helpful tourist information centre inside the municipal offices is a good place to visit. It is just off the main Okavango road, two blocks east of Hage Geingob Street (Kaiser Wilhelm Street).

What to see and do
There's not much to do here. The museum is the only real attraction during the day, and in the evenings things are even more limited. The bars at the Nord and Meteor hotels open all week, except Sunday, but are not inspiring.

Swimming pool
During the summer (October to May) the outdoor pool by the restcamp is open every day until 18.00.

Old Fort Museum

Also near the restcamp is Old Fort Museum (signposted as Das Alte Feste). This small, privately run museum is a few kilometres from the centre of town, past the Total service station and opposite the rugby stadium, on your left en route to Rundu. It centres on the original forge of a local blacksmith, and opens Tuesday and Friday 16.00–18.00, and Wednesday 09.00–11.00. At other times, phone 067 242456 to see it. Admission is free.

Excursions from Grootfontein

If you have a car, then there are several attractions in the area:

Hoba Meteorite

This famous lump of rock is signposted about 20km west of Grootfontein. Here, in 1920, the farm's owner discovered the world's heaviest metallic meteorite. It weighs about 50 tonnes, and analysis suggests it is mostly iron (about 80%) and nickel.

It was declared a national monument in 1955 and recently received the protection of a permanent tourist officer because it was suffering badly at the hands of souvenir hunters. The locals became particularly irate when even the UN's Transition Assistance Group (UNTAG) personnel were found to be chipping bits off for souvenirs as they supervised the country's transition to democracy. Now it is open full time, and there is a guard on duty. There is a picnic site and a small kiosk selling souvenirs, sweets and soft drinks.

Dragon's Breath cave and lake

This cave is claimed to contain the world's largest known underground lake. It is 46km from Grootfontein, just off the C42 to Tsumeb, on the farm Hariseb, owned by Mr Pretorius (identified by a roadside board with the head of a cow on it).

The lake has crystal clear, drinkable water with a surface area of almost two hectares, and lies beneath a dome-shaped roof of solid rock. The water is about 60m below ground level and to get to it currently requires the use of ropes and caving equipment, with a final vertical abseil descent of 25m from the roof down to the surface of the water. This perhaps explains why it is not open to visitors yet. It seems likely that it will be developed in the future, when an easier approach can be made.

Straussenfarm Ostrich Farm

Between the Hoba Meteorite and Grootfontein, on the D2859, the Straussenfarm Farm (PO Box 652, Grootfontein; tel: 06738 83130; fax: 067 242611) is about 10km west of town. It is run by Thekla and Udo Unkel and is an entertaining introduction to the recent boom in ostrich farming. They also serve a good lunch (normally smoked ostrich), and there's a curio shop with jewellery made from ostrich eggshells, ostrich leather, etc.

Nearby guest farms

Roy's Camp (5 rustic chalets and camping) PO Box 755, Grootfontein; tel/fax: 067 240302; email: royscamp@iway.na; web: www.swiftcentre.com or www.triponline.net
Situated on the main B8 to Rundu, only 55km north of Grootfontein, just past the C44 turn-off to Tsumkwe, Roy's is a super little lodge built in an artistic and very rustic style.

It was opened in '96 by Wimple and Marietjie Otto, whose ancestors were some of the first European settlers in Namibia. The camp is named after Wimple's father, Royal. The owners had originally planned to call it 'Royal Restcamp,' but the authorities didn't approve of that title, and so they cut it to Roy's Camp.

The accommodation comprises two 3-bedroom bungalows with en-suite shower and toilet and three 4-bedroom bungalows with the same facilities. All are wonderfully rustic to the point of being quite offbeat. All are serviced by elecricity although paraffin lamps light the way to your bungalow or campsite. Lunch and dinner (best arranged in advance) are served in the bar/dining area next to the swimming pool.

There are also eight green, well-watered lawns which function as campsites, complete with braai sites, little thatched roofs for shade, and ablutions with hot and cold water. All of this is set in 28km² of natural bush, which has been stocked with blue wildebeest, eland, kudu, zebra, duiker, steenbok and warthog. One walking trail (about two hours' leisurely stroll) has been made through this, on which many of the trees have been labelled.

Rates: single N$230; double N$185 per person; 3–4 beds N$270 person, including breakfast. Camping N$38 per person.

BUSHMANLAND

To the east of Grootfontein lies the area known as Bushmanland. (This is an old name, but I'll use it here for clarity; it is what most people call the area.) This almost rectangular region borders on Botswana and stretches 90km from north to south and about 200km from east to west.

Drive east towards Tsumkwe, and you're driving straight into the Kalahari. However, on their first trip here, people are often struck by just how green and vegetated it is, generally in contrast to their mental image of a 'desert'. In fact, the Kalahari isn't a desert at all; it's a fossil desert. It is an immense sandsheet which was once a desert, but now gets far too much rainfall to be classed as a desert.

Look around you and you'll realise that most of the Kalahari is covered in a thin, mixed bush with a fairly low canopy height, dotted with occasional larger trees. Beneath this is a fairly sparse ground-covering of smaller bushes, grasses and herbs. There are no spectacular sand dunes; you need to return west to the Namib for those!

This is very poor agricultural land, but in the east of the region, especially south of Tsumkwe, there is a sprinkling of seasonal pans. Straddling the border itself are the Aha Hills (see pages 439–40), which rise abruptly from the gently rolling desert. This region, and especially the eastern side of it, is home to a large number of scattered Bushman villages of the Ju/'hoansi !Kung.

The wildlife is a major attraction. During the late dry season, around September and October, game gathers in small herds around the pans. During and after the rains, from January to March, the place comes alive with greenery and water. Birds and noisy bullfrogs abound, and travel becomes even more difficult than usual, as whole areas turn into impassable floodplains. From April the land begins to dry, and during July and August the daytime temperatures are at their most moderate and the nights cold. But whenever you come, don't expect to see vast herds like those in Etosha or you will be disappointed.

The other reason for visiting is to see the Bushman people. The conventional view is that less than a century ago these people's ancestors were a traditional hunter/gatherer society using Stone-Age technology. Yet they possessed a knowledge of their environment that we are only just beginning to understand. Tourism is increasingly seen as a vital source of revenue for these people. In placing a high value on traditional skills and knowledge, it is hoped that it will help to stem the erosion of their cultural heritage.

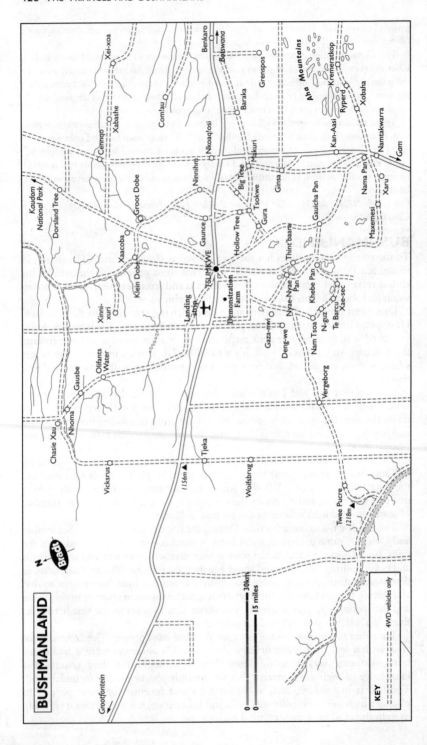

Getting there

The C44 road through to Tsumkwe is the main access route into the area. This is long, and continues a further 50km east to the new border post with Botswana at Dobe. From there it's a further 150km (3 hours' drive) of patchy gravel road to Nokaneng (a small town on the main tar road which runs down the western side of the Okavango Delta in Botswana).

Tsumkwe feels remote, but it is easily reached from Grootfontein by ordinary 2WD vehicle. From Nokaneng, an experienced driver should be able to get a high-clearance 2WD through to Tsumkwe, but doing this journey in a 4WD is recommended. Virtually all the other roads in Bushmanland require a sturdy 4WD and a good guide, or a GPS, or preferably both.

After travelling east from the B8 for about 31km there is a police station on the south side of the road.

Omatako Valley Restcamp is about 88km from the tar, and Tsumkwe about 226km. Around 89km before Tsumkwe, one of the turnings to the right is signposted 'Mangetti Duin', marking the way to one of the best stands of mangetti trees in the area – notable because mangetti nuts are one of the staple foods of the Bushmen.

Otherwise along this road there are a few turnings to villages, but little else. The area is not densely populated, and travellers coming this way should travel with water and some food, as only a handful of vehicles will use the road on any particular day.

One good way to visit is by combining it with a trip through Khaudum National Park, thus making a roundabout journey from Grootfontein to the Caprivi Strip. Alternatively, approaching Bushmanland from the south, via Summerdown, Otjinene, and the old Hereroland, would be an interesting and unusual route. Expect the going to get tough.

Tsumkwe

Though it is the area's administrative centre, Tsumkwe is little more than a crossroads around which a few houses, shops and businesses have grown up. Apart from the South African army, it's never had the kind of colonial population, or even sheer number of people, that led to the building of (for example) Tsumeb's carefully planned tree-lined avenues.

It is an essential stop for most travellers in the area though, even if only to get a few cans of cool drinks. It is also the location of the Conservancy Office and of Tsumkwe Lodge, the region's only real lodge for visitors.

Getting organised

To visit this area independently you must, as with Kaokoland, be totally self-sufficient and part of a two-vehicle party. The region's centre, Tsumkwe, has basic supplies but NOT fuel. The station referred to in older guidebooks is closed, so the nearest fuel stop is Grootfontein or at Divundu, as you leave the Caprivi Game Park. It is essential to set off for this area with supplies and fuel for your complete trip; only water can be relied upon locally.

Before embarking on such a trip, obtain maps from Windhoek and resolve to navigate carefully. Travel in this sandy terrain is very slow. You will stay in second gear for miles, which will double your fuel consumption. Directions can be difficult; if you get them wrong then retracing your steps will take a lot of fuel.

You'll need a minimum of about 100 litres of petrol to get from Tsumkwe to Rundu or Divundu. Because there's none in Tsumkwe, that means at least 150 litres to travel from Grootfontein via Bushmanland and Khaudum to Rundu or

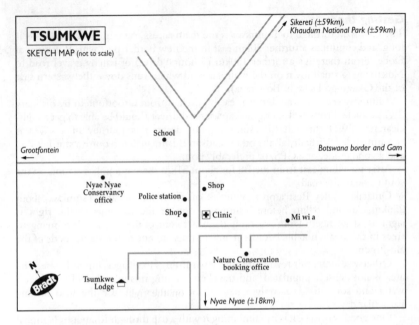

Divundu, or vice versa. You'll need more if you plan to do much driving around the area whilst here. So do plan ahead – arriving in Tsumkwe without enough fuel to get out again is *very* stupid.

If you are passing through Tsumkwe then, aside from the Lodge, two important places to stop are:

Mi wi a PO Box 1073, Grootfontein; tel/fax: (067) 244005; ngtsumke@iway.na; web: www.tsumkwe.com
'Mi wi a', which means 'thank you', is a shop run by the Reverend Hendrik van Zyl, the minister of the local Dutch Reform Church Congregation, and his wife, Elize. This sells only Bushman crafts, which are sourced from the Bushman villages throughout the region. Hendrik buys all the authentic curios that the villages want to make and sell, regardless of their commercial value or otherwise. Thus this encourages the full range of traditional skills, and not just the artefacts that are currently in vogue with this year's visitors.

It's a trade that has built up over the last ten years, and virtually all of the region's villages are now involved in regularly supplying crafts for the centre. If the sellers earned cash, then they would have had to walk between ten and fifty kilometres to Tsumkwe just to buy food. Hence Hendrik takes food out to the villages, and exchanges it for crafts. Given the loss of the large areas used for traditional hunting and gathering, many people are now dependent upon this food source for the more difficult parts of the year. So this scheme provides much needed food relief to many of the poorest villages, and at the same time encourages the people to value their traditional crafts and skills.

It's well worth supporting, not only because it directly benefits the villages, but also because you won't find a larger range of authentic Bushman crafts for sale anywhere. These include axes that also function as adzes, various children's games, bags made from birds' nests woven with wild cotton, hunting bags (containing a dry powder from fungus as kindling), dry grass, flint, wooden sticks, acacia gum, poisons, a 'string bag' made from giraffe tendons (for carrying things home), love bows, witchcraft bows, hunting bows and arrows, necklaces, bracelets and containers for poison pupae. It's fascinating.

So... if you're one of the many visitors who see great poverty in Africa, and wring your hands saying: 'what can I do', now you have an answer. You can come here and buy as much craftwork as you can afford. (If you're being honest with yourself, that really is a lot of crafts!) Thus appeasing your conscience with a valuable donation, whilst finding endless fascinating curios to give to friends when you return.

Currently, the main problem of this trade is the limitation of current distribution channels for these crafts. Only a few visitors pass through Tsumkwe, and although it's possible to arrange for 'mail order' deliveries overseas, this is not yet happening on a large enough scale. Shame – as it's fascinating stuff which would sell superbly at small craft markets overseas. So if you're reading this from outside Namibia, take a look at their website (www.tsumkwe.com). Ignore the religious slant, but think of placing a small order!

Nyae Nyae Conservancy Office Tel: 067244011 (see page 433 for details of the headquarters of Nyae Nyae in Windhoek – though it's not possible to make any reservations through that office).

Travelling east from Grootfontein, this is on the right side of the road, just before you reach the main Tsumkwe crossroads.

Several villages in the Nyae Nyae Conservancy have basic campsites (usually without ablution facilities as yet), and warmly welcome paying visitors. To find out more about them, and what's possible, best to stop here at the conservancy office. (If it's closed, then ask for information at Tsumkwe Lodge.) This is also the place to arrange a local guide if you want one – which is highly recommended. If you're planning on just camping in the area for a few days, to explore a little, then a guide can help you get a lot more out of the area – whilst actively giving a little more back to the local commuinity.

Where to stay
On the way east to Tsumkwe there's one community restcamp beside the road, although this is quite limited in scope. If you are not travelling in a self-contained expedition, then Tsumkwe Lodge is the only real option in or near Tsumkwe. Fortunately, it's an excellent option.

Omatako Valley Restcamp (Omatako San Community Project) No telephone here, or other communications, so advanced bookings are not possible.
On the way to Tsumkwe, about 88km east of the B8, is a restcamp run by one of the local Bushman communities. Driving into Bushmanland, it is hard to miss, in a dip immediately on the right of the road 13km past the veterinary control.

If you are heading for Tsumkwe then stop here for cool drinks. A small craft shop sells locally made crafts with a good selection including beads, necklaces (around N$15), spears, various tools and baskets (around N$20–30).

If you stay, then the community have built a few basic mud and thatch rondavels for sleeping in (with your own bedding and mosquito net), and a camp site with a good shower and one toilet. There's firewood for sale, lamps for hire at N$5 per evening, and sometimes a whole variety of things to do are possible, all arranged and guided by the local people. These include guided village tours (half-day for N$60), horseriding (N$30 per person per hour) and bush walks (half-day for N$70) for game viewing or birdwatching. The more adventurous can also have bush food cooked and prepared for N$10, or attend a

'traditional magic dance evening' costing N$150 for a small group. However, all of these activities are dependent on which of the villagers are around when you are; so none are at all guaranteed.
Rates: N$10 per person camping.

Bushmanland Safari Camp radio number 2080, via Walvis Bay Radio (tel: 064 203581)
At time of going to press, this is a brand new place providing campsites, and also pre-erected, furnished tents. I would welcome more news of it, but believe that it's been set up in some old saw mills, about 80km west of Tsumkwe. They only have a radio-telephone at present and so can be reached, with some difficulty, by booking a call via Walvis Bay radio.

Tsumkwe Lodge (9 bungalows and camping) PO Box 1899, Tsumeb; tel: 067 244028; fax: 067 244027; email: tsumkwel@iway.na; web: www.tsumkwel.iway.na
Run by Arno and Estelle Oosthuysen, this is the area's only lodge. It is well signposted a kilometre or so from the centre of Tsumkwe: just turn right at the crossroads, then right again opposite Nature Conservation. It is the best place to base yourself for visits to surrounding Bushman villages. At the lodge you'll find five large wooden guest bungalows with solid stone floors, and four brick rooms with solar-powered lights. Their floors have rugs on them, and there's also chairs, a table and wardrobe, with sliding glass or netting (for ventilation) windows, and twin beds surrounded by large mosquito nets. Each has an en-suite bathroom with a powerful shower, a toilet and a washbasin; they are simple but comfortable and very spacious.

The main building has a relaxed dining room/bar area, and adjacent is a small swimming pool. The team of Damara-speaking women at the lodge cook some wonderful food. However, the lodge's attraction lies in its activities, as Arno has been running trips into this region for years. He knows the local people well and has a very sensitive attitude to working with them and introducing tourists.

The lodge is also surprisingly good at taking children, as Arno and Estelle have two of their own. It's also fascinating that when visitors go to villages together with their own children, the local youngsters will relax and start playing with the young visitors very quickly – integrating far more easily than the adults. So if your children are active and not shy, expect to have difficulty dragging them away from Tsumkwe when it's time to leave.

If you do stay here before venturing into the bush, then it is often a good idea to tell Arno and Estelle where you are planning to visit, and when you'll be back. Then at least someone will know if you go missing. The lodge will organise trips, including trips into Khaudum National Park, and visits to a Ju/'hoan village. These cost N$1,800 per day and are usually arranged in advance. Camping out overnight is sometimes possible.
Rates: single N$345; double N$285 per person for accommodation only; single N$520; double N$460 per person including all meals.

Nyae Nyae Conservancy

Stretching east, north and south from Tsumkwe is the new Nyae Nyae Conservancy area. First established in 1988, it is really still in its infancy, and under development, but it is important to realise that now, when you visit Bushmanland, you are within a conservancy where the local people set the rules. Here the communities have won the right to manage their wildlife and tourism as they wish. One possible way forward is that whilst they have always hunted the wildlife here using traditional methods, now they can also derive income from trophy hunting in the area.

Having achieved the funding of a conservancy for the area, the Nyae Nyae Foundation is concentrating on helping to promote the region. As part of this, it has set up a tourism office (see page 431) in Tsumkwe. This should be your first stop in the region. Here you may have to pay entrance or conservancy fees in the

NYAE NYAE DEVELOPMENT FOUNDATION

Based just east of Tsumkwe, the Nyae Nyae Farmers Cooperative has been established since 1986 with a charter to support and encourage the Ju/'hoansi of Eastern Otjozondjupa to return to their historical lands known as Nyae Nyae.

Historically, this group of Bushmen has been in a difficult position. The South African army (SADF) moved into what was Eastern Bushmanland in 1960, to occupy the region as part of its war against SWAPO and the destabilisation of Angola. It formed a battalion of Bushmen to track down guerrilla fighters – using the Bushmen's tracking ability to lethal effect. Many of these people moved to Tsumkwe; whole families were dependent on the SADF.

This social upheaval, with lifestyles changing from nomadic hunter-gathering to dependence on an army wage, led to social problems amongst the people, including crime, alcohol and prostitution. Towards the end of the war, it was decided to improve their quality of life by taking them back to ground they had come from, a move initiated by the Nyae Nyae Development Foundation and its founder, John Marshall.

So in the late eighties and early nineties the Nyae Nyae Farmers Cooperative focused on grass-roots self-help projects, encouraging the Bushmen to start farming, rearing cattle, and growing their own food. Boreholes were provided, but few made a success of these projects. The Bushmen are not natural farmers or pastoralists. They seem to have a different approach to survival than most other ethnic groups in Africa.

The Nyae Nyae Development Foundation continues to run various education programmes to train teachers for the five newly built schools in the Nyae Nyae area (lessons are in English and Ju/'hoansi). They also run a workshop for mechanics and some agricultural programmes, but their focus has now changed.

In the last few years a craft programme has been set up, which is trying to improve the quality of the locally made crafts, whilst buying them to sell across the country and often across the world. Locally, this combines with a mobile shop, where people can buy food and other basics.

However, perhaps the most interesting project was initiated by the WWF in 1994. This has aimed to set up a conservancy for sustainable utilisation and management of the wildlife in the eastern area of Bushmanland – which was finally put into place in December 1997. This is being administered by the Nyae Nyae Development Foundation, who can be contacted in Windhoek on tel: 061 236327; fax: 061 225997, email: nndfn@iafrica.com.na.

future, but currently they are only coordinating visitors, helping with information and supplying guides on request. (You should pay any camping fees to the village nearest the campsite.)

Where to stay

For years camping has been possible anywhere in Bushmanland, with no permits necessary, provided you had a party with several 4WDs. However, as the area has just become a conservancy and tourism is seen as an important earner for the local people – so this is about to change.

In the past campers have set up their sites randomly, left litter behind them and caused many problems for the local people and the wildlife. They often used to camp close to water, frightening the area's already skittish animals, and even go swimming in reservoirs meant for drinking. Visitors were unaware that they were staying in an area used for hunting or gathering, and didn't realise the effect that their presence was having on the wildlife, This 'free camping' has now been banned. Instead head for one of the (increasing number of) village sites, where you'll find a place to camp for which you pay the nearby community directly.

In the last edition of this book – just three years ago – I listed three such sites. Now many more villages have simple adjacent sites and welcome visitors. Ask at the Conservancy Office in Tsumkwe and they'll give you a map of these and advise you of their cost, or better still a local guide.

Guidelines for visiting villages

Wherever you camp, you must take great care not to offend local people by your behaviour. It is customary to go first to the village and ask for permission to stay from the traditional leader (n!ore kxao). This is usually one of the older men of the village, who will normally make himself known. Never enter someone's shelter, as this is very rude.

Often the headman will be assisted by someone who speaks Afrikaans or even English, and if he's not around then somebody else will normally come forward to help you. If your Afrikaans is poor, then you may have to rely upon sign language. If you wish to take photographs of the people or place, this is normally fine – provided you ask in advance, and pay for the privilege.

Remember that you are in a wilderness area, where hyena, lion and leopard are not uncommon, so always sleep within a tent. Try not to scare the wildlife, or damage the place in any way. Keep fires to a minimum, and when collecting fuel use only dead wood that is far from any village.

If you wish to buy crafts from the village, then do not try to barter unless specifically asked for things; most people will expect to be paid with money. Similarly, if one of the villagers has been your guide, pay for this with money. Remember that alcohol has been a problem in the past, and do not give any away.

Some local people have been designated as community rangers, with a brief to check on poaching and look out for the wildlife. They may ask what you are doing, and check that you have paid your camping fees.

Water is essential for everybody, and in limited supply for most of the year, so be very careful when using the local waterholes or water pumps. Often there will be someone around who can help you. Never go swimming in a waterhole or reservoir.

Cultural sensitivity and language

Cultural sensitivity isn't something that a guidebook can teach you, though reading the section on cultural guidelines, in *Chapter 2*, may help. Being sensitive to the results of your actions and attitudes on others is especially important in this area.

The Bushmen are often a humble people, who regard arrogance as a vice. It is normal for them to be self-deprecating amongst themselves, to make sure that everyone is valued and nobody becomes too proud. So the less you are perceived as a loud, arrogant foreigner, the better.

Very few foreigners can pick up much of the local Ju/'honasi language without living here for a long time. (Readers note that spellings of the same word can vary from text to text, especially on maps.) However, if you want to try to pronounce the words then there are four main clicks to master:

/   is a sucking sound behind the teeth
//   is a sucking sound at the side of the mouth, used to urge a horse
!   a popping sound, like a cork coming out of a bottle
≠   a sharper popping sound (this is the hardest).

What to do and what to see

Aside from coming here out of a general curiosity about the area's wildlife and culture, one area stands out: the Nyae Nyae Pan. This is a large complex of beautiful salt pans, about 18km south of Tsumkwe. During good rains it fills with water and attracts flamingos to breed, as well as dozens of other waterbirds including avocets, pygmy geese, grebes, various pipers and numerous plovers. Forty-six different species of waterbirds have been recorded here when the pan was full.

Towards the end of the dry season you can normally expect game drinking here, and the regulars include kudu, gemsbok, steenbok, duiker and elephant. Meanwhile black-backed jackals patrol, and the grass grows to 60cm tall around the pan, with a belt of tall trees beyond that.

Cultural activities

It's worth being realistic from the outset of your visit here: if you're looking for 'wild Bushmen' clad in loincloths and spending all day making poison arrows or pursuing antelope, you will be disappointed.

The people in this area have been exposed to the modern world, and often mistreated by it, for decades. None now live a traditional hunter-gatherer lifestyle. Walk into any village and its inhabitants are more likely to be dressed in jeans and T-shirts than loincloths, and their water is more likely to be from a solar-powered borehole pump than a sip-well.

However, many of the older people have maintained their traditional skills and crafts, and often their knowledge of the bush and wildlife is simply breathtaking.

Those that I met appeared friendly and interested to show visitors how they live, including how they hunt and gather food in the bush – provided that visitors are polite, and ask permission for what they want to do, and pay the right price.

This kind of experience is difficult to arrange without a local guide who is involved in tourism and speaks both your language and theirs. Without such a guide, you won't get very much out of a visit to a local village. So even if you have your own 4WD transport, start by dropping into Tsumkwe Lodge or, if it is open, the new conservancy office in Tsumkwe. Ask for a local guide to help you, who can travel around with you. You can pay them directly, around N$50 per morning or afternoon, and this will open up many possibilities at the villages.

None of the village activities is artificially staged. They are just normal activities that would probably take place anyhow, though their timings are arranged to fit in with your available time. However, because they are not staged, they will take little account of you. As a visitor you will just tag along, watching as the villagers go about their normal activities. All are relaxed. You can stop and ask questions of the guide and of the villagers when you wish. Most of the local villagers are completely used to photographers and unperturbed by being filmed

Ideally, for a detailed insight, spend a few days with a guide and stay beside just one village. If they are happy about it, see the same people for an evening or two as well as during the days. This way, you get to know the villagers as individuals, not simply members of an ethnic group. Both you and they will learn more from such an encounter, and so enjoy it a lot more. Typical activities might include:

BEADWORK
Irene Jessop

'I hope someone in the village remembers me from last year.' '*Ja, ja*.' Arno, my guide, was certain they would. 'You should have seen the excitement when they shared out the beads you sent. You remembered them: they won't have forgotten you.'

I walked through the circle of yellow, beehive-shaped huts to where the headman was sitting, the only one on a chair, a concession to his age. As he clasped my hand his son, Steve, translated, 'My father says he is very pleased you have come back to see us.' From across the village Javid stared at me briefly and then dashed across to shake my hand. People smiled spontaneously as they recognised me: I didn't know who to say hello to first.

My stay at Nhoma the previous year had been brief. A Ju/'hoan village in remote northeast Namibia, it is one of about 30 villages at the edge of the Nyae Nyae Conservancy. I was persuaded that visitors provided vital revenue to the villagers, but had also read about marginalised people with problems of poverty, unemployment, and ill health. I anticipated that a visit would be at best a glum affair, and perhaps even a voyeuristic intrusion on a suffering people. Instead I found fun. Women sat by small fires in front of their huts with tall wooden mortars and pounded protein-rich mangettis that tasted pleasantly nutty if a little gritty. Some boiled vivid scarlet beans: after eating the flesh the kernel is roasted. Waste nothing: sometimes there is only nothing. While the women prepared food the men made hunting necessities. With his *chop-chop*, the Bushman's axe, Sao scraped fibres from mother-in-law's-tongue; these are twisted to make rope for a bird trap. Abel cleaned a dried steenbok skin to make a kit bag for the hunt. With great concentration Joseph squeezed the grub of a beetle cocoon to put poison on some arrows. Care is needed, as there is no known antidote and to avoid an accidental scratch it is not put on the tip. Even with all this work going on, it was never quiet: all around was talking and laughter.

The previous year N!hunkxa made ostrich egg beads, painstakingly filing them to the same size with a stone. These, along with pieces of leather, wood, and porcupine quills, were threaded into necklaces and bracelets, all brown and white. But what the women really wanted, they told me, were small glass beads, especially red and yellow ones. A few of them already had brightly coloured glass-bead necklaces and bracelets. Some, mainly the older ones, had bead medallions fixed through their hair so that they hung down on to their foreheads. The beads I had sent had all been used. Not only were the women wearing more necklaces and bracelets than last year, but also rings. Some of the men too wore ornate beaded belts or had circles of beads embroidered on their *shonas*, leather loincloths.

This time I had brought more beads and I was going to learn how to make

Food collecting/hunting trips

Normally lasting about 3–4 hours in the bush, you'll go out with a guide and some villagers and gather, or hunt, whatever they come across. The Bushmen know their landscape, and its flora and fauna, so well that they'll often stop to show you how this plant can be eaten, or that one produces water, or how another fruits in season.

Even Arno (an expert on the area who runs Tsumkwe Lodge) comments that after years of going out with them, they will still often find something new that he's never seen before. It's an ethno-botanist's dream.

something. As N!hunkxa unwrapped the beads a dozen or so women stopped work to see what I had brought. We sat on the sand in a circle under the shade of a large tree. Pleasantly warm now; it would soon be too hot to be in the sun. In the middle of the group was a large canvas sheet and we made indentations in it to stop the beads rolling away. N!hunkxa chose an easy style for me to make, two parallel lines which crossed over at intervals. Other women made elaborately decorated coils or wide headbands with zigzag patterns. Steve kept my pattern correct by calling out the numbers and colours of beads, 'Two blue, one red...' Jewellery making was obviously the chance for a good gossip. Though I couldn't understand the words I could absorb the rhythms of the conversation, quick one-line repartee, and long stories with a punchline.

Everyone was generous in praise of my necklace when it was finished. As I tried it on I thought 'When I get home this will always remind me of Nhoma.' This was followed by the realisation that I had brought the beads because the women liked them: it seemed pointless to take them away. Did I really need an object to remind me of that morning? It was better if N!hunkxa had it.

'Steve, please can you tell N!hunkxa that I would like her to have this so that she always remembers me.'

'Gadsha,' (good) several of the women said, knowing this was one of the words I understood. The approval in their expressions too told me that inadvertently or instinctively I had done just the right thing. I was later to find out that in Ju/'hoan society, gift exchange, xaro, is important in bonding people together. What is significant is the act of exchanging of gifts, not their value: beadwork is often a preferred offering for exchange.

N!hunkxa disappeared, to return a few moments later with an ostrich-bead necklace with a leather medallion, which she fastened round my neck.

'N!hunkxa would like to give you a name,' Steve said.

'What is it?' I wondered, knowing that visitors are often very accurately if not always flatteringly likened to animals, for example 'Elephant man' for someone with a big nose.

'No, no, you don't understand. She wants to give you her name.'

'Mi-way-ha (thank-you),' I said, sensing that an honour had been conferred, but not quite understanding.

I now know that by taking N!hunkxa's name I had essentially taken on her relationships and obligations. Any customs governing her behaviour towards other Ju/'hoan would apply to me also: thus I would have obligations of care towards those she did. Those who would look after her would look after me too. I had become one of her kin. However, we live so many miles apart that it is difficult to nurture this relationship, to help in difficult times or take pleasure at the good things. So I send beads because I know how much pleasure they give, because beads to me represent the connections made that morning.

The hunting tends to be for the smaller animals, and in season the Bushmen set up trap-lines of snares to catch the smaller bucks, which need checking regularly and setting or clearing. Spring-hares are also a favourite quarry, hunted from their burrows using long (typically 5m), flexible poles with a hook on the end.

Don't expect to go tracking eland with bows and arrows in half a day, though do expect to track anything interesting that crosses your path. These trips aren't intended as forced marches, and the pace is generally fairly slow. However, if there's some good food to be had, or promising game to be tracked, then these walks through the bush can go for hours. Bring some water and don't forget your hat. Expect to pay around N$50 per person to each of your Bushmen hosts for about a 3–4-hour trip. (So if ten villagers come on a food-gathering trip, that's N500 to pay to the village!)

It's usually best to discuss the money in advance, and agree a cost. However, bear in mind that working with money is relatively new to many of these people and so don't expect any sophisticated bargaining techniques. As a *quid pro quo*, don't use any such ruses yourself, or try to screw the people into a hard bargain; just aim for a fair price (which you learned when you stopped and asked at the conservancy office!).

Traditional craft demonstrations
As part of a half-day trip into the bush, you'll often stop for a while at the village, and there the people can show you how they make their traditional crafts. The Bushmen have a particularly rich tradition of story-telling, and it shows clearly here if they also demonstrate how snares are made and set, and give animated re-enactments of how animals are caught. This would normally be included in a half-day bush trip, above.

Evening singing and dancing
In the evenings, you can arrange (in advance) to visit a local village, and join an evening of traditional dancing. This probably means driving to just outside a village, where those who want to take part will meet you. They will build a fire, around which the women and children will gradually gather. Eventually those sitting will start the singing and clapping, and men will start dancing around the circle sitting in the firelight. They will often have percussion instruments, like shakers, strapped to their ankles.

The singing is beautiful, essentially African, and it comes as no surprise that everybody becomes engrossed in the rhythm and the dancing. On rare occasions, such concentration amongst the dancers can induce states of trance – the famous 'trance dances' – which are traditionally used as dances to heal, or prevent illness.

As an observer, expect to sit on the ground on the edge of the firelight, outside of the dancers' circle. You will mostly be ignored whilst the villagers have a good time. They will have been asked to dance for your benefit, for which they will be paid, but everything else about the evening is in their control. This is the kind of dancing that they do for themselves, with nothing added and nothing taken away.

Note that they're used to most visitors just sitting and watching whilst they dance. If you want to join in it's often not a problem... but expect to be the source of a lot of amusement for the resident professionals.

Expect to pay about N$300 to the village for such an evening, which is very cheap for the experience. (That's worked out at N$20 for every villager present – so a bigger gathering will cost more, and is split between however many Western guests are present.)

Cultural questions
When you see the Bushmen in the Tsumkwe, it's tempting to lament their passing from noble savage to poor, rural underclass: witness the lack of dignified 'traditional' skins and the prevalence of ragged Western clothes, or see the PVC quivers that the occasional hunter now uses for his arrows.

While they clearly need help in the present, part of the problem has been our blinkered view of their past. This view has been propagated by the romantic writings of people like Laurens van der Post and a host of TV documentaries. However, modern ethnographers now challenge many long-cherished beliefs about these 'noble savages'.

Essential reading in this respect is *The Bushman Myth: The Making of a Namibian Underclass*, by Robert J Gordon (see *Further Reading*). It stands out as an excellent, scholarly attempt to place the Bushmen in an accurate historical context, and to explain and deconstruct many of the myths that we hold about them. In partial summary of some of his themes, he comments about the book:

> The old notion of these people as passive victims of European invasion
> and Bantu expansion is challenged. Bushmen emerge as one of the many
> indigenous people operating in a mobile landscape, forming and shifting
> their political and economic alliances to take advantage of circumstances as
> they perceived them. Instead of toppling helplessly from foraging to
> begging, they emerge as hotshot traders in the mercantile world market
> for ivory and skins. They were brokers between competing forces and
> hired guns in the game business. Rather than being victims of pastoralists
> and traders who depleted the game, they appear as one of many willing
> agents of this commercial depletion. Instead of being ignorant of metals,
> true men of the Stone Age, who knew nothing of iron, they were fierce
> defenders of rich copper mines that they worked for export and profit. If
> this selection has a central theme, it is to show how ignorance of archival
> sources helped to create the Bushmen image that we, as anthropologists,
> wanted to have and how knowledge of these sources makes sense of the
> Bushmen we observe today.

Gordon's book isn't a light or swift read, but it will make you think. See also my comments on the wider context, include the modern media's portrayal of the San, in *People and Culture*, pages 16–22.

Further information
For more information about the area and its people, contact either Arno at Tsumkwe Lodge or the Nyae Nyae Development Foundation (see page 433); both are closely involved with the welfare of the Bushmen.

Aha Hills
Look southeast of Tsumkwe on the maps and you'll find an isolated group of hills straddling the border between Botswana and Namibia: the Aha Hills. Named, it's claimed, after the onomatopoeic call of the barking geckos that are so common in the area, these are remote enough to have a certain mystique about them – like their counterparts in Botswana, the Tsodilo Hills.

However, there the similarity ends. The Aha hills are much lower and more flattened. Their rock structure is totally different: a series of sharp, angular boulders quite unlike the smooth, solid massifs of Tsodilo. So they' are quite tricky to climb, and have no known rock art or convenient natural springs. All of this means that though they're interesting, and worth a visit if you're in the area – they do not have the attraction of Botswana's Tsodilo Hills.

With a guide, the track past !'Obaha Village does lead onto the hills, and it's possible to climb up Kremetartkop (which has some lovely baobabs on the top) in an hour or so. The view from the top – across into Botswana and 360° around – is pure Africa.

Do leave at least a whole afternoon for this trip though. I didn't, and ended up driving back to Tsumkwe in the half-light, which wasn't ideal. However, I caught a rare glimpse of a caracal bounding through the long grass in the headlights.

KHAUDUM NATIONAL PARK

Minimum of two 4WD vehicles per party. Entrance fees: N$10 per person per day and N$20 entry for the vehicle.

Situated next to Botswana and immediately north of Bushmanland, Khaudum is a wild, seldom-visited area of dry woodland savannah growing on old stabilised Kalahari sand-dunes. These are interspersed with flat, clay pans and the whole area is laced with a life-giving network of omurambas.

Omuramba is a Herero word meaning 'vague riverbed', which is used to describe a drainage line that rarely, if ever, actually flows above ground but often gives rise to a number of waterholes along its course. In Khaudum, the omurambas generally lie along east–west lines and ultimately link into the Okavango's river system, flowing underground into the Delta when the rains come. However, during the dry season the flood in the Okavango Delta helps to raise the level of the water-table in these omurambas – ensuring that the waterholes don't dry up, and do attract game into Khaudum. The vegetation here can be thick in comparison with Namibia's drier parks to the west. Zambezi teak and wild syringa dominate the dunes, while acacias and leadwoods are found in the clay pans.

Flora and fauna

The bush in and around Khaudum is quite complex. Different areas have totally different types of vegetation; biologists say that there are nine different 'biotypes' in Bushmanland.

Towards the southern end of the park, and between Tsumkwe and Sikereti, the bush is thick. Umbrella-thorn, leadwood, and cluster-leafed terminalia (also known as silver-leaf terminalia) are the dominant vegetation. The dune-crests often have stands of mangetti and marula trees and, although spectacular baobab trees are dotted around the whole region, there is a particularly high density of them in the Chokwe area.

Inside the national park, Khaudum has spectacular forests of teak (especially prevalent in the southeast) and false mopane trees, which form a shady canopy

---

GPS REFERENCES FOR KHAUDUM NATIONAL PARK (opposite)

BDRYNE	18°22.961'S	21°00.015'E	SONCAN	19°03.211'S	20°43.010'E
BDRYNW	18°23.289'S	20°43.050'E	TARIKO	18°53.661'S	20°52.332'E
BDRYSE	19°09.833'S	21°00.016'E	TSGATE	19°09.903'S	20°42.310'E
BDRYSW	19°09.922'S	20°32.244'E	TSOANA	19°05.648'S	20°35.583'E
CWIBAO	18°26.331'S	20°42.964'E	TURNBA	19°00.440'S	20°53.954'E
CWIBAA	18°26.320'S	20°44.118'E	TURNBU	18°35.032'S	20°44.909'E
CWIBAB	18°28.740'S	20°49.967'E	TURNEL	18°47.192'S	20°39.125'E
CWIBAC	18°29.555'S	20°57.510'E	TURNK2	18°30.143'S	20°49.099'E
DORING	18°35.705'S	20°50.677'E	TURNKH	18°30.479'S	20°43.618'E
ELANDS	18°47.212'S	20°38.052'E	TURNKR	18°57.932'S	20°33.451'E
KHAUDU	18°30.131'S	20°45.253'E	TURNOM	18°57.342'S	20°43.314'E
KHAUNO	18°23.289'S	20°43.050'E	TURNTS	18°40.630'S	20°44.159'E
KREMET	18°57.459'S	20°37.721'E	TURNSW	19°01.720'S	20°32.222'E
LEEUPA	18°43.157'S	20°51.693'E	WESTRN	18°40.484'S	20°36.094'E
NHOMAO	18°55.898'S	20°44.347'E	XDUSSI	18°50.825'S	20°47.092'E
SIKERE	19°06.157'S	20°42.399'E			

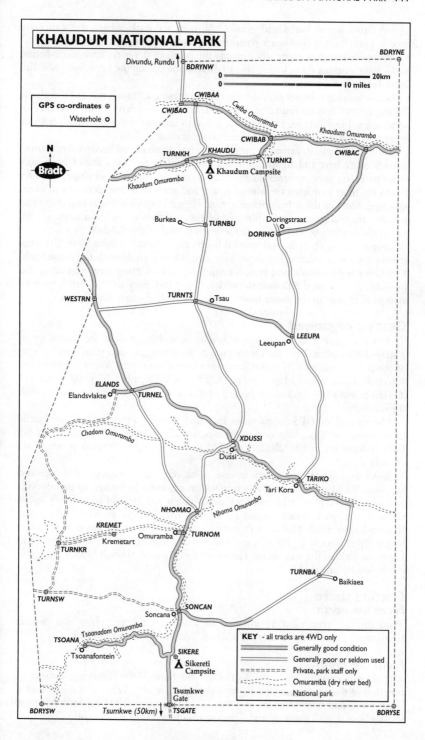

KHAUDUM NATIONAL PARK

Divundu, Rundu BDRYNW

BDRYNE

0   20km
0   10 miles

GPS co-ordinates ⊕
Waterhole ○

N

Bradt

CWIBAA
CWIBAO
Cwiba Omuramba
CWIBAB
Khaudum Omuramba
CWIBAC
TURNKH KHAUDU
TURNK2
⊕ Khaudum Campsite
Khaudum Omuramba

Burkea ○ TURNBU
Doringstraat ○
DORING

WESTRN
TURNTS
Tsau ○

Leeupan ○ LEEUPA

ELANDS
Elandsvlakte ○ TURNEL

Chadom Omuramba

XDUSSI
Dussi ○

TARIKO
Tari Kora ○

NHOMAO
Nhoma Omuramba

KREMET
Omuramba ○ TURNOM
Kremetart

TURNKR

TURNBA ○ Baikiaea

TURNSW

Soncana ○ SONCAN

TSOANA
Tsoanadom Omuramba
Tsoanafontein ○

SIKERE
⊕ Sikereti Campsite

Tsumkwe Gate

KEY - all tracks are 4WD only

━━━━ Generally good condition
──── Generally poor or seldom used
====== Private, park staff only
∙∙∙∙∙∙ Omuramba (dry river bed)
─ ─ ─ National park

BDRYSW
Tsumkwe (50km) ↓ TSGATE
BDRYSE

above low-growing herbs and grasses. All over the park, where the dunes are wooded you'll often find open expanses of grassland growing between them.

Many omurambas, especially towards the south of the park, have black-cotton soil – which makes them impossible to drive along during the rains, but good and hard during the dry season.

Game viewing is better here during the dry season, although most of the classic Kalahari game species found here are not strictly dependent on the presence of waterholes. Elephants are a notable exception to this rule, and they usually migrate away from sources of permanent water when it rains.

Though seldom occurring in numbers to rival Etosha's vast herds, there is some good wildlife here and Khaudum has a much wilder feel than any of Namibia's other parks. Its game includes the uncommon tsessebe and roan antelope, the latter noted for their penchant for lots of space, and areas with low densities of other antelope. Most of the subcontinent's usual big game species (excluding rhino and buffalo) are also represented – blue wildebeest, red hartebeest, kudu, oryx, giraffe, steenbok, duiker – as well as smaller animals typical of the Kalahari.

Leopard, lion, cheetah, and spotted hyena are the main predators and, though there are good populations of these, they are seldom seen through the dense bush. Khaudum is Namibia's best park for wild dog, which range over vast areas and probably criss-cross the Botswana border. (That said, they are very rarely seen by visitors here, due to the dense bush and relative lack of game-drive loops.)

Getting organised
Within the reserve, tracks either follow omurambas, or link the dozen or so waterholes together. Even the distinct tracks are slow going, so a good detailed map of the area is invaluable. Try the Surveyor General's office in Windhoek (see page 120) before you arrive. Map number 1820 MUKWE is only a 1:250,000 scale, but it is the best available and worth having – especially when used in conjunction with the one here.

The map with GPS locations is included here by kind courtesy of Estelle Oosthuysen, of Tsumkwe Lodge, who personally mapped it out and noted the GPS coordinates in late 2002. (In UTM format – so any translation errors are entirely mine!)

Water is available but nothing else, so come self-contained with fuel and supplies. Because of the reserve's remote nature, entry is limited to parties with two or more 4WD vehicles and each needs about 120 litres of fuel simply to get through the park from Tsumkwe to the fuel station at Mukwe, on the Rundu–Bagani road. This doesn't include any diversions while there. You'll need to use 4WD almost constantly, even in the dry season, making travel slow and heavy on fuel. In the wet, wheel chains might be useful, though black-cotton soil can be totally impassable.

Getting there
From the north
Turn off the main road 115km east of Rundu at Katere, where the park is signposted. Then Khaudum camp is about 75km of slow, soft sand away.

From the south
Khaudum is easily reached via Tsumkwe and Klein Dobe. Entering Tsumkwe, turn left at the crossroads just beyond the schoolhouse. This rapidly becomes a small track, and splits after about 400m. Take the right fork to Sikereti, which is about 60km from Tsumkwe and 77km south of the camp at Khaudum.

If you have a GPS with you, then Sikereti has co-ordinates 19° 6.318' S, 20° 42.325' E, whilst the crossroads at Tsumkwe is found at 19° 35.514' S, 20° 30.199' E.

Where to stay

Khaudum National Park has two camps: Sikereti camp in the south, and Khaudum in the north. Each has basic wooden huts with outside facilities, and campsites. The four-bed huts costs N$110 per hut at Khaudoum, and N$115 at Sikereti. The campsites are N$95 per day for up to four people, plus an extra N$10 per extra person. Advanced reservations, from Windhoek NWR, are essential here in order to be admitted – and you must arrive with an absolute minimum of three days' food and water.

Remember that neither camp is fenced, so leave nothing outside that can be picked up or eaten, and beware of things that go bump in the night. In an emergency, the park staff at Sikereti and Khaudum may have radios. If you can find them, they can usually help you.

Sikereti Restcamp Sikereti stands in a grove of purple-pod terminalia trees, one of several such dense stands in the park. There are three basic bungalows, with mattresses and communal showers and ablutions. Cold water, no lights or electricity. If you visit in winter, then there is a 'donkey' for heating water for the showers, but you'll have to stoke and light it for yourself.

Khaudum Restcamp Khaudum stands in a lovely spot on top of a dune, looking out over an omuramba. It is a great spot for sunsets, and there's a waterhole below the camp in the omuramba. Its facilities are rather battered, but there are two bungalows and four campsites here.

Owamboland

This verdant strip of land between Etosha and the Kunene and Okavango rivers is largely blank on Namibia's normal tourist map. However, it is highly populated and home to the Owambo people, who formed the backbone of SWAPO's support during the struggle for independence. The region was something of a battleground before 1990, and now the map's blank spaces hide a high concentration of rural people practising subsistence farming of maize, sorghum and millet.

Before independence this area was known as Ovamboland, and recently it has been split into four regions: Omusati, Oshana, Ohangwena and Oshikoto. Here, for simplicity, I will refer to the whole area as Owamboland. During the summer Owamboland appears quite unlike the rest of Namibia. It receives over 500mm of rain and supports a thick cover of vegetation and extensive arable farming.

The Owambo people are Namibia's most numerous ethnic group, and since independence and free elections their party, SWAPO, has dominated the government. Much effort is now going into the provision of services here. There are two main arteries through Owamboland: the B1/C46, and the smaller C45. The small towns that line these roads, like trading posts along a Wild West railroad, are growing rapidly.

Alongside the main B1 there is a canal – a vital water supply during the heat of the dry season. Driving by, you pass women carrying water back to their houses, while others wash and children splash around to cool off. Occasionally there are groups meeting in the shade of the trees on the banks, and men fishing in the murky water. Some have just a string tied to the end of a long stick, but others use tall conical traps, perhaps a metre high, made of sticks. The successful will spend their afternoon by the roadside, selling fresh fish from the shade of small stalls.

Always you see people hitching between the rural towns, and the small, tightly packed combi vans, which stop for them: the local bus service. If you are driving and have space, then do offer lifts to people; they will appreciate it. It's one of the best opportunities you will get to talk to the locals about their home area.

Owamboland has three major towns – Oshakati, Ondangwa and Ruacana – and many smaller ones. With the exception of Ruacana, which was built solely to service the big hydro-electric power station there, the others vary surprisingly little and have a very similar atmosphere.

There is usually a petrol station, a take-away or two, a few basic food shops, a couple of bottle stalls (alias bars) and maybe a beer hall. The fuel is cheaper at the larger 24-hour stations, in the bigger towns, and you can stock up on cold drinks

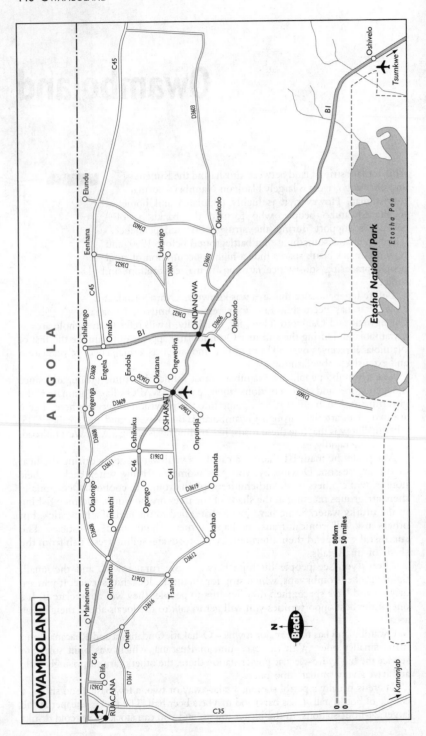

there also. The take-aways and bars trade under some marvellous names: Freedom Square Snack Bar, Music Lovers Bar and the Come Together Bar, to name but a few. These can be lively, friendly places to share a beer, but a word of warning: they are not recommended for lone women visitors.

Away from the towns, the land seems to go on forever. There are no mountains or hills or even kopjes – only feathery clumps of palm trees and the odd baobab tree break the even horizon. After a year of good rains, the wide flat fields are full of water, like Far Eastern rice paddies, complete with cattle wading like water buffalo.

Travelling eastwards and slightly south, towards Tsumeb, notice how, as the land becomes drier, the population density decreases, and maize becomes the more dominant crop. Where the land is not cultivated, acacia scrub starts gradually to replace the greener mopane bushes by the roadside. Keep your eyes open for raptors – especially the distinctive bateleur eagles that are common here.

Towards the edge of Owamboland, at Oshivelo (about 150km from Ondangwa and 91km from Tsumeb), you must stop to pass through a veterinary cordon fence. This is just a kilometre north of the bed of the Omuramba Owambo, which feeds into the Etosha pan.

OSHAKATI

By Namibian standards, this is a large sprawling town and is typical of the region. There are no tourist attractions here, but the town acts as the centre for several government departments.

Getting organised

Oshakati has all the major services that you might need. For car spares there is the large California Auto-spares dealer (tel: 065 221240), a branch of Cymot (tel: 065 220916), and many small garages. Towards the east of town, Phoenix Motors is the Nissan depot. There are lots of fuel stations, including Mobil and BP 24-hour stations. For food shopping, the market, on Main Street, has a fairly extensive range of supplies, and there's also a branch of Checkers, which is more basic than most, a Europa Wholesale (behind the First National Bank), and the Continental just east of town.

For money, there are major branches of Standard, First National and Commercial banks, both with hole-in-the-wall automatic cash dispensers. Don't expect credit cards from overseas to work.

If you need medicine there are several pharmacies including Oshakati Apteek (tel: 065 220964) on the main road which have good basic supplies.

In an emergency, the police are reached on tel: 065 210111, the ambulance on 065 200211, and the fire service on 065 221258. The hospital is on 065 220211.

Where to stay

The hotels in the area aim at business people, mostly aid-workers and visiting government employees. They are generally efficient, but don't expect to meet many other tourists here.

International Guest House PO Box 542, Oshakati; tel: 065 220175; fax: 065 221189
To reach this turn left at the Engen garage, and continue past the Yetu shopping centre until you reach the big white water-tower on your left. Turn left there. After a further 150m of tar, turn right on to a gravel road. After a further 250m take a left, and the guesthouse is right there. The last few turnings should be signposted with 'Coke'

signboards for the guesthouse. Its rooms have en-suite bathroom, air conditioning, TV and telephone, and there's a swimming pool and tennis court outside. It has improved since independence, and is as good a place to stay as anywhere in the region.
Rates: single N$270, double N$320, including breakfast.

Santorini Inn P Bag 5569, Oshakati; telfax: 065 220457/220506/221803; email: info@santorini-inn.com
Right on Main Road, on the right if arriving from Tsumeb, Santorini Inn has a pool, an à la carte restaurant, a squash court, a sports bar, and several different types of rooms. All have air conditioning and a telephone as well as DSTV. Despite its location, it feels very detached from the town.
Rates: single N$370–450, N$230–280 per person sharing, including breakfast.

Oshandira Lodge PO Box 958, Oshakati; tel: 065 220443/221171; fax: 065 221189; email: oshandira@iway.na
To reach this, follow the directions to the International Guest House, above. Then ask for Oshandira and someone will guide you to it. This has air-conditioned rooms with en-suite bathroom, a TV and a telephone. Elsewhere there's a sportsmen's bar with large-screen TV. Outside is a pool and the popular Garden Restaurant which is probably the best place to eat in town, so often gets busy; it also includes traditional Ovambo food on its menu. Oshandira Lodge has secure parking within a short walk of the airstrip.
Rates: single N$250, N$190 per person sharing, including breakfast.

Okave Club (8 bungalows) PO Box 1483, Oshakati; tel/fax: 065 220892
In the same part of town as the Santorini Inn, this is reached by turning left after the Engen station, then left again after the Bank of Namibia (on to a gravel road), and next right. The Okave Club started in 1990 and has eight bungalows with air conditioning, TV and telephone, as well as a pool, restaurant and bar.
Rates: single N$160–200, double N$125–150 per person sharing, including breakfast.

Continental Hotel and Restaurant (19 rooms) PO Box 6, Oshakati; tel: 065 220170; fax: 065 221233. Slightly west, out of town, the 'Continental number one' (as it's known) is run by Frans Indongo and has the widest range of rooms around. All are still clean, with en-suite bathrooms, and some are air conditioned.

Rooms are numbered 1–19, and generally the higher the number, the better the room. They are graded into three price brackets; rooms 1–5 are the smallest and most basic. These stand near the small casino, sharing toilets and showers. Rooms 8–13, 15 and 17 all have their own toilets and showers, as well as a TV and a telephone. The most expensive, 14, 16 and 19 (by far the largest) have all this plus air conditioning.

There's a busy beer garden in the centre of the hotel, and a simple restaurant for breakfast. It's not the plushest place in town, but it's fine for a night.
Rates: single N$180, double N$255, including breakfast.

Oshakati Country Lodge (50 rooms) PO Box 15200, Oshakati; tel: 064 500001; fax 064 500724; email: afrideca@mweb.com.na; web: www.namibialodges.com. Central reservations tel: 061 240375; fax: 061 256598.
Oshakati Country Lodge was built by Namibia Country Lodges, who also own De Duine at Henties Bay (page 325) and Aoub Lodge (page 198). It opened in 1999 and its main building has a large thatched structure under which you'll find a substantial public bar (with electronic gaming machines), as well as an à la carte restaurant and a conference centre that can accommodate 250 people.

All the rooms have air conditioning, TVs, telephones and a minibar/fridge, and there's also a decent swimming pool here.
Rates: single N$450, double N$310 per person sharing, including breakfast. Dinner N$86 (set menu) or N$94 (buffet).

Where to eat and drink

There is no shortage of places to eat which serve simple fare. There's a popular Kentucky Fried Chicken in the Yetu shopping centre, and Jotty's Fish & Chips take-away on the main road is a favourite. Club Oshandira (see above) probably has the best food in town, or at least the most pleasant surroundings in which to eat it.

For an evening out, Oshakati can be excellent – provided that you enjoy joining in with the locals and don't demand anything too posh. Club Fantasy (billed as 'Your Party Place') is perhaps the best place in town and has been going for years. Other contenders include Club Yellow Star and Moby Jack's, the Let's Push Bar, the Moonlight Bar, and the small Country Club – but don't take these names too literally.

ONDANGWA

This is the other main town of Owamboland, and in character it is very similar to Oshakati. There are Shell and Mobil fuel stations (24-hour), a couple of big supermarkets and even an outdoor market. Try the latter for fresh vegetables, and perhaps a cob of maize to snack on. As a last resort, there is always the aptly named Sorry Supermarket.

Getting there
By air
Ondangwa is serviced by a weekly flight that links it to Mokuti (N$205) and Windhoek (N$705), and connects to Oranjemund (N$1,780).

By road
Ondangwa is spread out along the main B1, and you'll find numerous local combi vans, sometimes referred to as taxis, stopping to pick up and drop passengers all along here.

Intercape Mainliner used to run a service between Windhoek and Oshikango, which stopped here, but as I write this is no longer operational. However, it might be worth checking the 'search' page on their website, www.intercape.co.za, to see if it's started up again.

Getting organised
If you need medicine there are several pharmacies including the Ondangwa Pharmacy, tel: 065 240361/240784. **In an emergency**, the police are reached on tel: 065 210111, the ambulance on 065 240111, and the clinic on 065 240305.

Where to stay
As with Oshakati's hotels, Ondangwa's cater mainly for business people. Most visitors will certainly wish to avoid the dubious 'private bar with sleeping rooms' next to the Caltex garage, leaving the choice of:

Punyu International Hotel (30 rooms) PO Box 247, Ondangwa; tel: 065 240556/240009; fax: 065 240660
One of the oldest hotels in the area, the Punyu is signposted off the main road near Ondangwa, north towards Eenhana. It has a central restaurant and bar, and each of its rooms has a TV, telephone and air conditioning.
Rates: single N$250, N$190 per person sharing, including breakfast.

Nakambale Museum Restcamp (3 huts, cottage and camping) c/o ELCIN, P Bag 2018, Ondangwa; tel/fax: 065 245668; email: olukonda.museum@elcin.org.na

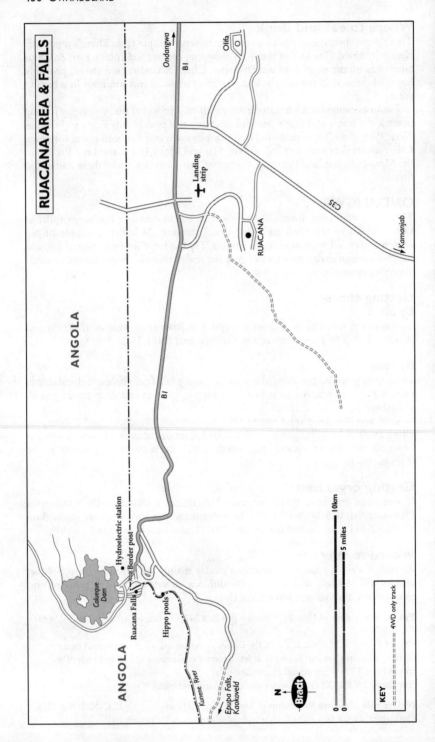

RUACANA AREA & FALLS

ANGOLA

Ondangwa

Olifa

B1

Landing strip

RUACANA

C35

Kamanjab

ANGOLA

B1

Calueque Dam

Hydroelectric station

Border post

Ruacana Falls

Hippo pools

Kunene River

Epupa Falls, Kaokoveld

N

Bradt

KEY

================ 4WD only track

0   5 miles

0   10km

Just 10km from Ondangwa, accommodation here is in traditional Owambo huts or in a missionary's cottage. While these are basic, they prove a point about life here a century ago, and this is reinforced by the availability of traditional Owambo food. There is also a campsite. Local guides are on hand to explain various traditional skills and practices.

Rates: Traditional hut N$50 per person; missionary cottage N$75 per person; camping N$35 per person.

Cresta Lodge Pandu Ondangwa (90 rooms) PO Box 2827, Ondangwa; tel: 065 241900; fax: 065 241919; email: ondangwa@crestanamibia.com.na; web: www.cresta-hospitality.com

This four-star hotel geared to the business community is typical of business hotels throughout the world. En-suire rooms have twin beds and air conditioning, while facilities include a swimming pool, restaurant, bar and free airport transfers.

Rates: single N$490, N$310 per person sharing, including breakfast.

At Olukonda, on the D3606, about 13km southeast of Ondangwa, are some of the oldest buildings in northern Namibia – a Finnish Mission built here in the late 1870s. (As an aside, Finland seems to have maintained its links with Namibia, forming a significant contingent of the United Nations' UNTAG force, which supervised the country's transition to democracy in 1990.) Here you'll also find the museum restcamp (see above).

RUACANA

This small town in the north of the country perches on the border with Angola, about 291km (mostly gravel) from Kamanjab and about 200km west of Oshakati. It owes its existence to the big hydro-electric dam that is built at a narrow gorge in the river and supplies over half of the country's electric power. This is of major economic and strategic importance, so the road from Tsumeb/Ondangwa is good tar all the way.

At Ruacana there's a BP petrol station, with the only fuel for miles, a general store and a large school. The town's nucleus feels quite modern, but there are no other facilities, and few visitors pass through.

The Ruacana Falls used to be an attraction for visitors, but now the water only flows over them when the dam upstream in Angola allows it to, and even then much is diverted through a series of sluices to the hydro-electric station on the border. The falls are well signposted in no-man's-land, so technically you have to exit the country to see them. However, at the large and under-used border post (opens 06.00–18.00) you can do so temporarily, signing a book rather than going through the full emigration procedures. Be careful when taking photographs: ask permission and don't take pictures of anything apart from the falls. This border area is still very sensitive.

West of Ruacana

West of Ruacana is the Kaokoveld, covered in *Chapter 15*. There is a road directly from Ruacana along the Kunene, for about 125km as far as Epupa Falls. However, its latter stages are very, very rough – taking me three days of painstaking driving on one occasion. Nothing west of Ruacana should be attempted without a self-sufficient two-vehicle party of rugged 4WD vehicles.

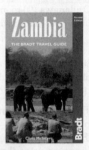

The Kavango and Caprivi Strip

The north of Namibia is generally very lush, watered by a generous annual rainfall. East of Owamboland – which means northeast of Grootfontein – lie the regions of Kavango and Caprivi.

These support a large population, and a surprising amount of wildlife. The wildlife has visibly increased in the national parks here in the last few years, helped enormously by various successful community-based game-guard and conservation/development programmes (see *Chapter 3*).

The main B8 road across the strip, or Golden Highway as it is sometimes called, is now completely tarred. It is destined to become an increasingly important artery for trade with Zimbabwe and Zambia, and hence a busier road. It has come a long way since the dusty gravel road that I first crossed in 1989, when many viewed it as *terra incognita*.

Unlike much of the rest of Namibia, the Kavango and Caprivi regions feel like most Westerners' image of Africa. You'll see lots of circular huts, small kraals, animals and people carrying water on their heads. These areas are probably what you imagined Africa to be like before you first arrived. By the roadside you'll find stalls selling vegetables, fruit, or woodcarvings, and in the parks you'll find buffalo hiding in the thick vegetation. This area is much more like Botswana, Zimbabwe, or Zambia than it is like the rest of Namibia. This is only what you'd expect if you look at a map of the subcontinent, or read the history of the area: it really is very different from the rest of Namibia.

Note Unrest in the last few years has meant that, at times, vehicles travelling across the Caprivi strip have been proceeding in convoy. Since the situation tends to change, check the Foreign Office website, www.fco.gov.uk/travel/namibia, for up-to-date advice. Note that it is the area to the north of the Golden Highway where disturbances tend to occur.

KAVANGO REGION

East of Owamboland, and west of Caprivi, lies the region of Kavango – which broadly corresponds to the old region of Kavangoland. Within this, Rundu is the main town. It is a useful stopover for most visitors, but an end in itself for few. Further east is Popa Falls, a set of rapids on the Okavango River. These mark an important geological fault, where the Okavango starts to spread out across the Kalahari's sands, to form its remarkable delta in Botswana. Popa Falls has only a small waterfall, but a lovely little restcamp.

Just downstream from Popa, on the border with Botswana, Mahango National Park is tucked into a corner of the country. Bounded on one side by the broadening Okavango, it encompasses a very wide range of environments in its

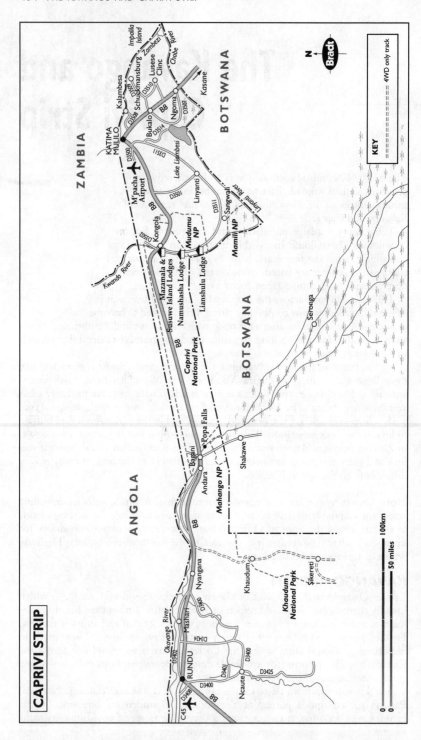

small area, and its game has improved vastly over the last decade. It now boasts Namibia's highest count of bird species in one park, and some prolific big game. With its expansive reedbeds, tall trees, and lush vegetation, Mahango is typical of the game parks further east.

Driving from Grootfontein to Rundu

Grootfontein to Rundu is about 250km of good tar road. Initially the only variation in the tree and bush thorn-scrub is an occasional picnic site by the roadside, or band of feathery makalani palms towering above the bush. About halfway to Rundu, you stop at a veterinary control post; a gap in the veterinary fence. This is the line where land-use changes drastically: from large, commercial ranches to small, subsistence farms. The fence is put there to stop the movement of cattle, and the transmission of foot-and-mouth and rinderpest disease. The difference is striking; the landscape changes drastically, becoming more like the stereotypical Western view of poor, rural Africa. Drivers should take care, as with more settlements there are now many more animals and people wandering across the road.

Gradually shops and bottle-stalls appear, and eventually stalls selling wood-carvings. Closer to Rundu, especially during the wet season, kiosks appear piled high with pyramids of tomatoes and exotic fruits – evidence of the agricultural potential in the rich alluvial soils and heavy rainfall.

Rundu

Northeast of Grootfontein and about 520km west of Katima Mulilo, Rundu sits just above the beautiful Okavango flood plain and comes as a pleasant relief after the long, hot journey to reach it. Perhaps because of this distance, it feels like an outpost. It certainly has few specific attractions. But these distances also make it a prudent stopover, and most of the lodges expect visitors to spend just one night with them. Perhaps because it is across the river from Angola, Rundu has a relaxed, slightly Portuguese atmosphere.

Orientation

The B8 is the main artery on which people arrive and depart, though it actually skirts the town. You must turn off at the buzzing Shell petrol station to get into Rundu itself.

Taking this turning brings you past the sports stadium on your right and to a four-way stop junction. Continue straight on, and you eventually meet the old river road at right angles, opposite the police station and Omashare River Lodge. Turn left here for the Kavango River Lodge, and right for all the others (except Hakusembe). This old road used to be the main gravel road to Katima, and it runs northeast, between the river and the new tar B8, for many miles. Occasionally it connects with the new tar B8 by access roads numbered DR3402, DR3421, etc.

Getting there

The main Engen fuel station is located at the four-way stop between the Shell garage (which is on the corner where you turn off the B8 and into Rundu) and town. If you are hitchhiking, then the Shell garage is the best place for lifts, as most people passing this will stop to fill up, or get a drink or food. Watch for thieves in the crowds here, as several problems have been reported in the past.

The Intercape Mainliner coach service (see pages 96–8), which links Windhoek with Victoria Falls, stops at the Engen garage on Sat and Tue at 04.10, en route for Victoria Falls. On the way back to Windhoek, it stops on Sun and Wed at 18.40. See page 98 for details or, better, check their latest timetable using the search facility at www.intercape.co.za.

The airport is signposted off the main road to Grootfontein, but no longer sees any regular, scheduled internal flights.

Where to stay

Rundu has boomed in the last few years. The Caprivi has opened up more to tourism, and visitors need to stop over on their way there and back. Now there is a wide choice of places to stay, dotted along 30km of riverfront. Most are clearly signposted off the road, towards the river.

Many offer activities like boating on the Okavango, though note that the river here is often so low from September to December that anything except, possibly, a shallow canoe will constantly ground on the sandbanks. In short, Rundu is a super place to stop over on the way to destinations where you will want to spend more time.

Hakusembe River Lodge (6 chalets) PO Box 1327, Rundu; tel: 066 257010, cell: 081 1222102; fax: 066 257011; email: hakusemb@mweb.com.na; web: www.namibianet.com/hakusembe

On the opposite side of town to virtually all the other lodges, Hakusembe is about 14km west of Rundu – off the main road to Nkurenkuru. To reach it, take a turning northwest off the main Rundu–Grootfontein road about 4km southwest of Rundu. Follow this towards Nkurenkuru for about 10km, until the lodge is signposted towards the river.

Hakusembe is managed by Lena and Henry Mudge as a restcamp, which also has activities available. All the chalets have been upgraded with 24-hour electricity, and en-suite shower and toilet. These are set amidst green lawns leading on to the river. There is also a swimming pool, and nearby, under thatch, the bar (popular with residents) and dining area.

Watersports and fishing are available January–October for N$50 per person per hour – options include waterskiing, parasailing, kneeboarding, birdwatching and sightseeing trips by boat. Sunset champagne cruises are also popular.

Rates: single N$600, N$480 per person sharing, including dinner, bed and breakfast..

Kavango River Lodge (14 chalets) PO Box 634, Rundu; tel: 066 255244; fax: 066 255013; email: kavlodge@tsu.namib.com; web: discover-africa.com.na

Situated in a superb (and very secure) spot on the western edge of Rundu, overlooking the river, Kavango River Lodge has been here for years, but was recently taken over by owners, Jackie and Tulio Parreira. Most of the camp's fully equipped bungalows are designed for two people – though a few are for families. These have AC and a ceiling fan, direct-dial telephones and a TV. All have en-suite facilities, and a small kitchen. Linen and cutlery are provided.

Although the chalets are fully equipped for self-catering, with braai facilities and braai packs, dinner and breakfast is available in the restaurant. That said, self-catering is easy here, and you can't beat your own braai overlooking the river for dinner. Simply pick up a few steaks and vegetables during the day, and get the fire going at sunset. The lodge is classed as a restcamp – and earned an award as Namibia's best restcamp in '97.

There's a small conference room below the chalets, and the tennis courts next door can usually be used by arrangement. Sundown cruises and canoeing can be organised when there's enough water in the river.

Rates: single N$240, double N$340, triple N$390, family N$440. Canoeing single N$25 per person/hour, double N$45; champagne cruises (when the water is high) N$130 per person/hour, including half a bottle of champagne and a snack platter,.

Omashare River Lodge (20 twin rooms) PO Box 617, Rundu; tel: 066 256101; fax: 066 256111; email: omashare@iway.na

Owned by a Namibian company, De Beers, Omashare is in the very centre of town, around where the old Kavango Motel used to be. Its rooms are laid out in a semi-circle, overlooking the Okavango and Angola beyond.

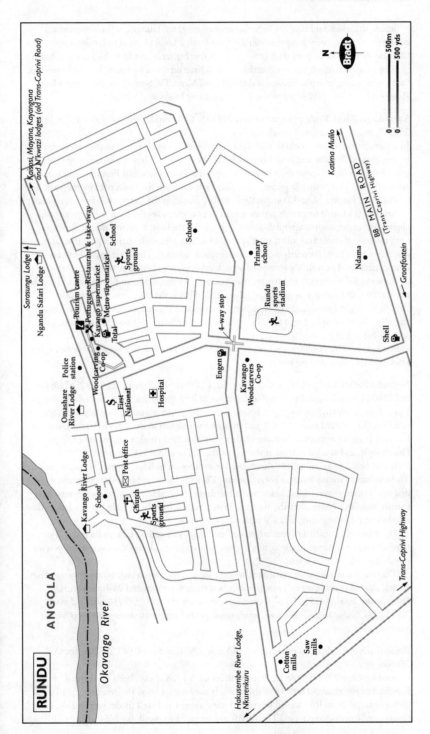

Inside the main building is a large 'ladies' bar, carpeted lounges, soft chairs, and a conference room; everything that you'd expect from a hotel catering to business people. Outside there's a large pool with little shade. A few big trees would make a great difference.

The rooms are small but comfortable, and all have direct-dial phones, tea/coffee makers, flasks with water, en-suite shower and toilets, and Mnet TV. Some have AC, others fans. *Rates: single N$340, N$240 per person sharing, including breakfast.*

Sarasungu River Lodge (9 bungalows) PO Box 414, Rundu; tel: 066 255161; fax: 066 256238; email: sarasungu@mweb.com.na
Just outside town, Sarasungu is well signposted by the river. It is one of the oldest and best lodges around Rundu, and is still run by Eduardo and Ines. They are welcoming hosts who, between them, speak fluent English, German, Portuguese and French – and make a good effort at a few other languages too! The turn-off from the main road by the river leads down a hill, passing Ngandu on your left, before reaching the lodge a kilometre or so later.

Sarasunga's nine bungalows are all spread out on green lawns. Each is individual and slightly different, named after a different animal. All are large reed and thatch structures with en-suite shower and toilet, usually a small sitting area with chairs and coffee table, and double or twin beds (beneath mosquito nets when needed). These are rustic but very comfortable, and beautifully furnished with local fabrics and African artefacts.

Sarasungu's restaurant and bar are the focal area for the lodge, and its pizzas and pastas are certainly the best for hundreds of kilometres. This is the most atmospheric place in Rundu for a good meal and a quiet drink; Eduardo and Ines are on hand and it is always friendly. Canoes can be hired for N$35 per person per hour, and boat trips arranged for around N$70 per person.
Rates: single N$290, N$200 per person sharing, N$540 for three beds in a bungalow, including full breakfast. Camping N$30 per person.

Ngandu Safari Lodge (28 rooms) Usivi Rd, PO Box 519, Rundu; tel: 066 256723; fax: 066 256726; email: ngandu@mweb.com.na; web: http://resafrica.net/ngandu-safari-lodge
Just off the main road by the river, beside the turn-off to Sarasungu, Ngandu is a large complex that opened around 1998, just in time for tourism to the Caprivi to nose-dive. It has very large whitewashed A-frame chalets with thatched roofs, reminiscent of Cape Dutch style, and is hard to miss at the top of the hill overlooking the river.

It was billed as an affordable alternative for visitors on holiday, especially South Africans. The ten luxury rooms have air conditioning, TV with Mnet and overseas channels, direct-dial telephones, stove, fridge, kettle and a hairdryer. A breakfast pack, to cook yourself, is usually supplied. More recently, six semi-luxury rooms have been added to the lodge; these also have air conditioning, and TV with Mnet.

Ngandu's six standard rooms are more basic, with just ceiling fans and a fridge. For families there are some simple family rooms, whilst there's always the campsite if you are travelling with your own tent.

The lodge has a separate restaurant, a curio shop, a laundry, a swimming pool, internet access, shaded parking spots, braai facilities, a conference room and 24-hour security.
Rates: luxury rooms N$290/170 single/sharing, semi-luxury rooms N$230/160, standard rooms N$180/135, budget rooms N$100/90, family rooms N$145 per person sharing. All prices include breakfast.

Kaisosi River Lodge (16 twin rooms) PO Box 599, Rundu; tel: 067 255265; fax: 067 256566
Owned by Global Food Services, Kaisosi River Lodge has always been on the east of Rundu, but has changed style over the years. It now competes with Omashare as a business person's stopover in Rundu. All the rooms are carpeted and well made, with high-quality fittings and direct-dial phones. The rooms are arranged in small, double-storey brick

chalets and each has patio doors and a sitting area outside, overlooking the river. The standard rooms have a fan, toilet and shower, whilst the luxury rooms are larger, with AC and a combined bath and shower.

The main building includes the reception, bar and dining area – all under a grand thatched roof. Just outside are a couple of pools overlooking the river, and a large area of wooden decking for just relaxing. Perhaps as a remnant of its past, there's still a campsite here. Whilst Kaisosi is efficient and ideal as a business hotel, it lacks the atmosphere that most visitors want for a holiday stopover.

Rates: Singles are N$320/N$360. Standard double/twin rooms are N$265, luxury ones N$295, per person sharing. Three-bed rooms N$640/N$710. Rates include breakfast. Camping is also available for N$40 per person.

Mayana Happy Lodge (8 basic thatched shelters)
Just a few hundred metres west of Kayangona, and almost 20km northeast of Rundu (follow the directions to n'Kwazi), this was not at all happy when last visited. Its eight simple chalets were just reed-and-thatch shells, with shared ablutions. Nobody there could advise if there was space available, or how much it would be. However, the grass was well-watered and Mayana Happy Lodge would be a very cheerful place to drop into if you were on an overland truck which takes over the whole place for an evening or two.

n'Kwazi Lodge (14 chalets) PO Box 1623, Rundu; tel/fax: 066 255409; email: nkwazi@iafrica.com.na
About 20km east of Rundu, n'Kwazi is well signposted (with fish eagle logos) just beyond both Mayana Happy Lodge and Kayangona. Leaving Rundu for Katima, take the tar for 10km before turning left. Then 3km later, turn right on to the old gravel Rundu–Katima road, then left after a further 3km. The lodge is about 4km along this dirt road, after Mayana Happy Lodge and Kayangona.

N'Kwazi was built in 1995 by Wynand and Valerie Peypers, and is still run by them and their family. Its design is impressive, with a couple of large thatched areas by the river – one a bar, with ample comfortable seating, and a central fire; the other the main dining room overlooking a pool and the river beyond.

The bungalows are large, comfortable wooden structures, with high thatched ceilings, large meshed windows and warm fabrics. They are lit by gas and paraffin lamps, making n'Kwazi the plushest lodge near Rundu.

Note that the Peypers also own **Vistas for Africa** tour operation, which concentrates on upmarket overlanding operations, and various activities are available from the lodge – boat and mokoro fishing trips, and even water-skiing if you're willing to dodge the hippos and crocodiles. N'Kwazi has a small campsite adjacent, which may transfer to Kayangona in the future.

Rates: single N$400, N$310 per person sharing, including breakfast. Camping N$30 per person per night.

Kayangona Lodge (8 chalets) PO Box 1623, Rundu; tel/fax: 067 255467
Kayangona is n'Kwazi's lower-budget neighbour, and is owned by the same family. Kayangona's simple en-suite chalets have reed walls and ceilings, twin beds, a basic toilet and a shower. They are clean and functional, with mesh windows (reed blinds) and a personal padlock on the doors.

A few others are similarly clean and functional, but share toilets and showers. None has electricity. The lawns around them are well kept, and there are braai sites dotted around for you to cook with. Meals are not available here, but can usually be arranged next door, at n'Kwazi.

Rates: single about N$140, N$85 per person sharing, for en-suite rooms. Others N$65 per person; camping N$15 per person.

Mayana Lodge (10 rooms plus dormitory) PO Box 519, Rundu; tel: 067 255911; fax: 067 255910

The turn-off to Mayana, not to be confused with Mayana Happy Lodge, is just 1km further northeast along the old gravel road than the turn signposted to n'Kwazi. It is about 4km off the gravel road, overlooking the river.

Mayana has five simple chalets, which share their showers and toilets, as well as a dormitory sleeping twelve, and a family room for four. All are basic thatch-on-brick structures with few frills. If arranged in advance, the lodge can do spit roasts (20 people or more), boat cruises, village hikes and fishing, and arrange 'tribal dancing' evenings – and hence is an ideal stop for large overland trucks, whose occupants find the small plunge pool irresistible.

Rates: single N$120, N$80 per person sharing, for en-suite rooms; others N$60 per person; camping N$15 per person.

Where to eat

Rundu has a few choices for eating out, but because the lodges are so spread out, most people tend to eat there rather than go to restaurants. Of these lodges, Sarasungu is central and worth the journey for its food, and n'Kwazi and Kaisosi also have good tables if you are there.

In town itself, on the old gravel road just east of the centre, **Casa Mourisca** (PO Box 617, Rundu; tel: 067 255487) is the only proper restaurant. It offers a mix of international cuisine and a promising chalkboard of daily specials.

For lower-budget bites, try the **Portuguese Restaurant & Take-away** (tel: 067 255240/255792) – almost opposite the Total service station in the centre of town, near the Woodcarving Coop. Alternatively, the **Hunter's Tavern** take-away at the Shell petrol station, on the main road, is the perfect choice for those just grabbing a bite on the run.

For buying supplies, the best supermarket in town is probably the **Kavango Supermarket**, which is large and has a good selection. It is opposite the Total garage in town.

Getting organised

There are several 24-hour **fuel stations** in town, including the main Shell station, and several **garages** including: Gabus Garage (tel: 067 255641/255541) for Mercedes; the Nova Tyre centre, in the industrial area, for tyres and retreads (tel: 255029, or 255503 after hours for emergencies); and Kavango Toyota for Toyotas (tel: 255071).

The **Tourism Centre** (PO Box 519; tel: 067 255911; fax: 067 255910) is a useful small curio shop and privately run booking agency, almost behind the Portuguese Restaurant & Take-away. It is also the base for the owners of Ngandu Safari Lodge.

Go slightly east along the river road from the main T-junction and there is a **First National Bank** (tel: 067 255057) on your left, amidst various government offices. This is open 09.00–15.30 weekdays, and 08.30–11.00 on Saturdays, but it's better to use the ones in Grootfontein if you can.

The **Mbangura Woodcarvers' Coop** (PO Box 86, Rundu; tel: 067 256170; fax: 067 256608) have their local outlet next to the Kavango Supermarket, in the centre of town. (The one at the four-way stop is not a retail outlet.) This is worth dropping into, but most of the carvings on display are larger items like tables and chairs. This large, thriving cooperative supplies many of the curio markets further south, including Okahandja's two large roadside markets.

Out of town, heading east on the old gravel road, 2km past the turning to Kaisosi River Lodge, is the **Vungu Vungu Dairy**. For those with a sophisticated line in camp cooking, this is a useful source of juices and fresh dairy produce like milk, butter and cream.

In an emergency, the hospital and ambulance service is on 067 405731 and the police on 067 10111.

Popa Falls

2WD. Entrance fees: N$10 per person plus N$10 per vehicle.
Popa Falls is a simple government restcamp next to some rapids in the Okavango River, which are pretty rather than spectacular. They mark where the river drops 2.5m over a rocky section, caused by a geological fault. After passing over this, the Okavango begins gradually to spread out across the Kalahari's sands until eventually, in Botswana, it forms its remarkable inland delta.

Getting there

The falls and the restcamp are right on the Okavango's western bank, south of the Divundu Bridge, near Bagani. Simply take the road signposted to Botswana which leaves the main B8 just west of the Caprivi Game Park, and the restcamp is on the left after about 3.5km. It is immediately beside the road. The only petrol in the area is found near here, on the left just after the turn-off from the B8 to Popa.

What to see and do

The camp's area by the riverside is thickly vegetated with tall riverine trees and lush green shrubs, which encourage waterbirds and a variety of small reptiles. Footbridges have been built between some of the islands, and it's worth spending a morning island hopping among the rushing channels, or walking upstream a little where there's a good view of the river before it plunges over the rapids. In a few hours you can see all of this tiny reserve, and have a good chance of spotting a leguvaan (water monitor), a snake or two, and many different frogs. The various birds include cormorants with a captivating technique of underwater fishing.

Note that Popa's gates usually open at sunrise and close at sunset, so don't get here after dark or you'll have to sleep somewhere else.

Where to stay

There are now several campsites in this area if you're camping, but if you want a good lodge you've less to choose from.

Popa Falls Restcamp Book via the NWR in Windhoek, page 118
This is a neat, organised restcamp with a well-tended office, good sites, and six excellent four-bed bungalows. The camp's office includes a small shop with a surprisingly wide range of foodstuffs, cool drinks (including some beer and wine) and postcards.

Popa's bungalows are well built of local wild teak and come with their own bedding and gas lamps, but use communal kitchens and ablutions. If you are camping then walk around before you pitch camp: there are secluded sites as well as the more obvious ones. Try taking the main track down to the river, and turning right along the bank. Beware of the mosquitoes, which are numerous.

Rates: Entry is N$10 per person, plus N$10 for the vehicle. Camping sites N$95; four-bed huts are N$210–230 in total.

Suclabo Lodge (11 bungalows) PO Box 894, Rundu; tel/fax: 066 259005; fax: 066 259026; email: suclabo@iway.na; web: www.suclabo@iway.na
Suclabo has stood for many years in a stunning position overlooking some rapids on a beautiful bend in the river, downstream of the main Popa Falls. It is well signposted a few

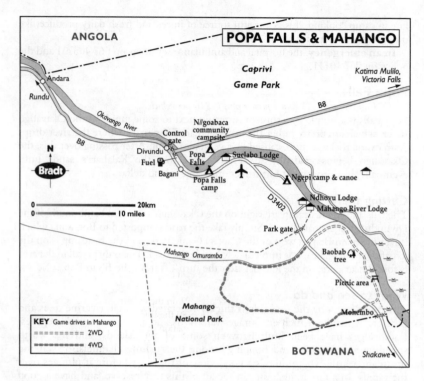

kilometres off the main road, just south of Popa, along with a proud sign boasting 'German hospitality'. It is unclear if this is intended as an enticement or a warning, but the author generally prefers Namibian hospitality.

Suclabo has a swimming pool, restaurant, bar, and a number of thatched bungalows, each with private deck and a view to go with it; there are also facilities for camping. . River trips and fishing excursions by motor boat can be organised by the lodge, as can drives into Mahango National Park. The paddle-yourself canoe trips sound like a treat, as the manager will tell you where the hippos are, presumably so you can avoid them. A boat is being converted into a floating bar, and eventually Suclabo will be a super camp.

Rates: single around N$550, N$357.50 per person sharing, including breakfast. Lunch N$65, buffet dinner N$98. Boat trips N$75 per person per hour. Camping N$55 per person.

Ngepi Camp Signposted from the road between Suclabo and Ndhovu, by two large red bananas on a signpost (perhaps canoes at one stage), this is 4km off the road, along a track that really needs negotiating with a high-clearance vehicle to avoid the sand traps.

Ngepi is a beautiful, green, grassy campsite by the river under some shady trees. Aside from the lawns, and shared ablutions, you can buy a cold drink at the bar, and hire a canoe.

Rates: N$45 per person camping, N$200 per person in some basic bush huts. Breakfast N$45, dinner N$80.

Ndhovu Lodge (8 twin tents/chalets) Bookings are now held at PO Box 559, Swakopmund; tel/fax: 064 463979; cell: 081 1249333; email: gogga4@mweb.com.na
The lodge is now ably run by Lee Dekker and Lance Wilson, after the owners, Roy and Lyn Vincent, moved to Swakopmund to run the office from there.

There are six Meru-style walk-in tents on one side of the lodge, and a further two small wooden chalets on the other. All are well kept with good fabrics and have en-suite facilities set back behind the bedroom. One of the chalets is a 'honeymoon' suite, and hence has a double bed and a bath (with a story belonging to it, if you ask Lance) rather than a shower.

All have solar electricity from battery-powered storm lanterns. Some of the tents are a little closer together than ideal. All have roofs that are shielded from the sun to keep cool in the summer. The wooden chalets come into their own during the winter though, when they are much warmer than the tents.

Activities available include boat trips down the river, and 4WD excursions into the nearby Mahango National Park.

Rates: single N$970, N$795 per person sharing, including breakfast. Activities are extra; expect about N$150 per person for a game drive.

Caprivi Community Campsites

With the backing of the government and the IRDNC (see page 44), several Caprivi communities are opening small campsites. These are broadly based on the *modus operandi* of the camps that have helped to rejuvenate both the game and the local communities in the Kaokoveld. Supporting these, by staying there and paying for their crafts, and by using their skills as guides to the local area, is a practical way in which visitors can help some of the poorest of rural communities raise both money and pride. Most of these sites only have rudimentary facilities and simple ablutions – so they'll only suit you if you have a self-contained 4WD with your own food and supplies.

One of the first, at N//goabaca, opened in May '97 on the eastern bank of the Okavango River, just south of Divundu. Its turn-off is 4km from the bridge, and the campsite is 3km from road. N//goabaca (see pages 434–5 for an explanation of the obliques in N//goabaca) has four private pitches, each with a flush toilet, hot shower and a tap for water. Two have viewing decks, and all overlook Popa Falls from the eastern bank. It's run by Kxoe Bushmen, many of whom worked as trackers and scouts for the South African Army during the war, but have subsequently been economically and politically marginalised. Tourism can not only pay them, but also encourages them to put a higher value on their traditional skills and bushcraft, so support them if you can. Book through IRDNC in Katima Mulilo (tel: 066 252518; fax: 066 252108) or see www.nacobta.com.na for more information.

Excursions into Botswana

At the southern end of Mahango lies Namibia's Mohembo border post, followed by a new Botswana customs and immigration post, just north of Shakawe. These are generally quiet posts; both sides seem pleasant and efficient, and open 06.00–18.00. Botswana's programme of tarring roads has been fast, and you can drive all the way to Maun on tar.

If you've thought of visiting Botswana's Okavango Delta, then when you drive across the Caprivi Strip it can feel so near, and yet so far. However, just south of Mahango, within Botswana, are a couple of small camps which are close enough to reach whilst crossing the Caprivi Strip. They offer a taste of the Okavango Delta, within easy reach of Namibia.

Prices within this section are in pula (£1 = P8.13, $1 = P5.16; € 1 = P5.56).

Mohembo border and ferry

Heading north about 13km after Shakawe, you reach the area of the border with Namibia. A left fork takes you to the neat, newly built customs and immigration area for those crossing into Namibia by road.

A right fork leads swiftly to the (free) Mohembo Ferry, which usually takes a few vehicles at a time across the river, including the occasional small truck. Expect

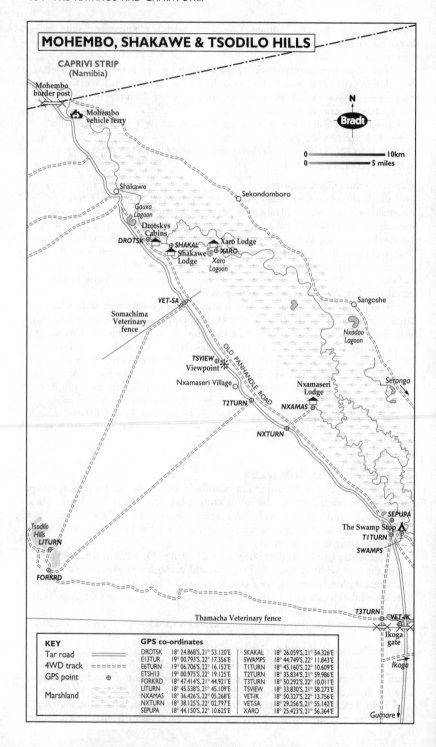

MOHEMBO, SHAKAWE & TSODILO HILLS

CAPRIVI STRIP
(Namibia)

Mohembo
border post

Mohembo
vehicle ferry

N

Bradt

0   10km
0   5 miles

Shakawe

Sekondomboro

Gauxa
Lagoon

Drotskys
Cabins

DROTSK

SHAKAL
Shakawe
Lodge

Xaro Lodge
XARO

Xaro
Lagoon

Sangoshe

VET-SA

Somachima
Veterinary
fence

Nxadao
Lagoon

TSVIEW
Viewpoint

OLD PANHANDLE ROAD

Nxamaseri Village

Setonga

Nxamaseri
Lodge

T2TURN

NXAMAS

NXTURN

Tsodilo
Hills
LITURN

SEPUPA

The Swamp Stop
TITURN

SWAMPS

FORKRD

T3TURN   VET-IK

Thamacha Veterinary fence

Ikoga
gate

Ikoga

Guthare

KEY		GPS co-ordinates			
Tar road		DROTSK	18° 24.868'S, 21° 53.120'E	SKAKAL	18° 26.059'S, 21° 54.326'E
4WD track		E13TUR	19° 00.793'S, 22° 17.356'E	SWAMPS	18° 44.749'S, 21° 11.843'E
GPS point		E6TURN	19° 06.706'S, 22° 16.152'E	TITURN	18° 45.160'S, 22° 10.609'E
		ETSH13	19° 00.975'S, 22° 19.125'E	T2TURN	18° 35.834'S, 21° 59.986'E
Marshland		FORKRD	18° 47.414'S, 21° 44.921'E	T3TURN	18° 50.292'S, 22° 10.011'E
		LITURN	18° 45.538'S, 21° 45.109'E	TSVIEW	18° 33.830'S, 21° 58.273'E
		NXAMAS	18° 36.426'S, 22° 05.268'E	VET-IK	18° 50.327'S, 22° 13.756'E
		NXTURN	18° 38.125'S, 22° 02.797'E	VET-SA	18° 29.256'S, 21° 55.142'E
		SEPUPA	18° 44.150'S, 22° 10.625'E	XARO	18° 25.423'S, 21° 56.364'E

to find a lot of people waiting around here – some to cross, others to meet those who have crossed, or to buy and sell things here.

Shakawe

This very large fishing village stands on the northern banks of the Panhandle of the Delta, some 281km north of Sehithwa and 13km south of the Mohembo border post on the Caprivi Strip. Driving into the village always used to feel like entering a maze of reed walls, each surrounding a small kraal, as the track split countless ways between the houses. The odd trap of deep sand was enough to stop you for an hour, and thus serve up excellent entertainment to numerous amused locals.

However, with the arrival of the tarred road, visiting Shakawe is less fraught than it has been previously. In the village you'll find a major police station, and a significant base for the army (the Botswana Defence Force), as you'd expect in one of the country's more sensitive border areas. If you're going to be doing anything unusual here, then stopping to ask at the police station if it is OK to proceed is always a good idea.

If you've the time, take a walk along the river that is just behind the police station. Sometimes there's a mokoro ferry shuttling local people to and from the eastern side of the river, full with their wares to sell or recent purchases to take back home.

There are also a few shops here, many concentrated within the small shopping centre around the bus stop. On the west side of town, just 400m off the tarmac, you'll find a good paved airstrip, with a very neat, round thatched terminal building.

If you can't leave the modern world behind you then Shakawe has cellphone coverage which usually extends to Drotsky's, but not much further.

Getting there and getting away

If you're not driving here, then there are good daily bus services to Maun via the rest of the western Panhandle from the centre of town. Alternatively, hitchhiking is relatively easy.

Where to stay

There's nowhere practical to stay in Shakawe itself, though there are several water-based camps on the river south of town. These cater mainly for fishing and birdwatching. In recent years, since Namibia's Caprivi Strip has been off-limits for many visitors, trade here has dramatically fallen and these camps have often relied on business from visiting road construction engineers and local government officials. Listed are the three main options, from north to south:

Drotsky's Cabins (6 chalets & camping) PO Box 115, Shakawe; tel: +267 6875035; fax: +267 6875043

Almost 8km south of the radio mast in Shakawe you'll find a left turn off the tar road. This sandy track will lead you east, crossing the old road up the Panhandle for about 3km to reach Drotsky's Cabins (⊕ DROTSK 18°24.868'S, 21°53.120'E). You should be able to drive across this in a normal 2WD car, though the sand can be very thick, so some driving skill is needed.

This long-established camp has been run by the delightful Jan and Eileen Drotsky, and their family, who have seen the Shakawe area change from a remote outpost to a thriving little town.

Drotsky's Cabins stands on a high bank, overlooking the river, which is already several kilometres wide. Below is a network of deepwater channels and large beds of papyrus. It's excellent for birdwatching or fishing, though there's little game around except for hippos and crocodiles.

Drotsky's six chalets are set amongst well-watered lawns in a shaded haven under a canopy of thick riverside trees. Colourful shrubs and banana trees have been planted between them, creating the welcoming impression of a green and tropical haven.

Two of the chalets sleep two people, whilst the other three are bigger and built on two levels, and so can sleep four. All are A-frame design with low brick sidewalls supporting a tall, steeply angled thatched roof. These are insect-proofed with mesh on the window and lit by mains electricity. They all have simple furnishings, rugs on the floor, and a tabletop electric fan. Central to the lodge is a bar (which often seems to play host to an eclectic selection of local characters) and a very large dining area, built over the river. Look out for the rather beautiful wooden top to the bar here!

Drotsky's is a very genuine old camp, where hospitality hasn't been learned from a manual. If you are willing to take it on its own terms, then it can be a super lodge, and offer you fascinating insights into the area, its history and its ecosystems.

Rates: P236/P385/P495 for a single/twin/4-person chalet, or P33 per person camping. Breakfast P35, lunch P50, dinner P60. Boat hire varies in cost depending on the size of the boat, and transfers to or from Shakawe airport are P25 per person.

Shakawe Lodge (10 bungalows) contact via Travel Wild in Maun; tel: +267 6860822/3; fax: +267 6860493; email: t.wild@info.bw
Shakawe Lodge (✪ SKAKAL 18°26.059'S, 21°54.326'E) has been known as the Shakawe Fishing Camp for decades. You'll find the turning to it on the main road about 5.5km north of the Somachima Veterinary Fence (✪ VET-SA 18°29.256'S, 21°55.142'E), and 12km south of the radio-mast in Shakawe Village.

The lodge stands on the bank of the Okavango River, a little less than 3km east of the main road. It was started as long ago as 1959; subsequently its present owners, Barry and Elaine Price, now very well-known local characters, took over the fishing camp in 1975. Now this offers ten large, thatched, brick bungalows. Each has a fan and mains power throughout, and an en-suite bathroom. All are carpeted, though very basic. There's a circular thatched boma, used as a bar/dining room, adjacent to a small lily-covered lagoon that's behind the splash pool.

Under shady trees on the river bank, a few metres south of the main lodge, is the campsite. This is a lovely, grassy site with simple ablutions and a few metal drums that act as braai stands for cooking.

Most visitors here come to fish, though birdwatching – through the riverside forest or from boats – is also popular. When Namibia's Caprivi is safe, the Mahango Game Reserve is within reach of a day-trip, though most visitors would opt to stay there as a separate destination.

Beside the bank at the lodge, look for the Okavango's only armoured boat. This is a relic of the Angolan war from the late 1970s. Apparently it was used by 32 Battalion of the South African forces, who were stationed in the Caprivi Strip, near the site where Ngepi Campsite is now. However, it broke loose and drifted south, and has been gentle rusting in Botswana ever since! Barry has some stories to tell you about this if you ask him.

Rates: chalet P275/P418/P637 for single/double/triple, camping P35 per person incl. tax. Breakfast P35, lunch P45, dinner P65. Boat hire is P85 per hour, plus fuel. Transfer to/from Shakawe airport is P75 per vehicle. Or it's US$250 per person per night, including everything except drinks, for overseas groups.

Xaro Lodge (8 chalets) Book via Drotsky's Cabins, above
Xaro (✪ XARO 18°25.423'S, 21°56.364'E) is about 8.5km downstream from Drotsky's Cabins, its parent camp, and is usually reached from there by boat – a 15-minute trip. The lodge is built on an outcrop from the mainland, amidst an old, established grove of knobthorn (*Acacia nigrescens*), mangosteen (*Garcenia livingstonei*) and jackalberry (*Diospyros mespiliformis*) trees.

Above Leopard at Okonjima Guest Farm (CM)
Below left Caracal cub (CM)
Below right Namibia has about a quarter of the world's cheetah population (CM)

Above Waterhole scene on the southern
edge of Etosha Pan (CM)

Right and below Both giraffe and elephant
are partial to acacia, which is common in
Etosha National Park (CM)

Once there, it's hard to escape the feeling that this was once an absolutely beautiful, old-style Okavango camp. It was originally built in about 1984 by Hartleys Safaris, before passing through several hands until it was acquired by Jan Drotsky, whose son now runs the camp. Here you'll still find a thatched, stone dining area with a large table in the centre and various old books on the bookshelves in the walls.

Accommodation is currently in Meru-style tents built on permanent concrete bases, each with a shaded veranda and a separate toilet and shower. These are adequate, though there are plans to build eight more modern, octagonal thatched rondavels with en-suite facilities to replace them in the future.

Look around and you'll also find a garden of succulents and cacti here, banana trees and even a small baobab tree (*Adansonia digitata*) on the left of the camp as you look out onto the river.

Talking to Royal, one of the marvellous staff who have been here for years, he recalled that the lodge has always been used for fishing and birdwatching from motor-boats, never from mekoro, and that's still the situation.

Rates: P247/P385 for a single/twin tent. Breakfast P35, lunch P50, dinner P60. Boat hire varies in cost depending on the size of the boat, and transfers to or from Shakawe airport are P50 per person.

Nxamaseri

Though the small village of Nxamaseri is not a stop for most visitors, I've included a section here because the area around Nxamaseri Camp is a very interesting one, and capable of providing a deep-water Delta experience which is as interesting as most of the reserves further east.

Specifically, the Nxamaseri Channel here is a side-channel of the main Okavango River. Like Guma Lagoon, further south, it's fairly easily accessible due to the presence of a lodge. If you want a real Delta experience in the Panhandle, then this should be high on your list of places to visit – though getting here either requires your own vehicle or a flight.

Flora and fauna highlights

The Nxamaseri Channel is north of the point where the main Okavango River divides at the base of the Panhandle, and is a stretch of open, clear water up to about 30m wide in places. Beside the edges you'll find stands of papyrus and common reeds, whilst its quieter edges are lined by patches of waterlilies, including many night lilies, *Nymphaea lotus* (aka lotus lilies) as well as the more common day lilies, *Nymphaea nouchali caerulea*. Look out also for the heart-shaped floating leaves, and star-shaped white or yellow flowers of the water gentian, *Nymphoides indica*.

As with the rest of the Panhandle, this isn't a prime area for game viewing. You may catch glimpses of sitatunga or the odd lechwe, and you're almost bound to see hippo and crocodile, but big game is scarce.

However, the channel is a super waterway for birdwatching; home to a tremendous variety of waterbirds. Without trying too hard, my sightings have included many pygmy geese, greater and lesser jacanas, lesser galinules, colonies of reed cormorants, darters, numerous species of bee-eaters and king-fishers, green-backed herons, a relaxed black crake, numerous red-shouldered widows and even (on a cloudy morning in February) a pair of Pel's fishing owls. Beside the channel are pockets of tall riverine trees and various real fan and wild date palms, whose overhanging branches house several colonies of weavers (masked, spotted-backed and brown-throated).

Upstream of the lodge, on the main Okavango River, there's a colony of carmine bee-eaters at a location known locally as 'the red cliffs'. This is occupied from around early September to the end of December, but is probably at its best in late-September/early-October (the best time for most migrant species here).

Getting there and getting away

About 19km north of Sepupa (over 37km south of Shakawe) there's an unmarked turning (✪ NXTURN 18°38.125'S, 22°2.797'E) onto a vague track through the bush which leads northeast, about 5.5km from the main road, to Nxamaseri Lodge (✪ NXAMAS 18°36.426'S, 22°5.268'E). This is little more than a number of confusing tracks in the deep sand which initially head slightly left of the straight-line direction to the lodge, before finally bending right.

If you're approaching from the north this is about 21.5km south of the Somachima Veterinary Fence (✪ VET-SA 18°29.256'S, 21°55.142'E). After 10km you'll pass a slight rise marked by a sign as 'Tsodilo View' (✪ TSVIEW 18°33.830'S, 21°58.273'E). From here, on a clear day, you can see the hills to the southwest. Less than 3km south of this viewpoint you'll pass a sign to Nxamaseri, which leads to the village of the same name. The camp's unmarked turning is almost 9km south of this.

Nxamaseri will only accept advanced bookings, and it is surrounded by water for most of the year. So you *always* need to make advance arrangements to stay here. You'll usually be met if you're arriving by vehicle, and a boat and mokoro are often needed to ferry you the final few kilometres – so this is not a lodge to try and drop into unannounced.

What to see and do

As mentioned, this isn't a lodge for big-game safaris, but the boat trips for birdwatching are first class, and whilst there tends to be less emphasis on mokoro excursions, these are also possible when the water levels are high and there are suitable areas of shallow water nearby.

Fishing is another major activity here, and is possible throughout the year. For enthusiastic anglers, the very best tiger-fishing months are from August to November, and the best times for bream are between March to June. During the first three months of the year the rain and new floodwaters are said to disturb the fish, which move out to the floodplains – and so fishing in the channels can be more difficult.

The record tiger-fish catch here is about 6.7kg, though in a normal season they'd expect to have 10–15 catches over the 6kg mark. Fly-fishing and lure/spinning fishing are done here, and Nxamaseri pride themselves in keeping their equipment in good condition. Like most Okavango lodges, Nxamaseri operates a 'catch-and-release' system with fishing, except for the occasional bream taken for the table. They have two large, flat, barge-like boats which provide a very stable platform for several people fishing, and is also ideal for photography.

Where to stay

Nxamaseri Lodge (6 chalets) PO Box 159, Maun; tel: +267 678016; fax: +267 678015; email: nxa.lodge@info.bw

Nxamaseri Lodge stands beside the Nxamaseri Channel, in an area where, when water levels are high, there are plenty of open marshy floodplains covered with an apparently unblemished carpet of grass, and dotted with tiny palm islands. It's very like the Jao Flats, and is one of the Okavango's most beautiful corners.

Nxamaseri is a long-established camp that has sometime in the past been written off as 'just a fishing camp'. That is how it started: built in about 1980 by PJ and Barney Bestelink, who now run Okavango Horse Safaris. It is claimed that fly-fishing in the Delta was pioneered here, and certainly it remains an attraction for people who fish seriously. However, given that much of the magic of the Delta, and especially its wetter parts, are the birdlife and the scenery, then Nxamaseri's environment and attractions are at least comparable to most of the other water camps in the Delta.

Accommodation is in one of six chalets. Looking from the river, there's a double (most camps would call this a 'honeymoon') chalet on the right of the main lounge/dining area, and five twin-bedded chalets on the left. All are brick with thatch and, above a waist-high wall, one side is largely open to the river. (A rainproof screen can be rolled down, but is seldom needed.) All have high thatched roofs and very simple, wooden furniture.

With a free flow of air from outside, a walk-in mosquito net protects the beds from insects. Each has an en-suite bathroom with flush toilet, hot shower and a washbasin. The camp has a generator running during the day, and that feeds batteries which supply power at night for two bedside lights in each chalet. They're very comfortable, but not luxurious.

The camp's central lounge/dining area is under a large thatched roof, with one side open to the river. Again, this is simple and comfortable though not ornate. What does strike one about the camp is the way that it's been built within a wonderfully thick and tropical patch of riverine vegetation. All around there are knobthorn (*Acacia nigrescens*), waterberry (*Syzygium cordatum*), sycamore fig (*Ficus sycomorus*) mangosteen (*Garcinia livingstonei*), jackalberries (*Diospyros mespiliformis*), sausage trees (*Kigelia africana*) and some of the most wonderfully contorting python vines (*Cocculus hirsutus*) that you'll see anywhere.

Rates: US$220/330 per person sharing/single per night from December to June; US$295/440 from July to November. Includes all meals, activities and local drinks – but excludes other drinks and transfers. Open: all year.

Mahango National Park

2WD/4WD. Entrance fees: N$10 per person and N$10 per vehicle. If you're going straight through on the main road, there is no charge.

This small reserve is tucked away in a corner of the Caprivi Strip, bounded by the Botswana border. It is bisected by one of the main roads between Namibia and Botswana, a wide gravel artery from which two game drives explore the area.

Though forming its eastern boundary, the Okavango River is also the focus of this reserve. The eastern loop road passes beside the river and is normally the better one for game. Here the river forms channels between huge, permanent papyrus reedbeds. Adjacent are extensive floodplain areas, where you're quite likely to spot red lechwe or sable, relatively scarce but beautiful antelope which seem to thrive here.

Beside these, on the higher and drier land of the bank, are wide belts of wild date palm-forest, as well as the lush riverine vegetation that you'd expect. Further from the river are dry woodlands and acacia thickets, dotted with a few large baobabs. This rich variety of greenery attracts an impressive range of animals including the water-loving buffalo, elephant, sable, reedbuck, bushbuck, waterbuck and the more specialist red lechwe and sitatunga. Good numbers of hippo and crocodile are also present.

Mahango is a great favourite with birdwatchers; more species can be found here than in any other park in Namibia. This variation should come as no surprise, as the reserve has one of Namibia's few wetland habitats, adjacent to large stretches of pristine Kalahari sandveld. Thus many water-loving ducks, geese, herons, plovers, egrets, kingfishers, and various waders occur here, along with the dry-country birds that you'll find in the rest of Namibia. Okavango specialities like the slaty egret can sometimes be spotted, and for many birds – including the lesser jacana, coppery-tailed coucal, and racket-tailed roller – Mahango marks the western limit of their distributions.

Amongst the larger species, the uncommon western-banded snake eagles occur, though black-breasted and brown snake eagles are more frequently seen. Similarly, the park's Pel's fishing owls are rare compared with its marsh, giant eagle, and spotted owls.

When to visit
As with most parks, the game varies with the season. The dry season, July to October, tends to be better as the riverfront is at its busiest with animals drinking. Sometimes the park is inundated with elephants and buffalo. During the summer rains (from November to April) the big game here can be disappointing. Visiting in early March in 1990, the highlight of my day's game viewing was a distant kudu, and a snatched glimpse of fleeing sable. Whilst game densities have improved since then, the vegetation is still thick and the animals elusive. However, summer migrants like the exquisite carmine bee-eaters are then in residence, making this the perfect time for birdwatching here.

Where to stay
There are no facilities in Mahango, so most people stay in one of the lodges or restcamps between the park and Popa. See pages 461–3.

What to see and do
Game drives
There are two game drives to explore, both branching from the main road about 800m south of the northern entrance to the park. The better, eastern road, which is good gravel, soon overlooks the floodplain, passing a picnic spot before returning to the main road farther south. The western course, suitable for high-clearance 4WDs only, follows a sandy omuramba away from the river, before splitting after about 10.7km. The right fork continues along the omuramba, terminating at a waterhole, while the left rejoins the main road again 19km later.

Bush walking
One real bonus is that walking in the park is officially encouraged. However beware – the summer's lush growth is far too thick to walk safely in, so better to visit when the plants and shrubs have died down during the winter and you are able to see for a good distance around you. Then you can get out of the car and go for it, but watch for the elephants, buffalo and occasional lion. (For comments on walking safely in the bush, see *Camping and Walking in the Bush*, pages 104–8.)

THE CAPRIVI STRIP
The Caprivi Strip's nerve-centre, Katima Mulilo, is closer to Lusaka, Harare or Gaborone than it is to Windhoek, and in many ways this region is more like the countries which surround it than like the rest of Namibia. For example, note the different designs of the rondavels and villages as you travel through. Some are identical to those in eastern Zimbabwe, while others resemble the fenced-in kraals in Botswana. Even the local language used in the schools, the Caprivi's *lingua franca*, is the Lozi language – as spoken by the Lozi people of Zambia.

Situated on the banks of the Zambezi, Katima Mulilo is a very lively, pleasant town with a bustling market and most of the facilities that you are likely to need. Away from the main town, the region has two established national parks, Mamili and Muumuu. These are both lush, riverside reserves with increasing numbers of animals, and a very bright future. Sadly, the Caprivi Game Park has still to live up to its name, having been badly abused during the war of independence and largely ignored since then. Right on the area's eastern tip, relying mainly on the riverside attractions of Botswana's Chobe National Park, several new lodges are now springing up.

History of the Strip

On the map, the Caprivi Strip appears to be a strange appendage of Namibia rather than a part of it. It forms a strategic corridor of land, linking Namibia to Zimbabwe and Zambia, but seems somehow detached from the rest of the country. The region's history explains why.

When Germany annexed South West Africa (Namibia) in 1884, it prompted British fears that they might try to link up with the Boers, in the Transvaal, and thus drive a wedge between these territories and cut the Cape off from Rhodesia. Out of fear, the British negotiated an alliance with Khama, a powerful *Tswana* king, and proclaimed the Protectorate of Bechuanaland – the forerunner of modern Botswana. At that time, this included the present-day Caprivi Strip. Geographically this made sense if the main reason for Britain's claim was to block Germany's expansion into central Africa.

Meanwhile, off Africa's east coast, Germany laid claim to Zanzibar. This was the end game of the colonial 'scramble for Africa', which set the stage for the Berlin Conference of July 1890. Then these two colonial powers sat down in Europe to reorganise their African possessions with strokes of a pen.

Britain agreed to sever the Caprivi from Bechuanaland and give control of it to Germany, to add to their province of South West Africa (now Namibia). Germany hoped to use it to access the Zambezi's trade routes to the east, and named it after the German Chancellor of the time, Count George Leo von Caprivi. In return for this (and also the territory of Heligoland), Germany ceded control of Zanzibar to Britain, and agreed to redefine South West Africa's eastern border with Britain's Bechuanaland.

At the end of World War II the land was again incorporated into Bechuanaland, but in 1929 it was again returned to South West Africa, then under South African rule. Hence it became part of Namibia.

Driving across the Strip

The main B8 road from Rundu to Katima, known as the *Golden Highway*, has always been gravel – which was fine for 2WD cars, though its bad potholes and fine dust cause many accidents. In the last year this has been tarred, and it is now possible to drive from Katima Mulilo to Rundu entirely on tar.

A word of warning though. Do not underestimate the distances on the Caprivi: they are deceptively long. Driving in one day from Victoria Falls or Kasane to Mudumu, or from Katima Mulilo to Popa Falls, or from Mudumu to Rundu, are the maximum distances that you should attempt as part of a normal holiday trip.

Rundu to Divundu: 204km

This section of the road makes a pleasant drive, as it is often surrounded by green, irrigated fields with the Okavango River as a backdrop. The entry point to the Caprivi Game Park is a bridge over the Okavango.

A few hundred yards before the river the road forks. The right goes to Botswana, via Popa Falls and Mahango. Just after the fork, on the left of the Popa road, is a useful service station which usually has petrol and diesel. This may not seem like a very important place, but it is the only reliable source of fuel for hundreds of kilometres.

Fork left on to the bridge (which always used to be referred to as the Bagani Bridge) and there's usually a small checkpoint. This puzzles many: why maintain it? It is just a hut by the bridge. But consider the importance of that one bridge over the Okavango, and you will realise why the checkpoint remains.

Okavango River View Restcamp Out on a limb, there's a restcamp about 5km north of the main B8. It is reached just opposite the turning south into Khaudum, signposted Khaudum and Sigaretti, about 111km from Rundu. The author would welcome any news on this new camp. It seems ideally situated for those (many) who misjudge just how bad the road going north, out of Khaudum, is going to be.

Divundu to Kongola: 191km

The map shows that a large chunk of the Caprivi Strip is taken up by the Caprivi Strip Game Reserve. The Golden Highway bisects this undeveloped park which, while it is home to much wildlife, has no facilities and no marked game-viewing side roads. Most visitors just pass through, saving their time for other parks, as the game seems to avoid the main road. The most that you can usually see is a few raptors aloft and the occasional elephant dropping on the road – but drive carefully in case something does appear on the road.

Because it borders on Angola, this area was very sensitive and controlled by the military for many years. Now only two control posts remain to remind you of Caprivi's past troubles: one at Bagani and another at Kongola. You do not need any permits to cross the strip and the people manning the control posts will usually just ask where you are going and wave you on with a smile.

There are only two larger settlements within this park: the Omega Shopping Centre, 70km from Bagani, and Babatwa (with a Baptist Mission Church), 23km further on. Neither township is large, and few visitors stop at either but they might be helpful in an emergency. Aside from these, this game reserve is very sparsely populated. One interesting stop should be:

Kxoe Cultural Village

This community development project, being built at Omega III (about 60km west of the Kwando), is due to open around the end of 1998. It is promised as a showcase for some aspects of the Kxoe people's traditional culture, probably including information and demonstrations of their food, medicines, dancing and traditional healing ceremonies. Like Lizauli, this is run by the people for the people's benefit, and so is well worth supporting.

Kongola to Katima Mulilo: 110km

Kongola used to be like Bagani, just a small hut by the bridge over the river Kwando. Now the bridge has become a large tar-and-concrete structure, so perhaps we should expect Kongola to expand similarly. About 5.5km east of the bridge is a small group of buildings, including a convenient bottle stall, and 1.5km later is the Engen fuel station and a turn-off to the south, signposted Sangwali and Lianshulu. The sign also notes that the next fuel stop along this road is at Linyanti, 122km away.

Continuing towards Katima the road becomes busier, with more people around. About 40km from Katima there is a collection of people selling wooden elephants, which is worth a stop if you have the time.

Kwando River area

The southern border of eastern Caprivi is defined rather indistinctly along the line of the Kwando, the Linyanti and the Chobe rivers. These are actually the same river in different stages. The Kwando comes south from Angola, meets the

Kalahari's sands, and forms a swampy region of reedbeds and waterways called the Linyanti swamps. (To confuse names further, locals refer to sections of the Kwando above Lianshulu as 'the Mashi'.)

These swamps form the core of Mamili National Park. In good years a river emerges from here, called the Linyanti, and flows northeast into Lake Liambezi. It starts again from the eastern side of Lake Liambezi, renamed the Chobe. This beautiful river has a short course before it is swallowed into the mighty Zambezi, which continues over the Victoria Falls, through Lake Kariba, and eventually discharges into the Indian Ocean.

To explore any of these areas on your own, ensure that you have the relevant 1:250,000 maps from the Surveyor General (Nos 1723, 1724, 1823 and 1824), a compass and the normal tourist map of Namibia. Combine these with local guidance and you will find some interesting areas. The NWR has staff in Katima, who may be able to help you with specific information: tel: 0677 3027. If you are really heading off into Mamili, then you should have some back-up help (eg: a second 4WD vehicle) and a GPS might be very useful.

Kongola

Though a large dot on most maps, this is a small settlement. About 7km east of the B8 bridge over the Kwando, there is a large Engen fuel station (incorporating a little post office and shop) at the main road's junction with the D3511. Nearby is **Mashi Crafts**, a local community craft centre selling curios made by the local Kxoe community. It specialises in traditional baskets, beadwork, and East Caprivian reed mats and carvings. The centre is open Monday to Friday from May to July, and on Monday, Wednesday and Friday during the rest of the year.

From here the D3511 heads south past a number of lodges that line the Kwando River, passing deep inside Mudumu National Park, and skirting Mamili, before turning back towards Katima. About 126km from the B8 turn-off is the village of Linyanti, where there's often petrol available, and it is then a further 90km or so back to Katima.

A few kilometres west of the Engen station is a turn-off south to Mazambala Island Lodge, and beyond that is a large, new bridge over the Kwando – tangible proof, in tar and concrete, that the Caprivi is regarded as a major trade artery of the future.

Susuwe Triangle area

To the west of the Kwando River and the east of the Caprivi Game Park is a narrow triangle of land. It is wide in the north, but becomes narrower towards the Botswana border. It is known as 'the triangle', 'the Susuwe Triangle' or 'the Golden Triangle', and though outside any current park, it is rich in game.

To explore this you'll need a 4WD, and some detailed maps. Before you start, turn north from the western end of the Kongola Bridge, following the sign to 'Information at Susuwe'. About 3km along this road is the NWR rangers' station. You must check in here and obtain permission before entering the area, and it's also wise to ask their advice on what you plan to do. There's also a bush airstrip here.

One of the most popular spots is Nambwe Campsite, 14km south of the main road, on the western bank of the Kwando. (The turn-off is opposite the turning north to Susuwe.) Just follow the track from near the bridge that runs south, parallel to the river. It has no facilities, but plenty of game.

Well worth visiting is Horseshoe Lagoon, about 5km south of Nambwe, which is a stunning ox-bow lake with excellent game. Note that there is no camping allowed here.

Where to stay

There are several lodges based on the eastern bank of the Kwando River – some are just campsites, others are much more comfortable. Some use the Susuwe Triangle area, and the eastern end of the Caprivi Game Park (now often called the Bwabwata National Park), for their game activities. The choice is:

Mazambala Island Lodge (4 twin chalets) PO Box 1935, Ngweze–Katima Mulilo; tel/fax: 066 250405, cell: 081 2511471
Mazambala opened in June '97, but closed for a while. Now it's back, the closest lodge to the main road. Its turn-off, a few kilometres east of the Kongola Bridge, leads about 4km south, along a dirt road. The lodge has a bar and dining area, and four simple thatched chalets. Each is small with netting windows, twin beds, nice fabrics, and an en-suite shower and toilet. Candles and a torch are provided, as there's no electricity anywhere. It also has several private campsites.
Rates: N$180/150 per person single/sharing, including breakfast. Camping N$30 per person.

Open Skies Campsite P Bag 1072, Ngweze–Katima Mulilo; tel/fax: 0677 2029. Alternatively PO Box 1791, Otjiwarongo; tel: 0651 4131; fax: 0651 4132
Open Skies Campsite is signposted 26km south of the Katima–Kongola road, along the D3511, and then 3km west from that. It has a few simple shades under which you can eat and drink, and its caretakers have been very helpful and pleasant whenever visited, but the owner has never been around.
Rates: Camping N$35 per person.

Susuwe Island Lodge (6 double chalets) PO Box 70378, Bryanston 2021, South Africa; tel: +27 11 706 7207; fax: +27 11 463 8251; email: info@impalila.co.za; web: www.islandsinafrica.com
Built, owned and run by the team responsible for Impalila Island Lodge (see page 483), Susuwe was constructed with impressive faith at a time of great uncertainty over the Caprivi's future for tourism. It's certainly the area's best lodge. Many fly in to Susuwe, but if you're driving then turn south at the Kongola filling station, and after 6km take a right, signposted to Kubunyana Camp. After 4km of sandy track, you'll have to leave your vehicle at Kubunyana and transfer by boat to the lodge.
   Susuwe has six large brick-and-thatch chalets complete with en-suite bathroom, bedroom and lounge. The canopied beds have mosquito nets, and electricity to power ceiling fans and even hairdryers. Outside each the wooden veranda contains a tiny private plunge pool.
   Activities include game drives, night drives, boating trips, birding walks and picnics in the bush.
Rates: US$195 per person (single or sharing) from Dec to Mar, US$275/355 per person single/sharing from Apr to Nov. Includes all meals, drinks, laundry and activities.

Kubunyana Camp Book via IRDNC in Katima Mulilo (tel: 066 252518; fax: 066 252108). See page 463 and www.nacobta.com.na for more details.
One of the Caprivi's community-run campsites, Kubunyana is reached by turning south from the Golden Highway at the Kongola filling station. After 6km the camp is signposted to the right, and you'll reach it a further 4km along that track.
   Kubunyana has three large pre-erected tents under thatched shade covers, with basic beds but no linen, and four private camping pitches. There's also a communal kitchen, and ablution block with flush toilets and hot showers. There's no food available, and you need to bring your own drinking water.
Rates: N$70 per person for the tents, N$35 for camping. Canoes are available for N$25 per person, and guides can be hired for N$30 per game drive.

Namushasha Lodge (15 chalets) PO Box 21182, Windhoek; tel: 061 240375; fax: 061 256598; email: afrideca@mweb.com.na; web: www.namibialodges.com
Standing above the Kwando, Namushasha overlooks the Caprivi Game Park. It is well signposted, 16km off the B8 along the D3511, and then 4km west off that, along its own drive. (The final kilometre of this is over a sandy ridge; saloon cars need to be driven carefully.)

Namushasha's two-person chalets all have en-suite facilities, as well as mosquito nets and netted windows with roll blinds. These are functional, although far from stylish. There's a comfortable bar/lounge area, partly under thatch, and a separate dining room, all overlooking the river and park beyond. Nearby is a large splash pool, with dugout canoes modified into poolside seats, surrounded by well-watered green lawns.

Activities include boat trips and game drives. More energetic visitors will also appreciate a self-guided walking trail that circles the riverbank near camp, extending about 2.5km. Namushasha is a good camp, although its rooms could easily be better. Note that it allows day visitors for lunch, game drives and boat trips.

Rates: single N$525, double N$860, including breakfast. Dinner N$86 per person. Game drive N$80.

Mudumu National Park

The more northerly of the region's two new reserves, Mudumu, covers 850km² of riverine forest south of Kongola, either side of the D3511. Bordered by the Kwando River on the west, the reserve has good populations of a large variety of animals. Together with Mamili and the Triangle, Mudumu is notable for its buffalo (otherwise uncommon in Namibia), roan and sable antelope (both generally uncommon species), the water-loving lechwe and sitatunga, and often large herds of elephant.

Mudumu can be explored on foot or by 4WD, though don't expect much organisation or many clearly marked game drives. To stay here, the choice is either an unfenced campsite with river water and basic sanitation, Nakatwa Nature Conservation Camp, or one of the lodges by the river. If you opt to camp, then follow the signs to the camp and note that the reserve, which is not fenced or clearly demarcated, borders on to hunting areas. Ask the scouts *exactly* where the boundaries are.

Mamili Reserve

This unfenced swampland reserve of about 350km² was created shortly before independence and consists largely of marshland, veined by a network of reed-lined channels. It includes two large islands: Nkasa and Lupala. Together with Mudumu National Park, it has the vast majority of Namibia's population of sitatunga, red lechwe and puku.

Mamili is located in the southwest corner of the eastern Caprivi Strip, where the Kwando sharply changes direction to become the Linyanti. As yet there are no facilities for visitors and few passable roads, even with a 4WD. The NWR issues camping permits, so check with them for the latest information and buy one before you leave Windhoek or Katima Mulilo.

Approaching along the D3511, the turn off to Mamili National Park is at Sangwali village. This community, together with the nearby villages of Samudono and Nongozi, are in the process of setting up a conservancy in their area just outside the park, and plan to develop a simple campsite there. There is already a small craft stall, Sheshe Crafts, about 4km from the D3511 as you head into Mamili. This sells locally produced baskets, carvings, reed mats and some very authentic fishing traps.

If you really want to see Mamili, and don't have a small expedition, then the easiest way is probably to stay on the other side of the river, in one of several exclusive camps in Botswana. Selinda, Linyanti, DumaTau and King's Pool are all in this area, overlooking the park from Botswana.

Where to stay

Some of the camps beside the Susuwe Triangle will run trips into Mudumu, but there is one long-standing camp within the park:

Lianshulu Main Lodge (11 chalets) PO Box 142, Katima Mulilo. Reservations: PO Box 90391, Windhoek; tel: 061 254317; fax: 061 254980; email: lianshul@mweb.com.na; web: www.lianshulu.com.na

Lianshulu was one of Namibia's first private lodges to be built inside a national park. In the 1970s there was an old hunting lodge here but, when Mudumu Reserve was created in 1990, the lodge was taken over and gradually made it one of the country's best lodges. It's since faded from those dizzy heights, but remains a good lodge.

The lodge stands on the banks of the Kwando River, about 5km down a good bush track off the D3511, 40km from the B8 turn-off. Accommodation at the main lodge is in one of 11 thatched A-frame bungalows, complete with en-suite facilities, a veranda overlooking the river, and lots of space. Meals are normally eaten together with the managers and guides in the dining-room/bar area.

Excursions vary from game walks and drives through Mudumu, to exploring the river's channels afloat.

Rates: N$1,390/1,740per person sharing/single including all meals, drinks and activities.

Lianshulu Bush Lodge (8 chalets) see the Main Lodge, above, for contact details
The Bush Lodge is essentially a slightly smaller version of the main lodge, and is built about 16km downstream. I'm told that this has been booked solidly for the whole year by an American tour company, OAT, so don't expect it to be accepting individuals. When available again, its rates should be the same as the main lodge.

Lizauli Traditional Village

This small village is well signposted on the D3511, just to the north of Lianshulu, and is an important attraction for visitors. N$20 is charged as an entrance fee, and visitors are guided around the village where traditional arts and crafts are being practised. Aside from the fascination of the actual attractions – an iron forge, a grain store, and various carvers and basket weavers – a visit here gives a good opportunity to sit down and talk to some local people about their way of life. This is just one of several important community projects in this area.

Conservation projects

The solution tried here is simple: to link the success of the lodge and the national park with direct economic benefits for the local community, and thus to promote conservation of the local wildlife.

The problem with many national parks in Africa has been that the surrounding local communities feel little benefit from the tourists. However, they are affected by the park's animals, which raid their crops and kill their livestock. Thus the game animals are regarded as pests, and killed for their meat and skins whenever possible.

In the Mudumu area the need to involve the communities in conservation is being directly addressed in at least four projects: the community game-guard scheme, the bed-night levy, the Lizauli Traditional Village, and the thatching grass project.

The first employs game-guards, recruited from the local villages, to stem poaching and educate about conservation. They are paid by grants from the US, WWF and Namibia's own Endangered Wildlife Trust.

Secondly, there is a nominal charge per bed-night on the reserve's visitors (already included in Lianshulu's prices) which goes directly to the communities most affected by the park. This aims to compensate for any loss of crops or stock caused by wild animals, and show that the wildlife can be of direct financial benefit to the local people.

Thirdly, Lizauli Traditional Village is an attraction by which the local people themselves can earn money directly from visitors. This inevitably depends upon the flow of visitors through the reserve. Thus more animals should mean more visitors and hence more income for the village – so the local people benefit financially if the area's wildlife is preserved.

Finally, in 1994 Grant from Lianshulu started a scheme to transport thatching grass from the area further south, where there is a strong demand for its use in thatching new safari lodges and chalets. Drive down the D3511 during the late dry season to see the success of this. Now people will come from all over Namibia to buy grass from the roadside here. The local communities all collect and bundle it, knowing that there's plenty of demand and it will sell. It is, of course, a truly sustainable resource, which can only be produced if the local communities continue to conserve the environment.

Katima Mulilo

Established originally by the British in 1935, Katima is the regional capital of the eastern Caprivi. It replaced the old German centre of Schuckmannsburg, which now consists of just a police post, a clinic and a few huts. Collectors of trivia note that the taking of Schuckmannsburg, on September 22 1914, was the first allied occupation of German territory during World War I.

Katima is a large town with good facilities, beautifully placed on the banks of the Zambezi. There is an open central square, dotted with trees and lined with useful places like the Katima Supermarket, the Ngwezi bottle stall, and the Ngwezi post office.

Recently, as western Zambia has started to open up, Katima has taken on the role of frontier town: a base for supplies and communication for the new camps on the Upper Zambezi River in Zambia. It has just a little of the wild-west air that Maun used to have a decade ago, when it was remote and the hub of the Okavango's safari industry.

Getting there
By air
About 18km west of town is the M'Pacha airport. This receives the odd private flight for Lianshulu or Namushasha, and several services a week from Air Namibia. These call at Windhoek and Katima Mulilo, before continuing to Victoria Falls. Flights from Katima to Windhoek cost N$1,140.

By road
Katima is about 69km from the Ngoma border post, and with only one road through the Caprivi Strip, hitching, at least as far as Grootfontein or Kasane in Botswana, is relatively easy. Lifts to Victoria Falls and Etosha have also been reported.

The Intercape Mainliner bus from Victoria Falls to Windhoek stops in the square at 12.10 on Wednesday and Sunday, and on its return to Victoria Falls on Monday and Friday at 11.55.

To and from Zambia
To reach the Zambian border, continue west past the Zambezi Lodge until the tar turns left towards Rundu. Instead of following it, continue straight on to a gravel

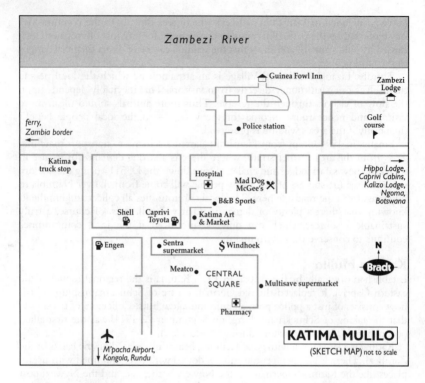

road for about 6km, passing the (unpleasant) rubbish dump. The border post here at Wenella opens 06.00–18.00 every day.

Sesheke, the small Zambian settlement near the border, is split in half by the Zambezi. Either side makes Katima look like a thriving metropolis in comparison. Namibian dollars can usually be changed into Zambian kwacha here (try the green building with the Coca-Cola sign, opposite the Chuma Kweseka grocers), before continuing on the long gravel road north to Ngonye Falls and ultimately to Mongu.

Getting organised

For those needing **car repairs**, Katima Toyota is next to the Caltex garage, just off the square. Just behind the square you will find the **Air Namibia** office, and the Butchy-Butchy **bakery** which sells good fresh bread.

The **Windhoek Bank** here even has an auto teller, but don't expect foreign credit cards to work. Note that none of the banks in Katima are good at dealing with Zambian currency; they usually refuse to either buy or sell kwacha. For this you will usually need to cross the border and exchange currency with local traders on the Zambian side.

Where to stay

Zambezi Lodge (27 twin/double rooms) PO Box 98, Katima Mulilo; tel: 066 253203; fax: 066 253631; email: katima@iafrica.com.na
Zambezi Lodge is a few hundred metres off the main road as it enters Katima from Ngoma. It is the area's best hotel, boasting a swimming pool, restaurant and even a floating bar (which closes lamentably early).

Flame trees and bougainvillaea line the lodge's drive, while to your right is the town's golf course. Inside, the hotel is bright, efficient and has expanded considerably since it began. It caters mainly for visitors who stop for a night, and though the service at its open-air restaurant is sharp and attentive, its chefs seem too used to mass catering to produce anything outstanding. But there's always a swim in the floodlit pool, or even a sauna, to make you feel better.

The rooms are spread out east in a long row along the river. The nearer rooms have been refurbished in a modern, quite German, style. Tiled floors and walls throughout, en-suite toilet/shower, basic AC, minimalist desk and chair, direct-dial phone and tea/coffee-making facilities. They are quite large and comfortable, with a wide double patio door overlooking the river. Family rooms are available, but of a much lower standard. We are assured that they are due to be refurbished soon.

The Zambezi Lodge is pleasant, efficient and ideal for a one-night stop. However, its activities are limited to short cruises on the river, and it lacks the character or activities to entice visitors to stay longer.

Rates: N$260 single, N$160 per person sharing, including breakfast.

Hippo Lodge (23 twin rooms) PO Box 1120; tel: 067352 685

Situated east of town (and just beyond the turn to Caprivi Cabins), Hippo Lodge opened in 1989 and is 2km off the main road. It has some of the lushest gardens in Namibia and a gaggle of aggressive geese, which don't reflect the lodge's relaxed atmosphere at all. This is a very laidback place.

Hippo's rooms are carpeted, with brick walls and thatched roof. All are built in a line overlooking the river, with a couple of chairs in front of each. The rooms have en-suite shower and toilet, mosquito nets and fans – perfectly adequate, but slightly dingy and in need of sprucing up.

Basic meals are available, and there is a pool to swim in, surrounded by green lawns and colourful herbaceous borders. Canoes are available for residents to explore the river, at their own risk.

Rates: N$180 single, N$130 per person sharing, N$340 for a family room taking four. Includes breakfast. Camping is also available for N$20 per person.

Guinea Fowl Inn Tel: 0677 3349

This seedy hotel is easily found by following the 'guinea fowl' signs behind the back of the police station, just west of the Zambezi Lodge.

Guinea Fowl Inn has a lovely situation, with its back facing lawns which slope down to the Zambezi. Unfortunately, its small rooms have thin, prefabricated walls, and often separate showers or baths. Mosquito nets and fans are provided, but little else. There is a simple restaurant here serving breakfast, lunch and dinner, to the lower end of the local market, and the odd budget traveller who has no camping equipment.

Though this inn has changed hands several times in the last few years, it has improved little. It still gives the impression that rooms may be hired by the hour.

Rates: N$110 single, N$70 per person sharing, including breakfast.

Caprivi Cabins (8 chalets) PO Box 2029, Ngwezi–Katima Mulilo; tel: 066 252288 or 252295; fax: 066 253158

Run by Trix van der Spuy, and well-signposted about 800m off the main road just east of the Zambezi Lodge, Caprivi Cabins opened over six years ago, and remains very good value. Outside its thatched chalets are set in inviting lawn areas. Inside the chalets have cool stone floors, twin beds with quilts, stocked minibar/fridges, clean tiled bathrooms, and even direct-dial telephones. The lodge seems to welcome children, offering to set up small igloo tents outside the chalets of parents.

Locals in Katima have discovered the cuisine on offer here, which is served in a large dining area with high thatched ceiling, TV, bar, and a captivating fish tank. (For evening meals starters are around N$15, main courses about N$40–50 for steaks with chips and vegetables.) So don't expect the place all to yourself.

For most of the year there is also the option of an open thatched area with tables overlooking the Zambezi. The energetic can use the small gym and plunge pool, or allow Trix to arrange fishing trips on the river, using the small twin-engined boat that is moored at the cabins. Caprivi Cabins is a super place to stop, provided its standards remain as high.

Rates: N$200 single, N$250 double, breakfast N$20 extra per person.

Zambezi Lodge camping PO Box 98; tel: 0677 3203; fax: 0677 3631
At present, campers can stay on the west side of the lodge for N$25 per person. With the lodge expanding, it was anticipated that the camping area would soon move, perhaps to where the golf club is now. In any case, expect to find some camping facilities somewhere around the Zambezi Lodge ...

Kalizo Restcamp (8 chalets, 3 rooms and camping) PO Box 1854, Ngweze–Katima Mulilo; tel/fax: 066 252 802; email: kalizo@mighty.co.za or bruno@iway.na; web: www.bruno.iway.na or www.natron.net/kalizo
Kalizo Restcamp is family-run and stands on the banks of the Zambezi, about 25km downstream from Katima. To reach it, drive 13km from Katima towards Ngoma (about 56km from Ngoma), until Kalizo is clearly signposted off left. Then follow the signs for an increasingly sandy 5km – inexperienced drivers may need a high-clearance vehicle.

Scattered around lovely green lawns, Kalizo's eight twin-bed thatched chalets are of an unusual octagonal design. They are well furnished and comfortable (one is a self-catering chalet, with cooking facilities), with reed mats, mosquito-netted windows and nice fabrics. Some of the chalets have en-suite facilities; others share separate, well-kept toilets and showers.

There's always a bar open and meals are arranged on request. Much of the restcamp's *raison d'être* seems to be tiger-fishing, and boats can be hired for N$70 per hour, or N$300 for a full day, including a guide and fuel. If you haven't brought your own equipment, then add N$25 per person per day. Those who have will be pleased that there's a good slipway. Other activities include birding and quad biking, while trips further afield can be organised as well. Kalizo makes a super sojourn if you have a 4WD and love fishing, but isn't the easiest or most comfortable stop for a trip with a normal 2WD vehicle.

Rates: single N$220, N$200 per person sharing, full board. N$390 per person including all meals and fishing activities. Camping N$20 per person.

Where to eat
If you are staying in Katima Mulilo, then you'll probably eat at your lodge. Those who are just passing through might also consider:

The Golf Club Close to the Zambezi Lodge, this serves breakfast, lunch, dinner and drinks. It is conveniently next to the place where the lodge's new campsite is likely to be.
Zambezi take-away and mini-market In the centre of town, near the stadium, this serves a wide range of snacks, pies and pre-prepared sandwiches.
Mad Dog McGee's (aka SOS club) PO Box 70, Katima Mulilo; tel/fax: 0677 2021
Tucked away down a side street, between the Zambezi Lodge and the main town shopping centre, Mad Dog McGee's appears reactionary at first. However, it's the busiest bar and restaurant in this frontier town, and attracts safari operators who come to Katima for supplies, as well as an assortment of interesting bush characters and travellers.
Good lunches and dinners are served every day except Sunday, steaks and burgers being the house speciality, though vegetarian travellers might just use the swimming pool, pool tables and bar – and eat elsewhere.

What to see and do

Katima has few intrinsic attractions, although the lodges along the Zambezi are very pleasant places to stay. If you do have time here, then use it for trips on the river, or as a base for longer expeditions into Mudumu, Mamili, the Upper Zambezi and Lake Liambezi.

Although closed when I last visited, the **Caprivi Arts Centre** (Olifant Street, Ngweze–Katima Mulilo, tel: 0677 3378) is a good outlet for the many local crafts and well worth visiting.

Lake Liambezi

This large, shallow lake is located between the Linyanti and Chobe rivers, about 60km south of Katima Mulilo. When full, it covers some 10,000ha, although it has been dry (something of a dustbowl) since 1985. People and cattle now populate its bed.

Lake Liambezi's main source of water used to be the River Linyanti, but after this has filtered through the swamps it seems unable to fill the lake, even in recent years of good rain. However, next time the Zambezi is in flood it may be able fill the lake either via the Bukalo Channel, which runs southwest from the river to the lake, or even via the Chobe River – which can actually reverse its flow.

There is one new community campsite planned in this area (page 485), in the new Salambala Conservancy.

Zambezi-Chobe confluence

Two rivers bound the eastern end of the Caprivi Strip: the Chobe to the south, and the Zambezi to the north. Their confluence is at the end of Impalila Island, at the eastern tip of Namibia. The Zambezi flows relentlessly to the sea but, depending on their relative heights, the Chobe either contributes to that, or may even reverse its flow and draw water from the Zambezi. Between the two rivers is a triangle of land, of about 700km², which is a mixture of floodplains, islands and channels which link the two rivers.

This swampy, riverine area is home to several thousand local people, mostly members of Zambia's Lozi tribe. (The main local languages here are Lozi and Sobia.) Most have a seasonal lifestyle, living next to the river channels, fishing and farming maize, sorghum, pumpkins and keeping cattle. They move with the water levels, transferring on to higher, drier ground as the waters rise.

Flora and fauna

The area's ecosystems are similar to those in the upper reaches of the Okavango Delta: deep-water channels lined by wide reedbeds and rafts of papyrus. Some of the larger islands are still forested with baobabs, water figs, knobthorn, umbrella thorn, mopane, pod mahogany, star chestnut and sickle-leafed albizia, while jackalberry and Chobe waterberry overhang the rivers, festooned with creepers and vines.

Because of hunting by the local population, large mammals are scarce. Most that do occur come over from Botswana's Chobe National Park. Elephants and buffalo sometimes swim over, and even lion have been known to swim across into Namibia in search of the tasty-but-dim domestic cattle kept there.

Even when there are no large mammals here, the birdlife is spectacular. Large flocks of white-faced ducks congregate on islands in the rivers, African skimmers nest on exposed sandbanks, and both reed cormorants and darters are seen fishing or perching while they dry their feathers. Kingfishers are numerous, from the giant to the tiny pygmy, as are herons and egrets. However,

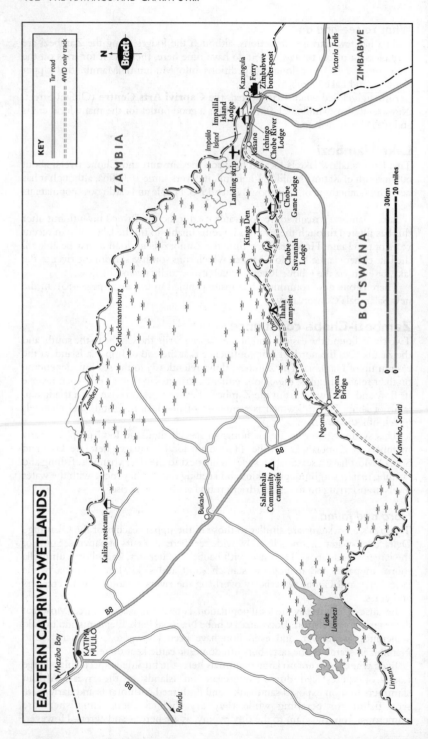

EASTERN CAPRIVI'S WETLANDS

KEY

———— Tar road
= = = = 4WD only track

N

Bradt

ZAMBIA

Kazungula
Ferry
Zimbabwe
border-post

→ Victoria Falls

ZIMBABWE

Impalila
Island

Impalila Island
Lodge

Landing strip

Kasane

Ichingo
Chobe River
Lodge

Chobe
Game Lodge

Kings Den

Chobe
Savannah Lodge

BOTSWANA

Schuckmannsburg

Zambezi

Ihaha campsite

Ngoma
Bridge

Ngoma

→ Kavimba, Savuti

B8

Salambala
Community
campsite

Bukalo

Kalizo restcamp

B8

→ Maziba Bay

KATIMA
MULILO

B8

→ Rundu

Lake
Liambezi

Linyanti

30km

20 miles

the area's most unusual bird is the unassuming rock pratincole with its black, white and grey body, which perches on the rocks of rapids, between hawking for insects in the spray.

Where to stay

The largest island in this area, Impalila Island, is at the very tip of Namibia. It gained notoriety during the '80s as a military base for the SADF (South African Defence Forces), as it was strategically positioned within sight of Botswana, Zambia and Zimbabwe. It still boasts a 1,300m-long runway of smooth tar, but now its barracks are a secondary school, serving most of the older children in the area.

There is a customs and immigration post on Impalila, which opens from 07.00 to 17.00. The lodges here all use this, and are usually reached by a short boat transfer from Kasane in Botswana.

Impalila Island Lodge (8 double chalets) PO Box 70378, Bryanston 2021, South Africa; tel: (27) 11 706 7207; fax: (27) 11 463 8251; email: info@impalila.co.za; web: www.islandsinafrica.com

Situated on the northwest side of Impalila Island, overlooking the Zambezi's Mowomba rapids, Impalila Lodge has in many ways brought the island to people's attention.

Accommodation is in one of eight wooden chalets, each with twin beds or a king-size double. Opened in 1994, it is fairly luxurious. Much is made of polished local *mukwa* wood, with its natural variegated yellow and brown colours. The raised-up chalets have a square design, enclosing a bathroom in one corner, giving blissfully warm showers from instant water heaters. Below the high thatch ceilings are fans for warmer days, and mosquito nets for most nights. Large adjacent double doors open from one corner of the room on to a wide wooden veranda, overlooking the rapids. These doors have an optional mosquito-net screen for when it's hot, though are more usually glass. Being next to the river can be quite cold on winter mornings.

Activities at Impalila include guided motor-boat trips on the Zambezi and Chobe: the Zambezi mainly for birdwatching and fishing, while the more distant Chobe also offers remarkable game viewing on the edge of Botswana's Chobe National Park. Mokoro trips explore the shallower channels, and even run the gentle rapids, whilst guided and independent walks are possible on the island. Superb fishing (especially for tiger-fish, best caught on a fly-rod) is all year round, and the guides are relaxed enough to take beginners or experts out to try their luck.

The main part of the lodge is a large thatched lounge/dining area built around two huge baobabs, including a pool table and comfortable couches. This is open to the breeze, though can be sheltered when cold. The wooden pool deck has reclining loungers, umbrellas, and a great view of the river. Impalila's food is excellent and candle-lit three- or four-course meals around the baobab make a memorable scene. It is a stylish, well-run lodge ideal for fishing, birding, or just relaxing, with the added bonus of game viewing from the river in Chobe.

Rates: single €355, €275 per person sharing, including all meals and activities. Open: all year.

Ichingo Chobe River Lodge (7 twin-bed tents) PO Box 55, Kasane, Botswana; tel/fax: +267 6250143 (on island); fax: +267 6250223 (in Kasane town); cell: +267 713 02439; email: ichingo@iafrica.com; web: www.ichingo.com

First set up in '93, Ichingo was the idea of Dawn and Ralph Oxenham. Ralph was originally working in Livingstone, when they both embarked upon their own canoe trip from Katima Mulilo to Livingstone for one holiday. Dawn overturned her canoe in the Muwomba rapids and, exhausted and frustrated, ended up staying on the island where she had scrambled ashore. That was Impalila Island, and the inspiration for starting a lodge here.

BATTLE FOR AN ISLAND

The precise boundary between Namibia and Botswana in this area has been defined to follow the deepest channel of the Chobe River – a kind of definition which works well for most river boundaries. However, the Chobe splits into many streams, whose strengths and depths seem to gradually alter over the years.

Kasikili Island is a small, very low, flat island that is frequently flooded and used mainly for grazing cattle. It was generally regarded as South West African and then Namibian territory. However, around the time of Namibian independence, it was annexed by Botswana, which calls it Sidulu Island and claims that it is south of the river's deepest channel.

Recently, it has been occupied by the BDF (Botswana Defence Force) who have built several watchtowers on it – chunky structures towering over the island's grassy plains, and cunningly disguised with a variegated military-pattern netting. The dispute has been referred to the international court in The Hague.

Initially managers ran Ichingo, but in '96 Dawn and Ralph decided to refurbish and run it themselves. It stands on the south side of Impalila, just east of the Cresta Mowana and a few kilometres from Kasane. It overlooks the quiet backwaters of some of the Chobe River's rapids, and there is no noise from the mainland.

Ichingo's accommodation is walk-in Meru tents, which are more rustic than Impalila's chalets. The shower/basin/toilet are en suite, at the back under thatch, and there's a balcony at the front, overlooking the river through thick vegetation.

Activities include game viewing, birdwatching and fishing from motor-boat trips, mokoro excursions, fly-fishing in rapids, and walks around the island and along nearby floodplains. Unusually for a bush lodge, the camp actively welcomes children, even when not accompanied by adults, as craft activities can usually be organised for them.

Ichingo's large thatched bar and dining areas overlook rapids on Chobe River, and this relaxed, rustic camp makes a super base for river trips and game-viewing from boats along the Chobe River.

Rates: single US$220, US$200 per person sharing, including all meals, drinks and activities. Open: all year.

Zambezi Queen & King's Den Lodge PO Box 98, Katima Mulilo; tel/fax: +267 650814 (Botswana); tel/fax 066 253 203 (Namibia); email: katima@iafrica.com.na
King's Den (10 twin-bed chalets by water, 5 on land thatched) PO Box 98, Katima Mulilo; tel: 0677 3203; fax: 0677 3631
Owned by the owners of Zambezi Lodge in Katima, King's Den overlooks the Chobe National Park. It is reached by taking a boat west from Kasane, and is nearer to this park than either of Impalila Island's lodges. However, it is larger than them, as in addition to its 10 chalets, there is a 13-cabin riverboat, the *Zambezi Queen*, anchored (some say stuck) there. So while its site has potential, King's Den fails to provide the intimate 'small-lodge' experience of Impalila or Ichingo.

Rates: single N$1,000, N$800 per person sharing, including all meals and activities.

Ngoma border

The conversion of the gravel road from Katima to Ngoma into tar has been taking years. When you reach Ngoma, there's little there apart from the border post, a smart office next to the bridge by the Chobe River. About 2km further on, over the river, Botswana's border post is a newer building perched high above the water. Both seem efficient, pleasant, and generally quiet. This crossing is fine for 2WD vehicles, and opens 06.00–18.00.

Beyond is a good gravel road to Kasane, which cuts through the Chobe National Park, or a choice of slower more scenic routes. One leads to Kasane, for game viewing along the Chobe riverfront; the other heads through forested and communal lands towards Savuti and Maun. Both the scenic options require park permits and a 4WD vehicle.

Salambala Community Campsite The turn-off for Salambala, off the main B8, is about 15km north of Ngoma or 46km south of Katima Mulilo. This is another of the Caprivi's excellent community campsites. It has three separate pitches for tents and a fourth better suited to larger groups, each with a private flush toilet and a shower with hot water. All profits from this camp go back to the community.
Rates: N$25 per person.

Bradt Travel Guides

Africa by Road Charlie Shackell & Illya Bracht
Albania Gillian Gloyer
Amazon, The Roger Harris/Peter Hutchison
Antarctica: A Guide to the Wildlife
Tony Soper/Dafila Scott
Arctic: A Guide to Coastal Wildlife
Tony Soper/Dan Powell
Armenia with Nagorno Karabagh Nicholas Holding
Azores David Sayers
Baghdad Mini Guide Catherine Arnold
Baltic Capitals: Tallinn, Riga, Vilnius, Kaliningrad Neil Taylor et al
Bosnia & Herzegovina Tim Clancy
Botswana: Okavango, Chobe, Northern Kalahari
Chris McIntyre
British Isles: Wildlife of Coastal Waters
Tony Soper/Dan Powell
Cambodia Anita Sach
Cameroon Ben West
Canada: North – Yukon, Northwest Territories, Nunavut Geoffrey Roy
Cape Verde Islands Aisling Irwin/
Colum Wilson
Cayman Islands Tricia Hayne
Chile & Argentina: Trekking Guide
Tim Burford
China: Yunnan Province Stephen Mansfield
Croatia Piers Letcher
East & Southern Africa: The Backpacker's Manual Philip Briggs
Eccentric America Jan Friedman
Eccentric Britain Benedict le Vay
Eccentric Edinburgh Benedict le Vay
Eccentric France Piers Letcher
Eccentric London Benedict le Vay
Ecuador: Climbing & Hiking in
Rob Rachowiecki/Mark Thurber
Ecuador, Peru & Bolivia: The Backpacker's Manual Kathy Jarvis
Eritrea Edward Denison/Edward Paice
Estonia Neil Taylor
Ethiopia Philip Briggs
Falkland Islands Will Wagstaff
Gabon, São Tome & Principe Sophie Warne
Galápagos Wildlife David Horwell/Pete Oxford
Gambia, The Craig Emms/Linda Barnett
Georgia Tim Burford
Ghana Philip Briggs
Iran Patricia L Baker
Iraq Karen Dabrowska
Kabul Mini Guide Dominic Medley/Jude Barrand

Kenya Claire Foottit
Latvia Stephen Baister/Chris Patrick
Lille Mini Guide Laurence Phillips
Lithuania Gordon McLachlan
London, In the Footsteps of the Famous
Nicholas Best
Macedonia Thammy Evans
Madagascar Hilary Bradt
Madagascar Wildlife Nick Garbutt/
Hilary Bradt/Derek Schuurman
Malawi Philip Briggs
Maldives Royston Ellis
Mali Ross Velton
Mauritius, Rodrigues & Réunion Royston Ellis/
Alex Richards/Derek Schuurman
Mongolia Jane Blunden
Montenegro Annalisa Rellie
Mozambique Philip Briggs/Ross Velton
Namibia Chris McIntyre
North Cyprus Diana Darke
North Korea Robert Willoughby
Palestine, with Jerusalem Henry Stedman
Paris, Lille & Brussels: Eurostar Cities
Laurence Phillips
Peru & Bolivia: Backpacking and Trekking
Hilary Bradt/Kathy Jarvis
River Thames, In the Footsteps of the Famous
Paul Goldsack
Rwanda Janice Booth/Philip Briggs
St Helena, Ascension, Tristan da Cunha
Sue Steiner
Seychelles Lyn Mair/Lynnath Beckley
Singapore John Nichol/Adrian Phillips/
Isobel Dorling
South Africa: Budget Travel Guide Paul Ash
Southern African Wildlife Mike Unwin
Spitsbergen Andreas Umbreit
Sri Lanka Royston Ellis
Switzerland: Rail, Road, Lake
Anthony Lambert
Tallinn Mini Guide Neil Taylor
Tanzania Philip Briggs
Tasmania Matthew Brace
Tibet Michael Buckley
Uganda Philip Briggs
Ukraine Andrew Evans
USA by Rail John Pitt
Venezuela Hilary Dunsterville Branch
Your Child's Health Abroad
Dr Jane Wilson-Howarth/Dr Matthew Ellis
Yunnan see *China*
Zambia Chris McIntyre
Zanzibar David Else

Bradt guides are available from bookshops or by mail order from:
Bradt Travel Guides, 19 High Street, Chalfont St Peter, Bucks SL9 9QE, England
Tel: 01753 893444 Fax: 01753 892333
Email: info@bradt-travelguides.com Web: www.bradtguides.com

Appendix 1

WILDLIFE GUIDE

This wildlife guide is designed in a manner that should allow you to name most large mammals that you see in Namibia. Less common species are featured under the heading *Similar species* beneath the animal to which they are most closely allied, or bear the strongest resemblance.

Cats and dogs

Lion *Panthera leo* Shoulder height 100–120cm. Weight 150–220kg.
Africa's largest predator, the lion is the animal that everybody hopes to see on safari. It is a sociable creature, living in prides of five to ten animals and defending a territory of between 20 and 200km². Lions often hunt at night, and their favoured prey is large or medium antelope such as wildebeest and impala. Most of the hunting is done by females, but dominant males normally feed first after a kill. Rivalry between males is intense and takeover battles are frequently fought to the death, so two or more males often form a coalition. Young males are forced out of their home pride at three years of age, and male cubs are usually killed after a successful takeover.

When not feeding or fighting, lions are remarkably indolent – they spend up to 23 hours of any given day at rest – so the anticipation of a lion sighting is often more exciting than the real thing. Lions naturally occur in any habitat, except desert or rainforest. They once ranged across much of the Old World, but these days they are all but restricted to the larger conservation areas in sub-Saharan Africa (one remnant population exists in India).

In Namibia, lions are occasionally reported in the Kaokoveld or in the central highlands, but Etosha and Caprivi's parks are the most reliable places to see them. Occasionally, they used to find their way down river valleys and take seals on the coast as prey. However, there are no reliable reports of this in recent years.

Leopard *Panthera pardus* Shoulder height 70cm. Weight 60–80kg.
The powerful leopard is the most solitary and secretive of Africa's big cats. It hunts at night, using stealth and power, often getting to within 5m of its intended prey before pouncing. If there are hyenas and lions around then leopards habitually move their kills up into trees to safeguard them. The leopard can be distinguished from the cheetah by its rosette-like spots, lack of black 'tearmarks' and more compact, low-slung, powerful build.

The leopard is the most common of Africa's large felines, yet a good sighting in the wild is extremely unusual – in fact there are many records of individuals living for years undetected in close proximity to humans. They occur everywhere apart from the desert, though they favour habitats with plenty of cover, like riverine woodlands and rocky kopjes. Namibia's central highlands are perfect for leopard, which are common on the farms there. Some lodges, like Okonjima, encourage sightings by offering them food.

Cheetah *Acynonix jubatus* Shoulder height 70–80cm. Weight 50–60kg.
This remarkable spotted cat has a greyhound-like build, and is capable of running at 70km per hour in bursts, making it the world's fastest land animal. Despite superficial similarities,

you can easily tell a cheetah from a leopard by the former's simple spots, disproportionately small head, streamlined build, diagnostic black tearmarks, and preference for relatively open habitats. It is often seen pacing the plains restlessly, either on its own or in a small family group consisting of a mother and her offspring. A diurnal hunter, cheetah favour the cooler hours of the day to hunt smaller antelope, like steenbok and duiker, and small mammals like scrub hares. Namibia probably has Africa's highest cheetah population – estimated at 25% of the world's population. This is largely due to the eradication of lion and spotted hyena

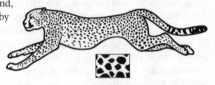

from large areas of commercial farmland, where cheetah are not usually regarded (by enlightened farmers) as a threat to cattle.

Etosha is Namibia's best park for cheetah in the wild, though there's probably a higher density of them on many farms.

Similar species: The **serval** (*Felis serval*) is smaller than a cheetah (shoulder height 55cm) but has a similar build and black-on-gold spots giving way to streaking near the head. Seldom seen, it is widespread and quite common in moist grassland, reedbeds and riverine habitats throughout Africa, including Owamboland, Etosha, Bushmanland and the Caprivi Strip. It preys on mice, rats and small mammals, but will sometimes take the young of small antelope.

Caracal (*Felis caracal*) Shoulder height 40cm. Weight 15–20kg.
The caracal resembles the European lynx with its uniform tan coat and tufted ears. It is a solitary hunter, feeding on birds, small antelope and young livestock. Found throughout the subcontinent, it thrives in Namibia's relatively arid savannah habitats, and occurs everywhere except the far western coastal strip of the Namib. It is nocturnal and rarely seen.

Similar species: The smaller **African wild cat** (*Felis sylvestris*) ranges from the Mediterranean to the Cape of Good Hope, and is similar in appearance to the domestic tabby cat. It has an unspotted torso, which should preclude confusion with the even smaller **small spotted cat** (*Felis nigripes*), a relatively rare resident of southeastern Namibia which has a more distinctively marked coat. Both species are generally solitary and nocturnal, often utilising burrows or termite mounds as daytime shelters. They prey upon reptiles, amphibians and birds as well as small mammals.

African wild dog *Lycaon pictus* Shoulder height 70cm. Weight 25kg.
Also known as the painted hunting dog, the wild dog is distinguished from other African dogs by its large size and mottled black, brown and cream coat. Highly sociable, living in

packs of up to 20 animals, wild dogs are ferocious hunters that literally tear apart their prey on the run. They are now threatened with extinction; the most endangered of Africa's great predators. This is the result of relentless persecution by farmers, who often view the dogs as dangerous vermin, and their susceptibility to diseases spread by domestic dogs. Wild dogs are now extinct in many areas where they were formerly abundant, like the Serengeti, and they are common nowhere. The global population of fewer than 3,000 is concentrated in southern Tanzania, Zambia, Zimbabwe, Botswana, South Africa and Namibia.

Wild dogs prefer open savannah with only sparse tree cover, if any, and packs have enormous territories, typically covering 400km² or more. They travel huge distances in search of prey and so few parks are large enough to contain them. In Namibia wild dogs are sometimes seen in Khaudum or on the Caprivi Strip. Botswana's nearby parks of Chobe and Moremi are one of their last strongholds, and so they certainly move across the border. Attempts to reintroduce them to Etosha have so far failed.

Black-backed jackal *Canis mesomelas* Shoulder height 35–45cm. Weight 8–12kg.

The black-backed jackal is an opportunistic feeder capable of adapting to most habitats. Most often seen singly or in pairs at dusk or dawn, it is ochre in colour with a prominent black saddle flecked by a varying amount of white or gold. It is probably the most frequently observed small predator in Africa south of the Zambezi, and its eerie call is a characteristic sound of the bush at night. It is found throughout Namibia, excluding the Caprivi Strip, and particularly common in Etosha, where it is frequently seen inside the restcamps at night, scavenging for scraps.

Similar species: The similar **side-striped jackal** (*Canis adustus*) is more cryptic in colour, and has an indistinct pale vertical stripe on each flank and a white-tipped tail. Nowhere very common; in Namibia it is found in the Caprivi Strip and occasionally Khaudum or Owamboland.

Bat-eared fox *Otocyon megalotis* Shoulder height 30–35cm. Weight 3–5kg.
This endearing small, silver-grey insectivore is unmistakable with its huge ears and black eye-mask. It is relatively common throughout Namibia, anywhere that the harvester termite is found. It is mostly nocturnal, but can sometimes be seen in pairs or small family groups during the cooler hours of the day, usually in dry open country. It digs well, and if seen foraging then it will often 'listen' to the ground (its ears operating like a radio-dish) whilst wandering around, before stopping to dig with its forepaws. As well as the termites, bat-eared foxes will eat lizards, gerbils, small birds, scorpions and beetle larvae.

Similar species: **The Cape fox** (*Vulpes chama*) is an infrequently seen dry-country predator which occurs throughout Namibia, but is absent from the Caprivi Strip. The Cape fox lacks the prominent ears and mask of the bat-eared fox, and its coat is a uniform sandy-grey colour. I once had a Cape fox approach me cautiously, after dusk, whilst camping at Bloedkoppie in the northern section of the Namib-Naukluft Park, but have never seen another.

Spotted hyena *Crocuta crocuta* Shoulder height 85cm. Weight 70kg.
Hyenas are characterised by their bulky build, sloping back, rough brownish coat, powerful jaws and dog-like expression. Contrary to popular myth, spotted hyenas are not exclusively scavengers; they are also adept hunters which hunt in groups and kill animals as large as wildebeests. Nor are they hermaphroditic, an ancient belief that stems from the false scrotum and penis covering the female hyena's vagina. Sociable animals, hyenas live in loosely structured clans of about ten animals, led by females who are stronger and larger than males, based in a communal den.

Hyenas utilise their kills far better than most predators, digesting the bones, skin and even teeth of antelope. This results in the distinctive white colour of their faeces – which is an easily identified sign of them living in an area.

The spotted hyena is the largest hyena, identified by its light-brown, blotchily spotted coat. It is found in the wetter areas of northern Namibia, most of the national parks and reserves devoted to game, and occasionally in eastern parts of the Namib Desert. Although mainly nocturnal, spotted hyenas can often be seen around dusk and dawn in protected areas like Etosha. Their distinctive, whooping calls are a spine-chilling sound of the African night.

Similar species: The secretive **brown hyena** (*Hyaena brunnea*) occurs in arid parts of Namibia, and has a shaggy, unmarked dark brown coat – not unlike a large, long-haired German shepherd dog. In contrast to the spotted hyena, brown hyenas tend to scavenge rather than hunt, and are generally solitary whilst doing so. They are the dominant carnivore in the drier areas of the Namib, and are even seen scavenging on the beaches and around seal colonies. Because of this, the local name for them is *strandwolf,* or beach-wolves.

Normally they forage for whatever they can, from small birds and mammals to the remains of kills and even marine organisms cast up upon the beaches. During drier, leaner periods they will eat vegetable as well as animal matter, and can go without water for long periods by eating nara melons.

Aardwolf *Proteles cristatus* Shoulder height 45–50cm. Weight 7–11kg.
With a tawny brown coat and dark, vertical stripes, this insectivorous hyena is not much bigger than a jackal and occurs in low numbers in most parts of Namibia. It is active mainly at night, gathering harvester termites, its principal food, with its wide, sticky tongue. These termites live underground (not in castle-like termite mounds) and come out at night to cut grass, and drag it back down with them.

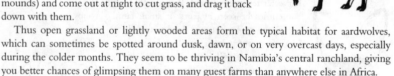

Thus open grassland or lightly wooded areas form the typical habitat for aardwolves, which can sometimes be spotted around dusk, dawn, or on very overcast days, especially during the colder months. They seem to be thriving in Namibia's central ranchland, giving you better chances of glimpsing them on many guest farms than anywhere else in Africa.

Primates
Chacma baboon *Papio cynocaphalus ursinus* Shoulder height 50–75cm. Weight 25–45kg.
This powerful terrestrial primate, distinguished from any other monkey by its much larger size, inverted 'U' shaped tail and distinctive dog-like head, is fascinating to watch from a behavioural perspective. It lives in large troops which boast a complex, rigid social structure characterised by a matriarchal lineage and plenty of inter-troop movement by males seeking social dominance. Omnivorous and at home in almost any habitat, the baboon is the most

widespread primate in Africa, frequently seen in most game reserves.

There are three African races, of which the chacma baboon is the only one occurring in Namibia. With a highly organised defence system, the only predator that seriously affects them is the leopard, which will try to pick them off at night, whilst they are roosting in trees or cliffs.

Vervet monkey *Cercopithecus aethiops* Length (excluding tail) 40–55cm. Weight 4–6kg.
Also known as the green or grivet monkey, the vervet is probably the world's most numerous monkey and certainly the most common and widespread representative of the *Cercopithecus* guenons, a taxonomically controversial genus associated with African forests. An atypical guenon in that it inhabits savannah and woodland rather than true forest, the vervet spends a high proportion of its time on the ground. In Namibia, it is found only around the narrow belts of woodland beside the Orange and Kunene rivers, and in the lush areas of Mahango and the Caprivi Strip.

The vervet's light grey coat, black face and white forehead band are distinctive – as are the male's garish blue genitals. The only animal that is even remotely similar is the baboon, which is much larger and heavier.

Vervets live in troops averaging about 25 animals. They are active during the day and roost in trees at night. They eat mainly fruit and vegetables, though are opportunistic and will take insects and young birds, and even raid tents at campsites (usually where ill-informed visitors have previously tempted them into human contact by offering food).

Lesser bushbaby *Galago senegalensis* Length (without tail) 17cm. Weight 150g.
The lesser bushbaby is the most widespread and common member of a group of small and generally indistinguishable nocturnal primates, distantly related to the lemurs of Madagascar. In Namibia they occur throughout the north, from northern Kaokoland and Etosha to Khaudum and the Caprivi Strip.

More often heard than seen, the lesser bushbaby is nocturnal but can sometimes be picked out by tracing a cry to a tree and shining a torch into the branches; its eyes reflect as two red dots. These eyes are designed to function in what we would describe as total darkness, and they feed on insects – some of which are caught in the air by jumping – and also eating sap from trees, especially acacia gum.

They inhabit wooded areas, and prefer acacia trees or riverine forests. I remember being startled whilst lighting a braai at Halali restcamp, in Etosha, by a small family of bushbabies. They raced through the trees above us, bouncing from branch to branch whilst chattering and screaming out of all proportion to their size.

Large antelope
Sable antelope *Hippotragus niger* Shoulder height 135cm. Weight 230kg.
The striking male sable is jet black with a distinct white face, underbelly and rump, and long decurved horns – a strong contender for the title of Africa's most beautiful antelope. The female is chestnut brown and has shorter horns, whilst the young are a lighter red-brown colour. Sable are found throughout the wetter areas of southern and East Africa. In Namibia, a thriving herd frequents the floodplain beside the Okavango River in Mahango National Park, and there are other groups further east in the Caprivi Strip's other parks.

Sable are normally seen in small herds: either bachelor herds of males, or breeding herds of females and young which are often accompanied by the dominant male in that territory. The breeding females drop their calves around February or March; the calf remaining hidden, away from the herd, for its first few weeks. Sable are mostly grazers, though will browse, especially when food is scarce. They need to drink at least every other day, and seem especially fond of low-lying dewy vleis in wetter areas.

Roan antelope *Hippotragus equinus* Shoulder height 120–150cm. Weight 250–300kg.

This handsome horse-like antelope is uniform fawn-grey with a pale belly, short decurved horns and a light mane. It could be mistaken for the female sable antelope, but this has a well-defined white belly, and lacks the roan's distinctive black-and-white facial markings. The roan is a relatively rare antelope; common almost nowhere in Africa (Malawi's Nyika Plateau being one obvious exception). In Namibia small groups of roan are found in Etosha, Waterberg, Khaudum and the Caprivi.

Roan need lots of space if they are to thrive and breed; they don't generally do well where game densities are high. Game farms prize them as one of the most valuable antelope (hence expensive to buy). They need access to drinking water, but are adapted to subsist on relatively high plateaux with poor soils.

Oryx or **gemsbok** *Oryx gazella* Shoulder height 120cm. Weight 230kg. This is the quintessential desert antelope; unmistakable with its ash-grey coat, bold black facial marks and flank strip, and unique long, straight horns. Of the three races of oryx in Africa, the gemsbok is the largest and most striking. It occurs throughout the Kalahari and Namib and is widespread all over Namibia, from the coast to the interior highlands.

As you might expect, gemsbok are very adaptable. They range widely and are found in areas of dunes, alkaline pans, open savannah and even woodlands. Along with the much smaller *springbok*, they can sometimes even be seen tracking across flat desert plains with only dust-devils and mirages for company. Gemsbok can endure extremes of temperature, helped by specially adapted blood capillaries in their nasal passages which can cool their blood before it reaches their brains. Thus although their body temperature can rise by up to 6°C, their brains remain cool and they survive. They do not need drinking water and will eat wild melons and dig for roots, bulbs and tubers when grazing or browsing becomes difficult.

Waterbuck *Kobus ellipsiprymnus* Shoulder height 130cm. Weight 250–270kg.

The waterbuck is easily recognised by its shaggy brown coat and the male's large lyre-shaped horns. The common race of southern Africa and areas east of the Rift Valley has a distinctive white ring around its rump, while the defassa race of the Rift Valley and areas further west has a full white rump. In Namibia, waterbuck are very uncommon, only occasionally seen on the eastern fringes of the Caprivi Strip. They need to drink very regularly, so usually stay within a few kilometres of water, where they like to graze on short, nutritious grasses. At night they may take cover in adjacent woodlands. It is often asserted that waterbuck flesh is oily and smelly, which may discourage predators.

Blue wildebeest *Connochaetes taurinus* Shoulder height 130–150cm. Weight 180–250kg. This ungainly antelope, also called the brindled gnu, is easily identified by its dark coat and bovine appearance. The superficially similar buffalo is far more heavily built. When they have enough space, blue wildebeest can form immense herds – as perhaps a million do for their annual migration from Tanzania's Serengeti Plains into Kenya's Masai Mara. In Namibia they naturally occur north of Etosha and east into the Caprivi Strip. They are also found in the Kalahari, Khaudum and the far eastern borders of Namibia. They are adaptable grazers, but prefer short grass plains and need access to drinking water. They have been introduced on to several game ranches.

Similar species: The **black wildebeest** *Connochaetes gnou*, endemic to South Africa's central highveld, now numbers a mere 4,000. It is seen most easily in South Africa's Golden Gate National Park, though has also been introduced into several private game areas in Namibia. It differs from the blue wildebeest in having a white tail, a defined black-on-white mane, and horns that slope sharply down then rise to form a 'U' when seen from the side.

Hartebeest *Alcelaphus buselaphus* Shoulder height 125cm. Weight 120–150kg.
Hartebeests are ungainly antelopes, readily identified by the combination of large shoulders, a sloping back, a glossy, red-brown coat and smallish horns in both sexes. Numerous subspecies are recognised, all of which are generally seen in small family groups in reasonably open country. Though once hartebeest were found from the Mediterranean to the Cape, only isolated populations still survive.

The only one native to Namibia is the red hartebeest, which is found throughout the arid eastern side of the country, and north into Etosha and Owamboland. They have been introduced on to the NamibRand Nature Reserve but are absent from the Caprivi Strip, and common nowhere. Hartebeests are almost exclusively grazers; they like access to water though will eat melons, tubers and rhizomes when it is scarce. Etosha's waterholes, especially those in areas of mopane sparse woodland, probably offer your best chance to see hartebeest in Namibia.

Similar species: The **tsessebe** *Damaliscus lunatus* is basically a darker version of the hartebeest with striking yellow lower legs. (Related subspecies are known as *topi* in East Africa.) Widespread but thinly and patchily distributed, the tsessebe occurs occasionally in the Caprivi Strip. Its favourite habitat is open grassland, where it is a selective grazer, eating the newer, more nutritious grasses. The tsessebe is one of the fastest antelope species, and jumps very well.

Bontebok *Damaliscus dorcas dorcas* Shoulder height 850–95cm. Weight 60–70kg.

Though endemic to the fynbos areas of the Western Cape in South Africa, bontebok have been introduced into many private reserves in Namibia. They look like particularly striking small hartebeest, with a distinctive white face, chestnut back, black flanks and white belly and rump. Bontebok were hunted close to extinction in the early twentieth century, and now they are largely found in private protected areas – like the grounds of Mokuti Lodge, or the NamibRand Nature Reserve.

Similar species: The duller but more common **blesbok** (*Damaliscus dorcas phillipsi*) is, in essence, the highveld race of bontebok native to eastern South Africa. That, too, has occasionally been introduced on to the odd private reserve in Namibia.

Kudu *Tragelaphus strepsiceros* Shoulder height 140–155cm. Weight 180–250kg.

The kudu (or, more properly, the greater kudu) is the most frequently observed member of the genus tragelaphus. These medium-sized to large antelopes are characterised by the male's large spiralling horns and dark coat, which is generally marked with several vertical white stripes. They are normally associated with well-wooded habitats.

The kudu is very large, with a grey-brown coat and up to ten stripes on each side. The male has magnificent double-spiralled corkscrew horns. Occurring throughout Mozambique, Zimbabwe, Zambia, Botswana and Namibia, kudu are widespread and common, though not in dense forests or open grasslands. In Namibia they are absent only from the Namib Desert – though they are found in the river valleys and are very common on farmland, where their selective browsing does not compete with the indiscriminate grazing of the cattle.

Sitatunga *Tragelaphus spekei* Shoulder height 85–90cm. Weight 105–115kg.

The semi-aquatic antelope is a widespread but infrequently observed inhabitant of West and Central African swamps from the Okavango in Botswana to the Sudd in Sudan. In Namibia it occurs in the Okavango River beside Mahango, and in protected areas of the Kwando–Linyanti–Chobe–Zambezi river system where there are extensive papyrus reedbeds. Because of its preferred habitat, the sitatunga is very elusive and seldom seen, even in areas where it is relatively common.

Eland *Taurotragus oryx* Shoulder height 150–175cm. Weight 450–900kg.

Africa's largest antelope, the eland is light brown in colour, sometimes with a few faint white vertical stripes. Its somewhat bovine appearance is accentuated by relatively short horns and a large dewlap. It was once widely distributed in East and southern Africa, but in Namibia it is now found only in isolated Kalahari areas, Etosha and Waterberg. Small herds of eland frequent grasslands and light woodlands, often fleeing at the slightest provocation. (They have long been hunted for their excellent meat, so perhaps this is not surprising.)

Eland are opportunist browsers and grazers, eating fruit, berries, seed pods and leaves as well as green grass after the rains, and roots and tubers when times are lean. They run slowly, though can trot for great distances and jump exceedingly well.

Medium and small antelope

Bushbuck *Tragelaphus scriptus* Shoulder height 70–80cm. Weight 30–45kg.
This attractive antelope, a member of the same genus as the kudu, is widespread throughout Africa and shows great regional variation in its colouring. It occurs in forest and riverine woodland, where it is normally seen singly or in pairs. The male is dark brown or chestnut, while the much smaller female is generally a pale reddish brown. The male has relatively small, straight horns and both sexes are marked with white spots and sometimes stripes, though the stripes are often indistinct.

Bushbuck tend to be secretive and very skittish, except when used to people. They depend on cover and camouflage to avoid predators, and are often found in the thick, herby vegetation around rivers. They will freeze if disturbed, before dashing off into the undergrowth. Bushbuck are both browsers and grazers, choosing the more succulent grass shoots, fruit and flowers. In Namibia they have a very limited distribution around the Okavango River in Mahango National Park, and beside the Chobe and Kwando rivers on the eastern side of the Caprivi Strip.

Impala *Aepeceros melampus* Shoulder height 90cm. Weight 45kg.
This slender, handsome antelope is superficially similar to the springbok, but in fact belongs to its own separate family. Chestnut in colour, and lighter underneath than above, the impala has diagnostic black and white stripes running down its rump and tail, and the male has large lyre-shaped horns. One of the most widespread and successful antelope species in East and southern Africa, the impala is normally seen in large herds in wooded savannah habitats. It is the most common antelope in the Caprivi Strip, and throughout much of the country further east, although it is absent from much of Namibia.

However, a separate subspecies, the **black-faced impala** (*A. m. petersi*), occurs in Etosha, the Kaokoveld and southern Angola. This is almost identical to the normal impala, and distinguished only by extra black stripes on its face, including a prominent one down the front of its nose. The total population of black-faced impalas is about a thousand individuals, but with a few days spent in Etosha you have a surprisingly good chance of spotting some.

As expected of such a successful species, it both grazes and browses, depending on what fodder is available.

Springbok *Antidorcas marsupilis* Shoulder height 60cm. Weight 20–25kg.
Springbok are graceful, relatively small antelope – members of the gazelle family – which generally occur in large herds. They have finely marked short coats: fawn-brown upper parts and a white belly, separated by a dark brown band. Springbok occur throughout Namibia; they are often the most common small antelope. They can be seen by the thousand in Etosha.

They favour dry, open country, preferring open plains or

savannah, and avoiding thick woodlands and mountains. They can subsist without water for long periods, if there is moisture in the plants they graze or browse; I have even seen springbok amongst the dunes at Sossusvlei on occasions.

Reedbuck *Redunca arundinum* Shoulder height 80–90cm. Weight 45–65kg.
Sometimes referred to as the southern reedbuck (as distinct from mountain and Bohor reedbucks, found further east), these delicate antelope are uniformly fawn or grey in colour, and lighter below than above. They are generally found in reedbeds and tall grasslands, often beside rivers, and are easily identified by their loud, whistling alarm call and distinctive bounding running style. In Namibia they occur only on the Caprivi Strip and a few riverine areas in the far north.

Klipspringer *Oreotragus oreotragus* Shoulder height 60cm. Weight 13kg.
The klipspringer is a stongly built little antelope, normally seen in pairs, and easily identified by its dark, bristly grey-yellow coat, slightly speckled appearance and unique habitat preference. Klipspringer means 'rockjumper' in Afrikaans and it is an apt name for an antelope which occurs exclusively in mountainous areas and rocky outcrops from Cape Town to the Red Sea.

They are common throughout Namibia, wherever rocky hills or kopjes are found – which means most of the central highlands and western escarpment, but not in the far north or the Caprivi Strip. Klipspringers are mainly browsers, though they do eat a little new grass. When spotted they will freeze, or bound at great speed across the steepest of slopes.

Lechwe *Kobus leche* Shoulder height 90–100cm. Weight 80–100kg.
Otherwise known as the red lechwe, this sturdy, shaggy antelope has a reddish coat and beautiful lyre-shaped horns. They are usually found only in moist, open environments and in Namibia they are found only beside the great rivers of the Caprivi Strip.

Lechwe need dry land on which to rest, but otherwise will spend much of their time grazing on grasses and sedges, standing in water if necessary. Their hooves are splayed, adapted to bounding through their muddy environment when fleeing from the lion, hyena and wild dog that hunt them.

Steenbok *Raphicerus cempestris* Shoulder height 50cm. Weight 11kg.
This rather nondescript small antelope has red-brown upper parts and clear white underparts, and the male has short straight horns. It is probably the most commonly observed small antelope; if you see a small antelope fleeing from you across farmland in Namibia, it is likely to be a steenbok. Like most other small antelopes, the steenbok is normally encountered singly or in pairs and tends to 'freeze' when disturbed, before taking flight.

Similar species: **Sharpe's grysbok** (*Raphicerus sharpei*) is similar in size and appearance, though it has a distinctive white-flecked coat. It occurs alongside the steenbok in the far eastern reaches of the Caprivi Strip, but is almost entirely nocturnal in its habits and so very seldom seen. The **Oribi** (*Ourebia ourebi*) is a widespread but very uncommon antelope, which is usually found only in large, open stretches of grassland. It looks much like a steenbok but stands about 10cm higher at the shoulder and has an altogether more upright bearing. In Namibia you have a chance of seeing these only on the Caprivi Strip, and you'll need to look hard.

The **Damara dik-dik** (*Madoqua kirki*) occurs in central-north Namibia, Etosha and the Kaokoland, as well as parts of East Africa where it is known as Kirk's dik-dik. It is Namibia's smallest antelope; easily identified from steenbok by its much smaller size. It is adapted to arid areas and prefers a mixture of bushes and spare grassland cover. Damara dik-diks are common in Etosha, and will often sit motionless beside the road whilst they are passed by without ever being seen. They are active during the cooler hours of the day as well as the night and are almost exclusively browsers.

Common duiker *Sylvicapra grimmia* Shoulder height 50cm. Weight 20kg.

This anomalous duiker holds itself more like a steenbok or grysbok and is the only member of its (large) family to occur outside of forests. Generally grey in colour, the common duiker can most easily be separated from other small antelopes by the black tuft of hair that sticks up between its horns. It occurs throughout Namibia, everywhere except the Namib Desert. Common duikers tolerate most habitats except for true forest and very open country, and are tolerant of nearby human settlements. They are opportunist feeders, taking fruit, seeds, and leaves, as well as crops, small reptiles and amphibians.

Other large herbivores

African elephant *Loxodonta africana* Shoulder height 2.3–3.4m. Weight up to 6,000kg.

The world's largest land animal, the African elephant is intelligent, social and often very entertaining to watch. Female elephants live in closely-knit clans in which the eldest female plays matriarch over her sisters, daughters and granddaughters. Mother-daughter bonds are strong and may last for up to 50 years. Males generally leave the family group at around 12 years to roam singly or form bachelor herds. Under normal circumstances, elephants range widely in search of food and water, but when concentrated populations are forced to live in conservation areas their habit of uprooting trees can cause serious environmental damage. Elephants are widespread and common in habitats ranging from desert to rainforest. In Namibia they are common in the Caprivi Strip and Etosha, and in Kalahari areas around Khaudum.

Read about the history of Etosha, and you'll realise that the park used to cover much of the present Kaokoveld. Until about 50 years ago Etosha's elephants used to migrate, spending the wetter parts of the year in the Kaokoveld and the drier months nearer to Etosha's permanent waterholes. Etosha's boundary fence has stopped that. However, the herds still tend to head to the hills of western Etosha during the rains, returning to the pan several months later as the bush dries out. Every year a few break out of the park's elaborate fences.

The isolated population which frequents the river valleys of the Kaokoveld are commonly known as 'desert elephants' – though desert-adapted might be a more accurate term. These family groups have learnt where the rivers and waterholes are, probably from their elders, and can navigate through the Kaokoveld's mountains and dunes to find water. The community game guard scheme, amongst others, has rescued this population from the edge of oblivion;

it is thriving to the point of conflict with the area's human population. After several decades of persecution by humans, these elephants are now (understandably) noted for their aggression. Even visitors in sturdy vehicles should treat them with exceptional respect (see *Driving near elephants*, page 88).

Black rhinoceros *Diceros bicornis* Shoulder height 160cm. Weight 1,000kg.

This is the more widespread of Africa's two rhino species, an imposing and rather temperamental creature. It has been poached to extinction in most of its former range, but still occurs in *very* low numbers in many southern African reserves; Namibia offers its best chance of long-term survival – thanks in no small measure to the work of Namibia's Save the Rhino Trust.

Black rhinos exploit a wide range of habitats from dense woodlands and bush, through to the very open hillsides of the Kaokoveld. Often (and descriptively) referred to as the hook-lipped rhino, the black rhino is adapted to browse. Over its range it utilises hundreds of different plants, though local populations are often more specific in their diet: in the Kaokoveld, for example, *Euphorbia damarana* is a great favourite.

Black rhinos are generally solitary animals and can survive without drinking for 4–5 days. However, they will drink daily if they can, and individuals often meet at waterholes – as visitors to the floodlit waterholes at Okaukuejo and Halali will usually see to their delight. They are often territorial and have very regular patterns of movement, which make them an easy target for poachers. Black rhinos can be very aggressive when disturbed and will charge with minimal provocation. Their hearing and sense of smell is acute, whilst their eyesight is poor (so they often miss if you keep a low profile and don't move).

White rhinoceros *Ceratotherium simum* Shoulder height 180cm. Weight 1,500–2,000kg.
No paler in colour than the black rhino – the 'white' derives from the Afrikaans *weit* (wide) and refers to its flattened mouth, an ideal shape for cropping grass. This is the best way to tell the two rhino species apart, since the mouth of the black rhino, a browser in most parts of its range, is more rounded with a hooked upper lip. (Note that there is *no colour difference at all* between these two species of rhino; 'white' and 'black' are *not* literal descriptions.)

Aside from a relic population of some 30 animals in the northern Congo, the white rhino is now restricted to southern African reserves. There are thriving populations in many South African parks, especially the Umfolozi and Hluhluwe parks, which have effectively saved the species and started to re-populate many of southern Africa's parks. They were reintroduced to Waterberg years ago, and about a dozen have recently been introduced back into Etosha – where they seem to frequent the areas between Namutoni and Springbokfontein waterhole. Unlike their smaller cousins, white rhino are generally placid grazing animals which are very rarely aggressive. They prefer open grassy plains and are often seen in small groups.

Hippopotamus *Hippopotamus amphibius* Shoulder height 150cm. Weight 2,000kg.
Characteristic of Africa's large rivers and lakes, this large, lumbering animal spends most of the day submerged but emerges at night to graze. Strongly territorial, herds of ten or more animals are presided over by a dominant male who will readily defend his patriarchy to the death. Hippos are abundant in most protected rivers and water bodies, and they are still quite common outside of reserves, where they are widely credited with killing more people than any other African mammal.

In Namibia they occur only in the great rivers of the Caprivi Strip, and occasionally in the Kunene River, at the north end of the Kaokoveld. Otherwise you won't generally see them.

Cape buffalo *Syncerus caffer* Shoulder height 140cm.
Weight 700kg.
Frequently and erroneously referred to as a water
buffalo (an Asian species), the Cape, or African, buffalo
is a distinctive, highly social ox-like animal that lives as
part of a herd. It prefers well-watered savannah, though also
occurs in forested areas. Common and widespread in sub-
Saharan Africa, in Namibia it is limited to the Caprivi Strip,
largely by the absence of sufficient water in the rest of the
country.

   Buffalo are primarily grazers and need regular access to water, where they swim readily.
They smell and hear well, and old bulls have a reputation for charging at the slightest
provocation. Lion often follow herds of buffalo, their favourite prey.

Giraffe *Giraffa camelopardis* Shoulder height 250–350cm. Weight 1,000–1,400kg.
The world's tallest and longest-necked land animal, a fully grown giraffe can measure up to
5.5m high. Quite unmistakable, the giraffe lives in loosely structured herds of up to 15 head,
though herd members often disperse and then they are seen singly or in smaller groups.
Formerly distributed throughout East and southern Africa, these great browsers are found in
the north of Namibia, from northern Damaraland and Kaokoland, to the Caprivi. Etosha has
a thriving population, many of which are very relaxed with cars and allow visitors in vehicles
to approach very closely.

Common zebra *Equus burchelli* Shoulder height
130cm. Weight 300–340kg.
Also known as Burchell's or plains zebra, this
attractive striped horse is common and widespread
throughout most of East and southern Africa, where it is often
seen in large herds alongside wildebeest. It is common in most
conservation areas from northern South Africa, Namibia and
Botswana all the way up to the southeast of Ethiopia. Southern
races, including those in Namibia, have paler brownish 'shadow
stripes' between the bold black stripes that are present in all races.

Similar species: The **Hartmann's mountain zebra** (*Equus grevyi hartmannae*), is confined to
Namibia's western escarpment and the plains nearby. It is very closely related to the Cape
mountain zebra which occurs in South Africa. Mountain zebra have a slightly lighter frame
than the Burchell's, their underparts are not striped, the striping on their legs extends all the
way to their hooves, and they have a dewlap which the Burchell's lack.

   They occur from the conservation area around the Fish River Canyon to the Harmann
Valley in the Kaokoveld, and have been introduced on to several private reserves away from
the escarpment area.

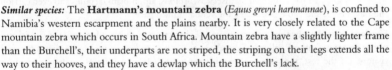

Warthog *Phacochoreus africanus* Shoulder height 60–70cm. Weight up to
100kg.
This widespread and often conspicuously abundant resident of the
African savannah is grey in colour with a thin covering of hairs, wart-
like bumps on its face, and rather large upward curving tusks. Africa's
only diurnal swine, the warthog is often seen in family groups, trotting
around with its tail raised stiffly (a diagnostic trait) and a determinedly
nonchalant air. They occur everywhere in Namibia apart from the far south
and the western desert areas, although I have often seen them grazing, on
bended knee, where the C36 cuts through the Namib-Naukluft National Park.

Similar species: Bulkier, hairier and more brown, the **bushpig** (*Potomochoerus larvatus*) is only known to occur in Namibia in the Caprivi Strip. It is very rarely seen due to its nocturnal habits and preference for dense vegetation.

Small mammals

African civet *Civettictis civetta* Shoulder height 40cm. Weight 10–15kg.

This bulky, long-haired, rather feline creature of the African night is primarily carnivorous, feeding on small animals and carrion, but will also eat fruit. It has a similarly coloured coat to a leopard, which is densely blotched with large black spots becoming stripes towards the head. Civets are widespread and common in many habitats, but very rarely seen. In Namibia, it is restricted to the far north.

Similar species: The **small-spotted genet** (*Genetta genetta*) and **large-spotted genet** (*Genetta tigrina*) are the most widespread members of a group of similar small predators. All of these are slender and rather feline in appearance (though they are *not* cats), with a grey to gold-brown coat marked with black spots and a long ringed tail. Most likely to be seen on nocturnal game drives or scavenging around game-reserve lodges, the large-spotted genet is gold-brown with very large spots and a black-tipped tail, whereas the small-spotted genet is greyer with rather small spots and a pale-tipped tail. Exact identification is a job for experts. The small-spotted genet is found all over Namibia, whilst the large-spotted genet is restricted to the Caprivi Strip and the area adjacent to the Okavango River.

Banded mongoose *Mungos mungo* Shoulder height 20cm. Weight around 1kg.
The banded mongoose is probably the most commonly observed member of a group of small, slender, terrestrial carnivores. Uniform dark grey-brown except for a dozen black stripes across its back, it is a diurnal mongoose occurring in playful family groups, or troops, in most habitats north and east of Okahandja. They feed on insects, scorpions, amphibians, reptiles and even carrion and bird's eggs, and can move across the veld at quite a pace.

Similar species: Another eight or so mongoose species occur in Namibia; some are social and gather in troops, others solitary. Several are too scarce and nocturnal to be seen by casual visitors. Of the rest, the water or **marsh mongoose** (*Atilax paludinosus*) is large, normally solitary and has a very scruffy brown coat; it's widespread along the Caprivi Strip, the Kunene and the Orange. The **white-tailed ichneumon** (*Ichneumia albicauda*) is another mongoose that is widespread in the Caprivi. It is a solitary, large brown mongoose, easily identified by its bushy white tail.

The **slender mongoose** (*Galerella sanguinea*) is as widespread and also solitary, but it is very much smaller (shoulder height 10cm) and has a uniform brown or reddish coat and blackish tail tip. It is replaced in the far south of Namibia by the **small grey mongoose** (*Galerella pulveruntela*), similar in size but grey with white flecks on its coat.

The **yellow mongoose** (*Cynitis penicillata*) is a small, sociable mongoose with a tawny or yellow coat, and is commonly found across most of Namibia. It normally forages alone and is easily identified by the white tip on the end of its tail.

Finally, **the dwarf mongoose** (*Helogate parvula*) is a diminutive (shoulder height 7cm), highly sociable light brown mongoose often seen in the vicinity of the termite mounds where it nests.

Meerkat or **suricate** *Suricata suricatta* Shoulder height 25–35cm. Weight 650–950g.

Found throughout the Kaokoveld and southern Namibia, meerkats are only absent from the driest western areas of the Namib and the wetter parts of northeast Namibia. These small animals are sandy- to silvery-grey in colour, with dark bands running across their backs. They are exclusively diurnal and have a distinctive habit of sitting upright on their hind legs. They do this when they first emerge in the morning, to sun themselves, and throughout the day.

Living in complex social groups, meerkats are usually seen scratching around for insects, beetles and small reptiles in dry, open, grassy areas. Whilst the rest forage, one or two of the group will use the highest mound around as a sentry-post – looking out for predators using their remarkable eyesight. Meerkats' social behaviour is very complex: they squeak constantly to communicate and even use different alarm calls for different types of predators. Because of their photogenic poses and fascinating social behaviour, they have been the subject of several successful television documentaries filmed in the southern Kalahari.

Honey badger *Mellivora capensis* Shoulder height 30cm. Weight 12kg.

Also known as the ratel, the honey badger is black with a puppyish face and grey-white back. It is an opportunistic feeder best known for its symbiotic relationship with a bird called the honeyguide which leads it to a beehive, waits for it to tear it open, then feeds on the scraps. The honey badger is among the most widespread of African carnivores, and also amongst the most powerful for its size; it occurs all over Namibia. However, it is thinly distributed and rarely seen, except when it has been tamed enough to turn up on cue to artificial feedings at safari camps (Okonjima's nightly feeding session used to get occasional visits from honey badgers).

Similar species: Several other mustelids occur in the region, including the **striped polecat** (*Ictonyx striatus*), a common but rarely seen nocturnal creature with black underparts and a bushy white back, and the similar but much scarcer striped weasel (*Poecilogale albincha*). The **Cape clawless otter** (*Aonyx capensis*) is a brown freshwater mustelid with a white collar, which is found in the Caprivi area, the Kunene and the Orange River. The smaller **spotted-necked otter** (*Lutra maculicollis*) is darker with light white spots on its throat, and is restricted to the Caprivi and Okavango River.

Aardvark (*Orycteropus afer*) Shoulder height 60cm. Weight up to 70kg.

This singularly bizarre nocturnal insectivore is unmistakable with its long snout, huge ears and powerful legs, adapted to dig up the nests of termites, on which it feeds. Aardvarks occur throughout southern Africa, except the driest western areas of the Namib. Though their distinctive three-toed tracks are often seen, and they are not uncommon animals, sightings of them are rare.

Aardvarks prefer areas of grassland and sparse scrub, rather than dense woodlands, and Namibia's ranchland suits them well – although their excavations into roads and dam walls are not appreciated by farmers.

Pangolin *Manis temmincki* Total length 70–100cm. Weight 8–15kg.

Sharing the aardvaak's diet of termites and ants, pangolins are another very unusual nocturnal insectivore – with distinctive armour-plating and a tendency to roll up in a ball when disturbed. Sometimes known as Temminck's pangolin, or scaly anteaters, these strange animals walk on their hindlegs, using their tail and front legs for balance. They occur in eastern and northern Namibia, but not in the Namib Desert, and are both nocturnal and rare – so sightings are exceedingly unusual.

In some areas further east, particularly Zimbabwe, local custom is to make a present of any pangolin found to the paramount chief (often taken to mean the president), which has caused great damage to their population.

Porcupine *Hystrix africaeaustralis* Total length 80–100cm. Weight 15–25kg.
This is the largest rodent found in the region, and occurs all over southern Africa, except for the western reaches of the Namib Desert. It easily identified by its black and white srtiped quills, generally black hair, and shambolling gait. If heard in the dark, then the rustle of its foraging is augmented by the slight rattle of its quills. These drop off fairly regularly, and are often found in the bush.

The porcupine's diet is varied, and they are fairly opportunistic when it comes to food. Roots and tubers are favourites, as is the bark of cetain trees; they will also eat meat and small reptiles or birds if they have the chance.

Similar species: Also spiky, the **southern African hedgehog** is found in north-central areas, including the Kaokoveld and Owamboland. This species is much smaller than the porcupine (about 20cm long), but is also omnivorous. They are not common.

Rock hyrax *Procavia capensis* Shoulder height 35–30cm. Weight 4kg.
Rodent-like in appearance, hyraxes (also known as dassies) are claimed to be the closest living relative of elephants. The rock hyrax and similar **Kaokoveld rock hyrax** (*Heterohyrax welwitschii*) are often seen sunning themselves in rocky habitats, and become tame when used to people.

They are social animals, living in large groups, and largely herbivorous, eating leaves, grasses and fruits. Where you see lots of dassies, watch out for black eagles and other raptors which prey extensively on them.

Scrub hare *Lepus saxatilis* Shoulder height 45–60cm. Weight 1–4.5kg.
This is the largest and commonest African hare or rabbit, occurring everywhere in Namibia except the far west and south. In some areas a short walk at dusk or after nightfall might reveal three or four scrub hares. They tend to freeze when disturbed.

Ground squirrel *Xerus inauris* Shoulder height 20–30cm. Weight 400–700g.
This terrestrial rodent is common of most arid parts of Namibia, except the far west of the desert. The ground squirrel is grey to grey-brown with a prominent white eye ring and silver-black tail. Within its range, it might be confused with the meerkat, which also spends much time on its hind legs. Unlike the meerkat, ground squirrels have a characteristic squirrel mannerism of holding food in its forepaws.

The ground squirrel is a social animal; large groups share one communal burrow. It can often be spotted searching for vegetation, seeds, roots and small insects, whilst holding its tail aloft as a sun-shade.

Appendix 2

LANGUAGES

Namibia's variety of languages reflects the diversity of its peoples – black and white. Amongst the indigenous languages there are two basic language groups which bear no relation to each other, Bantu (eg: Owambo, Herero) and Khoisan (eg: Bushmen, Nama). The only language that comes close to being a *lingua franca* is Afrikaans.

Most black townspeople speak both Afrikaans and English in addition to their 'mother' language. In the more rural areas, Afrikaans tends to be more widely used than English (which may not be spoken at all) – despite the widespread enthusiasm felt for the latter. In the farming areas of the central region, German is also commonly found, as many of the commercial farmers are of German origin.

Following independence, one of the new government's first actions was to make English Namibia's only official language (removing Afrikaans and German). This step sought to unite Namibia's peoples and languages under one common tongue ('the language of the liberation struggle'), leaving behind the colonial overtones of Afrikaans and German. This choice is also helping with international relations and education, as English-language materials are the most easily available.

There isn't the space here to include a detailed guide to Namibia's many languages, although, if you are staying in a community for longer than a few days, then you should try to learn a few local greetings from your hosts. Whilst travelling, you are likely to come across unfamiliar words that are in common use in southern African English, many of Afrikaans origin. These include:

apteek	chemist or pharmacy (most towns have one)
bakkie	pick-up truck, with open back
berg	mountain, or mountain range
boerewors (or *wors*)	sausage – an essential component of any *braai*
boma	traditional enclosure, often used at safari camps to mean the area around the fire where everyone gathers.
braaivleis (*braai*)	barbecue
the bush	generic term for any wild area, usually implying some thick vegetation cover
bundu	the bush (see above) – more often used in Zimbabwe
donga	small ravine, sometimes caused by water erosion
dorp	small rural town, though often implies a place with small-minded, reactionary attitudes
kantoor	an office
klippe	rock or stone (as used in *klip*springer)
kloof	ravine, often with a small river at the bottom
kopje (or *koppie*)	rocky hill, often alone in an otherwise flat area.
kraal	cattle enclosure or African huts (Owambo)
lekker	good, nice – now slang, typically used to describe food

mielie	corn or maize, the staple for most of the subcontinent
mieliepap	maize flour porridge, often eaten for breakfast
mokoro	dug-out canoe (others spellings also seen, including *mekoro*)
orlag	war
pad	road or track
ompad	diversion, often used on road signs
rivier	river
robots	traffic lights (ie: 'turn left at the *robots*, then…')
rondavel	traditional African hut (usually round)
tackies	running shoes or trainers
veld	grassland – like '*the bush*', this term is used for wide open wilderness areas, but implies mostly low vegetation cover
vlei	depression, valley, lake or low-lying place where water gathers, this term is used throughout the subcontinent
werft	traditional settlement (often Herero)

Bradt Travel Guides is a partner to the new 'know before you go' campaign, recently launched by the UK Foreign and Commonwealth Office. By combining the up-to-date advice of the FCO with the in-depth knowledge of Bradt authors, you'll ensure that your trip will be as trouble-free as possible.

www.fco.gov.uk/knowbeforeyougo

Appendix 3

FURTHER READING
History

Hansheinrich von Wolf and Duwisib Castle by Dr N Mossolow. Published in 1995 for the Society for Scientific Development, Swakopmund. ISBN 99916-30-13-9. This neat 20-page account of the castle and its founder is half in German and half in English, and often available from the castle itself. The middle eight pages are black-and-white photographs of the castle and its characters. Worth buying whilst you are there.

Africa: A Biography of the Continent by John Reader. Published in 1997 by Penguin Books Ltd, 27 Wrights Lane, London W8 5TZ, England. ISBN 0-241-13047-6. Over 700 pages of highly readable history, interwoven with facts and statistics, to make a remarkable overview of Africa's past. Given that Namibia's boundaries were imposed from Europe, its history *must* be looked at from a pan-African context to be understood. This book can show you that wider view; it is compelling and essential reading.

The Bushman Myth: the Making of a Namibian Underclass by Robert J Gordon. Published in 1992 by Westview Press Inc, 5500 Central Ave, Boulder, Colorado, 80301-2847. Also in the UK by Westview Press, 36 Lonsdale Road, Summertown, Oxford. ISBN 0-8133-1381-3. If you, like me, had accepted the received wisdom that Bushmen are the last descendants of Stone-Age man, pushed to living in splendid isolation in the Kalahari, then you must read this. It places the Bushmen in an accurate historical context and deconstructs many of the myths we have created about them.

Rivers of Blood, Rivers of Gold: Europe's Conflict with Tribal Peoples by Mark Cocker. Published in 1998 by Jonathan Cape, Random House, 20 Vauxhall Bridge Road, London SW1V 2SA. ISBN 0-224-03884-2. This highly readable book explores four colonial episodes: the conquest of Mexico, the British onslaught in Tasmania, the uprooting of the Apache in north America, and the German campaign in South West Africa during the early 20th century. It gives an excellent, detailed account of the 1904–7 war, and examines the conflict, and the main characters, in the context of contemporary world politics.

Lake Ngami and *The River Okavango* by Charles John Andersson. Originally published in the late 1850s, but republished as a facsimile reprint by C Struik of Cape Town in 1967. These two fascinating books record Namibia in the 1850s through the eyes of one of the first traders and hunters in the area.

Explorations in South-West Africa by Thomas Baines. Published 1864 in London. Although linked more with the countries further east, the travels of Baines, as he accompanied Livingstone and others, make fascinating reading.

Namibia – The Facts. Published by IDAF Publications Ltd, London, in 1989. Concentrates mainly on the liberation struggle over the last ten years. Highly emotive text and pictures.

History of Resistance in Namibia by Peter H Katjavivi. Co-published by James Currey, London; OAU in Addis Ababa; Unesco Press in Paris. Rather more scholarly than *Namibia – The Facts*, it's impressive in its detail.

The History of Rehoboth by Robert Camby. A very useful pamphlet for understanding Rehoboth's history.

The Price of Freedom by Ellen Ndeshi Namhila. A biographical account of 19 years spent in exile by a young Namibian woman.

'Why gossip is good for you' by R I M Dunbar. Article in *New Scientist*, November 21 1992.

'Franz or Klikko, the Wild Dancing Bushmen: A Case Study in Khoisan Stereotyping' by Q N Parsons. Published in the journal of the Botswana Society, Vol 20 (1989), pages 71–6.

Photography

The Skeleton Coast by Amy Schoeman. Published by Southern Book Publishers Ltd, Cape Town. ISBN 1-86812-593-9. Involving, well-informed text and superb photographs make this an excellent read, and easily the definitive work on the coast. Amy's late husband was the legendary Louw Schoeman, and she remains involved with Skeleton Coast Fly-in Safaris, though now does much travel writing on Namibia.

Namib by David Coulson. First published in 1991 by Sidgwick & Jackson Ltd, London. ISBN 0-283-99960-8. This stunning coffee-table book doubles as a readable travelogue. Published 18 years after Coulson's first visit, its insight tells much of his love for Namibia's wilderness.

Namibia – Africa's Harsh Paradise by Anthony Bannister and Peter Johnson. Published 1990 by New Holland Ltd, London. Yet another for the coffee table, this covers the whole country and concentrates on the Bushman and Himba people.

'Etosha: Namibia's Kingdom of Animals' article in *National Geographic*, Vol 163, No 3, March 1983. A general article about managing the park – with discussion of the problems of waterholes, anthrax, and too many lions!

'Elephant Talk' article in *National Geographic*, Vol 176, No 2, August 1989, pages 264–77. On infrasound communication in elephants, with some interesting comments about desert elephants in the Hoarusib River.

Guidebooks

Discovering Southern Africa by T V Bulpin. Published in South Africa by Discovering Southern Africa Productions, distributed by Book Sales. ISBN 0-9583130-1-6. Part guidebook and part history book, Bulpin covers mainly South Africa but also extends into Namibia and Zimbabwe. A weighty tome with useful background views and information, written from a South African perspective.

East and Southern Africa: The Backpacker's Manual by Philip Briggs. Second edition published in 2001 by Bradt Travel Guides Ltd. ISBN 1-84162 028 9. If you are venturing into southern Africa for a long budget trip, buy this book. It won't spoon-feed you with all the nitty-gritty details, but it will guide you to make your own discoveries and offer help when you really need it. An excellent manual.

Travelogues

The Lost World of the Kalahari by Laurens van der Post. First published by the Hogarth Press in 1958, subsequently many reprints published by Penguin. Laurens van der Post's classic account of how he journeyed into the heart of the Kalahari Desert in search of a 'pure' Bushman group – eventually found at the Tsodilo Hills. His almost mystical description of the Bushmen is fascinating, so long as you can cope with the rather dated turgid prose. You then need to read Robert J Gordon's very different book (see page 505) to put it in perspective.

Sheltering Desert by Henno Martin. First English edition published by William Kimber of London in 1957. ISBN 0-86852-150-7. The story of two German geologists who lived out World War II by hiding in the Kuiseb Canyon – holiday reading if you're visiting the Namib-Naukluft National Park.

Natural history

The Namib by Dr Mary Seely. Published by Shell Oil Namibia, PO Box 110, Windhoek. ISBN 0-620-11688-9. A detailed work on the desert's origins, with descriptions of many sites and the animals and plants that live there. This paperback is well worth getting when you arrive in Namibia.

Namib Flora by Patricia Craven and Christine Marais. Published 1986 by Gamsberg Macmillan, PO Box 22830, Windhoek. ISBN 1-86848-784-9. This delightful little hardback covers a small area 'from Swakopmund to the giant *welwitschia* via Goanikontes', though many of the plants that it so beautifully illustrates will be found elsewhere.

Damaraland Flora by Patricia Craven and Christine Marais. Published 1992 by Gamsberg Macmillan, PO Box 22830, Windhoek. ISBN 1-86848-784-9. Similar to the Namib Flora, and equally well illustrated, Covers Spitzkoppe, Brandberg and Twyfelfontein, but invaluable anywhere in the Kaokoveld.

Birds of Southern Africa by Kenneth Newman. Published in numerous editions from 1983 by Southern Book Publishers, PO Box 3103, Halfway House 1685, South Africa. Probably the best identification field-guide to birds in southern Africa, including Namibia.

The Living Deserts of Southern Africa by Dr Barry Lovegrove. Published 1993 by Fernwood Press, South Africa. ISBN 0-9583154-7-7. A beautifully illustrated book with a scholarly text that is both informative and accessible.

Fascination of Geology by Nicole Grunert. Published by Klaus Hess Publishers.

The Harsh and Forbidden Sperrgebiet Rediscovered by Sakkie & Theresa Rothmann.

Kalahari: Life's Variety in Dune and Delta by Michael Main. Published 1987 by Southern Book Publishers, PO Box 584, Bergvlei 2012, Johannesburg, South Africa. ISBN 1-86812-285-9. Though primarily concerned with Botswana, this is a superb, highly readable, treatise on the Kalahari. It covers the origins and ecology of this thirstland and even tackles some of the more sticky political and human questions facing the region. The many marvellous details in the book, and Main's general clarity on the issues, comes from personal experience – he's lived in Botswana and travelled there very extensively. But even if you're heading for Namibia's Kalahari, it's still worth getting a copy. The only problem is that it will, of course, captivate you and make a subsequent visit to Botswana essential…

Art and culture

The Rock Paintings of Southern Africa by the Abbé Henri Breuil. Published in 1955–60 by Trianon Press Ltd, in four volumes, and distributed through Faber and Faber. These large volumes cover some of Namibia's major rock-art sites, including the controversial white lady of Brandberg.

Rural Art in Namibia edited and published by the Rössing Foundation of Namibia (1993). A 25-page colour booklet, categorised by region, illustrating traditional Namibian arts and crafts, including interviews with artists about their work.

Peoples of Namibia by Professor J S Malan. Published in Pretoria by Rhino Press, 1995.

Art in Namibia by Adelheid Lilienthal. Published by the National Art Gallery of Namibia

Ongoma! – Notes on Namibian Musical Instruments by Minette Mans, published by Gamsberg Macmillan, Windhoek. Although written as a resource book for teachers, this practical little book contains a wealth of information on traditional instruments that deserves a wider readership.

General/reference

An Explorer's Handbook – Travel, Survival and Bush Cookery by Christina Dodwell. Published in 1984 by Hodder and Stoughton, 47 Bedford Square, London, WC1B 3DP. ISBN 0-340-34937-9. Over 170 pages of both practical and amusing anecdotes, including chapters on 'unusual eatables', 'building an open fire', and 'tested exits from tight corners'. Practical advice for both plausible and most unlikely eventualities – and it's a great read.

Bugs, Bites & Bowels by Dr Jane Wilson-Howarth. Published in the UK by Cadogan Books. Distributed in the US by Globe Pequot Press. ISBN 0-86011-045-2. An amusing and erudite overview of the hazards of tropical travel.

Your Child's Health Abroad: A Manual for Travelling Parents by Dr Jane Wilson-Howarth and Dr Matthew Ellis. Published 1998 in the UK by Bradt Travel Guides. ISBN 1-898323-63-1. Full of practical first-hand advice from two leading medical experts. An indispensable guide if you plan to travel abroad with young children.

Fiction

Meemulu's Children by Kaleni Hiyalwa, published by New Namibia Books, reads more like a biography of a child growing up during Namibia's struggle for independence than a novel. Powerful stuff.

The Purple Violet of Oshaantu by Neshani Andreas, published by Heinemann. A Namibian woman's perspective on love and marriage in the context of traditional values and beliefs.

Index

Page numbers in italics indicate maps.